Essential Linux Files

Hardware Access Files *(see Chapters 1 and 3 for details)*

Linux device files	in the /dev directory
Files holding data on hardware and drivers	in the /proc directory

Scanner Configuration Files *(see Chapter 3 for details)*

Main SANE configuration	/etc/sane.d/dll.conf
Scanner-specific configuration files	files in /etc/sane.d named after scanner models

Printer Configuration Files *(see Chapter 13 for details)*

Main BSD LPD and LPRng local printer configuration file	/etc/printcap
Main CUPS local printer configuration and remote access authorization file	/etc/cups/cupsd.conf
BSD LPD remote access authorization file	/etc/hosts.lpd
LPRng remote access authorization file	/etc/lpd.perms

Disk Mount Points *(see Chapters 2, 10, and 12 for details)*

Filesystem table file (defines where partitions and disks are mounted)	/etc/fstab
Floppy disk mount point	/floppy, /mnt/floppy, or /media/floppy
CD-ROM mount point	/cdrom, /mnt/cdrom, or /media/cdrom

Shell Configuration Files *(see Chapters 4 and 9 for details)*

bash system non-login configuration files	/etc/bashrc, /etc/bash.bashrc, or /etc/bash.bashrc.local
bash system login configuration files	/etc/profile and files in /etc/profile.d
bash user non-login configuration file	~/.bashrc
bash user login configuration file	~/.profile

Linux
Power Tools

Roderick W. Smith

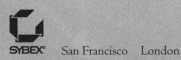

San Francisco   London

Associate Publisher: Joel Fugazzotto

Acquisitions Editor: Ellen L. Dendy

Developmental Editor: Brianne Agatep

Production Editor: Liz Burke

Technical Editor: Robert B. King

Copyeditor: Kathy Grider-Carlyle

Compositor: Maureen Forys, Happenstance Type-O-Rama

Graphic Illustrator: Jeff Wilson, Happenstance Type-O-Rama

Proofreaders: Emily Hsuan, Laurie O'Connell, Monique van den Berg, Amey Garber

Indexer: Ted Laux

Book Designer: Maureen Forys, Happenstance Type-O-Rama

Cover Designer: Richard Miller, Calyx Design

Cover Illustrator: Richard Miller, Calyx Design

Library of Congress Card Number: 2003101647

ISBN: 0-7821-4226-5

This book is for my sister Jennie.
What more can I say? She's my *sister!*

Acknowledgments

Although one person's name is most prominent on the cover, this book, like most, involves many peoples' input. At every point along the way from project beginning to finished product, many people other than the author have had their influence. Ellen Dendy, Acquisitions Editor, helped set the book on course at its inception. Brianne Agatep, Development Editor, guided the book's development throughout the process. Liz Burke, as Production Editor, coordinated the work of the many others who contributed their thoughts to the book. Editor Kathy Grider-Carlyle helped keep my grammar and spelling on track. Robert B. King, the Technical Editor, scrutinized the text for technical errors and made sure it was complete. I'd also like to thank Neil Salkind and others at Studio B, who helped get the project off the ground.

Contents at a Glance

Contents

Introduction

THE LAST DECADE has seen quiet and not-so-quiet technological revolutions. One of these many revolutions has been the emergence of Linux as a rival operating system (OS) to the likes of Windows, Mac OS, and Unix. Linux is a clone of the Unix OS, and so it has benefited from Unix's 30-year history. Just as important as its place in the Unix family is the fact that Linux is an *open source* operating system, meaning that its source code is freely accessible to all. Anybody can modify Linux and distribute these modifications. This fact has drawn a geographically diverse and enthusiastic group of developers into the Linux fold. The result has been tremendous technical advancements in Linux. These advancements have permitted the OS to develop into a competitor to both older Unix-like OSs and the popular Windows and Mac OS desktop OSs.

You may be reading these words while standing in a bookstore. If so, you can glance down and see plenty of other books on Linux. Most of these books are either general introductory books or books on very specific Linux programs. This book is designed to fit somewhere between these two general categories. *Linux Power Tools* is a general-purpose Linux book, but its goal is to go into greater depth than a typical introductory book on the OS. For this reason, *Linux Power Tools* omits coverage of some basic information. For instance, the book lacks a chapter on installing Linux—a popular topic in most introductory books. Instead, this book emphasizes more advanced options and tools, such as configuring fonts using Xft, modifying the system's startup scripts, setting up a network-based scanning system, and setting your system's time with the help of a time server.

One of the problems in the Linux world is that many Linux *distributions* exist. These distributions are collections of software (including installation routines) that together make a complete OS. Unfortunately, although all Linux distributions are Linux, no two distributions are exactly alike. This fact can be frustrating when you're trying to learn how something works, because what you read may be targeted at another distribution. This book aims to overcome this problem by providing explicit coverage of five of the most popular Linux distributions: Debian, Mandrake, Red Hat, Slackware, and SuSE. When I describe major configuration files or components, I describe distribution-specific differences. In some cases, this means that I describe two or more entirely different programs that fill similar roles. For instance, this book covers three mail servers: Exim, Postfix, and sendmail.

Who Should Buy This Book

This book is written for experienced Linux or Unix users who want to take their general knowledge of Linux to the next level. You should have already read a more introductory Linux book, such as Vicki Stanfield's and my *Linux System Administration, 2nd Edition* (Sybex, 2002). Alternatively, you might have gained knowledge in Linux or Unix through other means, such as reading web pages. Whatever the case, you now want to move beyond using a GUI environment's basic tools or every server's default configuration. Of course, this book can't cover specific servers or subsystems in any great depth, so if you want to learn about a specific tool, such as Apache or sendmail, you might be better off with a book on that topic. Instead, this book brings greater depth to a wide array of Linux system administration and use topics.

Like many OSs, Linux can be employed in a variety of environments. It can be a desktop OS in a home, a workstation in an office, or a server in a business. Linux users are equally diverse, but many of the needs of these users are the same. This book aims to cover these common needs first, but it also includes information relevant for specific user types. For instance, configuring fonts is a high priority for those running a desktop system or workstation, but it is not very important for most server administrators. Optimizing network configurations is more important to them. This book includes information on both fonts and network optimizations.

How This Book Is Organized

This book is divided into five parts—Hardware Tools, User Tools, System Administration Tools, Networking Tools, and Server Tools. The book also includes a Glossary.

PART I: HARDWARE TOOLS

This book hits the ground running with a look at the core of any computer: the hardware on which the OS runs. Linux runs on a broad range of hardware. Therefore, knowing how to configure the OS to handle the hardware is critically important. This section includes three chapters covering core hardware (the CPU, video hardware, sound hardware, drivers, and software/hardware interfaces), disk hardware, and external peripherals (including USB, RS-232 serial, and parallel ports; keyboards and mice; and scanners). Of course, hardware topics appear in other chapters of the book, as well, but these chapters cover the most critical hardware components, including Linux-specific issues when picking or configuring hardware.

PART II: USER TOOLS

The five chapters of Part II cover tools that ordinary users on a desktop system or workstation are likely to use. Specific chapters cover shells and shell scripting, using text-mode programs, using a desktop environment, using Linux office productivity tools, and miscellaneous user tools (sound editing, digital camera tools, the GIMP, web browsers, and e-mail clients). These areas have seen substantial development in the past couple of years, and they are likely to see more improvement in the future.

PART III: SYSTEM ADMINISTRATION TOOLS

This part of the book is quite large, with ten chapters that cover topics relating to local system administration—that is, keeping the system running smoothly for all users. The covered topics include modifying configuration files, using Linux alongside other OSs, managing software packages, managing filesystems and files, configuring print queues, managing programs and processes, recompiling the Linux kernel, improving your X configuration, backing up your system, and general system security measures. Most of these topics are important no matter how you use your Linux system.

PART IV: NETWORKING TOOLS

This section is fairly short, at just three chapters. It covers basic network configuration (including improving network performance), controlling remote access to your computer, and detecting when your system's security has been breached. These topics are all relevant to any computer that's connected to a network, whether it's a client or a server.

PART V: SERVER TOOLS

The final section of the book covers an assortment of servers. The chapters cover how to run servers, web servers, file servers, mail servers, remote login servers, and miscellaneous servers.

Conventions Used in This Book

This book uses certain typographic styles in order to help you quickly identify important information and help you to avoid confusion over the meaning of words. In particular:

- A normal proportionally spaced font is used for the bulk of the text in the book.

- *Italicized text* indicates technical terms that are introduced for the first time in a chapter. (Italics are also used for emphasis.)

- A `monospaced font` is used to indicate the contents of configuration files, messages displayed at a text-mode Linux shell prompt, filenames, and Internet URIs.

- *`Italicized monospaced text`* indicates a variable—information that differs from one system or command run to another, such as the name of a client computer or a process ID number.

- **`Bold monospaced text`** is information that you're to type into the computer, usually at a Linux shell prompt. This text can also be italicized to indicate that you should substitute an appropriate value for your system.

In addition to these text conventions, which can apply to individual words or entire paragraphs, a few conventions are used to highlight segments of text:

NOTE   A Note indicates information that's useful or interesting, but that's somewhat peripheral to the main discussion. A Note might be relevant to a small number of networks, for instance, or refer to an outdated feature.

TIP   A Tip provides information that can save you time or frustration, and that may not be entirely obvious. A Tip might describe how to get around a limitation or how to use a feature to perform an unusual task.

WARNING   Warnings describe potential pitfalls or dangers. If you fail to heed a Warning, you may end up spending a lot of time recovering from a bug, or even restoring your entire system from scratch.

SIDEBARS

A Sidebar is like a Note, but it is longer. Typically, a Note is one paragraph or less in length, but Sidebars are longer than this. The information in a Sidebar is useful, but it doesn't fit into the main flow of the discussion.

Help Us Help You

Things change. In the world of computers, things change rapidly. Facts described in this book will become invalid over time. When they do, we need your help locating and correcting them. Additionally, a 600-page book is bound to have typographical errors. Let us know when you spot one. Send your suggested improvements, fixes, and other corrections to support@sybex.com. Roderick W. Smith can be reached at rodsmith@rodsbooks.com. I maintain a web page devoted to this book at http://www.rodsbooks.com/linuxpower/.

Part I

Hardware Tools

## Chapter 1

Optimizing System Architecture Usage

ALTHOUGH LINUX IS A software product, it depends heavily on the hardware upon which it runs—and Linux runs on a very wide range of hardware. For this reason, knowing how to get Linux working best with your computer's hardware is a critically important skill, which is why this book begins with several chapters on hardware. This chapter begins the examination with several hardware components that reside on the motherboard or on boards attached directly to it—the CPU, video hardware, and audio hardware. This chapter also describes how to get Linux to recognize hardware devices, including many covered in subsequent chapters. Finally, this chapter concludes with a look at the /proc filesystem, which is a window onto the hardware. Knowing how to use /proc can help you diagnose and fix hardware problems.

Getting the Most from Your CPU

The CPU is the heart of your computer. It executes your Linux programs, including the Linux kernel. Therefore, picking the right CPU is important when you buy a new computer or upgrade an existing one. Even if you're not planning to upgrade your system soon, you can take steps to improve Linux performance on your existing CPU. In some cases, setting incorrect optimizations can prevent a program from running; but usually, the wrong optimizations merely degrade performance slightly.

Understanding and Choosing CPUs

The Linux kernel was originally written for the Intel 80386 (or *i386*) CPU. This CPU is part of a family of CPUs known as the *80x86*, *x86*, or Intel Architecture 32 (IA-32) family. These CPUs all have similar capabilities and run more-or-less the same programs, although there are exceptions to this rule. Other architectures are available, though, and Linux runs on many of them. If you're planning to buy a new computer, you may want to consider some of these alternatives to the ubiquitous IA-32 systems. First, I'll explain the architectures of the most popular desktop computer CPUs, followed by some tips on choosing the right CPU for your needs.

IA-32, IA-64, X86-64, PPC, AND MORE

The most popular CPU architectures for desktop computers in 2003 are the following:

IA-32   These CPUs power the vast majority of computers sold from the late 1980s to the present. Intel, AMD, VIA, and Transmeta are selling IA-32 CPUs in 2003, and other companies have sold them in the past. The most popular IA-32 CPUs of late are Intel's Pentium 4, Intel's Celeron, AMD's Athlon, and AMD's Duron. The *32* in *IA-32* refers to the fact that these CPUs have 32-bit data busses, meaning that they move data in 32-bit chunks. This 32-bit architecture has been adequate for over a decade, but increases in RAM capacity and new concepts in low-level CPU design make it desirable to retire this venerable CPU line. In 2003, both Intel and AMD are pushing new 64-bit CPUs. Time will tell how successful each is in this endeavor.

NOTE   *Linus Torvalds, the creator of the Linux kernel, now works for Transmeta. Therefore, the Linux kernel includes unusually good support for some Transmeta CPU features. These CPUs are uncommon in desktop systems, though; they're most popular in portable devices.*

IA-64   Intel's 64-bit CPU architecture is known as *IA-64*, and it is being sold under the *Itanium* name. Itanium is a high-performance 64-bit architecture that's being targeted initially at the high-end workstation and server markets. As such, IA-64 systems tend to be expensive. The IA-64 CPU is capable of running IA-32 programs in a compatibility mode, but performance suffers greatly in this mode, and you can't run IA-64 and IA-32 programs at the same time. Aside from the IA-32 compatibility mode, the IA-64 was intended in part to discard much of the historical baggage that's accumulated with the IA-32 architecture over the years.

x86-64   AMD's 64-bit architecture goes by the name *x86-64*, with chips sold under the names *Opteron* and *Athlon 64*. As the name implies, x86-64 is a 64-bit derivative of the 32-bit x86 (IA-32) architecture. As such, it's a less drastic deviation from IA-32 than is IA-64, and performance when running IA-32 programs doesn't suffer greatly. It's also possible to run x86-64 and IA-32 programs side-by-side, which should make the transition from IA-32 to x86-64 relatively painless.

PowerPC   This CPU (often called *PPC*) was developed jointly by Motorola, Apple, and IBM as a successor to Motorola's 680x0 CPU series, which were most commonly found in Apple Macintoshes from the 1980s and early 1990s. PPC CPUs are common in more modern Macintoshes, in some IBM workstations, and in a few less mainstream systems, such as the AmigaOne. The PowerPC was originally designed as a 32-bit architecture with little historical baggage, unlike the IA-32 and x86-64 CPUs. A 64-bit version is now available, as well.

Alpha   The 64-bit Alpha CPU was originally developed by Digital Equipment Corporation (DEC), but DEC went out of business and Compaq bought much of DEC, including the rights to the Alpha CPU. With the merger of Compaq and Hewlett-Packard (HP) in 2002, the Alpha CPU now belongs to HP, but it appears that HP intends to let the design die. Alpha CPUs found their way into many high-performance workstations and servers, but they never became a viable competitor to IA-32 or PPC for most consumers.

MIPS   The MIPS CPU line includes both 32- and 64-bit variants. These CPUs are most commonly found in embedded devices, such as dedicated routers, digital cable boxes, digital video recorders, and video game systems. Some of these devices run Linux; therefore, Linux and MIPS are closely related—but in ways that are not obvious to most people.

SPARC SPARC and UltraSPARC CPUs are used by Sun in its workstations, which usually run Solaris. Linux can also run on most Sun workstations, so if you want to use an UltraSPARC CPU for a Linux workstation or server, you can.

CHOOSING THE RIGHT CPU

For the most part, you must obtain software that's been compiled for a specific architecture in order to use software on that computer. For instance, to run Linux on an iMac, you need a PPC Linux distribution. The same applies to specific programs. For instance, if you want to run WordPerfect, you can only do so on the IA-32 architecture, because WordPerfect is a commercial program that's only been released for IA-32 systems. Most Linux software is available with source code, though, and so it can be readily recompiled for any CPU type. Therefore, in many ways, the CPU family you use doesn't matter; you can run common software such as Apache, sendmail, Mozilla, and KMail on any architecture.

One important consideration concerning Linux and different CPUs is the availability of Linux distributions for various CPU types. Table 1.1 summarizes the availability of some of the most popular Linux distributions on various CPUs. At the time of writing, x86-64 support is lacking, but it's likely to materialize in 2003. In most cases, the non-IA-32 versions of distributions lag behind their IA-32 counterparts by a version or two—for instance, Mandrake 9.0 for IA-32 versus 8.2 for PPC. Overall, if you want to run Linux on a non-IA-32 architecture, Debian is the safest choice, although there are other options for some CPUs.

TABLE 1.1: LINUX DISTRIBUTIONS AND CPUS

CPU	DEBIAN	MANDRAKE	RED HAT	SLACKWARE	SUSE
IA-32	Y	Y	Y	Y	Y
IA-64	Y	-	Y	-	-
x86-64	Likely in 2003	Likely in 2003	Likely in 2003	-	Likely in 2003
PowerPC	Y	Y	-	-	Y
Alpha	Y	-	Y (very old)	-	Y
MIPS	Y	-	-	-	-
SPARC	Y	-	Y (very old)	-	-

CPUs differ in some performance details. In particular, the IA-32 architecture is notorious for poor floating-point math performance, which makes it a poor choice for certain types of scientific simulations, ray-tracing graphics, and other tools that perform heavy floating-point math computations. Details differ by specific CPU model, though. For most desktop and even server purposes, this limitation is unimportant.

CPU manufacturers often make a big deal of whether their CPUs use a traditional complex instruction set computer (CISC) design or a reduced instruction set computer (RISC) design. IA-32 and its derivatives use a CISC design, whereas PPC, Alpha, SPARC, and MIPS use RISC designs. (The IA-64 uses a mixed design.) CISC CPUs feature more complex instruction sets, and they require more clock cycles to execute a single instruction than do the simpler instructions in RISC architectures. Therefore, RISC CPUs can often do more at any given clock speed, as measured in megahertz (MHz), than can CISC CPUs—but other factors come into play, as well. For instance, some tasks require more operations to perform with a RISC CPU than with a CISC CPU.

TIP *When comparing CPU speeds, you should examine benchmarks designed for this purpose, not the CPUs' speeds in megahertz. Even within a CPU family, design differences between models make directly comparing CPU speeds tricky at best.*

One other CPU design factor deserves mention: *endianness*. This word refers to the way that data are stored within a single 32- or 64-bit word. Data are broken up into 8-bit bytes, which may be stored with the least significant bit (LSB) first (aka *little-endian*) or the most significant bit (MSB) first (aka *big-endian*). IA-32, its derivatives, and Alpha are little-endian architectures, but SPARC is big-endian, and PPC and MIPS can work in either mode. Which mode a CPU uses is unimportant in terms of performance, but this feature can sometimes have consequences if programs are written to assume one encoding method or another. For instance, if a program stores data files by dumping data structures directly to disk, those files may not be readable by the same program compiled on another architecture. Most programs are smart enough to detect this difference and compensate, but some (mostly little-known and specialized tools) aren't, so you should be aware of the problem.

WITHIN-FAMILY DIFFERENCES

CPU design isn't static. Over the years, each architecture has spawned multiple CPU designs. New models frequently introduce new features, typically while maintaining compatibility with older designs. Therefore, old software can run on new CPUs, but to take full advantage of the new CPUs, software must be recompiled. This recompilation sometimes makes binaries incompatible with the older CPUs. The upcoming section, "Improving Performance with Compile-Time Options," describes some of the specifics of how to do this job.

Within the IA-32 family, there are several different general levels of performance, which are often referred to by numbers that relate to Intel's original naming convention for these CPUs. The lowest-numbered IA-32 CPU is the i386. (Earlier CPUs in this line, such as the i286, used 16-bit architectures. These CPUs are x86 CPUs but not IA-32 CPUs.) Intel, AMD, and Cyrix (now bought out by VIA) all produced i386 and i486 CPUs. With the next level, Intel began naming its CPUs, starting with the Pentium; therefore, this CPU is sometimes called the i586. AMD and Cyrix also produced i586-level CPUs, although their design details differed from the Pentium's.

Today, the best IA-32 CPUs are the Pentium 4 and the AMD Athlon, while Intel's Celeron and AMD's Duron occupy a slightly lower tier. Each of these CPUs is more than capable of running Linux. Because new CPU models emerge so quickly, your best bet for obtaining relative performance information is to check magazine reviews or online hardware sites, such as Tom's Hardware Guide (`http://www.tomshardware.com`).

Linux software packages (described in more detail in Chapter 11, "Managing Packages") often include an architecture code in their filenames. For IA-32 systems, this code is usually i386, but it may be i586, i686, or even something more specific, such as athlon. Installing a package with a code for a lower-grade CPU than you own isn't a problem, but installing a package intended for a higher-grade CPU or a specific CPU from another manufacturer may cause poor performance or program crashes. For instance, you shouldn't try to use an athlon package on a Pentium-class or Pentium 4 CPU.

Improving Performance with Compile-Time Options

If you compile your own software, you can pass options to the compiler to have it optimize the resulting source code for a specific CPU model. For instance, if you have an Athlon, you might compile your software with Athlon optimizations. For most programs, these optimizations will yield only trivial performance improvements, but for some programs, the benefits can be more important. These critical packages include the Linux kernel, common system libraries such as libc, any CPU-intensive programs that your system runs frequently, and for workstations your X server and other core GUI tools. Most IA-32 distributions ship with i386 optimizations, which means the distributions work even on very old computers, but they may experience modest performance improvements if you recompile some of these critical components. Some distributions offer prebuilt kernel packages with CPU-specific optimizations, so you may want to use these kernels. Mandrake is unusual in that it builds everything with i586 optimizations, which provides a small performance boost.

If you want to compile your own software with optimizations, you need to pass the appropriate options to the compiler. The GNU Compiler Collection (GCC) supports two options for IA-32 CPU optimizations: -mcpu and -march. The former optimizes code for a specific CPU model, but it does so in a way that allows code to run on other CPU models. The latter option does more complete optimizations for a CPU in such a way that the code may not run on other (and particularly on older) CPUs. Both options take the name of a CPU as a parameter, as in -march=pentium4. Options are i386, i486, i586, i686, pentium, pentium-mmx, pentiumpro, pentium2, pentium3, pentium4, k6, k6-2, k6-3, athlon, athlon-tbird, athlon-4, athlon-xp, and athlon-mp. The i586 option is equivalent to pentium, and i686 is equivalent to pentiumpro.

In order to use these options, you can either compile code directly using GCC (as in **gcc -march=pentium4 myprog.c -o myprog**) or edit the Makefile for a package. Typically, a Makefile includes a line in which various GCC flags are defined, such as this:

```
CFLAGS= -O2 -Wall -I/usr/X11R6/include
```

You should change this line to add the appropriate optimization, as in:

```
CLFAGS= -O2 -march=pentium4 -Wall -I/usr/X11R6/include
```

In some cases, a Makefile will already specify an optimization, in which case you can change that default. Some packages have configuration tools that enable you to specify an optimization. Consult the package's documentation for details. (The next section, "Setting Kernel Options," includes information on optimizing the Linux kernel.)

In addition to CPU-specific optimizations, it's possible to tell GCC to optimize code in less CPU-specific ways. These optimizations may increase compile time, reduce the reliability of the debugger, or increase program size. These optimizations are specified with the -O (that's an uppercase letter O) option, followed by a number from 0 to 3, as in -O2 in the preceding examples. Increasing numbers represent increasing optimizations for execution speed. In addition, the -Os option optimizes the code to reduce its size.

NOTE *Most distributions today use Red Hat Package Manager (RPM) or Debian packages. (Slackware is a notable exception.) Rebuilding such software from source code packages may or may not optimize them for your CPU, depending upon the build scripts included in the source package. You may need to edit these scripts in order to rebuild a package with CPU-specific optimizations.*

Setting Kernel Options

Because all Linux software runs atop the kernel, the kernel's performance, and hence its optimizations, is particularly important. What's more, the kernel's configuration tools enable you to set its optimizations from a menu. Figure 1.1 shows this menu, obtained by typing `make xconfig` in the kernel source directory, for a 2.5-series kernel.

FIGURE 1.1

The Linux kernel provides many options related to the CPU.

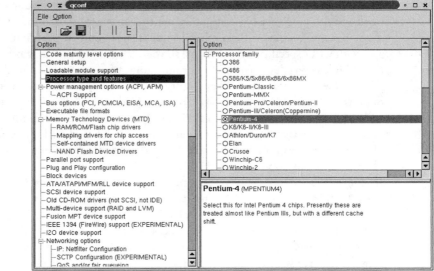

The Processor Type and Features option area contains kernel settings related to the CPU type and related options. Other options include:

SMP Support *Symmetric Multi-Processing (SMP)* refers to a computer with multiple CPUs. The kernel requires special support to take advantage of more than one CPU per computer.

APIC Support The *Advanced Programmable Interrupt Controller (APIC)* is an interrupt controller built into some CPUs, as opposed to built into the motherboard chipset. Select this option if your CPU supports this feature.

Machine Check Exception Motherboards and CPUs increasingly support hardware problem-detection circuitry. This option adds support for some such tools, such as temperature sensors that detect when the computer is overheating.

CPU Frequency Scaling   Some CPUs support changing their clock speeds "on the fly," which can be useful for conserving battery life on laptops. Select this option (in the Power Management Options area) to add support for this feature. Check `http://www.brodo.de/cpufreq/` for more information.

Laptop Support   Some laptops provide software "hooks" to enable an OS to check on the CPU's status and power management. You can compile support for these hooks into the kernel.

Device Interfaces   Some device files in the `/dev/cpu` directory provide access to the CPU, but only if you enable the appropriate support in the kernel.

High Memory Support   There are three settings for high-memory support: Off supports machines with less than one gigabyte of RAM, 4GB supports one to four gigabytes, and 64GB supports more than four gigabytes.

Math Emulation   The i386, some i486, and some early Pentium clone CPUs lacked a floating-point unit (FPU), aka a math coprocessor. Some Linux software relies upon the presence of an FPU, so the kernel includes an option to emulate one when it's not present. You only need to include this support if your CPU is a very old one that lacks an integrated FPU and if you haven't added a separate FPU chip to the motherboard.

MTRR Support   Intel's Pentium Pro and later CPUs offer a feature called *Memory Type Range Register (MTRR)*, which improves support for access to memory that's shared between the CPU and some other device. This configuration is most common on laptops and other computers with video hardware integrated into the motherboard. To enable this support, you must compile support for it into the kernel.

NOTE   *If you're using a 2.4.x or earlier kernel, the configuration tool looks different from the one shown in Figure 1.1, but it provides many of the same options.*

Kernel configuration is a very important topic in and of itself. Chapter 15, "Creating a Custom Kernel," describes the process in more detail.

Getting the Best Video Performance

Users interact with their workstations via their keyboards, mice, and monitors. The monitors, in turn, are controlled by the computer's video card. Today, use of GUI environments such as the X Window System (X for short) is ubiquitous on workstations. Such environments demand that the video card be capable of displaying high-resolution (typically 1024 × 768 or greater), high bit-depth (16-bit or greater) graphics. X uses this display to create windows and all the trimmings. All modern mainstream video cards can meet this minimal requirement. More critical means of differentiating hardware, therefore, include the extent to which video cards can exceed these minimum requirements and how fast the cards display text and graphics. These measures are influenced both by the cards' hardware and by their X drivers.

Important and Unimportant Video Card Features

Walk into a computer superstore, or even an office supply store, and you're likely to see shelves stacked with video cards costing $100 or more. What would such an expenditure buy, though? Is it really necessary? Features that are common on high-end video cards include:

Fast Video Bus   Most video cards sold today use the *Accelerated Graphics Port (AGP)* bus. This bus was designed for use by high-speed video cards, and modern motherboards include an AGP bus for video cards. Older video cards use the *Peripheral Component Interconnect (PCI)* bus, which is still used by most nonvideo plug-in cards; or even slower busses, such as the *Industry Standard Architecture (ISA)* bus.

Multiple Outputs   Some high-end video cards support multiple outputs—for instance, to handle both a monitor and a television. This feature is useful in certain specialized situations, but most Linux workstations don't need it.

2D Acceleration   Video cards use on-board memory to store a bitmap of the entire screen. X can modify this RAM more-or-less directly to create windows, display text, and so on; but this process consumes a lot of CPU time and bandwidth on the video bus. A quicker approach is to include enough smarts on the video board itself to draw specific shapes in response to simple commands from the X server. This feature is known as 2D acceleration, and it's present in all modern video cards. Some do better 2D acceleration than others, though.

3D Acceleration   The area of greatest improvement in video card designs over the past few years has been in 3D acceleration. This feature enables a video card to create a 2D representation of a 3D object. As with 2D acceleration, the computer's main CPU can perform this task, but it's more efficient to pass this task off to a dedicated video processor. This feature is most commonly used by video games, many of which present first-person views. In Linux, 3D acceleration requires support by a 3D graphics library such as Mesa (`http://mesa3d.sourceforge.net`), which in turn is an open-source implementation of the OpenGL (`http://www.opengl.org`) specification.

Lots of RAM   The larger your video display and the greater the color depth, the more RAM a video card requires to support the display. It's almost impossible to buy a new video card today that comes with less than 32MB of RAM. As Table 1.2 shows, this amount of RAM is more than enough for even very high-resolution 2D displays. Video cards with more RAM use the extra memory mainly to support their 3D acceleration features.

TABLE 1.2: RAM REQUIREMENTS FOR VARIOUS VIDEO RESOLUTIONS, IN KILOBYTES

RESOLUTION	8-BIT	16-BIT	24-BIT	32-BIT
640 × 480	300	600	900	1,200
800 × 600	469	938	1,406	1,875
1024 × 768	768	1,536	2,304	3,072
1280 × 1024	1,280	2,560	3,840	5,120
1600 × 1200	1,875	3,750	5,625	7,500
1920 × 1440	2,700	5,400	8,100	10,800

NOTE Color depth *is the number of bits of data devoted to describing the color of each pixel. An 8-bit display provides 2^8, or 256, possible colors per pixel; and a 24-bit display provides 2^{24}, or 16,777,216, colors per pixel. As a general rule, X works best with 16-bit (65,536-color) or greater color depth.*

Of these features, none is truly required for X operation. Even many ancient unaccelerated ISA video cards will work with X—although most modern motherboards lack the ISA slots needed by such outmoded cards! In practice, for basic desktop use in Linux, most modern video cards will work. RAM beyond 32MB (or even 10MB) and flashy 3D acceleration features aren't needed even for very large and color-heavy display modes. If you play first-person perspective video games or run some of the rare business or scientific applications that take advantage of OpenGL/Mesa 3D acceleration, you may want to examine video cards for which Linux Mesa support is available and pay attention to benchmark numbers for these video cards. Unfortunately, benchmarks in mainstream computer magazines are likely to use Windows applications, and Linux performance may not track Windows performance very closely. Fortunately, various people have posted Linux Mesa benchmarks online, including the Jongl benchmark page (`http://www.jongl.de/benchmarks.html`) and various reviews and articles at Linux Games (`http://www.linuxgames.com`).

Unfortunately, few reviews focus upon 2D performance, so if you're shopping for a card to use in a workstation, finding relevant performance information can be difficult. The good news is that 2D acceleration is common and very good on most video cards, so the lack of performance reviews isn't as serious a problem as it might be. You should, however, check on the status of X drivers for any card you're considering, as described in the next section, "Supported and Unsupported Video Card Features." Watch for words like "unaccelerated support" in X driver descriptions; this means that the card's 2D acceleration features are unused.

If a Linux computer is to be used as a server, even an ancient text-only video card should be fine. With the possible exception of initial setup, you don't need to run X on server computers. Therefore, you should buy the least expensive video card you can find.

Most laptop computers and even some desktop systems come with video circuitry integrated on the motherboard. Such systems can be convenient to buy, but they're risky because adding a video card to such a system can be tricky or impossible if the on-board video doesn't work. When buying such systems, you should be very careful to make sure your video hardware will be adequate, both in terms of features and in terms of X driver support. Also, some such systems use part of the computer's main memory as video RAM. For instance, if a computer has 128MB of RAM, you may have to set aside 4MB of that RAM to run a 1024 × 768 display at 32-bit color depth (see Table 1.2; the amount of RAM set aside is typically rounded up to the nearest power-of-two value in megabytes). Worse than this loss of RAM is the fact that the RAM on the motherboard is typically of a different type than the RAM on a video card. Standard motherboard RAM produces less-than-optimal performance with video card circuitry.

Supported and Unsupported Video Card Features

Overall, the most important criterion when purchasing a video card for use on a Linux workstation is the quality of the X driver support for the card. There are three main sources of drivers:

XFree86   The XFree86 package (`http://www.xfree86.org`) comes with all mainstream Linux distributions as the standard X server. XFree86, in turn, comes with drivers for a wide variety of video cards. These standard XFree86 drivers support 2D operation, including 2D acceleration modes for many cards. Not all drivers support 2D acceleration, though—even when those features are available on the hardware. As a general rule, support is best for cards that are a generation or more behind the latest models; this time lag enables XFree86 developers to implement acceleration features in their drivers. Consult the release notes for your version of XFree86 for details.

Video Card Manufacturers   Some video card manufacturers now release X drivers for their cards. These drivers may support acceleration before the official XFree86 drivers do, so it's worth checking with your video card manufacturer if you find you've got a video card that doesn't perform as well under Linux as you'd like.

Mesa   The Mesa project provides 3D acceleration under X. Mesa 3D acceleration drivers are available for just a small subset of the cards for which 2D acceleration drivers are available. Therefore, it's critically important that you check for these drivers before buying a card to be used with 3D Mesa applications.

Speeding Up X: Setting XFree86 Options

Chapter 16, "Optimizing X Configuration," describes how to set up X to get the most from your video card. It also includes many nonperformance tips, such as information on improving the appearance of fonts under X. For the moment, though, there are a few rules of thumb you can use to get X working at least tolerably well:

Try Multiple X Servers   XFree86 underwent a major architectural change between the 3.x and 4.x versions; with 3.x, drivers were integrated with *X servers*—programs that mediate the interaction between the display and individual programs. Therefore, you'd run a different X server for, say, an ATI board than for a Matrox board. With XFree86 4.0, a single X server was developed that loads drivers for specific video hardware. This change meant, though, that a lot of the old XFree86 3.x driver code had to be rewritten. As of XFree86 4.2, not all of the 4.x drivers are up to the standards of the older 3.x code. Therefore, you may want to try a 3.3.6 X server if you have problems with your video card under XFree86 4.x.

Research Driver Options   The `XF86Config` file (usually stored in `/etc` or `/etc/X11`) controls XFree86, including passing options to the video drivers. Some of these drivers may influence performance, and so you may want to study them.

Use Low Color Depths   X can run on a 1-bit display, but it's best to use at least 16 bits to get reasonable color fidelity from most programs. Beyond this value, improvements are modest for many purposes. Higher color depths, though, increase the work required to manipulate the display, and can therefore reduce performance. Reducing the color depth (done by setting the `DefaultDepth` option in the `Screen` section of the `XF86Config` file) may improve your video performance.

Taming Hardware via Drivers

All operating systems (OSs) use drivers to connect hardware to software. Drivers enable an OS to provide a consistent set of software interfaces for hardware to user programs, thereby simplifying application design compared to a direct-access approach. By requiring user programs to go through the OS to access hardware, drivers also help to keep multiple programs from interfering with each other's use of hardware devices. Unfortunately, the plethora of hardware available for modern computers, particularly in the IA-32 world, means that a huge number of drivers are required. This in turn can cause problems because sometimes it's difficult to identify and install drivers. Fortunately, knowing a bit about the Linux driver situation helps immensely.

NOTE *This section and its subsections describe drivers that are part of the Linux kernel. Some other devices—most notably video cards, mice, printers, and scanners—require driver support in user-space programs, such as XFree86, Ghostscript, or Scanner Access Now Easy (SANE). These drivers are covered in more detail in subsequent chapters of this book, including Chapter 3, "Using External Peripherals," Chapter 13, "Managing Printers," and Chapter 16, "Optimizing X Configuration."*

Identifying the Correct Drivers

The first hurdle that must be overcome when installing a driver is in identifying the correct driver to use. Modern Linux distributions go to great lengths to identify your hardware upon installation, but they sometimes miss or misidentify a component. You may also need to know what to use if you add a new device or recompile your kernel. Identifying the drivers actually involves two steps:

◆ Identifying the hardware

◆ Identifying the drivers that go with the hardware

IDENTIFYING HARDWARE

A *chipset* is a set of one or more chips that provide a device's core functionality. Typically, a manufacturer purchases a chipset from another company, attaches chips to a circuit board, and sells the product under its own name. Because devices from different manufacturers that use the same chipset require the same driver code, most Linux drivers are named after the chipsets they serve, not the individual device manufacturers. Some manufacturers develop their own chipsets and sell boards based on them. You can use several different strategies to identify your hardware's chipset:

Documentation If you're lucky, your device's documentation will identify the chipset it uses. This documentation may be a paper manual, a README file on a driver disk, or a web page. You might also be able to glean information from configuration files for another OS's drivers provided by a manufacturer. Some manufacturers provide Linux drivers for their products. These drivers are typically just the standard Linux drivers, sometimes renamed. If your manufacturer provides such drivers, look for similar drivers in the Linux kernel source tree.

Visual Inspection You can often learn a lot about a device by looking at it with your own eyes. Locate the largest chips and note any markings on them. For instance, Figure 1.2 shows a large chip on an Ultra100 ATA controller card. This chip is marked as a Promise PDC20267. Sometimes, chips are covered by paper stickers with the name of the board manufacturer. These stickers can be safely peeled away. Heat sinks appear on some motherboard and video card chips. They should *not* be removed; doing so could damage the chip, or make it difficult to reaffix the heat sink so that it does its job properly.

FIGURE 1.2

Device chips are
often marked to
identify the chipset.

Linux Identification   When Linux boots, it tries to identify most devices that are on or are connected directly to the motherboard. You can tap into these identifications in several ways. One is to use the `dmesg` command, which echoes startup messages. This command typically produces a lot of output, so piping it through `less`, as in **`dmesg | less`**, is a good idea. You can also use the `/proc` filesystem, which is described in more detail in the upcoming section, "Demystifying the `/proc` Filesystem." GUI interfaces to `/proc`, such as the `harddrake2` tool that ships with Mandrake (shown in Figure 1.3) or similar tools accessible from the GNOME or KDE systems in most distributions, can also be helpful. Unfortunately, none of these methods works well if you're having problems activating a device, but they might be useful if you want to record this information for future reference.

FIGURE 1.3

Most distributions
provide GUI inter-
faces to `/proc`
to enable you to
easily identify
most hardware.

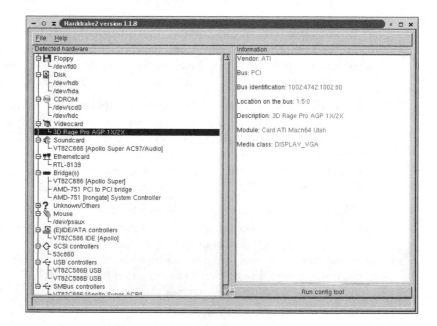

Alternative OS Identification   Non-Linux OSs provide tools similar to the `harddrake2` tool shown in Figure 1.3. For instance, Figure 1.4 shows the Windows 2000 Device Manager, which provides information on all the devices that are properly installed in Windows. One limitation of such tools is that they sometimes identify the device by the board's brand name rather than the chipset name.

FIGURE 1.4

Many non-Linux OSs provide GUI tools to enable you to identify most hardware.

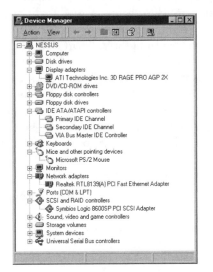

Web Searches   Some methods may provide incomplete or even potentially misleading information. You can improve matters by identifying your hardware in multiple ways and by performing web searches on whatever information you have. Use web search engines and Usenet archive sites, such as Google Groups (`http://groups.google.com`). With any luck, you'll be able to uncover some useful information.

MATCHING HARDWARE TO DRIVERS

After you've identified a chipset, you need to match that chipset to an appropriate Linux driver. If you're recompiling the kernel, this task usually involves reading the descriptions for various devices in the relevant category until you find a match. Even if you're not installing a new kernel, this approach can be useful. Locate your device in a kernel configuration tool and make note of what it's called in that tool. Your driver is probably called something similar to this.

You can also try searching through the kernel source code. For instance, suppose you want to identify the driver that supports the Promise PDC20267 chip shown in Figure 1.2. You could use `grep` to locate files in the `/usr/src/linux/drivers/ide` directory tree that contain this number:

```
$ cd /usr/src/linux/drivers/ide
$ grep -r "20267" ./
./pci/pdc202xx_old.h:  .device = PCI_DEVICE_ID_PROMISE_20267,
./pci/pdc202xx_old.h:  .name  = "PDC20267",
./pci/pdc202xx_old.c:  case  PCI_DEVICE_ID_PROMISE_20267:
```

> **NOTE**   *The* `/usr/src/linux` *directory is often a symbolic link to a directory named after a specific kernel version, such as* `/usr/src/linux-2.4.20`. *Red Hat uses* `/usr/src/linux-2.4` *instead of* `/usr/src/linux` *for its symbolic link to 2.4-series kernels.*

In this example, the `pdc202xx_old` driver should do the job. Given the filename, you might also try the `pdc202xx_new` driver, despite the fact that it doesn't contain the string `20267`.

As with chipset identification, matching hardware can benefit by a web search. This is particularly likely when you need to resort to third-party drivers, such as the alternative sound drivers described in the upcoming section, "When Standard Drivers Aren't Enough."

It's possible you'll find a match to a driver in the kernel source tree but you won't find a driver module precompiled by your distribution vendor. In some cases, this means that the driver's been compiled directly into the main kernel file. This practice is common with EIDE and SCSI drivers, because Linux needs access to these drivers when booting. Other times, the driver might be obsolete or might have been omitted because the device is very rare. In such cases, you may need to recompile your kernel, or at least that one device file, in order to use the device.

Brute Force: Building Drivers into the Kernel

One approach to loading drivers is to build them into the main Linux kernel file. When so configured, Linux should load the driver and detect the hardware when the system boots. In most cases, no other configuration is required for basic hardware functionality, although you may need to configure user software to take advantage of the hardware. For instance, you may need to add entries to `/etc/fstab` in order to use partitions on a SCSI hard disk, or you may need to tell your system its IP address and related information in order to use an Ethernet card.

To build a driver into the kernel, you must recompile the kernel. Chapter 15 describes kernel configuration in more detail. If the driver isn't part of the standard kernel, you must patch the kernel source code to include a new driver. Drivers that are designed to be used in this way come with instructions for performing this operation. Some drivers aren't designed to be so included, so you must compile and use them as modules.

On rare occasions, it's necessary to pass parameters to a driver for it to work correctly. This is most likely to be necessary when using old ISA cards, which sometimes aren't auto-detected by the kernel, especially if they're configured using unusual hardware settings. To pass parameters for drivers that are compiled into the main kernel file, you must modify your boot loader. The procedure for doing so depends on which boot loader you're using:

LILO   If you're using the older Linux Loader (LILO) boot loader, you can add an `append` line to the configuration for your Linux kernel in `lilo.conf`. This line looks something like `append="0,0x240,eth0"`.

GRUB   If you're using the Grand Unified Bootloader (GRUB), add the parameters to the end of the `kernel` line in the `grub.conf` file. For instance, this line might read `kernel /boot/bzImage ro root=/dev/hda6 0,0x240,eth0`.

The details of what you can pass to the kernel vary from one device to another, so you should consult the driver's documentation for details. These specific examples tell Linux to use I/O port 0x240 for the first Ethernet card. After you've compiled a new kernel, modified the configuration file, and in the case of LILO, reinstalled the boot loader by typing **lilo**, you must reboot your computer in order to use the new kernel and pass it the new parameters. The tedium of doing this can be a problem if you need to experiment with settings, which is one of the reasons that kernel modules are popular—you can load and unload kernel modules at will without rebooting the computer.

Subtle and Flexible: Loading Drivers as Modules

Most Linux distributions ship with as many drivers as possible compiled as modules. This approach saves memory, because unused drivers need not consume RAM as part of the kernel. Reducing the size of the main kernel file also makes it possible to fit the kernel on a single floppy disk, which is an important consideration for installation and emergency recovery systems. The use of kernel modules also makes for a more flexible system for handling drivers—the Linux installer can set itself up to use whatever drivers are appropriate, and adjusting the system for a new hardware configuration becomes a matter of changing configuration files. You can also add precompiled kernel modules to a computer without recompiling the kernel or even rebooting the system. You can load modules manually for testing purposes, or you can configure the system so that it automatically loads the correct modules when it boots or on an as-needed basis.

LOADING DRIVERS MANUALLY

Linux provides several commands for managing modules:

insmod   This command loads a single module. You can specify the module by its module name or by its filename. For instance, **insmod via-rhine** loads the via-rhine.o module (it may be compressed with gzip, and hence be called via-rhine.o.gz). Kernel modules are stored in subdirectories of /lib/modules/*version*, where *version* is the Linux kernel version. The problem with the insmod command is that it often fails because of unmet dependencies—the module may rely upon features that aren't present in the kernel or any loaded modules. To overcome such problems, you must load the missing modules. The modprobe command makes this task easier.

modprobe   This command loads a module and all the modules upon which it depends. It works much like insmod, but it's less likely to fail because of unmet dependencies.

depmod   In order to load all depended-upon modules, modprobe relies upon a catalog of module dependencies. This catalog is created with the depmod command. Specifically, typing **depmod -a** creates the catalog in /lib/modules/*version*/modules.dep, where *version* is the kernel version number. This command normally appears in a startup script, such as /etc/rc.sysinit or /etc/init.d/boot.localfs. Thus, you shouldn't need to type this command unless you update your modules and don't want to reboot.

rmmod   This command unloads kernel modules; it's the opposite of insmod. If you add the -r or --stacks option, the command deletes a set of modules—essentially, the command works as the opposite of modprobe rather than of insmod.

All of these commands support several options that influence their behavior. One of the most important of these options is the -k or --autoclean option to insmod and modprobe. This option sets the auto-clean flag on the installed module or modules. This flag causes the kerneld daemon, if it's running, to remove the module automatically after a period of time (generally about a minute) if it's unused. This practice can help keep modules from consuming memory if they're used for brief periods of time, but if you load modules manually, it can be an inconvenience to have to load them again.

Another important `insmod` and `modprobe` option is `-f` or `--force`. Ordinarily, Linux will load only modules that match the version of the running kernel. This option will attempt to force a module load even if the version number doesn't match. This option is often necessary when using drivers provided with commercial software such as VMware. It doesn't always work, though, particularly when the version numbers differ greatly, such as a driver for a 2.2.x kernel loaded on a 2.4.x kernel.

As a general rule, you'll load drivers manually only when you're testing them or debugging a system—for instance, if a driver fails to load, you might try loading it manually to identify the problem. You'll then configure the system to load the driver automatically, as described in the next section. In some cases, though, you might write a script to load a driver prior to performing some task, and then unload the driver afterward. You might do this if you have problems with the automatic kernel loading and unloading.

LOADING DRIVERS AUTOMATICALLY

The Linux kernel includes a configuration option called *kernel module loader*. If this option is compiled into the kernel, it will attempt to load modules on an as-needed basis. For instance, if you try to play an audio file, the kernel will attempt to load the appropriate sound card drivers for your system. In order for this feature to work, though, the kernel needs information on which modules to load for specific tasks.

The `/etc/modules.conf` file is the master control file for automatic handling of kernel modules. It's also used by `insmod`, `modprobe`, and `depmod`, although these tools aren't as dependent upon `modules.conf` as is the kernel module auto-loader. The `modules.conf` file is a text file that contains a series of lines that provide information on the modules to load for specific device types (such as sound or SCSI devices), options to pass to those modules, and so on. Listing 1.1 shows a simple `modules.conf` file.

LISTING 1.1: A SAMPLE `modules.conf` FILE

```
alias eth0 tulip
alias eth1 via-rhine
post-install via-rhine /usr/local/bin/setup-eth1
alias char-major-10-219 mwave
options mwave dspirq=10 dspio=0x130 uartirq=3 uartio=0x2f8
```

Debian uses a variant on this approach: It uses an `/etc/modutils` directory tree that contains a series of files for individual devices. (Most drivers are defined in files in `/etc/modutils/arch`.) After editing a file in this directory or creating a new one for a new device, type **update-modules** to update the module information, creating a new `/etc/modules.conf` file.

The `modules.conf` file supports a fairly large number of features, including conditional statements to configure certain drivers only if certain preconditions exist, such as only if the system is running a particular kernel version. The features illustrated by Listing 1.1 will accomplish a great deal, though. These features are

alias   The `alias` keyword at the start of a line maps a specific device type, such as an Ethernet interface, to a specific driver. The first two lines of Listing 1.1, for instance, tell Linux to use the `tulip` driver for `eth0` and the `via-rhine` driver for `eth1`. Not all device names are intuitively obvious, though; for instance, the fourth line of Listing 1.1 tells the system to use the `mwave` driver for `char-major-10-219`. This driver is for IBM's Mwave chipset, which provides both audio and modem functionality. It's mapped to specific major and minor device numbers rather than a device name like `eth0` or `scsi`.

options   You can pass options to drivers loaded as modules by including an `options` line in the `modules.conf` file. Listing 1.1 illustrates this capability with an `options` line for the `mwave` module. After the keyword `options` and the module name, the options passed to the module are very module-specific. You should consult your driver's documentation to learn what options it supports.

Outside Command Specifications   Listing 1.1's `post-install` specification is one of several keywords that can be used to run arbitrary programs before or after installing or uninstalling modules. The other keywords are `pre-install`, `pre-remove`, and `post-remove`. Begin a line with the keyword, then provide the module name, and then provide the external command. You could use this feature to automate features such as bringing up a network interface that's frequently not installed (for example, a USB network interface on a laptop) or to adjust mixer settings after loading a sound card's drivers.

If you're having problems with a driver for a device that should be supported by Linux out of the box, your best bet is to first use `insmod` or `modprobe` to try to get the appropriate module loaded. Checking on loaded modules in `/proc/modules`, as described in the upcoming section, "Demystifying the `/proc` Filesystem," can also be a useful diagnostic tool. Once you've discovered what modules need to be loaded, try creating entries for these modules in `/etc/modules.conf`. Assuming your kernel includes module auto-loader support, the drivers should then load automatically when you next boot or attempt to use the drivers in question.

If you've obtained drivers from a third-party source and need to integrate them into your system, the documentation that came with those drivers should include information on `/etc/module.conf` entries. Add those entries, and be sure your current `modules.conf` file doesn't include conflicting entries. If it does, comment those entries out by adding a hash mark (#) to the start of each conflicting line.

When modules depend upon other modules, it's important that `/etc/modules.conf` includes `alias` lines for all of the dependent modules. The `/proc/modules` pseudo-file can be very useful in finding all of these modules, assuming you've gotten the device working via `insmod` or `modprobe`. Type **cat /proc/modules**, and you'll see a series of output lines resembling the following:

```
parport      22528  2 (autoclean) [parport_pc lp]
```

The `lsmod` command produces similar output. The module names in square brackets (`[]`) at the end of the line are those that depend upon the main module (`parport` in this case). In other words, any `alias` line loading a driver for `lp` or `parport_pc` in this example must be preceded in `/etc/modules.conf` by a line that loads `parport`.

TIP   *If you create an* /etc/modules.conf *file and it doesn't seem to work, try manually loading each module the file references with* insmod *(not* modprobe*). If you receive a dependency error message when loading a module, track down the out-of-order or missing module and change or add its reference in* modules.conf.

Delivering Clear Sound

One perennial problem for Linux is sound. Sound hardware is quite varied, and as Linux often functions as a server OS, development of audio drivers and their integration into Linux distributions hasn't received the attention of some other hardware types. As a result, getting sound working can often be much tougher than getting other types of hardware working. The good news is that, by digging into a few configuration files, you can often get sound working. In a few cases, though, this isn't enough, and you'll need to locate nonstandard audio drivers or replace the sound card entirely.

Diagnosing and Fixing Sound Problems

Some Linux distributions, including Mandrake, Red Hat, and SuSE, attempt to detect and configure sound drivers upon system installation. Unfortunately, these attempts often fail. Desktop environments for such distributions sometimes include links to GUI utilities for configuring the sound card, but these tools seldom fare any better than the install-time detection and configuration. The result is that, if you don't get sound when you first start Linux, you'll almost certainly have to dig into the configuration files for sound modules, or perhaps even recompile your Linux kernel, as described in Chapter 15.

Before taking these drastic measures, though, you should take a few diagnostic steps. The most important of these steps relate to the presence of appropriate audio driver modules. Review the earlier section, "Taming Hardware via Drivers," and try installing drivers for your sound card using insmod or modprobe. If this step works and sound begins working, review your /etc/modules.conf file to be sure it includes appropriate alias lines for your hardware.

Be sure that /etc/modules.conf includes lines not just for the final sound driver, but for all those upon which it depends. Some sound card drivers depend upon many layers of sound-related drivers. This feature is particularly common with the Advanced Linux Sound Architecture (ALSA) drivers, which are described in more detail in the upcoming section, "ALSA Drivers."

Another common sound problem lies in *mixer* settings. A mixer is a tool that adjusts the volume of the various inputs and outputs on a sound card. It's possible that your system's sound drivers are loaded and working but that you're getting no sound because the mixer levels are set very low or the output channel is muted. Two common GUI mixers are KMix and GNOME Volume Control, which come with KDE and GNOME, respectively. Figure 1.5 shows the GNOME Volume Control mixer. Different sound cards and drivers support different inputs and outputs, so yours may not exactly match those shown the figure. The leftmost pair of sliders adjusts the master volume, and the other sliders adjust specific inputs and outputs. Be sure all levels are set high enough that they generate output and that the master, PCM, and any other levels are not muted. Similarly, be sure your speakers are plugged in, turned on, and (if applicable) that their volume knobs are set high enough for them to produce sound.

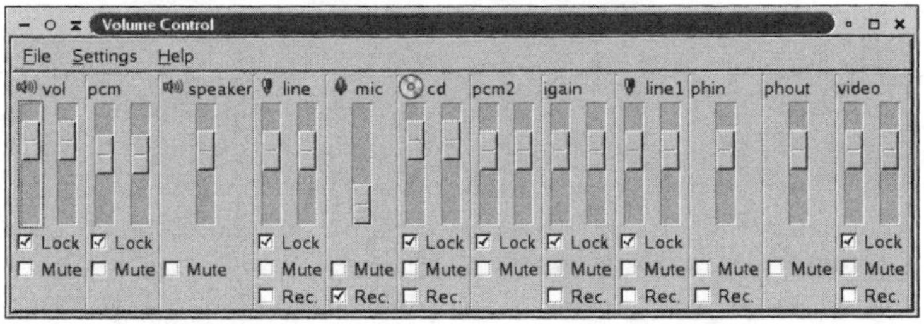

FIGURE 1.5

Mixers provide the means to adjust the volume coming from a sound card.

If you get output when you play a sound, but if it's too fast, too slow, or an obnoxious screech, it's likely that you're trying to play an audio file using a program that doesn't support the specific audio type. For instance, the audio player may not support the encoding bit rate, and so will play the sound back too fast or too slow. Try another program to play back the file; or if it's a test file, try another file, preferably from a different source. Sometimes, such problems can be caused by driver deficiencies. Switching drivers, as described in the next section, "When Standard Drivers Aren't Enough," may fix the problem.

When Standard Drivers Aren't Enough

Unfortunately, the Linux kernel doesn't ship with drivers for all sound cards; some aren't supported or are supported only minimally. For instance, a sound card might work only in 8-bit SoundBlaster mode, which will produce poor or no output from many audio files. In such cases, you may need to look to third-party sources for sound drivers or replace the sound card entirely.

COMMERCIAL OSS DRIVERS

The sound drivers included with the Linux kernel through the 2.4.*x* series are open source derivatives of drivers known collectively as the *Open Sound System (OSS)* drivers. The original OSS developers also make a set of drivers available commercially. These commercial OSS drivers are derived from the same code base that yielded the standard kernel drivers, but the two driver sets have diverged over time, so the commercial OSS drivers offer some advantages over the standard kernel OSS drivers. Most importantly, the commercial OSS drivers support some sound cards that aren't supported by the kernel drivers. The commercial drivers also ship with installation utilities that may (or may not) work better than the auto-detection tools provided with your Linux distribution.

You can obtain the commercial OSS drivers from 4Front Technologies (`http://www.opensound.com`). You can obtain an evaluation copy of the 4Front drivers from their web site. This copy will work for a limited period of time, then it will disable itself. The package includes an installer utility and precompiled binary kernel modules. If your sound card is a basic low-end model, the drivers may cost more than the card, but it may be simpler to install commercial OSS drivers than to replace the card, particularly if the sound card is integrated on the motherboard and you lack a free slot for a replacement card. The OSS drivers may also be worthwhile if your sound card is an expensive model with advanced features supported by the drivers.

ALSA DRIVERS

The ALSA project (`http://www.alsa-project.org`) has long provided an alternative to the kernel's standard OSS drivers. ALSA provides a low-level program audio interface that's different from that provided by the standard kernel and commercial OSS drivers, but ALSA also provides a compatibility layer so that it can work with software written with the OSS drivers in mind. ALSA also provides a different mix of supported devices than either the kernel or commercial OSS drivers, so it's possible ALSA is the only choice for your hardware.

Although ALSA is not part of the standard Linux kernel, as of the 2.4.x series, some distributions ship with ALSA support. Specifically, Debian, Mandrake, and SuSE deliver ALSA support. Therefore, if you use these distributions, using ALSA should be fairly straightforward—the ALSA drivers may be the default drivers, although in some cases the ALSA drivers are used only if kernel OSS drivers aren't available or are deficient in some way.

The 2.5.x development kernels have absorbed ALSA. With these kernels, you can select either the old open source OSS drivers or the ALSA drivers as part of the kernel configuration. Therefore, future versions of Linux should all include ALSA support out of the box.

If you're using a distribution that doesn't ship with ALSA and if you're using a 2.4.x or earlier kernel, you must install and configure the ALSA drivers to use them. This process can be a bit tedious, but in many cases it's worth doing. The procedure is as follows:

1. Recompile your kernel or install the kernel source package for your distribution. ALSA relies upon the presence of kernel source code, including all dependency information generated by compiling the kernel. If you recompile your kernel, be sure to select the sound core support, but do not build any drivers for your sound card into the kernel proper. If you recompile the kernel, reboot into your new kernel before proceeding.

2. Obtain the ALSA source code. You'll need three source code packages—`alsa-driver`, `alsa-libs`, and `alsa-utils`. Version 0.9.0 and later packages provide `alsa-tools` and `alsa-oss`, but these packages deliver supplemental tools that aren't needed for basic operation.

3. Extract all three source code packages into an appropriate location, such as `/usr/src`. For instance, from `/usr/src`, you might type **tar xvjf ~/alsa-driver-*version*.tar.bz2**, where *version* is the ALSA version number, to extract the `alsa-driver` source code.

4. Run the `configure` script in the `alsa-driver` source directory to configure the package. The `configure` script supports various options. Table 1.3 summarizes some of these options. For instance, to compile the drivers with support for ISA plug-and-play (PnP) devices, you would type **./configure --with-isapnp=yes**.

TIP   Compiling all of the ALSA drivers takes a long time. If you're positive you know which driver you need, use the `--with-cards` *option, as in* `--with-cards=via82xx`. *You can find a list of modules in the* `configure` *script itself; search for the string* `--with-cards` *to find the list. This practice speeds up compilation and reduces clutter in your compiled kernel modules directory.*

TABLE 1.3: POPULAR ALSA DRIVER CONFIGURATION OPTIONS

configure PARAMETER	TAKES OPTIONS	DEFAULT OPTION	EFFECT
--with-debug	none, basic, memory, full, or detect	none	Sets debugging level
--with-isapnp	yes, no, or auto	yes	Enables auto-detection of ISA PnP boards
--with-sequencer	yes or no	yes	Enables support for Musical Instrument Digital Interface (MIDI) sequencer
--with-oss	yes or no	yes	Enables OSS compatibility code
--with-cards	Driver names	All drivers	Compiles the specified set of drivers

5. Type **make** in the alsa-driver directory to build the driver source code.

6. Type **make install** as root in the alsa-driver directory to install the ALSA drivers.

7. Type **depmod -a** as root to create entries for the new ALSA drivers in the module dependency file. (This step isn't necessary for 0.9.0 and later versions.)

8. Type **./snddevices** as root in the alsa-driver directory to create device file entries for the ALSA drivers.

9. Repeat Steps 4 through 6 in the alsa-lib and alsa-utils directories, in that order. The configure scripts in these directories support fewer options than the one in the alsa-driver directory; in particular, there's no need to specify a sound card in any of these cases.

10. Type **modprobe *sound-driver***, where *sound-driver* is the name of your ALSA sound driver module, as root. This command should load the relevant ALSA sound driver and any dependent modules.

11. Type **modprobe snd-pcm-oss** and **modprobe snd-mixer-oss** as root to load the OSS compatibility modules, if desired.

12. Launch a sound mixer application and adjust the volume levels so that you can hear sounds. ALSA ships with all channels muted by default, so this step is critically important. It's also a step that many new ALSA users overlook.

13. Test the driver by playing a sound. The aplay command plays a simple sound, such as a .wav file, via the ALSA interface. You can use tools such as Ogg Vorbis players or CD players to test other features, including OSS compatibility. Once you're satisfied that everything is working, check the ALSA documentation (http://www.alsa-project.org/alsa-doc/) for information on the appropriate /etc/modules.conf entries for your driver. Alternatively, write a custom startup script that calls modprobe to load the drivers.

TIP *If your desktop environment doesn't automatically restore your mixer settings, try adding a* `post-install` *line to* `/etc/modules.conf` *to do the job with a command-line utility such as* `alsactl`. *Type* **`alsactl store`** *as* root *at a command prompt to store your current mixer settings, and then place a call to* `alsactl restore` *just after loading the ALSA drivers in* `modules.conf`, *as described earlier, in "Loading Drivers Automatically."*

Installing and configuring the ALSA drivers can be a tedious process, at least in pre-2.5.*x* kernels, but the results are often worthwhile. The standard kernel drivers provide limited or no support for some cards, and ALSA helps fill this gap.

REPLACING HARDWARE

Sometimes you have no choice but to replace audio hardware. Fortunately, basic sound cards are inexpensive; you can pick up a generic 16-bit sound card for $20 or less in many stores or from mail-order retailers. Unfortunately, a generic card can be a gamble from a Linux driver perspective, because it's seldom obvious from examining the box what chipset the card uses. You could try performing a web search on some models to find information on Linux driver support, or you could try cards in series until you find one that works. Another option is to step up a level or two in order to obtain a brand-name card with better-documented driver requirements. Consult the kernel configuration tools or the ALSA web page to learn what cards are supported.

Just because a card is supported under Linux doesn't mean that it will work *well* under Linux. In particular, features such as wavetable MIDI synthesis (which uses samples of instruments to play back good-sounding instrumentals from very small files) and surround sound features may not be supported. If these features are important to you, you'll have to do more extensive research to discover what Linux drivers support these features.

Demystifying the */proc* Filesystem

Programs use device files in the `/dev` directory tree to access most hardware for day-to-day use, but these interfaces typically provide only limited information on hardware features and configuration. To learn, say, whether an EIDE controller is configured to use direct memory access (DMA) mode, another tool is required: the `/proc` filesystem. This directory is entirely virtual—the files don't exist on your hard disk; they're created on-the-fly by the Linux kernel. By reading from these files, you can learn about hardware capabilities and settings. You can write to some of these files to change settings, as well.

NOTE *Many Linux system tools use* `/proc` *behind the scenes. Therefore, these tools are effectively interpreters for* `/proc`, *and are usually much easier and safer to use than direct access to* `/proc`.

The */proc* Directory Structure

To use `/proc` directly (as opposed to from a utility that accesses `/proc` and interprets its contents for you), you must understand something about what's in the `/proc` directory tree. For the most part, `/proc`'s files and subdirectories are named after the subsystems to which they interface. For instance, `/proc/pci` provides information on devices connected to the PCI bus, and `/proc/asound` delivers information on sound cards managed by ALSA. Some devices are complex enough that they merit entire subdirectory trees under /proc. You may find yourself digging into several layers of subdirectories to locate the information you want. There are also links within the /proc hierarchy. Some of the more important files and directories in the main /proc directory include:

The CPU   The most obvious CPU information resides in cpuinfo, which holds information on the CPU's brand, model, speed in megahertz, and so on. The loadavg and stat files also hold information relevant to the CPU, in the form of CPU load averages and related statistics. The loadavg file presents this information in a form that's more intelligible to humans. The uptime command displays this information, as well.

Busses   The bus directory holds subdirectories that interface to various system busses, such as the ISA (isapnp) and PCI (pci) busses. You'll also find an interface to information on USB devices (usb) here. The PCI and ISA busses also merit files in the base of /proc. These files deliver summary information on devices on their respective busses, whereas the bus/pci and bus/isapnp subdirectories deliver more detailed information on specific devices.

Interrupts, DMAs, and I/O Ports   In order to be useable, hardware must be accessible to the CPU. To do so, a unique set of hardware addresses is assigned to each device. These addresses are known as *interrupt requests (IRQs or interrupts), direct memory access (DMA) lines,* and *input/output (I/O) ports*. You can learn which of these critical resources are in use and by what drivers by examining the interrupts, dma, and ioports files. There's also an irq subdirectory that can provide more detailed information on devices using specific IRQs, but this information is usually scarce.

Memory   The meminfo file presents information on memory use, similar to that provided by the free command. The kcore file is essentially a window upon *all* of the system's memory; if you knew where to look, you could dredge any information from any running program by reading that file. The swaps file presents information on swap space usage, similar to that provided by typing **swapon -s.**

WARNING   The kcore file is unusually sensitive. It's set to be owned by root with 0400 permissions (read-only for root, no access for others). Even root cannot change these settings. If an unauthorized individual were to gain access to this file, no information on the computer would be safe—passwords, sensitive data files, and more would all be open to view.

The Kernel and Modules   The version file holds overview information on the kernel, including its version number, when it was compiled, and what compiler did the job. The cmdline file holds the kernel's boot parameters, as passed to the kernel from a boot loader. The modules file delivers information on modules that are loaded on the system. (This file does *not* present information on modules that are unloaded but available for manual or automatic loading.) The ksyms file presents kernel symbols—names given to kernel data structures and used to pass information back and forth between kernel subcomponents.

Network   The net subdirectory holds files related to network statistics. Most of the information presented by these files is much more readily interpreted with the aid of network utilities such as netstat and ifconfig, as described in Chapter 19, "Basic Network Configuration."

Filesystems and Partitions   The `filesystems` file presents a list of supported filesystems. Some of these filesystems are things you might not think of as such, such as `pipefs`. These filesystems are used internally by Linux to implement specific features. The `fs` subdirectory contains information on certain specific filesystems, should they be supported by your system, such as `nfs` and `reiserfs`. Not all filesystems create `/proc/fs` entries for themselves, though. The `partitions` file summarizes disk partitions. You can obtain the same information from the `fdisk` utility or its equivalent on non-IA-32 architectures, such as `pdisk` for Macintosh systems.

Disk Subsystems   The `ide` and `scsi` subdirectories contain information on EIDE and SCSI devices, respectively. (One or the other subdirectory may be missing if you lack that interface type.) Both subdirectories contain entire subdirectory trees themselves, giving access to information on the EIDE controller or SCSI host adapter as well as specific hard disks and other devices, such as tape drives.

Sound Cards   The ALSA drivers create a subdirectory called `asound`, which contains several files and subdirectories. These files provide information on the ALSA configuration and all of your system's sound cards.

Running Programs   If you type `ls /proc`, chances are that half or more of the entries you'll see will be numbered subdirectories. These contain files related to specific running processes; each is named after one process's process ID (PID) number. Some of the information provided by these files is accessible from the `ps` command and related commands, such as `top`.

Miscellaneous Information   Various additional files relating to specific subsystems, such as Advanced Power Management (APM; `apm`), supported devices (`devices`), and ttys (files in the `tty` subdirectory), are also available in the `/proc` directory.

NOTE   The /proc filesystem is generated by the kernel and its modules. As such, the layout of the /proc filesystem can change as you install and remove modules. The layout can differ from one system to another because of differences in hardware (say, the presence or absence of a SCSI host adapter) and because of differences in the kernel. Even given the same hardware, different kernels may produce different /proc filesystems.

Most of the files in `/proc` are reported as having a length of 0. Don't be deceived; most of these files actually contain data—or will generate it when accessed. One notable exception is `/proc/kcore`, whose length is equal to the amount of useable memory on your computer. This value is your installed memory minus a small amount (often 60KB, but sometimes more) reserved for I/O ports and the like.

WARNING   When you back up your computer, as described in Chapter 17, "Protecting Your System with Backups," be sure not to back up /proc! Backing up /proc will unnecessarily increase the size of your backup by something more than the amount of RAM you have installed. Even worse, a miscreant who obtains the backup might be able to extract information from the /proc/kcore backup file, or restoring over the working /proc filesystem could cause problems when settings are overwritten.

Learning About Your Hardware

The most common use of /proc is to obtain information about your computer. You can do this by reading the contents of /proc pseudo-files, typically by using cat or less to view them. For instance, to find information on your kernel, you could type the following command:

```
$ cat /proc/version
Linux version 2.4.19 (rodsmith@localhost.localdomain) (gcc version 3.2 20020903
➥(Red Hat Linux 8.0 3.2-7)) #3 Sun Nov 24 14:22:16 EST 2002
```

Although some files in /proc are intended for human consumption, others aren't—or at least, you need specialized skills to interpret the output. Various utilities, such as fdisk, free, ps, and netstat, help interpret /proc contents. These tools are described in the appropriate sections of this book. In some cases, other chapters also refer to specific /proc files and their contents.

Some /proc directories contain quite a maze of subdirectories. The ide, scsi, and asound subdirectories spring to mind as examples. Locating the correct file within these subdirectories can be a challenge, but most of the files and subdirectories are named in clear ways. For instance, /proc/ide/ide0/hda/model holds information on the manufacturer name and model number of the first EIDE hard disk. The ide0 subdirectory refers to the first EIDE channel, and hda is the Linux identifier for the first disk on this channel.

Modifying Hardware Settings

The most common use for /proc is to deliver information to you on a computer's configuration. This isn't the only use for /proc, though; it's possible to write to some of the pseudo-files in /proc, which causes them to change their settings. This practice is most commonly used to adjust hardware parameters, such as whether a hard disk uses DMA mode. Such tasks are almost always better performed via utilities designed for the purpose, however. For instance, although you can write to the /proc/ide/ide0/hda/settings file, doing so is tricky. It's better to use the hdparm utility (described in Chapter 2, "Improving Disk Performance") to tune EIDE disk performance. This utility provides parameters that are easier to use than writing raw data to /proc pseudo-files.

Summary

Understanding a few critical system components can help you get the most out of your computer. Knowing about CPUs can help you select the right one when it's time to buy a new computer, and it can also help you tune Linux to get the most from the CPU you've got. The video hardware can also greatly influence your perception of the utility of a computer. Although sound cards aren't truly critical components on most systems, they do connect directly to the motherboard and can be tricky to configure in Linux. In all of these cases and in others, knowing how to identify hardware and install drivers is important when troubleshooting or upgrading hardware. One tool that can be useful in these tasks is the /proc filesystem. Although separate programs often mediate access to /proc, you can deal with it directly if you prefer. In fact, doing so is sometimes the best way to get the information that you need.

## Chapter 2

Improving Disk Performance

THREE MAJOR COMPONENTS ARE most important in determining your system's overall performance: the CPU, memory, and hard disks. Chapter 1, "Optimizing System Architecture Usage," described some steps you can take to optimize CPU performance. Optimizing memory performance is fairly straightforward—you add RAM to the computer when it doesn't have enough memory, pick the fastest type of RAM your computer supports, and don't run extraneous programs. Optimizing disk performance, though, is a tricky subject—tricky enough that it deserves an entire chapter.

This chapter begins with a look at basic disk technologies—the hardware that's used to connect disks to computers. Your choice of interface can have profound effects on your system's disk performance, and in some cases a fairly inexpensive hardware upgrade can go a long way toward improving overall system speed. This chapter then proceeds to a look at how you can optimize disk performance through software means, including tweaking disk driver settings and modifying partition layout. (Chapter 12, "Filesystems and Files," further examines this topic by covering the merits and problems associated with specific filesystems.) This chapter concludes with a look at removable media—floppies, Zip disks, CD-Rs, and so on.

Understanding ATA and SCSI

In 2003, two interface standards dominate the hard disk market: *Advanced Technology Attachment (ATA)*, aka *Enhanced Integrated Drive Electronics (EIDE)*, and *Small Computer System Interface (SCSI)*. Each standard includes various "sub-standards" that deliver differing levels of performance. Disks and disk-like devices (CD-ROM drives, tape drives, and so on) attach to an ATA controller or SCSI host adapter. You can use both ATA and SCSI interfaces on one computer, if you need both.

NOTE *Floppy drives interface to computers through a third type of connection, generally referred to as a floppy controller. This interface is very low-speed and isn't good for much except handling floppy disks, although some early tape drives used this interface.*

Why Two Disk Standards?

Prior to ATA and SCSI, most microcomputer hard disks used the ST-506 standard, which required the computer to understand various disk-specific timing parameters, how the hard disk laid out data on its platters, and so on. Both ATA and SCSI created data abstractions in order to present a simpler and more uniform hard disk interface to the computer. They did this by shifting some of the burden of managing low-level disk details onto the drive itself.

SCSI is the more sophisticated of the two disk standards. Some of the features that differentiate SCSI and ATA include the following:

Devices Per Bus   In the context of disk devices, a *bus* is a means of connecting disk devices to a computer via a single cable or daisy-chained set of cables. ATA supports just two devices per bus, with most ATA controllers providing two busses. SCSI supports up to seven or 15 devices, depending upon the SCSI variety. On most systems, each bus consumes one interrupt request (IRQ) line, and because the number of IRQs in an IA-32 computer is limited, this gives SCSI a strong advantage for systems that need many disks. In practice, though, SCSI's advantage isn't as great as it might seem, because cable-length limits make it difficult to support more than half a dozen SCSI devices on most types of SCSI busses. Also, modern systems usually allow multiple devices to share a single IRQ, so the IRQ limitation isn't as severe as it once was.

Termination   SCSI busses must be *terminated* by using special resistors. This requirement caused early SCSI systems to be tricky to configure when compared to ATA busses, which don't require special termination. More recent SCSI systems help automate termination, so this problem is less severe than it once was. Restoring complexity to SCSI, though, is the fact that different variants require different types of termination, which can be confusing and troublesome.

Multitasking   The SCSI bus was designed to support multiple simultaneous transfers. For instance, if a specific type of SCSI bus is capable of 80MB/s transfers, and if two devices are connected to that bus, each of which is capable of 40MB/s transfers, then both devices can handle full-speed (40MB/s) transfers at once, saturating the SCSI bus's 80MB/s speed. Neither device is slowed down by the other's transfer. ATA, by contrast, is fundamentally single-tasking; in the same situation, only one device can transfer data at once, resulting in an overall system slow-down. Of course, because ATA supports only two devices per controller, this limitation isn't as severe for ATA as it would be for SCSI.

TIP   To improve the performance of a two-disk system, put each disk on its own ATA bus. For instance, one bus might have the main hard disk and a CD-ROM drive, and the second bus might have a second disk and a tape backup drive. With this configuration, the system can access both disks simultaneously, improving performance in some multitasking situations.

Range of Devices   Historically, more devices have been available for SCSI than for ATA. The original ATA specification was intended only for hard disks, whereas SCSI has long supported other devices. Through the 1990s, though, ATA has acquired standards for handling many nondisk device types. (ATA still doesn't support most external device types, such as scanners and printers.)

Speed and Capacity   Historically, SCSI drives have been faster and available in higher capacities than ATA drives. These features haven't been so much a matter of the interfaces themselves as they've been ones of drive marketing; manufacturers have released their fastest and largest drives in SCSI form first. Today, this difference is smaller than it once was, and in fact it's easier to find ATA drives in very high capacities than to find similarly large SCSI drives.

Price   SCSI devices have traditionally been more expensive than ATA devices of similar capacity. This price premium has increased in the last few years.

In the mid-1980s, SCSI found favor on Unix workstations and servers, and it was also Apple's favored disk type for its Macintosh computers. IA-32 systems, by contrast, generally used ATA drives. As IA-32 systems have gained prominence in the marketplace, ATA disks have gained a similarly dominant position. Today, even many Macintoshes and non-IA-32 workstations use ATA drives. You can still use SCSI devices, even on IA-32 computers, but this is definitely the less common approach.

When to Use Each Disk Type

All modern IA-32 motherboards come with at least two built-in ATA controllers. Therefore, using an ATA disk is just a matter of setting a jumper or two, connecting the disk to the motherboard via an ATA cable, and attaching a power connector to the hard disk. Because most motherboards have only two ATA controllers, and each controller can handle just two drives, most motherboards can support only four ATA devices. Most computers have a hard disk and a CD-ROM drive. Adding a Zip or other removable-media drive and a tape backup drive leaves no room for expansion. In order to move beyond the four-drive limit, you must add a separate ATA controller, as described in the next section, "Controllers and Host Adapters." In this situation, SCSI offers the advantage of supporting more devices per chain, and hence per IRQ.

SCSI's multitasking nature is potentially important on large servers with many hard disks that are accessed simultaneously. As with resource use, though, these benefits are most important when you have many disks. When you have only one hard disk, or you have disks on separate chains, SCSI's advantages are slim or nonexistent.

Overall, SCSI devices have traditionally been good choices for high-end servers and workstations, but not for typical desktop productivity systems or small servers. ATA has been slowly eroding SCSI's advantages over the past decade, so today even most mid-sized servers can do quite nicely with ATA drives. Today, SCSI is most worthwhile if you need hundreds of gigabytes of disk space spread over several disks. Such a configuration is likely to be quite expensive. You might also consider using a low-end SCSI host adapter to drive nondisk SCSI devices, such as a tape backup unit or CD-R drive, particularly if you've run out of ATA positions.

NOTE   *To implement some functions, Linux provides an ATA-to-SCSI driver, which provides SCSI device interfaces that link to ATA devices. This feature is used to support ATA CD-R drives, for instance. You don't need an actual SCSI drive or SCSI host adapter to use this feature.*

ALTERNATIVES TO ATA AND SCSI

ATA and SCSI are the dominant hard disk interfaces today, but there are alternatives. One is the Universal Serial Bus (USB), which is a popular means of connecting external Zip drives, CD-R drives, and the like. USB 1.*x* is very slow (1.5MB/s), and so isn't suitable for hard disks except for some low-performance functions. The newer USB 2.0 is fast enough to support hard disks (60MB/s), and may become important for this function in the future. Linux creates USB-to-SCSI interfaces for USB disk devices, so USB drives look like SCSI drives to Linux software.

Another alternative is *IEEE-1394*, aka *Firewire*. Like USB 2.0, IEEE-1394 is a fast interface (up to 100MB/s) and so is useful for hard disks as well as other disk-style devices. IEEE-1394 is becoming popular as a means of attaching external hard disks, and Linux provides an IEEE-1394-to-SCSI driver so that these devices look like SCSI devices. This support is still fairly new in the 2.4.*x* kernels, though.

USB 2.0, IEEE-1394, and more exotic variants such as Fibre Channel are all most important as means of connecting external drives. ATA is likely to dominate the internal drive market for desktop computers for the next few years, although ATA is likely to be extended. One ATA extension that's emerging is *serial ATA*, which uses serial cables rather than parallel cables.

Controllers and Host Adapters

Hard disks interface to computers via components known as *controllers* or *host adapters*. (The former term is usually applied to ATA interfaces, whereas the latter applies to SCSI interfaces.) Until the mid-1990s, these devices were usually separate cards that plugged into motherboards. Today, though, all new IA-32 motherboards ship with ATA controllers built in, and some motherboards include SCSI host adapters, as well. Even when a motherboard includes a controller or host adapter, though, you may want to add another one or replace an existing one.

When to Add or Upgrade Hardware

In most cases, your motherboard's ATA controller will work just fine for handling ATA devices. For a typical setup, then, there's seldom any need to change the configuration. There are reasons you might want to add to or replace your motherboard's ATA controller, though:

Lack of Linux Driver Support   All ATA controllers work to a minimal extent using an old compatibility mode that dates back to the days of the ST-506 interface. By today's standards, though, this mode is extremely slow; to get the most out of an ATA controller, you need Linux support for it. Linux includes such support for most ATA controllers, but occasionally this support may be missing or buggy. This is particularly likely to be true if you buy a motherboard that uses a brand-new chipset for which Linux ATA drivers haven't been written. In such a case, you might want to disable the built-in ATA controller and use an add-on card instead.

Too Many Disks   As noted earlier, it's easy to consume all four devices that can be controlled by a typical IA-32 motherboard. In this situation, you must add a second controller to supplement, rather than replace, the motherboard's controller. A typical expansion ATA controller can handle two additional chains, for a total of eight devices. Alternatively, you could use SCSI devices for expansion and use a SCSI host adapter.

Need for SCSI Support   If you've got a SCSI device that you want to use, such as a SCSI scanner or tape drive, you must add a SCSI host adapter to your system. Some SCSI devices ship with low-end SCSI host adapters that may not work under Linux, so replacing them is a necessity. Even if you don't currently have any SCSI devices, you might prefer the features of SCSI models to non-SCSI models for some nondisk devices, in which case adding a SCSI host adapter is required.

Speed Upgrade   If your motherboard is more than a year or two old, it may not support the speeds that a modern hard disk can support. In such a situation, you may want to disable the motherboard's ATA controller in favor of one on a more modern controller card. You're not likely to see any benefit of such an upgrade unless you also buy a new hard disk, though; at any given point in time, the best available ATA controllers exceed the sustained data transfer speeds possible with the best ATA hard disks.

Fundamentally the same rules apply to upgrades for SCSI host adapters as for ATA controllers, although some details differ. Only the largest systems will exceed SCSI's device limit, although past half a dozen or so devices, it's often much easier to configure a second SCSI host adapter than it is to add more devices to the primary SCSI bus. You might also want two SCSI host adapters to support both recent and older SCSI devices, because it's sometimes difficult to get SCSI devices of wildly differing ages to coexist on a single SCSI bus.

Picking the Correct Hardware

When you pick an interface, matching the card to the disks and other devices it will control is important. Both ATA and SCSI come in several different levels, each of which provides better performance than earlier levels. In theory, new interfaces can manage older devices; however, in practice complications sometimes arise. Older devices may degrade the performance of newer devices attached to the same bus, particularly in the case of ATA devices. Differing termination and bus width requirements can make mixing SCSI devices of radically different ages a real nightmare.

PICKING THE CORRECT ATA HARDWARE

ATA hardware is known by several names and comes with varying capabilities. Many names are largely marketing hype or unofficial names assigned to indicate the device's maximum transfer speed. Table 2.1 summarizes the names and basic characteristics of these devices. Note that the Added PIO Modes and Added DMA Modes columns are cumulative; later standards support all of the modes of earlier standards, plus the modes listed in their entries in these columns. Unlike SCSI's 50- and 68-pin cables, ATA's 40- and 80-wire cables are physically compatible, so you can use a new cable to attach an old device to a new or old controller.

NOTE   *At the time of this writing, an ATA-7 standard is under discussion, but it has not yet been finalized. It's likely to include support for 133MB/s transfers and UltraDMA mode 6. In practice, hardware often leads standards, so devices with these features are already on the market.*

Table 2.1: ATA Hardware Types

Official Name	Unofficial Names	Maximum Speed	Added PIO Modes	Added DMA Modes	Cable Type
ATA-1	IDE	11.1MB/s	0, 1, 2	0, 1, 2, Multiword 0	40-wire
ATA-2	EIDE	16.6MB/s	3, 4	Multiword 1, Multiword 2	40-wire
ATA-3		16.6MB/s			40-wire
ATA-4	UltraDMA/33, ATA/33	33.3MB/s		UltraDMA 0, UltraDMA 1, UltraDMA 2	40-wire or 80-wire
ATA-5	UltraDMA/66, ATA/66	66.6MB/s		UltraDMA 3, UltraDMA 4	80-wire
ATA-6	UltraDMA/100, ATA/100	100MB/s		UltraDMA 5	80-wire

In addition to the standards outlined in Table 2.1, many ATA devices support the *ATA Packet Interface (ATAPI)*, which is a set of software extensions to support CD-ROM drives, tape drives, removable disks, and other non-hard-disk devices. ATAPI is a matter of drive and software communication, though; the ATA adapter doesn't need explicit ATAPI support.

When considering an upgrade, check your existing devices' documentation to learn which speeds they support. You can buy a more capable ATA controller than you need now, but try to put devices of similar levels on the same bus whenever possible. For instance, if your motherboard supports 33MB/s transfers and you buy an ATA-6 (100MB/s) card to supplement it, put slow devices on the motherboard and fast ones on the expansion card.

Some very high-end ATA controllers support *Redundant Array of Independent Disk (RAID)* technology. RAID enables you to link together multiple hard disks for improved speed, improved reliability, or both. RAID controllers tend to be rather expensive, but they're well worth the cost for high-end applications such as busy servers. They may require special Linux drivers, though, so check on driver availability, as described in Chapter 1, before buying a RAID controller. Also, the Linux kernel supports software RAID, which is adequate for many purposes.

Before you buy an ATA controller, check on Linux driver availability. The Linux kernel configuration tool provides information on supported ATA controllers. These drivers should be built into the Linux kernel itself, at least if you intend to boot from a disk connected to a controller you buy.

Picking the Correct SCSI Hardware

Three different types of SCSI cable are commonly used: 25-pin, Narrow (50-pin) and Wide (68-pin). Wide SCSI host adapters typically include at least one Narrow and one Wide connector. Three types of termination are in common use:

◆ Passive, which is used on the oldest and low-end devices

◆ Active, which is used on mid-range devices

◆ Low-voltage differential (LVD), which is used on the latest high-end devices.

Active and passive terminations are known collectively as single-ended; they're somewhat interchangeable, although active almost always works better. High-voltage differential, or HVD, termination is also an option on some more obscure SCSI variants. As a general rule, you shouldn't mix termination types, although you can usually get away with mixing active and passive termination. Different SCSI variants support different maximum cable lengths, which you should never exceed. Table 2.2 summarizes the features of different SCSI varieties.

TABLE 2.2: SCSI HARDWARE TYPES

SCSI TYPE	SPEED	TERMINATION	CABLE TYPE	MAXIMUM CABLE LENGTH
SCSI-1	5MB/s	single-ended	25- or 50-pin	6m
SCSI-2	5MB/s	single-ended	50-pin	6m
Fast SCSI-2	10MB/s	single-ended	50-pin	3m
Fast/Wide SCSI-2	20MB/s	single-ended	68-pin	3m
UltraSCSI	20MB/s	single-ended	50-pin	3m or 1.5m[1]
UltraWide SCSI	40MB/s	single-ended	68-pin	3m or 1.5m[1]
Ultra2 Wide SCSI	80MB/s	LVD	68-pin	12m
Ultra3 SCSI or Ultra160 SCSI	160MB/s	LVD	68-pin	12m
Ultra320 SCSI	320MB/s	LVD	68-pin	12m
Ultra640 SCSI	640MB/s	LVD	68-pin	12m

[1] *Maximum cable length is 3m for four or fewer devices and 1.5m for five or more devices.*

Picking an appropriate SCSI host adapter can be tricky if you need to mix device types, especially those that use different types of termination or cable widths. Some high-end SCSI host adapters support two SCSI chains, which can make such mixtures easier to implement; otherwise, you may do well to buy a low-end SCSI adapter for low-end devices and a high-end adapter for faster devices.

Unlike ATA controllers, SCSI host adapters have no lowest-common-denominator mode; Linux *must* support your model adapter to provide even minimal functionality. If you want to boot from a SCSI disk, the driver must be compiled directly into the kernel. In this case, the SCSI adapter must also include a SCSI Basic Input/Output System (BIOS), which enables the computer's BIOS to see the hard disk to begin the boot process. Most high-end and mid-range SCSI adapters include a BIOS, but many low-end adapters don't.

Testing and Optimizing Disk Performance

Aside from replacing hard disks or related hardware, what can you do to improve disk performance? Linux occasionally fails to set disk parameters optimally, so disk performance sometimes suffers on a default installation. Identifying and correcting this condition is usually fairly straightforward, once you know how. Additional fine-tuning can also help, but it is sometimes riskier. This is particularly true if you decide to enable experimental driver options for your hardware.

Identifying Poor Disk Performance

One clue to poor disk performance is poor overall system performance, particularly at disk-intensive tasks such as launching large programs. Unfortunately, there are so many differences between computers that it may not be obvious when a system's performance is just slightly lacking. A severely mistuned system, though—say, one using the ancient ATA-1 mode—is likely to catch your attention as being sluggish.

To test your disk's performance, use the hdparm utility. This program's main purpose is to display and set various ATA parameters that influence performance. The program can also run basic performance tests. The -t parameter tests disk read speed, while the -T parameter tests Linux's disk cache performance. Essentially, -T is a test of the computer's memory and CPU speed. The cache speed is important to overall disk performance, but for purposes of testing, you don't want the cache to interfere with raw disk performance tests. You can combine the two tests, and hdparm will apply correction factors to separate the two measures. Following the -Tt parameter, you specify the hard disk you want to test as follows:

```
# /sbin/hdparm -Tt /dev/hdb
```

```
/dev/hdb:
 Timing buffer-cache reads:  128 MB in 0.58 seconds =220.69 MB/sec
 Timing buffered disk reads: 64 MB in 2.36 seconds = 27.12 MB/sec
```

In order to get reliable results, you should perform these tests on a system that's otherwise not doing much, and especially not performing any disk-intensive tasks. It's also best to perform the test at least three times so that you can spot any outliers that might be caused by events such as cron jobs causing aberrant performance on a single run.

What's poor performance, though? This depends on the disk. You should be able to find detailed specifications for your disk on the manufacturer's website. You need to find the specification for sustained transfer speeds to and from the disk's media (aka "internal" speeds). In early 2003, most new drives nominally produce maximum speeds of 30–100MB/s. Actual speeds are likely to be between 50 percent and 75 percent of the nominal speed, though, because manufacturers report absolute best-case speed scenarios. Speeds also vary from one part of the disk to another; the outermost tracks produce better speeds than the innermost tracks, because disk manufacturers place more sectors on outer tracks than inner ones.

WARNING   *Disk manufacturers often prominently advertise their disk interface speeds, such as 100MB/s. Media transfer rates are more important, though, and manufacturers often hide this information on data sheets. Also, manufacturers sometimes measure disk performance in megabits per second (Mbps), but* hdparm *reports its results in megabytes per second (MB/s). Divide megabits per second by 8 to obtain the value in megabytes per second.*

If you believe your disk speed is deficient, you should search for a reason for the problem. In the case of ATA disks, the -v parameter to hdparm produces a summary of disk settings:

```
# /sbin/hdparm -v /dev/hdb
```

```
/dev/hda:
 multcount    = 16 (on)
 IO_support   = 1 (32-bit)
 unmaskirq    = 1 (on)
```

```
using_dma    = 1 (on)
keepsettings = 0 (off)
readonly     = 0 (off)
readahead    = 8 (on)
geometry     = 9729/255/63, sectors = 156301488, start = 0
```

The most important setting displayed by this output is the using_dma item. This setting reveals whether the controller is using *direct memory access (DMA)* mode, in which the controller directly transfers data between the disk and the computer's memory. The alternative is *programmed input/output (PIO)* mode, in which the computer's CPU mediates all transfers. DMA mode is generally faster than PIO mode, and DMA transfers impose a lower CPU load, so disk accesses need not slow down CPU-intensive programs as much.

You can also check pseudo-files in the /proc/ide directory tree for information on disk configuration. In particular, examine the /proc/ide/hdx/settings file, where hdx is the code for the drive in question, such as hda for the first drive. You'll find the settings shown by hdparm -v, as well as more, such as current_speed, which reveals the current top speed setting for the drive. Even if the system is set to use DMA mode, if the current_speed setting is very low, it may be the cause of a performance bottleneck.

Improving Disk Performance

If Linux isn't running your disks in an optimal mode, you can use hdparm to adjust its settings. In some cases, you can apply driver-specific options to your ATA driver. Finally, one issue of disk performance doesn't relate to speed, but it is important to laptop users: energy use. You can configure the disks to spin down when they haven't been accessed for some time, thereby saving energy.

ADJUSTING DISK PARAMETERS

Just as hdparm can read disk parameters, it can write them. Table 2.3 summarizes some of the parameters you can pass to ATA disks to modify their settings.

TABLE 2.3: hdparm PARAMETERS FOR IMPROVING DISK PERFORMANCE

PARAMETER	VALUES	EXPLANATION
-c	0, 1, or 3	Enables (1 or 3) or disables (0) 32-bit data transfers between the CPU and ATA controller. Mode 1 is a normal enabling; 3 enables the mode using a special sync sequence required by some chipsets.
-d	0 or 1	Enables (1) or disables (0) DMA transfer mode.
-E	Positive integers	Sets the speed of a CD-ROM. This parameter normally isn't needed. Its main use is in *lowering* a drive's speed to better read a scratched disc.
-m	Power-of-two integers (2, 4, 8, etc.)	Sets the number of sectors exchanged per transfer cycle. Most drives work best with a value of 16 or 32, but some drives require lower values (4 or 8, typically). A value of 0 disables multisector transfer, causing transfers of one sector at a time.

Continued on next page

TABLE 2.3: hdparm PARAMETERS FOR IMPROVING DISK PERFORMANCE *(continued)*

PARAMETER	VALUES	EXPLANATION
-p	0 to 5	Sets the PIO mode used by the drive. Higher modes produce better performance, but not all drives support all modes. *Setting the wrong mode may hang the computer.*
-u	0 or 1	Enables (1) or disables (0) the ability of the system to unmask the IRQ of a drive. In general, enabling this feature results in increased system responsiveness, but it's been known to cause unreliable operation with some controllers. *Do not* capitalize this option; the capital -U option unregisters (disables) an interface!
-X	sdmax, mdmax, or udmax	Sets the ATA transfer mode. On modern systems, a value of udmax, where x is the UltraDMA mode, enables that mode, which produces the best performance. Older drives may require use of the mdmax or sdmax modes to set multiword or simple DMA modes, respectively. (Again, x is the DMA mode number.) Table 2.1 summarizes DMA transfer modes.

As a general rule, drives power up in a mode that's optimal, and most distributions have configuration scripts that either don't change these settings or that also set drives for optimal performance. Occasionally, though, this isn't the case, so you may need to experiment with hdparm options and then set up a local configuration script to do the job automatically when you reboot, as described in Chapter 9, "Bypassing Automatic Configurations to Gain Control." In these cases, a line such as the following should do the trick:

```
hdparm -d1 -X udma5 /dev/hda
```

Of course, you may need to adjust the ATA transfer mode (udma5 in this example) to suit your drives and host adapter. In some cases, including additional options from Table 2.3 can improve performance further.

WARNING Both the -d and -X parameters are potentially very dangerous. Don't play with them idly unless you're prepared to hang your computer.

NOTE The hdparm performance-tweaking parameters apply only to ATA devices; you can't use these options to improve the performance of SCSI devices. SCSI host adapters are much smarter than ATA controllers, so SCSI devices don't need these tweaks. You may be able to use driver options to improve the performance of some SCSI devices, though.

ADJUSTING DRIVER PARAMETERS

Chapter 1 described the process of passing parameters to the kernel or to individual modules. Although rare, some ATA and SCSI drivers support options that can affect performance. Consult the driver's documentation for details. Check for documentation files in the /usr/src/linux/Documentation directory. (Red Hat uses linux-2.4 rather than linux in this pathname.)

SPINNING DOWN A DISK TO SAVE ENERGY

Normally, a computer's hard disks spin whenever the computer is turned on. This feature makes disk access swift, because there's no need to begin spinning the disk to access a file; however, it consumes a fair amount of power. Therefore, as an energy-saving measure, spinning down a disk when it's not in use is sometimes desirable. Doing so is particularly helpful on laptop computers, on which a spinning hard disk can greatly reduce battery life. Therefore, `hdparm` supports the `-S` option to set this feature. Unfortunately, the encoding of this feature is rather odd, as outlined in Table 2.4.

TABLE 2.4: POWER-SAVING OPTIONS SET WITH `hdparm -S`

VALUE	MEANING
0	Power-saving mode disabled; disk never goes into low-power mode.
1–240	Time in 5-second multiples; for instance, 12 means 60 seconds.
241-251	Units of 30 minutes (241), 60 minutes (242), and so on through 5.5 hours (251).
252	21 minutes.
253	Drive-specific timeout value.
255	21 minutes and 15 seconds.

For instance, to set the disk to power down after ten minutes of inactivity, you could type the following command:

```
# hdparm -S120 /dev/hda
```

You can place this command in a startup script, as described in Chapter 9, to have it run automatically whenever you boot. One caveat concerning disk power-saving options is that Linux is a very disk-intensive OS. The system may need to access the disk at unexpected times, even if nobody is actively using the computer. Thus, power savings may be smaller under Linux than under some OSs. Powering up a drive also takes time, but typically it takes well under 10 seconds. For this reason, you may prefer to forego the energy-saving mode on desktop systems or when a laptop is plugged into a power supply.

Optimizing Disk Partitions

Even if your disk hardware is working optimally, poor placement of data on your disks can degrade performance. Understanding the issues will help you design a partition layout that can help maximize your disk performance. The downside is that you may need to move data around in order to do this job. The best way to do it is when you first install Linux—setting up optimal partitions from the beginning is far easier than doing so after the fact.

Why Does Partition Placement Matter?

Hard disks store data on circular disk platters. Each platter contains a large number of *tracks*, which are in turn broken up into *sectors*. The disk platters rotate at a high velocity (typically 5,400 to 10,000 revolutions per minute, or rpm). A pivoting arm carries a *head* that reads and writes data from individual sectors as they pass beneath it. Most modern disks have two or three platters stacked atop one another. The tracks in these drives are logically grouped into one mass that's called a *cylinder*. The read/write heads for the drive move in a synchronized fashion so that all the tracks that make up a cylinder are accessed at once. Outer tracks are broken into more sectors than are inner tracks, in order to make better use of the greater area in outer tracks. This arrangement is illustrated in Figure 2.1.

FIGURE 2.1

Hard disks are built from platters, each of which is broken into tracks, which are broken into sectors.

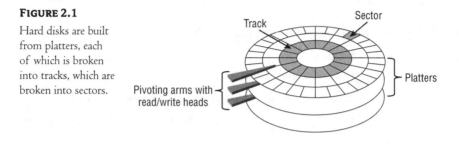

NOTE *In order to retrieve data from a disk, the disk must be told which cylinder, head, and sector to read. This is the basis of the so-called* cylinder/head/sector (CHS) *geometry that IA-32 computers have traditionally used. Modern drives create a fictitious CHS geometry to satisfy IA-32 BIOSes, because standard IA-32 BIOSes aren't set up to handle the variable number of sectors per track used by modern drives. Modern drives can also use a* linear (or logical) block addressing (LBA) *mode in which sectors receive sequential numbers and the drive determines the correct cylinder, head, and sector. LBA mode is slowly taking over from CHS mode, but CHS mode must still be supported to keep everything working together.*

You can think of partitions as occupying concentric rings of a hard disk. In order to access data from one partition or another, or indeed from different areas within a single partition, the disk head must move to read the appropriate cylinder. This movement takes time, which reduces disk throughput immediately after such an operation, which is known as a *seek*. Seeks take differing amounts of time depending upon the distance that must be traversed; moving from the innermost cylinder to the outermost cylinder takes more time than seeking just halfway, for instance.

The result is that, for optimal performance, you should place partitions so that most data accesses are within as narrow a range of cylinders as possible. This practice will minimize seek times, thereby improving performance. Another important feature is that the data density is greater on outer cylinders than on inner cylinders, which results in better disk performance on outer cylinders. The outer cylinders are the early ones, from the point of view of the operating system. You can use this fact to your advantage when placing partitions.

Tips for Placing Partitions for Best Performance

The physical layout of sectors on a hard disk and the characteristics of data transfer speeds from inner and outer cylinders lead to potentially conflicting rules for optimizing disk performance. These factors also interact with your specific needs; for instance, you might want to favor one type of data over another one for optimal performance. Some of the rules of thumb you can use to improve performance include:

Put often-used data near the center of the disk.   On average, the time to seek to the middle of a disk is the lowest of any seek time. Therefore, you should put frequently accessed files near the center of the disk. Such partitions are likely to include your Linux root (/) partition and, if you separate any of them, your /var, /tmp, /usr, and /home partitions. Partitions you can move aside include any partitions you use for archival storage, infrequently used binaries, /boot, and non-Linux OSs.

Put the swap partition near the center of the disk.   In many cases, the swap partition is a *very* heavily used partition. Therefore, as a corollary to the preceding rule, swap should sit as close to the center of the disk as possible.

Put data for which high throughput is important at the start of the disk.   Large data files that you read or write in large blocks can benefit from the superior performance of the outer cylinders (early-numbered sectors) of the disk. For instance, if you maintain large database files, you're likely to see a performance boost if you put them early on the disk. Partitions with lots of small files, such as web pages served by a web server, benefit less from this advantage and, therefore, can go later on the disk.

Keep related partitions near each other.   If a pattern of disk activity is likely to keep the disk head moving between two partitions with few accesses to other partitions, those two partitions should be placed next to each other. The biggest consequence of this rule of thumb is that partitions belonging to one OS should be kept in sequence on the disk. An exception might be a seldom-accessed partition, which could be split off from the rest if some other factor intervenes.

Address special requirements for the boot partition.   The IA-32 BIOS has historically imposed limits on where boot files (namely, the Linux kernel and any boot loaders you use) reside. This issue isn't nearly as much of a problem today as it once was, but if you have a computer that's more than a few years old, you might need to create a separate /boot partition to hold the kernel and place it in the first 1,024 cylinders (about 8GB) of the disk.

Split OSs across multiple disks.   "Two heads are better than one," the saying goes, and in the case of hard disks, using two can improve performance by reducing the number of head seeks. For instance, if your /home partition is on one disk while /usr is on another disk, head seeks required to access files in /home won't budge the head resting in /usr, which can speed the next access to files in /usr.

As noted in the lead-in to this list, these rules sometimes conflict. For instance, you might want a partition to reside early on the disk to improve throughput, but you also might want it near the center to minimize seek times. Deciding how to resolve these conflicts is usually a matter of guesswork; without running experiments, it's not easy to know which configuration will work best. You may want to compromise; for instance, you could put the partition on which you want fast access near the center of the disk, but put it at the beginning of a group of such partitions.

Moving Data via Sneakernet: Removable Media

The vast majority of Linux's disk accesses involve hard disks, but hard disks aren't the only type of disk. In fact, removable media are more important in some ways than hard disks—they enable you to easily move data from one computer to another when a conventional wired or wireless network is not available or is awkward. (This method of data transport is sometimes called a *sneakernet* because of the role that feet, and hence athletic footwear, play in the operation.)

If you're in the market for new hardware, the first step is evaluating your needs. With this information, you can pick appropriate Linux-compatible hardware. You must then settle upon what filesystem or filesystems you'll use on these disks. Finally, you can configure your system to actually use the hardware.

Evaluating Your Removable Media Needs

Fully understanding your needs can help lead you to a decision regarding the best type of removable disk to buy. In the end, you'll have to do some research on available media to determine which specific products will work best for you. Linux compatibility, described in the upcoming section, "Picking Linux-Compatible Hardware," is also a potential issue, although most removable-media devices work well with Linux. Some of the features you may want to consider include:

Capacity   One of the most obvious factors is the capacity of the media. You may want to use two or three removable media devices in order to support multiple capacities.

Speed   As a general rule, higher-capacity media produce faster speeds, but there are exceptions to this rule.

Interface   Several methods of interfacing removable-media drives exist: floppy port, ATA, SCSI, USB, IEEE-1394, PC-card (most commonly used on laptops), and parallel port. As a general rule, ATA, SCSI, USB 2.0, and IEEE-1394 are the fastest and most reliable interface methods, although Linux IEEE-1394 support is not as mature as support for most other interfaces. Older USB 1.*x* interfaces produce modest speed; they're fine for floppy disks, tape drives, and even Zip disks, but not for portable hard disks or 1GB or larger removable disks.

Internal versus External   Devices that connect via the floppy or ATA ports are usually internal, although internal-to-external adapters are available. Most SCSI host adapters support both internal and external devices. The other interface methods all support external devices. External units are portable, so you can easily use them on multiple computers. External devices tend to be pricier than their internal counterparts, though, and they add to the cabling mess around your computer.

Media Durability   For archival storage or if you move media around a lot, durability is important. CD-R and recordable DVD media are likely to be the most long-lasting, assuming they're properly stored. Estimates of their lifetimes range from 10 to 100 years. Floppies are notoriously unreliable as long-term storage media, and tapes aren't much better, although individual experiences differ substantially. Removable hard disks are sensitive to physical shocks, and so shouldn't be moved unnecessarily. For long-term storage, you may also want to consider the durability of the standard. For instance, CD-ROM and DVD-ROM drives are likely to be available for at least another decade or two, but less common and proprietary formats such as Castlewood Orb drives may not be.

Sequential versus Random Access Most removable media are *random access* devices, meaning that you can read data from any point on the medium without reading intervening data. You can write a normal Linux filesystem to such a device and treat it much as you would a hard disk. Tapes are *sequential access* devices, meaning that you must read all intervening data before reading the targeted data. This feature makes tapes a good choice for backups, but not for archives that should be random access.

Access Programs and Procedures Most media use ordinary Linux filesystem handling tools, such as the `mount`, `umount`, `cp`, and `mv` commands. CD-R and recordable DVD media require the use of special programs, such as `cdrecord`, to write data, but work with ordinary commands for reading data. This issue is described in the upcoming section, "Burning CD-Rs." Tapes also require special access methods. Typically, you use `tar`, `dump`, or some other tape backup tool to read and write tapes.

Cost Two costs are important to consider when choosing removable-media devices: the cost of the drive and the cost of the media. The total cost is the cost of the drive plus however many media you expect to need over its lifetime. You may want to consider both the absolute cost and the cost per megabyte or gigabyte stored. Because costs are constantly dropping, it's hard to summarize what's best in this arena, although CD-R drives and media are usually both well priced.

Table 2.5 summarizes some of the important characteristics of various popular removable media. Remember that these technologies keep improving, so you may find something with superior specifications to what's shown in Table 2.5.

TABLE 2.5: CHARACTERISTICS OF POPULAR REMOVABLE MEDIA TECHNOLOGIES

DEVICE TYPE	CAPACITY	SPEED	INTERFACES
Floppy Disk	180KB–2.88MB	Depends on capacity; typically 30KB/s	Floppy, USB
Iomega Zip Disk	100–750MB	0.6–2.4MB/s	ATA, SCSI, USB, parallel, PC-Card
LS-120 & LS-240	120–240MB	4.0MB/s	ATA, USB, parallel, PC-Card
Iomega Jaz	1–2GB	5.4MB/s	SCSI
Castlewood Orb	2.3–5.7GB	12.2—17.35MB/s	ATA, SCSI, USB, IEEE-1394
Magneto-Optical	128MB–9.1GB	2–6MB/s	SCSI
Iomega Peerless	5–20GB	15MB/s	IEEE-1394, USB
Removable Hard Disk	100MB–300GB	2–100MB/s	ATA, SCSI, IEEE-1394, USB
CD-R and CD-RW	700MB	150KB/s–7.5MB/s	ATA, SCSI, USB, IEEE-1394
Recordable DVD	4.7–9.4GB	4–8MB/s	ATA, SCSI, IEEE-1394, USB 2.0
Tape	40MB–160GB	0.5–16MB/s	Floppy, ATA, SCSI, USB, parallel

Picking Linux-Compatible Hardware

Fortunately, the vast majority of removable-media devices are compatible with Linux, with the caveat that the IEEE-1394 and USB 2.0 interfaces are still fairly new. You'll find the best support for ATA and SCSI devices.

Linux treats most removable-media devices as if they were hard disks. This is true of all of the Iomega, magneto-optical (MO), Castlewood Orb, and removable disk drives shown in Table 2.5. These devices are often partitioned like hard disks and mounted via entries in /etc/fstab, as described in the upcoming section, "Configuring Removable Media." Floppy disks usually aren't partitioned, and indeed removable-media devices in general don't need to be partitioned and sometimes aren't.

CD-R and recordable DVD drives are generally accessed via the SCSI generic device driver. There are standards for such devices, so all modern drives should work with Linux CD-R packages.

Most tape drives use standard tape-device protocols. These should work for almost all SCSI and ATA devices, but other interface types are riskier. I recommend doing a web search to check on compatibility of specific devices. The floppy and parallel ports aren't used by modern tape drives; they're used only for old low-capacity units. The ftape kernel drivers support them, if you happen to have an old legacy drive.

Choosing a Filesystem for Removable Media

To use a removable disk to its fullest, you must use it in conjunction with a filesystem. Chapter 12 describes filesystems in more detail, including information on the advantages and disadvantages of specific filesystems. Some removable media have unusual features that make using some filesystems necessary and using others inadvisable, though, and these issues deserve attention.

NOTE   *Tapes are an exception to the filesystem rule; tapes are normally accessed "raw." Typically, you send a* tar *or similar archive file directly to the tape device, and then you read it back through the same or a companion program. Floppies are occasionally used in the same way, particularly when transferring data between different Unix-like systems that may not share a common filesystem.*

Aside from tapes, the most unusual removable media formats, from a filesystem requirement perspective, are CD-R, CD-RW , and recordable DVD media. (From now on, I will refer to all three as *CD-R* media for simplicity's sake.) Most removable media enable random reading or writing of individual sectors of the disk. Although it's possible to randomly read individual CD-R sectors, randomly writing them is tricky at best, and it is frequently impossible. Instead, these media are normally written all at once; you write an entire filesystem to the disk, complete with all the data that filesystem will ever contain. Subsequent accesses are read-only. In the case of CD-RW and some recordable DVD media, the disc can be erased and rewritten, but this operation wipes out all the existing data on the disc. With some filesystems, it's possible to append new data to an already-written disc.

The read-only nature of the created CD-R media means that many normal read/write filesystem features are unnecessary. Therefore, a special read-only filesystem exists for CD-R media: ISO-9660. The upcoming section, "Burning CD-Rs," describes how to create an ISO-9660 filesystem and write it to a CD-R. CD-RW and recordable DVD discs also often use another filesystem, *Universal Disk Format (UDF)*, which supports more in the way of features useful for adding data to an already-created disk. Linux UDF support is not as mature as its ISO-9660 support, though. Two extensions to ISO-9660 are common: *Rock Ridge*, which adds support for Unix-style file ownership, permissions, and file types, as well as long filenames; and *Joliet*, which adds support for long filenames as used by Microsoft Windows. Linux supports both Rock Ridge and Joliet, and depending upon your specific needs, you may want to create CD-Rs that use neither, one, or both of these ISO-9660 extensions.

On more conventional removable-media disks, you can theoretically use any of the standard Linux filesystems you might use on a hard disk. One important concern with many media, though, is their limited capacity. Journaling filesystems require the creation of a *journal file*, which may be quite large. Therefore, most people don't use journaling filesystems on low-capacity removable media. Instead, the four most popular filesystems for non-CD-R removable media are as follows:

FAT   The *File Allocation Table (FAT)* filesystem is the primary filesystem for DOS and Windows 9*x*/Me. It's also supported by Windows NT/2000/XP and most other OSs. Therefore, FAT makes an excellent choice as a lowest-common-denominator filesystem. FAT is low in overhead, so you can often squeeze more files onto a FAT disk. Typically, you'll mount a FAT disk using the vfat filesystem type code, which enables support for long filenames. This usage doesn't support Linux ownership or permission information, though, so you shouldn't use FAT if preserving this information is important. (The umsdos FAT extension can preserve this information, but its use is rare.)

HFS   Apple's *Hierarchical File System (HFS)* is the Macintosh equivalent to FAT. If you need to exchange files with Mac OS users, HFS is a good choice. Linux's HFS support is not as mature as is its support for many other filesystems, though. Most Macintoshes include FAT support, so you may prefer to use FAT even when exchanging disks with Macintosh users.

The Minix Filesystem   Linux's first filesystem was borrowed from the Minix OS, and in Linux bears its name (minix). This filesystem has severe limitations on partition size (64MB) and filename length (30 characters), so it's a poor choice for use on Linux hard disks. It's useful for floppies, though. Because the Minix filesystem imposes very low overhead, you may be able to fit a few more files on a Minix-filesystem floppy than on an ext2fs floppy.

Ext2fs   The Second Extended Filesystem (ext2fs) has long been the standard Linux filesystem, and it can be a good choice for use on removable media when they'll be accessed only from Linux systems. By using ext2fs, you preserve all file attributes, including long filenames, ownership, and permissions. Most other OSs have limited support for ext2fs, though, so this filesystem isn't the best choice if you need to exchange files with other OSs.

TIP   When creating an ext2 filesystem with the mke2fs command, the -m option specifies the percentage of disk space that's to be reserved for use by root. The default value is 5, meaning 5 percent of disk space. This feature is an important safety measure on certain hard disk partitions, but it's unimportant on removable disks. Thus, passing the -m0 parameter to mke2fs will increase the amount of disk space accessible to ordinary users of a removable disk.

As a general rule, FAT and ext2fs are the best choices for removable media—FAT is the best when you're exchanging data with non-Linux systems, and ext2fs is best when you're sure the data will be read only by Linux systems. On rare occasions, you might want to use the Minix filesystem, HFS, tar, or even something more exotic.

Configuring Removable Media

Before you can begin using external media, you must configure them for use. For traditional disk media (floppies, Zip disks, and so on), this process involves either creating /etc/fstab entries, much as for hard disk filesystems; or using special access programs for some non-Linux filesystems. The upcoming section, "Burning CD-Rs," describes how to create CD-Rs in Linux. Chapter 17, "Protecting Your System with Backups," describes tape backups in more detail.

Prior to creating /etc/fstab entries or using other access methods, you must ensure that your computer can recognize the hardware itself. Some devices, including floppies and ATA drives, may need to be enabled in the computer's BIOS settings, so check there if you have problems seeing the device. For other devices, including SCSI devices if this is your only SCSI device, USB devices, and IEEE-1394 devices, you'll need to compile the appropriate support into the kernel to handle the controller or device. In particular, be sure you enable the support for SCSI disk devices (even for USB and IEEE-1394 devices), as well as for the appropriate SCSI, USB, or IEEE-1394 interface hardware.

USING ACCESS PROGRAMS FOR QUICK ACCESS

Two packages enable quick access to FAT and HFS media without actually mounting a drive. These packages are mtools for FAT (http://mtools.linux.lu) and HFS Utilities for HFS (http://www.mars.org/home/rob/proj/hfs/). Both packages enable you to insert a removable disk and copy files to and from the disk without mounting the disk with mount. Table 2.6 summarizes some of the commands offered by these packages.

TABLE 2.6: FAT AND HFS ACCESS COMMANDS

mTools COMMAND	HFS UTILITIES COMMAND	ACTION
–	hmount	Tells HFS Utilities what device to use.
–	humount	Tells HFS Utilities to stop using a volume.
mformat	hformat	Writes a new filesystem.
mcopy	hcopy	Copies a file to or from the disk.
mdir	hdir	Displays a directory listing.
mdel	hdel	Deletes a file.
mmove	hrename	Moves or renames a file.
mmd	hmkdir	Creates a new directory.
mrd	hrmdir	Removes an empty directory.

The mtools programs use DOS-style drive letters to determine what device to access. By default, a: and b: refer to the first and second floppy disks. Therefore, immediately after inserting a floppy disk, you could type **mcopy prog.zip a:** to copy prog.zip to the floppy. To use additional devices, you can edit the /etc/mtools.conf configuration file. (If you install mtools from source code, this file may be in /usr/local/etc.) If you want to create a custom configuration for a specific user, place it in the user's .mtoolsrc file, which overrides the global default file. These files link drive letters to specific device files using lines such as the following:

```
drive n: file=/dev/sda4
```

This line maps the n: drive to /dev/sda4 (a common identifier for the standard partition used by SCSI Zip disks). The standard file includes several examples, although some are intended for use under non-Linux OSs.

HFS Utilities requires that you first use hmount to tell the tools to access the disk. For instance, you might type **hmount /dev/sda** to tell the system to use an HFS-formatted SCSI Zip disk. Some commands, such as hcopy, require that you use the name of the disk volume as part of the command, or at least a colon (:) to indicate which filename is a local Linux filename and which applies to the HFS disk. For instance, you might type **hcopy prog.sit.hqx xfer:** to copy prog.sit.hqx to a volume with the disk label xfer. When you're done, you must use humount to finish all operations and stop using the removable disk. This step may be necessary to eject some removable disks. In addition to the standard text-mode tools, HFS Utilities includes a GUI front-end, xhfs, which enables point-and-click file transfers.

Both mtools and HFS Utilities provide access to their supported filesystems even when the Linux kernel lacks that support. HFS Utilities has the advantage of being a bit less trouble-prone than the Linux kernel's HFS support. Both suffer from one disadvantage, though: They're fundamentally just file-transfer tools. That is, you can't launch a Linux program and directly access files on the removable disk from that program. You must first copy the files to your hard disk, then copy them back to the removable disk when you've finished making changes. These tools also do no good if you want to access other filesystems, such as ext2fs or ISO-9660. In order to enable ordinary users to directly access any filesystem supported by the kernel, you must create /etc/fstab entries.

CREATING /etc/fstab ENTRIES FOR REGULAR ACCESS

The /etc/fstab file tells Linux where to mount specific filesystems. Entries for removable media are just like those for hard disk partitions. Most Linux distributions set up a few standard removable-media entries in /etc/fstab upon installation, so you may not need to modify these entries. Typical entries resemble the following:

```
/dev/cdrom   /mnt/cdrom   iso9660   user,noauto,ro        0 0
/dev/sda4    /mnt/zip     auto      user,noauto,uid=500   0 0
```

There are, however, some changes you might want to make:

Mount Points   Some distributions, such as Slackware and Debian, place mount points in the root (/) directory, as in /cdrom for the CD-ROM drive. Others, such as Red Hat and Mandrake, place mount points for individual drives within the /mnt directory, as in /mnt/cdrom. SuSE places mount points in subdirectories of /media, as in /media/cdrom. By altering the second column of the /etc/fstab entry for a device, you can change these assignments as you see fit.

Filesystem Type Codes   The filesystem type code tells Linux what filesystem to use when mounting a device. Common removable-media filesystem type codes include ext2 (ext2fs), minix (Minix filesystem) msdos (FAT with short filenames), vfat (FAT with long filenames), hfs (HFS), and iso9660 (ISO-9660, with auto-detection of Rock Ridge or Joliet extensions). It's sometimes not possible to specify in advance what filesystem a removable medium will use, so one common practice is to use the `auto` specification, which tells Linux to auto-detect the filesystem type. This feature usually works correctly, but on occasion it doesn't. You may want to specify different options for different filesystem types. In such cases, you can create separate entries, using different mount points, for each filesystem type.

Filesystem-Neutral Options   The `mount` man page details many filesystem-neutral options, which appear in a comma-separated list in the fourth column of `/etc/fstab`. Common options for removable media include `ro` (to force read-only access), `noexec` (to prevent users from executing program files on removable media), `user` (to enable ordinary users to mount and unmount the filesystem), and `noauto` (which tells Linux not to mount the filesystem when it boots). The last two options are particularly common for removable media, which normally aren't mounted until a user wants to access them.

Filesystem-Specific Options   Many filesystems include options unique to themselves or to just a few filesystems. The `uid=user-ID` and `gid=group-ID` options are common on non-Linux filesystems. These options set the user ID and group ID, respectively, to be assigned to all files on a mounted filesystem. Similarly, the `umask=umask` option sets the umask. These options are useful in fine-tuning who may access files on a mounted filesystem that doesn't support standard Unix-style ownership and permissions.

Some GUI environments attempt to auto-mount a filesystem when a CD-ROM disk is inserted. This setup is the default in Red Hat's GNOME configuration, for instance. If you prefer to manually mount your volumes, you can disable the automatic setup using tools such as the CD and DVD Properties tool in Red Hat, accessible from the GNOME Menu ➢ Preferences ➢ CD Properties menu option.

Burning CD-Rs

CD-R media are an extremely popular means of exchanging moderately large files. Most CD-R and CD-RW media hold 700MB of files (older discs held 650MB), while recordable DVD formats have capacities of several gigabytes. Plain write-once CD-R discs cost $0.50 or less and are likely to remain readable for several decades, given proper storage, so they're an excellent low-cost archival medium. You can't simply mount a CD-R disc and write files to it as you would a floppy disk, though; you must create a complete filesystem and then copy (or *burn*) that filesystem to the disc. This process requires using two tools, `mkisofs` and `cdrecord`; or variants of or front-ends to these tools.

NOTE   *This section describes creating CD-Rs. To read a CD-R, you can treat it like a CD-ROM and mount it using a standard removable-media mount point, as described earlier in "Creating /etc/fstab Entries for Regular Access." CD-Rs created by Macintosh users sometimes use HFS, so you might also be able to use HFS Utilities, as described in "Using Access Programs for Quick Access."*

Linux CD-R Tools

The Linux CD-R-creation process involves three steps:

1. **Collect source files.** You must first collect source files in one location, typically a single subdirectory of your home directory.

2. **Create a filesystem.** You point a filesystem-creation program, `mkisofs`, at your source directory. This program generates an ISO-9660 filesystem in an image file. Alternatively, you can create another filesystem in an appropriately sized partition or image file and copy files to that partition or image file. This latter approach can be used to create ext2fs, FAT, or other types of CD-Rs, but there's seldom any advantage to doing this.

TIP   If you install an OS to a partition that's less than 700MB in size, you can back it up by burning the partition directly to CD-R. The result is a CD-R that uses the OS's native filesystem. You can restore the backup by using `dd`, *assuming the target partition is exactly the same size as the original.*

3. **Burn the CD-R.** You use a CD-R burning program, such as `cdrecord`, to copy the CD-R image file to the CD-R device.

The traditional three-step approach to CD-R creation is a bit on the tedious side. One way to minimize this tedium is to use GUI front-ends to `mkisofs` and `cdrecord`. These GUI tools provide a point-and-click interface, eliminating the need to remember obscure command-line parameters. Popular GUI Linux CD-R tools include:

X-CD-Roast   This program, headquartered at `http://www.xcdroast.org`, was one of the first GUI front-ends to `mkisofs` and `cdrecord`, although the latest versions are substantially improved over earlier versions.

ECLiPt Roaster   This program, which is also known as *ERoaster*, is part of the ECLiPt project (`http://eclipt.uni-klu.ac.at`), which aims to support various Linux tools and protocols, frequently through the use of GUI front-ends.

GNOME Toaster   This program, which is also known as *GToaster*, is tightly integrated with GNOME, although it can be used from other environments. Check `http://gnometoaster .rulez.org` for more information on this package.

K3B   This program, based at `http://k3b.sourceforge.net`, is a front-end that uses Qt (the KDE toolkit). It's the default CD-R tool for some distributions.

All of these programs work in similar ways, although the details differ. X-CD-Roast must first be run by `root` before ordinary users can use it. Other programs may require setting the SUID bit on the `cdrecord` executable, and ensuring it's owned by `root`, if ordinary users are to use them. In order to work, a GUI front-end must be able to detect your CD-R drive or be told what it is. On my test system, X-CD-Roast, ECLiPt, and K3B had no problem with this task, but GNOME Toaster failed to detect my CD-R drive. The moral: If one tool doesn't work, try another.

All of these CD-R tools provide a dizzying array of options. For the most part, the default options work quite well, although you will need to provide information to identify your CD-R drive and burn speed, as described in the next section, "A Linux CD-R Example." Some `mkisofs` options can also be important in generating image files that can be read on a wide variety of OSs, as described in "Creating Cross-Platform CD-Rs."

A Linux CD-R Example

If you're unfamiliar with Linux CD-R burning, the gentlest introduction is usually to try a GUI tool. Here is how to do the job using X-CD-Roast:

1. Start the program by typing **xcdroast** in an **xterm** window or by selecting the program from a desktop environment menu.

NOTE   The first time you start X-CD-Roast, it may inform you that you lack sufficient privileges. If so, start the program as **root**, *click Setup, click the Users tab, and ensure that Allow All is selected in the Access by Users area (alternatively, add specific users who should be given CD-R writing privileges to the list). Click Change Non-***root** *Configuration and confirm that you want to enable non-***root** *mode. After you quit, ordinary users should be able to run X-CD-Roast.*

2. Click the Create CD button in the main window.

3. Click the Master Tracks button. The result is the X-CD-Roast track-mastering window, shown in Figure 2.2.

4. Add files and directories to the file list. Do this by selecting the files or directories you want to add in the File/Directory View pane and clicking Add. X-CD-Roast will ask what part of the path to the files or directories you want to keep. Make a selection and click OK. Your selection will appear in the Session View pane.

5. Click the Create Session/Image tab, which brings up the display shown in Figure 2.3. Check in the New Session Size field in the Session Information area to be sure you haven't exceeded the capacity of your media. If you have, go back and remove files.

FIGURE 2.2

X-CD-Roast provides GUI tools for specifying what files to include on a CD-R.

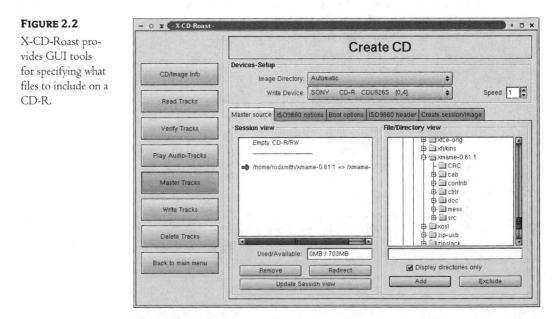

FIGURE 2.3

Additional CD-R creation options are available on additional program tabs.

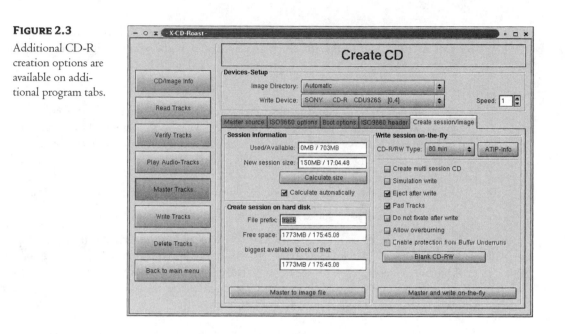

6. Click the ISO-9660 Options tab in the main window. This action displays a large number of options you can set. The defaults are usually fine, but you should be sure that both the Joliet Extension (for Windows) and Rock Ridge (Anonymous) options are selected. You may also want to check the options on the ISO-9660 Header tab, in which you can set a volume title and similar information.

7. From the Create Session/Image tab (see Figure 2.3), Click the Master and Write On-the-Fly button. The program displays a dialog box asking for confirmation that you're ready to continue. If you haven't already inserted a blank CD-R in your drive, do so, and then click OK. The program displays a progress dialog box summarizing the burn operation.

NOTE *You may need to adjust the permissions on your CD-R device file to use a GUI CD-R package. Alternatively, you can set the set-user-ID (SUID) and set-group-ID (SGID) bits on the* cdrecord *binary. For instance, as* root, *type* **chmod 6755 /usr/bin/cdrecord** *to give all users access to* cdrecord, *including* root *privileges while running it. Change* 6755 *to* 6750 *to limit access to those users who belong to whatever group owns* cdrecord.

There are many additional options in X-CD-Roast, of course. For instance, you can create a bootable CD-R by using the Boot Options tab (shown in Figures 2.2 and 2.3), selecting the El Torito (for IA-32) or Sparc (for Sun workstations) option, and entering the path to a bootable floppy disk image in the Boot Image field. You can create audio CD-Rs by placing .wav or other supported audio files in the temporary storage directory (specified from the setup area's HD Settings tab; typically /tmp). Click Write Tracks and use the Layout Tracks tab to select which audio files you want to burn and in what order. You can also burn an existing image file in much the same way—copy the file to the temporary storage directory and tell X-CD-Roast to copy it using the Write Tracks option.

Despite their wide range of options, X-CD-Roast and other GUI tools aren't always the best way to create a CD-R. Sometimes, the command-line tools are the solution. To create an image file, you use the mkisofs command:

```
$ mkisofs -J -r -V "volume name" -o ../image.iso ./
```

This command creates an image file called *image.iso* in the parent of the current directory, using the contents of the current working directory (./) as the image contents. The -J and -r options enable Joliet and Rock Ridge extensions, respectively, and the -V option sets the volume name to whatever you specify. Dozens of other options and variants on these are available; check the mkisofs man page for details.

Once you've created an image file, you can burn it with a command such as the following:

```
$ cdrecord dev=0,4,0 speed=2 ../image.iso
```

In this example, dev=0,4,0 option specifies that SCSI host adapter 0 is used, burning to the CD-R drive on SCSI ID 4, with logical unit (LUN) 0. The speed is set using the speed option, and the final parameter specifies the source of the file to be burned. As with mkisofs, cdrecord supports many additional options; consult its man page for details. If the SUID bit isn't set on this program, with ownership set to root, you must run it as root.

TIP   You can use the loopback option to verify the contents of an image file before burning it. For instance, typing **mount -t iso9660 -o loop image.iso /mnt/cdrom** *mounts the image.iso file to /mnt/cdrom. You can then check that all the files that should be present are present. You must be* **root** *to use this option, or you must have created an appropriate /etc/fstab entry.*

Creating Cross-Platform CD-Rs

You may want to create a CD-R that works on many different OSs. If so, you may want to create a CD-R that uses a wide range of filesystems and filesystem extensions. Such CD-Rs contain just one copy of each file; the filesystems are written in such a way that they all point their unique directory structures at the same files. Thus, the extra space required by such a multiplatform CD-R is minimal. Features you may want to use on such a CD-R include:

Follow Symbolic Links   The -f option to mkisofs causes the tool to read the files that symbolic links point to and include them on the CD-R, rather than to write symbolic links as such using Rock Ridge extensions. Following symbolic links can increase the disk space used on a CD-R, but this option is required if you want symbolic links to produce reasonable results on systems that don't understand Rock Ridge, such as Windows.

Long ISO-9660 Filenames   Normally, mkisofs creates only short filenames for the base ISO-9660 filesystem. Long filenames are stored in Rock Ridge, Joliet, or other filesystem extensions. You can increase the raw ISO-9660 name length to 31 characters with the -l (that's a lowercase *L*) option. This option yields a CD-R with some files that may not be readable on MS-DOS, but some OSs may display the full filenames when they otherwise wouldn't.

Joliet Support   The -J option to mkisofs, as noted earlier, creates an image with Joliet extensions. These extensions do *not* interfere with reading the CD-R from OSs that don't understand Joliet.

Rock Ridge support   The -R and -r options both add Rock Ridge extensions. The -R option adds the extensions, but it doesn't change ownership or permissions on files. Using -r works the same, except that it changes ownership of all files to root, gives all users access to the files, and removes write permissions. These features are usually desirable on a CD-R that's to be used on any but the original author's computer.

UDF Support   You can add support for UDF by including the -udf option. As of mkisofs 1.15, UDF support is considered experimental, and the generated filesystem doesn't support all UDF features.

HFS Support   To create a CD-R that includes Mac OS HFS support, add the -hfs option. When you insert the resulting CD-R into a Macintosh, the computer will read the HFS filenames. A slew of options are related to this one. These options include -map *mapping-file* (to point mkisofs at a file to map filename extensions to HFS file and creator types), --netatalk (to include file and creator types stored on directories used by a Netatalk server), and -probe (which tells mkisofs to try to determine the creator and type codes by examining the files' contents).

Translation Table   You can pass the -T option to have mkisofs create a file called TRANS.TBL (or something else you specify with the -table-name option). This file contains the mapping of long (Rock Ridge) filenames to short (ISO-9660) filenames. This file can be useful if the CD-R will be read on a DOS system or something else that doesn't understand your long filename extensions.

Because mkisofs supports so many filesystems and options, it can be an excellent way to create a CD-R that's maximally accessible on as many platforms as possible. For instance, you can add all the filesystem options and have a CD-R that will be readable, complete with long filenames, on Linux, other Unix-like OSs, Windows, and Mac OS. Few other CD-R programs can make this claim.

Summary

Disk performance is very important to overall system performance, so being able to optimize disk performance is a valuable skill to possess. Doing so begins with understanding the benefits of both of the major disk interface standards, ATA and SCSI. Knowing how to select and configure disk interface hardware can also help you get the most out of your disk. Even partition placement can play a role; by putting heavily used partitions where they'll yield the best performance, you can improve overall disk performance, even without tweaking the hardware settings. Linux treats removable media differently than do many other OSs, so picking the appropriate media and setting them up properly are very important skills.

Chapter 3

Using External Peripherals

THE PRECEDING TWO CHAPTERS described configuring various devices (such as the CPU, video card, and hard disks) that usually reside inside the computer's case. Many computer devices, though, are external—they sit outside of the computer and connect to it via a cable, or sometimes even an infrared or radio link. Examples include keyboards, mice, scanners, cameras, modems, and printers. Most of these devices connect through one of three types of *ports*, or interfaces: the *Universal Serial Bus (USB)*, *RS-232 serial* ports, or *parallel* ports. A few devices, including many keyboards and mice, as well as some scanners, interface through other ports. This chapter begins with a look at the three main ports; you'll need to know about them even when you're dealing with devices (such as cameras, modems, and printers) that aren't explicitly covered in this chapter. This chapter then looks at three different external devices: keyboards, mice, and scanners.

Configuring USB, RS-232 Serial, and Parallel Ports

No matter what external device you use, the computer communicates with it via some sort of port. USB, RS-232 serial, and parallel ports all have their own unique configuration requirements, ranging from kernel settings to utilities that enable you to optimize the performance of the devices attached to the port.

NOTE *Some devices use other types of external ports. Most Small Computer System Interface (SCSI) host adapters, for instance, have external connectors, used to connect external hard disks, tape drives, scanners, and so on. IEEE-1394 devices are usually external, but they're still fairly rare in 2003. Many keyboards and mice connect through dedicated keyboard and mouse ports, as described in the upcoming sections, "Overcoming Keyboard Quirks" and "Using a Mouse to the Fullest."*

The devices described in this chapter usually interface through connectors on an IA-32 system's motherboard, as depicted in Figure 3.1. These connectors are accessible from the back of a typical computer. The port connectors on some older systems were placed on expansion cards. Even today, such cards may be used to add extra ports, should you need more than the standard mix. Some systems place one or more USB connectors on the front of the computer, instead of or in addition to the back-panel USB connectors. Some very old RS-232 ports, as well as the RS-232 connectors on most external devices, use wide 25-pin connectors rather than the 9-pin connectors shown in Figure 3.1.

FIGURE 3.1

The port connectors on modern IA-32 computers are placed in a standard arrangement and are accessible from the back of the computer.

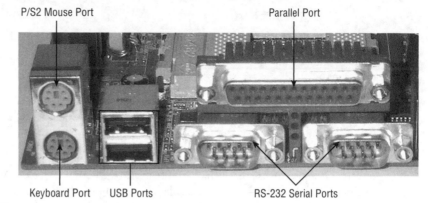

P/S2 Mouse Port

Parallel Port

Keyboard Port   USB Ports

RS-232 Serial Ports

Recognizing USB Devices

Introduced in the late 1990s, USB took a while to take hold, but it's now become an extremely popular device interface. Some computers, particularly Macintoshes, have discarded RS-232 serial and parallel interfaces entirely in favor of USB ports, which are faster than RS-232 serial ports and more flexible than parallel ports. USB's flexibility, though, comes at a cost: Linux requires dozens of distinct drivers to support the many available USB devices. Therefore, configuring USB support can be tricky. Unfortunately, Linux doesn't support all USB devices, although Linux does support many of the most popular USB devices.

USB DRIVER REQUIREMENTS

In order to use a USB device, your computer requires at least two types of drivers. In some cases, you may need additional drivers, as well:

USB Host Controller Drivers   The *host controller driver (HCD)* is the driver for USB itself, as implemented by a chipset on your motherboard or a USB expansion card. As of the 2.5.54 kernel, Linux supports three HCDs: *Enhanced Host Controller Interface (EHCI)*, *Open Host Controller Interface (OHCI)*, and *Universal Host Controller Interface (UHCI)*. EHCI handles the USB 2.0 protocol (which is capable of speeds of up to 60MB/s, as opposed to 1.5MB/s for USB 1.*x*). UHCI is the USB 1.*x* controller used by Intel and VIA motherboard chipsets. OHCI is the USB 1.*x* controller used by most add-on cards and motherboards that use chipsets from manufacturers other than Intel or VIA. If your system has USB 2.0 support, you need both the EHCI driver and either the UHCI or OHCI driver.

USB Device Drivers   Each USB device is uniquely addressable and supports its own commands. For instance, Linux must be able to treat a USB Zip disk as a block device (to transfer 512-byte blocks in one operation), whereas a USB keyboard must be configured as a character device (to transfer data in single-byte chunks). Furthermore, Zip disks require sector addressing, disk-lock commands, and other features that are not needed by keyboards. Thus, each USB device requires its own drivers. Some of these drivers, such as those for keyboards, mice, and printers, work for an entire class of device. Others, such as mass storage drivers for disk and disk-like devices, are often written for specific brands and models of devices, although generic drivers sometimes work with devices that aren't explicitly supported.

Non-USB Support Drivers   Some USB drivers tie into older non-USB portions of the kernel's device driver hierarchy. Most notably, USB mass storage drivers make the USB devices look like SCSI devices to Linux programs. There are also USB-to-RS-232-serial and USB-to-parallel adapters, which link into RS-232 serial and parallel systems in the kernel, respectively; and USB speakers that look like sound cards to software. In all of these cases, you need to activate at least basic support for the mimicked device type. For instance, to use a USB Zip drive, you need both basic SCSI and SCSI disk support. The USB mass storage driver then works much like a driver for a specific SCSI host adapter.

Non-Kernel Drivers   Some devices—most notably scanners, cameras, printers, and mice—require non-kernel drivers in support software. Scanners need drivers in the *Scanner Access Now Easy (SANE)* package, as described in the upcoming section, "Getting a Scanner to Work." Cameras are supported by camera packages, as described in Chapter 8, "Miscellaneous User Tools." Printers usually need drivers in Ghostscript, as described in Chapter 13, "Managing Printers." Mice require drivers in X or in text-based mouse packages. USB mice use the PS/2 mouse protocol or variants of it, as described in the upcoming section, "Using a Mouse to the Fullest."

In addition to these drivers, the Linux USB kernel options include some features that tweak performance or modify the way Linux interfaces with USB devices. For instance, the USB Device Filesystem option creates a `/proc/bus/usb/devices` virtual file that contains information on USB devices.

NOTE   The USB Device Filesystem option doesn't create any files or subdirectories in the `/dev` directory. If you activate the `/dev` Filesystem Support option in the Filesystems kernel configuration area and activate this filesystem at boot, though, Linux will automatically create device file entries for your USB devices, which can greatly simplify locating them.

Most Linux distributions ship with support for most USB devices available as modules. If you recompile your kernel, though, you'll need to be sure to compile support by selecting the options you need in the USB Support section of the kernel configuration, as shown in Figure 3.2 for a 2.5.54 kernel. Chapter 15, "Creating a Custom Kernel," describes kernel compilation in more detail.

TIP   New USB drivers are constantly being written and added to the kernel. Thus, if a USB device doesn't work with Linux as installed, do a web search or simply try the latest kernel. Your device might be supported in a more recent kernel. You should also check `http://www.linux-usb.org`, which hosts information on the latest Linux USB developments.

USING A USB DEVICE

Because USB devices are so varied, it's impossible to present simple and complete instructions on their use. The general outline for using USB devices is as follows:

1. Plug the USB device into the computer.

FIGURE 3.2

The Linux kernel provides a large number of USB driver options.

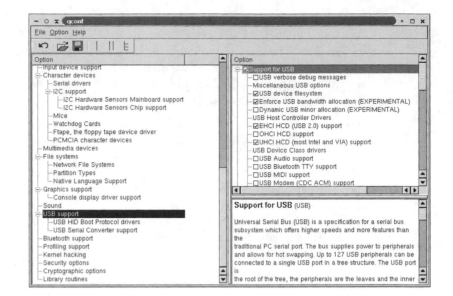

2. If applicable, turn on the device.

3. Load the Linux kernel modules for the driver, as described in Chapter 1, "Optimizing System Architecture Usage." In most cases, the drivers will load automatically when you plug in the device or power it on.

4. Use the device just as you would any other device of its class. For instance, create an appropriate entry for a USB mouse in /etc/X11/XF86Config; or mount a USB Zip disk with mount.

If you opted to create a /dev filesystem, most USB devices will be accessible through files in the /dev/usb subdirectory. For instance, a Kodak DC-240 digital camera appears as /dev/usb/dc2xx0 and a USB scanner is /dev/usb/scanner0. Some devices—mainly those that mimic older hardware types, such as USB mass storage devices—appear under other names. For instance, a USB Zip disk is likely to be accessible as /dev/sda, with partitions numbered /dev/sda1 and up, assuming the system has no true SCSI disks or other USB mass storage devices. Mandrake and Slackware use a /dev filesystem by default, but other common distributions don't.

If you don't use the /dev filesystem, your distribution will have shipped with a large number of device files, most probably including a /dev/usb subdirectory for common USB devices. Unfortunately, naming and placement of device files in /dev isn't entirely consistent across distributions— particularly for USB devices, although most bear common names, such as /dev/usb/scanner0 for a scanner. You may need to locate your driver's documentation for instructions on creating device-specific device files, particularly for less common hardware.

Using *setserial* to Optimize RS-232 Serial Performance

RS-232 serial ports are general-purpose communication ports; in theory, you could design any number of devices to use these ports. In practice, though, they're limited by slow speed—115,200bps on standard hardware, although some designs can manage twice or more of that value. This speed compares to 12Mbps (12,000,000bps) for USB 1.*x* or 480Mbps for USB 2.0. For this reason, RS-232 is used only by relatively low-speed peripherals. Common RS-232 devices include external telephone modems, low-speed text-only dumb terminals, mice, and digital cameras. It is possible to link two computers via their RS-232 serial ports using the *Point-to-Point Protocol (PPP)* or *Serial Line Interface Protocol (SLIP)*, but this application is very rare.

NOTE *Older internal modems typically included both modem and RS-232 circuitry on one circuit board. These modems are indistinguishable from regular RS-232 serial ports from a software point of view. Most newer internal modems are so-called WinModems or software modems. These modems don't include serial port hardware and require special drivers to function in Linux. Check* `http://www.linmodems.org` *for information on such modems.*

Most programs that use the RS-232 serial port, such as gPhoto when it communicates with an RS-232-interfaced camera or `pppd` for initiating dial-up modem connections to an ISP, provide tools to set the speed of the RS-232 serial port, as well as other relevant options. Sometimes, though, it's necessary to set RS-232 serial port options before launching a communication program or to do so at boot time. You can do this using the `setserial` program, which reads and writes RS-232 serial port parameters. You pass one or more parameters to this program, as well as the device filename of the interface; for instance, to obtain a listing of the current RS-232 serial port parameters, you would type:

```
$ setserial -a /dev/ttyS0
/dev/ttyS0, Line 0, UART: 16550A, Port: 0x03f8, IRQ: 4
        Baud_base: 115200, close_delay: 50, divisor: 0
        closing_wait: 3000
        Flags: spd_normal skip_test
```

The -a option tells the program to display all the device's information. The *universal asynchronous receiver/transmitter (UART)* is the core of the RS-232 serial port. Most UARTs today are 16550A models, but others exist. If `setserial` reports that your system has a 16450, or especially an 8250, then either the system has erred in detecting your hardware or you have a truly ancient RS-232 serial port. Such old ports may not function well at speeds above 38,400bps, so you should probably replace the hardware.

If you want to change an RS-232 serial port's parameters, you can do so by following the device identifier (such as `/dev/ttyS0` for the first port) with options such as the following:

port *port-number* This option changes the hardware port associated with the device identifier. The *port-number* is typically expressed as a hexadecimal value, such as `0x03f8`.

irq *irq-number* You can assign the interrupt request (IRQ) line used by a device using this option.

uart *uart-type* If the system has misidentified the UART, you can correct the matter with this option. Legal *uart-type* values are 8250, 16450, 16550, 16550A, 16650, 16650V2, 16654, 16750, 16850, 16950, and 16954. Specifying `none` disables the port.

autoconfig This parameter tells the kernel to try to determine the RS-232 serial port type. This option requires you to also use the `port` option.

skip_test   Use this parameter in conjunction with `autoconfig` to tell the system to skip the UART detection test, which can cause problems with some brands of UART.

baud_base *rate*   You can set the RS-232 serial port's speed, in bits per second, to the specified *rate* with this option.

These options are just a sample of those available. If you're using a very timing-critical RS-232 serial port application (say, a scientific data acquisition tool), you may want to read the `setserial` man page to study the many options that can influence RS-232 serial port performance. For the most part, none of these options are required. You're most likely to need to use these options with some inexpensive internal modems, which may use oddball UARTs that aren't auto-detected correctly; or with unusual multiport RS-232 serial cards, which support more than four ports. (Linux tries to auto-configure just the first four RS-232 serial ports.)

A typical motherboard ships with two RS-232 serial ports, but sometimes you may need more than this—for instance, if you're running an ISP's modem dial-in bank. In these cases, you probably want to purchase a dedicated multiport RS-232 card. These devices are unusual pieces of equipment that require special drivers, so check for Linux driver availability before buying. If you add an internal ISA bus modem that hosts its own RS-232 serial hardware, you may run into a problem: Traditionally, the first two RS-232 serial ports use IRQs 4 and 3. Many internal modems come preconfigured as the third RS-232 serial port and attempt to "share" IRQ 4. This configuration may not work well in Linux, though, because interrupt sharing of ISA devices is a tricky proposition at best. Therefore, if you add an internal modem, your best bet is to disable one of the two standard RS-232 serial ports and reconfigure the modem to assume its identity. This way, there's no conflict over the IRQ. Alternatively, leave the modem configured to be the third RS-232 serial port (`/dev/ttyS2` in Linux), but configure it to use an IRQ that no other device claims. Type **cat /proc/interrupts** after you've booted to obtain a list of interrupts—but be aware that this list will omit interrupts that aren't in use because the driver hasn't been loaded, such as a floppy port if you've not used the floppy disk recently. Similarly, you can configure the modem on the standard first or second port's settings and reconfigure the displaced motherboard port as the third port.

Improving Printing with Interrupts

Most IA-32 computers provide one parallel port, which is most commonly used to drive a printer. Occasionally, you'll find other parallel port devices, such as scanners or Zip drives. In theory, parallel ports are capable of speeds approaching 2MB/s, but in practice this optimum speed is seldom obtained. Several causes of this deficit are common:

Sub-Optimal Port Settings   Modern parallel ports support several different operating modes: *standard parallel port (SPP)*, *enhanced parallel port (EPP)*, and *enhanced capabilities port (ECP)*. For ports built into the motherboard, you set the mode from the BIOS's setting screen, typically accessed by pressing Delete or some other key early in the boot process. For the best performance, select ECP mode, or at least EPP; SPP produces distinctly lower transfer rates than other modes.

Poor Cables   Some cables don't work well with EPP or ECP modes, or they may not work at all with some printers. For the best results, be sure you're using an IEEE-1284 cable.

Interrupt Settings   Parallel ports can work either without an interrupt (IRQ) or with one. IRQ-less operation consumes more CPU time and is usually slower than IRQ-driven operation; however, there are cases in which use of IRQs can impair performance. You may need to experiment to determine the optimal settings.

Linux's parallel port drivers have changed substantially over the years. With 2.4.*x* and later kernels, these drivers have several layers. For typical use with a printer on the IA-32 architecture, there are three drivers:

◆ `parport`, which provides basic parallel-port operation

◆ `parport_pc`, which handles the parallel port as implemented on IA-32 systems

◆ `lp`, which uses the parallel port to communicate with a printer

Other parallel-interfaced devices use drivers other than `lp` atop the `parport` and `parport_pc` drivers.

To determine whether your system is currently using interrupts for printing, type the following command, which displays a list of interrupts used by the parallel port driver:

```
# grep parport /proc/interrupts
  7:         0          XT-PIC  parport0
```

If this command produces no output, either your system isn't configured to use interrupts or the parallel port drivers aren't loaded. Check the contents of `/proc/modules` for the `parport`, `parport_pc`, and `lp` modules. If they aren't present, review your kernel configuration to see if the drivers are compiled into the kernel.

If your printer performance isn't what you'd like it to be, you might try changing from IRQ-less to IRQ-driven printing, or vice-versa. This change isn't guaranteed to have a dramatic impact on printing speed, but it might help.

In order to change the interrupt settings using 2.4.*x* and later kernels, you need to change the parameters passed to the `parport_pc` driver, as described in Chapter 1. Specifically, you might use a line such as the following in `/etc/modules.conf` to enable interrupt-driven printing:

```
options parport_pc io=0x378 irq=7
```

This line tells the system to use I/O port 0x378 and IRQ 7 for the parallel port. IRQ 7 is typical for the first parallel port. I/O port 0x378 is also typical, but some systems use 0x3bc. Check your BIOS settings or the jumpers on the parallel port card to determine what `io` setting to use. You should also check `/proc/interrupts` to be sure that IRQ 7 isn't already in use by another device. If it is, you may need to reconfigure that device or the parallel port before proceeding.

After modifying `/etc/modules.conf`, you can remove the parallel port drivers by using `rmmod` to remove each of the modules. You can then type **modprobe lp** to reload these drivers with the new settings. Check `/proc/interrupts` to see if the parallel port is now using the IRQ.

WARNING   *It's possible, but unlikely, that the new parallel port settings will hang the computer. If this happens, you'll need to use an emergency recovery system to restore your original `/etc/modules.conf` before rebooting the computer.*

Factors other than the interrupt setting can influence printing speed or reliability. One common problem relates to the use of Ghostscript when printing common document types. Linux doesn't use most non-PostScript printers' built-in fonts, so even many plain-text files are sent as huge bitmap graphics, which can be time-consuming. Chapter 13 addresses these high-level printing issues in more detail.

Overcoming Keyboard Quirks

In most cases, keyboards just plain work. On IA-32 platforms, the keyboard support is so standardized and necessary that it doesn't even appear as an option in the kernel configuration menus—it's compiled into the kernel as a matter of course. Behind the scenes, though, a lot happens in Linux's keyboard processing, so quirks can emerge. These quirks include odd mappings between keys and characters in text mode or in X. Such quirks are particularly common when using non-U.S. keyboards or unusual keyboards, such as those that use the Dvorak layout. Finally, if you use a USB keyboard, you may need to take special steps to ensure that it works under Linux.

Understanding Keyboards in Linux

In order to manage a keyboard in Linux, it helps to understand what happens to keyboard input data. Figure 3.3 illustrates this process. The keyboard sends a *scan code* to the computer. This code maps to a physical key, but any given scan code might represent a different symbol depending upon the keyboard type. For instance, a Russian keyboard might return more-or-less the same scan codes as a U.S. keyboard, but the Russian keyboard's scan codes map to Cyrillic letters, whereas the U.S. keyboard's scan codes map to Roman letters. This mapping to individual symbols is done in different ways depending upon whether the computer is running in text mode or in X.

Figure 3.3

Keyboard input processing in Linux can take one of two paths.

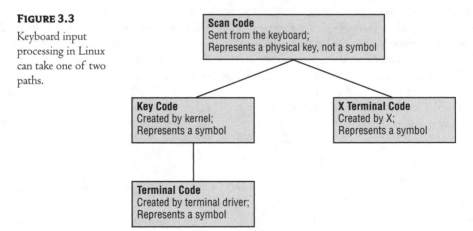

In text mode, the kernel interprets the scan code and creates a *key code*. Most text-based Linux programs, though, are designed to work both from the console and from remote logins—dumb terminals, network logins, xterm windows, and so on. Therefore, a terminal driver converts key codes into a final code type that I refer to as a *terminal code*. This code is a uniform representation of the symbol on the keyboard, no matter what device generated the keypress.

When you run X, the X server reads scan codes directly and does its own conversion into an X-based terminal code. X-based programs work from this terminal code. When you run a text-mode program in an xterm window, the xterm must generate a conventional text-mode terminal code from the X terminal code.

In summary, three major key mapping conversions take place. You can modify any of these mapping operations by running the appropriate utilities or modifying configuration files. When you installed Linux, one of the questions you were asked was what type of keyboard you use. The installation program used your answer to this question to set up appropriate keyboard maps for both text mode and X. You might have cause to adjust this map, though. For instance, you might have given the wrong information when you installed Linux, or the map might be incorrect as delivered by the distribution provider. You might also want to change the map to individualize the keyboard to your liking. The next two sections, "Getting a Keyboard to Work in Text Mode" and "Getting a Keyboard to Work in X," describe how to do this.

Getting a Keyboard to Work in Text Mode

The `loadkeys` program loads a keymap that modifies the kernel's mapping of scan codes to key codes. You normally pass the name of a mapping file to this program; if you omit a mapping filename, the program uses a default mapping. Most distributions call `loadkeys` as part of the system startup process, as summarized in Table 3.1.

TABLE 3.1: KEYMAP CONFIGURATION FILES

DISTRIBUTION	`loadkeys` CALLED FROM	DEFAULT KEYMAP SPECIFIED IN	KEYMAP FILE STORAGE DIRECTORY
Debian	`/etc/init.d/keymap.sh`	`/etc/init.d/keymap.sh`	`/etc/console` and `/usr/share/keymaps`
Mandrake	`/etc/rc.d/rc.sysinit` and `/etc/rc.d/init.d/keytable`	`/etc/sysconfig/keyboard`	`/usr/lib/kbd/keymaps`
Red Hat	`/etc/rc.d/rc.sysinit` and `/etc/rc.d/init.d/keytable`	`/etc/sysconfig/keyboard`	`/lib/kbd/keymaps`
Slackware	N/A	N/A	`/usr/share/kbd/keymaps`
SuSE	`/etc/init.d/kbd`	`/etc/sysconfig/keyboard`	`/usr/share/kbd/keymaps`

Most distributions point `loadkeys` directly at a keymap file in a subdirectory of the directory specified in the Keymap File Storage Directory column of Table 3.1. Debian is an oddball in this respect; when you install it, it copies a keymap file from `/usr/share/keymaps` to the `/etc/console/boottime.kmap.gz` file. Slackware is even more odd; it doesn't call `loadkeys` at all during its boot process; it uses the default keymap and requires you to modify a startup file, such as `/etc/rc.d/rc.local`, if you want to load a custom keymap.

Even if your keymap is set up correctly, you may be vexed by peculiar keyboard repeat rate settings. If you find that too many or too few characters appear each second after you hold down a key for a brief period, then you need to adjust the keyboard repeat rate. You can do this with the `kbdrate` program, which takes rate and delay parameters, as shown here:

```
# kbdrate -r 12 -d 250
```

The rate (-r) setting is specified in characters per second, and the delay (-d) setting is specified in milliseconds. Thus, the preceding example sets the keyboard repeat rate at 12 characters per second after a 250ms (1/4-second) delay. This command must be typed by root, or it can be included in custom startup scripts. In fact, the script that calls loadkeys, as specified in Table 3.1, often calls kbdrate, so you can modify that call instead of creating a new one. Some distributions pass parameters in this file that are stored elsewhere, such as in /etc/sysconfig/keyboard.

Getting a Keyboard to Work in X

X's keyboard mapping is set up in the main X configuration file, which is called XF86Config or XF86Config-4 and is stored in /etc or /etc/X11. This file contains a section that includes various keyboard parameters:

```
Section "InputDevice"
    Identifier "Keyboard1"
    Driver  "Keyboard"
    Option  "XkbModel"     "pc105"
    Option  "XkbLayout"    "us"
    Option  "XkbOptions"   ""
    Option  "AutoRepeat"   "250 12"
EndSection
```

TIP   *You can type* **setxkbmap -v** *to view your current X keyboard settings, even if they've been changed since starting X.*

You can ignore some of these entries. The most important are listed here:

Option "XkbModel" "pc105"   This line tells X what set of scan codes to expect from the keyboard. In the U.S., pc101, pc104, and pc105 keyboards are common. The macintosh setting is appropriate for Linux running on Macintoshes, and you should use sun if you've got a Sun keyboard. You can use the setxkbmap -model *name* command to change the keyboard model name after X has started.

Option "XkbLayout" "us"   This option tells the system how to map scan codes to X terminal codes. Most options are two-letter country codes, such as us for the U.S., de for Germany, and so on. You can find a list of codes and their meanings in the /usr/X11R6/lib/X11/xkb/symbols.dir file. You can load a new keyboard layout with the setxkbmap -symbols *layout-name* command, where *layout-name* is the name of an appropriate layout.

Option "AutoRepeat" "250 12"   This line isn't present in most configurations, but you can add it to adjust the keyboard repeat rate. The 250 in this example is the delay before the keys begin repeating, in milliseconds; and 12 is the repeat rate in characters per second. You can also change the repeat rate after logging in or launching X by using the xset r rate *delay repeat-rate* command, where *delay* is the delay period and *repeat-rate* is the repeat rate. The GNOME desktop environment includes a GUI control to adjust the keyboard repeat rate as part of its Control Center, but KDE lacks an equivalent.

If you want to modify just a few keys, you can use the -e option to xmodmap to modify a single key in the keyboard map. For instance, if your Tab key is mapped incorrectly, you could use the following command to fix it:

```
$ xmodmap -e 'keycode 23 = Tab'
```

If you collect several such corrections, you can put them in a file and load them all by typing **xmodmap *filename***, where *filename* is the name of the file holding the modification. Many X configurations automatically load the .Xmodmap file from the user's home directory in this way whenever a user logs in or starts X.

If you need to modify your keyboard configuration because you're using a keyboard for a non-English language, one additional step may be helpful, although it's not technically a keyboard issue: Set the LANG environment variable in the .bash_profile file in your home directory. This variable tells many programs what language to use for menus and on-screen displays. (Some programs, such as Mozilla, rely upon their own unique language settings, though.) You can find a set of language codes in the /usr/X11R6/lib/X11/locale directory.

USING A DVORAK KEYBOARD LAYOUT

If you're willing to invest some time in learning a new keyboard layout, the Dvorak layout may be worth investigating. Experienced typists who learn Dvorak often report being able to type faster with Dvorak than with the traditional QWERTY layout. You can load a Dvorak layout in Linux's text mode by typing **loadkeys dvorak**, or by modifying your startup scripts to run this command.

In theory, you should be able to specify dvorak as the XkbLayout option to use a Dvorak layout in X. In practice, though, this may not work correctly. The http://home.xyzz.org/dvorak/ site includes a file that can be used as a .Xmodmap file to create a Dvorak layout.

USB Keyboard Quirks

Recently, USB keyboards have emerged as an alternative to the more common PS/2 keyboards. USB keyboards can work quite well, but they do carry some caveats. The first of these is that the keyboard may not work until after Linux has booted. This can be a serious problem because you may not be able to select your OS from your boot loader if you boot multiple OSs. You can often overcome this problem by enabling *legacy USB support* in the BIOS. This support enables the BIOS to treat a USB keyboard as if it were a regular PS/2 keyboard.

Another problem with USB keyboards is that they require support in the Linux kernel. This support comes with most modern distributions, but you should enable human interface device (HID) support if you recompile your kernel. Some kernel versions separate out support for different HID tools—keyboards, mice, and joysticks. You can use HID support compiled as a module, but if there's a problem loading the module or if it gets unloaded, you may have no way to control the computer. Therefore, I recommend you compile this support directly into the main kernel file.

Using a Mouse to the Fullest

Next to keyboards, mice are the most important human input devices. Most distributions enable you to configure and test your mouse during installation, so chances are it'll work correctly as soon as you've installed Linux. Sometimes you may need to adjust this configuration, though. The installer might have gotten it wrong or didn't run it at all during installation, or you might need to tweak the configuration to get the most out of your mouse. Some features beyond basic configuration that you might want to set include using a two-button mouse, using a scroll mouse, and using buttons beyond the traditional three.

Basic Mouse Configuration

XFree86 treats mice and keyboards in basically the same way—you define their operation in an `InputDevice` section of the `XF86Config` file. A typical mouse configuration looks like this:

```
Section "InputDevice"
  Identifier    "Mouse1"
  Driver        "mouse"
  Option        "Device"      "/dev/mouse"
  Option        "Name"        "Autodetection"
  Option        "Protocol"    "ps/2"
EndSection
```

NOTE   *I use the word* mouse *to refer to any pointing device, be it a mouse, a trackball, a touch pad, or more exotic devices. All of them function identically as far as* X *is concerned.*

The most critical options in this section are as follows:

Option "Device" "/dev/mouse"   This option identifies the mouse device file. Frequently, /dev/mouse is a symbolic link to the true mouse device, such as /dev/psaux (for a PS/2 mouse), /dev/usb/mouse0 (for a USB mouse), or /dev/ttyS0 (for an RS-232 serial mouse). If this option is set incorrectly, X won't start at all or it will start but the mouse won't work.

Option "Protocol" "ps/2"   This option sets the software protocol used by the mouse. Most PS/2 and USB mice sold today use the ps/2 protocol or variants of it, such as Microsoft's IntelliMouse extension (imps/2). Older RS-232 serial mice use protocols named after the manufacturers who originated them, such as logitech or microsoft. The protocol type auto often works; this keyword tells XFree86 to auto-detect the mouse type. A mouse configured with the wrong protocol may not work at all, or the pointer may move about in a very erratic fashion. Check http://www.xfree86.org/current/mouse4.html for more protocols to try if you have problems getting a mouse to work.

Using a Two-Button Mouse

Many mice sold today have only two buttons. Such mice work fine under Windows, but X programs frequently assume that a mouse has three buttons. When presented with a two-button mouse, X uses the left and right buttons as such, but the middle button's functions are inaccessible. If you intend to use a desktop computer under X for any extended period of time, replacing a two-button mouse with a three-button model is worthwhile. Very expensive mice typically sell for only about $50, and even some sub-$20 models come with three buttons.

Sometimes, though, you have no choice but to live with a two-button mouse—for instance, you can't easily replace the built-in touch pad on a laptop computer. (You may be able to supplement the touch pad with an external mouse, though, and this action is quite worthwhile whenever it's practical.) Other times, it may not be worth the bother—for instance, you might intend to use a computer as a server, and will use X very rarely. In such situations, you may need to configure the mouse to support *chording*—pressing both buttons simultaneously to mimic the effect of pressing the middle button. In order to enable chording, you need to add a line or two to the mouse's `InputDevice` section in `XF86Config`:

```
Option "Emulate3Buttons"
Option "Emulate3Timeout" "60"
```

The first of these lines tells XFree86 to enable the chording feature. The second line sets a timeout value—the amount of slop, in milliseconds, that X tolerates between pressing the two buttons before it declares the button press to be the middle button. In this example, you could press the two buttons as much as 60ms apart and XFree86 will register it as a click of the middle mouse button. If you omit this line, XFree86 assumes a default value of `50`.

Configuring a Wheel Mouse

Many mice sold since the late 1990s include wheels or rollers. Typically, you can use the wheel to scroll the contents of windows or to perform application-specific tasks. You need a special configuration to implement these features, though. First, you need to specify the `imps/2` mouse protocol in `XF86Config`. Second, you need to add the following line to the mouse `InputDevice` section:

```
Option "ZAxisMapping" "4 5"
```

This line tells X to treat movement of the wheel in its two directions as equivalent to presses of a fourth and fifth button. It's then up to the program to interpret these virtual button presses appropriately. Most programs released since the late 1990s do so. If you encounter a program that doesn't respond to the wheel, consult the next section, "Configuring Extra Mouse Buttons."

NOTE   Most scroll wheels replace the middle mouse button. This fact isn't a concern, because the wheels can typically be depressed, thereby functioning as a regular middle mouse button.

Configuring Extra Mouse Buttons

A few mice have more than three buttons. You can often configure these buttons to do interesting things in X programs, but the configuring is done on a program-by-program basis. You can use the same techniques to assign meanings to a scroll wheel for programs that don't support it natively; just assign a button 4 action to one wheel direction and a button 5 action to the other wheel direction.

The basic procedure is to modify a program's configuration file to assign meaning to these extra mouse buttons. Unfortunately, there's no single central repository of such configuration files. You may be able to locate information on how to accomplish this task in a program's documentation. If not, check the following websites, which focus on using wheel mice under X:

```
http://koala.ilog.fr/colas/mouse-wheel-scroll/
http://jcatki.dhs.org/imwheel/
```

These sites provide instruction and tools for configuring programs to use wheel mice. Because X handles the wheel by emulating a fourth and fifth button, these instructions can also be used to implement support for more than three true buttons.

Getting a Scanner to Work

Think of a typical office computer and you're likely to imagine a system that runs certain types of programs, such as word processors and spreadsheets. A prototypical desktop office system has a monitor, a keyboard, and a mouse for human interaction, and it is connected to a printer for output. One component is missing from this stereotypical office desktop computer, though: a scanner. Not every computer has or needs a scanner; however, for many applications, scanners are indispensable. With a scanner, you can load printed photographs into files you can manipulate with graphics programs, convert textual documents into word processing files, and even (with the help of a printer and a modem) turn a computer into a photocopier and fax machine.

Scanners require two main types of support in Linux: support for the underlying interface, such as SCSI or USB; and drivers for the specific scanner model. Linux's main scanner package is *Scanner Access Now Easy (SANE)*, which includes drivers for many scanners. You can configure and use SANE as a stand-alone program or call it from other software. You can even configure SANE to operate over a network, enabling many computers to share a scanner much as computers can share a printer.

Locating Scanner Support

SANE ships with all of the major Linux distributions. If you want to get something more recent, you can check the main SANE web page, `http://www.mostang.com/sane/`. This site also holds information on supported scanners. Support categories are *stable* (tested and known to work), *beta* (seems to work fairly well), *alpha* (very new support that may contain major bugs), *untested* (should theoretically work, but hasn't been tested), and *unsupported* (doesn't work). Some devices may be unsupported by one driver, but they will work with others.

If you can't find support for your scanner on the official SANE web page, do a web search; you may turn up an experimental driver that hasn't yet been integrated into the main SANE package. If your scanner is a USB model, you should also check `http://www.linux-usb.org`, which hosts information on USB developments, including links to new drivers. Many new and experimental drivers aren't very stable, though, and they may require you to recompile SANE from source code. You might do better to retire your existing scanner and buy a new one.

Configuring Scanner Software

Fundamentally, SANE is an application programming interface (API); it provides a set of routines that programs can call to use a scanner—*any* scanner. SANE effectively has three major parts:

- ◆ The libraries that implement the API (aka the *middleware* or *meta back-ends*)

◆ The drivers that access the scanner (aka the *back-ends*)

◆ The programs that call the SANE API (aka the *front-ends*)

Two front-ends can be very different from one another. For instance, text-mode front-ends can enable scanning from the command line, and X-based front-ends provide GUI preview scans and other common scanning features.

Much of the task of configuring SANE involves setting up the correct back-end for your scanner. This task is accomplished by editing two files:

/etc/sane.d/dll.conf   This file holds a list of the SANE back-ends for which SANE should search when it's called upon to do some work. Back-ends are typically named after the scanner's manufacturer, sometimes with a model number appended, such as mustek or umax1220u. Lines that begin with a hash mark (#) are comments, and are ignored.

Scanner-Specific Configuration Files   In addition to dll.conf, the /etc/sane.d directory holds configuration files for specific scanners. These files are named after the back-ends, with .conf appended, such as mustek.conf or umax1220u.conf. In most cases, you don't need to adjust these files. Sometimes, though, you can improve a scanner's performance by tweaking the settings. Most files include comments describing the parameters; uncomment the sample configurations or make the changes described in the comments to alter the scanner's performance.

NOTE   All major Linux distributions place SANE configuration files in /etc/sane.d; *however, If you build SANE from source code without changing the defaults, these files will be in* /usr/local/etc/sane.d.

You can discover which scanners are available by typing two commands. First, type **sane-find-scanner.** This command searches likely local scanner interfaces to locate scanners. The result should be one or more output lines identifying the device filename at which a scanner resides, such as /dev/usb/scanner0. (Symbolic links between device files or duplicate device files sometimes make a scanner appear twice.) If sane-find-scanner doesn't find a scanner that you know exists, be sure it's connected and, if applicable, turned on. Also verify that you've loaded the appropriate drivers. USB scanners require the scanner driver, SCSI scanners need the driver for your SCSI host adapter and the SCSI generic (sg) driver, and parallel-port scanners require Linux parallel port support (parport and, on IA-32 systems, parport_pc). The sane-find-scanner program won't detect networked scanners (see the upcoming section, "Network Scanning," for more information on this topic).

Once you're sure that the scanner hardware is accessible, you can check to see if SANE correctly identifies the scanner model. You can perform this task by typing **scanimage -L.** This command calls the scanimage front-end, which is normally used to scan an image; however, with the -L parameter, this program merely identifies available scanners. If all is working, you'll see output such as this:

```
device `umax1220u:/dev/usb/scanner0' is a UMAX Astra 1220U flatbed scanner
```

Most distributions ship with SANE configurations that disable most or all scanners. Thus, if scanimage -L doesn't yield the results you expect, you should check /etc/sane.d/dll.conf and uncomment the line corresponding to your back-end. If you need to add a very new back-end, follow the instructions that came with it to learn how to do this. Red Hat is unusual in that it ships with uncommented configurations for many common scanners; therefore, it may work without modification as soon as it's installed. This setup may slow down scanner detection slightly, though.

One other configuration detail may need attention: device file permissions. The device file (such as `/dev/usb/scanner0`, as returned by `scanimage -L` in the preceding example) must be readable and writeable by anybody who'll use the scanner. Many distributions give world read/write access to this file by default, but you should double-check this detail to be sure it's set appropriately. If the file doesn't have world read/write permissions, use `chmod` to change the permissions. If the file is owned by a special scanner group that has read/write permissions, add any users who should have scanner access to this group.

Doing Basic Scans

Once `scanimage -L` has found your scanner, you probably want to begin using the scanner in a more meaningful way. Because SANE is technically an API, not a program, the manner in which you use SANE depends upon the program you use to access it. One detail you may need for some of these programs is the scanner *device name*. This name isn't merely the device file (in the `/dev` directory tree), although it includes this identifier. The device name is a concatenation of the back-end name, a colon (`:`), and the device filename. For instance, this name might be `mustek:/dev/sg2` or `umax1220u:/dev/usb/scanner0`. This name is returned by `scanimage -L`.

Here are some popular basic scanning packages:

scanimage   This program is a text-mode front-end to SANE. It accepts a large number of options (consult its man page for details), but a basic scan can be performed by typing **scanimage -d *device* > *scanfile.pnm***, where *device* is the device name, such as `mustek:/dev/sg2`. The output file is in Portable Anymap (PNM) format unless you change this detail with the `--format` *format* option. Despite the fact that this program is a front-end, it's typically distributed in the SANE back-end package.

xscanimage   This program is a basic GUI SANE front-end program. It does many of the same things as `scanimage`, but it uses GUI controls to access most options. It's usually part of a SANE front-end package (`sane` or `sane-frontends`).

XSane   This program isn't part of the main SANE package, but it's closely related. It's a more feature-filled X-based front-end to SANE, headquartered at `http://www.xsane.org`. Most distributions ship it in a package called `xsane`.

Kooka   This program is a GUI front-end to SANE that's affiliated with the K Desktop Environment (KDE). Kooka features image management and libraries to help provide Kooka-mediated scans to other KDE applications. You can learn more at `http://www.kde.org/apps/kooka/`.

There are also more specialized SANE-based scanning applications, such as `xcam` (which uses SANE as a method of interfacing to cameras) and `scanadf` (which provides support for scanning via automatic document feeders). The upcoming section, "Network Scanning," describes another unusual use of SANE.

As an example of SANE in use, consider XSane. You can scan a document using XSane by following these steps:

1. Launch the program by typing **xsane**. It may respond by asking you to select which of several scanners to use. This may happen even if you have just one scanner, should the program detect the scanner using two or more redundant device files. In this case, it doesn't matter

which you use. XSane should bring up four windows, as shown in Figure 3.4. In that figure, clockwise from the bottom-left corner, are the options window, the main control window, the color histogram window, and the preview window. You can open or close windows, including a couple that don't open by default, from the View menu in the main control window.

FIGURE 3.4

XSane provides several windows in which you can enter options and control a scan.

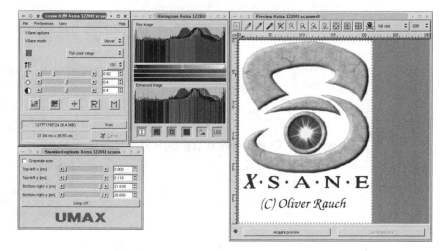

2. XSane starts up in Viewer mode by default. This means that if you begin a scan, the program opens another window to display the scan. You can then manipulate and save the image from the viewer window. You can select other modes from the XSane Mode option at the top of the main control window. For purposes of this demonstration, select Save. This option enables you to save the scan to a file. The main control window expands to provide a field for entering the filename and format of the file.

3. If the default out.pnm isn't a suitable filename, type a better name in the filename field, or click the icon of a floppy disk to pick a filename using a file selector dialog box.

4. Select a scan resolution in the resolution selection button in the main control window. (This button is set to 150 in Figure 3.4.) Some scanners use sliders to set the scan resolution.

5. If the document is grayscale, such as a black-and-white photograph, click the Grayscale Scan box in the options window. Some scanners may provide additional bit depth or line-art options.

6. Place the document to be scanned on the scanner's bed.

7. In the preview window, click the Acquire Preview button. Your scanner should spring into action and scan a low-resolution preview that will appear in the preview window.

8. If you don't want to scan the entire page, select the area you do want to acquire with the mouse in the preview window, much as you would in a graphics program.

9. Click the Scan button in the main control window. XSane should scan your document and save it to the file you specified in Step 3.

10. Repeat Steps 3 through 9 if you want to scan more documents, or select File ➤ Quit to exit from the program.

You can set several additional options in XSane. For instance, you can select destinations to which to send the scan using the XSane Mode option (make a photocopy with the Copy option, fax a document with Fax, or e-mail a document with Email); you can adjust brightness, contrast, and gamma values with the sliders in the middle of the main control window; and so on. Some options apply only to specific scanners, so you may see different options than those shown in Figure 3.4.

NOTE   *With some scanners, SANE shuts off the scanner's lamp whenever you quit from a SANE front-end. Many SANE front-ends also provide a means to shut off the lamp manually, such as the Lamp Off button in the options window in Figure 3.4. Other scanners shut off their lamps only when you turn off the scanners.*

Integrating a Scanner with Other Software

Because SANE is an API, it's theoretically possible for any program to call SANE in order to acquire scans. Of course, doing this makes more sense for some programs than for others. The programming effort involved in calling SANE, including giving users access to SANE options, means that programs that provide direct scanner access often use an interface toolkit provided by another package. For instance, the GNU Image Manipulation Program (GIMP) uses the XSane interface, and Kooka provides tools to enable KDE-based programs to interface to a scanner.

The details of how scanning works from nonscanner applications vary. In the GIMP, you select a scanner option from the File ➤ Acquire menu (there may be several options for various scanners). The result is the usual collection of XSane windows shown in Figure 3.4; however, there's no XSane Mode option in the main control window. Anything you scan in this way goes straight into a GIMP window, where you can manipulate it as you would any other image. (Chapter 8 covers the GIMP in more detail.)

Converting Graphics to Text: OCR

Scanners are fundamentally graphics devices—their product is a bitmap graphics stream, which is easily displayed in an X window or saved in a graphics file. Sometimes, though, the purpose of scanning a document is to convert it to text in order to edit it in a word processor, load data into a spreadsheet, or otherwise manipulate it in a nongraphical way. To accomplish this goal, *optical character recognition (OCR)* programs exist. These programs accept a graphics file as input and generate a text file that corresponds to the characters in the input file. Essentially, the OCR package "reads" the characters out of the input file. This is an extremely challenging task for a computer program, though; the software must overcome many obstacles, including streaks and blotches in the input file; the varying sizes and appearance of characters in different fonts; and the presence of nontextual information, such as embedded graphics. Therefore, OCR software tends to be imperfect, but it's often good enough to be worth using. Typically, you'll scan in a document and then proofread it against the original, making whatever corrections are appropriate. Here are the main Linux OCR packages:

Clara   This program, based at `http://www.claraocr.org`, is intended for large-scale OCR projects, such as converting out-of-print books to digital format. The program includes an X-based GUI, but it doesn't interface directly to scanners. Thus, you must scan your documents into files and then use Clara on them.

GOCR   This program is headquartered at `http://jocr.sourceforge.net`, and it is an OCR program that works from the command line. As such, it can be called by other programs, such as XSane or Kooka, to provide them with OCR capabilities.

OCR Shop   This is a line of commercial OCR packages for Linux. It's a much more mature product than the open-source Clara or GOCR packages, but OCR Shop is also a very pricey product, with the entry-level package going for close to $1,500. OCR Shop doesn't use SANE as a back-end, so you must be sure that your scanner is supported before you buy the program. Check `http://www.vividata.com` for more information.

As an example of OCR in action, consider using GOCR from XSane. Follow these steps:

1. If necessary, install the GOCR package from your distribution or from the GOCR web page.

2. Launch XSane. Leave the XSane Mode set to Viewer; you'll acquire an image into the viewer and then have the viewer run GOCR.

3. Be sure that XSane is set to acquire a grayscale or a line-art image.

4. Acquire a preview by clicking the Acquire Preview button in the preview window.

5. Select the portion of the document you want to scan in the preview window.

6. Set the scanning resolution to between 150dpi and 300dpi; this range tends to produce the best OCR results.

7. Click Scan to scan the document. XSane should open a window in which the document is displayed. Chances are this window will be very large.

8. In the scanned document window, select File ➢ OCR - Save as Text. The program displays a file selection dialog box in which you enter a filename.

9. Type in a filename, and click OK in the file selection dialog box. XSane doesn't show any indication that GOCR is working, but it is. Within a few seconds, the file you specified should be created and contain the text equivalent of the scanned file.

Unfortunately, GOCR's output isn't always as good as you might hope. As I write, GOCR is at version 0.37—in other words, it's a very early work. Its accuracy is likely to improve as its version number climbs, so check back with the GOCR website frequently if accurate OCR is important to you. You may also be able to improve GOCR's accuracy by adjusting various scanning parameters, such as the resolution, contrast, and brightness.

Network Scanning

SANE was designed with flexibility in mind. In particular, the implementation of SANE as separate back-ends, SANE libraries, and front-ends makes it fairly easy to link together components in unusual ways. The existence of text-mode scanning tools such as `scanimage` is one example of this effect. Another example, and a more dramatic one, is the ability of SANE to handle scanning over a network. For instance, suppose you're configuring a small group of computers, such as public workstations in a university computing center or a pair of computers used by two people who share an office. You've got a scanner, and the small size of the room means that it's easy for everybody in the room to physically access the scanner. Using SANE, you can connect the scanner to one computer and yet make it available to every computer in the room as if the scanner were connected directly to each of the computers.

WARNING   *Network scanning requires running a server on the computer to which the scanner connects. This activity imposes certain risks. You should exercise caution when implementing a network scanning configuration. Use a firewall, TCP Wrappers, or* xinetd *security options to limit who may access the scanner server. Chapter 20, "Controlling Network Access," describes network security in more detail.*

Setting up network scanning requires different configurations on each of the computers. The trickiest part of this configuration is on the server side—the computer to which the scanner connects most directly. This system must run a SANE server, which is effectively *middleware*—that is, it sits between the back-end that talks to the scanner and the front-end on the client computer. This SANE server is called `saned`, and most Linux distributions place it in /usr/sbin. You configure it to run from a super server, such as `inetd` or `xinetd`, both of which are described in more detail in Chapter 22, "Running Servers." To do this, take the following steps:

1. Configure the scanner so that it works on the server system, as described earlier in "Configuring Scanner Software."

2. Check that `saned` is installed. It's usually part of the `sane` or `sane-backends` package. If it's not installed, locate and install the appropriate package.

3. If necessary, add an entry for the SANE port to /etc/services. Some distributions ship with this entry present, but others don't. Look for it, and if it's not present, add it:
   ```
   sane   6566/tcp   # SANE network scanner access
   ```

4. Create a super server configuration for `saned`. Consult Chapter 22 for more information on super server configuration.

   A. Debian, Slackware, and SuSE all use `inetd` by default. An /etc/inetd.conf line for `saned` looks like this, although you should use a username and group that's present on your system:
   ```
   sane stream tcp nowait saned.saned /usr/sbin/saned saned
   ```

   B. Mandrake and Red Hat both use `xinetd` as a super server. For these distributions, you should create an /etc/xinetd.d/saned file that contains the following lines:
   ```
   service sane
   {
       disable      = no
       socket_type  = stream
       protocol     = tcp
       wait         = no
       user         = saned
       group        = saned
       server       = /usr/sbin/saned
   }
   ```

5. Pass a SIGHUP signal to the super server. Type **ps ax | grep inetd** to find the process ID (PID) number, and then type **kill -SIGHUP** *pid*, where *pid* is the PID number, to do the job. This process is described in more detail in Chapter 22.

6. Be sure that the user or group you've configured the super server to use when launching **saned** exists and has access to the scanner's file. It's best if this user has no other privileges on the computer and cannot log in at all.

7. Add the hostnames of all the computers that should have access to the scanner to the /etc/sane.d/saned.conf file, one per line. This file is the primary access control method used by **saned**.

At this point, the **saned** server should respond to queries, but you need to tell clients how to access the server. To do this, you need to perform the following configuration steps:

1. Include the **net** option in the /etc/sane.d/dll.conf files on the clients. This option tells the SANE libraries on the clients to look for network scanners.

2. Edit the /etc/sane.d/net.conf files on the clients, and include the hostname of the SANE server system.

At this point, the scanner should work from the clients. The **sane-find-scanner** program won't work, but **scanimage -L** should turn up the network scanner:

```
$ scanimage -L
device `net:scan.luna.edu:umax1220u:/dev/usb/scanner0' is a UMAX Astra 1220U
➡flatbed scanner
```

Note that the scanner device name has two additional elements: The keyword **net** leads the identifier, and that keyword is followed by the hostname of the server system. You can pass this entire scanner device name to front-ends that require it, or you can rely on the auto-detection mechanisms of programs such as XSane.

TIP   You can access a SANE-served network scanner from OSs other than Linux. You can find pointers to SANE front-ends for various OSs at http://www.mostang.com/sane/sane-frontends.html. *Of particular interest, front-ends for Windows are available, and they can work with many Windows scanning applications.*

Summary

External peripherals can be connected through a wide variety of ports, but three of the most widely used and flexible ports are USB, RS-232 serial, and parallel ports. Collectively, these three ports support keyboards, mice, modems, scanners, printers, removable disks, and many other devices. Knowing how to optimize each port type can help you get these peripherals working at their best. As basic input devices, keyboard and mouse configuration are particularly critical to your system's operation. You can adjust factors such as keyboard repeat rate, keyboard layout, and support for wheel mice using a few configuration files and commands. Scanners are just one of many types of external peripherals, but their configuration is often less obvious than that of other devices, such as printers. Fortunately, Linux has good support for scanners in its SANE package. Making a few small changes to configuration files should enable you to scan images in Linux, provided you have a supported scanner.

Part II

User Tools

Chapter 4

Mastering Shells and Shell Scripting

MANY PEOPLE USE NOTHING but GUI tools for manipulating files, launching programs, and so on. This approach certainly has its merits—GUI tools tend to be easy to learn, and they fit the needs of some tasks, such as graphics programs, very well. There is an older method of interacting with computers, though, which still has advantages: text-based *shells*. They are programs that accept typed commands and respond to these commands by launching programs or performing actions. Linux supports many text-based shells, and knowing how to select a shell and use it to its fullest can help you work with Linux. Shells work even when GUI tools are unavailable. They provide some features that are difficult for GUI equivalents to match—for example, the ability to operate on a collection of files that meet some arbitrary naming convention (say, all files whose names begin with A or Q and that end in .txt).

Shells are also extremely important because they're the basis for *shell scripts*. These programs are written in a language that's provided by the shell. (Most shell-script constructs can be used directly on the command line, which can be a quick way to test them.) Shell scripts use many common programming features, but they provide particularly easy access to features that are of great interest for everyday computer use, such as launching external programs. You can use a shell script to tie together several simple programs to accomplish much more complex tasks than any of these programs could manage by itself. Ordinary users can create shell scripts to work on their own files, but they're also important for system administration. In fact, common Linux startup files are most often shell scripts. This makes these scripts easy to customize—if you know how to write and modify shell scripts.

NOTE *Shells, and particularly shell scripting, are potentially quite complex subjects. For more information, consult your shell's man page or a book on your shell of choice, such as Newham and Rosenblatt's* Learning the bash Shell *(O'Reilly, 1998) or Kochan and Wood's* UNIX Shell Programming, Revised Edition *(Sams, 1989).*

Selecting an Appropriate Shell

For casual use, many shells work equally well. All shells allow you to run external programs. Even most basic commands, such as ls, are actually external programs. Shells differ in some details of their scripting languages, as well as in some interactive features. Some shells are very unusual and may be suitable for use by less-experienced users who nonetheless need to use Linux over text-mode connections.

TIP   You normally specify a user's shell in the user's account configuration, as described shortly. You can change shells temporarily by typing the shell's name; after all, a shell is just a program and as such it can be launched from another shell.

Some of the many shells available in Linux include:

bash   The *Bourne Again Shell (bash)* is the default shell for most installations and accounts. It's an open source extension to the original Bourne shell (sh), which is popular on many Unix-like platforms. Linux distributions make sh a link to bash, so that scripts intended for sh run on bash.

tcsh   This shell is an enhanced variant of a "classic" Unix shell, the C Shell (csh). Both csh and tcsh use a scripting language that resembles the C programming language, although csh/tcsh scripts are by no means C programs.

pdksh   The *Public Domain Korn Shell (pdksh)* is an implementation of the Korn shell. It's similar to the Bourne shell, but it borrows some features from the C shell, as well.

zsh   The *Z Shell (zsh)* is modeled after the Korn shell, but it adds some extra features.

sash   The *Stand Alone Shell (sash)* is a small shell that incorporates many programs, such as ls, that are normally external, into the main sash executable. The goal is to have a shell that functions even on a system that's otherwise badly corrupted.

Any of these shells will serve well as your primary Linux shell, although you might prefer to reserve sash for emergency systems. In the end, shell choice is a highly personal matter; one person may have a strong preference for one shell, but somebody else may prefer another. I recommend that you try several of them. Because covering all of these shells would be impractical, the rest of this chapter focuses on bash, which is the default shell for most Linux distributions.

NOTE   Differences between shells are most noticeable in relatively advanced features, such as command completion and details of the scripting language. As such, you probably won't notice much difference if you just use a shell's basic features.

The default shell is part of the user's account configuration. This information is stored as the final entry in the account's /etc/passwd line, which looks like this:

```
sandro:x:523:100:Sandro B.:/home/sandro:/bin/bash
```

To change the default shell, you can edit this file directly or use the usermod command, as shown here:

```
# usermod -s /bin/tcsh sandro
```

Editing /etc/passwd and running usermod both require superuser privileges. Ordinary users can change their shells by using the chsh program:

```
$ chsh -s /bin/tcsh
```

If the shell is omitted, the program prompts for it. The program also asks for a password as a security measure, to ensure that a passerby can't change a user's shell if the user leaves a terminal unattended for a minute.

Making Efficient Use of a Shell

Basic use of a shell is fairly straightforward: Type a command and the shell responds by executing that command. To get the most out of any text-mode interaction with Linux, though, you need to know how to use a shell's more advanced features. Ultimately, most interactive shell features boil down to ones that save you time, but some features enable you to change the shell's appearance and the names of its commands.

Time-Saving Shell Tricks

Unix shells support many features that system administrators and programmers have found valuable. These features help save time by automatically completing commands, by enabling you to run commands you've run before with minimal effort, and by supporting editing of commands you're typing. From early in Unix history, shells have supported features that enable capturing output from programs or sending a file as input to a program, as well as sending one command's output to a second one as input. Naturally, Linux's shells incorporate these features.

TYPING PARTIAL COMMANDS: COMMAND COMPLETION

Typing long commands or filenames can slow down command-line operations, both by adding to typing time and by increasing the odds of a typo, thereby causing a command to fail or have unintended consequences. Thus, bash and many other shells support a feature known as *command completion*. Type the first few letters of a command or filename and then press the Tab key. The shell locates all of the possible matching commands on the path or filenames that match. If just one command or filename matches, the shell fills out the rest of the command. If more than one command or filename matches, the shell beeps, displays all the matching names, or both, depending on the shell's configuration. If no files match the specified letters, the shell beeps.

For instance, at a command prompt, try typing chm and then the Tab key. The shell should respond by completing the command name: chmod. You can then enter a parameter for the command, making the text you see chmod 0644. If you then type a single letter for a filename and press Tab again, the shell may beep, display a list of files that begin with that letter, or fill in a complete filename.

You can configure whether the shell displays all of the matching filenames or simply beeps by adjusting the /etc/inputrc file. If you want bash to display a list of files, add the following line to inputrc:

```
set show-all-if-ambiguous on
```

If this feature is turned off, bash merely beeps when more than one file matches; pressing the Tab key again causes the display of matching files to appear.

Rerunning Commands: History

As you work in a shell, chances are you'll find yourself wanting to issue the same commands, or minor variants of them, again and again. For instance, you might try to install a package (as described in Chapter 11, "Managing Packages"), only to discover that you first need to add another package. After you add the depended-upon package, you'll want to add the first one. You can use a popular shell feature to simplify this task: *history*. Most modern shells maintain a record of the most recently typed commands. You can move through these commands by pressing the Up Arrow and Down Arrow keys. For the benefit of Emacs fans, the Ctrl+P and Ctrl+N keys perform these same actions. When you find the command you want to use, press the Enter key or edit the command, as described in the next section, "Modifying Commands: Editing."

You can also search through the history. Type Ctrl+R, and `bash` will display the following prompt:

```
(reverse-I-search)`´:
```

Type the first few characters of the command you want to find, and the system will locate the best match. Type Ctrl+R again to search further back in the history.

NOTE *In theory, Ctrl+S should perform a forward search; however, many text consoles intercept this keystroke as a means of pausing output, so Ctrl+S doesn't have the desired effect.*

Modifying Commands: Editing

Shells include simple editing features for commands you type. You can use these features to correct errors as you type commands, or you can use them to modify commands retrieved from the shell history, further expanding the utility of the history feature. The editing features in `bash` are modeled after those in Emacs. Table 4.1 summarizes the most important of these commands.

TABLE 4.1: Common bash Editing Commands

Keystroke	Effect
Ctrl+A	Move cursor to start of line.
Ctrl+E	Move cursor to end of line.
Ctrl+F or Right Arrow	Move cursor one position right.
Ctrl+B or Left Arrow	Move cursor one position left.
Esc+F	Move cursor one word right.
Esc+B	Move cursor one word left.
Backspace	Delete the character to the left of the cursor.
Ctrl+D or Delete	Delete the character under the cursor.
Ctrl+T	Transpose the character on which the cursor rests and the preceding character.
Esc+T	Transpose the word on which the cursor rests and the preceding word.
Ctrl+K	Delete from the cursor to the end of the line.
Ctrl+X Backspace	Delete from the cursor to the start of the line.

NOTE   *Some editing features depend on appropriate keyboard handling, as described in Chapter 3, "Using External Peripherals." In particular, some keymaps may not handle the Backspace and Delete keys in the way described here. Also, some keyboards label the Backspace and Delete keys differently; for instance, most Macintosh keyboards label Backspace as Delete, and Delete as Del.*

Mastering these commands can be quite useful. For instance, suppose you discover that you've mistyped the second character of a command. Instead of retyping the entire command, you can press Ctrl+A to move the cursor to the start of the line, move the Right Arrow key to move forward one character, press Delete to delete the flawed character, type the correct character in its place, and press the Enter key to enter the new command. Instead of retyping potentially dozens of characters, your correction takes just five keystrokes.

RUNNING MULTIPLE PROGRAMS: BACKGROUND OPERATIONS

Even in text mode, you can run multiple programs in Linux. One tool for doing this is the ampersand operator (**&**). Append this character to the end of a command and Linux launches the program in the background; the program runs, but you retain control of the terminal from which you launched the program. Of course, this action makes more sense for some programs than for others—launching a text-mode text editor in this way doesn't make much sense, for instance, because you need to interact with the program. A program that just processes data and doesn't produce any console output, though, may be profitably launched in the background. You could launch dd in this way, for instance, to copy a floppy disk image to a file while still retaining control of your console:

```
$ dd if=/dev/fd0 of=floppy.img &
```

You can also launch X programs in this way; when so launched, the program doesn't take over your xterm window, although it may still direct some output to the xterm. If you omit the ampersand, you can't use the xterm window until the X program finishes its work.

Once a program is running, you can usually kick it into the background by pressing Ctrl+Z. The program suspends operations (it stops whatever it was doing, even if it was a CPU-intensive computation), and you can type new commands at your shell. Typing **bg** at this point puts the program in the background, much as if you'd launched it with an ampersand. Typing **fg** brings the program back to the foreground.

MANIPULATING INPUT AND OUTPUT: REDIRECTION

Text-mode Linux programs operate on three input/output *streams*, each of which is treated much like a file: *Standard input (stdin)* is normally tied to the keyboard and is the method programs use to accept input from the user. *Standard output (stdout)* is normally tied to the screen, xterm window, or other text-mode display tool, and it displays normal program output. *Standard error (stderr)* is also usually tied to the text-mode display, but it handles high-priority messages such as error reports. Linux can readily redirect these input and output streams. Therefore, you can capture the output of a text-mode program in a file or send the contents of a file to a program as input. You do this by using redirection operators, as detailed in Table 4.2.

TABLE 4.2: COMMON REDIRECTION OPERATORS

OPERATOR	ACTION
<	Redirects stdin to use the specified file.
>	Redirects stdout to the specified file, overwriting the existing file's contents.
>>	Redirects stdout to the specified file, appending to the existing file's contents.
2>	Redirects stderr to the specified file, overwriting the existing file's contents.
2>>	Redirects stderr to the specified file, appending to the existing file's contents.
&>	Redirects both stdout and stderr to the specified file, overwriting the existing file's contents.

Each operator takes a filename as a parameter. You can combine multiple operations. For instance, to pass the contents of data.txt to numcrunch and to save the program's output in out.txt, you could type:

```
$ numcrunch < data.txt > out.txt
```

TIP   *Redirection is often used as a way to quickly obtain "junk" data or throw away data. Specifically, if you want a lot of empty input, you can use input redirection to obtain data from /dev/zero, which generates a limitless supply of binary 0 values. To get rid of a program's output, redirect it to /dev/null; the output vanishes forever.*

COMBINING COMMANDS: PIPES

Pipes are a way to link programs together. The first program's standard output is redirected to the second program as standard input. The chain can continue for as many programs as you like. The pipe operator is a vertical bar (|), so a piped series of commands looks like this:

```
$ ps ax | grep gdm
```

This example takes the output of ps ax and pipes it into grep, which searches for lines containing the string gdm. Using grep in this way can be a good way to trim a verbose program's output down to size. You may also want to pipe textual output through the less pager, enabling you to peruse the output at a human pace.

Customizing Your Shell

People don't have the same preferences, and Linux's shells were designed with this fact in mind—they support customizations through a variety of configuration options. You can modify system defaults to suit your needs as a site and modify user-specific options to change the behavior in your account alone. Two common types of customization are using *aliases*, which enable you to create shortcuts or effectively change the defaults of a command, and setting *environment variables*, which provide information to shells and to other programs you run from shells.

FINDING CONFIGURATION FILES

Each shell has its own unique set of configuration files. System-wide configuration files usually reside in /etc, and user-specific configuration files are found in users' home directories. Both system-wide and user-specific configuration files come in two varieties: *login* configuration files and *non-login* configuration files. Login files apply only to shells launched by a login process, such as a remote Secure Shell (SSH) login or a login at a text-mode console. Non-login configuration files apply to shells that aren't login shells, such as xterm windows launched from a GUI environment or a shell obtained by using su to change the login user's identity. Table 4.3 summarizes the locations of bash configuration files.

TABLE 4.3: COMMON bash CONFIGURATION FILES

TYPE OF FILE	LOGIN FILE LOCATION	NON-LOGIN FILE LOCATION
Global Configuration File	/etc/profile and files in /etc/profile.d	/etc/bashrc or /etc/bash.bashrc
User Configuration File	~/.profile	~/.bashrc

In practice, Table 4.3 is just a starting point; it's possible for a configuration file to *source* another file, meaning to call the additional file. This is possible because these files are really shell scripts, so you can do anything in these files that you can do in any shell script. One example of sourcing is in the common practice of placing program-specific configurations in the /etc/profile.d subdirectory. Programs that require particular environment variables can place appropriate scripts to set those variables in this directory. Mandrake, Red Hat, Slackware, and SuSE all use this approach, but Debian doesn't by default.

In addition to these common login files, other files can run programs when you log out. Specifically, ~/.bash_logout does this for individual users. You might use this file to run programs that delete sensitive temporary files, shut down any open Point-to-Point Protocol (PPP) links to the Internet, or perform some other task.

USING ALIASES

One common shell customization is setting aliases, which enable you to type shorthand versions of commands or configure the shell to automatically add certain parameters to commands. For instance, the default behavior of the cp command is to overwrite files that match the target filename without prompting. If you prefer to have cp prompt you before overwriting an existing file, you could enter the following line in a bash startup script:

```
alias cp='cp -i'
```

This line tells bash to silently substitute cp -i whenever you type **cp.** You can also create a shorthand for a command; for instance, if you prefer to type **lo** instead of **logout**, you could create an alias like this:

```
alias lo='logout'
```

You normally place aliases in non-login file locations—/etc/bashrc, ~/.bashrc, or the like. This practice ensures that the aliases will be available whenever you launch a shell, whether or not it's a login shell. If you don't want to use an alias on a one-time basis, you can do so in a couple of ways. First, you can surround the command in double quotes, as in **"cp" file1 file2** to use cp without -i to copy the file. Second, you can type the complete path to the original executable, as in **/bin/cp file1 file2**.

SETTING ENVIRONMENT VARIABLES

Environment variables are pieces of data that Linux makes available to programs you run. For instance, a Usenet news reader needs to know the address of the news server from which it should retrieve messages. Some programs use program-specific configuration files for this purpose, but others rely on environment variables. The NNTPSERVER environment variable, for instance, holds the name of a Usenet news server. Using environment variables for this purpose makes sense when there are several programs that might use the information—you only need to set the environment variable once, and if all the programs know to access that variable for the relevant information, you're done. Some programs rely on environment variables even for program-specific settings, so you might need to set environment variables even for individual programs.

To set an environment variable, use the export command in a bash startup script, as in:

```
export NNTPSERVER=news.luna.edu
```

You can reference existing environment variables when setting a new one by preceding the existing environment variable with a dollar sign ($). For instance, one important environment variable is PATH, which specifies the directories in which Linux searches for programs when you type their names. Each directory is separated from its neighbors by a colon (:). You can add a directory to PATH with a command like this:

```
export PATH=$PATH:/opt/OpenOffice.org/program
```

By convention, environment variables are all-uppercase. Variables used by a single bash script, as described in the upcoming section, "Using Variables," are lowercase or mixed case. If you need to set an environment variable for a program, you should describe that variable in its documentation. You can then add the variable to a global or local configuration file, as appropriate.

CHANGING THE PROMPT

A shell presents a prompt when it's ready to receive input. You can change this prompt by setting the PS1 variable. For instance, if you want a simple $ prompt with no other adornment, you could type the following command:

```
$ PS1="$ "
```

NOTE   *There's no need to use the* export *keyword to set the prompt, because this variable is used internally to the shell;* export *makes a variable available to programs launched from a shell.*

Chances are you'll want to use assorted variables in defining your prompt. Table 4.4 summarizes some of these (check the bash man page for more). A backslash (\) identifies the following character as a variable. Most Linux distributions use [\u@\h \W]\$, or something similar, as their default prompt. This string results in a prompt ending in a dollar sign for ordinary users, and a hash mark (#) replaces the dollar sign for root logins.

TABLE 4.4: COMMON VARIABLES USED IN SETTING THE SHELL PROMPT

VARIABLE	MEANING
\d	The date in "weekday month day" format, such as Fri Nov 18.
\h	The computer's hostname without the domain name.
\H	The computer's hostname with the domain name.
\s	The shell's name.
\t	The time in 24-hour format.
\T	The time in 12-hour format.
\@	The time in 12-hour format with AM/PM indication.
\u	The username of the current user.
\w	The current working directory.
\W	The final directory of the current working directory.
\$	A dollar sign for most users, but a hash mark for root.

Saving Time with Shell Scripts

Both ordinary users and system administrators can use shell scripts to simplify life with Linux. Shell scripts enable you to combine multiple programs to create a potentially much more complex whole. You can also use features such as variables, conditional expressions, and loops to create complex programs. Most Linux system startup scripts are actually shell scripts; therefore, the ability to understand and modify shell scripts is critical to effective Linux system administration.

Key Features of Shell Scripts

Shell scripts are one specific subclass of *interpreted* programs, meaning that a special program (the *interpreter*—in this case, the shell program) reads the program file (the shell script) and implements the operations it specifies every time the program is run. This procedure is in contrast to *compiled* programs, in which a *compiler* reads the program file (the *source code*) and generates a new file (the *object code* or *binary file*) that the computer can run without further help from the compiler. Interpreted programs, and hence shell scripts, tend to be easier to develop because you can make a change to the program and run it immediately. Interpreted programs can also be run on any CPU, provided the appropriate shell exists and that the program doesn't depend upon specific hardware or CPU features. Compiled programs, by contrast, tend to run faster, because the compiler can generate object code that's optimized for the CPU; however, the resulting object code runs only on the target CPU or CPU family.

Shell scripts typically begin with a line that identifies them as such. This identification line begins with the characters #!, followed by the path to the interpreter (the shell itself). The Linux kernel knows to interpret these characters as identifying a script, and scripting languages all use a hash mark

(#) as a comment character, so the shell ignores this line. Many shell scripts identify themselves as being run by /bin/sh, but some specify /bin/bash or some other shell. Some simple scripts can run on a wide variety of shells, but others use shell-specific features. For instance, bash and tcsh use different methods of assigning values to variables, so any script that does this will run under one shell or the other, but not both.

In order to run a shell script, you must either launch it by passing it explicitly to the shell (as in /bin/bash *scriptname*) or change the permissions on the script file so that it's executable. Thereafter, you can launch it just as you would any other executable program, by typing its name (possibly preceded by the complete path to the file). To make a file executable, you use the chmod command:

```
$ chmod a+x scriptname
```

NOTE   *See Chapter 5, "Doing Real Work in Text Mode," for more information on file permissions and the* chmod *command.*

Launching External Programs

One of the most basic uses of shell scripts is to launch external programs. You do this by placing the name of the external program, possibly preceded by its complete path, in the script, just as you would type the command at a shell prompt. If you include an ampersand (&), the command launches in the background and processing continues to the next command; otherwise, the first command must finish before the next command executes. As an example, consider Listing 4.1, which launches a few X programs—specifically, two xterm instances, xeyes, and icewm. The first three programs are launched in the background, but the final program isn't. Consequently, the script won't finish executing until the final program terminates. This specific example could be used as a simple X startup script, such as an ~/.xinitrc file, because icewm is an X window manager. Therefore, the effect is that the X session lasts until the user quits from the window manager—an action that's normally performed to log out or shut down X.

LISTING 4.1: A SIMPLE SCRIPT TO LAUNCH SEVERAL X PROGRAMS

```
#!/bin/bash
xterm &
xterm &
xeyes &
icewm
```

You can also combine programs in a pipe or use redirection. Consider Listing 4.2, which shows a script that passes the output of dmesg through the less pager. This script is trivial, but it demonstrates a very powerful principle: By combining individual commands via pipes, you can create a script that performs more complex tasks. If you find yourself regularly typing a long compound command, you may want to place that command in a script and give it a shorter name. You can even use parameters passed to the script as variables to handle variable data required by the commands.

LISTING 4.2: A DEMONSTRATION OF PIPES IN A SCRIPT

```
#!/bin/bash
dmesg | less
```

NOTE   When calling a program from a script, you can use a command alone (such as dmesg*), use the complete path to a command (such as* /bin/dmesg*), or create a variable that includes the complete path and use it (as in* DMESG=/bin/dmesg*, and then use* $DMESG *to call the command). The first option is most readable and may ease porting the script to another distribution or non-Linux OS. The second option may be more secure because a miscreant can't manipulate the path to have victims run the wrong program. Using the complete path to a program also ensures that the script will work even if the* PATH *environment variable in the ultimate running environment omits the directory in which a program resides. The third option is a good compromise, and is frequently used on large scripts, but complicates the development of very simple scripts. For readability, I omit the path from most sample scripts in this chapter, but you may want to include them in your own scripts.*

Many Linux commands are most useful when they are launched from scripts. Table 4.5 summarizes these commands. Some of them are very complex, so you should consult their man pages for more details. Of course, you can also use commands you might normally type at a shell prompt, such as cd, cp, dd, and so on.

TABLE 4.5: COMMANDS FREQUENTLY FOUND IN SHELL SCRIPTS

COMMAND	EFFECT
awk	Simple programming language that produces results based on pattern matches. Linux ships with GNU awk, or gawk; it responds to either name.
cut	Removes portions of an input line.
echo	Sends a constant or variable to stdout.
false	Does nothing and returns a failure code.
find	Searches for files matching specified criteria, such as filename or creation date. Sends matching filenames to stdout.
grep	Searches for files containing a specified string. Normally sends the matching lines to stdout.
pidof	Returns the process ID (PID) matching a specified running program.
read	Requests input from the user or from a file.
sed	The stream editor; edits files based on commands passed to sed on the command line or in a script.
sort	Sorts lines of stdin or from a file and sends the sorted version to stdout.
uniq	Removes duplicate lines from a sorted file or from stdin.
true	Does nothing and returns a success code.

Using Variables

Programs, including shell scripts, frequently must work with data that's unknown to the programmer. For instance, you might write a script to convert a data file from one format to another by calling a series of conversion utilities. When you write the script, you don't know the original file's name, so your script uses one or more variables to hold this information. Environment variables, described earlier, in "Setting Environment Variables," are one type of variable you can use and set in shell scripts. In bash, you set a variable with the equal sign (=) operator, as shown here:

```
variable=value
```

Be sure there aren't any spaces surrounding the equal sign operator. The *value* can be an alphanumeric string, such as hitchhiker.txt, or a numeric value, such as 42. If you surround a text string in quotes, you can include spaces in the variable's value.

To use a variable, you use its name preceded by a dollar sign ($), much as you would use a constant value. For instance, Listing 4.3 shows a script that manipulates a variable. This script prompts for and accepts input (using the echo and read commands) and then displays the result of a manipulation. This manipulation passes the variable to the cut command using a pipe, and then it extracts the second field (-f 2), as defined by spaces in the input (-d " ").

LISTING 4.3: EXAMPLE SCRIPT DEMONSTRATING USE OF VARIABLES

```
#!/bin/bash
echo "Please type three words, separated by spaces:"
read inputline
echo -n "The second word is: "
echo $inputline | cut -d " " -f 2
```

If you type this script into a file called vardemo, make it executable, and then run it, the result might look like this:

```
$ ./vardemo
Please type three words, separated by spaces.
one two three
The second word is: two
```

You can also use the variables $1, $2, and so on to refer to parameters passed to the script when you launch the program. For instance, if you type **./vardemo aparam**, $1 takes on the value aparam. You can use this feature to easily send data to a script. For instance, if you want to write a script to convert one file format to another using various file-conversion utilities, you might pass the name of the original file as a parameter and refer to it as $1 throughout the script. The $0 variable refers to the name you used to launch the script, which can be useful for printing error messages or for changing the script's behavior depending upon how it's called.

Using Conditional Expressions

A *conditional expression* is an expression that evaluates to true or false. For instance, an expression might test whether a file exists or whether two variables are equal to each other. These expressions are encased in square brackets ([ ]) and are used by several commands described in the next few sections, including if, while, and until. The use of conditional expressions enables shell scripts to perform actions only when a condition exists or perform actions multiple times until an ending condition exists.

Table 4.6 summarizes conditional expressions. Because these expressions aren't useful except in conjunction with other commands, specific examples of their use will follow in upcoming sections.

TABLE 4.6: CONDITIONAL EXPRESSIONS AND THEIR MEANINGS

CONDITIONAL EXPRESSION	MEANING
-a *file*	True if *file* exists.
-b *file*	True if *file* exists and is a block file.
-c *file*	True if *file* exists and is a character file.
-d *file*	True if *file* exists and is a directory.
-e *file*	True if *file* exists.
-f *file*	True if *file* exists and is a regular file.
-g *file*	True if *file* exists and has its SGID bit set.
-h *file*	True if *file* exists and is a symbolic link.
-k *file*	True if *file* exists and its "sticky" bit is set.
-p *file*	True if *file* exists and is a named pipe.
-r *file*	True if *file* exists and can be read.
-s *file*	True if *file* exists and is not empty.
-t *fd*	True if file descriptor *fd* refers to a terminal and is open.
-u *file*	True if *file* exists and has its SUID bit set.
-w *file*	True if *file* exists and can be written.
-x *file*	True if *file* exists and can be executed.
-O *file*	True if *file* exists and is owned by the effective user ID.
-G *file*	True if *file* exists and is owned by the effective group ID.
-L *file*	True if *file* exists and is a symbolic link.
-S *file*	True if *file* exists and is a socket.
-N *file*	True if *file* exists and has been modified since its last access.
file1 -nt *file2*	True if *file1* has a more recent modification date than *file2*.
file1 -ot *file2*	True if *file1* has a less recent modification date than *file2*.
file1 -ef *file2*	True if *file1* and *file2* have the same inode and device numbers.

Continued on next page

TABLE 4.6: CONDITIONAL EXPRESSIONS AND THEIR MEANINGS *(continued)*

CONDITIONAL EXPRESSION	MEANING
-o *optname*	True if the option *optname* is enabled in the shell.
-z *string*	True if *string*'s length is zero.
-n *string*	True if *string*'s length is not zero.
string1 = *string2*	True if the strings are equal.
string1 != *string2*	True if the strings are not equal.
string1 < *string2*	True if *string1* comes before *string2* lexicographically.
string1 > *string2*	True if *string1* comes after *string2* lexicographically.
arg1 -eq *arg2*	True if *arg1* is equal to *arg2*. Both must be integers.
arg1 -ne *arg2*	True if *arg1* is not equal to *arg2*.
arg1 -lt *arg2*	True if *arg1* is less than *arg2*.
arg1 -le *arg2*	True if *arg1* is less than or equal to *arg2*.
arg1 -gt *arg2*	True if *arg1* is greater than *arg2*.
arg1 -ge *arg2*	True if *arg1* is greater than or equal to *arg2*.

Using *if* and *case*

Scripts must frequently perform different actions depending upon certain conditions. For instance, you might want a script to abort if it can't find a file the user specified, but continue processing if the file exists; or you might want to display information that's customized for each of several possible inputs. The if and case statements handle these situations.

MAKING BINARY CHOICES: *if*

The if keyword uses a conditional expression to determine whether or not to perform some action. Its basic syntax is given here:

```
if [ condition ]
then
    actions
else
    other-actions
fi
```

NOTE *Indenting lines within* if, case, *and looping statements to help improve the readability of scripts is common. This indentation isn't required, though, and different people have different styles of indentation.*

You can omit the else clause and the *other-actions* if you don't want the script to do anything should the condition not be met. As an example of if in action, consider Listing 4.4. This script checks for the presence of a /proc/ide/ide0/hdb directory, which should be present if and only if a slave hard disk is present on the primary ATA controller. If that directory is present, the script displays information on the attached hard disk. If not, the script tells you there's no drive.

LISTING 4.4: SCRIPT DEMONSTRATING USE OF if

```
#!/bin/bash
if [ -d /proc/ide/ide0/hdb ]
then
    echo "The drive's model is:"
    cat /proc/ide/ide0/hdb/model
else
    echo "Sorry, there isn't a primary slave disk."
fi
```

Although the identified drive model will vary from one system to another, Listing 4.4 produces output like this:

```
$ ./ifdemo
The drive's model is:
Maxtor 91000D8
```

MAKING MANY CHOICES: *case*

You can use if to make binary decisions—to take one action if a condition is true and another action if the condition isn't true. You can also nest if statements inside each other—in fact, the optional elif statement is built for this situation; use it after then but before else to perform a second test. Sometimes, though, a more flexible multiple-condition test is in order. That's where case comes in. You pass a variable to this statement and then specify a series of actions to be taken depending on the value of the variable. The case syntax looks like this:

```
case variable in
    value1) commands1
            ;;
    value2) commands2
            ;;
    [...]
esac
```

You can include an arbitrary number of values that might match the variable. The shell executes the commands associated with the first value that matches the variable. The values you specify may include wildcards, much like wildcards in matching filenames. One of the most useful of these is a value that consists of a single asterisk (*). This value matches any variable, so when it's the final option in a case statement, it works much like the else clause of an if statement.

Listing 4.5 shows case in action. This script launches one of three programs in response to the user's input. When a user runs this script, the text specified in the first two echo lines appears on the screen and the script accepts an input letter. If that input is anything but e, 1, or m, the script displays the default error message and exits; otherwise, the script launches the specified user program.

LISTING 4.5: SCRIPT DEMONSTRATING USE OF case

```
#!/bin/bash
echo "Type the first letter of a program name:"
echo "emacs, lynx, or mutt"
read progletter
case $progletter in
   e) emacs
      ;;
   l) lynx
      ;;
   m) mutt
      ;;
   *) echo "You didn't type e, l, or m; exiting!"
esac
```

Using Loops

One scripting tool is the *loop*—a way to execute the same code again and again. There are two broad classes of loops in shell scripts. A `for` loop will execute code for a fixed number of times. This number may not be known when you write the script, but it can be determined when entering the loop. By contrast, `while` and `until` loops execute while or until some condition is met, respectively.

for LOOPS

The basic syntax of a `for` loop is shown here:

```
for variable in list
do
    commands
done
```

The *variable* and *commands* are what you might expect. The *list* is a variable or expression that produces a list of elements—frequently, a command or set of commands enclosed in single back-quote marks (`` ` ``), a symbol that appears to the left of the 1 key on most keyboards. The *commands* execute once for each element in the *list*, and the *variable* takes on the value of each element in the *list* for each run through the loop. For instance, consider Listing 4.6, which is a variant on Listing 4.4. Instead of identifying just one drive, though, this script identifies all of a computer's ATA devices.

LISTING 4.6: SCRIPT DEMONSTRATING A for LOOP

```
#!/bin/bash
for drive in `ls -d /proc/ide/hd?`
do
    echo "The model of drive $drive is:"
    cat $drive/model
done
```

In use, Listing 4.6 produces output that varies from one system to another. In general, it will resemble this:

```
$ ./fordemo
The model of drive /proc/ide/hda is:
SAMSUNG SV6003H
The model of drive /proc/ide/hdc is:
MATSHITA CR-173
```

while AND *until* LOOPS

The `while` and `until` loops are very similar, but they differ in their exit conditions: A `while` loop executes for as long as the specified condition remains true. An `until` loop executes for as long as the specified condition remains false (that is, until it *becomes* true). Therefore, the two loop types are interchangeable, except that you must reverse the nature of the conditional expression. Their syntax is also quite similar. Here it is for the `while` loop:

```
while [ condition ]
do
     commands
done
```

Replace `while` with `until` to implement an `until` loop. Consider Listing 4.7, which is a variant of Listing 4.5. When run, this script repeatedly asks for an input letter. When you type an acceptable response, it launches the program in question or exits. When you quit from the target program, you see another prompt for a program to run. This script could be written using `while` just as well as `until`; but the conditional expression would use `!=` rather than `=` to determine when to exit.

LISTING 4.7: SCRIPT DEMONSTRATING USE OF `until`

```
#!/bin/bash
progletter=t
until [ $progletter = q ]
do
    echo "Type the first letter of a program name:"
    echo "emacs, lynx, or mutt"
    echo "(Type 'q' to exit)"
    read progletter
    case $progletter in
       e) emacs
          ;;
       l) lynx
          ;;
       m) mutt
          ;;
       *) echo "You didn't type e, l, or m; exiting!"
    esac
done
```

As demonstrated by Listing 4.7, it's often necessary to set the variable being tested in a `while` or `until` loop before the loop begins. Listing 4.7 sets this variable to a dummy value (`t`). Any value (aside from `q`) will do in this case; the goal is simply to keep the looping logic from terminating early or printing an error message because of a variable that hasn't been initialized.

Summary

Text-mode shells are an important part of any Linux system. They enable you to run text-mode programs from text-based login tools such as a text-mode console, dumb terminal, or network SSH session. Most Linux shells, including the popular `bash`, provide features that can help make text mode very productive. These features include command completion, history, command editing, redirection, and pipes. You can also customize your shell to your liking by creating aliases, setting environment variables, and modifying the prompt.

Shells provide an important additional feature: scripting. You can further enhance your productivity in Linux by writing scripts, which combine several commands, possibly using conditional expressions, loops, and other features to increase their power. Scripts can help automate tasks that would otherwise be quite tedious. Furthermore, many Linux startup scripts are written in the `bash` shell scripting language, so understanding this language is key to modifying startup scripts.

Chapter 5

Doing Real Work in Text Mode

THE PRECEDING CHAPTER, "Mastering Shells and Shell Scripting," described how to get the most out of a Linux text-mode shell. The shell is just part of the text-mode tool set, though. In order to be productive in a text-mode environment, you need to know how to use a variety of text-mode commands. These commands help you manipulate filesystems and files, and provide information about the system. These tools enable you to manage your home directory and support productivity in your ultimate applications. You may also want to customize your environment in various ways. Some customizations relate to the shell or even to hardware settings, such as the keyboard repeat rate (described in Chapter 3, "Using External Peripherals"), but others don't fall in these categories. These miscellaneous adjustments include telling Linux what terminal type to use and changing the font it uses to display text.

Running Multiple Programs in Virtual Terminals

When you log into a text-mode console, you're using a *virtual terminal*. To understand virtual terminals, remember that Linux was designed as a clone of Unix, which is a multiuser OS. Traditionally, Unix systems have supported dozens, hundreds, or even thousands of users, each working from a physical *terminal*—a device consisting of a keyboard, a monitor, and perhaps a mouse—that enables a user to access a computer remotely. You can use terminals with Linux, but a standard IA-32 PC has one primary keyboard and monitor. In order to improve usability, Linux supports configuring the system so that these devices can act like several physical terminals—that is, they're virtual. Each virtual terminal can run a separate program, or even support logins under different usernames. This feature enables you to run many programs and easily switch between them.

Most standard installations define six virtual text-mode terminals, reached by pressing Alt+F1 through Alt+F6. These terminals are defined in the /etc/inittab configuration file, using lines like the following:

```
1:2345:respawn:/sbin/mingetty tty1
2:2345:respawn:/sbin/mingetty tty2
3:2345:respawn:/sbin/mingetty tty3
4:2345:respawn:/sbin/mingetty tty4
5:2345:respawn:/sbin/mingetty tty5
6:2345:respawn:/sbin/mingetty tty6
```

These lines tell the system to run `mingetty` on `tty1` through `tty6`—that is, the first six virtual terminals. The `mingetty` program is one of several programs known collectively as `getty` programs. These programs manage the interactions between a terminal (either real or virtual) and the `login` program, which accepts user logins. Several `getty` programs are available, and different distributions favor different `getty`s. Mandrake, Red Hat, and SuSE use `mingetty`; Debian uses the original `getty`; and Slackware uses `agetty`, for instance.

NOTE   *When you run X, it starts up in the first unused virtual terminal—typically, number 7. Therefore, to switch to X from text mode, you can press Alt+F7, assuming X is running. To switch from X to a text-mode terminal, you must add Ctrl to the key sequence, as in Ctrl+Alt+F1 to switch to the first text-mode terminal.*

You can make effective use of virtual terminals by logging into several and running a different program in each. For instance, you might examine a man page in one virtual terminal and type commands based on what you read in another.

Mastering Important Linux Commands

Linux includes many text-based commands for doing real work. Many of these tools are extremely specialized and complex, so I can't present more than a bare introduction to these programs in this chapter, which covers some of the most important general-purpose text-mode tools. If you have specific needs, they might be described in other chapters of this book, or you might be able to find helpful information in a specific program's documentation or web page.

NOTE   *You can use any of the programs described in this chapter from a text-mode login or from a shell run in a text-based window, such as an* `xterm`, *in a GUI environment. Utilities that change text-mode settings, such as the resolution, are best run from text mode, though.*

Accessing Media: Filesystem Manipulation Tools

One common requirement when using a Linux workstation is the need to access removable media— floppy disks, Zip disks, CD-ROMs, and so on. If you're familiar with DOS or Windows, you're probably used to accessing these media using drive letters, such as `A:` for the floppy disk. This approach doesn't normally work in Linux, although the `mtools` package enables limited access in this way, as described in Chapter 2, "Improving Disk Performance." Instead, you must *mount* a removable disk to a *mount point*—that is, make it available at a specific directory set aside for this purpose. Chapter 2 describes editing `/etc/fstab` to create mount points for your removable media disks. If you include the `user` option, ordinary users can mount and unmount the filesystem, but only the user who mounted it can unmount it. The `users` option works in the same way, but anybody can unmount the filesystem once it's mounted.

To mount a filesystem, you use the `mount` command, followed by the mount point or device filename, as shown here:

```
$ mount /mnt/floppy
```

This command mounts the device with a defined mount point of `/mnt/floppy` in `/etc/fstab`— presumably the floppy drive. Assuming permissions allow, you can then read, write, and otherwise manipulate files on the floppy disk. When you're done, you should unmount the disk using the umount command:

```
$ umount /mnt/floppy
```

NOTE *The* umount *command really does have just one* n; *if you type* **unmount**, *it won't work.*

These commands work as shown only if you've defined a mount point in /etc/fstab; if you haven't, you must also specify the device file used to access the partition or disk, as in **mount /dev/fd0 /mnt/floppy**. Only root can mount a filesystem for which no /etc/fstab entry exists.

Sometimes you need to prepare a disk to hold files. You use one or both of two commands to do this job:

fdformat This command performs a *low-level format* of the floppy disk. This format defines the low-level data structures, such as sectors and tracks. This tool can *only* be used on floppy disks; hard disks are low-level formatted at the factory.

mkfs This tool writes a filesystem to a disk or partition, an operation that's sometimes called *high-level formatting*. In reality, mkfs calls other programs, such as mkfs.ext2 and mkdosfs, to do the real work.

Suppose you have a new unformatted floppy disk you want to use to exchange data with a Windows user. You could use the following commands to prepare the disk:

```
$ fdformat /dev/fd0
$ mkfs -t msdos /dev/fd0
```

NOTE *These commands only work if you have write access to the device file—*/dev/fd0 *in this example. Some distributions give the user logged into the console ownership of* /dev/fd0 *and some other device files. Others have a group called* floppy *or* disk *and grant read/write access to these files to that group, so you can add any authorized user to the appropriate group.*

After creating a filesystem, you can mount the floppy and copy files to it. If you prefer to use a filesystem other than FAT, you can do so—substitute the other filesystem's name, such as ext2 or minix, for msdos. Because fdformat is used only for floppy disks, you won't type that command when using Zip disks or other non-floppy removable media. You also don't need to use fdformat on floppies that have already been used.

Chapter 12, "Filesystems and Files," describes filesystems and more advanced filesystem tools in more detail. Check there if you need to decide what filesystem to use on a hard disk, recover a corrupted filesystem, or perform other advanced tasks.

Accessing Files: File Manipulation Tools

Much of the work you do with any computer and in any environment relates directly to manipulating files—copying them, moving them, changing their ownership and permissions, and so on. Linux provides a wide variety of tools for performing these tasks. They may seem peculiar and even intimidating to the uninitiated, but Linux's text-mode file-manipulation commands are very powerful.

Wildcard Specifications

One aspect of file manipulation in Linux is the use of *wildcards*, which are special characters or character groups that stand in for other characters. Using wildcards, you can tell the system to operate on a large number of files that meet certain name criteria. Table 5.1 summarizes some of the most common wildcards.

Table 5.1: Common Wildcards in File Operations

Wildcard	Meaning
*	Any collection of zero or more characters.
?	Any single character.
[ABC]	Any character from the specified set, ABC, of characters, where ABC can be any collection of characters, of any length.
[A-C]	Any character from the set of characters between A and C in the character set.

You can combine wildcards in various ways. For instance, `*.[co]` matches any filename that ends in `.c` or `.o`, such as `inet.c` or `load.o`; but not names that end in any other string, such as `sound.h`. Wildcards are expanded by the shell; therefore, programs called from a shell and passed wildcards as arguments actually receive the complete list of matching files as arguments, not the wildcard.

Copying Files

One of the workhorse Linux file-manipulation commands is `cp`, which copies files. The syntax for this command is deceptively simple:

```
cp [options] source destination
```

In this case, *source* is one or more source files, possibly expressed using wildcard operators. The *destination* can be either a file, in which case the original is copied to the new filename; or a directory, in which case the original is copied to the new directory using its original filename. If you specify multiple *source* files, either explicitly or via a wildcard, the *destination* *must* be a directory.

The complexity of `cp` emerges in the use of its many options, some of which are summarized in Table 5.2. This table isn't comprehensive; consult the `cp` man page for more options.

Table 5.2: Common cp Options

Option	Effect
-a	Archive a directory; copy recursively (as in -r) and preserve ownership, permissions, and symbolic link status.
-b	Make a backup of any destination file the operation replaces.
-f or --force	Replace any matching destination file without asking for confirmation.

Continued on next page

TABLE 5.2: COMMON cp OPTIONS *(continued)*	
OPTION	**EFFECT**
`-i` or `--interactive`	Query before replacing any existing destination file.
`-l` or `--link`	Create hard links rather than copies.
`-p`	Preserve ownership, permissions, and time stamps.
`-r`, `-R`, or `--recursive`	Copy directories recursively.
`-s` or `--symbolic-link`	Create symbolic links rather than copies.
`-u` or `--update`	Copy only when the destination file doesn't exist or is older than the source file.
`-x` or `--one-file-system`	Don't recurse into mounted filesystems (used in conjunction with `-r`)

LINKING FILES

Linux supports two types of *links*, which are ways to reference a single file by multiple names:

Hard Links This type of link creates two or more directory entries for each file. No directory entry is more "real" or "official" than the others, although one will necessarily be created first. If you delete any link, the others continue to work, until you delete the last link, at which point the file is deleted. All hard links to a file must reside on the same filesystem; you can't create, say, a hard link from your home directory to a file on a CD-ROM, floppy, or even another hard disk partition. Hard links between directories aren't permitted.

Symbolic Links This type of link, also known as a *soft link*, creates a special file whose contents point to another file by name. The soft link stops working if the original file is deleted, but the original file is unaffected if you delete any soft links pointing to it. You can create cross-filesystem soft links, as well as soft links to directories. Soft links impose an extra filesystem lookup and, therefore, are very slightly slower than hard links, although you won't notice this tiny difference in common operations.

You can create hard or soft links using the `-l` and `-s` options to cp, as noted in Table 5.2. You can also create links using the ln command, which uses a syntax that's identical to that of cp. The two commands also share many options, including `-b`, `-f`, and `-i`. Ordinarily, ln creates a hard link; but passing it the `-s` option causes it to create a symbolic link. In either case, you can create links on any Linux-native filesystem, such as the Minix filesystem, ext2fs, ext3fs, ReiserFS, JFS, or XFS. The Rock Ridge extensions to ISO-9660 also support soft links, although some mkisofs options cause them to be ignored or converted into duplicate files. A few non-Linux filesystems support soft links, such as OS/2's High-Performance File System (HPFS). The soft links are encoded as HPFS Extended Attributes and aren't useable from OS/2. You can't create links on most other filesystems, including FAT, although you can create soft links that reside on Linux filesystems that point to files on filesystems that don't support links.

Linux makes extensive use of links—especially symbolic links—in its standard system files. Many commands are available under multiple names via symbolic links, and symbolic links are also critical in most distributions' startup script systems. News server software typically makes heavy use of hard links.

WARNING *Some backup programs don't cope well with hard or symbolic links. The standard* tar, *for instance, handles symbolic links well, but it creates one file in its archive for each hard link. When restored, each file takes up its own share of disk space.*

RENAMING AND MOVING FILES

The mv command does double duty: It renames and moves files. Its syntax is much like that of cp:

    mv [*options*] *source destination*

When you specify a complete filename for the destination, mv renames the file. When the destination is a directory, mv moves the file (keeping the old filename). When the destination is a complete filename in another directory, mv moves and renames the file.

You can use many of the same options with mv that you use with cp or ln. In particular, from Table 5.2, -b, -f, -i, and -u all apply. The -p option isn't available because mv doesn't alter permissions, ownership, or time stamps.

You can apply mv to a directory, but only when the target location is on the same filesystem as the original. If you want to move an entire directory tree from one partition to another, you'll have to use cp with its recursive option (or better, -a, to preserve permissions, symbolic links, and so on), tar, or some other tool to copy the files, and then delete the original files with rm and its recursive option.

DELETING FILES

The rm command deletes (removes) files. Its syntax is shown here:

    rm [*options*] *files*

This command accepts many of the same options as cp, ln, and mv. Specifically, from Table 5.2, -f, -i, and -r work with rm. Unlike some operating systems' file-deletion tools, rm is permanent; Linux doesn't store deleted files in any sort of "trash can" folder. Chapter 12 provides pointers to tools and utilities you can use to recover deleted files or to implement a holding area to prevent files from being immediately deleted.

The rm command doesn't normally delete directories, but if you pass it the -r or -R option, it will delete an entire directory tree, whether or not there are files in the target directory.

WARNING *The* rm *command is potentially dangerous, particularly when used with its recursive (-r or -R) option or in the hands of* root. *If you're not careful, you can easily wipe out all the files on the computer by misusing this command. For instance, consider* **rm -r / home/nemo**. *You might type this command to delete a former user's (*nemo's*) home directory—but there's a stray space between the leading* / *and* home, *so the effect is to delete all the files in the entire directory tree. Always pause and examine an* rm *command before typing it as* root!

CHANGING OWNERSHIP

In Linux, all files have owners. This information is encoded in the form of a user ID (UID) number, but most utilities work with the associated username. For instance, a long file listing might look like this:

    $ ls -l report.*
    -rw-r--r-- 1 homer users   5271 Dec 12 12:07 report.tex

The username in this case is homer. The file is also associated with a specific group—users in this example. It's sometimes necessary to change the ownership of a file—for instance, a system administrator may want to move files into a specific person's account for that person's exclusive use. Ordinary users can't change the ownership of a file, but root can, by using the chown command, which has the following syntax:

```
chown [options] owner[:group] files
```

You can specify the *owner* as a username or as a UID number. The optional *group* specification can also be a name or a group ID (GID) number. This command accepts several options, the most important of which is -R, which initiates a recursive ownership change. You can use this option to change ownership of an entire directory tree.

Although only root has the power to change a file's ownership, ordinary users can change a file's group, within certain limits. Specifically, the user must belong to the target group and must own the file in question. For instance, if homer is a member of the users, horse, and bow groups, homer can assign a file to any of these groups, but not to the library group. The tool to change a file's group is chgrp, and it works much like chown:

```
chgrp [options] group files
```

As with chown, you can use the -R option to perform a recursive change.

CHANGING PERMISSIONS

Linux file security is based upon both ownership and permissions. Three permissions are paramount: *read*, *write*, and *execute*. The first grants the ability to read the contents of a file; the second enables the ability to modify a file's contents; and the third grants the right to run a file as a program (of course, it must be a program file for this access to be meaningful). These three permissions can be set differently for three increasingly broad classes of users: the file's owner, the file's group, and all others (that is, *world* permissions).

The combination of three permission types and three scopes to which they apply means that there are nine primary permission bits. These permissions are frequently expressed as a nine-character string, such as rwxr-x---. The first three characters represent read, write, and execute permissions for the owner. If these characters are letters matching the type of permission (r for read, w for write, and x for execute), then the owner has the specified permission. If the character is a dash (-), then the owner lacks the specified permission. The next block of three characters represents the access granted to the file's group, and the final block of three characters represents world access. Thus, in the case of rwxr-x---, the owner has full read, write, and execute permission; the group has read and execute but not write access; and everybody else has no access. These nine characters are sometimes preceded by another that represents the file's type—a dash (-) for an ordinary file, d for a directory, s for a symbolic link, and so on.

NOTE   Linux treats directories as files. Therefore, to add files to a directory, a user must have write access to the directory. Likewise, deleting files from a directory requires write access to the directory, but this action doesn't require write access to the files in question. One exception is if a special permission bit, known as the sticky *bit, is set, as described shortly; in this case, only* root *or the owner of a file may delete it.*

These permissions can also be expressed by using octal (base 8) numbers. An octal 0 represents no access; a 1 means execute permission; a 2 means write permission; and a 4 means read permission. These numbers can be added together when more than one permission is present. The result is a single octal digit for each permission scope, and these numbers are displayed one after another. For instance, rwxr-x--- is equivalent to 750.

You can change permissions using the chmod command, which takes the following syntax:

```
chmod [options] mode files
```

The *mode* specification is potentially complex. You can specify the mode as an octal number, such as 750. You can also use a symbolic format in which you specify whose permissions are to be affected; whether you're adding, deleting, or setting permissions; and what permissions you're changing. Table 5.3 summarizes the options for symbolic modes. Pick one or more elements from the Affects Symbol column, one from the Operation Symbol column, and one or more from the Permission Symbol column.

TABLE 5.3: SYMBOLIC MODE COMPONENTS

AFFECTS	AFFECTS SYMBOL	OPERATION	OPERATION SYMBOL	PERMISSION	PERMISSION SYMBOL
Owner	u	Add permission	+	Read	r
Group	g	Subtract permission	–	Write	w
World	o	Set permission	=	Execute	x
All	a			Execute for directories or if any execute permission exists	X
				Set user ID or set group ID	s
				Sticky bit	t
				Existing owner's permission	u
				Existing group permissions	g
				Existing world permissions	o

You can combine multiple symbolic mode options by separating them with commas (,). As an example of chmod's symbolic modes, Table 5.4 presents some before-and-after scenarios. As a general rule, you can achieve the same goals using either symbolic or octal modes; however, there are exceptions. For instance, you can use the u, g, and o permission symbols to set permissions on a group of files uniquely for each file, depending on their existing permissions for a specific user set. The uppercase X permission symbol can also be useful in setting permissions on directories, which normally have execute permissions set whenever their read permissions are set. (Execute permission for a directory enables searching the directory's contents, not executing code in the directory.)

TABLE 5.4: EXAMPLES OF chmod SYMBOLIC MODE COMMANDS

PERMISSIONS BEFORE	SYMBOLIC MODE	PERMISSIONS AFTER
rwxr-x---	a-x	rw-r-----
rwxr-x---	o=g	rwxr-xr-x
rw-r--r--	a+x	rwxr-xr-x
r--r--r--	u+wx,g+x	rwxr-xr--

A couple of special permission settings deserve attention:

SUID and SGID Bits　The *set user ID (SUID)* and *set group ID (SGID)* bits can be set on executable files by applying the s permission symbol to owner or group permission, respectively. Ordinarily, when you run a program, that program runs with the permissions of the user who launched the program. With the SUID or SGID bit set, though, the program runs with the permissions associated with the program file's owner or group, respectively. This feature is used by a handful of key system programs to enable users to do things that they otherwise wouldn't be able to do, such as access a CD-R drive's device files. You should use this feature sparingly, though; a bug in a program that's run with its SUID bit set (particularly if its owner is root) can be a security risk if the program has a bug or enables users to write arbitrary files. For instance, an SUID root editor would enable any user who can run the editor to edit key configuration files. You can spot SUID or SGID programs by the presence of an s rather than an x as the execute permission symbol in their permission strings, as in rwsr-sr-x.

Sticky Bit　Ordinarily, write permission on a directory enables any user to create and delete any file within a directory. Sometimes, though, this isn't desirable; for instance, you probably don't want to let users delete each others' temporary files in /tmp or similar shared directories. You can set the *sticky bit* on such directories by using the t symbolic permission symbol. This bit keeps users from deleting files they don't own. You can tell when a directory has its sticky bit set by the presence of a t rather than an x in the world permission string, such as rwxrwxrwt.

WORKING WITH DIRECTORIES

Many Linux commands for working with files also apply to directories. For instance, chown, chmod, cp, mv, rm, and ln (with some restrictions on some of these commands) all apply to directories. Directories present their own unique needs, though. For instance, you need a special command to create a directory. Some directory-centric commands include:

mkdir　This command creates a new directory, as in **mkdir reports** to create a directory called reports.

rmdir　This command deletes an empty directory. If you want to delete a directory tree that contains files, you're better off using rm -r.

cd　This command changes the current working directory. For instance, typing **cd /etc** moves you into the /etc directory, so that you can more easily work on files in this directory.

pwd　This command displays the current working directory, so that you know where you're working.

Using System Information Tools

Sometimes you need to know things about your computer—where partitions are mounted, how much memory is in use, and so on. Linux provides a number of commands that provide this information. Examples include:

df   This command displays information about all of the mounted filesystems. If you pass a mount point or partition identifier as a parameter, df displays information about the specified filesystem only. Information includes the device filename, total filesystem size, used space, free space, percentage of disk space used, and mount point. This tool is extremely useful in tracking disk use and in planning disk expansions.

du   The df command is very useful for tracking disk use on a partition-by-partition basis, but it's not good for tracking finer-grained disk use. That's where du comes in; it tells you how much disk space each subdirectory in a directory tree uses. This command accepts many options, one of the most useful of which is --max-depth=*n*; this option trims the report so you don't see details of subdirectories below a specific depth. For instance, **du --max-depth=1 /home** will tell you how much disk space your users are consuming in their home directories. (Depending on the permissions users have set, this particular example might work only if it is typed by root.)

stat   This command displays information on a file, including the filename, file size, ownership, permissions, three dates (last access, last modification, and last file status change), and some low-level data structures such as the inode number. This information can be useful in determining when files have been used or modified and in performing some low-level file maintenance.

lsof   This command lists all the open files on a computer, and it lists information on the user and process that is accessing the files. As such, lsof produces copious output. You'll probably have to pipe the output through less or grep to make sense of it, or you might use various lsof options to trim its output. This command is very useful in finding processes that are using files on removable media you want to unmount but can't because of open files.

uptime   This command reports how long the computer has been running. It also displays three *load averages*, which give you an idea of how much demand there is for CPU time. A load average of 0.0 means no programs are requesting CPU time; 1.0 means the CPU is being used to its fullest; and values above 1.0 mean that the kernel has been rationing CPU time because programs want more CPU time than the system can deliver. Some systems, such as busy servers, run with load averages of well over 1.0, but on others, load averages should be below 1.0 most of the time.

free   This command summarizes the system's memory use. The total column displays available memory; used reports memory that's in use; and free summarizes free memory. The most important line is the one labeled -/+ buffers/cache; this line reports memory use by system processes, and so is a good measure of the demand for memory on the system. The Mem line is likely to show very little free memory because this line includes memory that is used by buffers and caches, which are allocated dynamically by Linux to improve disk performance, consuming most memory not being used by programs. The Swap line reports the demand for swap space. If the used entry for this line approaches the total entry, you may need to add memory or swap space to improve performance.

hostname   Typed by itself, this command returns the computer's TCP/IP networking hostname. The system administrator may change the hostname by typing a new name after the command.

who This command returns a list of the users who are logged onto the computer. The users command is similar to who, and finger provides additional information.

dmesg This command displays the Linux kernel message buffer. Soon after starting Linux, this buffer contains startup messages, which can be useful in system debugging. As the system runs, the message buffer will accumulate messages on normal operations and the startup messages will be lost.

TIP Because startup messages can be such useful diagnostic tools, you may want to create a startup script that saves these messages as part of the startup process. Debian, Mandrake, and Red Hat all do this by default, storing the results in /var/log/dmesg.

Managing the Text-Mode Environment

When using text-mode tools, chances are you want to take best advantage of your video hardware. Many Linux tools are written with a display of roughly 80 characters by 25 lines with monochrome text in mind. Even very old IA-32 hardware, however, can display more and wider lines than this, and can display text in various colors. GUI xterm windows are also much more flexible in their display capabilities. Knowing how to take advantage of these modes can make text mode much more appealing.

Using an Appropriate *termcap* or *terminfo*

One of the problems faced during the early development of Unix was the wide array of terminal hardware with which the OS had to cope. The codes that would clear the screen on one terminal might have no effect on another, and they would cause a third to perform some wholly inappropriate action. Because of this, programs couldn't be written to use specific terminal codes to perform specific actions. The solution to this problem was to create a database of information on terminal types. Originally, this database was known as termcap, and it relied on data stored in /etc/termcap. Newer programs use a more recent database known as terminfo, which stores data in files in the /usr/share/terminfo directory tree.

In both cases, programs rely upon the TERM environment variable to identify the terminal type. Examples of values this variable might hold include linux (for text-mode Linux logins), xterm (for xterm windows under X), and vt100 (for the popular DEC VT-100 terminal or any terminal or program that emulates it). Type **echo $TERM** in a shell to learn what terminal your system believes it's using.

In most cases, Linux auto-detects the terminal type, so you don't need to adjust it. Sometimes, though, this auto-detection doesn't work correctly. In these cases, you may need to set the terminal type manually. If the /etc/termcap file and /usr/share/terminfo directory tree contain appropriate entries, you can do so by setting the TERM environment variable, as shown here:

```
$ export TERM=vt100
```

Of course, you should change vt100, if necessary, to whatever value is appropriate. Try browsing through /etc/termcap and the filenames in the /usr/share/terminfo directory to try to find one that matches the terminal or terminal emulator you're using. If you can't find a match, consult the terminal or terminal emulator's documentation; it may support another model's codes. Failing that, the hardware or software may come with an appropriate `termcap` or `terminfo` database entry that you can add to your system.

Modifying Console Fonts

Most IA-32 computers boot up in a basic video mode that displays 80 columns and 25 rows of text. By default, Linux works in this mode, but it's possible to change it in two ways. First, you can load a new font. You might do this in order to support language-specific characters or simply because you don't like the default font. Second, you can alter the screen resolution, yielding more or fewer columns or rows of text. You could do this to take better advantage of a large screen by displaying smaller text— or to help you see the text on a small screen or to enlarge the fonts if you're visually impaired.

SETTING THE CONSOLE FONT

You can adjust the size and appearance of text by altering the fonts displayed by the video card. Linux provides several tools designed to do this: `consolechars`, `setfont`, and `fontconfig`. Which tools are available depends upon which distribution you're using, as specified in Table 5.5. The first two programs work in a very similar way. Both take a number of options, but you can usually run them by passing a font filename to the command with `-f` (for `consolechars`) or `-v` (for `setfont`):

```
$ setfont -v /usr/lib/kbd/consolefonts/t.psf.gz
```

TABLE 5.5: CONSOLE FONT UTILITY AND FONT FILE LOCATIONS

DISTRIBUTION	FONT-SETTING UTILITIES	PACKAGE HOLDING FONT-SETTING UTILITIES	PACKAGE HOLDING FONT FILES	LOCATION OF FONT FILES
Debian	consolechars	console-tools	console-data and fonty	/usr/share/ consolefonts
Mandrake	consolechars and setfont	console-tools	console-tools	/usr/lib/kbd/ consolefonts
Red Hat	setfont	kbd	kbd	/lib/kbd/ consolefonts
Slackware	setfont and fontconfig	kbd	kbd	/usr/share/kbd/ consolefonts
SuSE	setfont	kbd	kbd	/usr/share/kbd/ consolefonts

The `fontconfig` utility is unique to Slackware. It presents a menu of font choices and enables you to try a font before setting it for your login session. If you want to make the change permanent, `fontconfig` writes a startup script, `/etc/rc.d/rc.font`, which calls `setfont` to do the job every time the system boots. The location of the console font files and the packages from which they're installed vary substantially from one distribution to another, as Table 5.5 shows.

Most console fonts are eight or nine pixels wide and between eight and sixteen pixels high. An 8 × 16 font yields 25 lines of text. You can double the number of lines of text displayed in text mode by switching to an 8 × 8 font, or you can set an intermediate value with a font of another size.

Setting the Text Resolution

One key attribute of graphical video modes as used by X is their resolution—how many pixels are displayed, both horizontally and vertically. Text mode, too, sets a specific resolution. The combination of this resolution and the size of the characters that make up the font determine how many characters can be displayed on the screen. Therefore, one way to adjust the number of characters displayed on the screen is to adjust the underlying resolution. There are two ways to do this:

Modifying the Kernel   You can alter a kernel to use a specific video mode using the `vidmode` command. You pass numerical codes to be used as video modes; for instance, `-2` enables an extended VGA mode that doubles the number of lines of the display. To use this mode, you'd type **`vidmode /boot/bzImage -2`**, where */boot/bzImage* is your Linux kernel filename. One problem with this approach is that it's difficult to test, because you must reboot before the new mode takes effect.

Passing Kernel Options   You can pass options to the kernel using your boot loader to enable a specific video mode at system startup. For instance, if you use the Linux Loader (LILO), you can use the `vga=`*mode* line in `lilo.conf`, where *mode* is `normal` for an 80 × 25 display or `ext` for an 80 × 50 display. Like modifying the kernel, passing kernel options requires a reboot.

Using SVGATextMode   The `SVGATextMode` program (headquartered at `http://freshmeat.net/projects/svgatextmode/`) is a flexible program for setting text modes without modifying the kernel. You can set up text modes that aren't available in any other way using this tool, and you can change the text mode without rebooting the computer. Using this program overrides any options set in the kernel or by passing options to the kernel.

Because `SVGATextMode` is so flexible and complex, it deserves more explanation. This program comes with Debian, Mandrake, and SuSE in the `svgatextmode`, `SVGATextMode`, and `svgatext` packages, respectively. This tool uses a configuration file, `/etc/TextConfig`, that's similar to the XFree86 configuration file. The default configuration file is set up to support video modes that should work with any modern video card; but to get the most out of the package, you must reconfigure several details:

Chipset   The `Chipset` line sets the video card chipset. The default value of `VGA` works with most modern video cards, but you may be able to get more or better options by selecting your true video card. Comment out the `Chipset "VGA"` line by placing a hash mark (#) at the start of the line, then locate the appropriate line for your video card and uncomment it. If you can't find an appropriate line, you may need to use the generic VGA configuration. You must also change the chipset clocks configuration when you change the chipset.

Chipset Clocks   Different video cards support different *dot clocks*, which are low-level timing parameters. The VGA configuration includes a single `Clocks` line that sets two dot clocks. The configurations for specific video chipsets include one or more `Clocks` lines that specify many additional video clocks. Comment out the VGA configuration's `Clocks` line and uncomment the `Clocks` lines for your target video card.

Default Video Mode The `DefaultMode` line specifies the video mode the program sets if it is not given an explicit mode—80 × 25 is the default value. Change this line to read something else that you prefer, such as `132x50x8`. Most modes are specified by the number of columns of characters by number of rows of characters by the character width in pixels. (The assumption is that characters are 16 pixels in height.) You can sometimes omit the character width, and some modes are preceded by special characters, such as `v116x48`. Most of the latter half of the `TextConfig` file is devoted to defining video modes, so you can pick a name from among these modes. You may want to leave this option alone until you've tested several modes and found the one you like.

Disk Synchronization A line that reads `Option "SyncDisks"` flushes your disk cache before doing anything. This is a safety measure in case the program causes a system hang. Once you've tested the program, you can comment this line out to speed up operation.

Font Selection The `FontProg` line points the system at a tool to set console fonts. These tools are described in the previous section, "Setting the Console Font." You can also specify the location and names of font files that `SVGATextMode` will load to create various display sizes. Some distributions, such as SuSE, may override these values with others specified in other files, such as `/etc/sysconfig/console`.

Video Refresh Rates Locate the lines, which are commented out by default, that set the `HorizSync` and `VertRefresh` values. Uncomment these lines and enter the values used in your XFree86 configuration file (`XF86Config` or `XF86Config-4`, in `/etc` or `/etc/X11`). These values tell the system about your monitor's capabilities. You can also find the horizontal and vertical refresh rate values for your monitor in its manual.

WARNING *Setting incorrect* `HorizSync` *or* `VertRefresh` *rates can damage some monitors, so be sure to set these values correctly. Most modern monitors ignore out-of-range signals, but you shouldn't count on this happening.*

There are many other configuration options in `/etc/TextConfig`, but most of these relate to very advanced settings, such as definitions for new video modes. You can select from any video mode you like by specifying it when you call the program; for instance:

```
# SVGATextMode 132x50x9
```

WARNING *If you've set options incorrectly in the configuration file,* `SVGATextMode` *can yield a garbled display or no display at all. I recommend you try setting the basic* `80x25` *mode first. If a subsequent call fails, you can then use the Up Arrow key to retrieve the first call via your shell's history and replay it, restoring the screen to legibility.*

This example call configures the system to use a 132 × 50 display, using a 9-character-wide font. Try a few configurations using modes defined in the final half or so of the `TextConfig` file until you find one you like.

TIP *If you have an LCD monitor, you can set a text mode using* `SVGATextMode` *so that the resolution in pixels exactly matches the capability of the monitor. For instance, consider a 1024 × 768 monitor and an 8 × 16 font. Dividing the horizontal and vertical resolutions by the horizontal and vertical font dimensions yields an optimal size of 128 × 48. This configuration will produce crisper text on an LCD monitor than you probably get by default. On the other hand, most LCD monitors accept a narrow range of refresh rates, so this approach may not work without creating custom resolution definitions, which is a tricky undertaking.*

Once you've found a text mode that you like, you can set it as the default in the `DefaultMode` line in `/etc/TextConfig`. You may also want to create a custom startup script, as described in Chapter 9, "Bypassing Automatic Configurations To Gain Control," to set this mode whenever the system boots.

Using Color in Text Logins

Modern video cards can all produce color displays, even in text mode. Many text-mode programs, though, don't take advantage of this fact; they display plain text, possibly with a few effects such as bold or blinking text.

One common use of color in text mode is in file listings as produced by `ls`. You can see this effect by typing `ls --color`. Some distributions configure themselves to use this option by default whenever you type `ls`. If yours doesn't, but if you want to use this feature, edit your `~/.bashrc` file or a global shell configuration file, such as `/etc/bashrc`, to include the following line:

```
alias ls='ls --color'
```

As described in Chapter 4 an alias such as this modifies the way the system responds to the original command (`ls` in this case).

Summary

Linux supports a wide variety of text-mode programs, many of which are quite powerful. Using these tools to their fullest without running X, though, requires that you be able to configure your text-mode environment to take advantage of your terminal, including setting features such as your video mode and font. Using multiple virtual terminals can also improve your productivity, as can knowledge of the many Linux file-manipulation commands, such as `cp` and `mv`. Combined, these tools make a text-mode Linux installation a powerful system. Of course, you can also use text-mode programs from an `xterm` window under X, and get all the advantages of X in that way, too.

## Chapter 6

Getting the Most from a Desktop Environment

ALTHOUGH IT'S POSSIBLE TO be quite productive using nothing but text-based Linux tools, most Linux workstations operate in graphics mode much of the time. A GUI environment is superior for tasks such as image editing, and many people prefer GUIs even for tasks such as text editing and web browsing. You can run text-mode programs from a GUI environment using the xterm program or one of its many competitors; therefore, a GUI provides you with the ability to run both GUI and text-based applications.

Since Linux's creation, its support for GUI environments has grown substantially. Linux relies on the *X Window System* (or X for short), as implemented by the XFree86 package, for its GUI underpinnings. (Chapter 16, "Optimizing X Configuration," describes how to improve the low-level X configuration, such as video modes and fonts.) Atop X proper are several sets of programs—*window managers*, which handle the borders around windows; *widget sets*, which are programming tools that handle buttons, menus, and so on within windows; *file managers*, which provide GUI tools for manipulating files; and *desktop environments*, which combine window managers, file managers, and assorted smaller tools into one coherent whole.

This chapter is devoted to Linux desktop environments. Although you can use Linux without a desktop environment, these packages provide enough useful tools that many people would be lost without them. Several desktop environments are available for Linux, and the first step in using one to the fullest is in picking one. This chapter goes into further detail about two popular desktop environments, it looks at the possibility of building your own, and it discusses distribution-specific quirks of the standard desktop environments.

Selecting an Appropriate Desktop Environment

Depending on your Linux distribution and installation options, chances are good your system has more than one desktop environment available. The most common desktop environments are:

KDE   The K Desktop Environment (KDE; http://www.kde.org) is one of the most popular desktop environments for Linux. It's the default desktop environment for Mandrake and SuSE. It's built atop the Qt widget set, and it includes many powerful tools that integrate together very well. It's described in more detail in the upcoming section, "Mastering KDE."

GNOME   The GNU Network Object Model Environment (GNOME; http://www.gnome.org) is KDE's primary rival in the Linux desktop environment arena. GNOME is slightly newer than KDE and is built atop the competing GIMP Tool Kit (GTK+) widget set. Like KDE, GNOME includes many powerful tools that work together. It's described in more detail in the upcoming section, "Mastering GNOME."

CDE   The Common Desktop Environment (CDE) is a commercial desktop environment that has long been the standard on Unix systems. CDE isn't as complete as either KDE or GNOME, and it's losing ground even on commercial Unix systems (Sun has announced that it will be using GNOME on its Solaris, for instance). CDE is less memory-intensive than KDE or GNOME, and is built atop the commercial Motif widget set. A version for Linux is available from Xi Graphics (http://www.xig.com) under the name DeXtop.

XFce   This desktop environment, headquartered at http://www.xfce.org, is modeled loosely on CDE, but it is built using the GTK+ widget set. XFce sports fewer features than KDE or GNOME, but it also consumes less memory.

XPde   The XP-like Desktop Environment (XPde) is a very new desktop environment for Linux. It aims to reproduce the appearance and behavior of Windows XP's desktop as closely as possible. You can learn more at http://www.xpde.com.

Roll-Your-Own   It's possible to build a desktop environment of your own from components you like. At a minimum, you need a window manager (dozens are available), but for the configuration to truly be a desktop environment, you'll need other components, such as a file manager and small productivity tools. All of the components need to be accessible from some sort of menu system. The upcoming section, "Creating a Desktop Environment That's Just Right," describes this approach, which can yield a much snappier system than KDE or GNOME would create—albeit with much greater investment in picking components and putting them together.

Unfortunately, it's impossible to give a simple set of rules for when one desktop environment works better than another, although there are some generalities that do apply. New users who are accustomed to Windows or Mac OS will probably be happiest with GNOME or KDE; these environments are most like these traditional desktop operating systems' environments. Users who are familiar with commercial Unix OSs might give XFce a try or buy CDE for Linux. These environments are also good choices on systems that have less than copious RAM or less than blazing CPUs—as a general rule, KDE and GNOME both need 128MB of RAM and 500MHz IA-32 CPUs to feel useable. People who like to customize everything or who have less-capable computers should investigate the roll-your-own approach.

Making a recommendation between KDE and GNOME is difficult. Each environment has its adherents, but the reasons for using one over the other are matters of personal preference or highly individual needs. I recommend you try both. You may want to start with whichever environment your distribution favors. Red Hat uses GNOME by default, while Mandrake and SuSE use KDE. Debian and Slackware don't favor either environment. Even in the case of Red Hat, Mandrake, and SuSE, it's easy to use the other environment. You'll need to install its packages, and then it should appear as an option in the GUI login screen, as shown in Figure 6.1. (The exact appearance of this login screen varies substantially from one distribution to another.) Some systems, including the one shown in Figure 6.1, show several window managers as options alongside the full desktop environments. When you select these options, the bare window manager runs, and you can run other programs from it.

FIGURE 6.1

GUI login managers usually provide a selection of environments from which you can choose what to run.

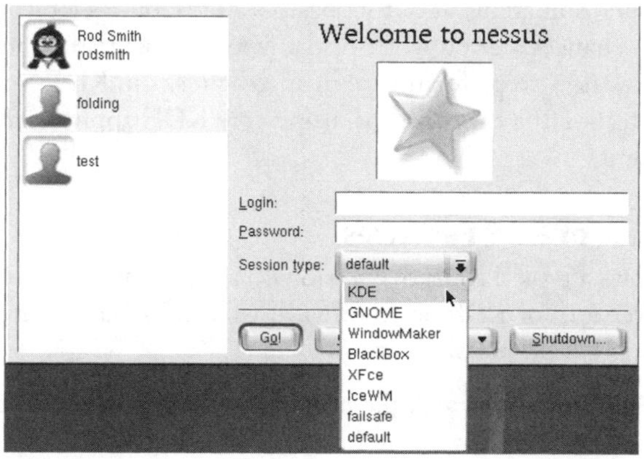

If you start X from text mode or are using the original X Display Manager (XDM) login program, you must launch your chosen desktop environment by specifying it in an X configuration file. The most common of these files are .xsession and .xinitrc, both of which are in your home directory. The .xsession file is the login file for XDM, and .xinitrc is the file that's run when you type startx from a text-mode login. Either file typically ends with a call to the desktop environment's startup program—startkde for KDE, gnome-session for GNOME, or startxfce for XFce. For a roll-your-own environment, chances are you'll start your window manager last, possibly preceded by calls to other utilities, such as a file manager. Chapter 9, "Bypassing Automatic Configurations to Gain Control," covers X startup files in more detail.

Some desktop environments—particularly KDE and GNOME—provide features designed to help integrate applications that use the environment's underlying libraries and services. For instance, you can set some user interface styles, default fonts, and so on, to apply to all supported applications. These features go beyond the raw mix of applications, and such integration is something you won't be able to accomplish in a roll-your-own solution. That said, most KDE and GNOME applications work fine outside of their parent environments, although they may be somewhat diminished by lack of integrative features. For instance, a KDE mail client and GNOME word processor might not be able to share the same address book data.

TIP Linux desktop environments store users' configurations in subdirectories of users' home directories, typically named after the environment itself, such as ~/.kde *or* ~/.gnome2. *(GNOME creates about half a dozen such directories, including some that aren't obvious, such as* ~/.themes.) *If you like your desktop configuration, back up this directory or directories. If you experiment and wind up with a completely unworkable configuration, you can restore your backup; or if you prefer, delete the backup entirely to return to the default configuration for your distribution.*

Mastering KDE

KDE is a mature desktop environment that's roughly comparable to desktop environments from Microsoft or Apple in overall functionality. As I write, the current version is 3.1. Using KDE requires knowing something about its basic features, but as KDE is modeled after other desktop environments, chances are you won't find any major surprises in its general use. Nonetheless, it's helpful to know how to perform certain specific tasks in KDE, such as managing files, changing the look and feel of the environment, using core KDE applications, and configuring new ways to launch programs.

An Overview of KDE Features

Figure 6.2 shows a typical KDE 3.1 session on a Mandrake 9.1 system. Some features will be different on other versions of KDE or on other distributions, but the main features should resemble those shown in Figure 6.2. Important features include

Konqueror File Manager A file manager is integral to most desktop environments. In KDE, Konqueror is the file manager, and it doubles as a web browser. This component is described in more detail in the upcoming section, "Managing Files with Konqueror."

Desktop Icons These icons launch Konqueror or other applications in order to access your home directory, system tools, websites, and so on. Most distributions provide a number of distribution-specific icons by default. You can, however, add or delete icons at will by right-clicking on a clear piece of the desktop and selecting an appropriate sub-option from the Create New context menu item, such as Create New ➤ Link to Application to create a new icon for launching a program.

Panel The KDE Panel is the strip of icons and tools at the bottom of the screen in Figure 6.2, but you can move it to other locations if you prefer. You can shrink the Panel to a small icon by clicking the triangular button on its left edge in Figure 6.2. This button may appear on the right edge or be so narrow it's not easily identified as a button on some installations.

Kicker The Kicker is part of the Panel that enables you to launch programs. Most icons in the Kicker launch individual programs, and some common tools come preconfigured in most KDE distributions. One particularly important Kicker icon is the K menu (aka the Application Starter), which is the leftmost icon in the Panel in Figure 6.2. The K menu provides an access port for many user programs, including all standard KDE programs and, frequently, many non-KDE programs. The upcoming section, "Adding Programs to the Kicker," describes how to edit the Kicker's and K menu's applications.

FIGURE 6.2

A KDE session delivers the types of tools most users expect in a GUI desktop environment.

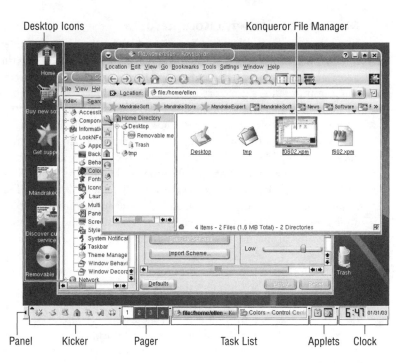

Pager KDE, like most Linux desktop environments and window managers, supports an arbitrary number of *virtual desktops*. These are semi-independent screens you can switch between, much like text-mode virtual terminals. Figure 6.2 shows a system with four virtual desktops accessible through a *pager*; click a desktop you're not using and a new set of windows appears. This feature is very useful for keeping your desktop uncluttered.

Task List The task list enables you to bring a window to the front even if it's minimized or completely hidden behind other windows.

Applets Most KDE installations deliver a couple of small applets in their Panels. In Figure 6.2, these enable you to view the contents of the clipboard and bring up a simple organizer program.

Clock The far right of the Panel usually contains a clock that displays the date and time. It can be configured to display the time in various formats, to omit the date, and so on.

In addition to these features that have clear accessibility from the desktop, KDE provides many additional features. These include integration between KDE components, a Control Center that lets you modify many KDE and system operation details, and numerous small and not-so-small applications that help make working with Linux easier. Some of these KDE applications are described elsewhere in this book; for instance, Chapter 7, "Using Linux for Office Productivity," introduces KOffice, a suite of office-productivity tools.

Managing Files with Konqueror

Konqueror performs double duty in KDE: It's both a file manager and a web browser. The Konqueror window in Figure 6.2 is typical—it shows the contents of the home directory in the right pane, which dominates the window, and the left pane shows a diagram of available subdirectories. You can move into a directory by double-clicking its folder icon in the main directory pane or by clicking the folder in the subdirectory list. The arrow buttons just below the menu bar enable you to go back to directories you've already seen or to move up one level in the directory hierarchy.

As with most other file managers, you can manipulate files by double-clicking them or by right-clicking them and selecting an option from the resulting context menu. Typically, double-clicking a file opens it in an appropriate application, as determined by the file's Multipurpose Internet Mail Extension (MIME) type. The next section, "Changing KDE's MIME Type Mappings," describes how to configure Konqueror to launch specific applications for specific MIME types. Right-clicking a file produces a context menu with many options, including deleting the file, renaming the file, setting the file's properties (its filename and permissions), and opening or previewing the file in a variety of applications.

You can click and drag files from one directory to another. When you do so, Konqueror asks if you want to copy the file, move the file, or create a link to the file. The desktop is just another directory as far as Konqueror is concerned, so you can create links to important files or programs on the desktop by dragging the originals and choosing to create links. If you drag a file to the trash can, Konqueror asks if you want to move it to the trash, and if you respond in the affirmative, Konqueror does so. Trashed files remain accessible until you right-click the trash can icon and select Empty Trash Bin from the context menu.

You can change many defaults of Konqueror's behavior by selecting Settings ➢ Configure Konqueror from its menu bar. The resulting dialog box provides many options in assorted categories. Most of the ones that are important for Konqueror's use as a file manager appear in the Behavior, Previews, and File Associations categories. You can change whether Konqueror opens new windows when you double-click a directory, whether it asks for confirmation before moving files to the trash, which applications to associate with particular file types, and so on.

Changing KDE's MIME Type Mappings

If you want to change the application that Konqueror or other KDE applications associate with particular types of files, you need to use KDE's File Associations tool. This tool can be accessed in several ways, including:

◆ From the main KDE desktop, launch the File Associations tool. In Mandrake 9.1, this option is under K Menu ➢ Configuration ➢ KDE ➢ Components ➢ File Associations. This direct-access method isn't present on all installations, though, or it may fall under another menu path.

◆ Launch the KDE Control Center (typically by selecting K Menu ➢ Control Center, K Menu ➢ Configuration ➢ Control Center, or something similar) and then select the KDE Components ➢ File Associations item in the list on the left of the window. (KDE Components may be just Components on some systems.)

◆ From Konqueror, select Settings ➢ Configure Konqueror and click the File Associations item in the list on the left of the window.

Figure 6.3 shows the File Associations tool. Some methods of launching it will produce a window that includes additional elements. In any event, this tool enables you to edit MIME types, which have two elements separated by a slash (/). The first element is a general type descriptor, such as `application` or `text`. The second element narrows the field to a specific file type, such as `pdf` or `html`. You can browse existing MIME types in the left pane of the window; for instance, Figure 6.3 shows the `text/html` type selected.

FIGURE 6.3

KDE ships with an extensive set of MIME types predefined.

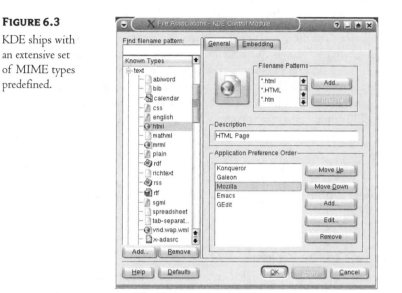

NOTE *Most of the* `application` *types actually describe files created by applications. Thus, you should always check the* `application` *area if you can't find a file type description in another area.*

Once you've selected a MIME type, you can make several changes to KDE's handling of that type, including:

♦ You can add or change the filename extensions associated with the MIME type. For instance, to make KDE treat files whose names end in .web as Hypertext Markup Language (HTML) files, you would click Add in the Filename Patterns area of the window shown in Figure 6.3 and then type `*.web` in the Add New Extension dialog box.

♦ You can change the description that appears in the Description field. This text appears in certain information dialog boxes.

♦ You can add an application that can support the file type by clicking Add in the Application Preference Order area of the window. The result is an expandable list of applications; select one and click OK, or type the complete path to the application in the provided field.

♦ You can change how KDE treats an existing application by selecting it and clicking Edit in the Application Preference Order area. The result is a dialog box in which you can specify where the application is located, what its icon is, what other MIME types it handles, and so on.

◆ You can change which application is the default for a particular MIME type by selecting applications and using the Move Up and Move Down buttons. The first application in the Application Preference Order list is the default one.

◆ You can change the icon associated with a file type by clicking the icon to the left of the Filename Patterns area. This action brings up an icon selector dialog box, which shows a number of icons from a standard location. Select one of these icons, or click Other Icons and browse to a new location to pick any icon you can find on the computer.

If you want to create a mapping for a file type that's not present in the standard list, you can do so; click Add at the bottom of the list. This action brings up a dialog box in which you specify a new MIME type. Enter your type, and the system creates it and enables you to enter information for it much as you can for an existing MIME type. Before you do this, though, try typing a filename pattern into the Find Filename Pattern field. For instance, type *.wp if you want to find a MIME type for WordPerfect files. This procedure may turn up a MIME type that you didn't find when searching for it manually.

TIP   If you don't know what an appropriate MIME type is for an application, check `http://www.iana.org/` `assignments/media-types/`. *This site lists official MIME type assignments. You might also try a web search for your file type and the keyword MIME, or check the application's documentation. If all of these resources fail, you'll have no choice but to make up a MIME type.*

Adding Programs to the Kicker

The simplest way to add programs to the K Menu is to type **kappfinder** in an xterm window. The kappfinder program attempts to locate all known user programs installed on your system and add them to appropriate locations on the K Menu. This tool displays a list of found applications with check boxes next to each, so you can tell it which programs to add to the K Menu. To trim the list of programs without performing a new search, rearrange programs on the menu, or add obscure programs, you must edit the Kicker in another way.

KDE provides a program called the K Menu Editor (kmenuedit) to edit items on the K Menu. You can usually access this tool from the K Menu ➢ Menu Editor, K Menu ➢ Settings ➢ Menu Editor, or a similar menu item. Figure 6.4 shows this tool in operation. The left pane of this window presents an expandable view of the items on the K Menu. Right-click an item to see a list of options, such as deleting or copying the entry. You can also click and drag an item to move it to another area of the menu tree. If an application has moved on disk or you want to change the options with which it's launched, you can do so by filling out the appropriate fields in the right pane of the editor.

NOTE   Some distributions provide alternative tools for editing the K Menu. For instance, Mandrake ships with a tool called MenuDrake, which works much like the K Menu Editor but provides a few additional options. MenuDrake simultaneously edits the menus for KDE, GNOME, and several window managers.

If you want to add an application to the Kicker, you must first add it to the K Menu. You can then right-click in the Kicker and select Panel Menu ➢ Add ➢ Application Button. This action brings up a duplicate of the K Menu. Select your application from this duplicate, and it will appear

Figure 6.4

The K Menu Editor
enables you to edit
the K Menu entries.

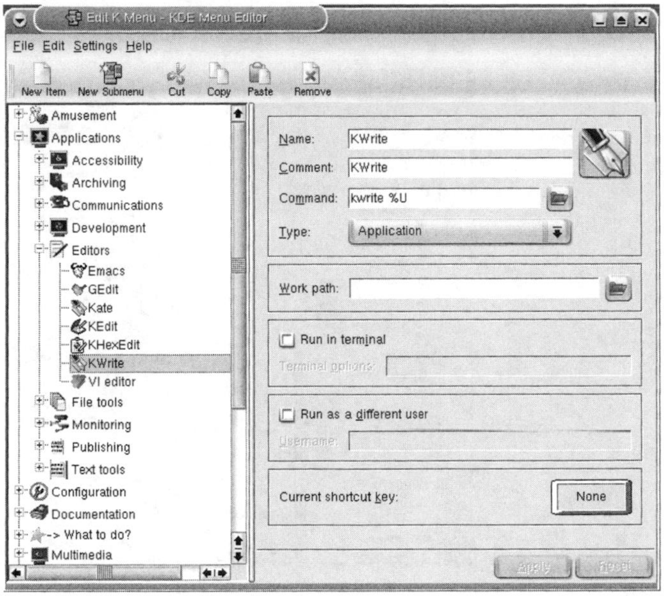

somewhere on the Panel. It may not appear exactly where you want it to be, though. If so, right-click the new icon and select Move *Appname* Button (*Appname* should be your application's name). The mouse pointer changes to a four-headed arrow; you can then move the icon around until it's positioned where you want it.

Setting a KDE Theme

People have wildly varying preferences in terms of the appearance of their desktops, menu buttons, and so on. Therefore, KDE ships with the ability to change the appearance of these elements. The simplest way to do this is to select a *theme*—an integrated set of desktop backgrounds, window manager borders, and so on. To do this, follow these steps:

1. Select K Menu ➤ Control Center, K Menu ➤ Configuration ➤ Control Center, or a similar menu item to launch the KDE Control Center.

2. In the index list on the left of the Control Center, pick Appearance & Themes ➤ Theme Manager or LookNFeel ➤ Theme Manager. The result is the Theme Manager, as shown in Figure 6.5.

3. Select a theme from those appearing in the list near the middle of the window. For instance, Figure 6.5 shows the Nostalgy theme selected. You'll see a miniature preview of the theme to the right of the theme list.

4. Click Apply to see your theme applied.

5. Select File ➤ Quit to exit from the Control Center.

FIGURE 6.5

The KDE Theme Manager lets you select a set of appearance options for the desktop.

Most distributions ship with just a handful of KDE themes. You can find many more on various websites, such as `http://www.kdelook.org`, `http://www.fwnetwork.com/kde/`, and `http://kde.themes.org`. To use a theme, download it and check the contents of the file. If it includes a file with a `.ktheme` extension, unpack it. If the archive has no such file but does have graphics files (with `.jpg`, `.xpm`, or other graphics file extensions) and a `.themerc` file, rename the tarball to use a `.ktheme` extension. You can then click the Add button in the KDE Theme Manager and locate the `.ktheme` file in the file browser. Your new theme should now appear in the list of themes, and you can select and use it. To make a theme available to all users, copy the `.ktheme` file to the `/usr/share/apps/kthememgr/Themes` directory. Some themes need to be compiled and installed like programs distributed as source code; follow the instructions in these themes' tarballs for details.

If you want to fine-tune your theme, you can do so by using various other KDE Control Center options in the Appearance & Themes or LookNFeel area; specifically:

- The Background area lets you set a background image or use a solid or gradient color.

- The Colors area lets you control the colors of the drag bar, the interior colors for most Qt and some non-Qt applications, and so on.

- The Style area controls the appearance of various Qt widgets—buttons, tabs, sliders, and so on. These changes affect only Qt-derived applications.

- The Window Decorations area sets the appearance of the window borders and title bars.

Adjusting the Mouse and Keyboard

It's not uncommon to find that the mouse and keyboard don't behave quite as you'd like. The mouse may drag along so slowly that you can't track from one side of the screen to another without running the mouse off of your desk, or it may zip along so quickly that you can't accurately position the pointer. Likewise, you may discover that keys repeat so quickly that you can't type anything without seeing a string of repeated letters, or they may repeat so slowly that keyboard repeat is useless. KDE provides controls to modify the mouse tracking speed, but the keyboard repeat rate is less flexible. Fortunately, there are alternatives to using KDE's own tools to adjust the keyboard repeat rate.

To adjust the mouse tracking speed, open the KDE Control Center by selecting K Menu ➤ Control Center, K Menu ➤ Configuration ➤ Control Center, or a similar menu item. You should then pick the Peripherals ➤ Mouse item, which produces a tool in which you can adjust how KDE treats the mouse. You can switch between right-handed and left-handed operation, choose to require double-clicks or use single-clicks to open files in Konqueror, and so on. The Advanced tab (shown in Figure 6.6) includes a couple of sliders that affect mouse tracking speed. The Pointer Acceleration slider affects how fast the mouse accelerates when you move it quickly, and the Pointer Threshold slider affects how soon this acceleration begins after you start moving the mouse. This tab has other mouse options, as well, such as the timing of double-clicks and the distance you must drag an icon before KDE accepts the action as a drag.

The Peripherals ➤ Keyboard area in the KDE Control Center provides tools for adjusting the keyboard, including one to enable or disable keyboard repeat. This tool, however, doesn't provide an option to adjust the keyboard repeat rate, beyond turning the feature on or off. For that, you must edit your XF86Config file, as described in Chapter 3, "Using External Peripherals." Alternatively, you can type **xset r rate *delay repeat-rate*** in an xterm, where *delay* is the delay in milliseconds before a key begins repeating and *repeat-rate* is the repeat rate in repeats per second.

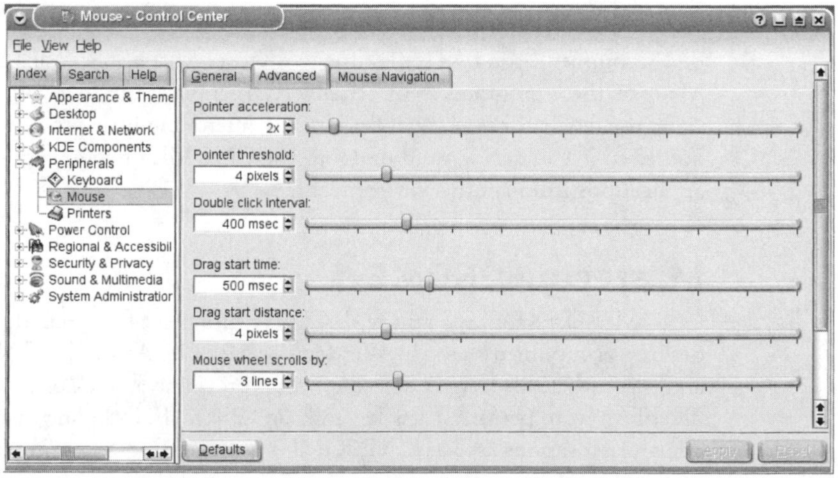

FIGURE 6.6

KDE provides configuration tools to adjust your mouse's responsiveness.

Some Important KDE Applications

KDE ships with a substantial number of applications. Most of these tools are small, but some are much larger. Some of the more noteworthy of these tools include:

KDE Control Center   This tool is KDE's main configuration program. I've referred to it in preceding sections as a way to adjust various KDE defaults, but those sections have barely scratched the surface of what the tool can do.

Konsole   This program is KDE's version of the veritable `xterm` program. From within the Konsole, you can run a shell, run text-based programs, and launch GUI programs by name.

KMail   This program is KDE's default mail reader. It supports local mailboxes, the Post Office Protocol (POP), and the Internet Message Access Protocol (IMAP) for receiving mail. It handles attachments and other modern e-mail features.

Games   KDE includes a large number of games, most of which are fairly simple, such as KAsteroids and KPoker.

KEdit and KWrite   These programs are two KDE-based text editors. KWrite is the more sophisticated of these two editors, but neither is as powerful as a behemoth like Emacs.

KPaint   This program is a simple graphics package. It supports the creation of simple shapes, drawing lines, and so on. It can't hold a candle to the power of the GIMP (described in Chapter 8, "Miscellaneous User Tools"), but it's quicker and may be adequate for some relatively straightforward tasks.

KPPP   This program is a GUI interface to handle the initiation and termination of Point-to-Point Protocol (PPP) Internet connections, as used with dial-up ISPs.

KOffice   This is a collection of programs that provide common office tools—a word processor, a spreadsheet, and so on. Chapter 7 covers these tools in more detail.

I recommend you take some time to discover what applications are available from the K Menu. Many of these programs aren't actually KDE applications, but you shouldn't let that deter you from using them. Chances are you'll find lots of interesting little programs, both associated with KDE and not. Even if you decide you'd prefer to use GNOME or some other environment, you can use KDE applications from another environment.

Mastering GNOME

GNOME, like KDE, is a mature desktop environment for Linux that's roughly comparable to the desktop environments used by Windows or Mac OS. As I write, GNOME 2.2 is the current version, and that's what this chapter describes. After providing a quick orientation to the GNOME desktop, I describe how to perform a few key tasks in GNOME, including managing files, setting MIME types, configuring various aspects of GNOME's user interface, and using important GNOME applications.

An Overview of GNOME Features

Figure 6.7 shows a typical GNOME desktop. This desktop has many of the same components as a KDE desktop (see Figure 6.2), but some details differ

FIGURE 6.7

The GNOME desktop provides all the familiar features of modern computer desktop environments.

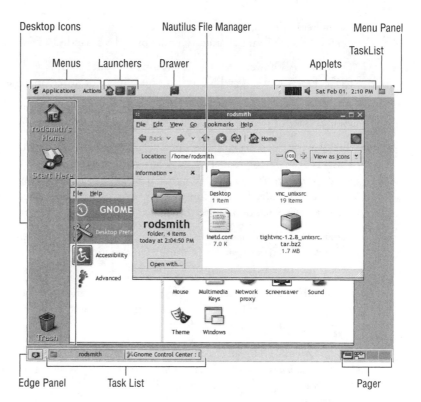

Important GNOME components include the following:

Nautilus File Manager   GNOME uses a program called Nautilus as its file manager. Unlike KDE's Konqueror, Nautilus doesn't double as a web browser, but it's similar to Konqueror and other file managers in general operating principles.

Desktop Icons   GNOME desktop icons open Nautilus windows on specific directories or launch programs, sometimes with specific configurations. You can create new icons by right-clicking on the desktop and picking an appropriate option, such as New Launcher to create a new program-launching icon.

Panels   GNOME uses two Panels by default, compared to KDE's one: a Menu Panel, which appears at the top of the screen; and an Edge Panel, which appears at the bottom. Subsequent components in this list appear in one of these two Panels. (Red Hat's default GNOME configuration uses only the Edge Panel, which takes over some of the duties of the Menu Panel.)

Menus   Menus usually appear in the Menu Panel, and they provide access to many user programs, including all the GNOME programs installed on the system. The Applications menu provides access to most programs, and the Actions menu causes GNOME to perform certain actions, such as running a program, taking a screen shot, or logging out.

Launchers   These enable you to directly launch programs without using an intervening menu. A default GNOME installation typically provides a handful of launchers for common tools.

Drawer   A Drawer acts as an extension to a Panel; click it and a sub-Panel appears at right angles to the first. Drawers can be handy if you run out of space on a Panel.

Applets   These are mini-applications that use space in the Panel as their primary presence on your desktop. Figure 6.6 shows a CPU use meter, a volume control tool, and a clock.

Task Lists   Two task lists exist in a default GNOME installation. In the far right of the Menu Panel is a small icon that changes to reflect the currently active application. Click it to obtain a list of all programs running on all virtual desktops. You can then switch to the desired application. Much of the Edge Panel is consumed by a set of buttons you can click to bring applications on the current virtual desktop to the front.

Pager   The Pager enables you to switch between virtual desktops, just like the equivalent tool in KDE. GNOME's pager shows a tiny representation of the windows that are open in each desktop, which may help you remember in which desktop critical applications are running.

GNOME's basic features are the same as those of KDE. The two environments differ from one another in fairly subtle details. Your best hope of learning which you prefer is to try both. Use one for a few days, then try the other for a few days.

NOTE   *Since version 8.0, Red Hat Linux has created themes for GNOME and KDE to make both environments look and work as much alike as possible. Thus, if you're using Red Hat, the surface differences between these two environments will be particularly slim. Configuration tools, such as those for modifying styles and mouse actions, still differ between these two environments, though.*

Managing Files with Nautilus

Nautilus works much like most other file managers on Linux, Windows, or Mac OS. You can double-click directories to move into them, use the arrow buttons in the icon bar to move back to directories you've already seen or to move up in the hierarchy, drag and drop files between folders to move them, and so on. To copy a file or create a link, middle-click it and drag it to a location; GNOME then asks if you want to move the file, copy it, or create a link. As with KDE's Konqueror, Nautilus treats the desktop as another folder, so you can move, copy, or create links to files on the desktop. If you want to create an icon on the desktop to launch a program, right-click on a free part of the desktop and pick New Launcher from the resulting context menu. Nautilus presents a dialog box in which you enter the program's name, a path to the filename, and so on.

Nautilus includes a Trash icon. When you drag files to the Trash, they aren't immediately deleted, so you can easily recover them. Right-clicking the Trash icon produces a context menu on which one option is Empty Trash; selecting this option deletes all the files in the Trash.

You can modify how Nautilus displays files or allows you to interact with them in various ways. In particular, the View menu supports enabling or disabling the detail pane on the left side of the window, changing the icon sort order, changing the size of the icons, and so on. You can change the default behavior for many of these features by selecting Edit ➢ Preferences, which brings up a dialog box in which you can modify various Nautilus defaults.

Changing GNOME's MIME Type Mappings

Like KDE, GNOME relies on MIME types to determine what type of data a file contains and, therefore, what to do when you double-click an icon. GNOME ships with an extensive database of MIME types and associations to applications and filename extensions, but if you need to modify this database, you can. To do so, pick Applications ➢ Desktop Preferences ➢ Advanced ➢ File Types and Programs from the Menu Panel. (This tool's location can vary substantially from one distribution to another, though.) The result is the File Types and Programs window shown in Figure 6.8. Like the equivalent KDE tool, this program organizes document types into categories; but the File Types and Programs tool's categories don't exactly correspond to MIME types.

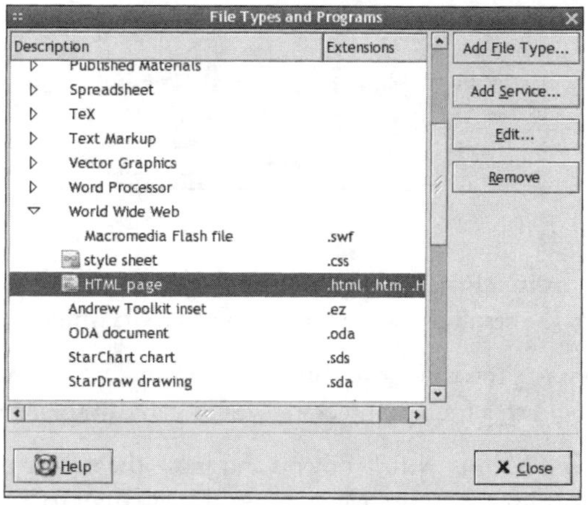

FIGURE 6.8

The File Types and Programs tool enables you to edit GNOME's file type associations.

If you can find an entry for your file type, double-click it or click it and then click Edit. The result is the Edit File Type dialog box shown in Figure 6.9. You can enter or modify the description, MIME type, associated filename extensions, and so on. GNOME uses an internal database of applications associated with common file types, but if your file type isn't handled correctly, you can enter the path to an appropriate program in the Program to Run field. If the appropriate program is text-mode, be sure to check the Run in Terminal check box.

Adding Programs to GNOME's Panels

You can add or modify elements on a GNOME Panel or its menus in various ways:

Creating or Deleting Panels   Right-click a Panel and select Delete This Panel to delete it. To create a new Panel, select an option from the New Panel submenu.

Adding Items to a Panel   Right-click the Panel and use the Add to Panel menu. This menu presents various options, including many common applets in assorted categories. If you want to add a launcher for a regular application, use the Launcher from Menu sub-option; this provides access to all the tools available from the GNOME Applications menu. To add a launcher for an application that's not listed on this menu, select Add to Panel ➢ Launcher from the context menu; this action produces a dialog box in which you enter the name of the application, the path to its executable, an icon, and so on.

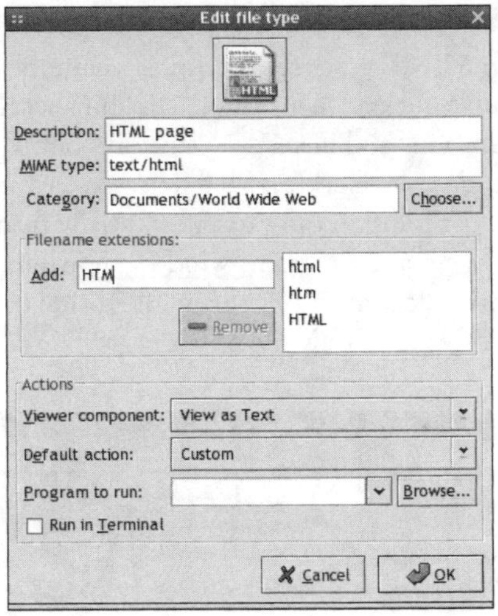

FIGURE 6.9

You can modify MIME types using the Edit File Type dialog box.

Deleting Items from a Panel   Right-click the element you want to delete, and select Remove from Panel from the resulting context menu. GNOME immediately removes the element.

Moving Elements   You can move Panel components by right-clicking them and selecting Move. The cursor changes to a four-pointed arrow, and you can then slide the element around the Panel.

Adding Items to a Menu   Click a menu and move the cursor to an item that's not a submenu, then right-click and select Entire Menu ➤ Add New Item to This Menu. GNOME displays a Create New Launcher dialog box—the same as it displays when you create a launcher for the desktop.

On the whole, GNOME's Panels are extremely flexible. With a bit of work, you can customize them to include almost any tool you like, making them launchable in almost any way you like.

Setting a GNOME Theme

GNOME supports themes to modify the appearance of assorted on-screen elements—window borders, button styles, and so on. Although they're not officially part of the theme, you can also modify other elements, such as the desktop background. To modify themes, select Application ➤ Desktop Preferences ➤ Theme from the Menu Panel. (Again, the exact location of this option varies from one system to another.) This action brings up the Theme Preferences dialog box shown in Figure 6.10. Click a theme and GNOME immediately changes the display to match your selection.

If you want to exercise greater control over a theme, select it and click Details. GNOME displays a Theme Details dialog box in which you can control three sets of options, each from its own tab:

Controls   These are the widgets that appear within GNOME windows—buttons, tabs, menu bars, and so on. Changing the controls doesn't affect most non-GTK+ programs, though.

FIGURE 6.10

The GNOME Theme Preferences dialog box lets you adjust the appearance of various window and desktop elements.

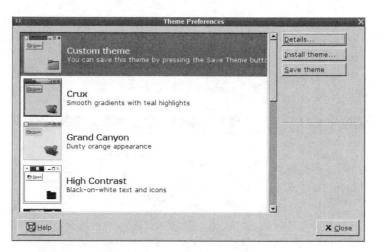

Window Borders   You can alter the appearance of window borders (particularly drag bars) by using this tab. This option affects both GTK+ and non-GTK+ applications.

Icons   Most distributions ship with several sets of GNOME icons you can select. These icons appear on the desktop, in GNOME menus, and so on.

In addition to adjusting these features, you can set the desktop background by selecting Applications ➤ Desktop Preferences ➤ Background from the Menu Panel. This action produces the Background Preferences dialog box, in which you can select a background image or set the background to a solid color or a gradient.

If you're dissatisfied with the selection of themes that came with your system, you can retrieve additional themes from various websites, such as `http://gtk.themes.org`, `http://art.gnome.org`, or `http://developer.ximian.com/themes/gtkthemes/`. These themes typically come as tarballs that expand into similarly named subdirectories. For instance, `silly-theme.tar.gz` might expand into a directory called `SillyTheme`. You should place this directory in the `/usr/share/themes` directory if all users should be able to access it, or you should place it in the `~/.themes` directory in your home directory if only you need to use it.

To make new background images available, place them in the directory that the Background Preferences dialog box uses by default. (This location varies from one installation to another.) You can select images from other locations if you prefer, but placing an image in the default location is the simplest course of action.

Adjusting the Mouse and Keyboard

Chapter 3 covers mouse and keyboard configuration in general, but GNOME provides tools that override many details of how these critical devices function. Because these GNOME tools change the default X settings, you probably want to be familiar with the GNOME-specific tools if you use GNOME.

To adjust the mouse's movement, button mappings, and so on, pick Applications ➤ Desktop Preferences ➤ Mouse. This action produces the Mouse Preferences dialog box shown in Figure 6.11.

The options you're most likely to want to change are on the Motion tab. The Acceleration slider changes how rapidly the mouse accelerates when you begin moving it quickly, and the Sensitivity slider changes how far you must move the pointer before acceleration begins. You can change the mouse for left-handed use or alter the timing required for double-clicks from the Buttons tab, and you can modify the appearance of the default mouse pointer from the Cursors tab.

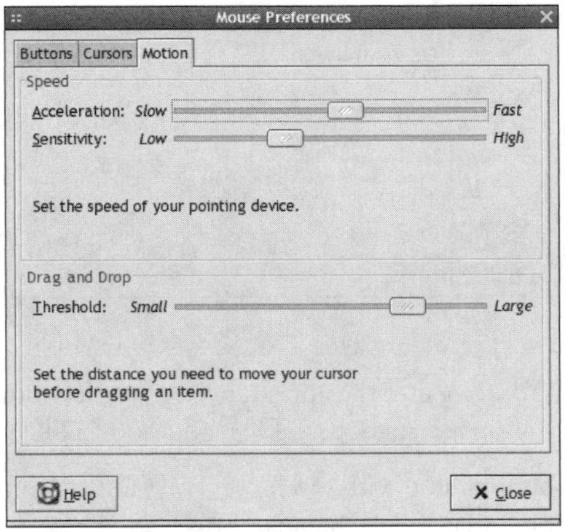

FIGURE 6.11

The Mouse Preferences dialog box provides tools for adjusting mouse behavior.

To adjust details of keyboard activity, pick Applications ➤ Desktop Preferences ➤ Keyboard, which brings up the Keyboard Preferences dialog box shown in Figure 6.12. If you want keys to produce repeated characters when held down, be sure the Keyboard Repeats When Key Is Held Down check box is selected. You can then adjust the Delay and Speed sliders to influence how long it takes before a key begins repeating and to regulate the speed of the repeats, respectively. The same dialog box enables you to set the cursor blinking speed for GNOME text-entry fields and whether or not applications that try to create a keyboard "bell" produce a beep (from the Sound tab). Clicking the Accessibility button brings up a new dialog box for setting more esoteric keyboard features, such as filters to help eliminate keybounce (a problem on some worn-out keyboards or for people with shaky fingers), tools to let the keyboard's numeric keypad substitute for the mouse, and so on.

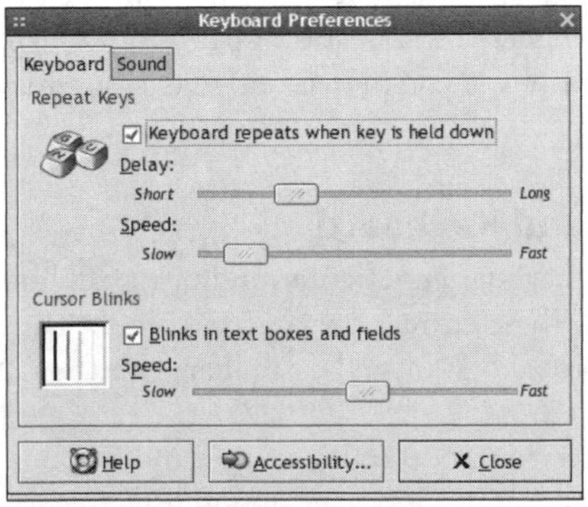

FIGURE 6.12

The Keyboard Preferences dialog box controls the keyboard repeat rate and other keyboard and text-entry options.

Some Important GNOME Applications

GNOME ships with many small and not-so-small programs that can help make using Linux a more productive and enjoyable experience. Some of these programs, such as Nautilus, have been alluded to earlier, and others are described in other chapters of this book. Some of the most important of these tools are listed here:

GNOME Control Center   This program (`gnome-control-center`) is essentially a launching tool for many of the configuration modules described earlier, such as Keyboard Preferences and Theme Preferences.

File Roller   Linux provides command-line tools, such as `tar`, `gzip`, and `zip`, to manage archive files such as tarballs. The File Roller (`file-roller`) is a GUI front-end to these tools, enabling you to preview what these files contain, create new archives, and so on. Some distributions call this tool the Archive Manager on their menus.

GNOME Terminal   This program (`gnome-terminal`) is a variant on the common `xterm`. It runs text-mode programs within a window on the GNOME desktop. By default, GNOME Terminal runs your login shell, such as `bash`.

gEdit   This program (`gedit`) is GNOME's editor. It is a fairly lightweight editor, so if you need something with lots of extras, look elsewhere.

Evolution   This program (`evolution`) is one of many e-mail packages based on GTK+. Others include Balsa and Sylpheed. E-mail readers are covered in more detail in Chapter 8.

Galeon   The web browser that's most closely associated with GNOME is Galeon (`galeon`). This package uses the same rendering engine as Mozilla and Netscape, but it is much slimmer.

Games   GNOME ships with a number of small games, such as GNOME Mines and Mahjongg.

The GIMP   This is the most powerful bitmap graphics package for Linux, and it's closely associated with GNOME. It's covered in more detail in Chapter 8.

GNOME PPP   This tool, also called the GNOME Dialup Utility (`gnome-ppp`), is a GUI PPP package. You can use it to initiate a connection to an ISP via an analog telephone modem.

GNOME Office   A sub-project of GNOME is GNOME Office, which is an effort to create a coherent whole out of a disparate group of office tools. A few of the programs just described are technically part of GNOME Office, but GNOME Office is most focused on office productivity tools such as word processors and spreadsheets. It's described in more detail in Chapter 8.

Most of these programs are accessible from the Applications menu on most GNOME installations. Many are installed from their own packages, though, so some may be missing from your menu; and any given distribution might or might not include a tool on its default menus. Many installations include a KDE Menu submenu off of the main Applications menu, so you can access KDE's tools from GNOME. As with KDE's tools, you can use most GNOME tools from other environments, as well. Therefore, if some of these tools appeal to you but you prefer KDE, XFce, or a roll-your-own solution, you can use the GNOME tools from your preferred environment.

Distribution-Specific Quirks

The preceding description of KDE and GNOME has glossed over an important issue: Most distributions don't ship standard KDE or GNOME installations. Instead, they create custom themes, modify Panel settings, alter menu contents, place distribution-specific icons on the desktop, and sometimes even replace components. Also, different distributions may ship with different versions of popular desktop environments. The net effect of these changes is to create a desktop that's identifiable as belonging to a particular distribution. Nobody who's familiar with the systems would mistake a SuSE KDE installation for a Mandrake KDE installation, for instance, although the same core features are available on both. Some of the issues with specific distributions include:

Debian   Debian runs on a longer release cycle than most other distributions, and it is more likely to include older but better-tested versions of its packages than are other distributions. Debian 3.0, for instance, ships with KDE 2.2 and GNOME 1.4, which are becoming fairly aged, although you can upgrade these packages to more recent versions. Debian tends not to make extensive changes to its default KDE or GNOME installations.

Mandrake   This distribution favors KDE but includes GNOME. The distribution makes modest changes to both environments, but it makes more to GNOME than to KDE. In both distributions, some menus are altered to include the Mandrake name. For instance, the GNOME Applications menu becomes the MandrakeLinux menu. Mandrake includes some distribution-specific hardware and software configuration tools, some of which replace desktop environment-specific tools, such as MenuDrake replacing the K Menu Editor. Most of the screen shots in the "Mastering KDE" section of this chapter were taken from a Mandrake 9.1 beta system, running a late beta of KDE 3.1.

Red Hat   Red Hat has made extensive changes to both its KDE and GNOME installations to make them look as much alike as possible. Unlike most GNOME systems, Red Hat's default GNOME includes no Menu Panel; instead, the Edge Panel takes on most Menu Panel elements, sometimes in slightly altered form. Most GNOME tools remain accessible, although their positions on menus may be altered from the default.

Slackware   Like Debian, Slackware tends not to make extensive changes to its desktop environments, and it doesn't jump on the bandwagon with the latest release as quickly as some others. For instance, Slackware 8.1 shipped with KDE 2.2 and GNOME 1.4, although KDE 3.0.5a was officially available as an upgrade in early 2003, and a late GNOME 2.2 beta was available from http://www.dropline.net/gnome/ (I used this beta to produce most of the screen shots in the "Mastering GNOME" section of this chapter). Slackware 9.0, released late in this book's development process, includes more up-to-date versions of both KDE and GNOME—3.1 and 2.2, respectively.

SuSE   Like Mandrake, SuSE favors KDE, and makes even more extensive changes to the default KDE themes and menu layouts. These changes include ready access to SuSE's system configuration tool, YaST. SuSE's default GNOME configuration is less heavily modified than is its KDE setup.

Because of these differences between distributions, some of the specific menu paths provided in earlier sections of this chapter may not apply to your system; nonetheless, the basic principles of operation and most or all of the utilities described should be available to you.

Creating a Desktop Environment That's Just Right

Some people aren't particularly enamored of either KDE or GNOME. Such people consider these environments to be bloated or they don't like certain details of their operation or they have specific needs that aren't met by these desktop environments. There may also be hardware-related reasons to favor other tools. Specifically, KDE and GNOME both consume a lot of memory, so they don't work well on low-memory systems. In these cases, an alternative environment may be in order. One such environment is XFce. XPde is another option, and may be a good one for those who are familiar with the Windows XP desktop. Another option is to create your own custom environment using just the components you need. Three main types of programs go into such an environment: a window manager, a file manager, and an assortment of small utilities for adjusting the environment, editing files, and so on. Locating and trying such tools can be a time-consuming task, though.

Selecting a Window Manager

The first piece of a do-it-yourself desktop environment is the window manager. Some newcomers to Linux confuse window managers and desktop environments. In fact, window managers are much more limited programs that handle a much more specific task: the maintenance of window borders, window controls, and the display as a whole. Window managers affect the appearance of window title bars and the widgets that enable you to minimize, maximize, and resize windows. Window managers also provide simple program-launch tools. These tools may be accessed by clicking, middle-clicking, or right-clicking the desktop or a control strip (similar to a KDE or GNOME Panel) along the bottom, top, or side of the screen. Most window managers provide the means to change the background of a screen to a color or picture, although a few lack this capability. Most window managers also provide virtual desktops, although a few lack this feature. Window managers do not include file managers, applications for setting keyboard repeat rates, or the like.

You can find literally dozens of window managers for Linux, but fewer than a dozen are truly popular. One good site that provides links to and information about many Linux window managers is http://www.xwinman.org. Check there for the latest developments and for pointers to many more window managers than I can describe here. In particular, the Others link points to a page that lists over seventy window managers. Some of the more popular options are listed here:

AfterStep This window manager is modeled after the NeXTSTEP environment developed by NeXT for its computer and OS. It features a *wharf*—a line of icons representing running or available programs, similar to NeXTSTEP's *dock*. AfterStep, like many window managers, is derived from fvwm. An assortment of programs have been written expressly for AfterStep, providing features such as audio CD players that integrate well with the window manager. The official AfterStep home page is http://www.afterstep.org.

Blackbox This window manager, headquartered at http://blackboxwm.sourceforge.net, is designed to consume little RAM, and so it is a good choice for those who need to run a slim desktop for RAM-consumption reasons. Blackbox is a from-the-ground up window manager that shares no code with others.

Enlightenment Some window managers feature lots of "eye candy"—the ability to customize the look of title bars, borders, icons, and so on, often in very unusual ways. Enlightenment is perhaps the ultimate in this expression. Early versions were derived from fvwm and developed a reputation for bloat and speed problems. More recent versions are entirely new rewrites and are much speedier, although they rely on fairly advanced graphics libraries. Early versions of GNOME used Enlightenment as the default window manager. You can learn more at `http://www.enlightenment.org`.

`fvwm` **and** `fvwm95`   In the mid-1990s, these window managers were the standard on Linux systems. They've since become less popular, although some derivative projects, such as AfterStep, retain popularity in some circles. These window managers were popular in part because of their extreme configurability, but this feature also led them to be somewhat larger than some competing programs. The original `fvwm` was modeled loosely on `mwm` and borrowed some code from `twm`, whereas `fvwm95` is designed to look somewhat like Windows 95's windows and includes a task bar similar to KDE's Panel. You can learn more at `http://www.fvwm.org`, and `fvwm95` is available from `ftp://mitac11.uia.ac.be/pub`.

IceWM   This window manager, headquartered at `http://www.icewm.org`, was designed as an independent and lightweight window manager that supports themes to alter the appearance of its windows. Many themes are available to make IceWM windows look like those from OS/2, Windows, Mac OS, `fvwm`, `mwm`, or entirely unique environments. IceWM also provides a task bar similar to KDE's Panel, and it can be used as a window manager for GNOME. GUI configuration tools can simplify IceWM configuration for the inexperienced.

`mwm`   The Motif widget set ships with a window manager called `mwm`, which has long been the standard on many commercial Unix systems. You can obtain the official `mwm` for Linux with Motif distributions, such as the freely available OpenMotif (`http://www.opengroup.org/openmotif/`). The Motif clone called LessTif (`http://www.lesstif.org`) also includes an `mwm` clone. This window manager isn't particularly packed with features by today's standards, but it may be a reasonable choice, particularly if you run other Motif-based programs.

Sawfish   This window manager was originally known as Sawmill, and its official website URL still reflects this fact: `http://sawmill.sourceforge.net`. Like Blackbox and IceWM, Sawfish was designed as an independent and slim window manager. Nonetheless, it includes support for themes, so its appearance can be customized. Until recently, it was the default window manager for GNOME. Recent versions of GNOME use Metacity by default, though, and Sawfish has lost a lot of development momentum lately.

`twm`   This window manager is very old and is no longer actively maintained. I mention it mainly because it's the window manager of last resort for many X startup scripts, and it is the default window manager for Virtual Network Computing (VNC) sessions.

Window Maker   Like AfterStep, Window Maker aims to reproduce the look and feel of NeXTSTEP; however, Window Maker does so with a new code base, rather than building atop `fvwm`. Window Maker is also associated with the GNUstep project (`http://gnustep.org`), which aims to implement the OpenStep API (as used by NeXTSTEP) on Linux and other Unix-like OSs. Window Maker can also serve as GNOME's window manager. You can learn more at `http://www.windowmaker.org`.

wm2 and wmx   These window managers, and especially wm2, are bare-bones compared to some others; they don't provide extensive theme options, task bars, or the like. They implement unusual side-mounted title bars. If you want virtual desktops, wm2 won't do, although wmx handles this feature. Read more at `http://www.all-day-breakfast.com/wm2/` and `http://www.all-day-breakfast.com/wmx/`.

NOTE   KDE and GNOME both include their own window managers. KDE uses KWM, and GNOME uses Metacity. Prior to version 2.0, it was easy to use another GNOME-compliant window manager with GNOME; however, the configuration tools for doing that were removed with GNOME 2.0, making the switch much more difficult. KDE has never officially supported other window managers, although if you dig into the configuration files, you can get some others to work with KDE.

Which window manager is right for you? That's a question only you can answer, and only after trying several. You can install as many window managers as you like on your system, and then change your login procedure, as described in the earlier section, "Selecting an Appropriate Desktop Environment," to launch each one for testing. Some window managers also provide an option to exit and launch another window manager instead, which can make it easy to test different window managers in quick succession.

As a general rule, for lightweight systems, Blackbox, IceWM, Sawfish, Window Maker, wm2, and wmx are the best choices. The first four of these provide a substantial feature set; wm2 and wmx (but particularly wm2) are extremely Spartan. Other window managers may appeal to you, though, particularly if you're putting together your own environment more to fill very specific needs than to minimize memory consumption.

Selecting a File Manager

A file manager is actually an optional component of a desktop environment. If you don't much like the idea of manipulating files with a mouse, you can use an `xterm` and text-mode commands, such as those described in Chapter 5, "Doing Real Work in Text Mode." Most true desktop environments do include file managers, though, and Linux provides plenty of choices. File managers can provide several different types of views of directories and ways of shifting those views:

Multiwindow Views   In this approach, the file manager displays icons or text representing files in a window, and when you select a subdirectory, the file manager opens another window on that directory. You can then drag files from one window to another to operate on them.

Single-Window Views   Another design is to open one window and replace its contents with another directory's contents when you select the second directory. This approach requires that you open a second file manager window to move files between widely separated directories, although you can usually move files to subdirectories by dragging them into a folder in the primary window.

Dual-Pane Views   Some file managers implement a two-window or two-pane view, with one window or pane showing one directory and the other showing another directory, to simplify moving files between directories. This approach is similar to that used by many FTP clients, and it is sometimes referred to as the Norton Commander style, after a popular DOS file manager from years gone by. This view style usually displays textual representations of files, not icons.

Triple-Pane Views   A variant on the dual-pane view is the triple-pane view, in which opening a directory in one pane causes it to be displayed in the next one, and so on. This view style was used by NeXT's file manager, and Apple's Mac OS X can also produce this display style, so users of these environments may like this approach.

Explorer-Style Views   Some file managers support a tree-like view in one pane and an expanded view of a selected directory in another pane. The Konqueror window in Figure 6.2 uses this approach, which is often referred to as an Explorer design, after the Windows Explorer file browser from Windows 95 and NT.

Some file managers support several of these view types. For instance, Konqueror uses Explorer-style views by default; however, you can shut off the tree view, reverting it to a single-window system. You can also select options to turn Konqueror into a multiwindow file manager.

Table 6.1 summarizes some of the major features of several popular Linux file managers. Some of these headings require explanation. The Desktop Icons column describes whether the file manager supports placing icons on the desktop. The drag-and-drop operations summarized in Table 6.1 work between windows or panes of a file manager, but drag-and-drop between the file manager and other applications may or may not work. The Object Oriented column reports whether the file manager supports taking actions based on the type of a file, such as launching an associated program based on the file type. The Multiple Execution column describes whether you can associate more than one application with a single file type (say, selectable from a menu by right-clicking a file).

TABLE 6.1: MAJOR FEATURES OF POPULAR LINUX FILE MANAGERS

FILE MANAGER	DISPLAY STYLES	DESKTOP ICONS	DRAG-AND-DROP	OBJECT ORIENTED	MULTIPLE EXECUTION
DFM	Multiwindow	✓	✓	✓	–
FileRunner	Dual-pane	–	✓	✓	–
Gentoo	Dual-pane	–	–	✓	✓
Konqueror	Multiwindow, single-window, Explorer	✓	✓	✓	✓
Nautilus	Multiwindow, single-window	✓	✓	✓	✓
Northern Captain	Dual-pane	–	✓	–	–
ROX	Single-window	✓	✓	✓	–
TkDesk	Single-window, triple-pane[2]	–[1]	✓	✓	✓
Xfm	Single-window	–[2]	✓	–	–
Xplore	Explorer-style	–	✓	✓	✓

[1] *TkDesk supports an application bar similar to the ones created by AfterStep or Window Maker.*
[2] *Xfm supports a dedicated application-launching window.*

Of course, file managers are complex programs, and a table can't convey all the important information about these programs. Additional details include:

DFM The Desktop File Manager (DFM; `http://www.kaisersite.de/dfm/`) uses GTK+ and is modeled after OS/2's WorkPlace Shell (WPS), although DFM doesn't implement all of WPS's features.

FileRunner This program, whose website is `http://www.cd.chalmers.se/~hch/filerunner.html`, is unusual in that it includes a built-in FTP client.

Gentoo This program is inspired in part by an Amiga program, Directory Opus 4. You can learn more at `http://www.obsession.se/gentoo/`.

Konqueror This file manager is part of KDE, and it is best used from within that environment. It's described in more detail in the earlier section, "Using Konqueror for File Management."

Nautilus This file manager is part of GNOME, and it is best used from within that environment. It's described in more detail in the earlier section, "Using Nautilus for File Management."

Northern Captain This program also goes by the name *XNC*, and in many ways it's the closest to an X-enabled clone of Norton Commander that's available. The Northern Captain website is `http://www.xnc.dubna.su`.

ROX Its developers bill ROX as a desktop environment, and there are indeed ROX components that fill many of the desktop environment software components; but ROX relies on a window manager you obtain elsewhere, so I classify it as a file manager. You can learn more at `http://rox.sourceforge.net`.

TkDesk This program, headquartered at `http://tkdesk.sourceforge.net`, is a fairly well-established Linux file manager. Because of its application bar, it fits well with window managers that provide limited or awkward program-launch tools.

Xfm This file manager is old and uses old widget sets, so it seems decidedly crude compared to modern programs based on Qt- or GTK+. Nonetheless, it can be a good choice if you need a minimal file manager. You can learn more at `http://www.musikwissenschaft.uni-mainz.de/~ag/xfm/xfm.html`.

Xplore This Motif-based program includes a few unusual features, such as a pane that displays the `stdout` output of programs it launches. Its home page is `http://www.musikwissenschaft.uni-mainz.de/~ag/xplore/`.

As with window managers, your best bet for determining what file manager is best for you is to try several. Most of the file managers described here come with most Linux distributions, so you should have several on your installation media.

Selecting Applications

To make a useable desktop environment, you need to collect several small and large programs—text editors, image viewers, web browsers, mail readers, calculators, `xterm` programs, and more. Precisely what programs are important is of course a very personal question, so I can't provide you with a list. Presumably you have some idea of what you need, though.

One place to look for these applications is in the established desktop environments—primarily KDE and GNOME, but also XFce and even others, such as ROX. Even if you don't use the entire environment, you can use small or large programs from these environments in your custom environment. For instance, I have, from time to time, used tools such as KDE's KPPP and GNOME's gEdit from custom environments.

Another way to locate applications is to use a GUI package management tool (such as the ones described in Chapter 11, "Managing Packages") to browse the programs that are installed on your system or that are available with your distribution. Chances are you'll be able to find packages for many of the small tasks you may need to do. The package manager provides tools to help you locate the executable file, so you can test the programs from an `xterm` and then modify your window manager or file manager configuration to provide an easy way to launch the program.

Many Linux websites provide guides to help you locate both major and minor programs. Two particularly useful starting points are `http://www.linuxapps.com` and `http://www.linux.org/apps/`, both of which list categories on their main pages and subcategories under that.

Once you've selected applications, you need an easy way to launch them. Window managers invariably provide some sort of configuration file or directory, usually dot files named after the window manager; for instance, `~/.icewm` is the configuration directory for IceWM. This file or directory contains, among other things, information on a list of programs that can be launched from whatever program-launch facility the window manager supports. Many, but not all, file managers support a similar feature. Some file managers enable you to configure their file-launch facilities from the running file manager rather than by editing a configuration file in a text editor.

WARNING *Some distribution configuration tools and program installation tools overwrite window manager and file manager configuration files without asking. For instance, Mandrake's MenuDrake is constantly overwriting my IceWM menu. Be sure to back up your configuration file so that you can recover from problems caused by overzealous automatic configuration tools.*

Summary

GUI environments are an important part of life for most people who use Linux workstations. Linux provides considerable choice in desktop environments, including both major integrated packages, such as KDE and GNOME, and roll-your-own solutions built around any of dozens of window managers and file managers. Linux distributions frequently customize their default environments with unique icons, background images, and desktop themes. You can accept these defaults or install your own themes and artwork.

Chapter 7

Using Linux for Office Productivity

LINUX HAS TRADITIONALLY BEEN a server OS and an OS for running fairly specialized work-station applications, such as scientific data analysis programs. Most people and organizations have bypassed Linux in favor of other OSs, such as Windows and Mac OS, for running desktop productivity tools such as word processors, office graphics programs, and spreadsheets. Linux does support these tools, though. The Linux offerings have been growing in capability; today, they're powerful enough to meet the needs of many people and organizations.

To use Linux for office productivity, you must first select the appropriate tools. Many packages are available, and which ones you choose will have a big impact on whether Linux works well for you. One common issue with Linux office productivity tools, and especially word processing, is that Linux's font handling is odd compared to most OSs; therefore, word processors frequently require special font configurations. Getting this detail right will greatly improve your word processing capabilities. Likewise, knowing how to configure printers in office tools can help you get the most out of a Linux workstation configured for office productivity uses.

NOTE   *This chapter is nowhere near long enough to cover every detail of the day-to-day use of even one Linux office productivity package. Most packages work much the same as their Windows or Mac OS counterparts, but some don't. If you need help on this detail, consult the specific package's documentation or purchase a book on the program, such as Haugland and Jones'* StarOffice 6.0 Office Suite Companion *(Prentice Hall, 2002) or Kopka and Daly's* A Guide to LaTeX: Document Preparation for Beginners and Advanced Users, *3rd Edition (Addison-Wesley, 1999).*

Selecting Appropriate Office Tools

Linux office productivity suites vary in complexity, completeness, compatibility with the ubiquitous Microsoft Office file formats, and other features. Most Linux office tools are open source, although a few, such as the now-defunct Corel WordPerfect Office for Linux, are not. This section presents an overview of some of the most popular and capable packages: OpenOffice.org, KOffice, GNOME Office, and LaTeX. This section concludes with a brief look at running other operating systems' office productivity tools under an emulator.

Most office productivity suites are broken into multiple components, each of which handles one task. Typical components are a word processor, a spreadsheet, a presentation program, and a graphics editor. Most suites include additional components, but the details of what's included vary from one suite to another. LaTeX is an exception to this rule; it's a document preparation system that's very different from a typical office suite. I describe LaTeX in this chapter because it's an extremely flexible tool, and because it's very useful in preparing scientific and technical documents.

TIP   *You can mix and match components from different office suites, although you'll lose some cross-tool integration abilities.*

Using OpenOffice.org

OpenOffice.org, shown in Figure 7.1, and its commercial twin, Sun's StarOffice, are the closest the Linux world has to Microsoft Office, short of running Microsoft Office in an emulator. One of this suite's strengths is its cross-platform nature—it's available for Linux, other Unix-like OSs (most notably Sun's Solaris), and Microsoft Windows. A Mac OS X version is available, but it requires an X server to run. Older versions of StarOffice were also available for OS/2, but OS/2 has been dropped with recent versions. Like Microsoft Office, OpenOffice.org is a big package that supports a wide array of features.

FIGURE 7.1

OpenOffice.org's components resemble those of Microsoft Office.

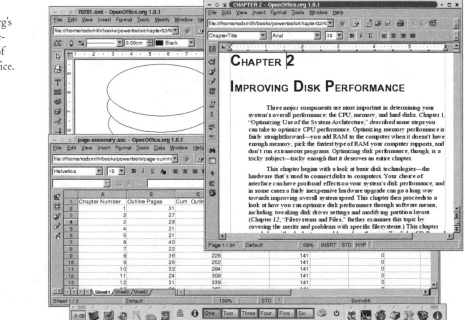

Major OpenOffice.org components include:

Writer   This is the word processing component of OpenOffice.org. It's a very powerful tool that supports all the usual features—fonts, styles, tables, macros, embedded graphics, and so on. OpenOffice.org Writer also features some of the best Microsoft Word import/export filters in existence. StarOffice includes additional import/export filters that are missing from Open-Office.org.

Calc   This spreadsheet is quite powerful and complete, and users who are accustomed to Microsoft's Excel should have little trouble adapting to this program.

Draw   The OpenOffice.org graphics package is a *vector* graphics program, meaning that it deals with shapes—circles, triangles, rectangles, lines, and so on. You can embed a bitmap graphic, such as a digital photo, but for the most part you deal with vector objects.

Impress   The Impress presentation manager helps you create material to support a presentation such as a lecture or sales pitch. You can combine elements created with the other OpenOffice.org components on *slides*—individual screens that can be displayed from a computer (if it's hooked up to the appropriate projection equipment) or printed on overhead transparencies, photographic slides, or plain paper.

OpenOffice.org has earned a reputation, based largely on its StarOffice 5.2 and earlier predecessors, for being a hugely bloated program. The program is indeed the largest office package for Linux, but OpenOffice.org 1.0 and StarOffice 6.0 are slimmer and quicker than the earlier StarOffice 5.2. Either is an excellent choice if you need a full-featured integrated office package for Linux, and especially if you need the best compatibility with Microsoft Office (and especially Microsoft Word) files. Although OpenOffice.org Writer's file import/export features are not 100 percent perfect, they're better than any other program's Microsoft Word import/export filters. In fact, some people say they're better than Microsoft Word itself in this respect, because Word sometimes has problems handling files created by earlier or later versions of itself.

NOTE   *OpenOffice.org is derived from Sun's StarOffice. Like Netscape and its Navigator, Sun decided to open the source code to its StarOffice product (which it acquired from a company called StarDivision). OpenOffice.org 1.0 was the result, and it's nearly identical to StarOffice 6.0, although the latter includes a database component, extra fonts, clip art, and a few other odds and ends. The peculiar OpenOffice.org name derives from the fact that "OpenOffice" was already taken by another product.*

Many Linux distributions, including Mandrake, Red Hat, and SuSE, ship with OpenOffice.org. For others, you must obtain the program from the main OpenOffice.org website, `http://www.openoffice` `.org`. Alternatively, you can buy the commercial StarOffice package, which comes with support and a few additional components and import/export filters. Unlike most Linux programs, OpenOffice.org comes with a GUI installation program; unless you install a package that ships with a distribution, you run this program to install OpenOffice.org. OpenOffice.org can be installed in two different ways:

Single-User Install   After you unpack the OpenOffice.org files, run the `setup` program as an ordinary user. This program will step you through the installation process. Typically, you'll install the entire OpenOffice.org package in your home directory.

Network/Multiuser Install   A more typical installation method for Linux involves a multiuser installation, often called a *network installation* in OpenOffice.org documentation. To perform this installation, run the `install` program as `root`, passing the `-net` parameter to `setup`. The installer puts the OpenOffice.org files wherever you specify (typically under `/usr/local`). You may want to create links in a directory on your system's default path to the program files (`swriter`, `scalc`, `sdraw`, `simpress`, and `setup`) so that users can most easily run these programs. Alternatively, you can add the Open-Office.org program directory to the system's path. Individual users then run the `setup` program to enter their personal information and create OpenOffice.org configuration files in their home directories.

Single-user installs of OpenOffice.org are uncommon. You could conceivably install OpenOffice.org this way on a single-user workstation, but performing a multiuser install is generally preferable for all the reasons that make Linux's multiuser security system desirable in general. For instance, you're less likely to accidentally destroy the OpenOffice.org installation when you install it as `root`.

Once they're installed, OpenOffice.org components are run by typing their names. Distributions that ship with OpenOffice.org often create desktop icons or menu entries that launch OpenOffice.org. Therefore, the package can be easy to run, at least from the popular GNOME and KDE desktops.

Using KOffice

The KDE Office (KOffice, shown in Figure 7.2) package is a popular open-source office package that's associated with KDE, although it's not wed to KDE—you can use KOffice even if you run GNOME, XFce, or a "bare" window manager as your desktop environment. KOffice runs on Linux and most other Unix-like platforms. You can learn more about the package at `http://www.koffice.org`. This section describes KOffice 1.2.1.

FIGURE 7.2

KOffice provides many of the same features as Open-Office.org, but it isn't quite as sophisticated.

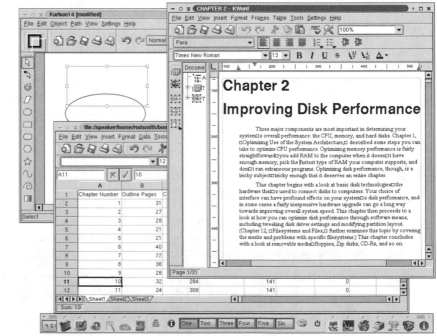

Major KOffice components include:

KWord   This program is the KOffice word processor. It's a *frame-based* program, which means that text and other features are entered in elements called *frames* that you can move around on the page. KWord's Microsoft Word import/export filters are competent for simple documents, but they tend to fall down with more complex files.

KSpread   This spreadsheet is not as complex as OpenOffice.org's Calc, but it's good enough for many less-demanding uses.

KPresenter   As the name implies, this program is a presentation program. Several examples of presentations created with KPresenter are available at `http://www.kde.org/kdeslides/`.

Kivio   This program is similar in concept to the Windows program Visio; it creates flowcharts.

Kugar   This program helps generate business reports. This function is rare in Linux office suites.

Karbon14   Roughly equivalent to OpenOffice.org's Draw, Karbon14 creates vector graphics. As of KOffice 1.2.1, Karbon14 is rudimentary compared to many other vector graphics programs. This program used to be called Kontour, so you may see references to it by that name.

Krita   This program is a bitmap graphics tool. The KOffice web page likens it to the GNU Image Manipulation Program (GIMP; described more fully in Chapter 8, "Miscellaneous User Tools"), but Krita is not nearly as mature as the GIMP.

KChart   KOffice's graphics tools are rounded out by KChart, which generates charts, graphs, and so on from data files.

The KOffice suite includes more major components than OpenOffice.org but fewer than GNOME Office (as described next). To some extent this fact is an arbitrary matter; programs don't need to be part of the same suite to work together, and even programs that are part of the same suite can sometimes be installed separately and used without their suite-mates. The KOffice tools were developed as an integrated group; as such, they tend to work well with each other and present very similar user interfaces. These tools are packaged together, so installing one without the others isn't practical, but of course you can use one component without the others.

KWord is gaining respectability as a major Linux word processor. Although not as sophisticated as OpenOffice.org's Writer, the program is quite capable for many tasks, and it's slimmer and faster than Writer. These characteristics make it a good choice for use on systems that are a year or more behind the times, in terms of memory and CPU speed. Its frame-based nature also makes it a good choice for light desktop publishing. As a general rule, other KOffice components aren't as sophisticated, but many are useable, and they're improving all the time. KOffice 2.*x*, 3.*x*, or some other future version, could possibly compete strongly with OpenOffice.org in terms of its feature list.

Using GNOME Office

GNOME Office (shown in Figure 7.3) is the Borg of office suites—it assimilates other projects into its collective, turning each component into just one part of a greater whole. Most GNOME Office projects began life independently, and some still maintain independent web pages. In fact, according to the official GNOME Office website (`http://www.gnome.org/gnome-office/`), OpenOffice.org is becoming part of GNOME Office. For the moment, though, I think of OpenOffice.org as a separate project.

FIGURE 7.3

GNOME Office is built from independent components—note the different icons in the icon bars of each application.

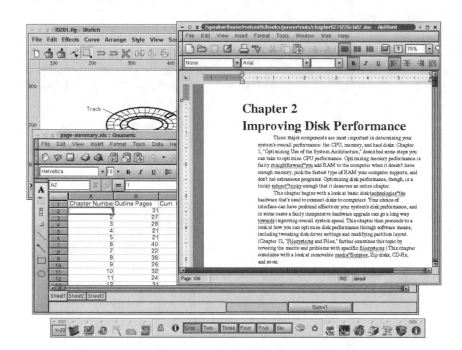

Whereas KOffice is built with KDE in mind, GNOME Office is designed around GNOME. Like KOffice, you can use GNOME Office or its components even in other environments—KDE, XFce, or anything else. Unlike KOffice, GNOME Office components are installable separately. This fact is very fortunate, because the sheer number of GNOME Office components is huge. Some of the more important of these include:

AbiWord   AbiWord is the least sophisticated of the major Linux word processors, but it's still good enough to be used daily on many systems, and it's improving rapidly. This program was originally developed as a cross-platform tool, and you can obtain versions for Windows, Mac OS X (with an X server), and others.

Gnumeric   This program is a powerful spreadsheet program; the developers claim to have implemented 95 percent of Microsoft Excel's functions. Although Gnumeric isn't a clone of Excel, users of Microsoft's spreadsheet shouldn't have trouble adapting to Gnumeric.

GNU Cash   This program is the only major Linux entry in a field that's very important to home users and small businesses: personal financial management. GNU Cash is roughly equivalent to Microsoft Money or Quicken, but it uses a somewhat different model. Specifically, it uses the double-entry accounting instead of the single-entry approach used by most personal financial packages.

Agnubis   This program is GNOME Office's presentation manager. It's a very new program and, therefore, it isn't very mature as I write these words.

GFax   GFax is an unusual office component, but it is an important one for many businesses—it helps manage faxes. Specifically, GFax provides a uniform GUI interface for sending faxes from applications that can print. You can use GFax even from programs that aren't part of the GNOME Office suite.

The GIMP   The *GNU Image Manipulation Program* is one of the most sophisticated programs in the GNOME Office suite. It's a powerful bitmap graphics editor that closely approaches Adobe Photoshop in power.

Sketch   The GIMP handles bitmap graphics for GNOME Office, and Sketch does the same for vector graphics. Sketch isn't nearly the dominant player in this field that the GIMP is for bitmap graphics, though.

Eye of GNOME   This program is a simple graphics file viewer. You might configure your desktop environment to launch this program whenever you double-click on a graphics file.

Evolution   This program is the Linux world's answer to Microsoft's Outlook package. Evolution handles e-mail, address book, and scheduling functions.

Galeon   This web browser is based on the Gecko engine (used by Mozilla and Netscape, among others), but it is much slimmer than Mozilla or Netscape.

In addition to these major components, GNOME Office claims many others, even including multiple entries in specific categories. For instance, in addition to Evolution, the Balsa mail client is part of GNOME Office. Of these components, the most mature and powerful are the GIMP, Gnumeric, GNU Cash, and Evolution. Other programs are often useable, but they are usually not the leaders in their fields. Of course, you might not want the feature leader. For instance, if you just want a basic mail reader, Evolution is overkill.

GNOME Office's scope is such that many of its components have no counterparts in other office suites, but this fact isn't terribly important. For instance, KDE's Konqueror web browser is similar to Galeon in many ways. Konqueror isn't officially part of KOffice, but it is part of KDE. Whether the web browser is part of the desktop environment or office suite is unimportant to most users.

Using LaTeX

LaTeX (pronounced "lay-tek") is an unusual entry in this rundown of Linux office suites because LaTeX really isn't an office suite; rather, it's a document preparation language, similar in principle to the Hypertext Markup Language (HTML) that's commonly used for web pages. To use LaTeX, you create a document in a text editor—Emacs, NEdit, vi, or any other text editor you like. Certain symbols and strings within a LaTeX document carry special meaning. Most importantly, the backslash (\) character marks the beginning of most commands, and braces ({}) surround the text on which operations are to occur. For instance, the string `\emph{strongly}` emphasizes the string *strongly* in the output. To create output, you pass the LaTeX document file through one or more programs that convert your file into PostScript, which you can then print using `lpr`.

Listing 7.1 presents a simple but complete LaTeX file. This file begins with a declaration of the class of document (an article), which defines various default settings, such as the default font. The `\begin{document}` line marks the start of the document, as opposed to the preamble, where global settings are defined. The `\Huge` line tells LaTeX to use an extra-large font. Ordinary text isn't marked out in any extraordinary way, so the next couple of lines print in the final document much as you would expect, with the exception of LaTeX keywords, which begin with a backslash. Therefore, `\today` is replaced in the final output by the current date, and the text delimited by `\itshape{...}` is printed in italic. Of course, this example is trivial. The true power of LaTeX emerges with its more complex options, including a very powerful syntax for handling mathematical equations. This facility makes LaTeX a favorite among mathematicians, scientists, and computer professionals. LaTeX is centered strongly around the use of predefined and extensible styles; you set up a style to handle some type of document element, such as bulleted lists or embedded graphics with their captions. Thereafter, you call the style to have LaTeX apply it, and you don't worry about the formatting details; LaTeX does that for you.

LISTING 7.1: A SAMPLE LaTeX DOCUMENT

```
\documentclass{article}
\begin{document}
\Huge
Today, \today, I formally declare my candidacy for the
position of \itshape{town dogcatcher.}
\end{document}
```

In order to fully master LaTeX, you must invest some effort in learning its complexity. This effort may not be worthwhile if you write typical business documents and are already familiar with the GUI approach to writing; but if you need LaTeX's powerful layout features, you may want to pick up a book on the subject or browse the documentation available at `http://www.latex-project.org`.

If you type Listing 7.1, or some other LaTeX document, into a file, you can convert it into other formats by passing it through the `latex` program. This program converts the LaTeX document, which typically uses a `.tex` filename extension, into a device independent (DVI) file, which is actually an intermediate format. To produce a useful output file, you'd use a program such as `dvips` or `dvipdf`, which create PostScript or Portable Document Format (PDF) files as output, respectively. Other conversion programs are available to convert into other formats, as well. After creating `announce.tex`, you might type these commands to create a PDF:

```
$ latex announce.tex
$ dvipdf announce.dvi
```

The result is a file called `announce.pdf`, which is shown in Figure 7.4 as displayed by Xpdf. This output file demonstrates the fact that LaTeX is free to reformat lines as it sees fit—note that indentation and line breaks in the output don't match those on the input. To control these details, you must use special LaTeX commands that set these options globally, or that set overrides in specific cases. One of LaTeX's strengths is that it handles these details, making consistent formatting more likely than would be the case if you were using a typical GUI word processor.

FIGURE 7.4

LaTeX output matches the description provided in the input, not the formatting of the raw text file.

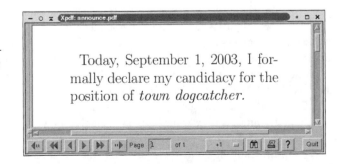

If you like GUI word processors but want to take advantage of LaTeX's power, you should consider a compromise program: LyX (`http://www.lyx.org`). This program, shown in Figure 7.5, is essentially a GUI text editor with direct links to call LaTeX and with the ability to parse a limited subset of LaTeX commands to present a GUI display. LyX is not a what-you-see-is-what-you-get (WYSIWYG) word processor, though. Although LyX displays some text attributes, such as italics, on-screen as they'll appear on the printed page, features such as line breaks, page breaks, and more advanced LaTeX features aren't displayed as they'll appear. In fact, even the on-screen font doesn't necessarily display as you might expect. Nonetheless, LyX can be a useful bridge if you want to obtain some of LaTeX's power without spending hours poring over LaTeX documentation.

FIGURE 7.5

LyX provides a GUI face to LaTeX.

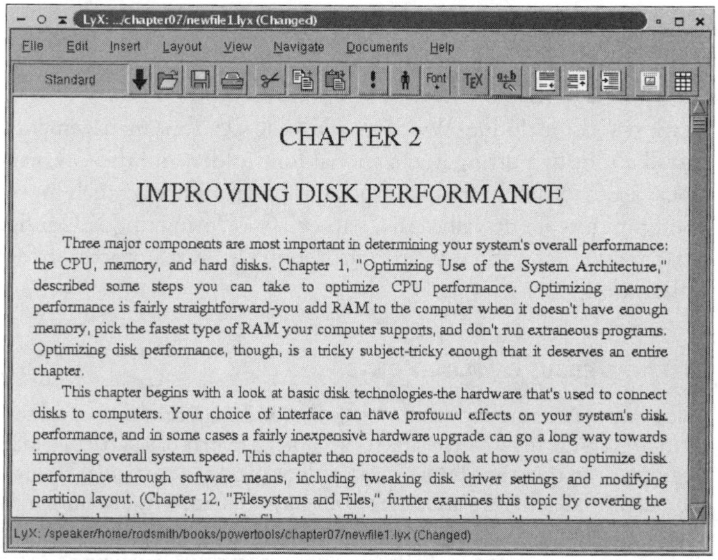

Using Emulators

Some people need to use programs that aren't available for Linux. This is frequently the case when you must exchange files in a proprietary Windows format, such as Microsoft Word files. Although many Linux programs support proprietary file formats, compatibility is seldom perfect, so you may have to use the "genuine article" to do your job. If this is the case, emulators can help you use Linux while also getting work done. Chapter 10, "Using Multiple OSs," includes more information on emulators. In brief, on IA-32 systems, you can use Windows emulators, such as Win4Lin (`http://www.netraverse.com`) or WINE (`http://www.winehq.com`) to run Windows programs. You can use machine emulators, such as VMWare (`http://www.vmware.com`) or Plex86 (`http://savannah.nongnu.org/projects/plex86`) to run an entire host OS—Windows, Linux, or others. (Win4Lin also runs Windows itself under Linux, but it can *only* run Windows, not other OSs.) On PowerPC systems, the Mac-on-Linux (MoL; `http://www.maconlinux.org`) program lets you run Mac OS from Linux. You can use Bochs (`http://bochs.sourceforge.net`) to boot Windows or some other OS. Most of these packages require you to have a copy of the target OS, such as Windows. These programs vary in their degree of integration with Linux; for instance, you might not be able to cut-and-paste between Linux and Windows programs. As a general rule, WINE integrates best with Linux, but WINE is also the least successful emulator in terms of its ability to run a wide variety of programs. Some of the best emulators, including Win4Lin and VMWare, are commercial products.

TIP   *The commercial Crossover Office package (*`http://www.codeweavers.com`*) is a WINE variant with a user-friendly installation routine and the ability to run all but the latest versions of Microsoft Office, as well as several other common office productivity packages. If you really need to run Microsoft Office and want it to integrate well with other Linux programs, using Crossover Office may be the best solution.*

Managing Fonts in Office Tools

In most OSs, including Windows and Mac OS, font management is fairly straightforward—you install a font by putting it in a special font folder, and the OS makes it available to all your applications. Unfortunately, font management under Linux is much more complex. Some aspects of this configuration are described in Chapter 16, "Optimizing X Configuration." Word processors are particularly picky about their fonts, though, so word processor font management requires some elaboration.

BITMAP VERSUS OUTLINE FONTS

Two types of fonts are common: *bitmap fonts* and *outline fonts*. The former are defined as bitmaps, much like bitmap graphics files; each character occupies a matrix of a particular size, with individual bits set on or off. Designers can fine-tune bitmap fonts to look good at a particular resolution, using human aesthetic judgments. Bitmap fonts are also quick to display; a character's bitmap can be copied to the screen or a printer file very speedily. On the downside, bitmap fonts require distinct font files for each resolution and size. For instance, a 12-point font displays only at 12 points; if you want a 10-point font, you need another font file. (It is technically possible to scale these fonts, but the results usually look very bad.)

Outline fonts, by contrast, use mathematical descriptions of the fonts' outlines, in terms of lines and curves. The computer can map these outlines onto a matrix of a given resolution to create a bitmap for display. This characteristic means that one outline font file can serve many different resolutions, vastly simplifying font administration. On the downside, outline fonts require more CPU power to display, and computers tend to do a poor job of creating good-looking results at low resolutions.

Most fonts you buy on font CDs or download from the Internet today are outline fonts, usually in Apple's TrueType or Adobe's PostScript Type 1 (aka Adobe Type Manager, or ATM) format. Linux can handle both font formats, although XFree86 4.0, a special TrueType-enabled font server, or the new Xft library, is required for TrueType fonts. All Linux distributions ship with collections of fonts in these formats, as well as in various bitmap formats. These fonts are usually stored in subdirectories of `/usr/X11R6/lib/X11/fonts`.

Word Processor Font Issues

X was designed with displaying fonts on the screen in mind; the core X protocols give little consideration to mapping screen fonts to printed fonts. In some cases, this isn't a big deal. For instance, a web page can usually be displayed on the screen or on a printout using almost any font, so the screen and print fonts don't need to match. In the case of a WYSIWYG word processor, though, screen and printer fonts must match. The best way to achieve this effect is to use the same font files for both on-screen display and printing. X's font model, though, doesn't give word processors direct access to the source font files; X delivers font bitmaps to applications, even when the font is an outline font. This break means that applications are limited in what they can do with a font. For instance, to download a font to a printer, the application would have to know the printer's resolution, request the font in a size appropriate to create output at that resolution, and send the resulting bitmap to the printer. X applications may not know the printer's resolution, though. Even if they did, X doesn't provide the precise font spacing information that's often needed to produce the best-looking displays at printer resolutions.

In order to work around these problems of linking display to printed fonts, word processors have adopted various strategies. Each strategy is unique, but there are certain commonalities. The strategies include:

Mapping Display and Printer Fonts   One approach is to create detailed and explicit maps between the fonts that X provides and the fonts in the printer or installed in the word processor for delivery to the printer. For instance, if you choose to use Times, X delivers a bitmap Times to the word processor, which tells the printer to display *its* version of Times. Times is one of the standard PostScript fonts, so the printer has it available. If you pick a font that's not available in the printer, X still displays the font correctly, and the word processor downloads its own copy to the printer. In both cases, the X font and printing font may not derive from the same source, which can cause printed and displayed fonts to not match if the fonts are misconfigured. AbiWord and KWord both use this approach, but their implementation details differ substantially.

In-Application Font Handling   In order to avoid mismatched screen and printer fonts, some word processors have taken the task of font handling entirely upon themselves. You install your fonts in the application, which displays text on the screen without using X's font-rendering code. The application then sends the font to the printer when it's time to print. OpenOffice.org is one package that uses this approach.

Decoupling Screen and Printer Fonts   Some programs ignore font matching. LaTeX and LyX, for instance, don't make any attempt to have screen and printer fonts match. This approach may make it hard to judge how a final printed page will look, but it greatly simplifies screen font configuration. These programs still require you to install fonts for printing, though.

Using an Expanded Font Server   A *font server* is a program that delivers font data to one or more computers. Some Linux distributions, such as Mandrake and Red Hat, use local-only font servers as their X font delivery mechanism. Some commercial programs, such as Anyway Office (`http://www.vistasource.com/page.php?id=7`) and WordPerfect Office 2000, use an expanded commercial font server, Bitstream's FontTastic, to deliver outline font data as well as bitmaps. This solution enables the programs to display X fonts on the screen but still deliver outline fonts to the printer. Unfortunately, there's no open source expanded font server similar to FontTastic, so no open source word processor uses this approach.

Xft   Another solution is *Xft*. This library is a new font-handling tool that's being used by the latest versions of KDE and GNOME and by some other applications. Xft can deliver both bitmaps and outlines for a font, so the word processor can use Xft to display text and to send an outline font to a printer. As I write, KWord is the only major word processor that can use Xft in this way, but others are likely to follow. Chapter 16 covers Xft configuration in more detail.

NOTE   *Some word processors use variants or multiple techniques. For instance, OpenOffice.org, although best thought of as using in-application font rendering, can map its fonts to standard printer fonts.*

All of these approaches to font handling have one feature in common: In order to use a font in a word processor, you must install that font in the word processor or in an affiliated application. In the case of decoupled fonts, the installation affects only printed fonts; and in the case of expanded font servers and Xft, the font must be installed in the font server or Xft rather than the word processor *per se*. Nonetheless, this fact makes word processor font configuration another hassle. If you want to use a font both in a standard X application (say, your web browser) and in a word processor, you must install it both in X and in the word processor. Indeed, the mapping approach requires that you install the font in both X and the word processor even if you only want to use the font in the word processor. In the future, Xft is likely to simplify matters, as many applications will use Xft. Xft is still new enough that this simplification is only beginning; and as Chapter 16 details, Xft's configuration has itself undergone changes, which has added to confusion in the short term.

Adding Fonts to Word Processors

Each word processor provides its own font management facilities. You may need to consult your word processor's documentation for details on how to do the job. In broad outline, the procedures for the more popular programs are described here:

OpenOffice.org Writer   You run the `spadmin` program to administer fonts and printers. (You may need to change into the directory in which this program resides to run it or it will get confused.) Click the Fonts button to enter the font manager (as shown in Figure 7.6). You can then add TrueType or PostScript fonts by clicking Add and selecting the fonts you want to add in the resulting file selector. Unfortunately, OpenOffice.org's font installer tends to be very finicky; sometimes it won't install a font, or will appear to install a font but not make it available, or display a similarly-named X font instead.

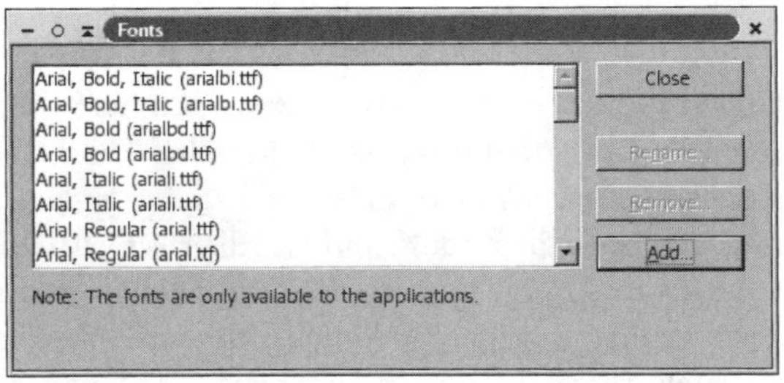

FIGURE 7.6

OpenOffice.org provides a GUI font management tool.

KWord   If you check the KWord font list, you'll see all your standard X fonts; however, if you try to print in anything but a standard PostScript font, chances are you'll find that your font has been replaced with another. To avoid this problem, you must install the target font in your Post-Script printer or, if you're using a non-PostScript printer, in Ghostscript. (The upcoming section, "Ghostscript Font Management," covers this procedure in more detail.) It may be helpful to generate a sample PostScript file that uses the fonts in question so that you can identify the names that KWord uses for them. Recent versions of KWord also support Xft fonts for both on-screen display and printing.

TIP   If you use a PostScript printer and you don't have the ability to easily add a font to the printer, you can create a print queue that prints to the PostScript printer using Ghostscript's PostScript output driver. This is an ugly solution in many ways, but it enables you to add fonts to Ghostscript rather than to the printer.

AbiWord   This program ships with a basic set of fonts, which it stores in `/usr/share/AbiSuite/fonts` or a similar location. You can add fonts by placing them in this directory and modifying the `fonts.dir` and `fonts.scale` files. These files have the same format as the files of the same name in X font directories, as described in Chapter 16. When you run AbiWord, it tells X to add this font directory's contents to its list of fonts, so both X and AbiWord have access to the same fonts. AbiWord works best with Adobe Type 1 fonts. TrueType fonts may work, but they require both X and your printer (or Ghostscript) to have TrueType support, and you must also jump through extra configuration hoops.

NOTE   AbiWord's developers plan to change its font-handling system to use Xft in the near future. The preceding description is accurate as of version 1.0.2.

Ghostscript Font Management

Linux's printing system has traditionally worked under the assumption that the printer understands PostScript, but most printers sold for the home and small business markets don't meet that requirement. To fill the gap, Linux uses Ghostscript to convert PostScript into a format that the printer understands. Essentially, Ghostscript is a PostScript interpreter that resides on the computer rather than on the printer. As such, Ghostscript is responsible for printer font management.

PostScript printers all ship with a standard set of fonts available, including Times, Helvetica, and Courier, and Ghostscript makes them available, as well. All Linux systems also ship with these fonts installed in X. Some word processors, though—most notably KWord—require that you install additional fonts in your PostScript printer or in Ghostscript in order for them to be used. Consult your printer's documentation for information on installing a font in your printer. If you're using Ghostscript, you can install a font by storing the font file in an appropriate directory and adding an entry to a configuration file.

NOTE   You don't need to add fonts to Ghostscript when using OpenOffice.org, AbiWord, or some other word processors; these programs send the font to the printer along with the file being printed.

Most distributions place Ghostscript fonts in the `/var/lib/defoma/gs.d/dirs/fonts`, `/usr/share/fonts/default/ghostscript`, or `/usr/share/ghostscript/fonts` directory. Ghostscript works best with Adobe Type 1 fonts, but Ghostscript also supports TrueType fonts—if the program was compiled with this option, which not all Ghostscript executables include. When installing Type 1 fonts, you need to copy two files per font, one with a `.pfb` or `.pfa` filename extension and one with a `.pfm` or `.afm` extension. TrueType fonts come in single files, all of which have `.ttf` extensions.

TIP *If you want to use the same fonts for printing and for X screen displays, you can save some disk space by either using symbolic links between the X font directory's files and the Ghostscript font directory's files or by using the same directory for both locations. For instance, you can add the Ghostscript font directory to X's font path and place X* `fonts.dir` *and* `fonts.scale` *configuration files in this directory.*

Once you've copied font files to a directory, you need to tell Ghostscript to use them by editing a file called `Fontmap` or `Fontmap.GS`, which is usually in the `/var/lib/defoma/gs.d/dirs/fonts` or `/usr/share/ghostscript/`*version*`/lib` directory, where *version* is the Ghostscript version number, such as `7.05`. Fundamentally, this file consists of a series of name assignments of one of the following two forms:

```
/PostScript-Font-Name (font-filename.ext) ;
/New-Font-Name /PostScript-Font-Name ;
```

The first form assigns a font file stored in the font directory to a PostScript font name. (This directory's location is hard-coded in the Ghostscript executable, but it varies from one distribution to another.) The second form defines an alias—when a PostScript file requests a font called `/New-Font-Name`, Ghostscript looks up the font associated with `/PostScript-Font-Name`. To add fonts, you add definitions of this form. An alias might or might not be useful. They're common in the default font file because many of Ghostscript's fonts are clones of more common fonts—for instance, instead of Adobe Times, Ghostscript uses a similar font called Nimbus Roman. Thus, Ghostscript defines Nimbus Roman (or `/NimbusRomNo9L-Regu`, to be precise) as the primary font and sets up Times (or `/Times-Roman`) as an alias. For most purposes, the configuration would work as well with `/Times-Roman` pointing directly to the target font file.

TIP *If you want to add a lot of fonts, you can use the* `type1inst` *program, described more fully in Chapter 16, to create a* `Fontmap` *file with entries for all the Type 1 fonts in a directory.*

Managing Printers in Office Tools

Just as font management in word processors can pose unique challenges, so too can printer handling. In most cases, office programs generate PostScript output and print using standard Linux printer queues; however, there are some exceptions to this rule, as well as quirks in setting up office tools to print. Some of these details are actually font issues, especially in configuring Ghostscript's fonts, as described in the earlier section, "Ghostscript Font Management." Some printer configuration details are different or more subtle than this, though. These issues relate to mapping printer queues to lists in office programs and selecting the correct printer model when the application gives you a choice.

Mapping Linux Printer Queues to Printer Lists

Most X-based Linux applications, when you select the option to print, display some sort of dialog box in which you pick your printer from a list of options or enter the printer queue name. For instance, Figure 7.7 shows the KWord print dialog box. You can select a printer from the Name widget. In the case of Figure 7.7, the first three selections are printers, and the final four are specialty options.

FIGURE 7.7

Most X applications present dialog boxes to aid selecting a printer and printer options.

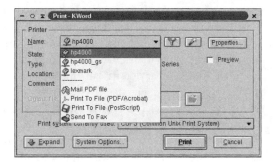

Sometimes a program requires special configuration to locate the printers. This need is particularly likely to arise if your printing configuration is odd in some way. For instance, some programs look for a list of printers in /etc/printcap, but this file may not exist if you use the Common Unix Printing System (CUPS). If you don't see any printer options, you can try creating a dummy /etc/printcap file, such as Listing 7.2, which presents entries for the same printers shown in Figure 7.7. (In fact, CUPS usually generates a dummy /etc/printcap file automatically.)

LISTING 7.2: DUMMY /etc/printcap FILE

```
hp4000_gs:
hp4000:
lexmark:
```

A few programs require you to configure a printer's features before they'll present the printer. This is true of WordPerfect 8, for instance, although the major open source office packages don't need such configuration for basic printing. Nonetheless, OpenOffice.org enables you to define odd printer characteristics using the same spadmin program you use to add fonts. If you find you can't take advantage of your printer's features, you may want to run this utility and click the New Printer button, which will guide you through configuring a new printer. You can also set up a fax queue or PDF output generator using this utility.

Selecting a Printer Model

Some programs generate quite generic PostScript output. This output should work on any PostScript printer, or by extension, any printer that's driven via Ghostscript. Sometimes, though, you need to take advantage of printer-specific features, or even just features of a class of printers. For instance, your printer might have a duplexer (hardware that enables you to print on two sides of a sheet), or your printer might print in color but you get black-and-white output even from documents that contain color. In such cases, you may need to define the printer's characteristics, and this task is usually accomplished by telling your software that you have a specific brand and model of printer. For instance, you do this in one of the first steps of defining a printer in OpenOffice.org's `spadmin` program. Typically, you'll see a large list of printer models, and you pick the one that's closest to your printer.

A few programs, including WordPerfect 8 and the GIMP, support printing to non-PostScript printers. For such programs, printer selection is particularly critical; you don't want to pick an inappropriate driver type for your print queue. If you use a non-PostScript printer for which Ghostscript drivers exist, you have a choice in such cases: You can print PostScript and let Ghostscript create printer-specific output; or you can generate printer-specific output directly. The latter option requires creating a special "raw" printer queue that doesn't call Ghostscript. It may or may not generate better output than a traditional Linux printer queue that uses Ghostscript.

If you use Ghostscript and need to select a printer model from a list, the question of which model to select arises. In most cases, Apple LaserWriter drivers work well with Ghostscript-driven printers. I've also had good luck with QMS magicolor drivers with color printers in many applications. In some programs, some drivers may generate output that includes mode-switching code to kick the printer into an appropriate mode. Such code will usually confuse a Linux printer queue, so it's best to use a printer driver that doesn't generate such code, just raw PostScript.

In theory, CUPS can simplify printer configuration by delivering information on printer capabilities to applications. The applications can then present appropriate printer options—for instance, they might display a duplexing option for printers that are so equipped. In practice, though, most applications aren't CUPS-aware, so they don't take advantage of these features. Some programs are beginning to add at least rudimentary CUPS support, though—for instance, note in Figure 7.7 the option for the printing system, which is set to CUPS.

Summary

Linux has long been gaining power as a desktop productivity OS. Today, application suites such as OpenOffice.org, KOffice, and GNOME Office provide the tools you need to perform typical office tasks such as word processing and presentations. Linux also offers more traditional Unix tools such as LaTeX, which remains the tool of choice for many scientific, engineering, and other technical endeavors. When using office tools, you must be aware of peculiarities relating to Linux's handling of fonts and printers. Using more than basic fonts from Linux office tools often requires installing the fonts twice—in X and in the office program. You may also need to tell your office program about your printer, or fine-tune your printer configuration to enable the program to use specialized features such as duplexers or multiple sheet feeders.

## Chapter 8

Miscellaneous User Tools

DESKTOP USES OF A COMPUTER are extremely broad in scope. The previous chapter covered one of the most important classes of such use—office productivity tools. This chapter covers an assortment of additional programs. Most of these tools can be either critical for business use of Linux or more recreational in nature. The topics covered in this chapter are manipulating sound files, using a digital camera, creating and manipulating graphics, using advanced web browsing options, and configuring e-mail.

Working with Sound Files

Computers have become multimedia centers in many homes and offices. One important component of this role is the ability to record and process pure audio files. Linux provides several tools (including sound recorders, file format converters, and multimedia players) to help you with this task.

NOTE   *Most of the tasks described here require that you have a working sound card. Chapter 1, "Optimizing System Architecture Usage," describes sound card configuration, so you should read it before proceeding if the sound isn't working on your system.*

Recording Sounds

As with many types of programs, Linux sound recording programs can be classified into one of two categories: text-based and GUI. The most common text-based sound recording program is rec, which is installed as part of the sox package. (In fact, rec is a symbolic link to play; the program records or plays sounds depending upon the name you use to call it.) Here is the basic syntax for rec:

```
rec [options] filename [effects]
```

The *filename* is, of course, the filename to be used. The *options* affect the basic file format—the sample rate, number of channels, and so on. The *effects* modify the recorded sound—they create echoes, fades, and so on. Table 8.1 summarizes some of the more important options. Consult the sox man page for information on effects.

TABLE 8.1: IMPORTANT OPTIONS FOR rec

OPTION	MEANING	VALUES
-c num or --channels=num	The number of channels recorded	Typically 1 or 2
-f format or --format=format	Bit format of the recording	s (signed linear), u (unsigned linear), U (U-law logarithmic), a (ADPCM), A (A-law logarithmic), or g (GSM)
-r rate or --rate=rate	Number of samples per second	Typically 8000 through 48000
-s size or --size=size	Size of each sample	b (8-bit), w (16-bit), l (32-bit), f (32-bit floating-point), d (64-bit floating-point), or D (80-bit floating-point)
-t type or --type=type	Audio file format	Common audio filename extensions, such as wav or au
-x or --xinu	Reverses the byte order when size is w or l. Necessary when transferring some files across platforms	N/A

If some of the options in Table 8.1 seem unfamiliar, don't be overly concerned. You can use the defaults, or use common values: signed linear (s) or unsigned linear (u) format, sample sizes of 8-bit (b) or 16-bit (w), and wav files. The most important options in determining the quality of reproduction are the sample rate and sample size. For reference, audio CDs use a rate of 44,100 with a 16-bit sample size. For stereo recordings, of course, you must specify two channels. For instance, you can create a recording (and then play it back) with commands such as the following:

```
$ rec -t wav -r 44100 -s w -c 2 sample.wav
$ play sample.wav
```

These commands have some caveats associated with them:

◆ You must have the appropriate audio inputs to your sound card. This includes mixer levels, which must be set to record from your chosen input source. Chapter 1 provides more information on mixers.

◆ The rec program doesn't know when to stop recording; therefore, you must press Ctrl+C when you've finished.

Using GUI Sound Editors

If you prefer to use a GUI sound recorder, you can do so. Two common tools to do this are GNOME Sound Recorder (gnome-sound-recorder, part of the gnome-media or gnome-media2 package on most distributions) and krecord or krec, part of KDE and distributed in a package called krecord or kdemultimedia on most distributions. The GNOME Sound Recorder is typical of these simple programs: Click the Record button to begin recording, and click Stop when you're done. The program displays its current recording settings near the bottom of its window. You can change them by picking Edit ➢ Preferences and using the Sound tab.

To do more with your recorded sounds, you need a more powerful package. Examples of such tools include GNU/Linux Audio Mechanics (GLAME; http://glame.sourceforge.net) and Sweep (http://www.metadecks.org/software/sweep/). These packages are full-featured audio editing tools. Figure 8.1 shows GLAME in action. This program uses a main window in which all of the open files are summarized and another window for each file. These editing windows display the sound files visually as waveforms. Using this display, you can select part of the sound file and apply various operations to it—you can cut the fragment, modify its volume, boost its bass level, and so on. These options are all available from a menu you obtain by right-clicking in the editing window. You can also zoom in and out. This fact makes it possible to zoom in on a very short sound, such as a pop in a recording taken from an old LP record. You can then modify that sound; for example, you could reduce the volume of the pop to an inaudible level.

FIGURE 8.1

GUI sound editors let you modify sounds using visual representations of the audio waveform.

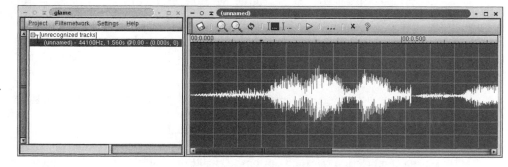

Creating MP3 or Ogg Vorbis Files

In the past, people have used a variety of media and formats for storing music—LP records, cassette tapes, and audio CDs being three of the most popular. Since the late 1990s, a new class of formats has emerged: compressed digital audio files, which can be stored on a variety of media for different players. Several specific file formats have emerged to fill this role, but one of the most popular is the Moving Picture Experts Group Layer 3 (MP3) format. A wide variety of hardware and software, ranging from dedicated portable MP3 players such as the popular Rio to MP3-enabled CD players to software multimedia players such as those described in the next section, "Using a Multimedia Player," can handle MP3 files. A simpler but related format, MP2, is also available.

One problem with MP3 is that the algorithms used to manage MP3 compression are covered by patents, so creating and using MP3 files can be a legal minefield for open source software. For this reason, many Linux users prefer using a competing file format, Ogg Vorbis (http://www.vorbis.com). Unfortunately, although Ogg Vorbis is a perfectly good format for computer-only use, portable Ogg Vorbis players similar to the Rio are rare, at least as of early 2003.

Both MP3 and Ogg Vorbis are *lossy* compression schemes, which means that they throw away some of the input data. Lossy compression is useless for storing program files, database files, and so on, but it can be very useful when applied to graphics, sound, or multimedia files—the compression scheme can be designed to throw away data that humans are unlikely to notice. Lossy compression schemes, including MP3 and Ogg Vorbis, typically enable you to set a level of compression. Low compression reproduces the input well enough that you're unlikely to object to the compression artifacts. High compression throws away more data, so even with good compression algorithms, you're likely to notice the effect.

Many Linux programs to create MP3 and Ogg Vorbis files exist; some of the more popular include:

lame   This program may be the most popular MP3 encoder for Linux. It's headquartered at http://lame.sourceforge.net. Because it is open source software, using it in the United States and other countries in which patents on MP3 algorithms are valid requires a special license, which is impossible for individuals to obtain.

mp3enc   This is a commercial MP3 encoder for Linux. A demonstration version is available from http://www.iis.fraunhofer.de/amm/download/index.html.

toolame   This program, headquartered at http://toolame.sourceforge.net/, is an MP2 encoder.

oggenc   If you don't need to play your files on portable MP3 players, MP3-enabled CD players, and the like, you can create Ogg Vorbis files with oggenc, which is based at http://www.vorbis.com.

Each of these programs has its own syntax and quirks, so you should consult your program's documentation for details on how to use it. Most provide a large number of options to encode information such as the album title, track title, performer, and date in the output data file. You can also set options that affect how the lossy compression scheme works, including one or more methods of setting compression rates and options to enable or disable particular compression features. As an example of one of these tools in use, consider the following command, which creates an Ogg Vorbis file from a standard .wav file:

```
$ oggenc -a "Linus Torvalds" -t "Linux" english.wav
```

This example converts a file called english.wav to english.ogg, adding information to the file specifying the title as Linux and the performer as Linus Torvalds. Similar commands can convert other audio files. Of course, you must have an audio file before you can convert it. In practice, chances are you'll want to encode an audio file derived from an audio CD, in order to convert the CD for playback on your computer or using a portable MP3 player. To do this, you must use a *digital audio extraction* (*DAE*, aka a CD *ripping*) tool, such as Cdda2wav (http://www.escape.de/users/colossus/cdda2wav.html) or cdparanoia (http://www.xiph.org/paranoia/). Like the MP3 and Ogg Vorbis encoders, these are command-line tools. In most cases, use of cdparanoia is simple: Type its name followed by the track or tracks you want to extract (enclosing them in quotes will protect them from being mangled by the shell). Some systems require that you have root privileges to run cdparanoia, even if you own the relevant device files. An example of cdparanoia in use is:

```
$ cdparanoia "1-4"
```

WARNING *In most countries, including the United States, performing DAE is legal, but only for personal use. For instance, you can create a backup CD, copy tracks to a personal MP3 player, or the like. It's not legal to distribute extracted files.*

For extracting anything more than one or two isolated tracks, chances are you'll want to use a GUI front-end to a DAE and compression tool. One very popular front-end is Grip (`http://www.nostatic.org/grip/`). This program includes `cdparanoia` code compiled into its binary, but it can use Cdda2wav or another DAE tool if you prefer. It requires an external encoder, such as `oggenc`, to do encoding. When you launch Grip and insert a CD, it reads the CD's contents and tries to identify it using an online database (at `freedb.freedb.org`, by default). If this operation is successful, Grip displays the CD's title, performer, and track titles, as shown in Figure 8.2. If not, track numbers are displayed. In either case, you can edit track titles and artist names by clicking the disc editor button in the main window (it resembles a pencil, near the middle of the bottom row of icons). The first time you run Grip, you may need to configure it from the Config tab, which in turn presents several sub-tabs. Of particular interest, the CD sub-tab enables you to specify what device to use to read CDs, the Rip sub-tab tells Grip what program to use for DAE functions, and the MP3 sub-tab configures the MP3 or Ogg Vorbis encoding software.

FIGURE 8.2

Grip is a powerful and popular MP3 and Ogg Vorbis encoder front-end.

To create MP3 or Ogg Vorbis files, right-click the titles you want to encode, click the Rip tab, and click the Rip+Encode button. This will do the job, but you must have a fair amount of space available on your disk—potentially a gigabyte or so, depending on the speed of your CD-ROM drive at DAE and the speed of your CPU for encoding.

NOTE Most computer CD-ROM drives aren't optimized for DAE, and some won't do DAE at all. Most take longer to perform DAE than they'd take to play the audio CD as such. Ripping and encoding a single CD can take several hours, even on a fast computer.

Using a Multimedia Player

Once you've created digital audio files, you probably want to play them on your computer. You can do so with the help of any of several multimedia players. Examples include:

ksmp3play This program is a text-based MP3 player. Read more about it at `http://www.xanadunet.net/ksmp3play/`.

mp3blaster This program is a text-based MP3 and Ogg Vorbis player. Read more about it at `http://www.stack.nl/~brama/mp3blaster.html`.

XMMS The X Multimedia System (XMMS) is a popular X-based MP3 and Ogg Vorbis player, similar in many ways to the popular Windows program WinAmp. It's based at `http://www.xmms.org`.

NOTE *Although the MP3 patent-holders allow free distribution of open-source MP3 players, some Linux distributions, including Red Hat, have removed all MP3 players. If you want to play MP3 files, you must add the appropriate software. Some players, such as XMMS, are modular, so you can either replace the entire package (which supports Ogg Vorbis but not MP3 files) or add a plugin to support MP3 files. The XMMS web page provides instructions.*

GUI audio players are usually modeled after conventional physical stereo hardware. Figure 8.3 shows XMMS in operation. This program uses three separate windows, which are arranged together as shown in Figure 8.3. Click the EQ (equalizer) and PL (play list) buttons in the main window to open and close the other two. You can open a play list (a file containing references to individual audio files) by clicking the Load List button in the lower-right corner of the play list window and selecting a play list from the file-selector dialog box. (Grip creates play list files as part of its operations.) You can then click the play button, which looks like a right-facing triangle, in the main XMMS window to begin playing the selections.

FIGURE 8.3

XMMS displays information about the files it plays and enables you to control playback using GUI tools.

Using Digital Camera Tools

Digital photography is displacing traditional film photography for many applications. You can buy a digital camera for anywhere from around $50 to well over $1000, depending on your needs. You can then download images from the camera to your computer, manipulate them in a graphics editor, and print the results to a high-resolution color printer. Many drug stores and malls now feature digital photography kiosks for even higher-quality prints, too. Unfortunately, most digital cameras ship only with Windows and Mac OS software, so to take advantage of these devices from Linux you need to locate an appropriate package. Fortunately, the Linux gPhoto program (`http://gphoto .sourceforge.net`) does an excellent job supporting a wide variety of cameras.

Picking a Digital Camera Package

There are several ways to extract digital photos from a camera. Many cameras use Compact Flash (CF) media, and Linux supports many CF media readers, treating them much like hard disks. Thus, you can move the CF card from a camera to a CF reader and use the reader to extract photos from the CF media. The cameras invariably use the FAT filesystem, so you should be able to mount the camera's media as if it were a FAT disk.

A few cameras are supported by tools that are tailored to specific digital cameras or chipsets—for instance, cameras built on a Fujitsu chipset are supported by code at `http://photopc.sourceforge.net`. You may need to search for packages for your specific camera if you can't get it to work with one of the major digital camera programs. A few digital cameras are supported by the Scanner Access Now Easy (SANE) package, which was described in Chapter 3, "Using External Peripherals."

The main Linux digital camera package is gPhoto. There are actually two variants of gPhoto: the original package (version 0.4.3) and a newer version, gPhoto2. The original gPhoto is a mono-lithic X-based program. The newer gPhoto2 breaks support down into multiple components—`libgphoto2` provides the underlying camera drivers and data transfer routines, `gphoto2` provides a command-line interface, and `gtkam` is an X-based interface program.

Both gPhoto and gPhoto2 support cameras that interface via the RS-232 serial port or the Universal Serial Bus (USB) port. To use the original gPhoto with USB cameras, you need support for your USB camera in the Linux kernel. Most Linux distributions ship with a number of camera drivers compiled as modules, but you may need to check this detail. By contrast, gPhoto2 requires that the kernel driver for your USB camera *not* be loaded; instead, gPhoto2 uses the USB device filesystem to directly access the USB camera. Using either package with an RS-232 serial port is comparatively straightforward—you need just standard RS-232 serial port drivers.

In all cases, you need to ensure that the user who accesses the digital camera has appropriate permissions on the interface. For RS-232 serial cameras, these are usually `/dev/ttyS?`, where `?` is a number—typically 0 or 1. USB cameras are usually accessible as files under `/dev/usb` (for example, `/dev/usb/dc2xx0` for a Kodak DC200-series camera). Many distributions ship without the appropriate device files defined for digital cameras, so you may need to create them using `mknod`, as in **mknod /dev/usb/dc2xx0 c 180 80**. Consult your driver's documentation (usually in `/usr/src/linux/Documentation/usb`) to learn what major and minor numbers (180 and 80 in the preceding example) to use. When using gPhoto2 with a USB camera, you need to enable USB access using the USB device filesystem. Unfortunately, this is a tedious process. It's described at `http://gphoto.sourceforge.net/doc/manual/permissions-usb.html`.

The gPhoto developers have officially abandoned the original gPhoto package in favor of gPhoto2; however, not all of the original gPhoto drivers are available in gPhoto2, as of version 2.1.1, and the `gtkam` program is still on the simple side. Configuring gPhoto2 to use a USB camera is an extremely tedious proposition, and it doesn't always work smoothly. For these reasons, I describe the use of the original gPhoto in the following pages. Eventually, gPhoto2 and `gtkam` will probably become the predominant digital photo package for Linux, though.

If you're in the market for a digital camera, you should take care to buy a model that's supported by gPhoto, gPhoto2, or some other program. A list of cameras supported by gPhoto2 is available at `http://gphoto.sourceforge.net/proj/libgphoto2/support.php`. The list for the original gPhoto is similar but not identical; a partial list appears in the `README` file distributed with gPhoto. Searching on Google Groups (`http://groups.google.com`) may turn up information on supported models, too.

Configuring gPhoto

Before launching gPhoto, you should connect your camera to your computer and turn on the camera. In the case of USB cameras, be sure you've got an appropriate device file entry for the camera. Mandrake with its device filesystem should create an entry in /dev/usb automatically; with other distributions, you may need to create one. When you first launch gPhoto, it will display a dialog box informing you of the fact that it couldn't find a configuration and that you must tell the program what camera you're using. You do this by selecting the Configure ➢ Select Port-Camera Model menu item, which brings up the Select Model/Port dialog box. Select your camera model from the drop-down list on the left of the dialog box and select the port used by your camera from the options on the right of the dialog box. If your camera uses a USB interface, you must type the device filename in the Other field. When you're done, click Save. If you see a dialog box advising you to check the device permissions, then the device file you specified might not exist or it might not have permissions that enable you to read from and write to it. You should correct this matter before proceeding further.

Some cameras provide additional options, which you can set from the Configure ➢ Configure Camera menu. These options may include functions such as the RS-232 serial port speed or the ability to set the camera's clock from your computer's clock. Other cameras provide no such options, so selecting this menu item displays a dialog box informing you of this fact.

Retrieving and Saving Photos

In most cases, you'll want to preview the photos stored on the camera before retrieving them. You can then select only those photos you want to retrieve, saving on transfer time. To view small thumbnail images, select Camera ➢ Download Index ➢ Thumbnails or click the Download Thumbnail Index item on the gPhoto icon bar. After a few seconds, a series of numbered preview images should appear, as shown in Figure 8.4.

To retrieve photos from your camera, you must first select the images you want to save. Click each image, or type Shift+A to select all of the photos. The borders around the images you select turn red. You can then retrieve the full photos in either of two ways:

- To retrieve images for subsequent manipulation within gPhoto, choose Camera ➢ Download Selected ➢ Images ➢ Open in Window or click the Download Selected Images icon. The program loads the images and makes them available via numbered tabs next to the Image Index tab. (Figure 8.4 shows two such tabs.)

- To retrieve images and store them directly on disk, choose Camera ➢ Download Selected ➢ Images ➢ Save to Disk or type Ctrl+G. The program responds by displaying a variant on a standard file selector dialog box, but instead of entering a single filename, you select a target directory and specify a filename *prefix*. gPhoto adds an index number and filename extension to each filename, enabling you to save multiple files in a single directory.

If you pick the first option, you can view the images by clicking their tabs. Many cameras produce pictures with resolutions higher than those produced by most monitors, though. Therefore, you may need to scroll to see the entire image, even if you maximize your gPhoto window. If you decide you want to keep an image, you can select File ➢ Save ➢ Opened Image(s) or click the Save Opened Image(s) icon. Using the resulting file selection dialog box, you can choose to save just the image you're viewing or all the images downloaded to that point. If you choose the former option, gPhoto saves the image to the filename you select; if you choose the latter option, gPhoto treats your filename as a prefix, as when downloading from the camera directly to disk.

Another method of saving photos is to print them. You can do this by selecting File ➢ Print, clicking the Print Image icon, or typing Ctrl+P after viewing an image by clicking its tab. gPhoto asks for a print command, which defaults to `lpr -r`. This command works fine in most cases, but you may need to add a printer destination or other options. For instance, to print to the `epson` printer, you would change the print command to `lpr -r -Pepson`.

FIGURE 8.4

gPhoto presents an index of images stored on the camera.

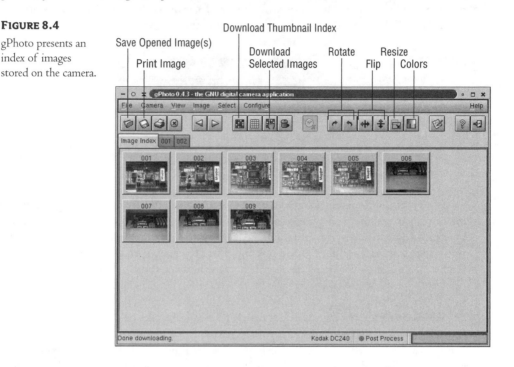

Manipulating Photos

Photos taken with digital cameras can frequently benefit from manipulations of various types. gPhoto provides facilities for performing some common manipulations. To make any of these changes, you must download an image into gPhoto and select it by clicking its tab. Changes you can make to photos before saving them include:

Rotations   You can use the Image ➤ Orientation ➤ Rotate Clockwise and Image ➤ Orientation ➤ Rotate Counter-Clockwise menu options, or the Rotate icons, to rotate an image if it appears sideways in the image preview window.

Flips   You can create a mirror-image reversal of the photo by using the Image ➤ Orientation ➤ Flip Horizontal and Image ➤ Orientation ➤ Flip Vertical menu options, or the equivalent Flip icons.

Resize   Three options under the Image ➤ Size menu enable you to resize the image: You can double the image's size, halve it, or change it to any value you like. (The final option is also available from the Resize icon.)

Color Balance   Sometimes the colors in a photo don't look right. You can adjust the color of the image by selecting the Image ➤ Color Balance menu item or by clicking the Colors icon. The result is the Color Adjustment dialog box shown in Figure 8.5. Click on one of the four color graphs on the right side of the image (one each for gray, red, green, and blue). You can then adjust the gamma, brightness, and contrast values for that color by moving the sliders under the color graphs. The miniature image on the left side of the dialog box displays the results of your manipulations. When you're satisfied, click Apply and then Close.

FIGURE 8.5

You can make basic color balance adjustments prior to saving a photo to disk.

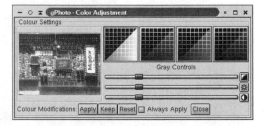

One common desirable manipulation is missing from gPhoto: cropping. In order to crop an image (say, to remove a telephone pole at the edge of a photo), you must use an external image manipulation program. Such programs frequently offer more obscure and sophisticated manipulations, too, such as the ability to add text and filters to create special effects. Therefore, it's well worth learning to use such programs, as described in the next section.

Using the GIMP

The GNU Image Manipulation Program (GIMP) is the premiere bitmap graphics program for Linux. It's very close to Adobe Photoshop in power, although of course the two programs have different strengths and weaknesses. The GIMP supports only the *red/green/blue (RGB)* color encoding used by monitors, whereas Photoshop also supports the *cyan/magenta/yellow/black (CMYK)* color encoding system used by printers. On the other hand, the GIMP supports a powerful scripting tool, Script-Fu, to help automate complex transformations.

This chapter describes some of the GIMP's basic features, including initial setup, loading and saving images, adding elements to images, working with layers, and applying filters. The GIMP is powerful enough that entire books have been written about it. If you need a more complete reference than I can provide here, read a book such as Bunks' *Grokking the GIMP* (New Riders, 2000), or consult the program's online manual (`http://manual.gimp.org`).

Launching the GIMP

You can launch the GIMP by typing **gimp** in an **xterm** window. Many distributions also create icons or menu entries in their GNOME and KDE setups to launch the GIMP from a desktop environment or by double-clicking graphics files in file browsers.

The first time you launch the GIMP, it runs through a setup routine in which the program creates various configuration files. During this process, the program creates a directory called `.gimp-1.2` in your home directory (this subdirectory name will be different if you're not using a 1.2.*x* version of the GIMP). This directory in turn holds a large number of subdirectories in which you can store scripts, patterns, and so on.

The GIMP will also ask you to set system-specific parameters, including:

Tile Cache Size The *tile cache* is a fixed-size area of memory in which the GIMP manipulates images. If this size is too large for your system, the GIMP may cause a lot of swap activity. If it's too small, the GIMP may perform poorly on complex images. The default value of 32MB is fine in most cases, but you may want to increase or decrease this value if your system has lots or very little RAM.

Swap Directory Data that doesn't fit into the tile cache is stored on disk in a swap directory. The default value is `~/.gimp-1.2`, but you might want to change this to `/tmp` or `/var/tmp`. Doing so will enable your distribution's automatic routines for cleaning up these temporary directories to remove any files that are left over in the event of a program crash. On the other hand, if space on the `/tmp` or `/var/tmp` partition is limited, leaving the swap directory at its default may be wiser.

Monitor Resolution If you want to have the GIMP display images at precise on-screen sizes, the program must know your monitor's resolution, in terms of horizontal and vertical dots per inch. The easiest way to do this is to click the Calibrate button. The GIMP then displays a large dialog box with horizontal and vertical rulers, which you measure with a physical ruler. You enter the actual measurements and the GIMP sets its monitor resolution data accordingly.

Once the GIMP has collected this information, it displays a set of windows, as shown in Figure 8.6. Clockwise from the top-left corner, these dialog boxes are the main GIMP window; the Tool Options dialog box; the Brush Selection dialog box; the Layers, Channels, and Paths dialog box; and the Tip of the Day dialog box. If you uncheck the Show Tip Next Time GIMP Starts option in the Tip of the Day dialog box and click Close, it won't appear on subsequent startups. Some of these dialog boxes will change as you select different tools and options in the main window.

FIGURE 8.6

The GIMP provides several windows to control its many features.

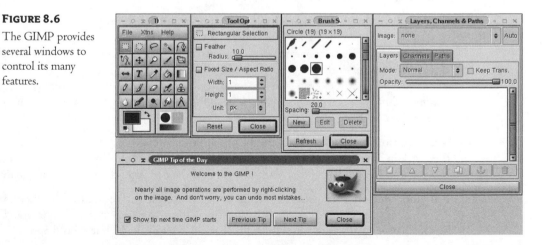

Loading Images

If you want to work on an existing image, you can do so by picking File ➢ Open from the main window's menu. The GIMP displays a file selection dialog box in which you pick a file. Alternatively, you can launch the GIMP and specify a filename at the same time, as in typing `gimp image.jpg` to work on `image.jpg`. Many file managers support linking graphics to file types or drag-and-drop operations, and you can use these features to launch the GIMP and have it load a file automatically.

The File ➤ Acquire menu is likely to present one or more options for acquiring images directly from some source. One option that's almost certain to be present is File ➤ Acquire ➤ Screen Shot, which loads the contents of a window or of the entire screen as an image. Another series of options that may be present load an image from a scanner. Chapter 3 describes this option in more detail.

If you want to create a new image, pick File ➤ New from the main menu. The GIMP responds by asking for an image size, which may be expressed in pixels or in a physical measurement (inches, centimeters, or so on). You can also specify that the image is to be color (RGB) or grayscale.

However you load or create an image, the GIMP opens it in a new window. If the image is too large to fit on the screen, the GIMP scales the image downward to fit, but it retains the entire image in memory. Many image-specific options are accessible only by right-clicking in the image window. This action presents a context menu with several options and more sub-options.

Painting with the GIMP

If you examine the GIMP's main window in Figure 8.6, you'll see that it's composed of a menu bar, a 5 × 5 array of icons, and two color-selection areas. You can use the icons to select tools with which to "paint" on and otherwise manipulate an image. The tools can be grouped into several categories:

Region Selectors   The top row of five icons and the leftmost icon on the second row enable you to select a region in several different ways. You can select rectangular or elliptical regions, irregular hand-drawn regions, auto-detected regions by borders, regions defined by Bezier curves, or shapes defined by a combination of control points and image contours. After you select a region, you can apply operators to that region alone, such as filling only a region with a color or removing the contents of that region from the image.

Region Operators   The second and fifth icons on the second row and the first icon on the third row enable you to manipulate regions in various ways—you can move them, rotate them, or flip them horizontally or vertically. These three operators require that you first select a region with one of the region selector tools. The fourth icon on the second row, which resembles a scalpel, enables you to crop or resize an image. Unlike the other region operators, cropping requires you to select the region *after* selecting the crop operator. You can only crop to a rectangular region.

Text Addition   The second icon on the third row (a letter *T*) adds text. Select this operator and then click in the image where you want text to appear. The GIMP displays a dialog box in which you select a font, font style, and font size. You also type the text you want to appear in the Preview field.

Fills and Gradients   The last two icons on the third row enable you to fill a region with a solid color or with a gradient. Fills operate on parts of the image that are clearly bordered by other areas. To apply a gradient, you must first select the region to which it should apply.

Freehand Drawing   Most of the icons on the final two rows enable you to create freehand drawings using various tools, each of which emulates the effect of a common physical art tool—a pencil, a paint brush, an eraser, and so on. You can adjust various parameters for each of these tools, such as the opacity and thickness of the lines they create, using the Tool Options and Brush Selection dialog boxes.

Color Selectors   You can use the two large fields at the bottom of the GIMP's main window to select colors and patterns. The left icon enables you to set foreground and background colors; it defaults to black and white. Click the black or white rectangle to open a color selector, in which you can pick a new color. The bottom-right area in the GIMP's main window lets you select a brush (it opens the Brush Selection dialog box that opens by default when the GIMP starts), a fill pattern, and a gradient type. The middle icon in the 5×5 icon matrix is a color picker; select it, then click anywhere in an image to "pick up" that color as the foreground color.

Miscellaneous Tools   The third icon on the second row (resembling a magnifying glass) zooms or shrinks the image. You can use this tool to better handle detailed pixel-by-pixel work. The fifth icon on the fifth row activates a measurement tool. You can use this tool to measure distances and angles.

Hands-on experience is best when learning to use the GIMP's tools. Therefore, I recommend that you create a new image and experiment with these tools. You'll soon learn much of what you can accomplish with the GIMP, in terms of creating new graphics from scratch. These tools, though, are just the beginning; much of the GIMP's power derives from its use of more advanced techniques, including layers and filters. With these techniques, you can modify an image you create or acquire from another source in ways that would be tedious to the point of impossibility with ordinary drawing tools such as those accessible from the GIMP's main window.

Working with Layers

One of the problems with most bitmap graphics formats is that it's difficult to manipulate individual components in the image. For instance, you can't easily move a circle from one location to another. Although many graphics programs, including the GIMP, do provide cut and paste operators, they cut and paste everything in the selected area—for instance, both the circle you want to move and any objects "beneath" the circle. If the circle is opaque, cutting it and moving it elsewhere will leave a big gap in the image.

One solution to this problem is to use a drawing program that operates on discrete objects. Drawing programs are frequently components of office suites, as described in Chapter 7, "Using Linux for Office Productivity," and there are also stand-alone drawing packages, such as Xfig (`http://www.xfig.org`). Drawing packages are seldom well adapted to working with bitmap graphics, though. If you want to manipulate digital photos, scans, screen shots, or other bitmap graphics, another solution is needed, and the GIMP provides one: layers.

Layers are individual bitmaps that you can move and otherwise manipulate within an image. For instance, if you want to create a screen shot with added text to highlight specific windows, buttons, or other features, you can use one layer for the screen shot proper and one layer for each text element or line. You can then move the text elements around on the display until they look good. The GIMP remembers the entire underlying screen shot and so can restore the part of the image that had been under the text elements when you moved them. Essentially, each layer is an independent bitmap image that combines with others into a greater whole.

One of the primary tools in manipulating layers is the Layers, Channels & Paths window (the upper-right window in Figure 8.6). Operations you can perform with layers include:

Creating New Layers   To create a new layer, you can right-click on an existing layer in the Layers, Channels & Paths window and select New Layer from the context menu, or click the New Layer button, which resembles a single sheet of paper. The result is the New Layer Options dialog box, in which you set the size of the layer, its name, and its fill type (how it interacts with other layers). When you first create text, the text is in a special type of layer known as a *floating selection*. You can click this layer in the Layers, Channels & Paths dialog box and click New Layer to make it a regular layer, or select Anchor Layer to tie the text to the background layer.

Moving Layers   To move a layer, pick the Move Layers & Selections tool in the GIMP's main window (the second icon on the second row). You can then select the layer in the Layers, Channels & Paths dialog box, hold down the Shift key, and move the layer by clicking it and moving it in the drawing window.

Change Layer Order   When more than two layers are present in the Layers, Channels & Paths dialog box, you can select one and move it in relation to the others by clicking the up and down arrow buttons. This action will affect which layers obscure which others in the final image.

Changing Layer Opacities   Select a layer in the Layers, Channels & Paths dialog box and adjust the Opacity slider to make it more or less opaque.

Merging Layers   You can merge the visible layers (those with eye icons next to them in the Layers, Channels & Paths dialog box) by picking the Layers ➤ Merge Visible Layers option from the context menu. You can merge all layers by using the Layers ➤ Flatten Image option.

You can use layers in many different ways. Layers of varying opacity can create double-exposure effects or add one image to another—for instance, you can add an image of the full moon to the sky in a night photograph, or create many other special effects. You can merge layers created from cut-out portions of one image to create special color effects for only parts of an image. Layers enable you to easily position elements such as text callouts on an image.

One important detail relates to saving images with layers. The GIMP's native file format, XCF, supports layers; but most other file formats, including common ones such as the Joint Photographic Experts Group (JPEG) and Tagged Image File Format (TIFF), don't support layers. Therefore, you must *flatten* an image to a single layer before saving in these formats. To do so, right-click in the image and pick Layers ➤ Flatten image from the context menu. You'll then be able to save the image in these common file formats. Recent versions of the GIMP can flatten an image automatically while saving it to a format that doesn't support layers, so you can save to such a format without flattening the original.

TIP   *Before flattening an image, save it in the GIMP's native format. That way, if you need to further manipulate the layers, you can do so.*

Applying Filters

The GIMP includes many built-in *filters* that enable you to easily create assorted special effects. These filters fall into several categories:

Blur   Blur filters introduce a controlled blurring of the image. You might use these to soften the outline of an artificial shadow or to de-emphasize wrinkles or other imperfections in a portrait.

Colors   Color filters add or modify colors throughout the image. Some of these effects can also be achieved through items on the Image ➤ Colors context menu.

Noise   These filters add random elements to the image, simulating effects such as film grain or television static.

Edge Detect   Edge detection creates an image that emphasizes the edges of an object, similar to a line drawing. Using edge detection can be an important first step in some advanced uses of layering; you use the original image as one layer and the edge-detected image as another that you can manipulate.

Enhance   Enhancements allow you to correct some types of problems in the original image. Examples include despeckle (which softens film grain and similar effects) and sharpen (which sharpens a blurry image).

Generic   This category is devoted to advanced filters best described through mathematics.

Glass Effects   You can distort your image so that it looks as if it had been photographed through an extreme wide-angle or other type of lens or mirror with these effects.

Light Effects   These effects apply simulated lens flare, glare, and similar light effects.

Distorts   These filters twist, warp, and otherwise distort the image. You can create artificial water ripples, curve text into a circular shape, and so on with these filters.

Artistic   You can make an image look like a painting in various media or styles with these filters.

Map   These filters map one image onto another using complex rules. For instance, you can take an image such as a two-dimensional world map and wrap it around a virtual sphere, creating what is effectively an image of a globe.

Render   This category is broad; it includes assorted effects that create new layers or impose elements designed to resemble common natural features on the image.

Web   The Web Image Map filter is designed to help create an image map for web page navigation.

Animation   Various filters support creating animations—files that consist of several images designed to be viewed in succession, creating an animation effect.

Combine   You can merge multiple files together in various ways with these filters.

These filters deliver a lot of power, and learning what they do takes time and experience. I recommend you try these filters out on a variety of images. Also, keep in mind that you can apply most filters to just part of an image by first selecting the target portion. For instance, you might warp some text to create an unusual effect for a poster, but leave a photograph for the same poster untouched.

Saving Images

When you're done modifying your image, you should save it. You can do this by right-clicking in the image and selecting File ➢ Save or File ➢ Save As. The former option saves the file to its original filename, while the latter enables you to enter a new filename. You can choose to save to any of a wide variety of file formats, but some formats don't save all of the information. Specifically, most file formats don't preserve the GIMP's layers, so you must flatten the image before saving a multilayer image.

NOTE   The GIMP's save option is accessible only from individual images' context menus, whereas the load option is also accessible from the GIMP's main window's menu bar.

Some file types present you with additional save options after you click the OK button in the Save Image dialog box. For instance, JPEG images use a lossy compression scheme, so when you save an image as a JPEG, you must specify the quality (on a scale from 0.00 to 1.00) and various other options. Setting a higher quality (say, 0.90) results in less loss of detail, which may be important for images that should be reproduced as close to perfectly as possible. Lower quality settings (say, 0.40) may be acceptable for web page graphics, which don't usually need to be perfect reproductions of the original and should be kept small to reduce load time and network bandwidth use.

Optimizing Linux Web Browsers

Many users find web browsers to be indispensable. The World Wide Web (WWW or Web for short) has become a valuable research tool; many companies and organizations place a great deal of information on their web pages. The Web has also become an important channel for commerce, with retailer websites popping up all over the world. Getting the most from the Web begins with choosing a web browser; a bad choice can make for a bad Linux web browsing experience. One common problem with web browsing in Linux is the use of poor web fonts, but you can take steps to improve this matter. Finally, for all its power and utility, the Web has also become a security minefield. If you're not careful, your private information, including very sensitive data such as credit card numbers, can fall into the wrong hands. Many organizations also try to track your online activities in ways you might not like. You can avoid a lot of problems by understanding these privacy and security issues and configuring your web browser to avoid problems.

Choosing a Web Browser

Web browsers differ in several respects. Most critically, web browsers use a variety of *rendering engines*—the core routines that interpret the Hypertext Markup Language (HTML) files that make up most web pages. Some web pages rely upon HTML features or even quirks of particular rendering engines, and such web pages may not look good on other web browsers. Different browsers also differ in the features that surround their rendering engine cores, such as their method of displaying multiple open pages, tools for manipulating bookmarks, and so on.

January of 1998 marked a watershed event for Linux web browsers: At that time, Netscape announced that it would make the source code for its Navigator web browser available under an open source license. Netscape is a huge program, and so it took the open source community as a whole a while to digest this code, but Netscape's rendering engine (Gecko) has been adopted by many other browsers. Therefore, in effect there are two classes of web browsers for Linux: those built atop Gecko and those with their own unique engines. Some of the most important browsers in both categories are listed here:

Galeon This program, headquartered at `http://galeon.sourceforge.net`, is a Gecko-based web browser that's officially part of the GNOME Office suite. It's designed as a lightweight GUI web browser.

Konqueror This KDE program serves a dual function: It's both a web browser and a file manager. Konqueror does a good job with most web pages. It's fairly lightweight, and so is well worth trying, particularly if you use KDE. You can read more at `http://www.konqueror.org`.

Lynx Most web browsers are GUI programs that display text in multiple fonts, show graphics inline, and so on. Lynx (`http://lynx.browser.org`) is unusual in that it's a text-based web browser. As such, it's a useful choice if you run Linux in text mode or if you don't want to be bothered with graphics. Lynx is also useful as a test browser when you develop your own web pages—if a page is readable in Lynx, chances are visually impaired people who browse the Web with speech synthesizers will be able to use your page.

Mozilla   This program, headquartered at `http://www.mozilla.org`, is the open-source version of Netscape. This Gecko-based browser may be the most popular Linux web browser. It's also a huge program that can take many seconds to launch, even on a fast computer.

Netscape Navigator   This program is the commercial version of Mozilla, and it too is a huge Gecko-based program. Netscape is still free in the sense of being available at no cost, but most Linux distributions ship with Mozilla. If you'd rather run "real" Netscape, you can find it on the main Netscape website, `http://www.netscape.com`.

Opera   An unusual commercial entrant in the Linux web browser sweepstakes, Opera (`http://www.opera.com`) claims to have the fastest rendering engine available. Opera features a scaling feature that enables you to enlarge or shrink a web page, which is great for ill-behaved sites that set their margins to absolute values wider than your browser window. You can download a free version that displays banner ads in its icon bar or pay a registration fee to rid yourself of the ads.

Notably absent from this list is Microsoft's Internet Explorer, which overtook Netscape in popularity in the late 1990s. Unfortunately, some websites just won't work with anything but Internet Explorer. If you must access such sites, you may need to run Internet Explorer in an emulator, as described in Chapter 10, "Using Multiple OSs." Other sites are somewhat picky, but they can work with at least one Linux browser. Thus, you should probably install at least two Linux web browsers. If you install just two, I recommend one Gecko-based browser (such as Galeon, Mozilla, or Netscape Navigator) and one non-Gecko browser (such as Konqueror, Lynx, or Opera).

Those interested in slim browsers should stay away from Mozilla and Netscape, both of which are quite memory-hungry. Although Opera claims to have the fastest rendering engine, you're not likely to notice huge differences between it and other browsers. All of these browsers offer a wide array of configuration options, some of which are important and some of which aren't.

Improving Web Fonts

One common complaint from new Linux users is that the fonts look bad when browsing the Web. To some extent, this matter can be remedied by improving the quality of the fonts made available by X, as described in Chapter 16, "Optimizing X Configuration." Once you improve your X fonts, your web browsing fonts should improve as well.

One other problem is web-specific, though: Many web pages refer to fonts that may not be installed on your system. When a browser encounters a request for such a font, it substitutes another font—often the rather ugly Courier. Many web pages refer to fonts that are common on Windows systems, such as Times New Roman and Verdana. Microsoft commissioned some of these fonts specifically for use on the Web, so they look very good at typical screen resolutions. Originally, Microsoft made the fonts freely available on its website, but it withdrew them from this form of distribution in August of 2002. You can install these fonts in Linux if you also run Windows on the same computer or you are otherwise licensed to use them—say, if you've installed and run Microsoft Office via an emulator. Doing so can be tedious, though. Various websites, such as `http://corefonts.sourceforge.net`, provide instructions and files to help with this process.

Another approach is to map the standard Microsoft fonts onto fonts that are likely to be installed in your system. Specifically, the standard Microsoft fonts Times New Roman, Arial, and Courier New are quite similar to the standard Linux fonts Times, Helvetica, and Courier. You can perform this mapping by creating new entries for existing fonts, changing only the font name to match the name provided by the web pages that aren't displaying properly. When you encounter such a page, use your browser's "view page source" option to view the HTML it's rendering. You should then search for a font face tag, which might look like this:

```
<font face="comic sans">
```

This tag specifies that a font called *Comic Sans* should be used, so you should create a definition for such a font, even if it points to another font. Your web browser will then display the font you specified.

Another fix for this problem is to tell your browser to ignore web pages' font-change tags. This option is usually in the font configuration area for your browser. For instance, in Mozilla, you would pick Edit ➢ Preferences from the main menu, then go to the Appearance ➢ Category area of the Preferences dialog box (as shown in Figure 8.7) and uncheck the Allow Documents to Use Other Fonts option. This configuration will set your browser to use only the fonts you specify, which may be preferable to attempting to match the potentially wide array of fonts specified by web pages.

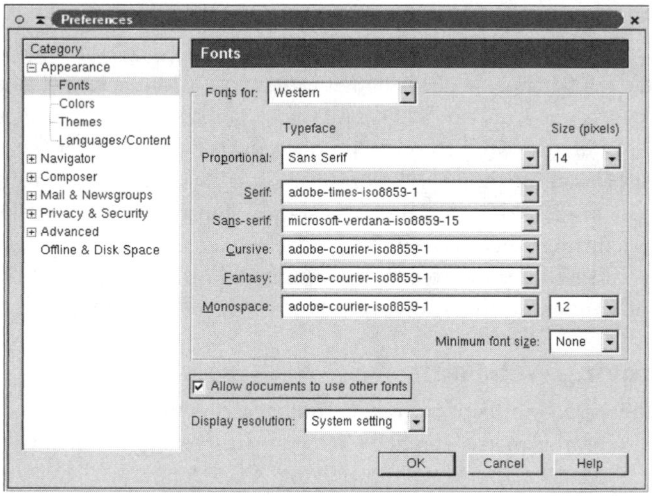

FIGURE 8.7

Most web browsers enable you to specify default fonts and disable use of other fonts.

Protecting Your Privacy and Security

Fundamentally, the Web is a file-transfer medium: Your web browser asks a web server for a document, which the web server delivers to your computer. At this level of analysis, there's very little to concern you regarding security and privacy. Unfortunately, the Web has grown very complex, and those with ill intentions can abuse complex web browser features to break into your computer, steal sensitive data, display unwanted and annoying content, or track your online activities. You can take some steps to improve your chances of avoiding abuse, but some of these actions can be limiting or complicated to set up. At the very least, though, you should be aware of the issues and the risks you take when you browse the Web.

MINIMIZING JAVA AND JAVASCRIPT RISKS

Most modern web browsers support Java and JavaScript, which are programming languages often associated with web pages. JavaScript code can be embedded within a web page, and a JavaScript-enabled web browser will run the JavaScript code automatically. Java programs aren't embedded within web pages, but they are run from them via links. In both cases, enabling their use is a potential landmine; a malicious individual could create a web page that does unfriendly things and make it available to the public.

If you would like to reduce the risk from unfriendly Java or JavaScript code, you must locate the options that enable these features in your browser and disable them. For instance, in Mozilla, pick the Edit ➤ Preferences menu item to bring up the Preferences dialog box. The Java option is in the main Advanced category, and the JavaScript option is in the Advanced ➤ Scripts & Plugins area. The latter area is shown in Figure 8.8.

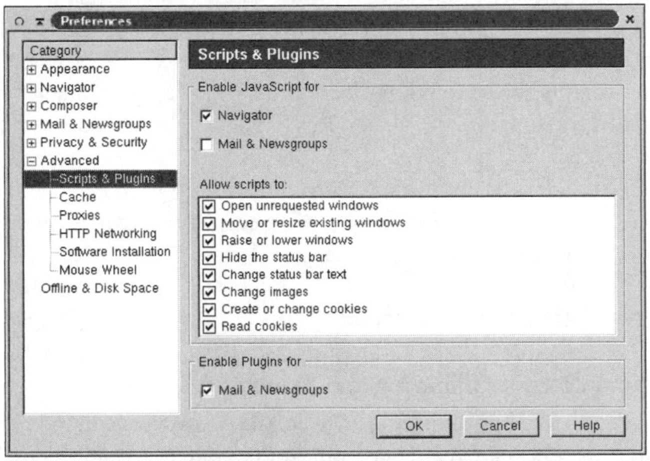

FIGURE 8.8

You can disable features such as Java and JavaScript in a web browser's configuration dialog box.

Unfortunately, disabling Java and JavaScript will likely render some web pages useless. A large number of web pages rely on JavaScript for routine operations, and some use Java for vital features, as well. Some web browsers enable you to fine-tune some Java or JavaScript features. For instance, the Mozilla Preferences dialog box shown in Figure 8.8 provides options to allow or disallow certain Java-Script actions, such as opening unrequested windows or reading cookies. If you leave Java and JavaScript enabled, you might want to disable at least some of these actions. Some features, such as opening unrequested windows, are used primarily by a rising bane of web surfers everywhere—*pop-up ads*, which appear in windows atop your browser window.

TIP   You may want to lock down one web browser and use it whenever possible. You can leave another one configured to use Java and JavaScript, and use it only for those sites that require these features.

ATTENDING TO ENCRYPTION

Some websites—particularly online retailers, banks, and other sites that deal with financial data—provide the option to encrypt data transfers. This encryption uses the Secure Sockets Layer (SSL) protocol. Most web browsers provide a small padlock icon, usually in a status bar near the top or bottom of the window, to indicate whether a page uses SSL encryption. If the padlock icon is closed, encryption is enabled; if it's open, encryption is disabled. Many browsers also come configured to pop up a dialog box that informs you whenever you enter or leave an encrypted site.

Before you send sensitive data, such as credit card numbers, you should check to be sure that the site is using encryption. If it's not, somebody at a site between you and the web server could intercept the communication and steal your data. If a retailer doesn't offer an encrypted order form, you should consider ordering by telephone or buying from another retailer.

WARNING *Sensitive data can be stolen even if you use a secure website. For instance, retailers' databases have been compromised and credit card numbers stolen from them. Of course, similar risks exist even when you shop at brick-and-mortar retailers. The point is that SSL encryption is not a security panacea.*

SSL encryption works through the use of encryption *keys*. These keys are digital "signatures" provided by one of a handful of companies set up to provide them. Web browsers ship with a number of certificate authorities' (CAs') keys built in. If a website uses one of these CA's keys, the web browser accepts the encryption. Sometimes, though, you'll run across a site that uses a CA that's not recognized by your browser. When this happens, your browser will display a dialog box informing you of this fact and giving you the option of proceeding with the transaction or aborting. As a general rule, it's safest to abort the transfer; an unrecognized key could signal a compromised server—somebody could have broken in or redirected web traffic in an effort to steal sensitive data. It's also possible that the key is valid, but that your browser doesn't recognize it—say, because your browser is old and hasn't been updated with the latest keys. Therefore, you may want to use a more recent browser to perform the transaction.

FILTERING CONTENT USING A PROXY SERVER

The Web is becoming an increasingly hostile environment in many respects. Some of these relate to security, but others are matters of obnoxious content. Examples include banner ads, pop-up ads, pornography, and graphic violence. You might want to filter such content from your web browsing, to save your own sanity, to prevent your children from being exposed to inappropriate material, or to reduce employee time wasted on such material. The question is how to do this. Some web servers provide partial solutions. For instance, Mozilla can prevent JavaScript from opening unrequested windows, which are used almost exclusively by pop-up ads, as described in the earlier section, "Minimizing Java and JavaScript Risks." For the most part, though, the solution lies in the use of a *proxy server*, which is a server program that sits in-between your web browser and the ultimate web server system. The proxy server can then filter out certain types of content, typically based on sites that it knows serve the objectionable material or on Uniform Resource Locators (URLs) that contain giveaway keywords, such as `ads`.

The first step in using a proxy server is in setting one up. Many are available, each tailored to a specific need. Popular examples include:

Privoxy This content-filtering proxy server is based on the older Internet Junkbuster and is designed to eliminate banner and pop-up ads as well as tame cookies (see the next section, "Managing Cookies") and other privacy-degrading web features. Read more at `http://www.privoxy.org`.

Squid   The Squid proxy (`http://www.squid-cache.org`) is designed primarily as a speed enhancer for midsized to large sites. By retaining recently accessed web pages, the proxy can return subsequent requests for the same site more rapidly than a true site access. Squid is extremely flexible, though, and add-on packages enable it to serve as a content filter.

SquidGuard   This package is an add-on that adds content filtering features to Squid. You can use it to filter ads, porn, Java, and even JavaScript. You can read more at `http://www.squidguard.org`.

DansGuardian   This program is another Squid add-on that can be used to filter ads, porn, hate speech, and other objectionable content. Rather than use a list of "banned" URLs, DansGuardian works by scanning each web page for content, which means it requires less frequent updates to its rules than some other filters. Its web page is `http://dansguardian.org`.

You should read the instructions for the proxy server to learn how to configure and install it. If you want to block access by people who might want to get around the proxy (say, employees or children), you should run the proxy server on a separate computer and use `iptables` (described in Chapter 20, "Controlling Network Access") to prevent direct access to web servers from anything but the proxy server computer.

TIP   *You can use a Linux proxy server to protect non-Linux systems running on the same network as the Linux system.*

Once the proxy server software is running, you must normally reconfigure your web browser to use it. You can do this from your browser's configuration tool. For instance, in Mozilla, you would pick Edit ➤ Preferences to open the Preferences dialog box, and then select the Advanced ➤ Proxies category within that dialog box, as shown in Figure 8.9. Select Manual Proxy Configuration, enter the hostname of the proxy server in the HTTP Proxy field, and enter the port on which the proxy server runs in the matching Port field. (Most proxy servers run on port 8000 or port 8080 by default.) Some proxy servers handle SSL (secure web server) transactions, FTP transactions, and so on, so you should enter the server's hostname and port number for these protocols, if appropriate. If you're not blocking all normal outgoing web access, you can enter exceptions in the No Proxy For field. Some websites simply don't work well through a proxy, so these exceptions may be necessary.

FIGURE 8.9

All major web browsers enable you to specify one or more proxy servers to use instead of direct access.

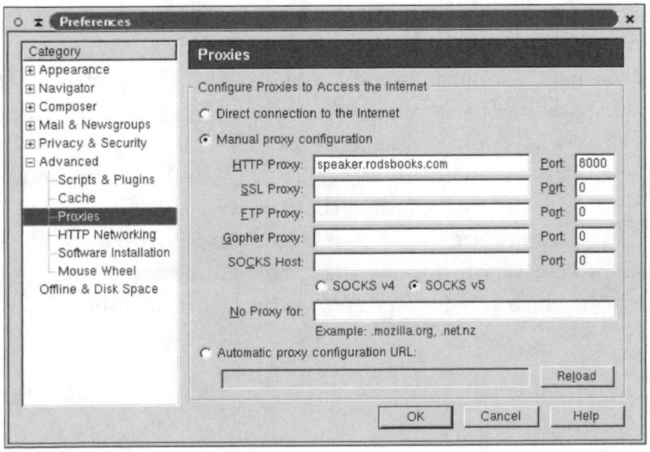

MANAGING COOKIES

Some types of web transactions require that the server be able to track a user, at least over a limited period of time. For instance, when you buy a product at a web-based retailer, the retailer must know that the person who submits a credit card number is the same person who ordered the copy of *Moby Dick* and *Heathers*. One way to perform this tracking is to use a feature known as a *cookie*. This is a code that the web server asks your browser to store, either temporarily or permanently, as a means of identification. When you begin entering items into a web page's shopping basket, the retailer's web server asks your browser to store a cookie. When you perform subsequent actions, the web server asks for the cookie back, enabling it to track who's ordering what. Cookies can also be used over the long term to enable identity tracking in order to simplify or even eliminate the need to "log in" to web pages that require authorization, such as subscription-based sites.

Unfortunately, cookies can be a powerful tool for those who wish to track your online activities across many sites. For instance, an advertiser might associate cookies with its banner ads, which appear on many sites. The advertiser can then tell which of those sites you've visited. What's more, a handful of companies dominate web-based advertising, so you can be tracked in this way even when the sites you visit carry very different ads. Many people consider the collection of such a database of information on their activities intrusive at best.

One way to manage cookies is to examine the cookie files themselves. For instance, Mozilla stores cookies in the `cookies.txt` file in the `~/.mozilla/default` directory or an oddly-named subdirectory of that directory, such as `sysog9b8.slt`. You can examine this file to learn who's been planting cookies on your system, and edit it to remove unwanted cookies. Unfortunately, this step is temporary—when you revisit a site, its cookies will be added back to your system, although they'll be new cookies unassociated with your original cookies. Also, some web browsers' cookie files aren't easily interpretable. Opera uses a binary format for its cookies, for instance. A more extreme trick is to set up the cookie file as a symbolic link to `/dev/null`, but this practice is extreme—it means that your system won't remember any cookies. All of these techniques apply only to permanent cookies, which the website tells your browser to store on disk. Many sites also use temporary cookies, which last only as long as the browser is running. Modifying the cookie file won't affect these temporary cookies.

Some proxy servers, such as Privoxy, are designed to intercept and selectively filter cookies, thereby blocking their introduction on your computer. Sometimes these measures can go too far, though—they can block not only privacy-degrading cookies but those required for a web page's normal operation, such as those used by Internet retailers' shopping carts.

Yet another cookie-management tool is the web browser itself. Today's browsers include various cookie-management tools, such as those shown in Figure 8.10 from Mozilla's Preferences dialog box. You can enable all cookies, disable all cookies, or set various restrictions on them. For instance, you might enable cookies only for the originating website, which can foil some tracking done by third-party advertisers. In theory, having the browser ask you before accepting cookies may sound good, but in practice you'll see several cookie requests per page for some web pages if you pick this option, so it can become very tedious very fast. Some browsers, such as Opera, enable you to specify the servers from which you'll accept cookies, and refuse all others.

FIGURE 8.10

Setting the appropriate cookie options can help you protect your privacy on the Web.

Choosing and Using Linux E-Mail Clients

In years past, people used telephones, faxes, and physical mail to communicate with colleagues, friends, and family. Today, e-mail has taken over at least some of the roles of each of these earlier methods of communication. As Linux has long supported network communications, it shouldn't come as any surprise that Linux supports a wide array of e-mail packages. Configuring these tools is little different from setting up e-mail packages in other OSs. It's important to understand some features of e-mail as practiced in the early twenty-first century, though. These features include attachments and various issues relating to e-mail security.

Picking an E-Mail Reader

Dozens of e-mail clients exist for Linux, and they provide features to meet just about any need. Some of the more popular programs include:

Balsa   This program, headquartered at `http://balsa.gnome.org`, is officially part of the GNOME Office suite. Its user interface resembles that of the Windows program Eudora, and its features include all the standard fare for modern e-mail clients.

Evolution   The Ximian Evolution package (`http://www.ximian.com/products/evolution`) is another GNOME Office component, but Evolution's scope is much broader that that of Balsa. Modeled after Microsoft's Outlook, and even able to share data files with Outlook (via the use of intermediary file formats), Evolution includes scheduling, contact management, and other features not found in most e-mail clients.

KMail   The KDE project's main mail reader is KMail (`http://kmail.kde.org`), and it is normally installed as part of the `kdenetwork` package. This program is roughly similar to Balsa in overall scope, but it integrates well with other KDE packages; for instance, it uses the KDE address book.

Mutt   This program is a powerful text-based mail program. Many Linux users prefer using Mutt to the flashier GUI programs such as Evolution or KMail, but Mutt may be intimidating to new users or those who are uncomfortable with text-based tools. You can learn more at `http://www.mutt.org`.

Netscape E-mail   The Netscape Communicator package includes the Navigator browser and other components, including an e-mail client. Mozilla includes a similar e-mail client. Therefore, if you normally keep Netscape or Mozilla open, you may find these e-mail clients convenient.

Pine   Another popular text-based mail client is Pine (`http://www.washington.edu/pine/`). Pine is similar in general scope to Mutt, but Pine is the older program. It has been used on text-based Unix systems for a long time, so users of such systems should find it familiar.

Sylpheed   This mail reader, headquartered at `http://sylpheed.good-day.net`, is built using the GIMP Toolkit (GTK+), and it integrates well with GNOME. It's designed for speed, and it provides all the usual GUI mail reader features.

Configuring an E-Mail Client

GUI mail clients frequently launch into configuration screens the first time they're run. If yours doesn't, the configuration tool can be accessed from a menu option, such as Sylpheed's Configuration ➤ Create New Account (see Figure 8.11) or KMail's Settings ➤ Configure KMail. Text-based programs are typically configured through text files, such as Mutt's `~/.muttrc`.

FIGURE 8.11

You must tell your mail reader how to send and receive mail.

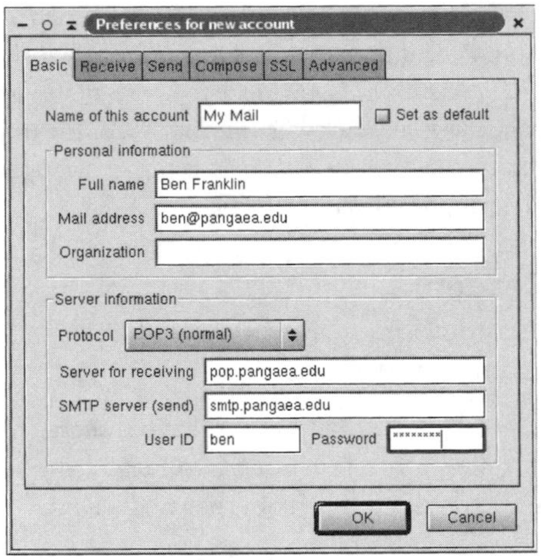

Mail readers must know how to send and receive mail. Some mail readers—especially text-based programs—default to using the local mail queue. This default setting works well if your Linux system is permanently attached to the Internet and runs its own mail server. Most desktop systems, though, don't run their own mail servers, or at most, run a mail server only for outgoing and local mail. Therefore, you must usually tell the mail program about yourself and your mail configuration. Specific data you may need to provide includes:

Account Information   You may need to tell the program what name and address to associate with outgoing mail. In Figure 8.11, you enter this information in the Full Name and Mail Address fields. You may also need to name the mail account you're configuring—that's the Name of This Account field in Figure 8.11. If you use multiple mail accounts—say, one for each of several ISPs you use—the ability to handle multiple accounts from one program can be handy.

Incoming Mail Server   You can configure most mail clients to read mail from the local mail spool, from a Post Office Protocol (POP) server, or from an Internet Message Access Protocol (IMAP) server. In the latter two cases, you must specify the server name (in the Server for Receiving field in Figure 8.11), a username (in the User ID field), and a password (in the Password field). Some mail readers and protocols provide additional receive options. These are accessible from the Receive tab in Figure 8.11.

Outgoing Mail Server   When you send mail, the mail reader must know how to do the job. Many mail readers default to using the `sendmail` program on the local computer, which is usually a mail server that can accept and send mail. Some workstations and networks aren't configured to allow such access, though, so you may need to specify another mail server. In Sylpheed (see Figure 8.11), this is done in the SMTP Server (Send) field. Some mail readers provide additional options on a tab such as Figure 8.11's Send or Advanced tabs.

NOTE   Not all mail readers provide all the primary options described here in a single dialog box or tab, as shown in Figure 8.11. You may need to open multiple dialog boxes or click multiple tabs to configure all the necessary features.

If you're not sure what to enter for any of this basic information, consult your ISP or network administrator. As described in the upcoming section, "Combining Many Mail Accounts: Fetchmail," you can configure your system to provide your mail via a local account even when you must use one or more external POP or IMAP servers.

Using and Abusing Attachments

E-mail is fundamentally a text-based medium. Mail messages are sent using normal alphanumeric characters, punctuation, and a few other symbols. Today, though, there's a great demand to send and receive non-textual data in mail messages—digital photos, sound files, spreadsheets, and so on. (Even word processing documents usually include non-text formatting bytes.) *Attachments* are a way around the text-only e-mail limitation. These use special types of encoding and separators to convert non-textual data into a textual form. All but the most primitive Linux mail programs support attachments. You can easily attach files you want to send or save attachments others send to you. There are some caveats, though:

HTML Issues   One common form of attachment is HTML text. Many mail readers can parse HTML, providing varied fonts, text colors, embedded graphics, and other features common on web pages. Unfortunately, HTML brings a host of problems with it, including privacy, size, and security concerns. For this reason, many people prefer not to receive HTML, and you should be cautious about HTML mail you receive from others—especially from strangers. Many mail readers provide options to enable or disable the parsing of HTML in mail messages.

Privacy Issues   If you enable HTML in your e-mail, and if your mail reader automatically displays graphics loaded from the Internet by HTML e-mail, your reading of e-mail may be tracked. This feat is accomplished by the sender incorporating an HTML *bug* in the mail—a reference to a small graphics file stored on a website. When your mail reader accesses the bug, the web server notes the fact, allowing the sender to track who's reading the mail and when.

Size Issues   Attachments can consume a lot of space. Binary files converted to attachments are larger than their originals; for instance, a 60KB file will be 80KB as an attachment. Therefore, if you want to transfer large files, using FTP or some other binary-transfer protocol will likely use less network bandwidth. HTML mail is frequently sent in both HTML and plain-text form, and the HTML tags take up space that wouldn't be used in the plain-text version.

Security Issues   Beginning in the late 1990s, e-mail readers regularly spawned security problems, and many of these issues are related to attachments. Many of these problems involve poor security settings in Microsoft's Outlook and Outlook Express programs, but Linux users shouldn't feel too smug; it's conceivable that somebody will eventually develop an e-mail virus that will exploit a weakness in a Linux mail client, especially one that's configured to automatically render HTML. You should never trust the contents of attachments sent from unknown sources, or even unexpected attachments from trusted sources; some e-mail viruses of the past have pillaged victims' address books to find subsequent victims. Security problems have been found even in nonprogram file types, so even graphics or audio files could harbor viruses.

Overall, attachments are very convenient tools for communication, but they pose security risks. I recommend using them with caution. You should disable HTML rendering in your mail reader, if it provides an option to do so. Don't blindly open an attachment, even if it's from somebody you know, unless you were expecting the attachment. If bandwidth is at a premium, choose another transfer method, or at least compress your files with `gzip` or `zip` before sending them. (Some file types, such as JPEG graphics, are precompressed.)

Combining Many Mail Accounts: Fetchmail

If you have many mail accounts, you may find configuring and checking them all in your mail clients to be tedious. You might also want to use two or more mail readers—say, a text-based client for when you're not using X, and a GUI client for other times. In such a situation, your mail-reading life would be much simpler if you could combine all your mail accounts into one. Linux provides a tool that enables you to do this: Fetchmail (`http://catb.org/~esr/fetchmail/`). This program is a mail client, but instead of enabling you to read the mail, it forwards it on to another account. A Linux computer that uses Fetchmail will typically use it to read mail from one or more external POP or IMAP accounts and inject the mail into the local computer's mail spool. You can then use mail readers configured to access the local mail spool, or even re-export the mail using your own POP or IMAP server.

For more information on Fetchmail, consult Chapter 25, "Delivering E-Mail."

Summary

Linux provides many tools that enable its use as a rich desktop productivity station. You can create and play audio files, extract images from digital cameras, edit graphics files, use web browsers, and handle e-mail from Linux. These tools supplement the core office productivity tools described in Chapter 7, making Linux an environment suitable for more than the dry server and scientific number-crunching tasks with which it's often associated.

Part III

System Administration Tools

## Chapter 9

Bypassing Automatic Configurations to Gain Control

As OSs HAVE GROWN more complex, configuration tools have become more commonplace. The average person who uses a computer to browse the Web, balance a checkbook, and send e-mail to Aunt Mathilda doesn't want to learn about dozens of configuration files, their syntax, their options, and so on. Much of the early success of Apple's Macintosh derived from the fact that it provided simple configuration tools—GUI control panels. By contrast, the Macintosh's main competitor at the time, DOS, used comparatively hard-to-configure text files such as CONFIG.SYS and AUTOEXEC.BAT. In its early years, Linux was configured exclusively by manually editing its configuration files. Today, though, a variety of text-mode and GUI configuration tools exist. These tools enable you to configure a Linux system by answering a few relatively simple questions, clicking option buttons, and so on.

Unfortunately, these automatic configuration tools aren't perfect. They sometimes get things wrong or don't let you configure the features you need to set. They also vary substantially from one distribution to another, which can make describing them in a cross-distribution book such as this one difficult. As a result, bypassing these automatic configuration tools is often desirable or even necessary. Once you do so, you can dig into the system's text-based configuration files to make the changes that are hard or impossible to make with the supposedly user-friendly default tools.

The Perils of Automatic Configurations

Standard Linux installations place a set of default configuration files on the system. Most of these files reside in the /etc directory tree and, except in cases of severely broken installation scripts, unsupported critical hardware, or similar serious problems, the default configuration files work well enough to boot the computer. Sometimes, though, these configurations fail seriously enough to cause problems, albeit not badly enough to prevent the system from booting. Likewise, the configuration tools provided with the distribution often work well enough to get a subsystem functioning partially, but not completely. Sometimes these tools fail altogether. Understanding these failures can help you to work around them, so this section summarizes four failure types:

- Incorrect identification of hardware or of another system component

- Incorrect configuration

- Inflexible configuration options

- Overzealous configuration tools

Incorrect Identification

Sometimes a configuration tool simply fails to recognize that your system has a particular hardware or software component. If you've installed a depended-upon package without the benefit of the package tool, this type of problem is common when installing software via package managers, as described in Chapter 11, "Managing Packages." This problem is also somewhat common when dealing with hardware configuration, particularly with older Industry Standard Architecture (ISA) cards, very new cards, or otherwise exotic hardware. Sometimes the system recognizes that you've got a given type of hardware, but it misidentifies the specific type. This problem can be particularly irksome when combined with inflexibility in options, as described in the upcoming section, "Inflexible Options."

Some configuration tools suffer from another problem: Incomplete identification. In this case, the problem isn't that the configuration tool has narrowed the field of options incorrectly, it's that the field isn't narrowed at all. For instance, Figure 9.1 shows the web-based configuration tool for the Common Unix Printing System (CUPS), which is described in more detail in Chapter 13, "Managing Printers." At the point shown in Figure 9.1, you're supposed to pick a printer port from the available options—all 25 of them. (Some systems present even more options.) This particular computer has just two printers attached to it, and it even lacks the device files associated with some of the options shown in Figure 9.1. Of course, this particular problem isn't alleviated by bypassing an automatic configuration tool. If anything, it's made worse—you must know more about your available devices than you would need to know when using a configuration tool. Nonetheless, as the configuration tool is supposed to make things easier for new administrators, presenting confusing or nonexistent options can be a problem.

As a general rule, bypassing an automatic configuration tool can help avoid problems with failure of identification by enabling you to force the issue. If the system insists on configuring your Mega-Sound audio card as a GigaSound card, you can dig into the configuration files and correct the matter. Of course, doing so requires that you know where to go digging—a topic that's covered in subsequent sections of this chapter. You must also know how to correct the problem—a topic that's covered in other chapters of this book.

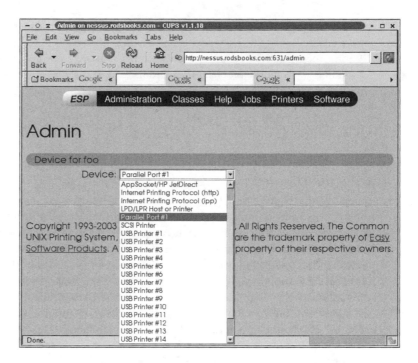

FIGURE 9.1

Some configuration tools present too many options to administrators.

Incorrect Configuration

Although misidentification can be a serious problem, one that's just as common is incorrect configuration. Many configuration files have sensitive formats—for some, a misplaced space or comma can spell the difference between a working configuration and one that doesn't work. As a general rule, computer programs are good at getting such details right, but this isn't always the case. Furthermore, some configurations rely on very specific information for particular hardware or software. For instance, you may need to pass particular options to a kernel module to get it to work, but other kernel modules may require different options. Therefore, automatic configuration tools often use databases of configuration options, and if these databases are flawed, the tool may fail.

As an example, consider Samba, which handles the Server Message Block/Common Internet File System (SMB/CIFS) file- and printer-sharing protocol that's common on Windows-dominated networks. Several GUI Samba configuration tools exist, the most flexible of which is the web-based Samba Web Administration Tool (SWAT). SWAT handles most configurations correctly, but it corrupts a specific type of configuration. Samba supports splitting configuration files into parts. The main file then uses an `include` directive to tell Samba to load referenced files. Unfortunately, SWAT doesn't know what to do with the `include` directive. Early versions of SWAT ignored that directive. Using such versions of SWAT, if you create a Samba configuration that relies on `include` and then try to modify that configuration using SWAT, you'll lose all the `include` references, which may cause subtle or not-so-subtle problems. Later versions of SWAT merge the included file into the main file but leave the `include` directive intact, which is likely to result in a working configuration;

however, if you fail to notice the change, you might make subsequent changes by hand that won't be implemented.

Some incorrect configurations are fairly small. These can be easy to fix—*if* you know where to look and how to fix the problem. Other tools tend to make a real mess of things, and such problems can be tedious to correct.

TIP   Once your system is working fairly well, back up the entire /etc directory tree, ideally to a removable disk. If an automatic configuration tool mangles a configuration file, you should then be able to restore the original relatively easily.

Inflexible Options

Some configuration tools are just overly simplistic—they don't support changing enough of the features of a product to make using the tool worthwhile. A similar problem is a tool that doesn't allow you to override its defaults. For instance, Figure 9.2 shows Red Hat's sound card detection tool. After launching this tool, the system returns information about any sound card that it has found. You can click the Play Test Sound button to hear if the system has detected the sound card correctly. If you don't hear a sound, the tool provides nothing in the way of options to try to correct the matter. You can't select another sound card from a list, modify driver module options, or take any other corrective measures. Your only choices at this point are to abandon any attempt to get the sound card working or to dig into configuration files and modify them manually.

FIGURE 9.2

Some configuration tools provide inadequate configuration options.

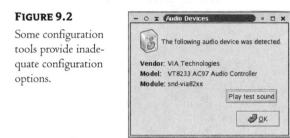

Even when a device works correctly in a simple case, it may present inadequate options for more complex configurations. For instance, many distributions include configuration tools that greatly simplify setting up Ethernet interfaces. Some of these tools, though, don't handle a second interface very well. They may lack any options for configuring a second interface, or they may provide some options but lack the finesse required to configure the second interface in the way that might be required for your application, such as setting up the computer as a router.

Overzealous Configuration Tools

Another class of problems relates to configuration tools that are overzealous in one way or another. Typically, these tools overwrite existing configuration files without just cause, and sometimes without asking you whether it's acceptable to do so. One common source of such problems is upgrading software packages, and especially servers and other system software. For instance, you may have spent hours creating the ideal Apache web server configuration. When you use `rpm`, `apt-get`, or some other tool to upgrade to the latest version, you discover that you've lost your changes because the replacement package included a new default configuration file that overwrote the original. Fortunately, both RPM and the Debian package system can mark configuration files as such. When the system installs a package, it backs up your existing configuration files by renaming them with a new extension, such as `.rpmsave`. Nonetheless, the need to go in and swap in your own working configuration file can be annoying. If a package is built incorrectly, it may lack the configuration file flag, causing your originals to be lost.

Some tools change the original configuration files, or other aspects of a system's configuration, when you run them—even if you don't ask for these changes to occur. For instance, Mandrake includes a package called Mandrake Security (`msec`), which periodically checks assorted directories for preconfigured levels of security. If the tool finds a problem, such as too-permissive permissions on a directory, the tool corrects the problem. This practice is a good one overall, but if you, as an informed and intelligent system administrator, don't want this tool changing your directory permissions without warning or even notification, you must dig into the tool's configuration and change it. Other tools might run even when you don't ask them to do so, or they might make changes beyond those you'd expect. For instance, it's becoming increasingly common for programs to try to add themselves to KDE, GNOME, and other environments' menus after they're installed. This practice might be fine if the tools do their jobs correctly, but sometimes they might delete entries for programs you've added manually, or they might create multiple entries for themselves if they run multiple times. Such problems can be difficult to track down, because it might not be obvious which program made the unauthorized changes. In the end, the best defense is to make backups of all your configuration files—both system files in /etc and user configuration files, which are generally dot-files in users' home directories.

Automatic Setup Mechanisms by Distribution

In order to bypass default configurations or those created by configuration tools, you must know where to look for these configuration files. All major Linux distributions place system configuration files in /etc, and there are certain commonalities beyond this detail. Each distribution's configuration has unique features, though, and you must understand these features to effectively configure your system.

Common Configuration Files

The traditional location for system configuration files in Unix-like systems is /etc, and Linux is no exception to this rule. Indeed, many obscure packages, including some that don't even ship with most distributions, install their configuration files in /etc. As a result, this directory's contents vary from one system to another, and I cannot describe every file or subdirectory it contains. Table 9.1 summarizes some of the most important files and subdirectories found in /etc on most distributions, though. Subdirectories are indicated by a trailing slash (/) in the name.

TABLE 9.1: COMMON FILES AND SUBDIRECTORIES OF /etc

FILE OR SUBDIRECTORY NAME	FUNCTION
bashrc, bash.bashrc, or bash.bashrc.local	System-wide default bash configuration file.
cron.d/, cron.daily/, cron.hourly/, cron.monthly/, cron.weekly/, crontab	Configuration files for system cron jobs; crontab controls cron, and the subdirectories hold scripts that execute on a regular basis.
csh.cshrc, csh.cshrc.local, csh.login, and csh.logout	System-wide default csh configuration files.
cups/	CUPS configuration files.
exports	Control file for Network File System (NFS) server.
fstab	Filesystem table file; describes filesystems, their mount points, and their options.
group	Specifies Linux groups and their options.
hostname or HOSTNAME	Holds the local computer's hostname.
hosts	Maps hostnames to IP addresses. Frequently used for local hostname/IP address mapping in lieu of a local DNS server.
hosts.allow and hosts.deny	Part of TCP Wrappers; specify what systems may or may not contact servers that use TCP Wrappers for security.
hosts.equiv	Lists computers that may access any of several servers, such as rlogin and BSD LPD print servers. Using this file is potentially dangerous; it should be empty, and more server-specific files used instead.
hosts.lpd	Lists computers that may access BSD LPD print servers.
httpd/ or apache/	Directory holding web server (Apache) configuration files.
inetd.conf	Configuration file for the inetd super server.
init.d/	Subdirectory holding SysV startup scripts. This is a subdirectory of /etc/rc.d on some systems.
inittab	Initial startup file; the kernel uses this file to control the very early stages of the boot process. After booting, this file controls the critical init process.
lilo.conf	The configuration file for the Linux Loader (LILO) boot loader program used by many Linux installations on IA-32 hardware.
logrotate.conf and logrotate.d/	Specify how the logrotate program, which is run daily via cron, is to handle log file rotation.

Continued on next page

TABLE 9.1: COMMON FILES AND SUBDIRECTORIES OF /etc *(continued)*

FILE OR SUBDIRECTORY NAME	FUNCTION
modules.conf	Defines the kernel modules that the system should attempt to load when programs try to access particular devices.
mtab	Holds information on mounted filesystems.
named.conf	Primary configuration file for the Berkeley Internet Name Domain (BIND) Domain Name System (DNS) server.
pam.d/	Directory holding configuration files for the Pluggable Authentication Modules (PAM) tool, which mediates most user login requests.
passwd	Primary user account definition file. (The shadow file usually holds actual passwords and additional data, though.)
ppp/	Directory in which Point-to-Point Protocol (PPP) dial-up networking account information and scripts are stored.
printcap	File specifying printer capabilities, used primarily by the BSD LPD and LPRng printing systems.
profile and profile.d/	Default bash login script and subdirectory with additional component scripts that may be called.
rc?.d/	Subdirectories holding SysV startup scripts for specific runlevels (? is the runlevel number). May be subdirectories of rc.d or init.d.
rc.d/	Subdirectory holding SysV startup scripts, possibly in their own sub-directories. Sometimes this is a symbolic link to /etc/init.d.
samba/ or samba.d/	Subdirectory holding configuration files for the Samba file and print server package.
services	File holding mappings of names to port numbers for common servers.
shadow	Shadow password file; holds encrypted user passwords and advanced account information in a file that's readable only to root.
ssh/	Holds configuration files for the Secure Shell (SSH) login server.
sysconfig/	Contains miscellaneous system configuration files, such as files holding network configuration options. SysV startup scripts typically reference these files.
X11/	Holds configuration files for the X Window System (X) and some related subsystems, such as X-based login tools.
XF86Config or XF86Config-4	Main XFree86 configuration file. This file often appears in /etc/X11.
xinetd.conf and xinetd.d/	Configuration file and subdirectory for the xinetd super server.

Table 9.1 is long, but even so, it doesn't present all of the configuration files and subdirectories in a typical Linux system. On the flip side, some of these files and directories aren't present on some Linux systems; for instance, if you haven't installed SSH, your system most likely won't have an /etc/ssh directory.

The /etc/inittab file is particularly critical for the system startup procedure. It defines certain processes that run constantly, such as getty or a similar program, which attaches itself to a text-mode console and runs the login program to accept text-mode logins. Just as important, inittab kicks off the rest of the startup process, through a line beginning with si. In a Red Hat system, this line is as follows:

```
si::sysinit:/etc/rc.d/rc.sysinit
```

Effectively, this line passes control of the startup process to /etc/rc.d/rc.sysinit—but the name of this script varies from one distribution to another, as detailed in the next few sections. Another detail set in /etc/inittab is the default *runlevel*—a number that serves as a code for a particular set of default servers and other programs to run. The runlevel is set in a line that begins with id, as in:

```
id:5:initdefault:
```

This line sets the runlevel to 5. Runlevels 0, 1, and 6 have special meanings and should never be specified in /etc/inittab. Most Linux distributions use runlevel 3 to mean a text-mode startup and runlevel 5 to mean a GUI startup. Slackware uses 4 instead of 5 for GUI startups, though, and Debian uses other means to determine when to perform a GUI startup.

Most Linux distributions use a startup script system borrowed from System V Unix, and hence referred to as *SysV startup scripts*. These scripts are stored in /etc/init.d, /etc/rc.d, or a subdirectory of one of these directories. Typically, subdirectories called rc?.d, where ? is the runlevel, hold symbolic links to the startup scripts for specific runlevels. Within each runlevel's directory, scripts whose names start with S are used to start a service, and those whose names start with K shut down (kill) a service when the system enters that runlevel. The upcoming section, "Creating New SysV Startup Scripts," describes the SysV startup script naming convention in greater detail. Some distributions use major or minor variants on this system, as detailed in the next five sections. Slackware is the most unusual of these variants.

Debian

Debian tends to shun specialized system administration tools. The Debian installer, of course, places a set of default configuration files in /etc, and some packages come with scripts that ask questions to help tune a configuration for your system. You can also use configuration tools that ship with or are written for specific packages, such as SWAT; or more general tools, such as Linuxconf (http://www .solucorp.qc.ca/linuxconf/) or Webmin (http://www.webmin.com). In general, though, when you administer Debian you do so by directly editing the relevant configuration files; there is, therefore, no need to bypass any automatic configuration tool that might try to modify your changes itself.

NOTE   *Commercial Debian derivatives, such as Libranet (http://www.libranet.com) and Xandros (http://www.xandros.com), generally include more in the way of GUI administrative tools that may modify configuration files.*

Of course, Debian has its own unique configuration quirks. Some of Debian's notable features that differ from some or all other Linux distributions include:

System Startup Procedure   Debian's `/etc/inittab` calls `/etc/init.d/rcS` as the system initialization script. This script calls the startup scripts in `/etc/rcS.d` and any scripts in `/etc/rc.boot` (the latter is intended for local startup scripts, but its use is officially discouraged). Debian's `init` then switches to the runlevel specified in `/etc/inittab` and runs `/etc/init.d/rc`, which runs the startup scripts in the appropriate SysV startup script directory.

Location of SysV Startup Scripts   Debian places its SysV startup scripts in `/etc/init.d` and places links to these files for specific runlevels in `/etc/rc?.d`, where `?` is the runlevel number.

Runlevels and Starting X   There are few differences between runlevels 3–5 in Debian, except that runlevels above 3 provide just one text-mode virtual terminal. Instead of using a runlevel as a code for whether or not to start X and present an X Display Manager Control Protocol (XDMCP) GUI login screen, Debian uses SysV startup scripts for each of the major display managers. You can set which to start by default in the `/etc/X11/default-display-manager` file.

cron   Debian's default `cron` configuration includes an `/etc/crontab` file that calls files in the `/etc/cron.`*`interval`* directories, where *`interval`* is `daily`, `weekly`, or `monthly`, at the stated intervals, and between 6:25 A.M. and 6:52 A.M.

Super Server   Debian uses `inetd` by default, although `xinetd` is also available.

Mail Server   Debian is the only major Linux distribution to use Exim as its default mail server. It's configured through `/etc/exim/exim.conf`. When you install Exim, the Debian package tools run a script that asks some basic questions to set up an initial Exim configuration.

Modules   One of Debian's few deviations from the automatic configuration rule is that it uses a tool called `update-modules` to create an `/etc/modules.conf` file. This tool assembles files it finds in the `/etc/modutils` directory tree into `/etc/modules.conf`. The easiest way to deal with this system is to change the files in `/etc/modutils` or add new files to it, rather than directly editing `/etc/modules.conf`. Consult the `update-modules` man page for more details.

Network Configuration   Debian uses the `/etc/init.d/networking` SysV startup script to start basic networking features. This script relies on variables stored in files in the `/etc/network` directory tree. Therefore, permanently changing some networking details requires editing these files.

Local Startup Files   If you want to change something about the system configuration that doesn't fit well in the default script set, you can create a script and place it in the `/etc/rc.boot` directory. Debian executes scripts in this directory after running the `/etc/rcS.d` scripts but before running the scripts for the startup runlevel. Debian's official documentation suggests creating SysV startup scripts and placing them in `/etc/rcS.d` or another SysV startup script directory, though.

As a general rule, Debian's configuration files are straightforward to adjust if you're used to text-based configuration. The SysV startup scripts work as they do on most Linux distributions. Local startup files are a bit odd if you're used to Red Hat, Mandrake, or SuSE; however, once you put a local startup script in `/etc/rc.boot`, you can modify it as you like.

Mandrake

Mandrake ships with a tool called the Mandrake Control Center, which can be launched from the standard menus in KDE or GNOME or by typing **drakconf** in a shell. If you launch it as an ordinary user, it prompts for the **root** password to continue. This program is a typical GUI configuration tool. It provides categories of configuration options in a list along the left side of its window. When you click one of these categories, the tool displays a set of specific configuration tools in the right side of the window, as shown in Figure 9.3. Click one of these tools, and it will open in the right side of the window or in a separate window, providing subsystem-specific options.

FIGURE 9.3

The Mandrake Control Center displays one or more configuration tools for each configuration category.

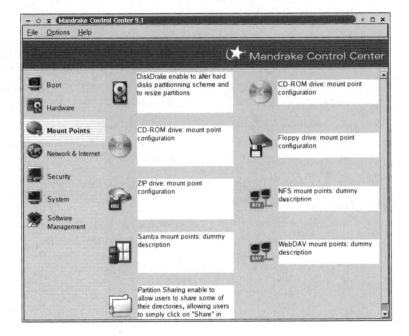

Mandrake also ships with a variety of more specialized configuration tools, such as the rpmdrake tool for managing packages. The Mandrake Control Center can launch many of these tools itself. Many of these tools can modify files in /etc, but you can modify these files manually if you prefer. Some Mandrake-specific details include:

System Startup Procedure   Mandrake's /etc/inittab calls /etc/rc.d/rc.sysinit as the system initialization script. This script performs a large number of basic initialization tasks, such as mounting the device filesystem, setting the system clock, and so on. Mandrake's init then switches to the runlevel specified in /etc/inittab and runs the startup scripts in the appropriate SysV startup script directory by calling /etc/rc.d/rc.

Location of SysV Startup Scripts   Mandrake places its SysV startup scripts in /etc/rc.d/init.d and places links to these files for specific runlevels in /etc/rc.d/rc?.d, where ? is the runlevel number.

Runlevels and Starting X   Mandrake uses the dm SysV startup script to start X and an XDMCP GUI login screen. This script is called using the name S30dm in runlevel 5 (causing the display manager to start) and using the name K09dm in runlevel 3 (causing the display manager to shut down). The dm script in turn calls /etc/X11/prefdm, which reads /etc/sysconfig/desktop and uses the variable DISPLAYMANAGER to determine which XDMCP server to run.

cron   Mandrake's default cron configuration includes an /etc/crontab file that calls files in the /etc/cron.*interval* directories, where *interval* is hourly, daily, weekly, or monthly, at the stated intervals. Except for the hourly run, these scripts run between 4:02 A.M. and 4:42 A.M.

Super Server   Mandrake uses xinetd by default. The /etc/xinetd.conf file is the master configuration file, while /etc/xinetd.d holds files for specific servers that xinetd is to handle.

Mail Server   Mandrake ships with Postfix as the default mail server. It's administered through files in /etc/postfix.

Network Configuration   Mandrake uses the /etc/rc.d/init.d/network SysV startup script to start basic networking features. This script relies on variables stored in the /etc/sysconfig/network and (for PC Card devices) /etc/sysconfig/pcmcia files and files in the /etc/sysconfig/networking and /etc/sysconfig/network-scripts directories. Therefore, you must edit these files to permanently change some networking details.

Local Startup Files   If you want to change something about the system configuration that doesn't fit in well in the default script set, you can edit the /etc/rc.d/rc.local script. This script executes after the conventional SysV startup scripts.

Using the Mandrake Control Center can help new administrators and those unfamiliar with Mandrake's version of Linux to configure some basic system features. If you launch this tool accidentally, be sure to tell it to ignore any changes (by clicking Cancel or other abort buttons), should it ask you about committing your changes to the system.

Red Hat

Red Hat uses a number of small configuration tools, most of which are accessible from the Server Settings, System Settings, and System Tools menu off of the GNOME Applications menu, as shown in Figure 9.4. These tools are also accessible from the Start Here icon on the default Red Hat desktop. Each of these tools provides a way to configure a specific feature, such as the network or sound card. (Figure 9.2 shows Red Hat's sound card detection tool.) If you log in as an ordinary user but need to administer the system, you can do so, but the tool will ask for the root password when you select it. The system remembers the password for a while, so calling other configuration tools soon after the first won't result in a new root password prompt.

Red Hat's startup procedure and configuration file locations are quite similar to those of Mandrake. This fact shouldn't be surprising because Mandrake used Red Hat as its starting point and, as a result, the two distributions share a common heritage. With every new release, though, Red Hat and Mandrake deviate more. Some of the important configuration files in Red Hat include:

System Startup Procedure   Red Hat's /etc/inittab calls /etc/rc.d/rc.sysinit as the system initialization script. This script performs a large number of basic initialization tasks, such as mounting the device filesystem, setting the system clock, and so on. Red Hat's init then switches to the runlevel specified in /etc/inittab and runs the startup scripts in the appropriate SysV startup script directory by calling /etc/rc.d/rc.

FIGURE 9.4

Red Hat makes its administrative tools accessible from menus on its default desktop configuration.

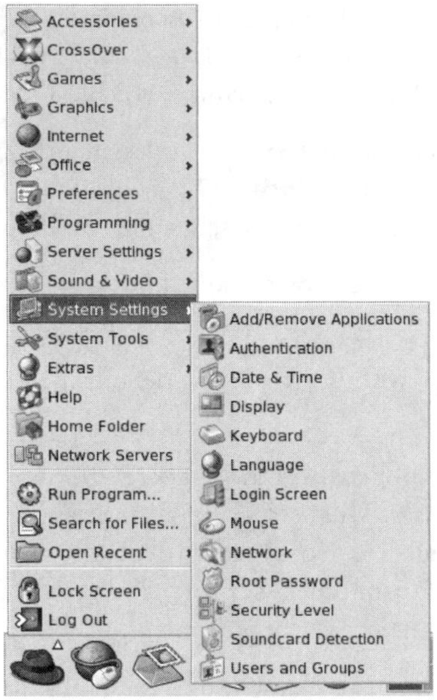

Location of SysV Startup Scripts   Red Hat places its SysV startup scripts in `/etc/rc.d/init.d` and places links to these files for specific runlevels in `/etc/rc.d/rc?.d`, where *?* is the runlevel number.

Runlevels and Starting X   Red Hat uses a line in `/etc/inittab` to start an XDMCP server, and hence X, in runlevel 5. This line calls `/etc/X11/prefdm`, which reads `/etc/sysconfig/desktop` and uses the variable `DISPLAYMANAGER` to determine which XDMCP server to run.

cron   Red Hat's default `cron` configuration includes an `/etc/crontab` file that calls files in the `/etc/cron.interval` directories, where *interval* is `hourly`, `daily`, `weekly`, or `monthly`. Except for the hourly run, these scripts run between 4:02 A.M. and 4:42 A.M.

Super Server   Red Hat uses `xinetd` by default. The `/etc/xinetd.conf` file is the master configuration file, while `/etc/xinetd.d` holds files for specific servers `xinetd` is to handle.

Mail Server   Red Hat ships with `sendmail` as the default mail server. It's administered through files in `/etc/mail`.

Network Configuration   Red Hat uses the `/etc/rc.d/init.d/network` SysV startup script to start basic networking features. This script relies on variables stored in the `/etc/sysconfig/network` file and files in the `/etc/sysconfig/networking` and `/etc/sysconfig/network-scripts` directories. Therefore, you must edit these files to permanently change some networking details.

Local Startup Files   If you want to change something about the system configuration that doesn't fit in well in the default script set, you can edit the `/etc/rc.d/rc.local` script. This script executes after the conventional SysV startup scripts.

For the most part, bypassing Red Hat's default or GUI-created configurations poses no special challenges; just edit the relevant configuration files by hand. If you accidentally launch a GUI configuration tool, select Cancel or another appropriate option to quit without saving the changes.

Slackware

Like Debian, Slackware doesn't rely on GUI configuration tools, although you can install tools such as Linuxconf or Webmin after the fact, just as with Debian. Some of Slackware's startup and configuration files are unusual compared to those of other Linux distributions, which can make moving from Slackware to another distribution or vice-versa a bit disorienting. Important Slackware configuration files include:

System Startup Procedure   Slackware's /etc/inittab calls /etc/rc.d/rc.S as the system initialization script, followed by /etc/rc.d/rc.M to initialize multiuser features. (When booting to single-user mode, Debian runs /etc/rc.d/rc.K.) Debian's init then switches to the runlevel specified in /etc/inittab, but unlike other distributions, Slackware's runlevels are controlled through single startup scripts called /etc/rc.d/rc.?, where ? is the runlevel number. In practice, the only runlevel of consequence is 4, as described next. (The rc.6 script reboots the system. A link to it, called rc.0, shuts down the system.)

Runlevels and Starting X   The standard Slackware startup scripts boot the system into text mode. If you want to start X and use an XDMCP login screen, change the runlevel to 4 in /etc/inittab. This action causes init to run /etc/rc.d/rc.4 on its next boot, which starts an XDMCP server. The script tries gdm first, followed by kdm and then xdm.

cron   Unlike most distributions, Slackware doesn't place a crontab file in /etc; instead, it relies on the root file in /var/spool/cron/crontabs. This file runs scripts in the /etc/cron.*interval* directories, where *interval* is hourly, daily, weekly, or monthly. Except for the hourly scripts, these run between 4:20 A.M. and 4:40 A.M.

Super Server   Slackware uses inetd by default, and it does not ship xinetd as an option. If you want to use xinetd, you must obtain it from another source, such as the xinetd home page (http://www.xinetd.org).

Mail Server   Slackware uses sendmail as its default mail server. The configuration files are in /etc/mail.

Network Configuration   Slackware uses the rc.inet1 and rc.inet2 files, both in /etc/rc.d, to initialize networking functions. The rc.inet1 file initializes network interfaces and includes information such as your IP address (if you use a static IP address), so you must edit this file to permanently change your network settings. The rc.inet2 file starts common network servers.

Local Startup Files   If you want to change something about the system configuration that doesn't fit well in the default script set, you can add commands to the /etc/rc.d/rc.local script, which is designed for system-specific configuration changes. This script is run from the end of the /etc/rc.d/rc.M script.

As a general rule, adding servers or other automatically run programs to Slackware entails adding entries to /etc/inetd.conf or /etc/rc.d/rc.local, rather than adding SysV startup scripts, as is common with other Linux distributions. In principle, you could edit other startup scripts, but it's usually cleaner to keep most startup scripts as they are and make changes to rc.local. One important exception to this rule is /etc/rc.d/rc.inet1, which holds local network configuration information.

SuSE

SuSE provides a pair of system configuration tools, YaST and YaST2. The former is text-mode, and the latter is GUI; however, they're quite similar in capabilities. I refer to them collectively as *YaST* for simplicity's sake. Navigating YaST is much like navigating Mandrake's Control Center; you select configuration tools from a hierarchical list. In YaST2 (as shown in Figure 9.5), tool categories appear in the pane on the left of the window, and individual tools are on the right.

A few of SuSE's features are a bit odd compared to most other Linux distributions, but they are not nearly as unusual as Slackware's files. You must be familiar with these oddities in order to modify configurations manually. Important scripts and configuration files include:

System Startup Procedure   SuSE's /etc/inittab calls /etc/init.d/boot as the system initialization script. This script calls the startup scripts in /etc/init.d/boot.d and the /etc/init.d/boot.local file (the latter is intended for local startup scripts—those created by the system administrator). SuSE's init then switches to the runlevel specified in /etc/inittab and runs the startup scripts in the appropriate SysV startup script directory.

Location of SysV Startup Scripts   SuSE places its SysV startup scripts in /etc/init.d and places links to these files for specific runlevels in /etc/init.d/rc?.d, where ? is the runlevel number.

FIGURE 9.5

YaST and YaST2 tools provide convenient access to many configuration options.

Runlevels and Starting X   Runlevel 3 produces a text-mode login prompt. Runlevel 5 starts an XDMCP server, and therefore X, at boot time. SuSE does this by providing a start link to `/etc/init.d/xdm` in the `/etc/init.d/rc5.d` directory. The `xdm` startup script in turn uses `/etc/sysconfig/displaymanager` to set several variables, including `DISPLAYMANAGER`, which tells the system which XDMCP server to run.

cron   SuSE's default `cron` configuration includes an `/etc/crontab` file that calls files in the `/etc/cron.interval` directories, where `interval` is `hourly`, `daily`, `weekly`, or `monthly`. Except for the hourly runs, these scripts run between 12:14 A.M. and 12:44 A.M.

Super Server   SuSE uses `inetd` by default, although `xinetd` is also available.

Mail Server   SuSE uses Postfix as the default mail server. Its configuration files reside in `/etc/postfix`.

Network Configuration   SuSE uses the `/etc/init.d/network` SysV startup script to start basic networking features. This script relies on variables stored in files in the `/etc/sysconfig/network` directory tree. Therefore, permanently changing some networking details requires editing these files.

Local Startup Files   If you want to change something about the system configuration that doesn't fit in well in the default script set, you can edit the `/etc/init.d/boot.local` script. SuSE executes this script after running the scripts in `/etc/init.d/boot.d` but before running the scripts for the startup runlevel.

As with other Linux distributions that use GUI configuration tools, you can modify configuration files to alter the system as you see fit; however, the automatic tools may choke or ignore your changes if those changes don't conform to the standards the tools expect.

Implementing Manual Configurations

When editing configuration files, you must of course conform to the standards of whatever files you modify. For instance, Linux startup scripts are usually written for `bash`. Therefore, they must use the syntax of a `bash` script, as summarized in Chapter 4, "Mastering Shells and Shell Scripting." In the case of distributions that use GUI configuration tools, it's also often important to create files or scripts that match those tools' expectations, lest subsequent uses of those tools create bizarre problems. You can change a configuration using the standard files or use local startup scripts to add to a configuration. It's also sometimes possible to achieve the desired results by creating or modifying individual users' configuration files.

Scripts versus Configuration Files

Quite a few Linux configuration files are actually scripts, generally written using the `bash` shell scripting language. Examples include whatever script `init` calls with the `si` line in `/etc/inittab` and SysV startup scripts. (The `/etc/inittab` file itself is not a `bash` script, though.) Scripts are typically used to launch programs, such as daemons and system configuration tools—`ifconfig`, `insmod`, and so on. Essentially, scripts leverage the power of ordinary text-mode Linux system administration tools, using them automatically during the system boot process or at other times, such as when you manually change the runlevel.

Chapter 4 introduces shell scripting with bash. You should consult that chapter if you're unfamiliar with shell scripting but you need to modify a startup script. For more detailed information, consult a book on bash shell scripting, such as Newham and Rosenblatt's *Learning the bash Shell* (O'Reilly, 1998).

Nonscript configuration files, on the other hand, simply store data that's used by other tools. For instance, the Postfix mail server uses /etc/postfix/main.cf as its configuration file. This file isn't a script, but its syntax resembles variable assignment operations in scripts. This file contains lines like this:

```
virtual_maps = hash:/etc/postfix/virtual
disable_dns_lookups = no
```

Each configuration file uses its own syntax. For instance, some use equal signs (=) to assign values to variables, but others don't. Some break the file into distinct sections, in which assignments or other operators apply only to specific features of the program. Because the rules for constructing and modifying configuration files vary from one program to another, you should consult the program's documentation, either provided with the program or in a book, third-party web page, or the like, before modifying these programs' configuration files.

Sometimes the line between boot scripts and configuration files is blurry. For instance, most Linux distributions use files in /etc/network, /etc/sysconfig/networking, or a similar location to store variables relevant to network configuration. These files frequently lack the first-line #!/bin/bash identification as scripts, but they're loaded by SysV or other startup scripts in order to assign values to variables that are used in the scripts' network-initialization calls. This practice enables you or the distributions' configuration tools to modify the configuration files without adjusting the sensitive SysV startup scripts.

Using Local Startup Scripts

One way to modify a system's configuration is to use local startup scripts. The preceding sections described these scripts and their locations. In summary, these scripts are as follows:

Debian   All scripts in /etc/rc.boot are local startup scripts. These scripts run after basic system initialization but before SysV startup scripts run. Debian's maintainers discourage use of this directory, and instead recommend creating genuine SysV startup scripts, possibly stored in /etc/rcS.d.

Mandrake, Red Hat, and Slackware   The local startup script is /etc/rc.d/rc.local. This script runs after all the SysV startup scripts for Mandrake and Red Hat but before any runlevel-specific scripts in the case of Slackware.

SuSE   The local startup script is /etc/init.d/boot.local. This script runs after basic system initialization but before SysV startup scripts run.

One critical difference between distributions is that their local startup scripts run at different times—before or after running the runlevel-specific SysV startup scripts. This fact can have important consequences. For instance, if a SysV startup script starts a server that must have basic networking features active, you can use a local startup script to start networking if your distribution runs the local startup script before the SysV startup scripts. If the local startup script runs after the SysV startup script, though, this may not work or it may require you to restart the server in the local startup script.

In a simple case, you can launch a program via a local startup script by adding the command to the script. For instance, if you've added a server called `bigserv` to your system by compiling source code, you might add a line like the following to a local startup script in order to launch the server:

```
/usr/local/bin/bigserv
```

Of course, you can add whatever options are appropriate. If the program you call doesn't put itself into the background, the script will stop execution until the program exits, unless you append an ampersand (&) to the command line. A halted startup script will halt the system boot process, so be sure to include this ampersand whenever necessary. Some programs you might call will exit quickly; for instance, the `play` command will play a sound and then exit, so failure to include the ampersand will delay the boot process only by however long it takes to play the sound file you specify.

Safely Changing Existing Configuration Files

Sometimes it's desirable to alter an existing configuration file or startup script. Doing so is potentially risky, though. An error could result in an unbootable system or in a system that doesn't work as you expect. Some rules to keep in mind when editing these files include:

Make a Backup   Be sure to make a backup of the file before you edit it. Some editors do this automatically, but if you save your changes more than once, the second save may overwrite the original backup.

Edit the File in Linux   Some other OSs, such as Windows, use different end-of-line conventions in their text editors than does Linux. Some configuration files are sensitive to these conventions, so editing a file in Windows may result in a file that doesn't work as you expect, possibly halting the boot process.

Note Ownership and Permissions   Before editing the file, notice who owns it and what the permissions are. Be sure that the edited file has the same ownership and permissions.

Make Minimal Changes   Don't change anything you don't understand, and try to change as little as possible of what you do understand.

Change Support Files, Not Core Files   If a SysV startup script or other file relies on variables loaded from another file, try to edit the support file rather than the primary file. As a general rule, you'll be less likely to introduce serious problems if you edit a support file.

Test the Changes   If possible, test the modified script or configuration file as soon as possible. For instance, shut down and restart a server. If you make extensive changes to startup scripts, you might even want to reboot the computer to be sure it boots correctly. With the changes fresh in your mind, you'll find it easier to correct problems than if you'd waited hours, days, or longer to test them.

Creating New SysV Startup Scripts

If you add a new server or other program that should launch whenever you start the computer, the easy way to get it to run is usually to add an entry to a local startup script, as described earlier in "Using Local Startup Scripts." SysV startup scripts exist for several reasons, though, and some of these apply even to locally compiled programs. Most importantly, SysV startup scripts enable you to configure a server to run in some runlevels but not others, and to start up and shut down using relatively simple commands—by passing the strings start or stop to the script.

The core idea behind a SysV startup script is fairly straightforward: It's a script to start, stop, and sometimes restart or check the status of a program. Most Linux distributions, though, add a lot of extras to their SysV startup scripts. These extra features include a summary of the startup status for programs as they're launched when the system boots, storage of process IDs (PIDs) in /var/run, and so on. Unfortunately, distributions have different methods of implementing these extra features. If you want to use similar features in your own SysV startup script, you may want to create yours by starting from an existing script. You can then replace calls to the original server with calls to your own. You should peruse several scripts to locate one that's best-suited to your modifications.

If you're willing to settle for a simpler SysV startup script, something like Listing 9.1 may fit the bill. This script starts and stops the fictitious bigserv program. Its method of stopping the server is to use killall, which kills all instances of the server. Some servers include provisions to store their PIDs in files. You can use this feature to store a PID when you start a server, and to kill only that instance when you shut it down, if you like.

LISTING 9.1: SAMPLE SYSV STARTUP SCRIPT

```
#!/bin/bash
case "$1" in
    start)
        /usr/local/bin/bigserv
        ;;
    stop)
        /usr/bin/killall bigserv
        ;;
    restart)
        $0 stop
        $0 start
        ;;
esac
```

Once you've created a SysV startup script, you should store it in the SysV startup script directory for your distribution, such as /etc/rc.d/init.d for Mandrake or Red Hat. If you want the server to start or stop automatically when you boot or change runlevels, you must then create links to the original file in the runlevel-specific SysV startup script directories, such as /etc/rc.d/rc?.d for Mandrake and Red Hat. These links' names should start with S if you want the server to start or K if you want the server to stop in that runlevel. Filenames also conventionally include a two-digit sequence number. For instance, to start the bigserv server, you might have a startup script link called S67bigserv and a shutdown link called K23bigserv in another runlevel directory. The runlevel management tools automatically pass a start parameter to files whose names begin with S and stop to those whose names begin with K. The sequence number determines the order in which the scripts run. For some packages, this isn't terribly important; but for others it is. For instance, most servers should start after the network or networking script runs, and they should be shut down before that script is run for shutting down the network in runlevels 0, 1, and 6. Each distribution uses its own set of sequence numbers, so you should study these sequences before inserting a new script into the sequence.

NOTE   *Chapter 22, "Running Servers," provides more information on SysV startup scripts. Chapter 22 also covers tools that can help you manage these scripts by helping you enable and disable SysV startup scripts.*

Bypassing and Overriding Configuration Files

Sometimes you may want to bypass or override a startup script or configuration file. In some cases, the easiest way to do this is to delete, rename, or move the file. For instance, removing a SysV startup script or its link in a relevant runlevel prevents that script from running. In this way, you can disable a server when the system starts. One potential risk to such actions is that automatic configuration tools may add the file back, particularly if you merely modified a link.

Sometimes you can edit a startup script to have it use a different configuration file than is the default. For instance, the -s option to smbd and nmbd (two programs that together compose Samba) specifies the configuration file. It's not used in most SysV startup scripts for Samba, but you could add it if you wanted to move the Samba configuration files to some location other than the default for your distribution.

Sometimes it's possible to use a local startup script to modify the actions of earlier startup scripts. For instance, if your system is obtaining a bizarre hostname from a Dynamic Host Configuration Protocol (DHCP) server at boot time, you can override that setting by using the hostname command in a local configuration file—*if* the local configuration file runs after the startup script that calls your DHCP client. If not, you may need to locate that startup script and modify it so that it doesn't accept the DHCP server's hostname or so that the script includes a call to hostname itself.

Creating User-Specific Configurations

Some configurations can be customized for individual users. Most of these settings relate to user-level programs, such as window managers, text editors, and web browsers. These configurations almost invariably reside in files or directories in the users' home directories, typically named after the program in question, but with a dot (.) at the start of the name to hide it from view unless you use the -a option to ls. For instance, the configuration file for the NEdit editor is ~/.nedit. Most of these files contain highly application-specific options, so you must consult the programs' documentation to learn more about them. Some of these programs also use system-wide defaults, often stored in /etc. These defaults may be copied to the user-specific files or may provide defaults that the user-specific files may override.

Two classes of user configuration files are particularly important. The first is shell configuration files, such as ~/.bashrc. Chapter 4 covers these files in more detail. They are essentially just shell scripts. Typically, you use them to set environment variables and aliases.

Another type of important configuration file is an X startup file. The most common of these files are listed here:

~/.xinitrc   X uses this file when you type **startx** from a text-mode login.

~/.xsession   The X Display Manager (XDM) XDMCP server uses this file. The KDE Display Manager (KDM) and GNOME Display Manager (GDM) XDMCP servers may also use this file if you select an appropriate login option.

~/.vnc/xstartup   This file is the Virtual Network Computing (VNC) X startup file, which is used by the VNC server and described in Chapter 26, "Providing Remote Login Access."

These files are usually bash scripts, and they typically launch programs the user wants to run when first logging in. The most important line in these files is usually the last line or at least something very near to the last line. This line launches the X *window manager*, which places decorative and functional borders around windows, including the title bar and the borders that enable you to resize windows. Instead of a call to a window manager, the script may launch a *desktop environment*, which includes a window manager and other helpful tools. Window managers and desktop environments are both described in more detail in Chapter 6, "Getting the Most from a Desktop Environment."

X startup scripts may include calls to other programs beyond window managers or desktop environments. For instance, if you want to launch an xterm when you log in, you would include a line that calls this program prior to the window manager call. Such calls typically end in ampersands (**&**) to launch the program in the background; otherwise, the script will stop executing until the program terminates. The call to the window manager, by contrast, lacks this feature; this way, the script doesn't continue executing until you exit from the window manager. After that point, X shuts down or your XDMCP server's login window reappears. On occasion, an X login script includes a few lines after the window manager call. These lines may clean up temporary files, play a logout sound, or what have you. Listing 9.2 shows a typical X login file. This file launches an xterm and plays a login sound before launching the IceWM window manager. (IceWM manages the xterm, even though the xterm was launched first.) When the user exits from IceWM, the system plays a logout sound.

LISTING 9.2: TYPICAL X LOGIN FILE

```
#!/bin/bash
xterm &
play ~/sounds/login.wav &
icewm
play ~/sounds/logout.wav &
```

Summary

Every Linux distribution has its own unique set of system startup scripts and configuration files, and many ship with tools to help you manage these files. If you don't want to use the configuration tools, though, you can dig into the configuration files to do things manually. There are potential problems with doing so, such as the risk of damaging a configuration or the risk that an automatic tool will undo your changes. Knowing where to go to make changes and how to make them most effectively can, therefore, be an important skill if you want to bypass these automatic tools.

## Chapter 10

Using Multiple OSs

SOME COMPUTERS RUN LINUX and no other OS. Others, though, run multiple OSs. Such configurations are particularly common where resources or desktop space are limited, and they present unique administrative challenges. This chapter covers these topics, which include installation issues, boot loaders, and exchanging data via foreign filesystems.

Even when a computer runs only Linux, it's sometimes necessary for it to interact with other OSs in a non-network manner. This is true when you need to read a floppy disk created on a Windows system, for instance. In addition to reading the disk, you may need to process the data on the disk, and that means understanding cross-platform and proprietary data formats. Finally, this chapter looks at emulation—running non-Linux programs in Linux.

Installation Tricks and Traps

You have a Linux CD-ROM in your hands and want to install it on the computer before you. That computer, though, already runs another OS, and it is packed with valuable data. Alternatively, you want to install Linux and one or more OSs on a blank hard disk, but you don't want to have to redo your effort because one OS's installer wipes out the first OS you install. In both cases, you need to be aware of potential multiboot pitfalls and ways to avoid them. Many of these pitfalls boil down to partitioning issues. You must be able to design a partitioning scheme and perhaps modify existing partitions. The order of OS installation can also be important, because some OSs are more respectful of existing installations than others.

NOTE *This section describes partitioning for IA-32 computers, which support the widest range of OSs. Multibooting on other platforms is usually simpler, although many of the basic issues described here still apply.*

Designing an Appropriate Partition Scheme

The "Optimizing Disk Partitions" section of Chapter 2, "Improving Disk Performance," includes information about creating partitions to optimize disk performance. Some of these rules impact multi-OS installations in that they suggest tradeoffs of one OS over another. Other rules suggest ways to harmonize OS configurations. Specific issues in a multiboot scenario include:

Prioritizing Disk Access Speed   Because of the way modern disks allocate sectors on their platters, early sections of the disk tend to produce faster throughput than later sections. Therefore, you should place partitions belonging to the OS you want to favor with faster disk access earlier on the disk.

Keeping OS Data Contiguous   Accessing new data files usually requires moving the disk head, and this action takes time. Thus, you should keep each OS's partitions contiguous. You might make exceptions for seldom-used partitions if other factors require it, though. For instance, the Linux /boot partition might be separated from other Linux partitions with little performance impact.

Boot Partition Requirements   Some OSs have specific requirements for their boot partitions. For instance, it's almost always necessary to store certain key files in a part of the disk that's accessible to the BIOS—a limit that's referred to as the *1024-cylinder* boundary. At various points in the history of the IA-32 architecture, the 1024-cylinder boundary has fallen at 504MB or 8GB. Modern systems and boot loaders usually don't suffer from these limits; they use more advanced calls that work around the 1024-cylinder limit. If in doubt, you may want to keep a Linux /boot partition, as well as boot partitions for other OSs, below the 8GB line. Some OSs must boot from primary partitions, as described next. A few, such as DOS, are limited to residing on the first 2GB of the disk.

Primary Partition Allotments   The partition table used by IA-32 computers provides only four "slots" for partitions. This is why the number of *primary* partitions is limited to four, one of which can be an *extended* partition that defines additional *logical* partitions. Some OSs, including the BSDs and all versions of Windows, must boot from a primary partition. Thus, you may want to allocate primary partitions only as boot partitions for such OSs and boot more flexible OSs, such as Linux and OS/2, from logical partitions. All logical partitions must be contiguous, because they're held within a single "carrier" extended partition.

NOTE   *It is possible to install Windows to a logical* D: *partition (or to a primary* D: *partition on the same or a different physical disk), but when you do so, Windows still requires a primary* C: *partition for some critical boot files. In some sense, Windows is actually installed on* C:, *and* D: *is used only for support files—albeit ones that make up the bulk of the OS.*

Another factor in a multiboot environment is data transfer. Typically, having a File Allocation Table (FAT) partition you can use for data exchange between the OSs is desirable. Each OS then uses its native format for its core OS files. If FAT is an OS's native filesystem, you might forgo having a separate exchange partition; however, using an exchange partition has certain data-isolation advantages. For instance, by not mounting a Windows C: partition in Linux, you minimize the risk of accidentally damaging critical Windows files from Linux.

As an example, consider a computer that boots DOS, Windows Me, and Linux. Its partition layout might resemble the following, as revealed by Linux's fdisk:

```
# /sbin/fdisk -l /dev/hda

Disk /dev/hda: 255 heads, 63 sectors, 1244 cylinders
Units = cylinders of 16065 * 512 bytes

   Device Boot  Start    End    Blocks   Id  System
/dev/hda1    *      1      8     64228+   16  Hidden FAT16
/dev/hda2    *      9    263   2048287+    b  Win95 FAT32
/dev/hda3         264   1245   7887316+    5  Extended
/dev/hda5         264    391   1028128+    6  FAT16
/dev/hda6    *    392    400     72261    83  Linux
/dev/hda7         401   1038   5124703+   83  Linux
/dev/hda8        1039   1059    168651    82  Linux swap
/dev/hda9        1060   1245   1493415    83  Linux
```

NOTE *Even if you were to try to reproduce the preceding partition table, you might notice some differences, particularly in partition sizes and type codes. For instance, two extended partition type codes exist, 0x05 and 0x0f. Multiple codes also exist for most FAT partition types. These different codes tell Windows whether or not the partition spans the 1024-cylinder boundary. If you use Linux's* fdisk, *type* l *in the utility to see a list of type codes. Those marked as being* LBA *codes are safest for use with Windows when that OS must access the disk past the 1024-cylinder mark.*

This configuration allocates one primary partition for DOS and another for Windows. The DOS partition (/dev/hda1) is 63MB in size and is described as "hidden" because the boot loader has modified its partition type number to "hide" it from OSs that rely on this number. This practice is sometimes required to boot multiple Microsoft OSs. The second partition is a 2GB FAT partition for Windows, and it holds all of the Windows software. After that comes an extended partition, including a 1GB FAT data exchange partition that's accessible from all OSs. Four Linux partitions, intended as a /boot partition, a root partition, the swap partition, and a /home partition, consume the end of the disk.

This configuration, like most multiboot partition layouts, is a mass of compromises. The DOS partition comes early because DOS has problems reading beyond the first 2GB of any disk. The Windows and exchange partitions come next to keep this block together and to avoid potential problems booting Windows from beyond the 1024-cylinder boundary. If you wanted to risk booting Windows from the end of the disk, you could move the Windows primary partition to the end, slightly improving Linux's disk performance.

TIP *Complex multiboot configurations often benefit from the use of two or more hard disks. You can place partitions intended for each OS on both disks, improving performance. The extra primary partitions may also come in handy when booting OSs that must boot from primary partitions but that aren't tied to the first physical disk, such as FreeBSD.*

Modifying Existing Partitions

If you're installing Linux on a computer that holds a working OS you want to preserve, you're faced with the daunting challenge of modifying that working configuration. You can proceed in one of three ways:

◆ You can add a disk for Linux.

◆ You can back up, repartition, and restore the data.

◆ You can use a dynamic partition resizer.

NOTE *A few Linux distributions support installation within an existing FAT partition, typically by using the UMS-DOS filesystem to add Linux filesystem features to FAT. This practice is convenient, and it can be a good way to test Linux, but UMSDOS is inefficient, so I don't recommend using this method for any but a temporary installation.*

ADDING A DISK

Adding a disk is the simplest and safest but most costly course of action. Suppose your existing configuration is typical—a single large primary C: partition for Windows. You can add a new hard disk, devote it entirely to Linux, and install the boot loader (described shortly, in "Picking an OS to Boot: Boot Loaders") to the original disk. Alternatively, you can split the new space between Linux and Windows.

Adding a disk poses little risk of data loss, and it isn't very tricky to do. Thus, if you have the money and aren't inclined to try anything more complex, it's the best way to install Linux. On the other hand, a backup/restore operation *shouldn't* be beyond your means—every computer *should* have adequate backup/restore hardware. Therefore, if you shy away from this option because you lack the hardware, that's a sign that your hardware is inadequate.

BACKING UP AND RESTORING

Traditionally, reconfiguring partitions has required backing up your data, repartitioning the disk, and restoring the data to the new partitions. To do this, you'll need adequate backup hardware and software. The hardware is likely to be a tape backup drive, an optical device such as a DVD-R, or a removable disk.

Software for this procedure is OS-specific. A variety of commercial backup programs exist for Windows, and many tape drives come with such software. Alternatively, you can use a bootable Linux emergency system to back up a Windows system. (Chapter 17, "Protecting Your System with Backups," covers Linux backup software and emergency recovery systems.) Whatever method you use, some caveats are in order:

Making Multiple Backups Backups sometimes fail, and Murphy's Law guarantees that if you make just one backup, it will fail after you repartition your computer. Therefore, you should make at least two backups before you intentionally destroy your original data.

Filename Protection Some backup methods don't back up both the short (8.3) and long filenames from FAT partitions. Both can be important. Linux tools, in particular, discard the short filenames and then re-create them at restoration. If the re-created short filename doesn't match the original, though, and if the short filename was used in a configuration file, bizarre problems may occur.

Restoring Windows Partitions   Some Windows backup tools—especially some older ones—use awkward DOS-based restore tools. These tools can make it difficult or tedious to recover a working system. Be sure you understand the procedures involved before proceeding. If possible, test the restore operation on a noncritical system.

Restoring Bootability   You may need to run a special utility to make your OS bootable again after restoring it. For DOS and Windows 9*x*/Me, you must boot from a floppy and type **SYS C:**. In Windows NT/2000/XP, the equivalent tool is called **FIXMBR**. Be sure you have a boot floppy and any tools you need to perform this operation before proceeding.

On the whole, the backup/repartition/restore juggling act is an awkward and time-consuming one. An error may yield a lost OS. If you're confident in your backup hardware and software, though, this may be the way to go.

USING DYNAMIC PARTITION RESIZERS

Some tools enable you to alter the size of a partition without deleting data on the partition. These *dynamic partition resizers* are popular tools for preparing a system to multiboot Linux and another OS, but they aren't without their risks. A bug, power loss, disk error, or other problem in operation could result in serious data loss—even an unusable OS. Thus, you should always create a backup before using such a tool. Because of the data-loss risks, the convenience of dynamic partition resizers does not offer as much of an advantage over backup/repartition/restore operations as it might at first appear. If you're interested in pursuing this course, you have several options, including:

FIPS   The First Interactive Nondestructive Partition Splitting (FIPS) program is a simple DOS tool designed to split a primary FAT partition in two. The target partition must be defragmented before operation, because FIPS can't move data around on the partition. FIPS comes with many Linux distributions.

GNU Parted   This program (`http://www.gnu.org/software/parted/`) is a multi-filesystem partition resizer. It's much more flexible than FIPS, but it runs only from Linux, which presents a chicken-and-egg problem if you're trying to install Linux on a system. You can obtain Linux boot floppy disk images with Parted at `http://ftp.gnu.org/gnu/parted/bootdisk/` to work around this problem. Parted can resize FAT, ext2fs, ext3fs, ReiserFS, and Linux swap partitions.

PartitionMagic   This program is a popular commercial partition resizer from PowerQuest (`http://www.powerquest.com`). It presents a friendly GUI (as shown in Figure 10.1) for manipulating partitions, even when it runs from DOS. PartitionMagic can resize FAT, New Technology File System (NTFS), ext2fs, ext3fs, and Linux swap partitions. Versions prior to 6.0 also supported OS/2's High-Performance File System (HPFS), but support for other filesystems is better in later versions. PartitionMagic runs from Windows or DOS.

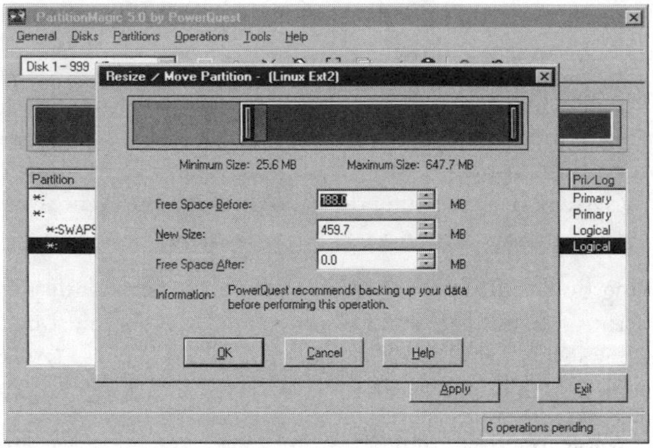

FIGURE 10.1

PartitionMagic pro-
vides a GUI inter-
face to simplify
partition resizing.

As a general rule, FIPS or GNU Parted may be worth using for a one-time installation of Linux
to a system that already runs Windows. These programs can't resize an NTFS partition, though, so
they may not be useful when installing Linux to a Windows NT, 2000, or XP system; for that, you'll
need PartitionMagic. As this software costs about as much as a new hard disk, you might prefer to
add a new disk rather than buy PartitionMagic. On the other hand, if you regularly juggle partitions,
PartitionMagic may be worth having.

Installing OSs in the Best Order

OS installation is inherently risky—installers typically include tools to delete and create partitions,
create filesystems, install boot loaders, and perform other actions that have the potential to damage
or destroy other OSs. Some OSs do a better job of alerting you to dangers or avoiding pitfalls than
others. For this reason, installing OSs in a particular order is often desirable and even necessary.

The most common source of problems is with boot loader installation. All OSs include boot
loaders. Microsoft provides a very simple boot loader that resides in the disk's Master Boot Record
(MBR) at the very start of the hard disk, with secondary code in the boot partition's boot sector.
This standard boot loader can boot only one OS, and most Microsoft OSs install the boot loader
automatically. (Windows NT, 2000, and XP include a secondary boot loader that can boot other
OSs.) Thus, if you install a Microsoft OS after any other OS, chances are your other OS will seem
to disappear. You can usually recover from this problem by using an emergency boot system to reinstall the other OS's boot loader in the MBR, or possibly by using DOS's FDISK to change which partition is bootable.

Another problem is partition type codes, which are numbers intended to identify which OS
"owns" a partition or what filesystem it contains. Unfortunately, not all partition type codes are
unique, which can cause confusion during installation. One such problem is with NTFS (used by
Windows NT, 2000, and XP) and HPFS (used by OS/2), both of which use a partition type code
of 0x07. When installing both of these OSs, you must be very careful when installing the second OS
so that you do not reformat the just-installed OS's partitions. Using a boot loader's partition-hiding
options, if available, can help you avoid problems after installation is complete.

Another problem code is 0x82, which is used both for Linux swap partitions and Solaris installation partitions. You may need to use Linux's `fdisk` on an emergency or installation boot CD to temporarily change the code of the first OS's 0x82 partitions before installing the second OS.

As a general rule, the best installation order is as follows:

1. DOS

2. Windows 9*x*/Me

3. Windows NT/2000/XP

4. Solaris or FreeBSD

5. OS/2

6. BeOS

7. Linux

I recommend preparing the disk by creating partitions for all of the OSs before you begin actual installation. You can use Linux's `fdisk`, run from an emergency or installation system, to do this. You'll then let each OS format its own partitions. DOS and Windows may require that the target installation partition be marked as bootable (you can do this using the `a` command from within Linux's `fdisk`).

Of course, you must be mindful of partition-formatting options with the later installations—most importantly, *never* select any option to use an entire hard disk. Most OSs provide options regarding boot loader installation. As you install multiple OSs, you may end up installing one boot loader over another until the end.

Picking an OS to Boot: Boot Loaders

On a single-OS computer, the boot process is fairly straightforward—on IA-32 systems, the BIOS searches for code on the hard disk's (or other bootable disk's) *boot sector*, aka the *Master Boot Record (MBR)*, which is the first sector on the disk. This code is often called the *primary boot loader*, and in some cases, it directs the boot process to just one OS or to any OS you select. In other cases, the primary boot loader relies on a *secondary boot loader*, which may reside in a partition of its own (as in OS/2's Boot Manager) or in the boot sector of a specific partition, in order to finish the job.

Three boot loaders ship with most Linux distributions: the *Grand Unified Boot Loader (GRUB)*, the *Linux Loader (LILO)*, and `LOADLIN`. Writing a Linux kernel directly to a floppy disk using `dd` and booting using the floppy is also possible, provided your kernel fits on a single floppy disk (it might not). This approach is useful for emergency situations and for testing a new kernel. Various third-party boot loaders are available, and you may want to use one of them. These tools require the help of GRUB or LILO (installed in a partition's boot sector) to boot Linux.

NOTE *This section describes boot loaders for IA-32 computers. Other architectures have their own boot loaders, such as Yaboot (`http://penguinppc.org/projects/yaboot/`) for PowerPC machines. The basic principles of configuring these tools are similar to those for LILO or GRUB, but many details differ.*

Picking the Right Boot Loader

For a simple configuration, just about any boot loader will do a good job. Certain exotic installations, though, have special needs. For instance, if you need to boot multiple versions of Microsoft Windows, you must set aside multiple primary partitions or use a boot loader that supports keeping several versions of Windows on a single primary partition. Booting from above the 8GB mark can also pose difficulties with some boot loaders. To perform a "normal" boot of Linux from a hard disk, either GRUB or LILO is required, although you can use another boot loader as a primary boot loader, relegating GRUB or LILO to secondary status to boot Linux alone. Some common boot loaders, and their advantages and disadvantages, include:

LOADLIN   This boot loader is a DOS program that only boots Linux. To use it, you boot DOS and run LOADLIN, passing it the name of the Linux kernel file (which must be stored on a FAT floppy disk or partition) and kernel parameters. For instance, you might type **LOADLIN C:\VMLINUZ root=/dev/hda7 ro**. This command boots the VMLINUZ kernel and tells it to use /dev/hda7 as the root partition, mounting it initially read-only (ro). Linux subsequently remounts the root partition for read/write access, assuming it's so configured in /etc/fstab. LOADLIN is most useful for testing new kernels without altering your standard boot procedure or for emergency boot situations (say, if you accidentally damage a boot loader configuration when installing a new OS). One important limitation of LOADLIN is that it has problems booting large kernels. Therefore, you may need to trim unnecessary options from a kernel before you can boot it with LOADLIN. Most distributions include LOADLIN in a directory called dosutils, tools, or something similar on their installation media.

GRUB   This boot loader was designed with support for tools that enable a computer to boot from beyond the 1,024th cylinder (roughly 8GB on modern systems), but older BIOSes may not support this option. GRUB is extremely flexible, and it is the default boot loader for some Linux distributions. Its configuration is controlled through a file that GRUB reads at boot time, so reconfiguring it doesn't require writing to the MBR or boot sector. GRUB configuration is described in more detail in the upcoming section, "Configuring GRUB."

LILO   This boot loader is older than GRUB. It didn't originally include the ability to boot anything from beyond the 1,024th cylinder, but modern versions can do so, provided the BIOS supports this feature. Although not quite as flexible as GRUB, LILO is still a powerful tool. To reconfigure it, you must alter a configuration file and type lilo, which rewrites the MBR or partition boot sector. This fact can complicate reconfiguring LILO if you can't get Linux to boot.

OS Loader   This boot loader, also known as NTLDR, ships with Windows NT, 2000, and XP. It's controlled through a file called C:\BOOT.INI, and it's designed to select between different versions of Windows. It can be configured as a primary boot loader, using LILO or GRUB as a secondary boot loader to boot Linux, but doing so requires extracting a Linux boot partition's boot sector into a file and placing that file on the Windows partition.

XOSL   This boot loader, headquartered at http://www.xosl.org, is a powerful open source boot loader. It installs partly to the MBR and partly to a FAT partition, and it provides GUI configuration tools. It's easier to configure XOSL to handle multiple Microsoft OSs than to do the same with LILO, so it can be a good choice for such systems.

System Commander This program, from V Communications (`http://www.v-com.com`), is a very powerful dedicated boot loader. It's stored on the MBR and a FAT partition, and it presents text-based or GUI menuing tools for reconfiguring from within the program itself. It can boot multiple Windows OSs (including booting two or more versions from a single partition), hide partitions when booting specific OSs, and more.

In most cases, you'll do well to stick with whatever boot loader is the default for your distribution—GRUB or LILO. Most Linux installations do a good job of setting up a system to boot Linux alone or to select between Linux and Windows. If your system is more complex, though, you may need to modify your GRUB or LILO configuration, or you may need to dedicate GRUB or LILO to a secondary role and use a third-party boot loader. XOSL and System Commander are both very powerful and easy-to-configure primary boot loaders, so they're both worth investigating for complex systems. OS Loader is awkward to reconfigure when you upgrade your Linux kernel, so I prefer to avoid it.

Configuring GRUB

To use GRUB, you must both install it on your system and configure it. GRUB installation involves more than just installing the GRUB package; you must run a command to copy the GRUB boot loader code to the MBR. Once installed, GRUB doesn't need to be installed to the boot sector again, unless you change the boot partition or need to reinstall GRUB because it has been wiped out by another OS. GRUB consults files on the hard disk to boot. These files must be on a supported filesystem and present options that enable GRUB to locate your Linux kernel or boot another OS.

INSTALLING GRUB

If necessary, you should install the GRUB package (generally called `grub`) using your distribution's package manager, or you should compile and install the package from source code, which is available from `http://www.gnu.org/software/grub/`. Once you've done this, you install GRUB to the MBR with the `grub` utility, which presents a command prompt at which you type a few commands:

```
# grub
grub> find /boot/grub/stage1
 (hd0,5)
grub> root (hd0,5)
grub> setup (hd0)
grub> quit
```

The `find` command locates the partition on which the GRUB configuration files reside. If the command as shown here returns a "file not found" error, try omitting the leading `/boot` in the pathname. GRUB searches partitions, not your fully mounted directory tree, so if `/boot` is a separate partition, you must omit the `/boot` specifier. The returned value (`hd0,5` in this example) is expressed in GRUB's own style. The first number (0) refers to the disk device—0 is usually `/dev/hda` in Linux terms. The second number (5) is the partition number, numbered starting from 0. Linux numbers partitions starting from 1, so `hd0,5` refers to `/dev/hda6`. The GRUB files normally reside in `/boot`, so if you know where that directory resides, you can forgo the `find` command; however, it's a useful double-check to use `find` even in this case.

The root command sets GRUB's root device. Note that the GRUB root device may not be the same as the Linux root partition; the GRUB root device is the partition on which GRUB's files reside. If your /boot directory is a separate partition, the GRUB root device will likely be different from your Linux root partition. A pointer to the GRUB root device is stored in the GRUB boot loader code, so that the code can find the GRUB configuration files when the system boots. You should pass the value returned by find to root.

The setup command writes the GRUB first-stage boot loader code—to hd0 (/dev/hda) in this example. If you want to use GRUB in conjunction with another primary boot loader, you should instead write GRUB to a Linux boot partition—probably the GRUB root partition, such as hd0,5 in this example.

Once this task is done, you can exit from grub. The system will attempt to boot using files stored in the GRUB root partition. This partition can be on any Linux native filesystem (Minix, ext2fs, ext3fs, ReiserFS, JFS, or XFS), on a FAT filesystem, or on a handful of other Unix-like operating systems' native filesystems, such as the Fast File System (FFS) used by FreeBSD and some others.

CONFIGURING GRUB

GRUB is configured through a file called /boot/grub/menu.1st. (Red Hat calls the file /boot/grub/grub.conf and also creates a symbolic link to this file from /etc.) Listing 10.1 shows a typical menu.1st file.

LISTING 10.1: TYPICAL GRUB CONFIGURATION FILE

```
default=0
timeout=10
splashimage=(hd0,4)/grub/splash.xpm.gz
title Linux (2.4.19)
        root (hd0,5)
        kernel /bzImage-2.4.19 ro root=/dev/hda7
title Windows
        unhide (hd0,1)
        hide (hd0,0)
        rootnoverify (hd0,1)
        chainloader +1
        makeactive
        boot
title DOS
        unhide (hd0,0)
        hide (hd0,1)
        rootnoverify (hd0,0)
        chainloader +1
        makeactive
        boot
```

The first three lines of Listing 10.1 set global options—the default OS to boot (numbered starting from 0, or the first definition in this example), the timeout in seconds before booting the default OS, and a graphics file to display as a background for selecting an OS. Many other global options are available, and many distributions set some of them. Consult the GRUB documentation (available as `info` pages, so type **`info grub`** to view them) for more details.

Subsequent lines are broken into sections beginning with the keyword `title`, which defines the name of the option that will appear in the GRUB boot menu. The first definition in Listing 10.1 is for Linux. The `root` keyword sets the GRUB root device, not the Linux root partition. The `kernel` keyword defines the kernel that's to be booted—`bzImage-2.4.19` in this example, defined relative to the GRUB root device. Because this root device is `/boot` from Linux's point of view, Listing 10.1 tells GRUB to use `/boot/bzImage-2.4.19` as the boot kernel. You can pass options to the kernel on this line. In Listing 10.1, `ro` tells the kernel to mount its root partition read-only (it's subsequently mounted read/write by the `/etc/fstab` entry) and the `root` parameter specifies Linux's root partition.

The `Windows` and `DOS` definitions in Listing 10.1 tell GRUB how to boot Windows and DOS, respectively. Because these OSs shouldn't be able to see each other's primary partitions, the `unhide` and `hide` keywords unhide the target partition and hide the one belonging to the other OS. Similarly, `makeactive` sets the target partition's bootable flag. The `chainloader +1` keyword tells GRUB to use the boot sector of the active partition (specified with `rootnoverify` on the preceding line) as a secondary boot loader. When GRUB hits the `boot` line, it passes control to this boot sector, thereby booting the OS that resides on this partition.

To reconfigure GRUB, you need only modify the `menu.1st` file. Thus, if you make a mistake when configuring GRUB, you can correct it from any OS that can read and write the filesystem on which it's stored. You don't need to reinstall GRUB in the MBR or partition boot sector, as you must do when reconfiguring LILO.

Configuring LILO

LILO uses a file called `/etc/lilo.conf` as its configuration tool. To install and use LILO, you must do three things:

1. Install LILO from the `lilo` package that comes with all major distributions. This job may have already been done when you installed Linux.

2. Edit the `/etc/lilo.conf` file, as described shortly.

3. As `root`, type **`lilo`** to install the LILO boot loader code in the MBR or partition's boot sector, as defined in `/etc/lilo.conf`.

TIP   If you want to experiment with LILO configurations, try installing LILO to a floppy disk. You can do this by specifying **boot=/dev/fd0***, instead of the usual hard disk or partition, in* /etc/lilo.conf. *You can then insert the LILO floppy to test the new LILO configuration without damaging your standard configuration.*

Listing 10.2 presents a typical `/etc/lilo.conf` file, which is similar in functionality to Listing 10.1's GRUB configuration. The first eight lines of Listing 10.2 set global options. These include the timeout period before LILO boots the default OS, in tenths of a second (`timeout=100`), the device to which the boot loader is installed (`boot=/dev/hda`—LILO installs in the MBR, as opposed to a partition boot sector such as `/dev/hda6`), and an option to use linear (or logical) block addressing (LBA) mode (`lba32`). The next eight lines (the `change-rules` section) define partition type codes, which will be used in the DOS and Windows setups. Listing 10.2 defines `DOS16` and `DOS32` partition types, each with a `normal` and `hidden` variant.

LISTING 10.2: TYPICAL *LILO.CONF* LILO CONFIGURATION FILE

```
prompt
timeout=100
default=linux
boot=/dev/hda
map=/boot/map
install=/boot/boot.b
message=/boot/message
lba32
change-rules
    reset
    type=DOS16
        normal=0x06
        hidden=0x16
    type=DOS32
        normal=0x0b
        hidden=0x1b
image=/boot/bzImage-2.4.19
    label=linux
    root=/dev/hda7
    read-only
other=/dev/hda2
    label=windows
    change
        partition=/dev/hda2
            activate
            set=DOS32_normal
        partition=/dev/hda1
            set=DOS16_hidden
            deactivate
other=/dev/hda1
    label=dos
    change
        partition=/dev/hda1
            set=DOS16_normal
            activate
        partition=/dev/hda2
            set=DOS32_hidden
            deactivate
```

The four lines beginning with the `image=` definition specify the Linux kernel image that's to be booted. Unless a `default=` line appears earlier in the file, the first `image=` or `other=` line is the default, so the Linux definition in Listing 10.2 is the default OS. The `label=` line sets a name for the image. Depending on other options and defaults for your version of LILO, you may type the name at a `boot:` prompt or select the OS by name from a menu that appears at boot time. The `root=` option tells LILO what the Linux root partition is, and the `read-only` option tells the kernel to mount that partition read-only (it's normally remounted read/write after the system reads `/etc/fstab`). Unlike GRUB, the kernel image specification is a regular Linux filename. Therefore, assuming the kernel image is stored in `/boot`, you must include that leading directory name whether or not `/boot` is a separate partition.

The two `other=` definitions set up Windows and DOS definitions, respectively. If you only have one DOS or Windows partition, these definitions can be much shorter than shown in Listing 10.2, and you can dispense with the earlier `change-rules` section, as well. The `change` subsections define how partition types are to be altered when booting one of these OSs. The `partition` subsections define the partition type to be set for the DOS and Windows partitions and whether to activate or deactivate the partitions (that is, mark them as bootable or not bootable). Listing 10.2 marks the partition that's to be booted as normal and active, and the other partition as hidden and inactive.

Exchanging Data via Foreign Filesystems

It's usually desirable to share or exchange data between the different OSs installed on a multiboot system. The simplest way to do this is to set aside at least one partition for data exchange. In some cases, one or more OSs can read other operating systems' native filesystems. Directly accessing another OS's main filesystems can simplify matters, but it also increases risks—a filesystem driver bug or user error can more easily wipe out another OS's data. In any event, you must configure one or more OSs to handle the data transfer or foreign OS's filesystems. Before doing this, though, you must decide which filesystem to use for data exchange.

NOTE   *If you want to further isolate Linux from other OSs, you can configure the OSs not to read each others' disks, and instead use removable media for file exchange. Chapter 2 includes information on filesystems for removable media, including exchanging data between Linux and non-Linux computers. This information is also applicable to transferring data between two "sides" of a single computer.*

Choosing a Filesystem for Shared Data

Support for most filesystems varies substantially between OSs. As such, a good shared filesystem for one pair of OSs may not be as good for another pair. Some possible filesystems for use in data exchange include:

FAT   This filesystem originated with DOS and was intended for use on floppy disks. In the years since, it has developed in two ways. First, FAT comes with different pointer sizes—12-bit, 16-bit, and 32-bit. These define the maximum partition sizes, and they sometimes appear after the *FAT* name, as in *FAT-32*, to indicate the pointer size. Second, the original FAT supports only short filenames of eight characters with a three-character extension (the so-called *8.3 filename limit*). An extension known as *VFAT* supports long filenames, though. Most OSs, including Linux, include excellent support for all of these FAT variants, although some OSs, such as DOS, don't support VFAT or FAT-32. Such OSs can read VFAT partitions, but they ignore the long file-names. If an OS lacks FAT-32 support, it won't read the partition at all. FAT lacks support for Linux ownership and permissions, although a special Linux-only variant known as UMSDOS adds these features. On the whole, FAT makes the best data-exchange filesystem because of its wide support, but you may want to use something else in some situations.

NTFS   Microsoft created NTFS for Windows NT. NTFS is highly proprietary; only Windows NT and its descendents include good NTFS support. Linux includes an NTFS driver, but it's reliable only for read access; the read/write support often corrupts data. Thus, you might use this driver to read data from a Windows partition, but you should not use it for writing unless and until the driver's reliability improves. Some distributions, including Red Hat, don't include even the read-only NTFS driver in their standard kernels, so you must add this driver from a third-party pack-age or recompile your kernel to get NTFS support.

HPFS   Microsoft created HPFS for OS/2 when Microsoft and IBM were still partners. Today, HPFS is used natively only by OS/2, although Windows NT 3.1 through 3.51 included HPFS support. Linux's HPFS drivers are fairly reliable, and they even support Linux ownership and per-missions, although OS/2 ignores this information. HPFS makes a good data exchange filesystem in a system with Linux and OS/2—better than FAT, in fact, because OS/2's native FAT support doesn't handle FAT-32 or VFAT, although both are available as third-party modules. HPFS isn't a good choice for data exchange with any other OS, except possibly Windows NT 3.1 through 3.51.

Ext2fs   Because the ext2fs code is freely available, implementations abound for other OSs, as described in more detail in the upcoming section, "Reading Linux Filesystems in Other OSs." Unfortunately, most of these implementations are limited in one way or another—they may not handle recent variants of ext2fs, they may be read-only, they may occasionally cause filesystem corruption, and so on. For this reason, ext2fs isn't a good choice for a data exchange partition, although you might want to read native Linux filesystems from other OSs if you find you need to read a file without rebooting. You might also set aside an ext2fs partition for data exchange with another Unix-like OS if you want to preserve ownership and permission information.

UFS and FFS   The *Unix File System (UFS)* was the original native Unix filesystem. More recently, a similar filesystem, the *Fast File System (FFS)* has emerged for FreeBSD, NetBSD, OpenBSD, and Mac OS X. Both FFS and UFS are handled by Linux's `ufs` driver, which includes an option (`ufstype`) to set the variant, as in `ufstype=44bsd` for a BSD system's FFS. Unfortunately, these filesystems aren't well supported outside of the Unix world. Indeed, even Linux's UFS/FFS driver is not completely reliable. Therefore, like ext2fs, it's useful mainly for exchanging data between Unix-like OSs when you need to preserve ownership and permission information. In that situation, you should create a separate data-transfer partition and not access other operating systems' main partitions from Linux.

HFS   Apple's *Hierarchical File System (HFS)* has long been the standard filesystem in the Macintosh world, although Mac OS X also supports FFS. Therefore, a multiboot Macintosh may use HFS as a data-exchange filesystem. Unfortunately, Linux's HFS support isn't as good as its FAT sup-port, so you should be very careful to create a separate data-transfer partition and not write to a Macintosh's boot and data partitions from Linux.

Overall, the best choice for data exchange is FAT, because of its excellent support in most OSs. FAT can even be a good choice for data exchange between OSs for which FAT isn't native, such as Linux and FreeBSD. Other potential choices for such combinations, such as ext2fs and FFS, are weak choices because neither OS's support for the other's native format is particularly reliable. Other filesystems that deserve attention are HPFS (only for Linux-OS/2 transfers) and HFS (on Macintosh systems).

Linux native filesystems beyond ext2fs are poor choices for data transfer because these filesystems are supported by few other OSs. Ext3fs is a partial exception because ext2fs drivers and utilities can sometimes handle ext3fs, although they ignore the ext3fs journaling features and may only provide read-only access. Another partial exception is the Journaled File System (JFS). IBM donated the OS/2 JFS code to Linux. JFS is also available on IBM's AIX OS. Silicon Graphics (SGI) donated XFS, but only SGI's IRIX supports XFS, although work is underway to port it to FreeBSD.

Reading Non-Linux Filesystems in Linux

Typically, any partition you want to access on a regular basis has an entry in /etc/fstab. Listing 10.3 shows a typical /etc/fstab file, including definitions for some non-Linux partitions. Each of this file's lines corresponds to a single partition. Each line has six fields, separated by spaces or tabs: the device identifier, the mount point, the filesystem, the filesystem options, the dump order, and the filesystem check order. Foreign filesystems have 0 entered for the final two fields, meaning that they're never backed up with the dump utility and aren't checked with fsck at boot time, respectively. The device field is typically a Linux device filename, but as Listing 10.3 shows, you can use a filesystem's volume name, preceded by LABEL=, for some filesystem types. Some distributions, such as Red Hat, use this form by default for Linux native filesystems. It has the advantage of surviving some types of partition table changes should you add or delete partitions in the future, but it may break if you reformat the partition in question—say, to change from ext2fs to ReiserFS.

LISTING 10.3: A SAMPLE /ETC/FSTAB FILE

```
LABEL=/       /                ext3      defaults                          1  1
/dev/hda9     /home            reiserfs  defaults                          0  0
/dev/hdb5     /other/shared    vfat      uid=500,umask=0                    0  0
/dev/hda3     /other/w2k-boot  ntfs      uid=500,umask=0,noauto,user,ro    0  0
/dev/hda8     /other/os2-data  hpfs      uid=500,umask=0,noauto,user       0  0
/dev/hdb4     /other/freebsd   ufs       noauto,user,ufstype=44bsd         0  0
/dev/fd0      /mnt/floppy      auto      defaults,user,noauto              0  0
```

The most interesting fields for configuring foreign filesystems are the filesystem type field and the filesystem options field. The filesystem type field contains the filesystem type code. Listing 10.3 demonstrates several of these codes, which are typically named after the filesystem in question, such as vfat for VFAT partitions. The auto filesystem type code is used mainly for removable media; it tells the kernel to try to auto-detect the filesystem type. This option is seldom used on hard disk partitions, which rarely change filesystem type.

The filesystem options field is a comma-separated list of filesystem options. Some options apply to most or all filesystems, but others are filesystem-specific. Table 10.1 summarizes the most popular filesystem options. Consult the mount man page or the documentation for a specific filesystem for more options. (The documentation for most filesystems is stored in the /usr/src/linux/Documentation/filesystems directory.)

TABLE 10.1: COMMON FILESYSTEM OPTIONS

OPTION	SUPPORTED FILESYSTEMS	DESCRIPTION
defaults	All	Uses the default options for this filesystem. It's used primarily to ensure that there's an options field in the /etc/fstab file.
loop	All	Uses the loopback device for this mount. Allows you to mount a file as if it were a disk partition. For instance, typing mount -t vfat -o loop image.img /mnt/image mounts the file image.img as if it were a disk.
auto or noauto	All	Mounts or does not mount the filesystem at boot time, or when root types mount -a. The default is auto, but noauto is appropriate for removable media.
user or nouser	All	Allows or disallows ordinary users to mount the filesystem. Default is nouser, but user is often appropriate for removable media. Allows users to type mount /mountpoint, where /mountpoint is the assigned mount point, to mount a disk.
users or nousers	All	Much like user and nouser, but changes the rules for unmounting a filesystem. When user is specified, only root or the user who mounted a filesystem may unmount it. When users is specified, any user may unmount a filesystem.
ro	All	Specifies a read-only mount of the filesystem. This is the default for filesystems that include no write access, and for some with particularly unreliable write support, such as NTFS.
rw	All read/write filesystems	Specifies a read/write mount of the filesystem. This is the default for most read/write filesystems.
uid=$value$	Most filesystems that don't support Unix-style permissions, such as vfat, hpfs, ntfs, and hfs	Sets the owner of all files. For instance, uid=500 sets the owner to whoever has Linux user ID 500. (Check Linux user IDs in the /etc/passwd file.)
gid=$value$	Most filesystems that don't support Unix-style permissions, such as vfat, hpfs, ntfs, and hfs	Works like uid=$value$, but sets the group of all files on the filesystem. You can find group IDs in the /etc/group file.

Continued on next page

TABLE 10.1: COMMON FILESYSTEM OPTIONS *(continued)*

OPTION	SUPPORTED FILESYSTEMS	DESCRIPTION
conv=*code*	Most filesystems used on Microsoft and Apple OSs: msdos, umsdos, vfat, hpfs, hfs	If *code* is b or binary, Linux doesn't modify the files' contents. If *code* is t or text, Linux auto-converts files between Linux-style and DOS-style or Macintosh-style end-of-line characters. If *code* is a or auto, Linux applies the conversion unless the file is a known binary file format. It's usually best to leave this at its default value of binary, because file conversions can cause serious problems for some applications and file types.
case=*code*	hpfs, hfs	When *code* is lower, Linux converts filenames to all-lowercase; when *code* is asis, Linux leaves filenames as they are. The default in recent kernels is asis.

Of course, in order to read any filesystem in Linux, the kernel needs to have the filesystem driver available. The driver can be compiled into the kernel proper or as a module. Most distributions ship with most or all common filesystems available, but there are exceptions and limitations. NTFS is usually compiled to provide read-only access; if you want to risk read/write access, you must recompile it. Red Hat ships with no NTFS support at all. UMSDOS support is often omitted, although two other FAT drivers (msdos, for support with 8.3 filenames; and vfat, for support with VFAT long filenames) are usually available. If you recompile your kernel, as described in Chapter 15, "Creating a Custom Kernel," you must ensure that you compile in support for the filesystems you need.

Reading Linux Filesystems in Other OSs

Sometimes being able to read a Linux filesystem in another OS is invaluable. You may want to use ext2fs because it provides the best cross-platform support for features such as long filenames or file ownership and permissions. Sometimes being able to retrieve a file from your Linux system on short notice and without rebooting is handy. On rare occasions, you may want to repair a broken Linux configuration file that's preventing the system from booting.

WARNING   Many non-Linux ext2fs drivers and utilities provide imperfect write support. Also, some Linux tools are sensitive to end-of-line conventions and will choke if they receive a file with DOS-style end-of-line characters. Therefore, you should use a non-Linux OS for Linux configuration file editing only in emergency situations. Even then, an emergency Linux boot system, as described in Chapter 17, is usually a better choice.

Because Linux's filesystems are available in source code form, they've been ported to a variety of OSs. Two of the recent Linux journaling filesystems, XFS and JFS, originate on other OSs; however, these and the other Linux journaling filesystems are not yet widely available outside of the Linux world. Some tools for accessing ext2fs include:

DOS   LTOOLS is a set of utilities for reading and writing ext2fs from DOS. It is available from http://www.it.fht-esslingen.de/~zimmerma/software/ltools.html. This package is a filesystem access utility, not a full driver; it doesn't provide arbitrary programs with access via a drive letter.

Windows 9*x*/Me   You can use LTOOLS with Windows 9*x*/Me. Another access tool is Explore2fs (`http://uranus.it.swin.edu.au/~jn/linux/explore2fs.htm`), which provides read/write access with a Windows GUI. For more seamless integration, you can use Fsdext2 (`http://www.yipton.demon.co.uk/content.html#FSDEXT2`), which enables you to mount an ext2fs partition as a Windows drive, complete with drive letter. The latest stable version, 0.16, is read-only, though.

Windows NT/2000/XP   You can use Explore2fs under Windows NT/2000/XP. A true filesystem driver is ext2fsnt (`http://www.chat.ru/~ashedel/ext2fsnt/`; but this site is slow and hard to reach from the U.S.), and another (ext2fsd) is available from `http://sourceforge.net/projects/ext2fsd`.

OS/2   OS/2 features one of the most complete non-Linux ext2fs drivers, EXT2-OS2 (`http://perso.wanadoo.fr/matthieu.willm/ext2-os2/`). It provides read/write access and even includes ports of ancillary utilities such as `e2fsck` and `mke2fs`. Unfortunately, the latest 2.40 version hasn't been updated since 1997, so it doesn't work with most new ext2fs partitions.

BeOS   A read-only ext2fs driver ships with recent versions of BeOS and was once available as an add-on for earlier versions; however, finding it has become difficult due to the decline of BeOS as a viable platform.

FreeBSD   FreeBSD ships with a read/write ext2fs driver, but it's not compiled into the kernel by default. To compile it, you must reconfigure and recompile the kernel. Consult FreeBSD documentation for more on this task. The read/write FreeBSD ext2fs support isn't entirely trustworthy, so I recommend using it for read-only access or on a dedicated data transfer partition.

A handful of drivers for other Linux filesystems are available in other OSs. For instance, a BeOS driver for ReiserFS is available from `http://www.bebits.com/app/3214`; JFS ships with AIX and some versions of OS/2, although cross-OS differences can complicate its use in this way ; and XFS is IRIX's native filesystem. If you use ext3fs, you may be able to use some ext2fs drivers and utilities, but some of these may disable read/write support.

Some of the older ext2fs drivers don't support the latest versions of ext2fs, as used in 2.4.*x* or even 2.2.*x* kernels. If you're planning a multiboot installation and you want to use a shared ext2fs partition, you can still do so, but you must create that partition with an old version of Linux's `mke2fs` or with another utility. For instance, you could use EXT2-OS2's `mke2fs` instead of Linux's `mke2fs` to create the shared filesystem. Both OSs should then be able to access the shared partition.

Exchanging Files: File Format Compatibility

If you mount a foreign filesystem but the data files you copy from it appear as gibberish in all the applications you try, mounting the filesystem will have proven useless. Thus, in any multiboot environment, you should give some consideration to your data file formats. Broadly speaking, there are two types of file formats:

◆ Cross-platform formats, which are based on open standards that can be implemented by anybody

◆ Proprietary formats, which are restricted to just one application

As a general rule, cross-platform file formats are better, but the lines can sometimes be blurry and there are a few exceptions.

Cross-Platform File Formats

Many tools exist to create files in most cross-platform formats. Linux tools to do so are described in other chapters of this book, such as Chapter 7, "Using Linux for Office Productivity" and Chapter 8, "Miscellaneous User Tools." Some important classes of such formats include:

Text Files   One of the simplest file formats is plain text, which is encoded using the *American Standard Code for Information Interchange (ASCII)*. Some minor variants on ASCII, most of which relate to the handling of end-of-line characters, also exist. Linux and other Unix-like OSs use a single character, which is often referred to as a line feed (LF) or new line (NL). DOS, Windows, and OS/2 all use two characters—a carriage return (CR) plus an LF. Mac OS uses a CR alone. The conv mount option (see Table 10.1) enables automatic translation of these features for some or all files, but this translation wreaks havoc for other file types. Some distributions ship with simple tools called dos2unix and unix2dos to perform these translations, too. Some file types are built using ASCII and so can be treated as such. For instance, the Hypertext Markup Language (HTML) that's at the core of the Web is nothing but ASCII with special formatting conventions.

Word Processing Files   Some word processors and other text-preparation tools, such as Anywhere Office and LaTeX, are built atop ASCII, much like HTML. Other word processors use binary formats. Most of these formats are proprietary in at least some sense, although of course the open source programs use formats that are public and well documented. One word processing format that's at least close to being cross-platform is Rich Text Format (RTF); most word processors can read and write RTF files. Unfortunately, the results are unpredictable. An emerging cross-platform standard is the Extensible Markup Language (XML). OpenOffice.org uses a compressed version of XML, and other word processors are adding XML support, as well.

Spreadsheet Files   Most spreadsheet programs use their own file formats. One common, but low-level, cross-platform format is the comma-separated value (CSV) format, which uses ASCII lines with commas separating spreadsheet fields. All modern spreadsheets can read and write CSV files, although they don't always support all spreadsheet features very well. Therefore, CSV is best used to transfer spreadsheet data—equations are likely to be lost.

Graphics Files   Many cross-platform graphics file formats exist. The most common are the Tagged Image File Format (TIFF), the Graphic Interchange Format (GIF), the Joint Photographic Experts Group (JPEG), the Portable Network Graphics (PNG) format, PostScript, and the Portable Document Format (PDF). All of these formats except PostScript are binary in nature, and all are supported by a wide array of graphics programs. Some of these formats are more open than others, though. Of particular note, GIF uses a compression algorithm that's covered by patents, so many open source software programs don't support GIF, or at most only support reading GIF files. The patents are scheduled to expire in 2003. PDF is a proprietary binary derivative of PostScript. I include it as a cross-platform format because both Adobe and third parties have developed PDF creation and viewing tools for a wide range of platforms.

Audio Files   Several audio file formats are commonplace. In the Windows world, `.wav` files are the standard, and many Linux audio tools handle these files quite well. Sun's `.au` format is common in the Unix world. Moving Picture Experts Group Layer 3 (MP3) files are an increasingly common format for music players, but MP3, like GIF, is covered by patents, so many Linux users favor the newer Ogg Vorbis file format.

Archive Files   Certain programs merge files into carrier files known as *archives*. Some of these formats are most common on one platform or another, but most are open and cross-platform. The most common archive file format is the `.zip` file, which is standard on Windows systems. You can create and extract files from a `.zip` archive with the `zip` and `unzip` Linux commands, respectively. The approximate Linux equivalent to a `.zip` file is a *tarball*, which usually has a `.tar.gz`, `.tgz`, or `.tar.bz2` extension. Most Linux distributions also support RPM Package Manager (RPM) files or Debian packages, both of which are open cross-platform formats, although they're not often used outside of Linux.

As a general rule, it's easy to exchange graphics and audio files across platforms because the many cross-platform formats are both extremely common and extremely well-supported. Plain text files also don't pose many problems. End-of-line handling is the most common issue with ASCII, but it can be handled with mount options, tools such as `unix2dos` and `dos2unix`, or even individual text editors—most can handle all three common end-of-line conventions.

WARNING   Some Linux configuration files are sensitive to end-of-line conventions; saving a file with DOS or Mac OS conventions may result in the file not working. In a critical startup configuration file, the result can be a system that doesn't boot. This is one of the reasons you shouldn't try editing Linux configuration files from DOS, Windows, or Mac OS unless you really need to do so.

Unfortunately, file formats for office productivity tools are not very well standardized, and the cross-platform formats that do exist are seldom adequate to the task. This is one of the reasons that people run emulators, as described in the upcoming section, "Improving Your Productivity with Emulators."

Proprietary File Formats

The most common proprietary file format is probably Microsoft Word's format (denoted by a `.doc` extension). Many businesses run on Microsoft Word; if you work with such a business, you'll have to exchange Microsoft Word files. In some fields, the file formats associated with other Microsoft Office components, such as Microsoft Excel (`.xls`) spreadsheets are equally or more important. Although Microsoft retains tight control over these file formats, most competing programs make at least some effort to support them. Chapter 7 describes some of the Linux programs that can handle these files. In brief, OpenOffice.org and its commercial twin StarOffice do the best job with Microsoft Word files. Unfortunately, no Linux program handles these files perfectly, so you may need to resort to emulation in some cases.

Many other programs outside the Linux world use proprietary formats. Office suites other than Microsoft Office, desktop publishing programs, tax-preparation software, advanced graphics tools such as Adobe Photoshop, and more all use proprietary formats. Some also support cross-platform formats, and as a general rule, if you want to exchange data files created with these programs, you should store them in a cross-platform format. In a few cases, you may be able to import the native file format using a Linux program, or even run a Linux version of the program.

TIP   Try saving files you must transfer in multiple formats. When you (or the files) get to the target system, if one format doesn't load, another might.

Many Windows programs are distributed as self-extracting archive files. These files have .exe extensions and are run as programs in Windows. The programs extract the files and install them on the system. Some of these programs are really just .zip or other cross-platform archive files with an executable wrapper, and these files can usually be handled by tools designed to process the core archive; but some self-extracting archives use formats that are harder to handle in Linux. Fortunately, you're not likely to need to access many of these files, although there are exceptions, such as font archives, clip-art collections, and so on.

Linux also has proprietary file formats, or at least formats for which support outside of the Unix world is rare. The GNU Image Manipulation Program (GIMP), for instance, uses its own file format, as do most Linux word processors. These file formats are all well-documented, but the big commercial players are, by and large, uninterested in implementing support for these file formats. Therefore, saving files from such tools in a cross-platform format, or in the proprietary format of the target program, may be the only way to load the files on a non-Linux system.

Improving Your Productivity with Emulators

Try as you might, sometimes you can't do what you want or need to do with Linux alone. This is one of the reasons for creating a multiboot system. An alternative or supplement to multibooting, though, is using an *emulator*—a program that enables you to run one OS's programs on another OS. Many different emulators are available, and they come with varying features and capabilities. Before exploring some of the specific emulators available, though, you should understand a little of how an emulator works and what the emulator's method of operation implies about its capabilities.

The Features and Limits of Emulation

Three main types of emulation are available in Linux:

CPU   Compiled software uses machine code that runs on only one CPU or CPU family, such as IA-32, IA-64, or PowerPC. If you want to run, say, an IA-32 executable on a Macintosh (which uses a PowerPC CPU), you must have software that translates the IA-32 CPU instructions in the executable to PowerPC instructions. This task is akin to interpreting the instructions in a script. Such emulation tends to be time-consuming, which substantially degrades performance.

Machine Environment   In addition to the CPU, computers have a host of hardware devices— video cards, hard disks, Ethernet interfaces, and so on. Linux takes full control of these interfaces, which means that to run another OS within Linux, some sort of indirection is necessary—that is, the emulator must present a fake hardware environment for the "guest" OS to use. Setting up this indirection is tricky from a programming point of view. It's also time-consuming, but not nearly as time-consuming as CPU emulation.

System Calls   Instead of running an entire guest OS within an emulator, you can create an environment of system calls that duplicate those of the emulated OS. This task is quite daunting in itself, but the challenges are different from those of CPU or machine environment emulation—instead of setting up a fake hardware environment that can fool software, a replacement software environment is required.

CPU emulation is most often used to run Macintosh programs on an IA-32 system, to run an IA-32 OS on a Macintosh, or to run software for older computers (such as Apple IIs, Ataris, or Commodores) or game systems on a desktop computer. Machine environment emulation lets you run an arbitrary OS for the same CPU that your computer has under Linux. Most commonly, you'll run Windows under Linux, but other options are available, too. A system call emulator can handle just one OS (Windows is the most common one). In theory, system call emulation can be slightly faster than machine environment emulation. In practice, the need to create a reimplementation of Windows without access to the original Windows source code makes system call emulation very difficult.

The main Linux system call emulator is WINE (Windows Emulator or WINE Is Not an Emulator, depending on who you ask). It does a good job with some programs, but a poor job with others. Machine environment emulators tend to run a broader range of programs, but they can be more limiting in terms of access to your Linux system. For instance, WINE uses the Linux filesystem, so you can load and save files in your Linux home directory as if you were using a native Linux program. Machine environment emulators, by contrast, generally use partitions or large files in which the emulator sets up a filesystem. You must use networking to save files in the Linux filesystem. (Win4Lin is an exception to this rule.)

You can use an emulator to run popular Windows or Mac OS programs such as Microsoft Office or various Windows games. Some games, though, use advanced video driver features that the emulators don't support, so some games don't work well (or at all) in an emulator. You should definitely check the emulator's website for information on whether any important programs you want to run will work. You may also need a fast CPU (especially for CPU emulators), lots of disk space, and a substantial amount of spare RAM, particularly for CPU and machine environment emulators. You may need to jump through a lot of hoops to use certain external peripherals, such as modems, printers, and scanners, and some may not work at all. Networking might or might not work well. Some CPU and machine environment emulators rely on nonstandard kernel drivers, so you may need to patch and recompile your kernel to use them.

Popular Emulators for Linux

Quite a few emulators are available for Linux. If you need to run a non-Linux program within Linux, chances are good you'll be able to do so, but picking the right emulator can be a daunting task.

CPU EMULATORS

The most important CPU emulator for Linux is arguably Bochs (`http://bochs.sourceforge.net`). This open source program sets up an emulated IA-32 environment in which you can run DOS, Windows 95, Windows NT, Linux, and probably other OSs. (Exact OS support varies from version to version, and the developers haven't tested every possible variation.) Bochs uses a disk file in which the emulator sets up a simulated hard disk. For instance, if you have an 80GB hard disk, you can create a 10GB file that the emulator will treat as a 10GB hard disk. As a CPU emulator, Bochs is quite slow.

It's most useful when you're running Linux on a non-IA-32 CPU such as a PowerPC or Alpha, and then it will be sluggish compared to running native programs. Despite these problems, Bochs can be a lifesaver if you really need to run a Windows program on a non-IA-32 system.

Other CPU emulators for Linux emulate older computers. A host of emulators, such as Executor (`http://www.ardi.com/executor.php`) and STonX (`http://stonx.sourceforge.net`), emulate 680x0-based systems such as early Macintoshes and Atari STs. These emulators tend to work reasonably well and, on modern hardware, can equal or exceed the original systems' performances. A wider range of emulators handle still older 8-bit computers and game systems. The most ambitious of these are the MAME and MESS projects, which are closely affiliated and handle a very wide range of systems from the 1970s through 1990s. Check `http://x.mame.net` for more information.

CPU emulators typically set up a window devoted to the host OS. The window may change in size as the host OS changes video resolution. Cutting and pasting between the host and guest OSs is typically not possible, but many emulators provide a screen shot option so that you can capture an image of the guest OS's display. Figure 10.2 shows a Bochs window as it boots Linux.

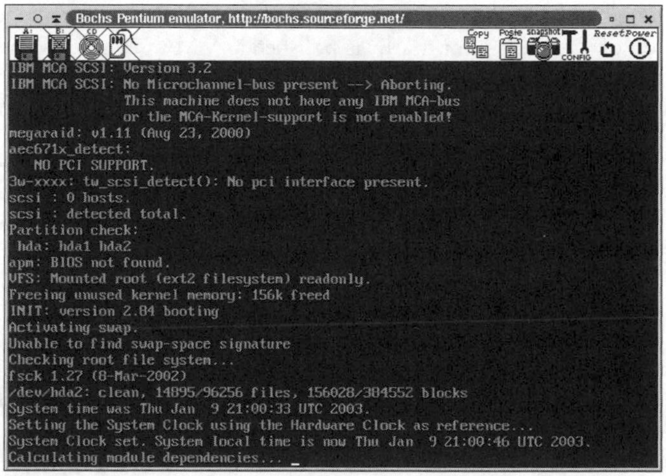

FIGURE 10.2

Most emulators run in windows that emulate a computer screen.

MACHINE ENVIRONMENT EMULATORS

Because they don't need to perform the costly CPU emulation, machine environment emulators typically run much faster than CPU emulators. They're usually about as tedious to set up, though, and they often require special kernel support to help the emulator interface with your real hardware. The five most popular machine environment emulators are listed here:

DOSEMU This open source emulator, headquartered at `http://www.dosemu.org`, is the simplest and most limited of the machine environment emulators. It supports just enough functionality to allow DOS to run. DOSEMU ships with most IA-32 Linux distributions, along with FreeDOS (`http://www.freedos.org`). DOSEMU works best using a file that it treats as a hard disk, but you can boot it from a DOS floppy if required.

Win4Lin   This commercial program, available from Netraverse (`http://www.netraverse.com`), is designed to run Windows 9x/Me only. It's available both in a desktop system and as the Win4Lin Terminal Server, which enables one Linux computer to deliver Windows functionality to many thin clients. Unlike most machine environment emulators, Win4Lin provides direct access to the underlying Linux filesystem. Because it's tailored so closely to Windows 9x/Me, Win4Lin is faster than other machine environment emulators—but of course, it's less flexible. Win4Lin requires a kernel patch to run.

VMware   This commercial emulator, available from a company of the same name (`http://www`
`.vmware.com`), is an extremely powerful and flexible program. VMware supports all versions of DOS, Windows, Linux, and FreeBSD. Other OSs might or might not run. VMware is slower than Win4Lin, and it requires a dedicated partition or a large disk file to serve as a virtual disk. (With some preparation, you can also boot the emulator from an existing standard Windows installation.) VMware requires a kernel patch to run.

Plex86   This open source emulator (`http://savannah.nongnu.org/projects/plex86`) can be thought of as either an open source version of VMware or a machine environment emulator version of Bochs. It's not nearly as polished as VMware. Like Bochs and VMware, Plex86 uses a large file as a virtual disk.

MoL   The Mac-on-Linux (MoL; `http://www.maconlinux.org`) project is roughly equivalent to VMware or Plex86, but it runs on PowerPC hardware. As such, MoL runs Mac OS or PowerPC versions of Linux rather than Windows. You can boot your regular Mac OS installation after running Linux, much as Mac OS X runs Mac OS 9 to enable compatibility with older Mac OS applications.

In general, Win4Lin, VMware, and MoL are the easiest of these emulators to use. DOSEMU's configuration can be tedious, and getting Plex86 to work is a real challenge. The commercial emulators pose a special hurdle, though, in keeping their kernel patches updated with a changing Linux kernel. You may be forced to pay for upgrades just to use a version for which modern kernel patches are available.

All of these emulators except for DOSEMU run in their own windows or take over the entire screen, much as do most CPU emulators. DOSEMU can run in much this way, but for text-mode applications, it can run in an `xterm` or from a text-mode login. This mode of operation simplifies text cut-and-paste operations for DOS programs.

WINE

The WINE project (headquartered at `http://www.winehq.com`) is an effort to develop an independent implementation of the Microsoft Windows application programming interface (API). WINE has two components. The first is a set of libraries (Winelib) that implement what are, in Linux terms, a widget set similar in scope to the popular Qt, GTK+, or Motif. Using this component of WINE, a developer can take Windows source code and compile it into a native Linux application. The second WINE component is a program loader. It launches unmodified Windows executables, enabling them to run with Winelib under Linux. In theory, Winelib could be used on any platform, but the program loader works only on IA-32 systems.

Unfortunately, WINE isn't yet complete, and probably never will be—Microsoft is likely to continue updating the Windows API until the Windows product dies, forcing WINE to play perpetual catch-up. Nonetheless, WINE has come a long way since its inception in 1993. WINE or its derivatives can run several versions of Microsoft Office, Internet Explorer, web browser plug-ins, many games, and assorted other programs. WINE's main problem is its tricky configuration (described in more detail shortly). Tweaking WINE for specific applications is often necessary, and doing so can take trial-and-error experimentation. In order to simplify configuration and fill in some of the gaps in WINE's source code, several commercial projects have arisen around WINE:

CrossOver CodeWeavers (`http://www.codeweavers.com`) markets three WINE spin-offs: CrossOver Office, CrossOver Office Server Edition, and CrossOver Plugin. The first two products are designed to run Microsoft Office on Linux workstations and servers, respectively. CrossOver Plugin runs Windows web browser plugins, such as QuickTime and Shockwave players. All of these products feature easy-to-use GUI installation and configuration tools. None ships with the target programs; you must obtain your own copy of Microsoft Office or other programs. You may be able to use these products to run programs not advertised by CodeWeavers, but they're fully tested and optimized only for their narrow ranges of programs.

WineX Transgaming (`http://www.transgaming.com`) provides a version of WINE that's optimized for use with popular Windows games. WineX is provided on a subscription basis to end users, or as a tool for game developers who want to release Linux ports of their games.

Lindows This system (`http://www.lindows.com`) is a Linux distribution that includes better WINE integration than most, with the goal of easing the transition from Microsoft Windows to Linux.

Assuming you install a stock WINE version on a traditional Linux distribution, you'll configure the program by editing a global configuration file called `wine.conf` or `config`, typically stored in the `/usr/local/etc` or `/etc/wine` directory. Alternatively, you can create a `.wine/config` file in your home directory to override the WINE defaults. Either way, the configuration file is structured much like the `WIN.INI` file from Windows 3.1—sections begin with names in brackets, and continue with lines that set important values. The WINE package comes with a sample `config` file, usually stored in the `documentation/samples` subdirectory of the directory in which you installed WINE. (If you install an RPM or Debian package, you can use the `rpm` or `dpkg` tool to locate the sample file, as in **`rpm -ql wine | grep config`** or **`dpkg -L wine | grep config`**.) Table 10.2 summarizes some of the more important sections and typical contents.

TABLE 10.2: IMPORTANT WINE CONFIGURATION FILE OPTIONS

CONFIGURATION FILE SECTION	FEATURES CONTROLLED	TYPICAL ENTRIES
`[Drive X]`	This section adjusts the mapping of Linux directories to Windows drive letters. It also sets drive volume labels and other features. *X* is the drive letter.	`"Path" = "/other/shared"` `"Type" = "hd"` `"Filesystem" = "win95"`
`[wine]`	This section sets the path to the Windows system directory, as required by many Windows programs, as well as some drivers and tools.	`"Windows" = "c:\\windows"` `"Temp" = "e:\\"`

Continued on next page

TABLE 10.2: IMPORTANT WINE CONFIGURATION FILE OPTIONS *(continued)*

CONFIGURATION FILE SECTION	FEATURES CONTROLLED	TYPICAL ENTRIES
[DllOverrides]	WINE includes built-in equivalents to many common Windows dynamic link libraries (DLLs), but sometimes a native DLL works better. This section lets you tell WINE which to use on a DLL-by-DLL basis.	"msvcrt" = "native, ➥ builtin"
[x11drv]	This section controls how WINE interfaces with X, including how many colors Windows programs can claim, whether or not to use the X window manager (the Managed setting), and so on.	"AllowSystemColors" = "100" "Managed" = "Y"
[fonts]	You can control the mapping of X fonts to Windows fonts in this section.	"Resolution" = "96" "Default" = "-adobe- ➥ helvetica-"
[FontDirs]	WINE can use TrueType fonts directly if you point it to appropriate directories.	"dir1" = "/usr/share/ ➥ fonts/TT"

The most important configuration file options are in the [Drive *X*] section. If these options are set incorrectly, Windows programs won't be able to locate the all-important windows directory, in which many store DLLs. You may also be unable to access your own user files. Typically, you should set aside a directory for C: (say, /usr/local/wine/c or perhaps a mounted Windows C: partition). If it's not already present, you should create windows and windows/system directories in this location. You may also want to create drive letters that point to your removable-media mount points, your home directory (the F: drive is usually so configured by default, using the ${HOME} variable), and any network filesystems you've mounted. The default settings usually work well, except that you may need to change the C: settings or create an appropriate directory. Defining Type as "hd" and Filesystem as "win95" is usually best. Be sure you have full read/write access to C: and any other directories that should be so accessible.

To run a program, type **wine** followed by the complete path to the program. You can specify this path either as a Linux path or in the equivalent Windows format. For instance, if D: is defined as /other/shared, then /other/shared/apps/someprog.exe and D:\\apps\\someprog.exe are equivalent. Note that when using Windows format, you use backslashes (\) rather than forward slashes (/) in the filename specification. To keep the Linux shell from interpreting the backslash as an escape character, you must double up these backslashes.

The first time you use WINE, it will spend some time parsing your fonts, so the program will launch very slowly. Subsequent launches will go much more rapidly.

WINE runs many Windows programs very well, but others it handles with quirks or not at all. In some cases, you may need to install the program in Windows and then copy some DLLs or other files from Windows to your WINE installation. You can try WINE on individual programs, or check the compatibility database at http://appdb.winehq.org; however, be aware that the compatibility database includes rankings from people with different skill levels and running different versions of WINE. A bad (or good) ranking from a year ago may not be relevant to a modern version of WINE.

WINE can either run all programs in a dedicated WINE window or run Windows programs side-by-side with Linux programs. Figure 10.3 shows the latter configuration, with Microsoft Word running on the Linux desktop using CrossOver Office, alongside the GIMP and other Linux programs. You can easily cut-and-paste between Linux and Windows programs.

FIGURE 10.3

WINE enables Windows and Linux programs to run on the same desktop.

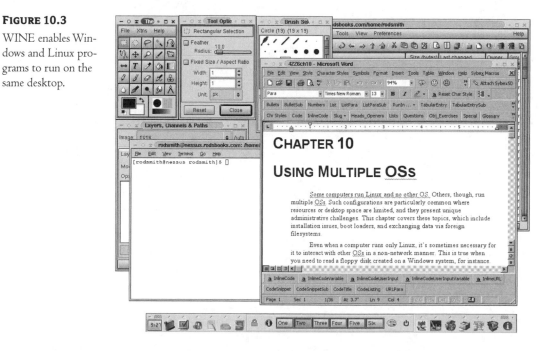

Summary

We live in a multi-OS world. This often translates into a need to run Linux alongside another OS on a single computer. Doing so presents certain challenges, but it can be done. Simple two-OS configurations are usually handled well by Linux installation routines, but doing more requires attention to details—partitioning issues, boot loader configuration, and filesystem handling. You should also know what file formats to use for the best cross-OS compatibility with the files you use. In some cases, the best compatibility can be achieved only by using an emulator. Fortunately, Linux supports many emulators, so chances are good you'll find one that'll do what you want.

Chapter 11

Managing Packages

MODERN OSs ARE COMPOSED of numerous files. These files include program files, configuration files, font files, and more. Many of these files come in collections that are often called *packages*, which consist of files that together make up a logical whole. For instance, a package might include a program file, its documentation, its configuration files, and other support files. Most Linux distributions today use one of two tools for managing packages: the *RPM Package Manager (RPM)* or Debian's package tools. Both systems enable distribution of packages as individual archive files and provide a set of tools for installing, removing, upgrading, and otherwise manipulating packages. Knowing how to use these tools is critical to basic system administration. After you have mastered the skills needed to use these tools, you can move beyond the basics. This chapter covers two advanced applications of these tools: how to convert between package file formats and how to use package management tools to help automate the upgrade process, thereby improving your ability to keep up to date with security and other important system upgrades.

NOTE   *A few distributions (notably Slackware) use* tarballs *as their package format. Tarballs are less sophisticated than other package formats, although Slackware builds a database of installed files using other means. Chapter 17, "Protecting Your System with Backups," covers* tar.

Basic Package Management Features

Both RPM and Debian packages rely on a database of information about installed packages for normal operation. This database includes the names of all installed files, checksum information on those files, the names and version numbers of the packages to which they belong, and the other packages upon which each package depends. This database is invaluable in managing software. For instance, suppose you want to install the manydep package. When you try to do so, the utilities note that manydep depends on several other packages, such as minorlib, obscurelib, and bizarrefonts. Without these packages, manydep won't function correctly, so if they aren't installed on your system, the package utilities complain and refuse to install manydep. If you install all of these packages and then try to uninstall minorlib, the system notes that manydep depends on minorlib, and so won't uninstall the latter package. Fitting with the Linux philosophy that people are smarter than computers, you can override the tool's refusal to perform an operation because of failed dependencies.

You might do this if you've installed the package in some way that's not reflected in the package management database. Particularly in the case of RPMs, you might also want to override the dependency checks when installing packages from one distribution on another, because different distributions sometimes use different names for equivalent packages.

The package database also allows detection of potential conflicts between packages. For instance, if `minorlib` and `majorlib` both provide a file called `/lib/mlib.so`, and if you try to install both packages, the system will refuse to do so without an explicit override. This feature can help prevent problems caused by different versions of libraries or support files being installed by multiple programs or by simple name conflicts. Such problems are rare unless you mix overlapping packages from different distributions. For instance, Distribution A might split up a set of programs into client and server packages, whereas Distribution B might use library and program packages for the same set of tools. Attempting to mix packages intended for Distributions A and B can then cause file conflicts.

When it comes time to remove or upgrade a package, package management tools help immensely; you don't need to track down all the files for a package, which may be installed in half a dozen or more directories and under names that aren't obviously related to one another. The package tool checks the database and can delete all the required files, and then delete the entries in the package database. When upgrading a package, the system uses these entries to delete any files that have been removed from the newer package, so as not to leave obsolete files lying around.

Package management tools also enable you to track down the package to which a file belongs, obtain descriptions of the package, obtain a list of all the files in a package, and more. Packages are generally built using specification files and original source code. *Source packages* are available for most RPMs. These packages contain source code, patches, and a compilation procedure. You can use a source package to build a new binary package. You might do this to work around some types of dependency problems or to rebuild a source package for a CPU for which a binary package isn't available. Debian packages aren't available as source packages, but you can find the specification file to do much the same thing, when combined with an original source code tarball. Because there's less variation in the Debian world than among RPM-based distributions, this is seldom necessary, though.

Avoiding Tedium with RPMs

The most popular package tool in the Linux world is RPM. Distributions that use RPM include Mandrake, Red Hat, and SuSE. The main text-based RPM program is `rpm`, which is used for adding, updating, deleting, and finding information on packages. Some distributions, such as Red Hat, use ancillary tools for some functions, such as rebuilding packages from source code. There are also GUI front-ends to `rpm`, which enable point-and-click access to RPM management features.

TIP   Even if you don't normally use GUI tools, GUI RPM utilities can be handy to "browse" a list of installed packages, enabling you to trim unnecessary packages from your system.

Understanding the *rpm* Utility

Basic RPM functionality resides in the `rpm` utility, which has the following syntax:

```
rpm operation [options] [package-names | package-filenames]
```

Table 11.1 summarizes the most common and important rpm operations, while Table 11.2 summarizes some common and important rpm options. Every rpm command requires one operation and often has one or more options. In most cases, you can specify multiple package names or package filenames. These two types of names are distinct. A package name is the name used by the package in the package database; it doesn't need to bear any resemblance to the filename used to store the package prior to installation, although in most cases the two are related. Recent versions of RPM support directly retrieving packages via the File Transfer Protocol (FTP) or from websites, so a package filename can be a URL; or it can be an ordinary local filename.

TABLE 11.1: COMMON rpm OPERATIONS

rpm OPERATION	DESCRIPTION
-i	Installs a package; the system must *not* contain a package of the same name.
-U	Installs a new package or upgrades an existing one.
-F or --freshen	Upgrades a package only if an earlier version already exists.
-q	Queries a package: Determines if a package is installed, what files it contains, and so on.
-V or -y or --verify	Verifies a package: Checks that its files are present and unchanged since installation.
-e	Uninstalls a package.
-b	Builds a binary package, given source code and configuration files. Split off into rpmbuild program as of RPM 4.1.
--rebuild	Builds a binary package, given a source RPM file. Split off into rpmbuild program as of RPM 4.1.
--rebuilddb	Rebuilds the RPM database, to fix errors.

TABLE 11.2: COMMON rpm OPTIONS

rpm OPTION	USED WITH OPERATIONS	DESCRIPTION
--root *dir*	Any	Modifies the Linux system having a root directory located at *dir*. This option can be used to maintain one Linux installation discrete from another one, say during OS installation or emergency maintenance.
--force	-i, -U, -F	Forces installation of a package even when it means overwriting existing files or packages.
-h or --hash	-i, -U, -F	Displays a series of pound signs (#) to indicate the progress of the operation.
-v	-i, -U, -F	Used in conjunction with the -h option to produce a uniform number of hash marks for each package.

Continued on next page

TABLE 11.2: COMMON rpm OPTIONS *(continued)*

rpm OPTION	USED WITH OPERATIONS	DESCRIPTION
--nodeps	-i, -U, -F, -e	Performs no dependency checks. Installs or removes the package even if it relies on a package or file that's not present or is required by a package that's not being uninstalled.
--test	-i, -U, -F	Check for dependencies, conflicts, and other problems without actually installing the package.
--prefix *path*	-q, -i, -U, -F	Sets the installation directory to *path* for relocatable packages. (Used with the -q operation, reports whether or not the package is relocatable.)
-a or --all	-q, -V	Queries or verifies all packages.
-f *file* or --file *file*	-q, -V	Queries or verifies the package that owns *file*.
-p *package-file*	-q	Queries the uninstalled RPM *package-file*.
-i	-q	Displays package information, including the package maintainer, a short description, and so on.
-R or --requires	-q	Displays the packages and files upon which this one depends.
-l or --list	-q	Displays the files contained in the package.

In most cases, the package filename takes the format *packagename-version-revision.arch*.rpm, as in manydep-2.31-6mdk.i586.rpm. The *version* is the official version number of the original program, such as 2.31 in this example. This version number corresponds to a release of the program from its official maintainer. The *revision* number refers to minor changes made to the official release to enhance it or add distribution-specific features. For instance, this number might go up if the package maintainer alters a configuration file default or applies a patch to fix a bug. Many distributions include a code to identify their distribution in this number, as in 6mdk for revision 6 from Mandrake. The *arch* in the filename is a CPU architecture code, such as i386 or i586 for IA-32 systems with varying CPU optimizations, or ppc for PowerPC. The noarch code stands for an architecture-independent package, such as fonts or a set of scripts. Source packages are identified by src architecture codes. A few SuSE packages use the nosrc architecture code, indicating a binary package for which a source package isn't available.

Investigating a Package

Sometimes you want to learn about a package. You might want to know what it does before you install it, find a list of files it contains before or after it's installed, or learn to what package a file on your computer belongs. You can do all of this and more with the -q operation, which takes several different options, as detailed in Table 11.2. For instance, you might issue commands like this to learn more about a specific file that you've found on your system:

```
# rpm -qf /usr/X11R6/bin/xv
xv-3.10a-15
# rpm -qi xv
Name          : xv                          Relocations: (not relocateable)
Version       : 3.10a                             Vendor: Red Hat Software
Release       : 15                            Build Date: Tue 07 Sep 1999 03:27:30 PM
EDT
Install date: Mon 13 Jan 2003 04:05:58 PM EST    Build Host: porky.devel.redhat.com
Group         : Amusements/Graphics         Source RPM: xv-3.10a-15.src.rpm
Size          : 4647951                        License: Shareware
Signature     : DSA/SHA1, Thu 23 Sep 1999 12:53:03 PM EDT, Key ID 219180cddb42a60e
Packager      : Red Hat Software <http://developer.redhat.com/bugzilla>
URL           : http://www.trilon.com/xv/xv.html
Summary       : An X based image file viewer and manipulator.
Description :
Xv is an image display and manipulation utility for the X Window
System.  Xv can display GIF, JPEG, TIFF, PBM, PPM, X11 bitmap, Utah
Raster Toolkit RLE, PDS/VICAR, Sun Rasterfile, BMP, PCX, IRIS RGB, XPM,
Targa, XWD, PostScript(TM) and PM format image files.  Xv is also
capable of image manipulation like cropping, expanding, taking
screenshots, etc.
```

Installing, Upgrading, and Removing Packages

The most important package management features enable installing, upgrading, and removing packages. With rpm, you can install packages using either the -i or -U operation. As Table 11.1 reveals, -i installs a package only if a package of the same name isn't already installed, whereas -U will install a package or upgrade an existing package. These operations are often combined with the -v and -h options to produce a series of hash marks as a progress indicator:

```
# rpm -Uvh xv-3.10a-15.i386.rpm
Preparing...                ######################################### [100%]
   1:xv                     ######################################### [100%]
```

FIXING A CORRUPT RPM DATABASE

If you kill rpm or the system crashes while it's working, the result can be a lock on the RPM database file and corruption of the database itself. The symptom is that you can no longer use rpm to upgrade, install, or remove packages. GUI tools may also complain or fail to run. In most cases, you can correct the matter by typing the following commands:

```
# rm -f /var/lib/rpm/__db*
# rpm -vv --rebuilddb
```

If this procedure fails to work, you may need to engage in a more lengthy recovery process, which is outlined at http://www.rpm.org/hintskinks/repairdb/.

If rpm responds to an installation attempt with a complaint of a dependency problem, you have several options for how to proceed, including:

Abandon the Installation The simplest, but least productive, solution is to abandon the attempt to install the program. This will leave the package uninstalled.

Fix the Dependency Problem You can attempt to correct the problem by installing additional packages, upgrading too-old packages, or uninstalling packages that hold conflicting files. Doing this will likely involve tracking down new packages and installing them. Particularly when your system has old versions of packages, you may find yourself in a nasty cycle of upgrades—upgrading a depended-upon package may require upgrading a package upon which it depends, and so on for several layers. These upgrades may break some already-installed packages. Installing new packages is usually easier, but you must locate them first.

TIP *If you can't figure out what package to install to meet a dependency, go to the RPM Find database (*http://www.rpmfind.net *or* http://rpmfind.net*). Enter the name of the depended-upon package or file, as reported by* rpm, *in the search field. You can download a matching file directly or try to find a package of the specified name on your distribution's installation media.*

Override the Complaint The --nodeps option disables dependency checks. You should use this option cautiously, if at all, and only when you're sure the dependency isn't critical or is met in a way that isn't reflected in the RPM database. The --force option enables you to install a package even if it means overwriting existing files. Doing so can cause problems down the line if and when you want to uninstall one package. It can also break the already-installed package if the new files aren't compatible.

Rebuild the Package Some dependency problems can be fixed by rebuilding a package. Specifically, if your system has an older version of a depended-upon package than the one a binary package requires, rebuilding the package from source code may fix the problem. This isn't a guaranteed solution, though, and even if it works, it may require installing additional development packages. Consult the upcoming section, "Rebuilding a Package," for more details.

If you install a package and subsequently decide you don't want to use it, you can remove it with the -e operation, as in:

```
# rpm -e xv
```

Note that this command takes a package name, not a package filename, as an option. Package filenames are needed for installation and upgrade operations because rpm must know where to look to find the package files; however, the original package filename is unimportant after it's installed, so the package name is used for uninstallation operations.

As with installation and upgrades, uninstallation can run into dependency problems. If you plan to uninstall depended-upon packages, you may as well add them to the list of packages and try again; rpm will check all dependencies and complain only if a package you didn't list depends on one you're trying to remove.

Verifying Package Integrity

The -V operation verifies a package—it checks various pieces of information concerning the package's files and compares them to information stored in the RPM database. The result looks something like this:

```
# rpm -V ntp
S.5....T c /etc/ntp.conf
```

Only files that differ from the original in some way are reported. The first eight characters are a code for the differences—a period (.) means that a feature hasn't changed, but an alphanumeric code indicates that it has changed. Specifically, the fields are the size (S), permissions (mode; M), Message Digest 5 (MD5; 5) sum, device numbers (D), readlink path mismatch (L), user ownership (U), group ownership (G), and time stamp (T). If a c appears after this eight-character string, the file is a configuration file. Changes in configuration files are not uncommon, but changes in other file types could spell trouble, such as disk errors, filesystem bugs, or security problems.

TIP   RPM wasn't intended as a security tool, but it can serve as a check of system integrity in a pinch. RPM isn't entirely reliable in this function, though—an intruder need only install a package using RPM to make it useless as a test. Chapter 21, "Detecting Intruders," includes information on far better intrusion-detection tools.

You can check the integrity of all the packages on your system by typing **rpm -Va**. Unfortunately, changes in some files—even some nonconfiguration files—are perfectly normal. Therefore, this command will produce a lot of output, making it hard to determine which deviations are important and which are not.

Using GUI RPM Tools

Several GUI RPM front-ends are available. Mandrake uses MandrakeUpdate (rpmdrake), Red Hat ships with one known as Package Management (redhat-config-packages), and SuSE's YaST and YaST2 include integrated RPM-management tools. An older tool called GNOME RPM is available on many distributions. Figure 11.1 shows GNOME RPM in use.

FIGURE 11.1

GUI RPM Tools enable you to browse and manipulate installed and uninstalled packages in a point-and-click environment.

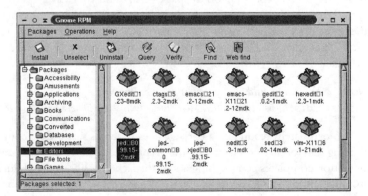

The details of how these tools operate differ somewhat, but typically, you can browse the installed packages using a hierarchical display. For instance, Figure 11.1 shows the packages that are installed in the Editors category. You can select an installed package, query its contents, uninstall it, and so on. You can install a package by clicking the Install button, clicking Add in the resulting Install dialog box, selecting a package in the resulting file selector dialog box, and then clicking Install in the Install dialog box. Mandrake's MandrakeUpdate, Red Hat's Package Management, and SuSE's YaST and YaST2 enable you to install any package that comes with the distribution from a list. The utility then locates depended-upon packages and prompts you for the disc or discs on which the packages reside. This feature can greatly simplify installation of new software, provided it comes with the distribution.

TIP   *GUI package management tools are very useful for browsing the installed packages. You can see what's installed, query packages to determine what they do, and uninstall packages you don't need. This capability enables you to save disk space and reduce the security threat posed by the presence of unnecessary servers or other potentially buggy software.*

Rebuilding a Package

Rebuilding a package is necessary if you can't find a prebuilt binary for your CPU architecture. It can sometimes help resolve dependency problems, too. If a package depends on newer versions of software than you have installed, rebuilding the package *may* work around that problem. Such dependencies sometimes originate in the source code, in which case rebuilding the package won't help; but if the dependency is an artifact of the chance fact that the original-build computer had a later library than you've got, then rebuilding will help.

With RPM versions 4.0 and earlier, you can rebuild a package using the `--rebuild` option to `rpm`. RPM 4.1, though, splits this functionality into a separate tool, `rpmbuild`. Other than the name of the executable, the procedure is identical. In its simplest form, you pass the name of the source RPM file to the RPM rebuilding utility:

```
# rpmbuild --rebuild manydep-2.31-6mdk.src.rpm
```

This command rebuilds the `manydep` package. The process takes anywhere from a few seconds to several hours, depending on the package size and your CPU speed. The result is a file for your architecture, such as `manydep-2.31-6mdk.i586.rpm`, stored in `/usr/src/`*distname*`/RPMS/`*arch*, where *distname* is a distribution-specific name (`RPM` for Mandrake, `redhat` for Red Hat, or `packages` for SuSE) and *arch* is a CPU architecture code. Once you've rebuilt a binary package, you can install it just like any other RPM.

NOTE   *You can rebuild most packages as an ordinary user, but only if that user has write permissions in the* /usr/src/*distname directory tree. Most distributions ship with this directory tree writeable only to* root.

Unfortunately, rebuilding a package doesn't always work. One common source of problems is missing development tools or libraries. Typically, you'll see an error message shortly before the build operation completes complaining about the lack of a library. With luck, you'll be able to locate it and install it using the RPM Find database or a search of your installation media. In most cases, you'll need to install a package with `devel` in the name. For instance, if the build aborts and complains about the lack of `obscurelib`, you'll need to install both `obscurelib` and `obscurelib-devel`.

Avoiding Tedium with Debian Packages

Debian packages are very much like RPMs in overall features and in the role that they fill in the distribution. Debian packages use different tools than do RPMs, though, and their options are unique. Also, a wider variety of command-line Debian package tools is available.

Understanding the *dpkg* Utility

The Debian package tool that's most similar to the rpm utility is dpkg. This tool's syntax is similar to that of rpm:

```
dpkg [options] action [package-filename|package-name]
```

Tables 11.3 and 11.4 summarize the dpkg actions (equivalent to the rpm operation) and options, respectively. Most of these actions and options are similar to their rpm counterparts, but there are some exceptions. For instance, there is no separate upgrade action in dpkg; the install action will also upgrade a package.

TABLE 11.3: dpkg PRIMARY ACTIONS

dpkg ACTION	DESCRIPTION
-i or --install	Installs a package.
--configure	Reconfigures an installed package: Runs the post-installation script to set site-specific options.
-r or -P or --remove or --purge	Removes a package. The -P or --purge action does a more complete job; it removes configuration files that -r and --remove don't delete.
-p or --print-avail	Displays information about a package.
-l *pattern* or --list *pattern*	Lists all installed packages whose names match *pattern*.
-L or --listfiles	Lists the installed files associated with a package.
-C or --audit	Searches for partially installed packages and suggests what to do with them.

TABLE 11.4: OPTIONS TO FINE-TUNE dpkg ACTIONS

dpkg OPTION	USED WITH ACTIONS	DESCRIPTION
--root=*dir*	All	Modifies the Linux system using a root directory located at *dir*. Can be used to maintain one Linux installation discrete from another one, say during OS installation or emergency maintenance.
-B or --auto-deconfigure	-r	Disables packages that rely on one being removed.

Continued on next page

TABLE 11.4: OPTIONS TO FINE-TUNE dpkg ACTIONS *(continued)*

dpkg OPTION	USED WITH ACTIONS	DESCRIPTION
--force-*things*	Assorted	Forces specific actions to be taken. Consult the dpkg man page for details of *things* this option does.
--ignore-depends=*package*	-i, -r	Ignores dependency information for the specified package.
--no-act	-i, -r	Checks for dependencies, conflicts, and other problems without actually installing the package.
--recursive	-i	Installs all packages matching the package name wildcard in the specified directory and all subdirectories.
-G	-i	Doesn't install the package if a newer version of the same package is already installed.
-E or --skip-same-version	-i	Doesn't install the package if the same version of the package is already installed.

Debian packages are named similarly to RPMs—the format is *packagename_version-revision*.deb, as in manydep_2.31-6.deb. An architecture code is sometimes added before the .deb extension, and the revision code is sometimes omitted.

Few independent sites carry Debian packages; the Debian site itself is the primary source of packages for this distribution. Check http://www.debian.org/distrib/packages for a search tool to locate packages by name. A few commercial distributions, such as Libranet (http://www.libranet.com) and Xandros (http://www.xandros.com), are built from Debian. In my experience, cross-distribution package compatibility is very good within this Debian family—much better than between RPM-based distributions.

Understanding the *dselect* Utility

The dpkg utility is useful if you've got a Debian package file in hand, ready to be installed. Another tool, which should be familiar to you if you've installed Debian, is dselect. This program is a text-mode utility that provides a list of available packages. The package list includes all those available from your chosen installation medium, and possibly from other sources as well, as described shortly.

When you first start dselect, it presents you with seven actions you can perform:

Access   You can set the media on which dselect looks for packages. You can specify CD-ROM, hard disk, and other local and network media. You can also tell dselect to use the Advanced Package Tool (APT) configuration, as described in the upcoming section, "Maintaining Debian with APT."

Update   This option tells dselect to check the packages available from the sources you specified using the Access option. If you select new sources or if they've been updated since your last run, you need to do this in order to update packages or install new packages.

Select This option leads to a text-mode package-selection tool, which you can use to locate and select packages for installation. Unfortunately, the list is *very* long, which can make finding a package difficult, particularly if you're unfamiliar with the keyboard navigation commands. Type a question mark (**?**) to get to the help system, which describes these commands.

Install This option installs any packages you've selected using the Select option. It also upgrades any packages that have been updated since they were installed, provided your installation source reflects those updates. The program provides you with a summary of upgrades before proceeding. On occasion, you may need to choose this option up to four times to install all the packages and their dependencies.

Config Some Debian packages include configuration scripts that run after they're installed. For instance, Debian asks you questions to help configure its mail server for your network. This option runs through any configuration scripts that haven't run.

Remove If you opted to remove packages, use this option to do so.

Quit This option exits from `dselect`.

If you want to select packages from the standard set of Debian options, `dselect` can be a useful tool. Because Debian includes so many packages (version 3.0 ships on seven CDs, not counting alternative first CDs for different countries), chances are you'll find what you need to install in the standard set of packages. If not, and if you can find a Debian package or create one using `alien` (as described in the upcoming section, "Converting Package Formats"), you should use `dpkg` to install the package. You might also prefer using `dpkg` to install isolated packages manually, because locating a package with `dselect` can be tedious. Yet another installation tool, APT, is described in the upcoming section, "Maintaining Debian with APT."

Using GUI Debian Package Tools

Commercial Debian derivatives have developed GUI front-ends to Debian's package utilities. One of these that's worked its way into the standard Debian package set is the Storm Package Manager (`stormpkg`), as shown in Figure 11.2. This program is essentially a GUI version of `dselect`; it provides an expandable list of installed and uninstalled packages. You can select a package to install or uninstall it. Picking Packages ➢ Update updates the package list, much like the `dselect` Update option. This tool is very useful if you're uncomfortable with `dselect`'s keyboard-based package navigation.

Converting Package Formats

For the most part, to install a package you must first find a copy of that package in the format supported by your distribution. Sometimes, though, doing this is difficult or impossible. When that's the case, your best course of action may be to convert a package in an alien format to whatever package format your distribution supports. The Debian developers have created a tool to do just this. Known as `alien`, this program ships with Debian and is also available in RPM format. (If you can't find it with your RPM-based distribution, check `http://rpmfind.net`.) Unfortunately, versions for RPM-based distributions are sometimes finicky to install or may not work correctly.

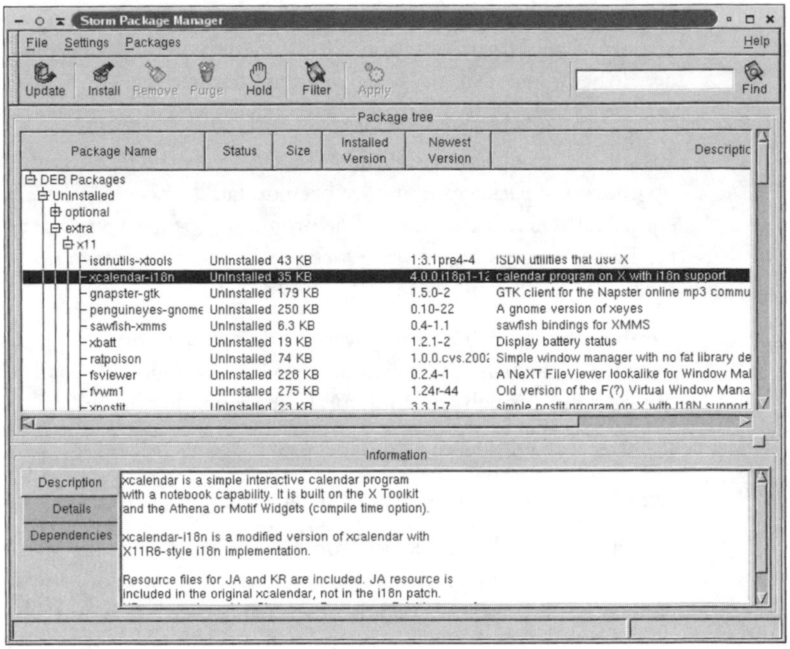

FIGURE 11.2

The Storm Package Manager is similar to GNOME RPM and other GUI RPM utilities.

Why Convert Package Formats?

Package databases work best when as many program and other system support files (fonts, icons, and so on) as possible are installed via the distribution's primary package system. It's possible to install both RPM and Debian package systems on one computer, but using both systems is inadvisable because the databases can't communicate with one another. Thus, when you go to install a package in your distribution's non-native format, chances are the database will flag many failed dependencies, even when appropriate packages are installed using the native system.

If you can't find a program in your primary package system, you may be tempted to install the program from a tarball. These are, after all, a "universal" package format, in that all Linux systems can extract tarballs. On most distributions, though, installing a tarball means that you won't have package information in your database, nor will you be able to check that you have the appropriate support libraries (at least, not through the package system itself).

In these cases, converting a package from one format to your native format is usually preferable to trying to install a tarball, install from source code, or install using a non-native package format. You can install the converted package and gain many of the benefits of your native package format—you'll be able to check for at least some dependencies, easily uninstall the package, and so on.

Using *alien*

The alien package relies on the presence of package tools for all of the package systems it's to support—normally at least tar, rpm, and dpkg. (One of the package databases will go unused, though;

`alien` just needs the foreign package system to extract or create archives, not to install the archives.) Here is the basic syntax for `alien`:

```
alien [--to-deb | --to-rpm | --to-tgz | --to-slp] [options] file[...]
```

Each of the `--to-` options specifies a target format—Debian package, RPM, tarball, or Stampede package. (Stampede packages are used by Stampede Linux.) Table 11.5 summarizes some of the options you can add to modify `alien`'s actions. In most cases, no options are required, aside from the target format specification. (Even this may be omitted if you're converting to the Debian package format.) The `--description` option can be useful if you're converting from a tarball, though; and `--install` automatically installs and then deletes the converted package.

TABLE 11.5: OPTIONS TO MODIFY `alien`'s ACTIONS

OPTION	EFFECT
`-i` or `--install`	Installs package after it's converted.
`-g` or `--generate`	Extracts files into a temporary directory without generating a package. You can then modify the files and generate a package using native package tools.
`--description=string`	Sets the package description to *string* when converting from a tarball.
`--version=version`	Sets the version number when converting from a tarball. (Displays the `alien` version number if you don't provide a package filename for conversion.)
`-c` or `--scripts`	Tries to convert scripts that run after installing or removing a package. These scripts are often distribution-specific, though, so this option may not have the desired effect.

Converting a package intended for one distribution for another one is fairly straightforward. For instance, consider converting an RPM to Debian package format:

```
# alien --to-deb icewm-themes-0.9.28-1.noarch.rpm
icewm-themes_0.9.28-2_all.deb generated
```

You might perform a conversion like this if you want to install an unusual package that's not available in your native package format. Such conversions are most likely to be successful for relatively straightforward applications and libraries. Servers and packages that are unusual in any way frequently cause problems because they rely on distribution-specific startup scripts, configuration files, and the like.

Another useful application for `alien` is to create a package from files that aren't normally distributed in package format at all. For instance, suppose you've found a `.zip` file with a set of fonts you want to use on several systems. You can create an RPM package with a series of commands:

```
$ mkdir -p ~/to-rpm/usr/X11R6/lib/X11/fonts/newfonts
$ cd ~/to-rpm/usr/X11R6/lib/X11/fonts/newfonts
$ unzip ~/newfonts.zip
$ cd ~/to-rpm
$ tar cvfz newfonts.tgz usr
$ su
# alien --to-rpm --description="New font collection" newfonts.tgz
```

NOTE *To convert to Debian format, you must run* alien *as* root. *You can create other formats as an ordinary user; however, file ownership in the resulting package may not be what you expect.*

The result of this series of commands is a new file, newfonts-1-2.noarch.rpm, which contains the fonts, set to install in /usr/X11R6/lib/X11/fonts/newfonts. You can then install the fonts using rpm and subsequently uninstall them using the same program, gaining all the benefits of the RPM database. In this specific example, you might also want to create fonts.dir and fonts.scale files, as described in Chapter 16, "Optimizing X Configuration," after extracting the original font archive and before creating the intermediary tarball. You can use a similar procedure for a commercial program that ships only as a tarball, or even that relies on an installation program—you can run the installation program, then package up the installed files (provided you know where to find them) to create an RPM or Debian package.

Automating Upgrades

For the most part, the tools described in this chapter so far are useful for installing and managing packages that you obtain in some other way. (One partial exception is dselect, which actually uses APT, described in "Maintaining Debian with APT.") The problem with this approach is that these tools cannot, by themselves, keep your system up to date. It's often desirable or even necessary to maintain at least some packages at the latest available versions. Several tools have been developed to help automate the software upgrade process. Examples include Debian's APT, Red Hat's Update Agent, and SuSE's YaST. Most of these tools are distribution-specific, although a version of Debian's APT has been developed to work with RPMs. No matter which of these tools you use, you should be aware of the potential risks they pose, as well as their substantial benefits.

Maintaining Debian with APT

APT is a powerful command-line tool installed from the standard apt package. Although it was developed for Debian systems, versions for RPM-based distributions are available. One such tool is APT4RPM (http://apt4rpm.sourceforge.net). APT for RPM-based distributions poses problems, though, because somebody must maintain the necessary network-accessible databases, and this maintenance is done on an unofficial voluntary basis. The Download Repositories link on the APT4RPM home page provides pointers to these databases.

Once you install APT, you must configure it. The most important APT configuration file is /etc/apt/sources.list, which holds information on the locations APT should search for installation files. Listing 11.1 shows a typical sources.list file. Each line in this file comprises three fields: a type code specifying the types of files to be found at a location; a universal resource identifier (URI), which specifies where the files can be found; and a list of arguments that describe the directories to be searched on the URI.

The first several lines of Listing 11.1 specify CD-ROMs, which are the original installation discs. These discs are identified by name so that APT can determine when you insert the correct disc. The last two lines specify network update sites. In Listing 11.1, both of these sites are websites, but you can also specify FTP sites, SSH servers, or other types of sites. You can obtain a list of official Debian mirror sites that you can list as URIs at http://www.debian.org/mirror/mirrors_full. Adding http://security.debian.org to sources.list, as in Listing 11.1, is also a good idea.

LISTING 11.1: A TYPICAL *SOURCES.LIST* FILE

```
deb cdrom:[Debian GNU/Linux 3.0 r0 _Woody_ - Official powerpc Binary-7
➡(20020719)]/ unstable contrib main non-US/contrib non-US/main
deb cdrom:[Debian GNU/Linux 3.0 r0 _Woody_ - Official powerpc Binary-6
➡(20020719)]/ unstable contrib main non-US/contrib non-US/main
deb cdrom:[Debian GNU/Linux 3.0 r0 _Woody_ - Official powerpc Binary-5
➡(20020719)]/ unstable contrib main non-US/contrib non-US/main
deb cdrom:[Debian GNU/Linux 3.0 r0 _Woody_ - Official powerpc Binary-4
➡(20020719)]/ unstable contrib main non-US/contrib non-US/main
deb cdrom:[Debian GNU/Linux 3.0 r0 _Woody_ - Official powerpc Binary-3
➡(20020719)]/ unstable contrib main non-US/contrib non-US/main
deb cdrom:[Debian GNU/Linux 3.0 r0 _Woody_ - Official powerpc Binary-2
➡(20020719)]/ unstable contrib main non-US/contrib non-US/main
deb cdrom:[Debian GNU/Linux 3.0 r0 _Woody_ - Official powerpc Binary-1
➡(20020719)]/ unstable contrib main non-US/contrib non-US/main

deb http://security.debian.org/ stable/updates main
deb http://http.us.debian.org/debian stable main contrib non-free
```

You can perform several actions with APT, including:

Database Updates   After configuring APT, one of the first actions you should perform is a database update. You can do this by typing **apt-get update**. The system contacts each of the URIs specified in sources.list to obtain a list of available packages. To be sure the system obtains the latest package available, you should always perform this action before installing or upgrading a package.

Individual Package Installations and Upgrades   You can install a new package by passing install and the package name to apt-get. For instance, typing **apt-get install nedit** installs the nedit package. If the requested package is already installed and a newer version is available, apt-get upgrades to the newer version.

Individual Package Removals   You can use the remove keyword to remove a package; for instance, **apt-get remove nedit** uninstalls the nedit package.

System Upgrades   If you want to upgrade all the packages on the computer to the latest version, type **apt-get upgrade** or **apt-get dist-upgrade**. These two commands are very similar, but the latter is more intelligent in handling dependencies. In theory, this makes dist-upgrade superior, but in practice it can sometimes break packages. Try upgrade first, and if you run into problems, use dist-upgrade.

Housekeeping   Typing **apt-get clean** removes package files from the /var/cache/apt/archives and /var/cache/apt/archives/partial directories where apt-get puts them prior to installing them. If you use apt-get much, it's important to use this option occasionally, lest your disk fill with original package files.

In addition to these major actions, apt-get supports numerous options. Of particular interest are -f, which attempts to fix broken dependencies on a system; -s, which causes apt-get to report on actions it would take without actually taking those actions; and -y, which enters an automatic yes response to most configuration prompts.

APT can be used in any number of ways. One is in routine package operations; you can use apt-get install to install a package, rather than use dpkg or dselect. A more powerful function relates to system upgrades; typing **apt-get update** followed by **apt-get upgrade** or **apt-get dist-upgrade** will upgrade all your packages to the latest version for your distribution. In principle, you could put these commands in a cron job to execute on a regular basis; however, doing so is a bit risky, because an undesirable automatic update could cause problems. Instead, you might want to use apt-get update; apt-get -s upgrade in a cron job. The result should be a regular report of any updated packages. You can then perform the upgrade at your leisure, at a time when you can cope with any problems that might arise.

Maintaining Red Hat with Update Agent

Red Hat uses a system upgrade tool known as Update Agent (up2date). This program is supplemented by a utility called the Network Alert Notification Tool, which displays an icon in the default GNOME Panel signifying whether the system needs an update. Specifically, an exclamation mark inside a red circle means that an update is available, and a check mark inside a blue circle signifies an up-to-date system.

NOTE *When I wrote this chapter, Red Hat allowed you to register one computer for free; but you need to pay a service fee to use the Network Alert Notification Tool with more than one computer. If you register, Red Hat will optionally send you e-mail about security-related updates.*

Click the red exclamation mark circle in the Panel to obtain a listing of available updates. If you want to update anything, click the Launch Up2Date button. Alternatively, you can type **up2date** in an xterm window to launch the tool directly. Either way, the result is the Red Hat Update Agent window, which guides you through the update process. After you click Forward a couple of times, Update Agent builds a list of available updates and enables you to pick which ones you want to install, as shown in Figure 11.3. The program then displays a series of progress dialog boxes as it resolves dependencies, transfers files, and installs the packages.

FIGURE 11.3

Red Hat's Update Agent presents a list of packages for which updates are available.

Assuming you register a computer with Red Hat and use it as a desktop system, the Network Alert Notification Tool makes it easy to keep up with system updates. Even without registration, Update Agent is convenient for workstations. As GUI tools, though, these utilities are less convenient for servers or systems that are used only from text-mode logins. There's little point to running Update Agent in a `cron` job, for instance, in the way you can run Debian's `apt-get`.

Maintaining SuSE with YaST

SuSE developed YaST and its GUI cousin, YaST2, for its distribution. These tools, both of which I refer to as YaST for convenience, are all-in-one system configuration tools. You can adjust startup scripts, set network options, and so on all from one user interface. One of the many options available from the YaST Control Center is an Online Update tool. This option is available from the Software configuration area on the main YaST page. Select it to update your packages to the latest versions available. YaST displays an Online Update window in which you select whether to perform an automatic or manual update, and in which you specify an update source. I recommend performing a manual update because this process enables you to opt out of upgrades that are unimportant or that might cause problems. If you select the manual update option, YaST displays a list of available updates, as shown in Figure 11.4. When you click Accept, YaST downloads information on the updates. You must then restart the Online Update tool to select and install the individual updates.

FIGURE 11.4

Like Red Hat's Update Agent, SuSE's Update Agent enables you to select packages to update.

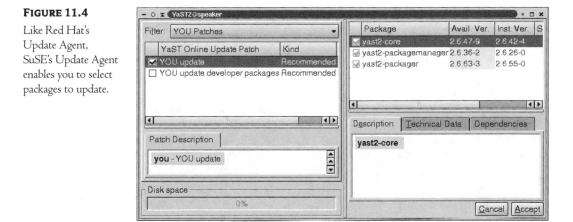

YaST's update options are very similar to those of Red Hat's Update Agent, considered broadly. Both tools present friendly GUIs that are best suited for use on desktop workstations, although they can be used on servers. SuSE doesn't offer an equivalent to Red Hat's Network Alert Notification Tool, though, so you should be careful to run YaST's Online Update from time to time.

Summary

Linux's package-management tools vary from one distribution to another. Most distributions use RPMs or Debian packages, which are conceptually quite similar to one another. Both tools provide command-line utilities for installing, upgrading, uninstalling, and otherwise managing packages.

Most distributions provide GUI front-ends to these tools. These GUI front-ends can help both inexperienced and experienced users manage the software on their systems. Additional tools, such as automatic update tools and package-conversion utilities, also help you to manage packages. Whether you use automatic software update tools or not, keeping your software packages up to date is important for security reasons.

Chapter 12

Filesystems and Files

EVERYTHING YOU DO WITH Linux involves files in one way or another. You launch programs from files, read program configurations in files, store data in files, deliver files to clients via servers, and so on. Therefore, the tools Linux provides for manipulating files are extremely important to overall system performance. At the core, these tools make up a *filesystem*—a set of data structures that allow Linux to locate and manipulate files. Several Linux native filesystems exist, the most important of these being the Second Extended File System (ext2fs), the Third Extended File System (ext3fs), the Reiser File System (ReiserFS), the Journaled File System (JFS), and XFS. The filesystem you use will affect your computer's overall performance and suitability for specific tasks.

Beyond picking a filesystem, you should be familiar with various filesystem tools. Filesystem creation options and performance enhancing tools can improve disk throughput, and partition resizers enable you to grow or shrink a partition to better suit your storage needs. Filesystems sometimes become corrupted, and fixing these problems is critical when they occur. Finally, one very common problem is that of accidentally or prematurely deleted files. Knowing how to recover such files can save you or your users a lot of time and effort.

Picking the Right Filesystem

When you installed Linux, the installation program gave you options relating to the filesystems you could use. Most distributions that ship with 2.4.x and later kernels support ext2fs, ext3fs, and ReiserFS. Some also support JFS and XFS. Even if your distribution doesn't support JFS or XFS, though, you can add that support by downloading the appropriate kernel patches or prepatched kernels from the JFS (http://oss.software.ibm.com/developerworks/opensource/jfs/) or XFS (http://oss.sgi.com/projects/xfs/) sites and compiling this support as a module or into the kernel proper. You can then convert a partition from one filesystem to another by backing up, creating the new filesystem, and restoring.

NOTE *Support for JFS has been added to the 2.4.20 and 2.5.6 kernels, and XFS has been added to the 2.5.36 kernel. Thus, these filesystems are likely to become options for most distributions at install time.*

Unfortunately, the best filesystem to use is not always obvious. For many installations, it's not even terribly important, but for some applications it is. Filesystem design differences mean that some perform some tasks better than others. Varying support tools also mean that advanced filesystem features differ. This section describes the pros and cons of the popular Linux filesystems in several different areas, such as filesystem portability, disk check times, disk speed, disk space consumption, support for large numbers of files, and advanced security features.

Maximizing Filesystem Portability

Chapter 10, "Using Multiple OSs," includes information on filesystem compatibility across OSs. As described there, ext2fs is the most portable native Linux filesystem. Drivers and access tools for ext2fs are available in many different OSs, meaning that you can access ext2fs data from many non-Linux OSs. Unfortunately, most of these tools are limited in various ways—for instance, they may be access utilities rather than true drivers, they may not work with the latest versions of ext2fs, they may be able to read but not write ext2fs, or they may run a risk of causing filesystem corruption when writing to ext2fs. Therefore, ext2fs's portability is limited.

Ext3fs is a journaling extension to ext2fs. (The next section, "Reducing Disk Check Times," describes journaling in more detail.) As such, many of the ext2fs access tools can handle ext3fs, although some disable write access on ext3 filesystems.

IBM wrote JFS for its AIX OS, and later ported it to OS/2. IBM then open sourced the OS/2 JFS implementation, leading to the Linux JFS support. This heritage makes JFS a good choice for systems that multiboot Linux and OS/2. There are compatibility issues, though. Most importantly, you must use 4,096-byte clusters to enable both OSs to use the same JFS partitions. There are also filename case-retention issues—OS/2 is case-insensitive, whereas Linux is case-sensitive. You can use JFS in a case-insensitive way from Linux, but this is only advisable on dedicated data-transfer partitions.

XFS, from Silicon Graphics' (SGI's) IRIX, is another migrant filesystem. Linux/IRIX dual-boot systems are rare, but you might want to use XFS as a compatibility filesystem on removable disks that move between Linux and IRIX systems. You can also use Linux's XFS support to read hard disks that originated on IRIX systems.

ReiserFS is currently the least portable of the major Linux-native filesystems. A BeOS version can be found at `http://www.bebits.com/app/3214`, but versions for other platforms have yet to appear, as of 2003. Therefore, you should avoid ReiserFS if you need cross-platform compatibility.

Reducing Disk Check Times

All filesystems necessarily write data in chunks. In the event of a power outage, system crash, or other problem, the disk may be left in an unstable condition as a result of a half-completed operation. The result can be lost data and disk errors down the line. In order to head off such problems, modern filesystems support a *dirty bit*. When Linux mounts a filesystem, it sets the dirty bit, and when it unmounts the filesystem, Linux clears the dirty bit. If Linux detects that the dirty bit is set when mounting a filesystem, the OS knows that the filesystem was not properly unmounted and may contain errors. Depending on `/etc/fstab` or `mount` command options, Linux may run `fsck` on the filesystem when its dirty bit is set. This program, described in more detail in the upcoming section, "Recovering from Filesystem Corruption," checks for disk errors and corrects them whenever possible.

Unfortunately, a complete disk check on a traditional filesystem such as ext2fs takes a long time, because the computer must scan all the major disk data structures. If an inconsistency is found, `fsck` must resolve it. The program can often do this on its own, but it sometimes requires help from a person, so you may have to answer bewildering questions about how to fix certain filesystem problems after a crash or other system failure. Even without answering such questions, disk checks of multi-gigabyte hard disks can take many minutes, or potentially even hours. This characteristic may be unacceptable on systems that should have minimal down time, such as many servers.

Over the past decade, *journaling filesystems* have received increasing attention as a partial solution to the disk check time problem. A journaling filesystem keeps an on-disk record of pending operations. When the OS writes data to the disk, it first records a journal entry describing the operation; then it performs the operation; and then it clears the journal. In the event of a power failure or crash, the journal contains a record of all the operations that might be pending. This information can greatly simplify the filesystem check operation; instead of checking the entire disk, the system can check just those areas noted in the journal as having pending operations. The result is that a journaling filesystem takes just a few seconds to mount after a system crash. Of course, some data might still be lost, but at least you won't wait many minutes or hours to discover this fact.

Linux supports four journaling filesystems:

Ext3fs   This filesystem is basically just ext2fs with a journal added. As such, it's quite reliable, because of the well-tested nature of the underlying ext2fs. Ext3fs can also be read by an ext2fs driver; however, when it's mounted in this way, the journal will be ignored. Ext3fs also has another advantage: As described in the upcoming section, "Converting Ext2fs to Ext3fs," you can convert an existing ext2 filesystem into an ext3 filesystem without backing up, repartitioning, and restoring.

ReiserFS   This filesystem was the first journaling filesystem added to the Linux kernel. As such, it's seen a lot of testing and is very reliable. It was designed from the ground up as a journaling filesystem for Linux, and it includes several unusual design features, such as the ability to pack small files into less disk space than is possible with many filesystems.

JFS   IBM's JFS was developed in the mid-1990s for AIX, then it found its way to OS/2 and then to Linux. It's therefore well tested, although the Linux version hasn't seen much use compared to the non-Linux version or even ext3fs or ReiserFS on Linux.

XFS   SGI's XFS dates from the mid-1990s on the IRIX platform, so the filesystem fundamentals are well tested. It's the most recent official addition to the Linux kernel, although it has been a fairly popular add-on for quite a while. XFS comes with more ancillary utilities than does any filesystem except ext2fs and ext3fs. It also comes with native support for some advanced features, such as ACLs (see the upcoming section, "Securing a Filesystem with ACLs), that aren't as well supported on most other filesystems.

For the most part, I recommend using a journaling filesystem; the reduced startup time makes these filesystems beneficial after power outages or other problems. Some of these filesystems do have drawbacks, though. Most importantly, some programs rely upon filesystem quirks in order to work. For instance, as late as 2001, programs such as NFS servers and the Win4Lin emulator had problems with some of these journaling filesystems. These problems have been disappearing, though, and they're quite rare as of the 2.5.54 kernel. Nonetheless, you should thoroughly test all your programs (especially those that interact with disk files in low-level or other unusual ways) before switching to a journaling filesystem. The safest journaling filesystem from this perspective is likely to be ext3fs, because of its close relationship to ext2fs.

ReiserFS and JFS are also somewhat deficient in terms of support programs. For instance, neither includes a dump backup utility. XFS's dump (called xfsdump) is available from the XFS development site but isn't shipped with the xfsprogs 2.2.1 package, although some distributions ship it in a separate xfsdump package. The xfsdump and the ext2fs/ext3fs dump programs create incompatible archives, so you can't use these tools to back up one filesystem and restore it to another.

Maximizing Disk Throughput

One question on many people's minds is which filesystem yields the best disk performance. Unfortunately, this question is difficult to answer because different access patterns, as created by different uses of a system, favor different filesystem designs. In *Linux Filesystems* (Sams, 2001), William von Hagen ran many benchmarks and found that every Linux filesystem won several individual tests. As a general rule, though, XFS and JFS produced the best throughput with small files (100MB), while ext2fs, ext3fs, and to a lesser extent JFS did the best with larger files (1GB). Some benchmarks measure CPU use, which can affect system responsiveness during disk-intensive operations. At small file sizes, results were quite variable; no filesystem emerged as a clear winner. At larger file sizes, ext3fs and JFS emerged as CPU-time winners.

Unfortunately, benchmarks are somewhat artificial and may not reflect real-world performance. For instance, von Hagen's benchmarks show ext2fs winning file-deletion tests and ReiserFS coming in last; however, von Hagen comments that this result runs counter to his subjective experience, and I concur. ReiserFS seems quite speedy compared to ext2fs when deleting large numbers of files. This disparity may be because von Hagen's tests measured CPU time, whereas we humans are more interested in a program's response time. The moral is that you shouldn't blindly trust a benchmark. If getting the best disk performance is important to you, try experimenting yourself. Be sure to run tests using the same hardware and partition; wipe out each filesystem in favor of the next one, so that you're testing using the same disk and partition each time. Install applications or user files, as appropriate, and see how fast the system is for your specific purposes. If this procedure sounds like it's too much effort to perform, then perhaps the performance differences between filesystems aren't all that important to you, and you should choose a filesystem based on other criteria.

Minimizing Space Consumption

Most filesystems allocate space to files in *blocks*, which are typically power-of-two multiples of 512 bytes in size (that is, $2^1 \times 512$, $2^2 \times 512$, $2^3 \times 512$, and so on). Common block sizes for Linux filesystems range from 1KB to 4KB (the range for ext2fs and ext3fs). XFS supports block sizes ranging from 512 bytes to 64KB, although in practice block size is limited by CPU architecture (4KB for IA-32 and PowerPC; 8KB for Alpha and Sparc). ReiserFS and Linux's JFS currently support only 4KB blocks, although JFS's data structures support blocks as small as 512 bytes. The default block size is 4KB for all of these filesystems except ext2fs and ext3fs, for which the default is based on the filesystem size.

You can minimize the space used by files, and hence maximize the number of files you can fit on a filesystem, by using smaller block sizes. This practice may slightly degrade performance, though, as files may become more fragmented and require more pointers to completely describe the file's location on the disk.

ReiserFS is unusual in that it supports storing file *tails*—the ends of files that don't occupy all of an allocation block—from multiple files together in one block. This feature can greatly enhance ReiserFS's capacity to store many small files, such as those found on a news server's spool directory. XFS uses a different approach to achieve a similar benefit—it stores small files entirely within the *inode* (a disk structure that points to the file on disk, holds the file's time stamp, and so on) whenever possible.

None of these features has much impact when average file sizes are large. For instance, saving 2KB by storing file tails in a single allocation block won't be important if a filesystem has just two 1GB files. If the filesystem has 2,000,000 1KB files, though, such space-saving features can make a difference between fitting all the files on a disk or having to buy a new disk.

Another aspect of disk space consumption is the space devoted to the journal. On most disks, this isn't a major consideration; however, it is a concern on small disks, such as Zip disks. On a 100MB Zip disk, ReiserFS devotes 32MB to its journal and ext3fs and XFS both devote 4MB. JFS devotes less space to its journal initially, but it may grow with use.

Ext2fs and ext3fs suffer from another problem: By default, they reserve five percent of their disk space for emergency use by root. The idea is to give root space to work in case a filesystem fills up. This may be a reasonable plan for critical filesystems such as the root filesystem and /var, but for some it's pointless; for instance, root doesn't need space on /home or on removable media. The upcoming section, "Creating a Filesystem for Optimal Performance," describes how to reduce the reserved space percentage.

Supporting the Maximum Number of Files

To some extent, storing the maximum number of files on a partition is an issue of the efficient allocation of space for small files, as described in the preceding section, "Minimizing Space Consumption." Another factor, though, is the number of available inodes. Most filesystems support a limited number of inodes per disk. These inodes limit the number of files a disk can hold; each file requires its own inode, so if you store too many small files on a disk, you'll run out of inodes. With ext2fs and ext3fs, you can change the number of inodes using the -i or -N options to mke2fs when you create the filesystem. These options set the bytes-per-inode ratio (typically 2 or 4; increasing values decrease the number of inodes on the filesystem) and the absolute number of inodes, respectively. With XFS, you can specify the maximum percentage of disk space that may be allocated to inodes with the maxpct option to mkfs.xfs. The default value is 25, but if you expect the filesystem to have very many small files, you can specify a larger percentage.

ReiserFS is unusual in that it allocates inodes dynamically, so you don't need to be concerned with running out of inodes. This fact also means that the -i option to the df utility, which normally returns statistics on used and available inodes, returns meaningless information about available inodes on ReiserFS volumes.

Securing a Filesystem with ACLs

Linux, like Unix in general, has traditionally used file ownership and permissions to control access to files and directories. Some of the tools for handling these features are described in Chapter 5,

"Doing Real Work in Text Mode." Another way to control access to files is by using *access control lists (ACLs)*. ACLs provide finer-grained access control than do ownership and permissions. ACLs work by attaching additional information—a list of users or groups and the permissions to be granted to each—to the file. For instance, suppose you have a file that contains confidential data. This data must be readable and writeable by you and readable by a particular group (say, readers). You give the file ownership and permissions such that only you can read or write the file and that anybody in readers can read it (0640, or -rw-r-----). You need to share this file with just one other user, though, and for purposes of security for other files, this user should not be a member of the readers group. ACLs enable you to do this by giving read permission to this one user, independently of the readers group. Without ACLs, you would need to create a new group (say, readers2) that contains all of the members of readers plus the one extra user. You'd then need to maintain this extra group. Also, ordinary users can manipulate ACLs, but this isn't usually the case for groups, so ACLs can greatly simplify matters if users should be able to give each other access to specific files while still maintaining restricted access to those files for others.

Few Linux-native filesystems support ACLs directly; this honor belongs only to XFS. If you need ACLs, though, you can obtain add-on packages for ext2fs, ext3fs, and JFS. Check http://acl .bestbits.at for pointers to these patches, instructions, and more. No matter what filesystem you use, you'll also need support utilities, which are available from the same site. These tools enable you to define and modify ACLs. For instance, getfacl displays a file's ACLs, and setfacl changes a file's ACLs.

ACLs are still quite new in Linux. As such, you may run into peculiar problems with specific programs or filesystems. Chances are you don't need ACLs on a typical workstation or a small server. If you're administering a multiuser system with a complex group structure, though, you might want to investigate ACLs further. You might be able to simplify your overall permissions structure by switching to a filesystem that supports ACLs.

Optimizing Filesystems

If you've already installed Linux, your partitions are already set up and configured with particular filesystems. You may decide you want to modify this configuration, though. Some changes are tedious to implement. For instance, changing from one filesystem to another requires you to back up, create a new filesystem, and restore your files. One exception to this rule is changing from ext2fs to ext3fs. If you switch filesystems, you may be able to use filesystem-creation options to improve the performance of the new filesystem. Other changes can also be done relatively painlessly. These include *defragmenting* a disk (that is, repositioning file contents so that they're not spread out over the entire partition) and resizing partitions to give you space where you need it.

Creating a Filesystem for Optimal Performance

Most filesystems support a variety of options that may impact performance. For instance, large allocation blocks can improve performance by reducing fragmentation and the number of operations needed to retrieve an entire file. Some of these options can be set only at filesystem creation time, but some can be changed after the fact. Not all of these features are available in all filesystems. Across all

Linux filesystems, important and popular performance-enhancing (or performance-degrading) options include:

Allocation Block Size   As noted in the earlier section, "Minimizing Space Consumption," small allocation blocks can facilitate more efficient use of disk space, but the cost is a small degradation in disk-access speed. Therefore, to improve performance slightly, you can increase your block size. This option is not easily changed after creating a filesystem. With ext2fs or ext3fs, you can use the -b `block-size` option to mke2fs; with XFS, the -b `size=block-size` option to mkfs.xfs does the job. For ext2fs and ext3fs, `block-size` must be 1024, 2048, or 4096; with XFS, the block size can theoretically be any power-of-two multiple of 512 bytes up to 64KB (65536 bytes), although in practice you can only mount a filesystem with block sizes up to 4KB or 8KB using common CPUs. ReiserFS and Linux's version of JFS do not yet support adjusting this feature.

Journaling Options   All the journaling filesystems support various journal options. One common option is the location of the journal. By placing the journal on a separate physical disk from the main filesystem, you can improve performance (provided the target disk isn't too sluggish itself). You can use the -J `device=journal-device` option in mke2fs or the -j `journal-device` option in mkreiserfs or mkfs.jfs to set this feature. Ext3fs also supports setting the journal size with the -J `size=journal-size` option, where `journal-size` is specified in megabytes and must be between 1,024 and 102,400 filesystem blocks. Specifying a too-small journal may degrade performance, but setting one too large may rob you of too much disk space. If in doubt, let mke2fs decide on the journal size itself.

Reserved Blocks   Ext2fs and ext3fs reserve a number of blocks for use by the superuser (or some other user you specify). The default value of 5 percent reserved space may be overkill on large partitions or on less critical partitions (such as /home). You can gain a bit more space by using the -m `reserved-percentage` option to mke2fs. Changing this percentage won't affect actual disk performance, but it may gain you just a bit more available disk space. You can change this option after you create a filesystem by passing the same parameter that mke2fs accepts to the tune2fs program, as in **tune2fs -m 1 /dev/hda4** to set the reserved blocks percentage to 1.

Check Interval   Ext2fs and ext3fs force a filesystem check after a specified number of mounts or a specified amount of time between mounts. The idea is to catch errors that might creep onto the filesystem due to random disk write errors or filesystem driver bugs. You can change these intervals by using the -c `max-mount-counts` and -i `interval-between-checks` options to tune2fs. For the latter option, you specify an interval in days, weeks, or months by providing a number followed by a d, w, or m, respectively. Altering the check interval won't modify day-to-day performance, but it will change how frequently the computer performs a full disk check on startup. This disk check can be quite lengthy, even for ext3fs; it doesn't restrict itself to recent transactions as recorded in the journal, as a forced check after a system crash does.

Directory Hash   ReiserFS uses a sorted directory structure to speed directory lookups, and mkreiserfs provides several options for the *hash* (a type of lookup algorithm) used for this purpose. You set this option with the -h *hash* option to mkreiserfs, where *hash* can be r5, rupasov, or tea. Some hashes may yield improved or degraded performance for specific applications. The

Squid Web proxy documentation suggests using the rupasov hash, whereas the qmail documentation recommends r5, for instance. One problem with the r5 and rupasov hashes is that they can greatly slow file creation in directories with very many (a million or so) files. In fact, rupasov is very prone to such problems, and so should be avoided on most systems. The tea hash is much less subject to this problem, but it is also much slower than r5 for directories with more typical numbers of files. In general, you should use the default r5 hash unless you know you'll be creating many files or the disk will be used by one performance-critical application, in which case checking the application's documentation or doing a web search for advice may be worthwhile.

Inode Options XFS enables you to set the inode size at filesystem creation time using the -i size=*value* option to mkfs.xfs. The minimum and default size is 256 bytes; the maximum is 2,048 bytes. (The inode size can't exceed half the allocation block size, though.) One impact of the inode size option relates to small file access times; because XFS tries to store small files within the inode whenever possible, specifying a large inode enables storing larger files within the inode. Doing so will speed access to these files. Therefore, if a partition will store many small files (under 2KB), you may want to increase the inode size. Depending on the exact mix of file sizes, the result may save or waste disk space. If few files will be smaller than 2KB, there's little point to increasing the inode size.

The default filesystem creation options usually yield acceptable performance. Modifying these options can help in some unusual cases, such as filesystems storing huge numbers of files or a computer that's restarted frequently. I don't recommend trying random changes to these options unless you intend to run tests to discover what works best for your purposes.

Converting Ext2fs to Ext3fs

One of the advantages of ext3fs over the other journaling filesystems is that it's easy to turn an existing ext2 filesystem into an ext3 filesystem. You can do this using the tune2fs program and its -j option:

```
# tune2fs -j /dev/hda4
```

If the filesystem to which you add a journal is mounted when you make this change, tune2fs creates the journal as a regular file, called .journal, in the filesystem's root directory. If the filesystem is unmounted when you run this command, the journal file doesn't appear as a regular file. In either case, the filesystem is now an ext3 filesystem, and it can be used just as if you created it as an ext3 filesystem initially. If necessary, you may be able to access the filesystem as ext2fs (say, using a kernel that has no ext3fs support); however, some older kernels and non-Linux utilities may refuse to access it in this way, or they may provide merely read-only access.

On rare occasion, an ext3 filesystem's journal may become so corrupted that it interferes with disk recovery operations. In such cases, you can convert the filesystem back into an ext2 filesystem using the debugfs tool:

```
# debugfs -w /dev/sda4
debugfs 1.32 (09-Nov-2002)
debugfs:  features -needs_recovery -has_journal
Filesystem features: dir_index filetype sparse_super
debugfs:  quit
```

After performing this operation, you should be able to use `fsck.ext2` with its `-f` option, as described in the upcoming section, "Filesystem Check Options," to recover the filesystem. The newly-deactivated journal will cause `fsck.ext2` to report errors even if the filesystem did not previously have them. If you like, you can then add the journal back by using `tune2fs`, as just described.

WARNING *Don't try to remove the journal from a mounted filesystem.*

Defragmenting a Disk

Microsoft filesystems, such as the File Allocation Table (FAT) filesystem and the New Technology File System (NTFS), suffer greatly from disk *fragmentation*—the tendency of files to be broken up into many noncontiguous segments. Disk fragmentation degrades performance because the OS may need to move the disk head more frequently and over greater distances to read a fragmented file than to read a nonfragmented file.

Fortunately, Linux's native filesystems are all far more resistant to fragmentation than are Windows filesystems. Therefore, most Linux users don't bother defragmenting their disks. In fact, defragmentation tools for Linux are hard to come by. One that does exist is called `defrag`, but this package doesn't ship with most distributions. Because it is an older tool, it won't work with most modern ext2fs partitions, much less any of the journaling filesystems.

If you think your system may be suffering from fragmentation problems, you can at least discover how fragmented your ext2 or ext3 filesystems are by performing an `fsck` on them. You may need to force a check by using the `-f` parameter. This action will produce, among other things, a report on the fragmentation on the disk:

```
/dev/hda5: 45/8032 files (2.2% non-contiguous), 4170/32098 blocks
```

This report indicates that 2.2 percent of the files are noncontiguous (that is, fragmented). Such a small amount of fragmentation isn't a problem. Unfortunately, the `fsck` tools for other journaling filesystems don't return this information, so you have no indicator of fragmentation on these filesystems. If you truly believe that fragmentation has become a problem, you may be able to improve matters by backing up the partition, creating a fresh filesystem, and then restoring the files. This procedure is likely to take far longer than the time saved in disk accesses over the next several months or years, though, so I only recommend doing it if you want to change filesystem types or have some other reason (such as replacing a hard disk) to engage in this activity.

NOTE *As a general rule, fragmentation becomes a problem only if your disk is almost full. On a nearly full disk, Linux may have trouble locating a large enough block of free space to fit a file without fragmenting it. If you almost fill a disk and then delete files, the remaining files may or may not be fragmented, depending on which ones you deleted. For this reason, keeping your partitions from filling up is best. As a general rule, anything less than 80 to 90 percent full is fine from a fragmentation perspective.*

Resizing Filesystems

All too frequently, you discover only after installing Linux that your partitions aren't the optimum size. For instance, you might have too much room in /usr and not enough room in /home. Traditional fixes for this problem include using symbolic links to store some directories that are nominally on one partition on another partition; and backing up, repartitioning, and restoring data. In many cases, a simpler approach is to use a dynamic partition resizer. These programs were described in Chapter 10 with respect to FAT and other non-Linux OSs. Fortunately, partition resizers exist for the most popular Linux filesystems, as well, so you can use these tools to manage your Linux installation.

WARNING *Dynamic partition resizers are inherently dangerous. In the event of a power outage, system crash, or bug, they can do serious damage to a partition. You should always back up the data on any partition you resize. Also, you should never run a dynamic partition resizer on a partition that's currently mounted. If necessary, boot a Linux emergency system to resize your partitions.*

RESIZING EXT2FS AND EXT3FS

Several tools exist to resize ext2 and ext3 filesystems:

resize2fs This program ships with the e2fsprogs package included with most distributions. The resize2fs program is fairly basic in terms of options. At a minimum, you pass it the device file associated with the partition, as in **resize2fs /dev/hda4**. This command resizes the filesystem on /dev/hda4 to match the size of the partition. You can also pass the partition size in allocation blocks, as in **resize2fs /dev/hda4 256000** to resize a filesystem to 256,000 blocks. The resize2fs program doesn't resize partitions, just the filesystems they contain. Therefore, you must use resize2fs in conjunction with fdisk to resize a partition and its filesystem. If you want to shrink a filesystem, you should do so first and then use fdisk to shrink the partition to match. If you want to grow a partition, you use fdisk first and then resize2fs. Because getting filesystem and partition sizes to match is tricky, it's usually best to forgo resize2fs in favor of GNU Parted or PartitionMagic.

GNU Parted This program provides both filesystem and partition resizing at once, so it's easier to use than resize2fs. It's described in more detail shortly, in "Using GNU Parted."

PartitionMagic This commercial program from PowerQuest (`http://www.powerquest.com`) supports integrated filesystem and partition resizing operations of FAT, NTFS, ext2fs, ext3fs, and Linux swap partitions. PartitionMagic is easier to use than other ext2fs and ext3fs partition resizers, but it runs only from DOS or Windows. (The package ships with a DOS boot floppy image and a bootable CD-ROM, so it's still useable on a Linux-only system.)

RESIZING REISERFS

Two tools are available for resizing ReiserFS:

resize_reiserfs This tool is ReiserFS's equivalent of the resize2fs program. Like resize2fs, resize_reiserfs resizes the filesystem, but not the partition in which it resides, so you must use this tool in conjunction with fdisk. If you only pass the program the partition identifier, it resizes the filesystem to fit the partition. If you pass an -s option and filesystem size, the program resizes the partition to the requested size, which you can specify in bytes, kilobytes, megabytes, or gigabytes (the last three options require K, M, or G suffixes, respectively). Alternatively, you can specify a change to the partition size by prefixing the size with a minus (-) or plus (+) sign. For instance, **resize_ reiserfs -s -500M /dev/sda5** reduces the size of the filesystem on /dev/sda5 by 500MB.

GNU Parted According to its web page, this program supports ReiserFS as well as other filesystems. Unfortunately, as of version 1.6.4, this support is more theoretical than real, because it relies on libraries that aren't present on most distributions, and that even a fresh build can't find when everything's installed according to directions. With luck, though, this support will improve in the future.

The ReiserFS resizing tools are not as mature as are those for resizing ext2 and ext3 filesystems. In fact, resize_reiserfs displays warnings about the software being beta.

RESIZING XFS

XFS has long included a partition-resizing tool, xfs_growfs. As the name implies, this program is designed for increasing a filesystem's size, not decreasing it. Unlike most partition-resizing tools, xfs_growfs is designed to work only on a mounted filesystem. The safest way to use it is to unmount the filesystem, delete the partition using fdisk, create a new partition in its place, mount the filesystem, and then call xfs_growfs:

```
# xfs_growfs /mount/point
```

As you might guess, /mount/point is the partition's mount point. You may also add the -D *size* option to specify the filesystem size in allocation blocks. Various other options are also available, as described in the xfs_growfs man page.

Although GNU Parted's web page doesn't mention XFS support, the source code does include an XFS subdirectory. Parted refuses to work on XFS partitions, but this may change in the future.

RESIZING JFS

JFS includes a rather unusual partition-resizing ability: It's built into the kernel's JFS driver. You can use this feature to increase, but not to decrease, the size of the filesystem. As with most other partition-resizing tools, you must modify the partition size first by using fdisk to delete the partition and then recreate it with a larger size. After you've done this, you should mount the partition as you normally do and then issue the following command:

```
# mount -o remount,resize /mount/point
```

This command resizes the filesystem mounted at /mount/point to occupy all the available space in its partition. No other partition-resizing tools are available for JFS, although there is a JFS subdirectory in the GNU Parted source code, suggesting that Parted may support JFS in the future.

USING GNU PARTED

Because Parted is the most sophisticated open source partition resizer, it deserves more attention. You can pass it a series of commands directly or use it in an interactive mode. The latter is more likely to be helpful for normal one-time uses. Passing commands to Parted enables you to write scripts to help automate partition resizing. Typically, you launch Parted in interactive mode by typing the program's name followed by the device on which you want to operate. You can then type commands to resize, create, delete, and otherwise manipulate partitions:

```
# parted /dev/sda
(parted) print
Disk geometry for /dev/scsi/host0/bus0/target5/lun0/disc: 0.000-96.000 megabytes
Disk label type: msdos
Minor    Start     End     Type     Filesystem  Flags
1          0.023   48.000  primary  ext2
2         48.000   96.000  primary  ext2
(parted) rm 2
(parted) resize 1 0.00 96.00
(parted) quit
```

This example deletes the second partition on the disk and resizes the first partition to fill all the available space. Unlike most Linux partition-management tools, Parted works in figures of megabytes. This fact can make translating Parted's partition start and end points to and from the cylinder boundaries upon which fdisk and other tools work tricky. Table 12.1 summarizes some of the most common and important Parted commands. Although many commands nominally require arguments, in practice they don't; instead, they prompt for the required information when Parted is run in interactive mode. The *part-type* code is p for primary partitions, e for extended partitions, and 1 for logical partitions.

TABLE 12.1: COMMON PARTED COMMANDS

PARTED COMMAND	EFFECT
help [*command*]	Displays information on how to use a command. If the *command* option is omitted, it displays a summary of all commands.
mkfs *partn fstype*	Creates a filesystem of *fstype* on partition number *partn*.
mkpart *part-type* [*fstype*] *start end*	Creates a partition, giving it the partition type code *part-type*, with *start* and *end* as its start and end points.
mkpartfs *part-type fstype start end*	Works like mkpart, but also creates a filesystem in the new partition.
move *partn start end*	Moves the partition to a new location on the disk.
print [*partn*]	Displays the partition table or, if *partn* is specified, more detailed information on the partition.
rescue *start end*	Attempts to recover a partition that was deleted.
resize *partn start end*	Resizes the specified partition to the specified size.
rm *partn*	Deletes the specified partition.
select *device*	Begins editing a new disk device.

RESIZING PARTITIONS

Most of the filesystem-resizing tools require that you modify the partition using `fdisk`. (GNU Parted and PartitionMagic are exceptions to this rule.) Precisely how you modify the filesystem's carrier partition depends on whether you'll be shrinking or growing the partition. The simplest case is growing a partition. When doing this, you should follow these steps:

1. Launch `fdisk` on the disk in question.

2. Type **d** in `fdisk` to delete the partition you want to grow. You'll be asked for the partition number.

3. Type **n** in `fdisk` to create a new partition in place of the old one. You'll be asked for the partition number and the start and end cylinders. The start cylinder must be the same as it was originally, and of course the end cylinder should be larger than the original.

4. Type **w** in `fdisk` to write your changes to disk and exit.

5. Follow the procedure for your filesystem-resizing tool to increase the filesystem size.

Of course, in order to grow a partition, there must be free space on the disk into which to expand the partition. This normally means that you'll have already deleted or shrunk a partition that follows the one you want to expand. If you want to expand a filesystem into space that's before it on the disk, your job is much harder. It's possible to expand the carrier partition as just described, but specifying an earlier starting point, and then use `dd` to copy a filesystem from later in the new partition to earlier in the partition. This task is tricky, though, because you must compute precisely how far into the newly expanded partition the existing filesystem begins. An error can easily wipe out all your data. Thus, I don't recommend attempting this task; instead, try creating a new filesystem in the earlier space and mount it at some convenient place in your directory tree. If the empty space is larger than the partition you want to move, you can create a new partition, move the original, verify that the copied partition is intact, delete the original partition, and expand the copied partition and the filesystem it contains.

In order to reduce the size of the filesystem, you must match the size of the partition to the filesystem, which can be a tricky task. Fortunately, there is a procedure that can make this task less error-prone:

1. Shrink the filesystem, using your filesystem-resizing tool, to a value that's smaller than you intend. For instance, if you want to shrink a 700MB partition to 500MB, shrink it to 400MB.

2. Use `fdisk` to resize the partition to the target size, such as 500MB. This target size should be larger than the filesystem by a wide enough margin to be comfortable.

3. Use the partition-resizing tool to expand the filesystem into the extra space on the partition, filling it exactly.

As with increasing the size of the filesystem, the start point of the filesystem must remain untouched. When moving space between filesystems, this requirement can create an awkward situation: You can shrink an earlier partition, but expanding the next partition into the freed space is risky.

Recovering from Filesystem Corruption

A common nightmare among all computer users is losing data due to filesystem corruption. This can happen because of errors introduced during a system crash, filesystem driver bugs (particularly when using non-Linux drivers to access Linux partitions), human error involving low-level disk utilities, or other factors. All Linux filesystems include disk-check tools, but they differ in many details.

The Filesystem Check Process

Most filesystems provide utilities that scan the filesystem's contents for internal consistency. This tool can detect, and often correct, errors such as mangled directories, bad time stamps, inodes that point to the wrong part of the disk, and so on. In Linux, the `fsck` utility serves as a front-end to filesystem-specific checking tools, which usually have names of the form `fsck.filesystem`, where `filesystem` is the filesystem name, such as `jfs` or `ext2`. If you need to check a filesystem manually, you can either call `fsck`, which then calls the filesystem-specific utility; or you can call the filesystem-specific program directly.

NOTE *On some distributions, such as Mandrake,* `fsck.reiserfs` *is actually a symbolic link to* `/bin/true`. *This prevents startup delays should the system try to check a filesystem at boot time, but the arrangement is otherwise potentially confusing. To check a ReiserFS partition on a Mandrake system, you must call the program by the* `reiserfsck` *name. XFS ships with an* `fsck.xfs` *program, but it does nothing. If you need to force a true consistency check, you must use the* `xfs_check` *program instead.*

Precisely what each `fsck` program does is highly filesystem-specific. These programs often perform multiple passes through the filesystem. Each pass checks for a particular type of problem. On a badly corrupted partition, you may need to run `fsck` several times to fix all the problems. You may also need to answer questions posed by `fsck` for some types of errors. Unfortunately, these questions tend to be cryptic to any but experienced filesystem gurus. Fortunately, they usually accept yes/no responses, so you can guess (the default value generally produces acceptable results).

TIP *If your partition is badly corrupted, and if you have enough unused space on another partition or hard disk, try copying the entire partition's data with* `dd` *as a backup prior to running* `fsck`. *For instance, typing* **dd if=/dev/sda5 of=/dev/hda7** *backs up the* `/dev/sda5` *partition to* `/dev/hda7`. *You can then restore that image and try other options if* `fsck` *doesn't work properly. You can also try adding the* `noerror` *option to a* `dd` *command to copy a partition on a drive that's producing physical read errors. It's possible that* `fsck` *will then be able to recover data from the copied partition even if it fails on the original because of the read errors.*

During system startup, Linux examines the filesystem entry in `/etc/fstab` to determine whether to run `fsck` automatically. Specifically, the final field for a filesystem entry is a code specifying when to check the filesystem. A value of 0 means not to run `fsck` on startup. This setting is appropriate for non-Linux filesystems. The root (`/`) filesystem should normally have a value of 1, meaning that it's checked first. All other Linux native filesystems should normally have values of 2, meaning that they're checked after the root filesystem. Filesystem checks at boot time can cause problems in some distributions and with some journaling filesystems, though. Specifically, the filesystem check tool may slow down the bootup process because it unnecessarily forces a thorough disk check. For this reason, these checks are sometimes disabled (with a 0 value in the final `/etc/fstab` field), particularly for ReiserFS, and sometimes for ext3fs and XFS. These filesystems are all capable of automatically replaying their journals when mounted, so an explicit filesystem check at boot time normally isn't necessary.

Filesystem Check Options

The main `fsck` program supports several options, which it passes on to the filesystem-specific programs as necessary. Table 12.2 summarizes these options. You use these options in the following syntax:

```
fsck [options] [-t fstype] [device] [extra-options]
```

TABLE 12.2: COMMON `fsck` OPTIONS

`fsck` OPTION	EFFECT
`-t fslist`	Specify the type(s) of filesystem to be checked. You can check multiple filesystems with one command, so `fslist` can be a comma-separated list of filesystem types.
`-A`	Check every filesystem specified as one to be checked in `/etc/fstab`.
`-R`	Skip checking the root filesystem (used in conjunction with `-A`).
`-C`	Display a progress indicator for filesystems that support this option (currently only ext2fs and ext3fs).
`extra-options`	Options not recognized by `fsck` are passed on to the filesystem-specific programs.

Most of the interesting options are filesystem-specific. Some of the things you can specify for particular filesystems include:

Backup Superblocks   The ext2 and ext3 filesystems use *superblocks*, which contain many vital filesystem details. Because the superblocks are so important, these filesystems store backup superblocks on the disk. If the main superblock is damaged, `fsck.ext2` can use a backup whose location you specify with `-b`. You can learn the location of the backup superblocks by typing **mke2fs -n /dev/file**, where `/dev/file` is the device file for the partition. Be sure to include the `-n` option or `mke2fs` will create a new filesystem, destroying the old one!

Detecting Bad Blocks   You can have `fsck.ext2` scan for physically bad sectors on the disk and mark them as such by passing it the `-c` option. Doubling up this option (that is, using `-cc`) performs a non-destructive read/write test, which may catch problems that a read-only test will miss.

Forcing a Check   Normally, most `fsck` utilities perform only minimal checks if the filesystem is marked as clean. You can force a check with the `fsck.ext2` and `fsck.jfs` utilities by passing them the `-f` option. In `reiserfsck`, the `--check` option causes it to check for errors but not correct them, while `--fix-fixable` causes it to automatically fix certain types of errors.

Journal Location   To tell `fsck.ext2`, `fsck.jfs`, or `reiserfsck` where an external journal is located, pass the location with the `-j journal-location` parameter.

Minimizing User Interaction   The `-p` option to `fsck.ext2` and `fsck.jfs` minimizes the questions they ask. The `-n` and `-y` options to `fsck.ext2` cause it to assume answers of **no** or **yes**, respectively, to all questions. (A **no** response causes `fsck` to not make changes to the filesystem.)

The -s option to xfs_check causes it to report only serious errors. This option can make it easier to spot a problem that prevents mounting the filesystem when the filesystem also has less important problems.

Rebuilding the Superblock   The reiserfsck program supports rebuilding the superblock by using the --rebuild-sb option.

Rebuilding the Filesystem Tree   You can rebuild the entire tree of directories and files by using the --rebuild-tree option to reiserfsck. This option is potentially very risky, but it can fix major problems. Back up the partition using dd before using this option.

Omit Replaying the Journal   The -o option to fsck.jfs causes the program to omit replaying the journal. This option is most useful when the journal itself has been corrupted.

You don't normally need to use fsck except when it runs into problems after a reboot. In that case, Linux may drop you into a maintenance shell and advise you to run fsck manually. Of course, you can run this utility at your discretion, as well, and doing so may be advisable if your disk access is acting up—if files are disappearing or if the disk appears to have too much or too little free space, for instance.

WARNING   *Never run* fsck *on a filesystem that's mounted for read/write access. Doing so can confuse Linux and lead to more filesystem corruption. If necessary, shut down the system and boot from an emergency system to run* fsck *on an unmounted filesystem or to run on one that's mounted for read-only access.*

JOURNALING FILESYSTEMS: NOT A PANACEA

Many people seem to think of journaling filesystems as protection against filesystem errors. This isn't their primary purpose, though. Journaling filesystems are designed to minimize filesystem check times after a crash or other severe error. Ext2fs has a good reputation as a reliable filesystem. Linux's journaling filesystems also have good reputations, but you shouldn't assume they're any safer than ext2fs.

Because journaling filesystems minimize system startup time after power outages, some people have taken to shutting off Linux systems that use journaling filesystems without shutting Linux down properly. This practice is risky at best. Linux still caches accesses to journaling filesystems, so data from recently written files may be lost if you power off the computer without shutting it down first. *Always* shut down the computer with the shutdown utility (or a program that calls it, such as a GUI login screen) before turning off the power.

Recovering Deleted Files

Perhaps the most common type of filesystem problem is files that are accidentally deleted. Users frequently delete the wrong files or delete a file only to discover that it's actually needed. Windows system users may be accustomed to undelete utilities, which scour the disk for recently deleted files in order to recover them. Unfortunately, such tools are rare on Linux. You can make undeletion easier by encouraging the use of special utilities that don't really delete files, but instead place them in temporary holding areas for deletion later. If all else fails, you may need to recover files from a backup.

Trash Can Utilities

One of the simplest ways to recover "deleted" files is to not delete them at all. This is the idea behind a *trash can*—a tool or procedure to hold onto files that are to be deleted without actually deleting them. These files can be deleted automatically or manually, depending on the tool or procedure. The most familiar form of trash can utility for most users, and the one from which the name derives, is the trash can icon that exists in many popular GUI environments, including KDE and GNOME. To use a GUI trash can, you drag files you want to delete to its icon. The icon is basically just a pointer to a specific directory that's out of the way or hidden from view, such as ~/Desktop/Trash or ~/.gnome-desktop/ Trash. When you drag a file to the trash can, you're really just moving it to that directory. If you subsequently decide you want to undelete the file, you can click or double-click the trash can icon to open a file browser on the trash directory. This enables you to drag the files you want to rescue out of the trash directory. Typically, files are only deleted from the trash directory when you say so by right-clicking the trash can icon and selecting an option called Empty Trash or something similar.

When you're working from the command line, the rm command is the usual method of deleting files, as in `rm somefile.txt`. This command doesn't use anything akin to the trash directory by default, and depending on your distribution and its default settings, rm may not even prompt you to be sure you're deleting the files you want to delete. You can improve rm's safety considerably by forcing it to confirm each deletion by using the -i option, as in `rm -i somefile.txt`. In fact, you may want to make this the default by creating an alias in your shell startup scripts, as described in Chapter 4, "Mastering Shells and Shell Scripting." For instance, the following line in ~/.bashrc or /etc/ profile will set up such an alias for bash:

```
alias rm='rm -i'
```

This configuration can become tedious if you use the -r option to delete an entire directory tree, though, or if you simply want to delete a lot of files by using wildcards. You can override the alias by specifying the complete path to rm (/bin/rm) when you type the command.

Forcing confirmation before deleting files can be a useful preventive measure, but it's not really a way of recovering deleted files. One simple way to allow such recovery is to mimic the GUI environments' trash cans—instead of deleting files with rm, move them to a holding directory with mv. You can then empty the holding directory whenever it's convenient. In fact, if you use both a command shell and a GUI environment that implements a trash can, you can use the same directory for both.

If you or your users are already familiar with rm, you may find it difficult to switch to using mv. It's also easy to forget how many files have been moved into the trash directory, and so disk space may fill up. One solution is to write a simple script that takes the place of rm, but that moves files to the trash directory. This script can simultaneously delete files older than a specified date or delete files if the trash directory contains more than a certain number of files. Alternatively, you could create a cron job to periodically delete files in the trash directory. An example of such a script is saferm, which is available from http://myocard.com/sites/linker/pages/linux/saferm.html. To use saferm or any similar script, you install it in place of the regular rm command, create an alias to call the script instead of rm, or call it by its true name. For instance, the following alias will work:

```
alias rm='saferm'
```

In the case of saferm, the script prompts before deleting files, but you can eliminate the prompt by changing the line that reads `read answer` to read `answer=A` and commenting out the immediately preceding echo lines. (Consult Chapter 4 for more information on creating or modifying shell scripts such as saferm.) The script uses a trash directory in the user's home directory, ~/.trash. When users need to recover "deleted" files, they can simply move them out of ~/.trash. This specific script doesn't attempt to empty the trash bin, so users must do this themselves using the real rm; or you or your users can create cron jobs to do the task.

File Recovery Tools

Undelete utilities for Linux are few and far between. The Linux philosophy is that users shouldn't delete files they really don't want to delete, and if they do, they should be restored from backups. Nonetheless, in a pinch there are some tricks you can use to try to recover accidentally deleted files.

NOTE   Low-level disk accesses require full read (and often write) privileges to the partition in question. Normally, only root has this access level to hard disks, although ordinary users may have such access to floppies. Therefore, normally only root may perform low-level file recoveries.

One of these tricks is the recover utility, which is headquartered at http://recover .sourceforge.net/linux/recover/ and available with most Linux distributions. Unfortunately, this tool has several drawbacks. The first is that it was designed for ext2fs, and so it doesn't work with most journaling filesystems. (It may work with ext3fs, though.) Another problem is that recover takes a long time to do anything, even on small partitions. I frequently see network programs such as web browsers and mail clients crash when recover runs. Finally, in my experience, recover frequently fails to work at all; if you type **recover /dev/sda4**, for instance, to recover files from /dev/sda4, the program may churn for a while, consume a lot of CPU time, and return with a Terminated notice. In sum, recover isn't a reliable tool, but you might try it if you're desperate. If you do try to run it, I recommend shutting down unnecessary network-enabled programs first.

Another method of file recovery is to use grep to search for text contained in the file. This approach is unlikely to work on anything but text files, and even then it may return a partial file or a file surrounded by text or binary junk. To use this approach, you type a command such as the following:

```
# grep -a -B5 -A100 "Dear Senator Jones" /dev/sda4 > recover.txt
```

This command searches for the text Dear Senator Jones on /dev/sda4 and returns the five lines before (-B5) and the 100 lines after (-A100) that string. The redirection operator stores the results in the file recover.txt. Because this operation involves a scan of the entire raw disk device, it's likely to take a while. (You can speed matters up slightly by omitting the redirection operator and instead cutting and pasting the returned lines from an xterm into a text editor; this enables you to hit Ctrl+C to cancel the operation once it's located the file. Another option is to use script to start a new shell that copies its output to a file, so you don't need to copy text into an editor.) This approach also works with any filesystem. If the file is fragmented, though, it will only return part of the file. If you misjudge the size of the file in lines, you'll either get just part of the file or too much—possibly including binary data before, after, or even within the target file.

Restoring Files from a Backup

Chapter 17, "Protecting Your System with Backups," describes system backup procedures. That chapter also includes information on emergency recovery procedures—restoring most or all of a working system from a backup. Such procedures are useful after a disk failure, security breach, or a seriously damaging administrative blunder. System backups can also be very useful in restoring deleted files. In this scenario, an accidentally deleted file can be restored from a backup. One drawback to this procedure is that the original file must have existed prior to the last regular system backup. If your backups are infrequent, the file might not exist. Even if you make daily backups, this procedure is unlikely to help if a user creates a file, quickly deletes it, and then wants it back immediately. A trash can utility is the best protection against that sort of damage.

As an example, suppose you create backups to tape using `tar`. You can recover files from this backup by using the `--extract` (`-x`) command. Typically, you also pass the `--verbose` (`-v`) option so that you know when the target file has been restored, and you use `--file` (`-f`) to point to the tape device file. You must also pass the name of the file to be restored:

```
# tar -xvf /dev/st0 home/al/election.txt
```

This command recovers the file `home/al/election.txt` from the `/dev/st0` tape device. A few points about this command require attention:

Permissions   The user who runs the command must have read/write access to the tape device. This user must also have write permission to the restore directory (normally, the current directory). Therefore, `root` normally runs this command, although other users may have sufficient privileges on some systems. Ownership and permissions on the restored file may change if a user other than `root` runs the command.

Filename Specification   The preceding command omitted the leading slash (`/`) in the target filename specification (`home/al/election.txt`). This is because `tar` normally strips this slash when it writes files, so when you specify files for restoration, the slash must also be missing. A few utilities and methods of creating a backup add a leading `./` to the filename. If your backups include this feature, you must include it in the filename specification to restore the file.

Restore Directory   Normally, `tar` restores files to the current working directory. Thus, if you type the preceding command while in `/root`, it will create a `/root/home/al/election.txt` file (assuming it's on the tape). I recommend restoring to an empty subdirectory and then moving the restored file to its intended target area. This practice minimizes the risk that you might mistype the target file specification and overwrite a newer file with an older one, or even overwrite the entire Linux installation with the backup.

Unfortunately, `tar` requires that you have a complete filename, including its path, ready in order to recover a file. If you don't know the exact filename, you can try taking a directory of the tape by typing **tar tvf /dev/st0** (substituting another tape device filename, if necessary). You may want to pipe the result through `less` or `grep` to help you search for the correct filename, or redirect it to a file you can search.

TIP   You can keep a record of files on a tape at backup time to simplify searches at restore time. Using the `--verbose` option and redirecting the results to a file will do the trick. Some incremental backup methods automatically store information on a backup's contents, too. Some backup tools, such as the commercial Backup/Recover Utility (BRU; http://www.bru.com), store an index of files on the tape. This index enables you to quickly scan the tape and select files for recovery from the index.

Summary

Linux, like any OS, is built on its filesystems. The ext2 filesystem has long been the standard for Linux, but over the course of development of the 2.4.*x* kernels, new journaling filesystems have been added as standard equipment. These filesystems give you several options that vary in subtle ways—disk space consumption by different types of files, support for ACLs, and so on. Most systems will work well with any Linux filesystem, but if disk performance is critically important to you, you may want to research the options further to pick the best one for your need. You can also optimize filesystems in various ways, ranging from options at filesystem creation time to defragmenting and resizing filesystems. Unfortunately, filesystems don't always work perfectly reliably. Sometimes you may need to fix filesystem corruption, and various tools exist to help you do this. Users may also accidentally delete files, and recovering them can be a challenging task, although being prepared by using trash can utilities and performing regular backups can greatly simplify recovery operations.

Chapter 13

Managing Printers

DESPITE CLAIMS OF ITS impending arrival for the past couple of decades, the "paperless office" seems to be perpetually late. If anything, offices today seem to process more paper than ever before. In part, this may be due to an extremely powerful computer technology: the printer. With a printer's help, you can generate reams of output with a few simple commands. Unfortunately, configuring the printer to work properly isn't always easy.

Linux supports several popular printing systems. Knowing which system your distribution uses is critical to proper printer configuration, and you may want to switch systems under some circumstances. With all of these systems, the assumption is usually that you have a PostScript printer. If you don't have one, you can use Ghostscript. Ghostscript converts PostScript into a form your printer can understand, so knowing how to tweak your Ghostscript configuration can help you generate better or faster output. Today, network printing is a popular means of sharing resources, and so knowing how to configure Linux to share a printer or use a shared printer (including a non-Linux print queue) can help your printing situation immensely.

Choosing the Best Linux Printing System

The three Linux printing systems are the original Berkeley Standard Distribution Line Printer Daemon (BSD LPD), the next-generation LPRng, and the Common Unix Printing System (CUPS). Each system has its advantages and is configured in its own way. Each distribution favors one of these systems, as summarized in Table 13.1, so configuring printing on one distribution may not be the same as doing so on another. Understanding these differences will help you get printing working on your system, and perhaps help you improve your printing experience by switching from one system to another.

NOTE   *This chapter is light on the basics of configuring each of these printer systems. Most distributions include printer configuration utilities that will set up a printer queue that works tolerably well. Instead, this chapter focuses on improving the queue that your distribution's tools will set up.*

TABLE 13.1: PRINTING SYSTEMS FAVORED BY VARIOUS LINUX DISTRIBUTIONS

DISTRIBUTION	STANDARD PRINTING SYSTEM	ALTERNATIVE PRINTING SYSTEM
Debian GNU/Linux 3.0	BSD LPD	LPRng, CUPS
Mandrake Linux 9.1	CUPS	LPRng
Red Hat Linux 8.1	CUPS	LPRng
Slackware Linux 9.0	LPRng	none
SuSE 8.1	CUPS	none

When to Pick BSD LPD

BSD LPD is the oldest of the Linux printing systems, and Linux distributions have been moving away from it in recent years. Nonetheless, BSD LPD remains the default printing system for Debian 3.0, although this statement is somewhat misleading. Debian installs BSD LPD (via the `lpr` package) by default, but you can select another printing system at install time by picking the appropriate package. You can also replace BSD LPD after installing Debian by replacing the `lpr` package with the package for a more recent system (`lprng` or `cupsys`).

BSD LPD is the traditional Linux printing system, so older documentation describes it. If you have an old introductory book on Linux with extensive information on printer configuration, you may want to use BSD LPD simply so that your documentation will more closely match your system; however, LPRng uses some of the same configuration files as BSD LPD. LPRng can therefore be configured in much the same way as BSD LPD—at least for printing applications on the local computer. On the other hand, few modern distributions use BSD LPD as the default printing system, or even ship with BSD LPD as an option, as Table 13.1 shows. If you want to install it, therefore, you'll have to track it down. A copy for an older version of your target distribution may be your best bet; most distributions moved away from BSD LPD around 2000, give or take a year or so.

BSD LPD is limited in some important ways. The most notable of these is that it provides no feedback to applications about the capabilities of printers. For instance, if you have a wide-carriage printer, or one with a duplexer, BSD LPD can't communicate this information to applications. Therefore, you must configure every printing application that should be able to use advanced features to do so on an individual basis—a potentially very tedious proposition. BSD LPD also lacks any means of automatically propagating a list of available printers across a network, which means that every client needs to be individually configured to use a print server—again, a potentially tedious task.

BSD LPD is configured through the `/etc/printcap` file. This file's format is similar to the file of the same name used by LPRng. It defines printers in the local system's printer queue. These printers can be either local (that is, connected to the computer via a parallel port, USB port, or the like) or network printers (that is, connected to another computer and shared by that computer's printing system).

If you want to share printers on a BSD LPD system with other computers, you must edit `/etc/hosts.lpd`, as described in the upcoming section, "BSD LPD Access Control."

NOTE   All Linux printing systems function as daemons. On a workstation, these daemons should only accept local connections, but they use networking protocols even for local printing. Opening access slightly allows a local printing configuration to accept remote printing requests.

When to Pick LPRng

As Table 13.1 reveals, Slackware 9.0 is the only major Linux distribution that uses LPRng as its primary printing system, although several others still ship with LPRng as an alternative system. Just a version or so ago, several other distributions used LPRng as their primary printing systems, so it's likely to be found on many not-too-old Linux installations.

LPRng was designed as a drop-in replacement for BSD LPD. LPRng uses the same network printing protocols as BSD LPD, so computers running these two packages can use each others' printers if they're configured to allow this access. LPRng uses the same /etc/printcap file to define printers as does BSD LPD. Listing 13.1 shows a sample of this file. Technically, each entry is a single line with colon-delimited fields; however, to help make the file readable to humans, entries are typically broken up across multiple lines using backslashes (\), which tell the system to treat the subsequent line as a continuation of the first. Therefore, all lines for an entry except for the last one end in backslashes. All lines save the first are typically indented to help improve readability.

LISTING 13.1: SAMPLE *etc/printcap* **FILE**

```
lp|epson:\
        :sd=/var/spool/lp0:\
        :lp=/dev/lp0:\
        :mx#0:\
        :sh:\
        :if=/var/spool/lp0/filter:
lp1|hplj:\
        :sd=/var/spool/lp1:\
        :rm=pserver:\
        :rp=hplj:\
        :mx#0:\
        :if=/var/spool/lp1/filter:
```

Each /etc/printcap entry begins with one or more queue names, separated by vertical bars (|). In Listing 13.1, the first queue may be referred to as either lp or epson, while the second is known as lp1 or hplj. Subsequent lines set features such as the spool directory where printed files are temporarily stored (sd=); the printer device file for local printers (lp=); the remote print server hostname and print queue name for network printers (rm= and rp=, respectively); the maximum size, in kilobytes, of a file the queue will accept, with 0 being a code for no limit (mx#); a command to suppress a header that identifies the user who sent the print job (sh); and the *print filter* that processes files (if=). Many other options are available to help you fine-tune the behavior of the print queue; consult the printcap man page for further information.

LPRng directly supports both local and network printers. You'll generally include either an lp= entry in /etc/printcap or both rm= and rp= entries. In Listing 13.1, the epson (or lp) queue is local, using a printer attached to /dev/lp0. The hplj (or lp1) queue is remote, using a printer called hplj on the computer called pserver.

TIP   When naming your print queues, you should try to assign names that match those of the remote printer queue whenever possible. Doing so will minimize any confusion that might result if one printer's name varies depending on the computer from which it is used.

Overall, LPRng can be a convenient print spooler if you're already familiar with its configuration or with BSD LPD. Its default network configuration is not secure, though, as described in the upcoming section, "LPRng Access Control." Therefore, if you use LPRng, you should be sure to close that hole. Also, LPRng suffers from many of the same limitations as BSD LPD—it can't tell applications about a printer's features, and it can't automatically communicate a list of networked printers to potential clients.

When to Pick CUPS

CUPS was developed, in part, to address the shortcomings of BSD LPD and LPRng in terms of print queue/application communication and network print client/server communication. CUPS includes mechanisms to facilitate both tasks and has the potential to greatly simplify application and print client configuration. This potential is not yet fully realized, though. CUPS is still fairly new, and many applications continue to use older protocols and ignore the new CUPS features. Nonetheless, CUPS' client/server communication features can make it easier to configure many print clients if you use CUPS on both the server and the clients. This configuration is described in more detail in the upcoming section, "Simplifying Network Printing with CUPS."

Compared to other Linux print queues, CUPS configuration is quite complex; however, CUPS includes a built-in web-based configuration tool to help simplify matters. You can access this tool by browsing to `http://localhost:631` from the computer on which CUPS is installed, as shown in Figure 13.1. (You can also use your computer's hostname instead of `localhost`.) Click the Manage Printers link to create or modify printer definitions. The web-based configuration tool provides links that will guide you through the process, including specifying your printer model. CUPS can then provide information about your printer to applications that ask for this information, simplifying application setup—if the applications avail themselves of this information, which many don't yet do.

Most of CUPS' features, including its web-based configuration tool, can be accessed from the network. The official default configuration is to deny administrative access to anything but the local computer but to accept print jobs from any host. Some Linux distributions, though, restrict matters further, so you may need to loosen these restrictions to enable network printing. This issue is described in the upcoming sections, "CUPS Access Control" and "Simplifying Network Printing with CUPS."

One problem with CUPS is that its new features rely upon a new network printing protocol, the *Internet Printing Protocol (IPP)*. By itself CUPS can't accept print jobs from computers that run BSD LPD or LPRng, although CUPS does include support for submitting print jobs to such systems. If you want to run a CUPS print server that can accept jobs from systems that run older printing systems, you must add a tool called `cups-lpd`, which adds support for the LPD protocol used by both BSD LPD and LPRng. This program ships with CUPS and is launched through a super server (`inetd` or `xinetd`). The `cups-lpd` man page includes sample configurations for both of these super servers, and most distributions that use CUPS ship with these configurations set up but in a disabled state. When run, `cups-lpd` accepts LPD jobs and converts them to IPP jobs for CUPS.

FIGURE 13.1

CUPS provides a web-based tool for managing printers.

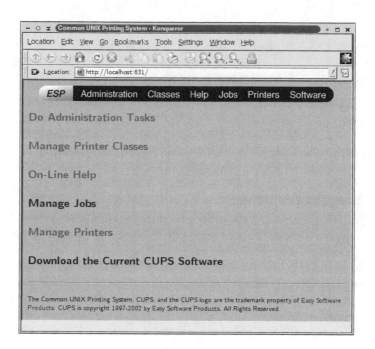

Whether or not you run `cups-lpd`, CUPS provides printing tools for local printer access that use the same names as the tools provided with BSD LPD or LPRng, such as `lpr`, `lprm`, and `lpq`. Some CUPS configurations also automatically generate an `/etc/printcap` file for the benefit of programs that check this file's contents; however, the CUPS `printcap` file is bare bones and isn't used to configure CUPS. Thus, editing the file is pointless. If your system doesn't generate an `/etc/printcap` file and some of your programs can't find your printers, you may want to try generating one. Listing each print queue name on a line of its own, followed immediately by a colon (`:`), should do the job.

Improving Ghostscript Output

Traditionally, Unix computers have used PostScript printers. This fact has greatly simplified the design of traditional Unix print queue systems such as BSD LPD and LPRng because these systems don't need to support extensive printer drivers, as are common in Windows and other OSs. Instead, applications produce PostScript output, which is fed more-or-less intact to the printer by the printer queue. This approach does have disadvantages, though, such as the fact that applications can't query a printer queue for detailed information about a printer's capabilities. One drawback that's more important for an average Linux system than for more traditional Unix workstations is that a Linux system is likely to be paired with a non-PostScript printer. Such inexpensive printers typically can't parse the PostScript output directly. Linux's solution is to call *Ghostscript* from the print queue. This program converts PostScript into a variety of other formats that can be displayed in graphics programs or processed by a printer. Effectively, Ghostscript becomes the printer driver on a Linux system. Another way of looking at the situation is that Ghostscript is a PostScript interpreter that runs on the Linux system rather than on the printer.

In order to get the most from Ghostscript, you must know how to configure it. This task includes knowing where to look to change the Ghostscript calls, knowing which Ghostscript driver to use, and knowing which driver options to use. You may also want to create multiple print queues to provide access to different printer features.

WARNING *Some printers that don't understand PostScript are marketed as PostScript printers. These printers use computer-based PostScript interpreters much like Ghostscript. Such a method does Linux no good, unless of course the drivers are available for Linux or the printer is used via a Windows print server. If you're shopping for a new printer and want PostScript capability, be sure the PostScript interpreter is built into the printer.*

Changing the Driver

A traditional BSD LPD or LPRng print queue calls Ghostscript and specifies the Ghostscript driver to be used with the help of a print filter. This filter is specified using the `if=` line in `/etc/printcap`, as described earlier, in "When to Pick LPRng." Unfortunately, several layers of indirection are usually involved, so you can't simply change the `if=` line to modify the driver or its options. Instead, you must locate documentation about the printer filter package that your distribution uses or that you've installed. One popular filter package is Apsfilter (`http://www.apsfilter.org`), which is often used in conjunction with BSD LPD or LPRng. CUPS uses its own printer filters. If your system uses another type of printer filter, you may need to backtrack from its `/etc/printcap` entry.

USING APSFILTER

Debian and Slackware both use Apsfilter. Typically, you use this tool to set up a complete printer queue—an `/etc/printcap` entry, spool directory, and filter script. To do this, type **/usr/share/ apsfilter/SETUP** to run the setup tool, which then runs through a series of informational screens and allows you to set various options, such as your printer type and location. Figure 13.2 shows the main configuration screen. If you haven't set all the necessary information, the (I) option won't appear on this menu. You use this item to finalize the installation. Before doing so, though, you should type **T** to print a test page to make sure the installation works.

FIGURE 13.2

The main Apsfilter Setup screen lets you change various printer options.

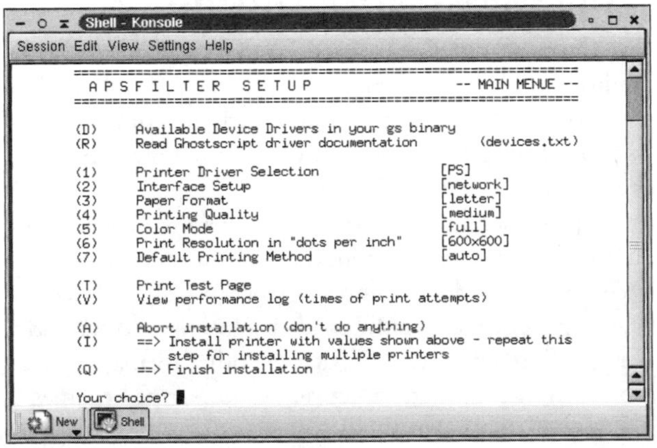

```
 -  □  x   Shell - Konsole                                          □ □ x
 Session Edit View Settings Help

   ===============================================================
     A P S F I L T E R   S E T U P              -- MAIN MENUE --
   ===============================================================

     (D)     Available Device Drivers in your gs binary
     (R)     Read Ghostscript driver documentation      (devices.txt)

     (1)     Printer Driver Selection              [PS]
     (2)     Interface Setup                       [network]
     (3)     Paper Format                          [letter]
     (4)     Printing Quality                      [medium]
     (5)     Color Mode                            [full]
     (6)     Print Resolution in "dots per inch"   [600x600]
     (7)     Default Printing Method               [auto]

     (T)     Print Test Page
     (V)     View performance log (times of print attempts)

     (A)     Abort installation (don't do anything)
     (I)     ==> Install printer with values shown above - repeat this
                  step for installing multiple printers
     (Q)     ==> Finish installation

   Your choice? ■

  New    Shell
```

Apsfilter provides many options for printer drivers when you type **1** in the main setup screen. Roughly speaking, these options fall into several categories:

PostScript Printer The first option is for a PostScript printer. Select this option if your printer understands PostScript natively, no matter what its brand or model.

Standard Ghostscript Drivers Option 3 on the driver page is for printer drivers built into Ghostscript. Most non-PostScript printers fall into this category, although a few don't. When you select this option, the program presents a long list of printers, and you select your model from this list.

Add-on Ghostscript Drivers Ghostscript ships with many printer drivers, but third parties have written additional drivers. Options 4 and up on the printer driver selection page enable you to use these drivers. Most of these drivers work with a small family of printers, so you pick the specific model from a list after selecting the family option.

NOTE *The upcoming section, "Finding the Best Driver," provides tips on locating the best printer driver for any given printer.*

Once configured, Apsfilter stores information on printer drivers in `/etc/apsfilter/`*queue*`/apsfilterrc`, where *queue* is the print queue name. Most importantly, the PRINTER variable holds the name of the printer driver. Therefore, you can change the driver a queue uses by modifying that variable. Drivers are stored in `/etc/apsfilter/basedir/driver` and its subdirectories. These drivers are actually Apsfilter configuration files, so you may be able to edit them to achieve unusual effects if you understand the Ghostscript configuration for your printer.

Apsfilter actually calls Ghostscript (the `gs` program file itself) from the `apsfilter` script, which is stored in `/etc/apsfilter/basedir/bin`. This script sets the `gs_cmd` variable to a Ghostscript command template, depending on the printer type. If you need to enable unusual Ghostscript options, you can modify this command template.

BACKTRACKING FROM /ETC/PRINTCAP

If you're using an unusual print filter with BSD LPD or LPRng, you may need to use your distribution's or print filter's configuration tool to create a new printer definition. You can then backtrack from its `/etc/printcap` entry to find the call to Ghostscript. The `if=` option in `printcap` points to the filter program. This program may be a do-it-all filter, such as Apsfilter, or a simpler filter that a filter package created for a specific printer. In either case, this filter is probably a shell script, so you can load it into a text editor and study it to learn how the printing system calls Ghostscript. Sometimes Ghostscript is called directly from the filter script. Other filters call still more scripts, or they place the Ghostscript command in another configuration file.

Once you've located the call to Ghostscript, you can change the driver by changing the `-sDEVICE` option to `gs`. In many cases, a filter script passes a variable to this option, so you may need to backtrack further to discover where this variable is set.

USING CUPS

When you use your web browser to access `http://localhost:631`, the system should display a summary of options, as shown in Figure 13.1. Click Manage Printers to manage existing printers or add new ones. The Add Printer link then lets you add a printer. This process is much like the Apsfilter process—you specify the printer's device or network location, its make and model, and so on.

If you want to modify an existing printer, you can do so by clicking the Modify Printer or Configure Printer option in a specific printer's listing. Modify Printer lets you change the printer driver, location, and so on. Configure Printer lets you set options such as the printer's resolution and paper size.

If you need to delve into configuration files, you can examine the `/etc/cups/printers.conf` file in which CUPS stores printer-specific information. This file includes information concerning the device file or network location of the printer, its current status, and so on. CUPS stores more detailed information on printers in the `/etc/cups/ppd` directory, which holds *PostScript Printer Description (PPD)* files. In the case of non-PostScript printers, these files include lines that begin with the string `*cupsFilter`, which identifies how CUPS should convert the file to a format the printer will understand. These lines don't correspond in any simple way to Ghostscript driver names, though, so they can be tricky to modify by hand; it's usually better to rely on the web-based configuration tool. If you want to tweak your Ghostscript configuration, though, check the final word on this line against the programs and scripts in `/usr/lib/cups/filter`—these CUPS print filters are responsible for calling Ghostscript. Many, but not all, drivers call `/usr/bin/foomatic-gswrapper`, which calls Ghostscript.

NOTE   *Some CUPS installations deliver a very limited set of printer choices by default. You can install GIMP-Print (as described in the next section), drivers from the Linux Printing website (`http://www.linuxprinting.org`), drivers available from many distributions as the `cups-drivers` package, or the commercial Easy Software Products (ESP) Print Pro (`http://www.easysw.com/printpro/`) to expand the range of options delivered by CUPS.*

Finding the Best Driver

The preceding discussion avoided one critical issue: How do you know which printer driver to select? If you're using a configuration tool such as Apsfilter or CUPS, you'll probably see a list of printers. If you're lucky, your printer will be on that list, so it should be obvious which one to pick. If you're unlucky, though, you might see two drivers for your printer or none at all.

If you see two drivers, I recommend that you try both. For both drivers, try printing both text and graphics output; one driver could produce better text and the other could produce superior graphics. If that's the case, and if both text and graphics quality are important to you, you can configure two printer queues, as described in the upcoming section, "Accessing Printer Options via Multiple Print Queues."

Most Ghostscript drivers work with many printers. For instance, Hewlett-Packard (HP) developed a printer language called the *Printer Control Language (PCL)*, which has been adopted by many printer manufacturers for their laser printers. Thus, picking an HP LaserJet model will work for many non-HP laser printers. If you don't see your printer model listed, select an earlier model from the same line or a compatible model. Most printers that emulate others come with documentation that should help you pick the right driver.

If you have no clue which driver to try, consult the Linux Printing website (`http://www.linuxprinting.org`). Click the Printer Listings link in the column on the left side of the window, and then use the selector buttons to locate your printer or all printers made by a given manufacturer. The resulting web page provides information on the overall level of support for a printer as well as details on specific drivers. The overall support is summarized as one of four levels: *perfectly* (printer works in all resolutions and with all major features), *mostly* (printer works, but has minor problems or limitations, such as lack of support for some resolutions), *partially* (printer works in a very limited way, such as black-and-white only on a color model), or *paperweight* (no support for this model). Below the summary information you'll find information on all the Ghostscript drivers that work with a printer, where appropriate. (Listings for PostScript printers note that you don't need to use Ghostscript.)

As a general rule, the standard Ghostscript drivers work well for most printers, particularly for printing text. One particular set of add-on drivers deserves mention, though: GIMP-Print (`http://gimp-print.sourceforge.net`). These drivers ship with most distributions, and you can select them from your printer setup tools. They derive from work done to support non-PostScript printers with the GIMP, and so their developers have optimized these drivers to get the best results on graphics files. Therefore, even if you get acceptable text printouts using a standard Ghostscript driver, you might want to investigate GIMP-Print for printing graphics.

One unusual alternative to any of these drivers is the TurboPrint package (`http://www.turboprint.de/english.html`), which is a commercial replacement for Ghostscript in the Linux printing queue. If you can't find regular Ghostscript support, or if the Ghostscript drivers are inadequate, TurboPrint may be worth investigating. The package also includes GUI printer management tools, so if you don't like your distribution's GUI tools, TurboPrint may be the answer.

A few applications support printing using printers' native modes rather than PostScript. The GIMP is the most notable of these programs, but there are other examples, such as WordPerfect 8.0 and Anywhere Office. To use the non-PostScript printing options of such programs, you must either have a printer queue that's smart enough to recognize the printer's native format and pass it through unmodified or you must configure a *raw* print queue. A raw queue doesn't use a print filter. You can create one for BSD LPD or LPRng by duplicating a conventional print queue entry in `/etc/printcap`, changing its name, and eliminating the `if=` line. (If the `if=` line is the last line in the entry, be sure to eliminate the trailing backslash on the end of the previous line, too.) If you're using CUPS, you can create a raw queue by selecting Raw as the printer make and Raw Queue as the model.

Raw queues can be useful for sharing a printer with Windows hosts, too. If you share a conventional printer queue, a Windows system may need to use a PostScript printer driver. This may work well, but it sometimes poses problems, particularly if Linux's support for the printer is weak. By using a raw print queue, you can use the printer's native Windows drivers, which may work better than using PostScript drivers. In fact, it's sometimes possible to share a printer using a raw queue even when no Ghostscript drivers exist.

Accessing Printer Options via Multiple Print Queues

In Windows, you can usually set various printer options from a printing dialog box. Depending on the printer's features, you can set the resolution, determine whether to print in color or black-and-white, specify whether or not to use a duplexing feature, and so on. Unfortunately, these options aren't always available when printing from Linux, because these options may be features of the Ghostscript configuration. For instance, Ghostscript includes an option (`-r`) to set the resolution, and conventional Linux print queues don't provide a way to pass this information to the printer. (CUPS provides means to pass some options on to printers, but most Linux programs still aren't

CUPS-enabled.) Fortunately, there is a way to access these options from Linux: You can create multiple print queues.

Linux print queues are logically unrelated to the physical printers—the queues are holding areas on disk and configurations for the printing software. It's entirely possible to link several queues to a single physical printer. For instance, suppose you've got an inkjet printer that supports several resolutions, ranging from 180 dots per inch (dpi) up to 1,440dpi. Inkjet printers usually print faster at lower resolutions, so you might want to use lower resolutions for draft printouts and higher resolutions for important final documents. In order to do this, you can create several queues for this printer, giving them names that indicate the intended resolution, such as `epson180`, `epson360`, `epson720`, and `epson1440`. Some smart filters and configuration tools enable you to set options such as the resolution when you create the filter; for instance, Apsfilter's option 6 (see Figure 13.2) does this job. Other tools let you change some of these options after creating the queue; for instance, this is one of the features of the CUPS printer configuration link that's available after a queue is created. With other tools or for some features, you may need to dig into the filter files, as described earlier in "Backtracking from `/etc/printcap`," to modify the call to Ghostscript or to add a feature in some other way.

In addition to accessing different print resolutions, you can create multiple queues to use a single printer via different Ghostscript drivers, to provide raw and Ghostscript-driven access, to provide options for features enabled through `/etc/printcap` such as the presence of a header page, and so on.

TIP *Some PostScript printers (especially old models) don't work well with all PostScript input. If yours chokes or produces odd output from some applications, you can create two queues: a conventional queue that relies on PostScript in the printer and a second queue that uses Ghostscript to convert PostScript into PostScript using the `pswrite` driver. The latter option will probably be slow, but it may work better for some files if your printer is low on memory, has a buggy PostScript interpreter, or has some other problem processing some print jobs.*

Sharing Printers on a Network

Both the IPP and LPD printing protocols are inherently network-enabled. Although they can be used for purely local printer control, they can also work over a network. Typical printer configuration utilities, including those provided with Apsfilter and CUPS, make configuring the use of a remote printer fairly straightforward—instead of listing a local printer device file, such as `/dev/lp0`, you specify the hostname and queue name of a remote printer. The tricky part of network printing involves controlling access to the print server. Each of the three print server packages described in this chapter has its own authorization procedures. Another potentially tricky topic is using printers that are shared via protocols other than LPD or IPP, such as printers shared from Windows or Mac OS computers.

Authorizing Remote Access to Printers

By default, the BSD LPD server is closed to outside access, so you must modify the system's configuration to enable this access. By contrast, both LPRng and CUPS ship with defaults that are more open, although individual Linux distributions sometimes modify these defaults. As a general rule, no matter what system you use, you should limit access as much as possible. With a completely open printing system, a miscreant could tie up your resources by printing large jobs, possibly with all-black pages so as to consume as much ink or toner as possible. If an intruder knows of a security bug in a printing system, the intruder might also be able to leverage an open server to provide greater access.

TIP   Security is best applied in layers. In addition to restricting access to your printers with the printer software's tools, you should consider creating `iptables` *firewall rules to block unwanted access. Chapter 20, "Controlling Network Access," covers this topic in more detail.*

BSD LPD ACCESS CONTROL

The BSD LPD system uses the `/etc/hosts.lpd` file as an access control mechanism. The simplest way to use this file is to fill it with hostnames or IP addresses, one per line. These computers are then authorized to print to any printer in the system's `/etc/printcap` file. If your network supports Network Information System (NIS) netgroups, you can specify a netgroup by preceding its name with a plus sign and an at-sign (`+@`). If you want to exclude specific hosts from an otherwise authorized netgroup, you can precede those hosts' names with minus signs (`-`). For instance, Listing 13.2 shows a sample `hosts.lpd` file. This file grants access to `gutenberg` in the server's own domain, `franklin.luna.edu`, `192.168.32.102`, and the `agroup` NIS netgroup. The host `bad.member.luna.edu` is explicitly denied printing access, though, even if that computer is in the `agroup` NIS netgroup.

LISTING 13.2: SAMPLE */ETC/HOSTS.LPD* FILE

```
gutenberg
franklin.luna.edu
192.168.32.102
+@agroup
-bad.member.luna.edu
```

As a general rule, the safest way to use the `/etc/hosts.lpd` file is to list hosts by IP address. Doing so means that a DNS failure can't cause printing problems and also minimizes the risk that a compromised DNS or NIS server could be used to provide bogus authorization for a miscreant.

WARNING   The `/etc/hosts.equiv` *file can also be used to authorize the use of a BSD LPD server; however, this file also authorizes the use of other servers, such as* `rlogind`*. These servers have their own access control mechanisms, and some (including* `rlogind`*) should generally be avoided. I recommend checking to be sure you don't have a* `hosts.equiv` *file at all or making sure that it is empty if you do have one. Use server-specific files, such as* `hosts.lpd`*, instead.*

LPRng ACCESS CONTROL

Unlike BSD LPD, LPRng doesn't use an `/etc/hosts.lpd` file to control remote access. Instead, it uses `/etc/lpd.perms`, which has a much more complex format. A typical default `lpd.perms` file consists mostly of comments describing its use, which can be helpful in figuring out the format if you're unfamiliar with it. Many `/etc/lpd.perms` files end with a line reading DEFAULT ACCEPT, which means that the default security policy is to accept print jobs from anywhere, if no earlier rules specify otherwise. Rules that can limit this default rule take the following forms:

```
ACCEPT criterion
REJECT criterion
```

These lines tell LPRng to accept or reject, respectively, connections that match certain criteria. Specification of these criteria can be quite complex, but typically involves providing a service code from Table 13.2 and a specification of who may or may not use the specified service, as summarized in Table 13.3. You can add the keyword NOT to the keys specified in Table 13.3 to reverse the meaning of a restriction. Most of these keys accept parameters, which you specify after an equal sign (=).

TABLE 13.2: LPRNG SERVICE CODES

LPRNG SERVICE CODE	AFFECTS SERVICE
X	Connections; affects all services
R	Job spooling; ability to submit jobs for printing via lpr
P	Job printing; ability to print jobs already in the queue
Q	Job queries; ability to obtain information about print jobs via lpq
M	Job removal; ability to delete jobs via lprm
C	Job control; ability to control jobs via lpc
S	Job status; ability to query job status via lpc

TABLE 13.3: LPRNG HOST AND USER SPECIFICATIONS

KEY NAME	EFFECT	PARAMETER ACCEPTED
USER	Sets user-by-user security based on a local username	Username
HOST	Specifies security based on the computer that originated the print job	Hostname
GROUP	Sets group-based security based on local groups	Group name
REMOTEPORT	Restricts access based on the originating port number	Port number
REMOTEUSER	Sets user-by-user security based on a remote username	Username
REMOTEHOST	Restricts access based on the computer that's attempting to access the server	Hostname
REMOTEGROUP	Sets group-based security based on a remote group	Group name
REMOTEIP	Restricts access based on the computer that submits the print job to the LPRng server	IP address
PRINTER	Restricts access based on the target printer	Queue name
SAMEHOST	True if HOST and REMOTEHOST are the same computer	none
SAMEUSER	True if REMOTEUSER is the one who owns the job	none
SERVER	True if the job originated on localhost	none

One way to limit remote connections is to add lines like the following before the DEFAULT ACCEPT line in /etc/lpd.perms:

```
ACCEPT SERVICE=X SERVER
REJECT SERVICE=X NOT REMOTEIP=172.22.0.0/16
```

These lines tell LPRng to accept connections (SERVICE=X) from the local computer (SERVER) and to reject connections from any other computer that's not on the 172.22.0.0/16 network. Because the X service applies to all connections, this rule effectively limits all access to the print server. This configuration should be useful if you want to share your printers locally, but not with the world at large. Of course, you must change 172.22.0.0/16 to an appropriate IP address and netmask for your network. If your printer shouldn't be shared at all, omit the second line.

You can create finer-grained rules to restrict access in important ways. For instance, you typically don't want users to be able to delete each others' print jobs. For this reason, the default /etc/lpd.perms file includes the following lines:

```
ACCEPT SERVICE=M SAMEHOST SAMEUSER
ACCEPT SERVICE=M SERVER REMOTEUSER=root
REJECT SERVICE=M
```

The first line tells LPRng to allow the job's owner on the submitting computer to submit a removal request. The second line enables root on the server computer itself to do the same. The third line blocks all other job-removal requests.

CUPS ACCESS CONTROL

CUPS models its access control rules after those provided by Apache. These rules reside in the /etc/cups/cupsd.conf file. Among other features, this file includes a series of multiline location specifications, which look like this:

```
<Location /printers>
Order Deny,Allow
Deny From All
BrowseAllow from 127.0.0.1
BrowseAllow from 192.168.1.0/24
Allow from 127.0.0.1
Allow from 192.168.1.0/24
</Location>
```

Each location applies to a particular type of resource. The printers location applies to all your printers. There's also a root (/) location that applies to all resources and an admin location that determines administrative access. If you want to restrict access differently for some printers than for others, you can create a location for a specific queue by providing the queue name after the /printers location name, as in Location printers/canon to modify the canon queue's accessibility.

Within each location specification, you'll find some combination of other rules that restrict or enable access, expressed as Allow, Deny, BrowseAllow, and BrowseDeny directives. The Allow and Deny directives grant or block access, respectively. The BrowseAllow and BrowseDeny directives determine whether or not other CUPS servers can automatically scan the server in question. All of these directives take a hostname or IP address as an option, following the from keyword. You can use wildcards or network specifications, such as `*.luna.edu` or `192.168.1.0/24`, to specify entire blocks of computers. The `@LOCAL` keyword stands for all local computer interfaces. The `Order` directive tells the system whether to apply `Allow` or `Deny` directives first—whichever type comes second takes precedence when there's a conflict.

Interpreting these rules, the preceding example specifies that computers on the 192.168.1.0/24 network, as well as the server computer itself, are given access to all of the printers. The `Deny from All` directive, in conjunction with the `Order Deny,Allow` directive, blocks all other computers from accessing this one's resources.

WARNING   The CUPS access control tools described here apply to IPP jobs, not to LPD jobs received via `cups-lpd`. *Once accepted by* `cups-lpd`, *these jobs look like local print jobs. Therefore, if you want to control LPD access to a CUPS-based print server, you must use other means, such as* `iptables` *firewall rules, TCP Wrappers, or* `xinetd` *access control rules. These topics are described in more detail in Chapter 20.*

Simplifying Network Printing with CUPS

One of CUPS' great advantages is that CUPS servers can communicate with one another and exchange lists of available printers. This process is known as *browsing*, and it can greatly simplify network printing configuration. Instead of manually defining print queues on each print client, you need only configure the clients to enable browsing and set up the print servers to share their printers. The second task is described in the preceding section, "CUPS Access Control"—you configure the `/printers` location so that all the clients can access the printers. Be sure to include both `Allow` and `BrowseAllow` directives in this definition. You must then enable browsing on both clients and servers. This task is accomplished by the following line prior to any location sections, on both the client and the server:

```
Browsing On
```

This directive is enabled by default with CUPS, but some distributions include a `Browsing Off` directive to disable it. On the server, you should also enable browsing for all the clients outside of the `/printers` location, using a line like this:

```
BrowseAddress 192.168.1.255
```

This line tells the system to accept browsing requests from the 192.168.1.0/24 network. As with other CUPS address specifications, you can provide this information in other forms, as well.

Once you have made these changes and have restarted the client and server print queues, you should see all the available network printers appear on the clients' printer lists, as revealed by the CUPS web-based configuration tools. It may take a few seconds, or potentially even minutes, for all these printers to appear, though, so be patient. CUPS is smart enough to keep printers from appearing multiple times. For instance, if you have two print servers, each server should detect the other's printer; however, the servers won't further propagate other servers' printer, so clients should show each printer just once. Printers shared through a non-IPP protocol, though, might conceivably appear multiple times if these printers are added to a print server whose printers are browseable via IPP.

NOTE   Both the client and the server must use CUPS for browsing to work. You can configure a CUPS client to print to an LPD server much as you'd configure the system to print to a local printer, but you must specify the server's hostname and print queue name instead of a local device filename.

Accessing Non-Linux Printers

Local networks today frequently contain multiple OSs. This fact can lead to complications, such as the need for one OS to understand the protocols intended for another OS. In the case of printing, the IPP and LPD protocols are native to Unix, and hence to Linux; you're most likely to use these protocols on a Linux print client when printing to a printer hosted on another Unix or Linux computer. Sometimes, though, you must print to a printer that's shared using another protocol. The two most common alternatives are the Server Message Block (SMB), aka the Common Internet File System (CIFS), which is used on Windows Networks; and AppleTalk, which is the native file- and printer-sharing protocol for Mac OS Classic. (The newer Mac OS X is Unix-based, but it still supports AppleTalk, and many network-enabled printers sold for the Macintosh market use AppleTalk directly.)

NOTE   This section describes using SMB/CIFS- or AppleTalk-shared printers from Linux. If you want to share a Linux printer with Windows clients, consult Chapter 24, "Sharing Files." You can share printers with Macintoshes using the Netatalk package introduced here, but its configuration for this role is beyond the scope of this book. As Mac OS X is Unix-based, you can easily configure it to use an LPD or IPP queue directly.

PRINTING TO WINDOWS PRINTERS

Most Linux printer packages, including Apsfilter and CUPS, enable you to create a print queue that sends its output to an SMB/CIFS server. You typically do so in much the same way you'd create a queue for another LPD server, but the information you provide is different: In addition to a hostname and queue name, you must provide a username and password. Depending on how the server is configured, these might belong to an ordinary user's account or to a special printer account. Consult the Window's system's administrator for details.

WARNING   Linux print queues that print to an SMB/CIFS print queue generally store the username and password in an unencrypted form somewhere in the print queue directory or in a configuration directory. This practice is a potential security risk, especially if the account is an ordinary user account. If possible, configure the server to share the printer using a special printing-only account, so as to minimize the risk of storing the password on clients.

Printing to Windows printers requires using the Samba (`http://www.samba.org`) package and, specifically, the `smbprint` or `smbspool` script. This script is usually part of a package called `samba-client`, `smbclient`, or something similar. The `smbprint` script calls another program, `smbclient`, which submits the print job. Thus, in order to print to an SMB/CIFS printer, you must install the Samba client package for your distribution.

PRINTING TO MACINTOSH PRINTERS

The Netatalk package (`http://netatalk.sourceforge.net`) enables a Linux computer to function as a file and print server for Mac OS computers. Although it's primarily a server package, Netatalk also includes utilities that enable Linux to print to and control AppleTalk printers. These programs are `pap`, `psf`, and `papstatus`.

To print to an AppleTalk printer, you can use `pap` much as you'd use `lpr` to print to a normal Linux print queue. For instance, to print `sample.ps` to the AppleTalk printer called `awriter`, you'd type:

```
$ pap -p awriter sample.ps
```

In many cases, you can use pap as a direct replacement for lpr in just this way. You can print from the command line or replace a call to lpr with a call to pap in GUI printing dialog boxes, such as the one for xv shown in Figure 13.3.

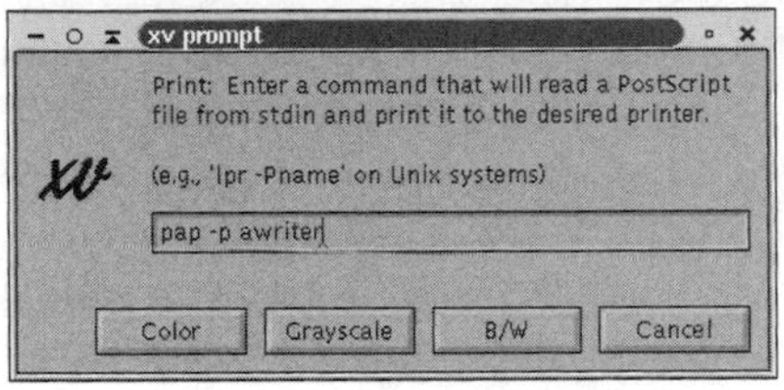

FIGURE 13.3

You can print to AppleTalk printers using the pap command, bypassing the Linux print queue.

Some applications don't enable you to easily replace calls to lpr, though. If you use such programs, you may want to create a conventional Linux print queue that redirects the print job via pap, much as you can create a queue that sends a print job using smbprint. The psf program is built for this task; it functions as an input filter for a BSD LPD or LPRng print queue. To use it in this way, you call it by an alternative name: ifpap. For instance, you might use this /etc/printcap entry:

```
awriter:\
        :sd=/var/spool/lpd/awriter:\
        :mx#0:\
        :sh:\
        :lp=/dev/null:\
        :if=/usr/sbin/ifpap:
```

This configuration requires a file called .paprc in the spool directory (/var/spool/lpd/awriter in this example). This file contains a single line with the name of the AppleTalk printer, such as awriter. Once this is configured, you can use lpr to submit a print job to an AppleTalk printer.

CUPS uses a system of *back-ends*—programs that handle delivering print jobs to local and remote printers. These back-ends are stored in /usr/lib/cups/backend, and they can be binary programs or shell scripts. Unfortunately, CUPS comes with no standard AppleTalk back-end, and I know of none that work reliably. (Mandrake's version of CUPS ships with a pap back-end, but it doesn't work on my network. Other CUPS pap back-ends I've found on the Internet also fail to work for me.) If printing using AppleTalk is vitally important to you, perhaps another printing system would be a better choice for you. Alternatively, you could delve into the CUPS documentation and write your own back-end.

Summary

Linux's printing system is different from that used by Windows, so if you've come from that environment, Linux may seem odd. Since the mid-1990s, Linux distributions have been migrating away from the traditional BSD LPD software to the updated LPRng, and now they're migrating to the totally redesigned CUPS. When printing to non-PostScript printers, all of these systems rely on Ghostscript to convert PostScript into a format the printer can understand; therefore, knowing how to tweak Ghostscript settings can be very helpful in optimizing a printing setup. Linux's printing model is very network-oriented, so sharing printers is relatively straightforward, at least in theory. In practice, the presence of three major printing systems, each with its own configuration tools, can make it tricky to get everything working together, particularly if your network uses more than one printing tool.

Chapter 14

Programs and Processes

In order to work with a computer, you run programs. A running program is known as a *process*. Once booted, a typical Linux system runs dozens of processes, even before a single user has logged in. Understanding how these processes relate to one another and how to learn about the processes on your system will help you manage them if problems arise. These problems usually boil down to poor performance caused by processes consuming too much CPU time or other system resources. In order to cope with these problems, you may need to scale back a running process's demands for resources or terminate it altogether. A variety of tools help you accomplish these tasks.

Understanding Relationships: The Linux Process Tree

Linux processes don't spring magically into being; they're started by other processes, via a mechanism known as *forking* or *spawning*—one process *forks* (or starts) another one, or *spawns* a thread. As a user or system administrator, you don't need to be too concerned with the details of how forking and spawning happen, but you do need to realize that this approach to process creation results in a series of relationships between processes. You can trace these relationships back to the first process the kernel runs, and hence to the kernel itself. Occasionally these relationships change or become mixed up, which can cause confusion or even problems.

The Parent/Child Relationship

Consider a user running a Linux shell, such as bash. This user may type a series of commands, launching some processes that terminate and others that don't. In a GUI environment, a single bash instance might be used to launch a mail reader and a multimedia player, both of which can run simultaneously. From the same shell, the user might run several commands in series, such as ls and cp. All of these programs are known as the *children* of the shell that launched them. The shell, in turn, is the *parent* of its children. These relationships can extend for an arbitrary number of generations. For instance, bash is the child of the xterm in which it's running, which in turn is the child of a window manager, another bash instance, or some other process. Any process in this tree can fork multiple children; for instance, the window manager is likely to launch several programs. This set of relationships is illustrated in Figure 14.1. The entire set of processes on a Linux computer is sometimes called the *process tree* because of the branching nature of these relationships.

FIGURE 14.1

Linux processes are arranged in a hierarchical structure similar to the structures of tree branches.

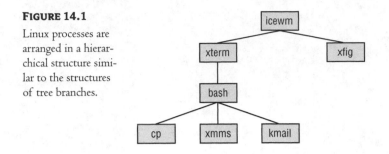

Unlike human relationships, the parent/child relationships among Linux programs require just one parent to create a child. Any given process can have no, one, two, three, or more children. Every process has a parent, although the first process has an unusual parent: the kernel. The Linux boot process begins with a boot loader launching the kernel. The kernel, in turn, is hard-coded to look for and run a program called init. This program loads and runs the /etc/inittab configuration file, which controls the rest of the boot process by launching additional programs and startup scripts.

Every process is identified by a unique number, the *process ID (PID)*. The task with a PID of 0 is the kernel, or more precisely the kernel's *idle task*, which runs when no other process demands CPU time. The PID of init is 1. Beyond init, the PID varies from one system to another, because startup procedures vary from one distribution to another and even from one installation to another. Nonetheless, Linux process management relies on the PID, so there are tools to help you locate the PID for any given process, as described in the upcoming section, "All You Ever Wanted to Know about Your Processes."

Dealing with Orphans and Zombies

Most Linux processes don't run forever. If they did, they'd consume memory, CPU time, and other resources, and Linux would soon become sluggish as a result. Processes can terminate for many reasons—because they've finished whatever finite job they're designed to do (as, for instance, cp terminates when it finishes copying a file), because a user has told a program to terminate via an exit command, because a user or administrator has told the process to terminate via a kill command (as described in the upcoming section, "Basic Use of kill"), or because a program has crashed. One complication of a process terminating is that it may leave behind children. For instance, in Figure 14.1, if the user exits from the bash shell (and hence the xterm in which it's running), the programs run from bash will be left without a parent—they'll be *orphaned*.

Because of the way Linux handles processes internally, the process tree must remain intact; orphaned processes can't simply be left running without parents. Linux solves this problem by having init "adopt" all orphaned processes. In order to help trace processes to their parents, each process has a *parent PID (PPID)*. For instance, the PPID of init is 0, indicating that init's parent is the kernel. When a process is orphaned, its PPID is set to 1. Because many programs are launched from scripts or other processes that terminate before the programs they launch, many Linux programs, including most servers, have PPIDs of 1.

Occasionally, something will go wrong when a process ends. Ordinarily, a parent is responsible for doing some of the work involved in cleaning up after its terminated children. If the parent doesn't do this work, though, the result is a *zombie*: a process that's been incompletely killed. Zombies consume little in the way of system resources, but they appear in process listings with a notation to the effect that they're zombies. Thus, zombies may be distracting, but they aren't really harmful—at least, not normally. If a buggy process spawns a lot of processes and then doesn't manage their termination properly, your process table might fill with zombies and system performance might even be impacted. Such occurrences are rare, though.

Because `init` adopts the children of a process that's terminated, you can rid yourself of zombies by locating the zombies' parents and killing them. When you do this, `init` adopts the zombies and does the housekeeping necessary to remove them from the process list.

All You Ever Wanted to Know about Your Processes

Most process management tools require you to know something about the processes you want to manipulate. If nothing else, you must know the process's PID number to use most process-management tools. Knowing how much CPU time, memory, or other system resources a process is using is also helpful; this information can point you to the source of system performance problems or help you head off such problems. Most of these tools are text-based, but some GUI tools serve much the same function as the more traditional tools.

Important *ps* Options

The most important tool for learning about your processes is `ps`. This tool displays a list of processes, along with assorted information about them, such as their PIDs, PPIDs, CPU time consumption, and so on. Precisely what information is displayed depends on the options you pass to `ps`. These options also determine what processes are displayed—those run from the current shell, those run by the current user, all processes, or some other set.

Although `ps` is a common Unix utility, it varies substantially from one OS to another, in terms of its options and output. Linux's `ps` supports several different option formats:

Unix98 Options   These options are single-character in nature and must be preceded by a dash, as in -a. You can combine multiple Unix98 options, as in -ax.

BSD Options   These options are single-character in nature and must *not* be preceded by a dash. You can combine multiple BSD options, as in ax.

GNU Long Options   These options are strings of several characters and are preceded by two dashes, as in --forest. You can combine GNU long options by separating them with a space, as in --forest --headers.

Some options from each format type produce similar effects, and even within a given class, different options may produce overlapping sets of information. Therefore, if you want to learn something specific, there may be many `ps` command variants that will do the trick. Some options take parameters, such as a user ID (UID) number. For Unix98 and BSD options, you separate these parameters from their options with a space; for GNU long options, you use an equal sign (=). Table 14.1 summarizes the most important `ps` options.

TABLE 14.1: IMPORTANT ps OPTIONS

OPTION	DESCRIPTION	REQUIRED PARAMETERS
-A or -e	Displays all processes	None
-N or --deselect	Reverses meaning of process-selection options	None
-a	Displays all processes on ttys except session leaders	None
-d	Displays all processes except session leaders	None
T	Displays all processes run from the current terminal	None
a	Displays all processes run from the current terminal, including those run by other users	None
r	Displays only actively running processes	None
x	Displays processes without associated ttys	None
-C	Displays processes by command name	Process name
-G or --Group	Displays processes by the real user's GID	GID number or group name
--group	Displays processes by the effective group ID	GID number or group name
-U or --User	Displays processes by the real user's UID	UID number or username
-u, U, or --user	Displays processes by the effective user ID	UID number or username
-g	Displays processes by session leader or GID	GID number or group name
-p, p, or --pid	Displays specified processes	Comma-separated PID list
-t, t, or --tty	Displays processes belonging to a tty	Tty number
-s or --sid	Displays processes by session number	Session number
-H, f, or --forest	Displays process parent/child relationships	None
-w or w	Displays wide (132-column) output	None
C	Uses raw CPU time rather than a decaying average for CPU time report	None
S or --cumulative	Includes dead child data in parent's report	None
c	Displays true command name instead of process name	None
e	Displays the environment following the command	None
h or --no-headers	Omits header from output	None
--headers	Displays header information every screen (usually 24 lines)	None
-m or m	Displays threads	None

Continued on next page

TABLE 14.1: IMPORTANT ps OPTIONS *(continued)*

OPTION	DESCRIPTION	REQUIRED PARAMETERS
`--cols`, `--columns`, or `--width`	Sets display width	Number of characters
`--lines` or `--rows`	Sets display height (used by `--headers`)	Number of lines
`-V` or `--version`	Displays ps version information	None
`--help`	Displays command use summary	None

NOTE *The Unix98, BSD, and GNU long options listed as equivalent in Table 14.1 don't always yield identical outputs.*

Many of the options in Table 14.1 modify the information that ps provides about each process. For instance, an option may add a PPID column to the output or change the command column to show options passed to the command. In addition, some options are designed expressly to modify the output. These options are summarized in Table 14.2. The -o, o, and `--format` options enable you to create your own custom output format by passing codes for the fields you want to see.

TABLE 14.2: ps OUTPUT FIELD OPTIONS

OPTION	CREATES OUTPUT FIELDS
`-f`	UID, PID, PPID, CPU utilization, start time, tty, CPU time, command
`-j`	PID, process GID, session ID, tty, CPU time, command
`-l`	Flags, state, UID, PID, PPID, CPU utilization, scheduling priority, nice value, process address, size in blocks, wait channel, tty, CPU time, command
`j`	PPID, PID, process GID, session ID, tty, controlling tty's process GID, status, UID, CPU time, command
`l`	Flags, UID, PID, PPID, scheduling priority, nice value, virtual memory size, resident set size, kernel process number, status, tty, CPU time, command
`s`	UID, PID, pending, blocked, ignored, caught, status, tty, CPU time, command
`u`	Username, PID, percentage of CPU time, percentage of memory, virtual memory size, resident set size, tty, status, start time, CPU time, command
`v`	PID, tty, status, CPU time, major page faults, resident text (code) size, data (stack) size, resident set size, percentage of memory, command

Because ps accepts so many options and produces so much output, it can be a challenge to use it to best effect. The fact that a Linux system can run dozens or hundreds of processes makes matters worse, because it can be hard to locate relevant information in a lengthy output. To some extent, you must learn to use ps through experience. Try experimenting with its options and studying its output. To that end, I will present a few simple examples. First, ps without any options:

```
$ ps
  PID TTY          TIME CMD
11716 pts/5    00:00:00 bash
21091 pts/5    00:00:01 nedit
29092 pts/5    00:00:02 xfig
 1597 pts/5    00:00:00 ps
```

This output includes just four columns, and ps displays information only on the portion of the process tree from which it's directly descended—that is, the shell from which it was run (PID 11716, bash), other processes run from that shell (PIDs 21091 and 29092, nedit and xfig), and the ps process itself (PID 1597). All of these processes are run from pts/5 (an xterm window), and none has used much CPU time (even a process that's been running for weeks might use almost no CPU time if it hasn't been called upon to do much work). In this particular example, the ps process has a lower PID than the other processes in the list because PID numbers can, and sometimes do, "loop back," much like a car's odometer ticking over to 0 miles. Despite the lower PID number, ps was run after the other processes.

The u option creates an output format with information geared toward evaluating the demands for system resources placed on the computer by a user's programs:

```
$ ps u
USER        PID %CPU %MEM   VSZ  RSS TTY      STAT START   TIME COMMAND
rodsmith 11716  0.0  0.3  2688 1216 pts/5    S    Jan23   0:00 bash
rodsmith 21091  0.0  0.9  6480 3204 pts/5    S    Jan27   0:01 nedit /home/rodsm
rodsmith 29092  0.0  1.1  6020 3632 pts/5    S    Jan28   0:02 xfig f1401.fig
rodsmith  1619  0.0  0.2  2684  780 pts/5    R    16:06   0:00 ps u
```

This output includes the same four columns as the prior example's output, although the COMMAND column includes command-line options, as well. Interspersed with these columns are others that provide additional information that you can use to help locate processes that are consuming too much memory or CPU time:

%CPU   This column displays the percentage of CPU time the process is currently demanding.

%MEM   This column displays the percentage of memory that the process is currently using.

VSZ   The virtual memory size is the total memory, both RAM and swap, that the process is using.

RSS   The resident set size is the amount of RAM that the process is using, not counting kernel data structures.

STAT   This column displays the status—S for a sleeping, or idle, process, and R for a running process.

START   This column displays the process start time, given as a time in 24-hour format or a date for processes that have been running for over a day.

One very helpful set of options is -aux; if you type **ps -aux**, ps produces output like that just described for every process running on the computer. Even a lightly loaded system is likely to have dozens of processes running, so you may want to pipe the output through less, redirect it to a file, or use grep to trim the output based on a process name you want to examine.

Using *top*

Although ps is a very flexible and useful tool, it has a major shortcoming: Its output is static. One common problem you may encounter is the need to determine which processes are consuming a lot of CPU time. Such resource consumption can spike momentarily, so running ps to locate over-consuming processes doesn't always work. What's needed is a dynamic tool—one that takes a reading, then takes another reading a short time later, and so on, updating its display with every reading. If this tool sorts its output according to the CPU time use, CPU-hogging processes become obvious because they'll appear consistently at the top of the list. Other processes may run up and down the list as they make momentary demands for CPU time. Linux provides a tool that does just this, and its name is appropriate: top.

Basic use of top is fairly straightforward: Type **top**. The result should be a display similar to the one shown in Figure 14.2. This figure shows that the FahCore_65.exe process is consuming huge amounts of CPU time—89.5 percent of CPU time at the moment the screen shot was taken, with a cumulative total of 1,948 minutes. The X process (XFree86) comes in a distant second, with 5.8 percent and a cumulative total of 86 minutes of CPU time.

NOTE   Several different top utilities are available, and produce output that's formatted slightly differently. For this reason, your output might have fields with slightly different names or positions than are depicted in Figure 14.2, but more-or-less the same information should be available.

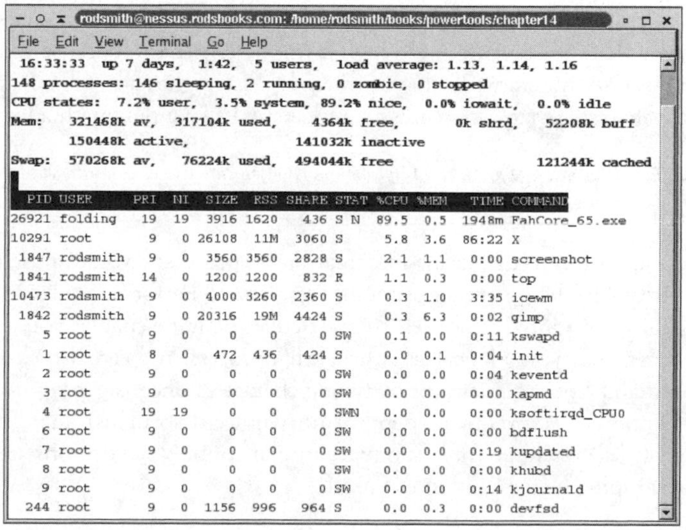

FIGURE 14.2

The top utility provides a dynamic display of resource use.

```
 - O x   rodsmith@nessus.rodsbooks.com: /home/rodsmith/books/powertools/chapter14      o □ x
 File  Edit  View  Terminal  Go  Help
 16:33:33  up 7 days,  1:42,  5 users,  load average: 1.13, 1.14, 1.16
148 processes: 146 sleeping, 2 running, 0 zombie, 0 stopped
CPU states:  7.2% user,  3.5% system, 89.2% nice,  0.0% iowait,  0.0% idle
Mem:   321468k av,  317104k used,    4364k free,      0k shrd,   52208k buff
       150448k active,          141032k inactive
Swap:  570268k av,   76224k used,  494044k free                121244k cached

 PID USER     PRI  NI  SIZE  RSS SHARE STAT %CPU %MEM   TIME COMMAND
26921 folding   19  19  3916 1620   436 S N 89.5  0.5  1948m FahCore_65.exe
10291 root       9   0 26108  11M  3060 S     5.8  3.6  86:22 X
 1847 rodsmith   9   0  3560 3560  2828 S     2.1  1.1   0:00 screenshot
 1841 rodsmith  14   0  1200 1200   832 R     1.1  0.3   0:00 top
10473 rodsmith   9   0  4000 3260  2360 S     0.3  1.0   3:35 icewm
 1842 rodsmith   9   0 20316  19M  4424 S     0.3  6.3   0:02 gimp
    5 root       9   0     0    0     0 SW    0.1  0.0   0:11 kswapd
    1 root       8   0   472  436   424 S     0.0  0.1   0:04 init
    2 root       9   0     0    0     0 SW    0.0  0.0   0:04 keventd
    3 root       9   0     0    0     0 SW    0.0  0.0   0:00 kapmd
    4 root      19  19     0    0     0 SWN   0.0  0.0   0:00 ksoftirqd_CPU0
    6 root       9   0     0    0     0 SW    0.0  0.0   0:00 bdflush
    7 root       9   0     0    0     0 SW    0.0  0.0   0:19 kupdated
    8 root       9   0     0    0     0 SW    0.0  0.0   0:00 khubd
    9 root       9   0     0    0     0 SW    0.0  0.0   0:14 kjournald
  244 root       9   0  1156  996   964 S     0.0  0.3   0:00 devfsd
```

Interpreting top's output isn't always easy. For instance, is the huge resource use of FahCore_65.exe excessive? Such a CPU hog might seem out of line at first glance, but in this case it's not; FahCore_65.exe is a distributed computing client for the Folding@Home project (http://folding.stanford.edu), which aims to help scientists better understand how proteins "fold" within cells. This project necessarily requires a lot of CPU time, and the Folding@Home project uses donated CPU time. If you examine Figure 14.2 again, you'll see that the FahCore_65.exe process is running with a nice value (the NI column) of 19. The nice utility and the meaning of nice values are described in the upcoming section, "Starting Processes with nice," but for now, know that a nice value of 19 means the process is using CPU time only when other processes don't need it. As a result, this process's impact on the system is minimal. Of course, somebody unfamiliar with the system whose top output appears in Figure 14.2, and unfamiliar with Folding@Home and its program names, wouldn't realize that nothing was wrong. The bottom line is that you must understand your own system in order to interpret CPU use information. It's also helpful to know something about typical resource use of common programs. For instance, it's not unusual to see X near the top of the CPU-use list, especially in terms of cumulative CPU use and when the system runs X continuously. If a small tool that normally terminates quickly, such as ls, starts racking up serious CPU time, though, something may be wrong.

In addition to the process-by-process data that dominates the lower two-thirds of Figure 14.2, top provides some overall usage information in the top third of its display. This information includes the time the system has been up, the number of users accessing it, the number of processes, total memory use, and three total CPU use figures (load averages), representing the load average over the past one, five, and fifteen minutes. A load average of 0.00 means that no processes are demanding CPU time (or that the demand is so low that it doesn't register). A load average of 1.00 means that programs are demanding exactly as much CPU time as the system can deliver. For instance, a single CPU-intensive program, such as the Folding@Home client, imposes a 1.00 load average all by itself. Load averages above 1.00 mean that Linux must ration CPU time. Such a situation may spell trouble on a small single-user workstation, but other systems should run with higher load averages. A multi-user system or busy server, for instance, is likely to have a load average of well above 1.00. Precisely how high a load average is too high is impossible to say, because it depends on the computer and its function. A system with a high-powered CPU might run with a load average of, say, 3.0, and be subjectively faster than a system with a weaker CPU running with a load average of 1.0 or less.

NOTE *Load average and system uptime information can also be obtained via the* uptime *and* w *commands. The* free *command returns memory use information.*

In addition to displaying information on processes, you can use top to effect many of the changes described in the upcoming sections, "Improving Performance by Modifying Process Priorities" and "Killing Unwanted Processes." In particular, typing **r** enables you to change the nice value for a process, and typing **k** enables you to kill a process. You can also change many display options with command-line arguments or by typing characters once top is running. For instance, typing **N** sorts by PID number, **M** sorts by resident memory usage, **T** sorts by total CPU time used, and **m** toggles the display of system memory summary information. More options are described in the top man page or by typing **h** from within top itself.

Obtaining Miscellaneous Information

Although ps and top provide a great deal of useful information, there are additional tools for learning about processes. These tools include:

pstree This program creates a process tree diagram, similar to what ps produces with its -H, f, or --forest options.

w This very short command displays load averages and information on resource use by user, including login time, idle time, cumulative CPU time used, and what process the user is currently running. If a user opens several xterm windows or run several remote login sessions, that user will appear in the w output several times.

jobs If you suspend a process by typing Ctrl+Z while it's running in a terminal, you may forget that it's suspended. If you're not sure if a terminal has any suspended processes, you can type **jobs** to find out. If there are no suspended processes, this command produces no output. If there are suspended processes, it names them. You can return to a suspended process by typing **fg**, optionally followed by a job ID number if you've suspended more than one process. (The job ID number is displayed by job and is not the same as a process ID number.)

lsof This program displays information on open files, including the filename, the PID of the process accessing the file, the name of the process accessing the file, and the user running the program. This command can be extremely useful if you can't unmount a removable disk because it's in use; type **lsof | grep */mount/point*** (where */mount/point* is where the disk is mounted) to learn what processes are accessing files on the disk.

netstat This program produces a plethora of information on network interfaces and connections. Of particular interest to this chapter is the -p option, which causes netstat to display the names of processes that are making network accesses, in addition to network-specific information such as socket numbers.

Both lsof and netstat tend to produce a lot of output, so they're best used in conjunction with less or grep to peruse the output or trim it if you know for what you're looking.

GUI Process Management Tools

The ps, top, and other text-mode utilities can be extremely useful, and they are very powerful tools in the hands of somebody who understands them. Less experienced users, though, may feel more comfortable with GUI process-management tools. Even experienced users may like some of the features of GUI tools. Linux provides these GUI tools, of course.

One of these utilities is the GNOME System Monitor, which is shown in Figure 14.3. You can launch this program by typing **gnome-system-monitor** or by selecting it from somewhere on the GNOME menu on most distributions. By default, the GNOME System Monitor displays processes using a tree-like view, but you can collapse parts of the tree by clicking the triangle to the left of a process's name. You can sort by different criteria by clicking the header names, such as User or Memory in Figure 14.3. If you right-click a process, a context menu appears from which you can change the process's priority, kill the process, and so on.

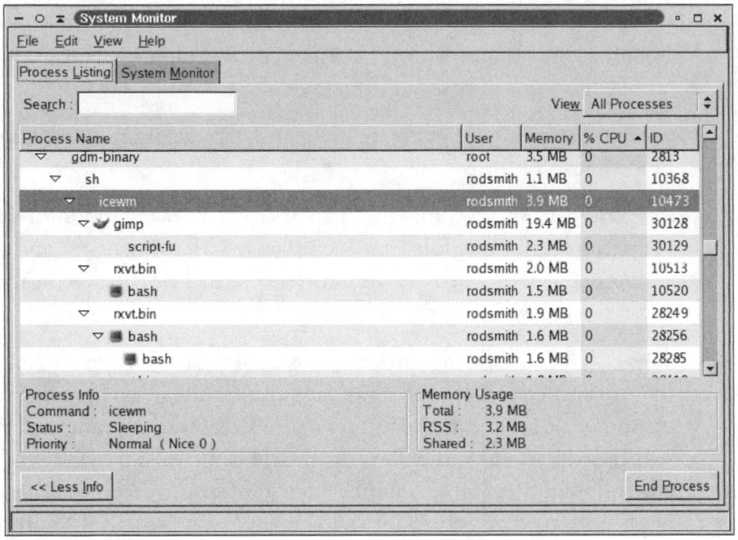

FIGURE 14.3

The GNOME System Monitor is a typical GUI process management tool.

FIGURE 14.3

The GNOME System Monitor is a typical GUI process management tool.

The System Monitor tab in the GNOME System Monitor provides access to additional information and features, including information on the demand for CPU time, memory, swap space, and disk space. Overall, the GNOME System Monitor is roughly comparable to top in its features.

KDE, like GNOME, provides a GUI process-management tool: KDE System Guard. This program is accessible from somewhere on the KDE menu, or can be launched by typing **ksysguard**. This tool can produce a process table akin to that displayed by the GNOME System Monitor, as shown in Figure 14.4. It can also produce graphs of resource use (on the System Load tab) and can display information on many other system resources. If you want to see only the process list, you can use a tool that KDE System Guard uses internally, KPM. You can launch this program by typing **kpm** in an **xterm** window or by selecting the process management option from the KDE menu. Right-clicking a process enables you to perform actions on it, such as killing it or changing its priority.

NOTE   *Like most programs that ship with KDE and GNOME, you can use KDE System Guard, KPM, and the GNOME System Monitor in environments other than the ones with which they're associated.*

Improving Performance by Modifying Process Priorities

When two programs both want to use the CPU simultaneously, the Linux kernel mediates this dispute, rationing CPU time. One critical question in this rationing system is how much CPU time to give to each process. Linux decides this question by associating a priority with each process. By default, Linux launches programs with a priority of 0. You can, however, change those priorities in one of two ways: You can launch programs with altered priorities or you can change the priority of an already-running process. The two programs that accomplish these tasks most simply are nice and renice, although other tools, including top and the GUI process management tools, can also do this job.

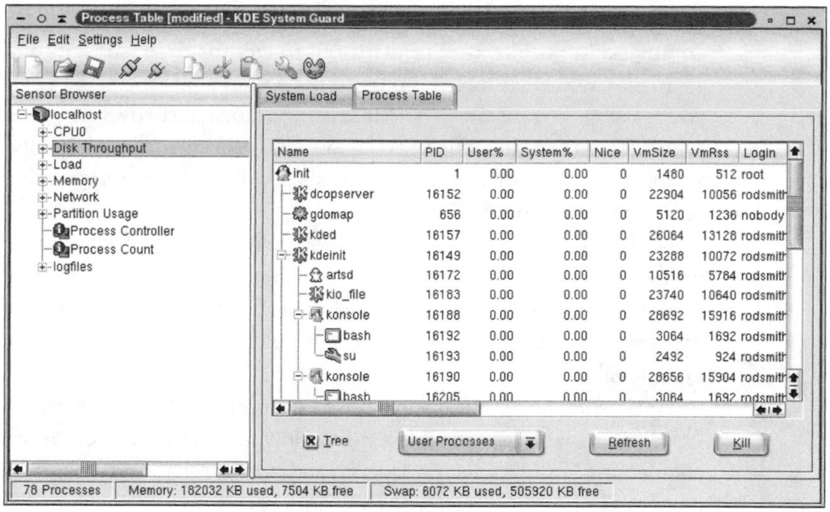

FIGURE 14.4

The KDE System Guard provides process monitoring tools and additional system information displays.

Starting Processes with *nice*

The nice command starts another program with an altered process priority. The nice command's syntax is simple but potentially a bit confusing:

```
nice [option] [command [argument]]
```

NOTE   Some shells, such as csh, include their own built-in implementations of nice. You can either use the shell's own nice or the standalone nice command with such shells. To use the standalone nice command, though, you must type its complete path, usually /bin/nice or /usr/bin/nice.

The program accepts just three options: --help, to display basic usage information; --version, to display the program's version number; and -n or --adjustment, to set the new process's priority. Instead of using -n or --adjustment, you can enter the new priority by preceding the number by a single dash (-), as in -12 to set a priority of 12. The *command* and *argument* are the command you want to run and any arguments it takes. If you pass no arguments to nice, it returns the priority of the shell from which you ran it.

The confusing part of nice is that the priority value seems backward. You can set a process's priority to anywhere from –20 to 19, but contrary to intuition, numerically higher priority values correspond to lower scheduling priority. For instance, if you run two processes, one with a nice value of 10 and the other with a value of –10, the process run at –10 will consume more CPU time. The default value when you run a program without nice is 0. (Figure 14.2 shows the nice value in the NI column of top's output, revealing that most processes are run at a 0 nice value.) If you don't pass any adjustment value to nice, it assumes a value of 10. Therefore, you can achieve a good reduction in CPU demand for an individual program by launching it with nice and no other options, as in **nice crunch**.

Adding to the confusion of specifying priorities with nice is the possibility of specifying a value without using -n or --adjustment. For instance, typing **nice -n 7 crunch** and typing **nice -7** crunch accomplish the same thing—both reduce the priority of the crunch program. The second command looks like a –7 priority, but in fact the dash isn't a minus sign in this context.

In all cases, the value you pass to nice is an adjustment—a change to the priority of the shell you're using. For instance, if you're using a normal shell in an xterm with a 0 nice value, and if you type **nice xterm**, the new xterm and shell will run with a nice value of 10. If you then type **nice xterm** in the new shell, the resulting shell will run with a nice value of 19. (It can't be 20 because the scale doesn't go that high.)

Ordinary users can use nice to reduce the priority of their processes (that is, apply positive nice values), but only root can increase the priority of jobs (that is, apply negative nice values). This rule applies relative to the priority of whatever process runs nice; for instance, if a user reduces the priority of a shell, the user cannot then restore the priority of programs launched from that shell to the default value of 0.

As a general rule, nice is best used to minimize the CPU-time demands of low-priority but CPU-intensive programs. Depending on your uses for the computer, you might run scientific or engineering simulations, ray tracers, audio manipulation tools, and so on with nice in order to minimize the impact of these programs on foreground processes, such as word processors, web browsers, and shells. Most interactive programs don't use much CPU time, but their responsiveness is important. Suppose you run a CPU-intensive program, such as a ray tracer, along with a less CPU-intensive program, such as a word processor. If you don't use nice, the ray tracer and word processor will compete for CPU cycles, and the word processor's performance will suffer, despite the fact that it uses far less CPU time than the ray tracer uses. If you run the ray tracer with a large nice value, though, the kernel will give priority to the word processor, so the word processor's performance won't be degraded much or at all by the ray tracer's CPU needs. Because the word processor needs relatively little CPU time overall, the ray tracer will still get the CPU time it needs, assuming no other CPU-intensive processes are running on the computer. Using nice to reduce the CPU time given to a CPU-intensive program will impact that program's performance if the system is running other CPU-intensive tasks, though. If your CPU load average, as revealed by top or uptime, is much above 0, you can expect use of nice to increase the run time of a CPU-intensive process.

On rare occasion, you may want to use nice to increase a process's priority (that is, give it a negative nice value). This practice is most likely to be desirable when you're launching a process that can't afford to miss the CPU time it requires. For instance, Linux audio recording tools work by sampling the output of a sound card at regular intervals. If one of these samples is missed because Linux couldn't give the recording tool CPU time at the critical moment, the resulting audio file will have audible artifacts. Such problems are most likely to occur on slower or heavily loaded systems. You may be able to improve matters by running the audio tool with a negative nice value, giving it priority over other processes. Another option is to shut down potentially competing processes.

Using *renice* to Change Priorities

You can use nice to change the priority of a process when you launch it, but sometimes you may need to change the priority of a process that's already running. For instance, if you find your system is running sluggishly because of some lengthy CPU-intensive process, you might want to reduce that process's priority without restarting it. To do so, you use a tool called renice, which has the following syntax:

```
renice priority [[-p] pid [...]] [[-g] group [...]] [[-u] user [...]]
```

In order to change the priority of processes, you must have some way to specify what processes to change. This is the purpose of the -p, -g, and -u options, which enable you to specify processes by PID, group (aka *process group*), or username, respectively. If you specify a group or user, renice changes the priority of all of that group's or user's processes.

The renice *priority* is specified in absolute terms, unlike the nice adjustment. There's also no -n or dash preceding this number. For instance, if a process is running with a nice value of 10 and you want to change it to a value of 15, you'd pass 15 as the *priority*, not 5. Nonetheless, only root may increase a process's priority (that is, reduce the nice value). Also, only root may modify the priorities of any process owned by another user.

A few examples of renice in action may be in order:

```
# renice -2 -p 24301
# renice 10 -p 1734 -u hoggy
# renice 5 -u hoggy piggy -g porcine
```

The first example sets the priority of the process with PID 24301 to −2, thereby giving that process precedence over most others. The second example sets the priority of PID 1734 and of all processes owned by the user hoggy to 10, in all probability reducing those priorities. The final example sets the priority of all processes owned by hoggy, piggy, or any member of the porcine group to 5, in all probability reducing the priority of those processes.

Many process-monitoring tools, including top, GNOME System Monitor, and KDE System Guard, also provide the ability to alter a process's priority. In top, you type **r** and the program prompts for a PID. In the GUI tools, right-clicking a process produces a context menu from which you can select an option to change the priority.

Killing Unwanted Processes

Sometimes a process goes so far out of control that you have no choice but to terminate it. Sometimes you can exit from a program in the normal manner, by selecting an exit option from its user interface. Some programs, though, such as most daemons, lack user interfaces in the conventional sense. (Most daemons can be shut down through their SysV startup scripts, though.) Programs may also become unresponsive to their user interfaces, or you might not have access to those user interfaces (as with programs run by remote users). In such cases, you can use the kill program to terminate the runaway processes. The same program can be used to pass nontermination *signals* to programs. These signals can tell a server to reread a configuration file, for instance. Other tools can be helpful or simpler to use than kill in some situations.

Basic Use of *kill*

Technically, kill is a tool that sends signals to processes. These signals may or may not cause the signaled processes to terminate. You can obtain a list of signals (both their numbers and their names) by typing **kill -l**. Table 14.3 summarizes the signals you're most likely to send via kill.

NOTE   Some shells, including bash and csh, include built-in implementations of kill. As with nice, you can bypass the built-in kill provided by these shells by typing the complete path to the kill binary, usually /bin/kill.

TABLE 14.3: COMMON SIGNALS

SIGNAL NUMBER	SIGNAL NAME	SIGNAL EFFECT
1	SIGHUP	Hang up—indicates that the terminal a process is using has closed. Daemons that don't run in a terminal often respond to this signal by rereading configuration files or restarting their logging tools.
2	SIGINT	Interrupt—end program operation. The kernel sends this signal when you press Ctrl+C.
3	SIGQUIT	Quit—terminate and leave a core file for debugging purposes. Normally initiated by a user action.
6	SIGABRT	Abort—terminate and leave a core file for debugging purposes. Normally initiated by a debugging process or self-detected error.
9	SIGKILL	Kill—end program operation ungracefully; the program may not save open files, etc.
10	SIGUSR1	User signal 1—Effect varies from one program to another.
12	SIGUSR2	User signal 2—Effect varies from one program to another.
15	SIGTERM	Terminate—end program operation gracefully (closing open files, etc.).
18	SIGCONT	Continue—resume processing; undo the effect of a SIGSTOP signal.
19	SIGSTOP	Stop—suspend program operation, similar (but not identical) to the effect of pressing Ctrl+Z.

The syntax for kill is shown here:

```
kill [ -s signal ] pid[...]
```

You can pass the signal by name or by number; for instance, **kill -s 9 6940** and **kill -s SIGKILL 6940** are equivalent. You can also usually omit the -s and add a dash to the signal name or number, as in **kill -SIGKILL 6940**. When you pass a signal name, the inclusion of the SIG portion is optional; for instance, KILL and SIGKILL are equivalent. (In practice, you may need to *omit* the SIG portion sometimes.) If you don't pass any signal specification, kill uses SIGTERM. Likewise, not all processes respond to all signals. If a process fails to respond to a signal, it will instead terminate, as if it had been passed a SIGTERM signal.

If a process is out of control (say, it's become unresponsive and is consuming excessive CPU time), you can try killing it. It's usually best to try SIGTERM first, which is the default, so typing **kill pid** is the usual first step. Programs that are out of control, though, frequently don't respond to this polite request to shut down, so you may need to take a firmer hand. You can do this by passing SIGKILL, which a process can't ignore. Only **root** or the owner of a process may terminate it.

One problem with kill is that you need a PID number. You can find a PID for a process by using ps, top, or a similar utility. If you know that the crunch process is out of control, for instance, you can type a command such as **ps -C crunch** to locate crunch's PID. Some daemons also store their PIDs in files, usually for the benefit of SysV startup scripts. These files typically reside in /var/run and are named after the process to which they refer, with names ending in .pid. For instance, /var/run/crond.pid holds the PID for crond. Unfortunately, sometimes a given program is running many times on a single computer, so isolating the instance you want to kill can be tricky. You may be able to use the user ID, as reported by many ps options, to help narrow the field. If the program is consuming inordinate amounts of CPU time, it may float to the top of the display in top.

If you're certain that only one instance of a program is running and if you know the process name, you can use killall instead of kill. This program works much like kill, but you pass it a program name instead of a PID, and killall kills all running instances of the specified program. For instance, **killall crunch** kills all processes called crunch.

WARNING *Some Unix-like OSs provide a program called* killall *that kills all running processes. Thus, you should not use* killall *on an unfamiliar system until you've checked the local system's documentation to be sure that* killall *does what you expect it to do.*

Additional Process Termination Tools

In addition to kill and killall, other tools can be used to terminate a process:

top   The top program includes a kill option. Type **k** while top is displaying its process list and the program will ask for a PID. Enter a PID to have top kill it.

SysV Startup Scripts   All major Linux distributions except Slackware use SysV startup scripts to start daemons and some other critical system tools. These scripts are typically located in /etc/init.d or /etc/rc.d/init.d, and you can call them manually, passing start, stop, or restart parameters to start, stop, or restart the service, respectively. These scripts generally use kill to terminate daemons, but they sometimes perform helpful shutdown housekeeping tasks, and so are usually preferable to using kill directly when shutting down a service.

GUI Process Monitors   GUI tools such as the GNOME System Monitor and KPM can kill processes. Typically, there's a button called Kill, End Process, or something similar (see Figure 14.3); highlight a process and click this button to kill the process.

Window Manager Tools   Window managers invariably provide close buttons on the windows they manage. Click or double-click this button to close the window. The underlying program should then terminate. This action doesn't always work as expected when a program is malfunctioning, though; and when the program isn't malfunctioning, it's usually better to terminate it through its usual exit mechanism, such as a File ➢ Quit menu option.

xkill   This program is a handy X-based process killer. Type **xkill** and X changes its cursor to a special pointer (sometimes a skull and crossbones, but not always). Click a window and X closes it. In response, the program that owned that window should shut down. This procedure has the benefit of enabling you to kill processes that you're running from another computer, using X's networking features. You can also terminate a window by passing a display name and resource ID to xkill, but of course you must know this information to do so. Consult the xkill man page for details. In my experience, xkill is usually quite effective at terminating misbehaving GUI applications.

Summary

The Linux kernel manages dozens or hundreds of processes, even on a lightly loaded system. These processes are related to one another in a tree-like structure, and each process has associated with it various pieces of information—its owner, a priority, and so on. You can learn about processes using ps, top, or various GUI tools. These tools can all be very useful diagnostic aids when a system isn't working as well as you'd like, and they can also be helpful in locating a specific process for more mundane purposes, such as terminating a server or telling it to reread its configuration file. The kill and killall programs send signals to processes, terminating them or causing them to perform other actions. You can also reprioritize programs, reducing the impact of CPU-intensive programs on interactive programs, by using the renice program, or you can start a program with a modified priority by launching it with nice. Other tools, including top, GUI process management programs, window managers, and xkill, can also help you modify the priority of or terminate running processes.

## Chapter 15

Creating a Custom Kernel

THE *KERNEL* IS THE heart of a Linux system. The kernel is a program, but it's a very special program: It serves as an interface between other programs and hardware, allocates CPU time, parcels out RAM, manages filesystems, and otherwise controls the computer as a whole. These tasks are quite basic and extremely important, so proper configuration of the kernel is critical.

NOTE *Technically, Linux is the kernel. Everything else on a Linux system—shells, servers, the X Window System, printing software, and so on—is available for other OSs, such as FreeBSD and often even Windows. For this reason, some people object to the use of the word* Linux *to refer to the entire OS. Some of these people refer to the OS as a whole as* GNU/Linux, *because many of these nonkernel components are derived from the* GNU's Not Unix (GNU) *project.*

Because Linux is an open source OS, you as a system administrator can customize the kernel. You can include or omit specific drivers or filesystems, change compilation options for particular kernel components, and even optimize the kernel for your particular CPU. Knowing how to do these things will enable you to improve your system's performance. This chapter covers these topics, beginning with information on how to obtain a kernel. The chapter then looks at the tools you use to modify the kernel's configuration. Next up is a broad look at the available kernel options, followed by a more in-depth examination of certain critical performance-enhancing options. Finally, this chapter looks at how to compile and install a kernel once you've configured it.

Obtaining a Kernel

All Linux distributions ship with a binary Linux kernel (or several kernels with different optimizations), and in most cases the kernel source code is also available. You can use your distribution-provided kernel source code if you like, and doing so has certain advantages. Distribution providers sometimes apply kernel *patches*—code that's not part of the original program but that improves or extends it in some way. It's possible your system relies on such patches to operate or to provide some function, such as drivers for an exotic piece of hardware. On the other hand, distribution-provided source code can be a problem for the same reason. Patches might contain bugs that aren't present in the official kernel source code, and they can create confusion if you go to others to get help, should a problem be related to a patch.

On the whole, I favor using the original unmodified Linux kernel source code. You can obtain this code from `http://www.kernel.org` or its mirrors; click the links to enter the archive areas and download the package. You should download a file whose name takes the form `linux-a.b.c.tar.bz2` or `linux-a.b.c.tar.gz`. This file holds the source code for kernel version *a.b.c* compressed with `bzip2` or `gzip`, as indicated by the extension. (The sidebar, "Kernel Version Numbering," describes how Linux kernels are numbered.)

Given the importance of the kernel, you may want to verify its integrity using the `gpg` utility. To do so, you must download a signature file along with the kernel. This file has the same name as your kernel file but adds an extension of `.sign`. Once you've downloaded the kernel and its signature file, type the following commands:

```
$ gpg --keyserver wwwkeys.pgp.net --recv-keys 0x517D0F0E
gpg: keyring `/home/rodsmith/.gnupg/secring.gpg' created
gpg: /home/rodsmith/.gnupg/trustdb.gpg: trustdb created
gpg: key 517D0F0E: public key "Linux Kernel Archives Verification Key
<ftpadmin@kernel.org>" imported
gpg: Total number processed: 1
gpg:               imported: 1
$ gpg --verify linux-a.b.c.tar.bz2.sign linux-a.b.c.tar.bz2
gpg: Signature made Mon 07 Apr 2003 01:59:12 PM EDT using DSA key ID 517D0F0E
gpg: Good signature from "Linux Kernel Archives Verification Key
<ftpadmin@kernel.org>"
gpg: checking the trustdb
gpg: no ultimately trusted keys found
gpg: WARNING: This key is not certified with a trusted signature!
gpg:          There is no indication that the signature belongs to the owner.
Primary key fingerprint: C75D C40A 11D7 AF88 9981  ED5B C86B A06A 517D 0F0E
```

The first command loads a key from `wwwkeys.pgp.net` as a baseline for comparison with the kernel's key. Be sure to type the key number (`0x517D0F0E`) correctly; if you mistype it, the next command won't work. You only need to type this command once; if you want to check multiple kernels, you don't need to type the command again. The second command (modified for your kernel, of course) checks the kernel's cryptographic signature. In this example, the `Good signature` message verifies that the signature and the actual file you downloaded match the information from `wwwkeys.pgp.net`. The warning message concerning the lack of a trusted signature certification relates to very high criterion of trust and shouldn't concern you unless you're building a *very* high-security system. Unless a miscreant manages to compromise the kernel you download, its accompanying signature key, and the signature file from `wwwkeys.pgp.net`, the `Good signature` message is sufficient indication of authenticity. Once you've downloaded the kernel tarball, extract it with a command like this:

```
# tar xvjf /path/to/linux-a.b.c.tar.bz2
```

Replace the `j` in `xvjf` with `z` if you downloaded a file that was compressed with `gzip`. This action creates a directory called `linux-a.b.c`. Typically, you type this command from the `/usr/src` directory, which is why I specified the `root` command prompt (`#`); normally, only `root` can write to this directory. If you make `/usr/src` writeable to all users, or at least to your own ordinary account, you can issue this command as an ordinary user. Another option is to extract the file in your home directory. In any case, you may want to simplify access by creating a symbolic link to the directory using the name `linux`: `ln -s linux-a.b.c linux`. (If you store the source code in your home directory, you must still type this command as `root` and adjust the source path appropriately.) Red Hat 8.0 and 9.0 use a link called `linux-2.4` rather than `linux`, so you may need to use `linux-2.4` instead of or in addition to `linux` if you're using Red Hat. If this link already exists (most likely pointing to an older kernel source directory), you should delete it first.

If necessary, you can download and install kernel patches. You might do this to use a very new hardware device or a development filesystem driver. Such projects include instructions on how to proceed. These instructions can vary somewhat from one project to another, so you should follow the directions for your particular patch.

NOTE   Although in most cases the latest stable kernel is the most appropriate one, on rare occasions you may want to use another kernel. For instance, an earlier kernel may be most compatible with a patch or be more stable for a specific purpose. Check resources such as `http://kt.zork.net/kernel-traffic/` *or* `http://www.ussg.iu.edu/hypermail/linux/kernel/` *for summaries and archives of Linux kernel mailing lists that may be relevant to discovering and working around such problems.*

KERNEL VERSION NUMBERING

Linux kernel numbering follows a precisely defined pattern. The kernel version number has three components—*a.b.c*, as in 2.5.67, which have the following meanings:

◆   The *a* component is the major version number. Changes to this number are quite rare. In mid-2003, this number is 2, and it's been at that level since 1996.

◆   The *b* component denotes major changes to the kernel's features or architecture. Even *b* numbers denote *stable* or *release* software. Such kernels are considered safe for use in production environments, at least when they're released. (Of course, bugs are sometimes found and corrected even in release kernels.) Odd *b* numbers signify *development* kernels. Kernel developers add new features to these kernels, make changes to internal kernel data structures, and so on. Development kernels, therefore, tend to be unsafe for use on production systems.

◆   The *c* component denotes changes made within a stable or development kernel series. For stable software, these numbers increase with bug fixes and occasionally with the addition of important new (but stable) drivers. For the development branch, the *c* number increases with bug fixes, new features, or other important changes. As the development kernel matures, it's eventually declared stable, its *b* value is incremented, and it becomes the basis for the next stable kernel.

As a general rule, you should use the kernel with the highest available *c* value in the highest-numbered stable kernel line. There are exceptions to this rule, though. For instance, if you need a new feature that's available only in a development kernel, you may have no choice but to use it. If you want to contribute to kernel development, you must obviously use the development kernel. Near the end of a development kernel series, the kernel tends to become useable, and in fact the general consensus is that development kernels as I write (the latest is 2.5.67) are very stable.

Prior to the official release of a new kernel, a number of development "snapshots" are distributed among kernel developers. You may occasionally run across such kernels. For instance, distributions occasionally use these kernels, and so may appear to have more recent kernels than the latest made available from `http://www.kernel.org`.

Kernel Configuration Tools

You can set some kernel options at boot time by adjusting your boot loader configuration, as described in Chapter 1, "Optimizing System Architecture Usage" and Chapter 10, "Using Multiple OSs." You can also adjust options related to kernel features that are loaded as kernel modules by adjusting the module options in /etc/modules.conf, as described in Chapter 1. Many other features, though, require adjusting the kernel's compilation options. These options determine whether or not a feature is compiled into the kernel, determine whether or not it's compiled as a module, and occasionally adjust settings that influence how a feature operates. Some of these features affect your system's overall performance or the ability of a driver (or of the kernel itself) to work at all on your system. This chapter is devoted to explaining these options, but you must first understand how to adjust them. The details of this process vary with your kernel version number and whether you're using text-based or GUI configuration tools. The kernel configuration tools changed early in the 2.5.x kernel series, so this chapter describes both the old and the new system.

The 2.4.x Kernel Configuration Tools

The 2.4.x kernel configuration procedure relies on the make facility, which also directs the kernel compilation process. To configure the kernel, change into the kernel source directory and type one of three commands:

make config   This command uses a simple text-mode interface. The system asks you whether or how you want to compile each kernel component, and gives you the ability to set particular options. Each option is presented precisely once, and there's no ability to jump back or forward in the sequence. As a result, this method of kernel configuration tends to be extremely tedious to use.

make menuconfig   This command presents a more sophisticated text-mode interface. Unlike make config, make menuconfig uses the curses library to present a text-based menuing system, as shown in Figure 15.1. When first started, the system presents the main configuration categories. Use the arrow keys to position the cursor on one and then press the spacebar to enter a submenu. (Figure 15.1 shows the Processor Type and Features submenu.) You can then select or deselect specific options, enter further submenus, and so on. Use the Tab key to pick between the Select, Exit, and Help functions at the bottom of the screen. When one of these is highlighted, press the Enter key to activate it. The Help function is particularly important when you want to know what an option does.

make xconfig   This command presents a menuing configuration system that's structured logically much like the make menuconfig options; however, make xconfig use the Tcl/Tk scripting language to present a GUI selection system, as shown in Figure 15.2. The main window (in the background in Figure 15.2) presents the general categories. Clicking one of these options brings up a new window in which specific options can be set, and this menu occasionally presents further submenus. Clicking Help displays information about the purpose of an option.

No matter how you select kernel options, many options have three possible values: Y to compile a feature directly into the main kernel file, M to compile an option as a module, or N to not compile a feature at all. (The make menuconfig procedure presents the Y option as an asterisk and the N option as an empty space, as shown in Figure 15.1.) The Y option ensures that the kernel feature will always be accessible when the system is running. This characteristic can be convenient, but it can be a big RAM-waster if you don't need the feature. Because of the wide variety of hardware available, therefore, most distributions ship with many features compiled as modules. The modules can be loaded or unloaded at will, as described in Chapter 1. On the other hand, a few features must be compiled into the main kernel file. Two examples are support for your boot disk's hardware and support for the root filesystem. Some features cannot be compiled as modules, and so don't present an M option. Many of these options are modifiers for other options, so the Y choice becomes available only after you select Y or M for the parent option. Other modifier options can be set to any of these values, but the Y choice is available only if you select Y for the parent option.

A few options can be set to numeric values or to any of several multiple-choice settings. For instance, you can pick your CPU type from a list (in the Processor Family option visible in Figures 15.1 and 15.2). The configuration utility won't allow you to enter an illegal value, although it can't protect you against all blunders. For instance, if you don't compile support for your root filesystem, the tool won't alert you to that fact.

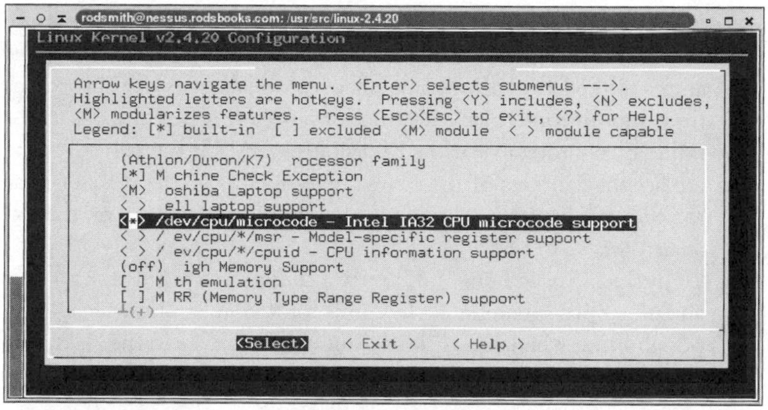

FIGURE 15.1

The make menuconfig kernel configuration command presents a text-based menuing system for selecting options.

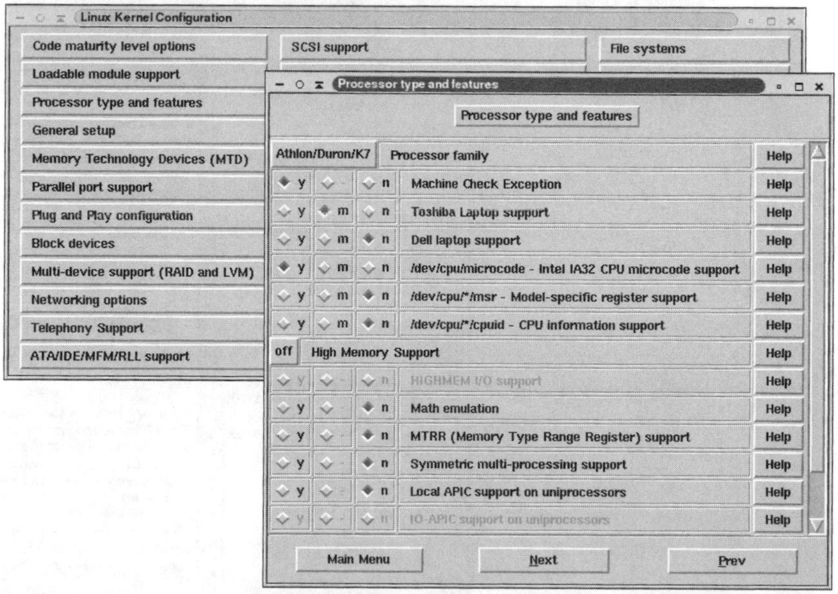

FIGURE 15.2

The make xconfig kernel configuration command presents a GUI menuing system for selecting options.

Whatever method you use, when you're finished you select an exit option. The utility asks if you want to save your changes. Answer in the affirmative and the program saves a configuration file in the .config file in the kernel source directory.

The 2.5.x/2.6.x Kernel Configuration Tools

One of the changes with the 2.5.x kernel series was an extensive revision to the kernel configuration system. The kernel is still configured using the same commands described in the previous section, "The 2.4.x Kernel Configuration Tools;" however, the underlying tools that perform the configuration are entirely new. If you use make xconfig to perform a GUI configuration, the appearance of the configuration utility has also changed. Figure 15.3 shows the make xconfig tool for kernel 2.5.67. The 2.6.x kernel series' GUI configuration tool will closely resemble the one shown in Figure 15.3. The list in the left pane shows the main categories of options, while the upper-right pane shows the options available in specific categories. The lower-right pane shows help text (the same text available from the Help button in 2.4.x kernels or available when using make menuconfig). Some of these options, denoted by triangles to the left of their names, have expandable sets of sub-options; click the triangle to hide or show these sub-options. (Some distributions may use different icons, such as plus and minus signs in a box rather than a rotatable arrow, to denote expandable categories.) Some options, when you click them, replace the contents of the entire upper-right pane with a series of additional options. You can return to the original display by clicking the tiny back arrow button on the topmost element of this display (such an arrow is visible in Figure 15.3).

In the 2.5.x and later GUI tool, a check mark stands for a Y response, a solid dot stands for an M, and an empty square or circle stands for N. Some options enable you to select between one of several possibilities; when you click one option, the others in the class are deselected. If you double-click an entry that supports numeric data entry, you can type a number to enter it.

FIGURE 15.3

The 2.5.x kernel series changes the appearance of the GUI configuration tool.

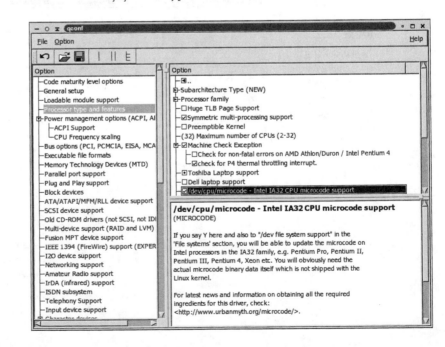

Duplicating an Old Configuration

One issue that crops up repeatedly when configuring a kernel is how to transfer a working kernel configuration to a new kernel. If you've already compiled a kernel once, or if you've installed your distribution's kernel source and want to duplicate that configuration in a new kernel, follow these steps:

1. Copy the .config file from the old kernel's source code directory to the new kernel's source code directory.

2. Type **make oldconfig.** This command works much like make config, except that it asks only about options that are supported by the new kernel but that aren't present in the .config file—that is, new options.

3. If you're uncertain about any of the new options, make a note about them and, when the make oldconfig process finishes, type **make menuconfig** or **make xconfig** and examine the help text for the option to help you decide whether to include it.

This procedure can greatly simplify configuring a new kernel if you've already configured an earlier kernel. The best feature of this procedure is that it reduces the odds of a configuration error creeping into the process—you're less likely to overlook a critical option while re-creating a configuration when you use this process, compared to using make config or some other conventional configuration process.

Duplicating the old configuration works best when you're moving between kernels that are not too different in version number. For instance, moving between kernels that differ by just one or two in their final (*c*) numbers is likely to work well and produce very few prompts. Moving between more widely separated numbers, such as a 2.0.*x* kernel and a 2.5.*x* kernel, will produce a huge number of prompts for new options. Performing such a transfer might conceivably produce a configuration that doesn't work, particularly if some of the new options are critical for your system but you pick the wrong value.

An Overview of Kernel Options

The Linux kernel supports a huge number of options. A .config file for recent kernels includes hundreds or even thousands of configuration options, depending upon your selections. Even the number of top-tier configuration areas is quite large—36 in a 2.5.67 kernel. Rather than try to cover every option, this section presents an overview of these major areas. The next section, "Optimizing Kernel Performance," provides information on the options that are most important if you want to improve the system's overall performance. Some other chapters of this book mention specific options in specific areas. In the latest kernels (2.5.67 and 2.4.20), the main kernel configuration areas are as follows:

Code Maturity Level Options This menu has just one option: Prompt for Development and/or Incomplete Code/Drivers. If enabled, the kernel configuration tool lets you select features that are considered "experimental." Such features are potentially risky, even in a stable kernel, but sometimes they're necessary. If you don't enable this option, the experimental features remain hidden or are grayed out in the configuration tool.

General Setup   This menu contains a few high-level options that don't fit neatly into other menus, such as support for process accounting systems. In the 2.4.20 kernel, this menu also includes options that, in the 2.5.67 kernel, appear under the Power Management Options, Bus Options, and Executable File Formats menus, described shortly.

Loadable Module Support   In order to support options compiled as modules, you must enable this support in the kernel, via the Enable Loadable Module Support option. This menu also provides a few additional options, such as Kernel Module Loader, which enables the kernel to run user-mode tools to load kernel modules when it needs them.

Processor Type and Features   This menu provides features that relate directly to the CPU and motherboard architecture, including the CPU type, support for symmetric multiprocessor (SMP) motherboards, and so on.

Power Management Options   This menu provides options relating to both Advanced Power Management (APM) and Advanced Configuration and Power Interface (ACPI) power management tools. These tools provide different ways to reduce CPU, disk, screen, and other system demands for power, and to turn off a computer's power when you select the shutdown option. Which options work best is very dependent upon your hardware, so you may need to experiment to learn what works best. These options are folded into the General Setup menu in the 2.4.20 kernel.

Bus Options   A computer *bus* is a set of data interfaces linking devices together. This menu covers mostly internal busses used by plug-in cards, such as the Industry Standard Architecture (ISA), MicroChannel Architecture (MCA), and Peripheral Component Interconnect (PCI) busses. This menu's contents are part of the General Setup menu in the 2.4.20 kernel.

Executable File Formats   This menu enables support for three types of executable file formats: The a.out format, which has been abandoned in the Linux world for several years, the Executable and Linkable Format (ELF), which is now the standard, and miscellaneous binaries (used by shell scripts and assorted other program types). You can safely omit a.out support unless you need to run very old binaries, but you should keep the others.

Memory Technology Devices   MTD devices are solid-state storage tools often used on embedded systems. If you're compiling a kernel for a desktop or laptop computer, chances are you don't need this support; it's most useful for Linux running on embedded devices such as cell phones and palmtop computers.

Parallel Port Support   This menu provides options for handling parallel (printer) ports. To use a parallel printer, you need to enable the Parallel Port Support and (on IA-32 systems) PC-Style Hardware options. Some printers may also require you to select Y to the IEEE 1284 Transfer Modes option. The Support Foreign Hardware option supports non-IA-32 or other exotic hardware. Chapter 3, "Using External Peripherals," covers parallel-port configuration in more detail. Chapter 13, "Managing Printers," covers printer configuration in more detail.

Plug and Play Support   This menu (called Plug and Play Configuration in the 2.4.20 kernel) enables Linux to automatically configure Plug and Play (PnP) devices—particularly ISA PnP cards.

Block Devices   This menu enables support for generic *block devices*—devices that perform input and output in multibyte blocks. The devices enabled on this menu include the floppy disk, old-style hard disks, parallel-port hard disks, the *loopback* device (which enables access to a file as if it were a disk), and *RAM disks* (which enables access to memory as if it were a disk). Some important block devices, such as most hard disk interfaces, have their own main menu entries—the ATA/ATAPI/MFM/RLL Device Support and SCSI Device Support options.

ATA/ATAPI/MFM/RLL Device Support   This menu, which is called ATA/IDE/MFM/RLL Support in the 2.4.20 kernel, includes submenus in which Advanced Technology Attachment (ATA), ATA Packet Interface (ATAPI), and some older disk hardware can be enabled. Options include support for specific device types (disks, tape backup units, CD-ROM drives, and so on), and support for specific ATA interfaces. One unusual item is the SCSI Emulation Support option, which makes ATA devices look like SCSI devices. This feature is useful for a few devices, such as recordable CD and DVD drives, for which Linux's SCSI support is stronger than its ATA support. This option can also be handy sometimes if you want to get multiple ATA controllers to coexist, by enabling you to bypass some types of device conflicts. If you boot from an ATA hard disk, you must normally include the appropriate ATA options in the kernel itself (compiled with the Y option), both for the basic disk support and for your ATA chipset. One way around this requirement is to use a RAM disk as part of the boot process, but it's usually easier to compile support into the main kernel file.

SCSI Device Support   This menu contains options equivalent to those on the ATA/ATAPI/MFM/RLL Device Support menu, but for Small Computer System Interface (SCSI) rather than ATA. If you boot from a SCSI hard disk, you must normally include both the SCSI Disk Support option and the option for your specific SCSI host adapter in the kernel file proper (that is, compiled with the Y option). As with ATA support, you can bypass this requirement by using a RAM disk, but it's usually easier to compile the support into the main kernel file.

Old CD-ROM Drivers   This menu provides drivers for assorted old CD-ROM drives. These devices are mostly 4× speed or slower, and they interface through sound cards or dedicated ISA cards. No modern computers ship with these devices, but you might be using one on an old system or if you scavenged parts from an old computer.

Multi-Device Support   Redundant Array of Independent Disks (RAID) technology enables you to tie together multiple physical disks and treat them as a single disk, in order to improve reliability, improve transfer speed, or both. This menu provides support for software RAID, as well as for Logical Volume Manager (LVM), aka Device Mapper, which enables mapping of disk sectors in a way that can aid in advanced partition management.

Fusion MPT Device Support   This menu is devoted to an exotic piece of hardware known as the Fusion Message Passing Technology (MPT), which provides both SCSI and networking features.

IEEE 1394 (FireWire) Support   This entire menu is considered experimental. It enables support for IEEE-1394 devices, aka FireWire. This protocol is becoming popular as a means of connecting external hard disks and video sources such as video cameras. Once activated, many IEEE-1394 devices look like SCSI devices to the kernel; therefore, you should activate support for the appropriate SCSI features, such as SCSI disk support.

I2O Device Support The Intelligent Input/Output (I2O) protocol is a way to break device drivers into two parts: an OS-specific component and a hardware-specific component. In theory, an I2O-enabled device can ship with an I2O hardware driver that works with any I2O-enabled OS. You can add the Linux side of I2O support using this menu. I2O is not common in 2003.

Networking Support This menu is called Networking Options in the 2.4.20 kernel, and it provides a way to activate support for TCP/IP, AppleTalk, and other network stacks. Many of the options on this menu relate to specific TCP/IP options. The 2.5.67 kernel incorporates the Network Device Support menu as a submenu of this one.

Network Device Support This menu hosts drivers for most network interfaces—Ethernet, Token Ring, Point-to-Point Protocol (PPP), and so on. This menu is a submenu of the Networking Support menu in the 2.5.67 kernel, but it is an independent top-level menu in the 2.4.20 kernel.

Amateur Radio Support Protocols exist to enable computers to communicate over amateur radio frequencies. If you want to use such equipment, look for support in this menu. Note that this menu does *not* contain drivers for conventional wireless networking hardware, which is available from the Networking Device Support menu (under Networking Support in the 2.5.67 kernel).

IrDA (Infrared) Support Some computers (particularly laptop and palmtop systems) support infrared communications. You can enable support for such hardware in this menu.

ISDN Subsystem Integrated Services Digital Network (ISDN) is a type of digital telephone service. ISDN modems exist and can operate at up to 128Kbps, compared to 56Kbps for conventional dial-up modems. ISDN is moderately popular in Europe, but it has never caught on in North America. ISDN devices are supported from this menu.

Telephony Support Linux supports one line of dedicated telephony cards, the QuickNet Internet. This device enables you to plug a telephone into the computer to use voice-over-IP (VoIP) applications in Linux, but you must enable the drivers in this menu to do so.

Input Device Support This menu (called Input Core Support in the 2.4.20 kernel) provides support for miscellaneous input devices, such as keyboards, mice, and joysticks. Normally, you should activate at least keyboard support, which is usually built into the kernel proper. The 2.5.67 kernel provides substantially more options in this menu than does the 2.4.20 kernel.

Character Devices This menu provides drivers for an assortment of character devices. The most important of these are the RS-232 serial driver options, which include drivers for standard RS-232 serial ports and for various nonstandard multiport cards. This menu also includes options for the I2C interface used by various hardware sensors, drivers for some mice, support for the Direct Rendering Interface (DRI) used for 3D support in XFree86, and more. In the 2.4.20 kernel, support for PS/2 mice appears here rather than in the Input Device Support menu; but the 2.5.67 kernel moves PS/2 mouse options to Input Device Support and puts only bus mouse options in this menu. Chapter 3 covers RS-232 serial configuration in more detail.

Multimedia Devices If you want to use a video capture card, a digital video broadcast card, or a radio card in Linux, you must activate the appropriate drivers in this menu.

File Systems   Activate support for filesystems from this menu. In the 2.5.67 kernel, the main menu provides support for most disk-based filesystems, such as ext2fs and ReiserFS, while submenus provide support for various specialized filesystems, such as CD-ROM filesystems and network filesystems. You must normally compile the filesystem used on your root (/) partition into the kernel itself—that is, using the Y option. You can get around this requirement by using a boot-time RAM disk, but setting this up is usually more effort than compiling the filesystem support into the kernel.

Graphics Support   This menu is called Console Drivers in the 2.4.20 kernel. It provides drivers to support *frame buffer* devices. These devices enable you to access high-resolution graphics modes on video cards in a device-independent manner. In theory, you could then use a single driver in XFree86 for all cards. In practice, frame buffer drivers are usually slower than direct drivers. Some systems (particularly non-IA-32 systems) require the frame buffer drivers to function in X or to present legible text modes. You may also need to activate some of these options to support special boot-time video modes that are set in your boot loader.

Sound   This menu provides sound card driver options. The 2.4.20 kernel supports only the original Open Sound System (OSS) drivers, but the 2.5.67 kernel delivers separate submenus for OSS and Advanced Linux Sound Architecture (ALSA) drivers. (You can add ALSA support for 2.4.*x* kernels by compiling it from a separate package, as described in Chapter 1.) Indications are that the OSS drivers will eventually disappear, but probably not in the 2.5.*x* or 2.6.*x* kernels' lifetimes. The arrangement of drivers in the 2.4.20 kernel and in the OSS section of the 2.5.67 kernel is chaotic. Some drivers appear only if you select the OSS Sound Modules option. These are the original OSS drivers, whereas others were written by other people but follow the OSS model. I consider all of these drivers to be OSS drivers, compared to the radically different ALSA model.

USB Support   The Universal Serial Bus (USB) has become a very popular means of connecting devices ranging from keyboards to external hard disks. Linux provides USB support, which is accessible from this menu. You must activate support for both the low-level interface used on your system (EHCI, OHCI, or UHCI) and for the device type (keyboard, scanner, camera, mass storage, etc.). Chapter 3 covers USB devices in more detail.

Bluetooth Support   Bluetooth is a wireless protocol designed to replace IrDA and short-range wires, such as those used to connect printers and keyboards to computers. Linux provides limited Bluetooth support, accessible from this menu.

Profiling Support   *Profiling* is a technique used by programmers to determine what sections of a program are consuming the most CPU time. The 2.5.67 kernel includes a profiling option that enables programmers to profile anything running on the system, including the kernel itself. You will probably need this support only if you're a kernel hacker.

Kernel Hacking   This menu provides options that are primarily of interest to kernel hackers. You can tell the system to include assorted facilities that can be helpful in debugging drivers or other kernel features.

Security Options   This menu, which is present on the 2.5.67 kernel but not the 2.4.20 kernel, adds support for various security *hooks* (kernel code that can be used to simplify implementation of security features). In 2003, this facility isn't used much, but it might become important for firewalls, virtual private networks (VPNs), access control, or other facilities in the future.

Cryptographic Options　This menu is another one that's present in 2.5.67 but not 2.4.20. It adds kernel-level support for various cryptographic tools, which may be used in creating network security tools in the future.

Library Routines　This menu provides 32-bit Cyclic Redundancy Check (CRC32) functions in the 2.5.67 kernel. In the 2.4.20 kernel, this menu provides options for zlib compression and decompression. In either case, the option is available so that the features will be available when no in-kernel modules need the support but kernel modules from another source do require these functions.

If you've never compiled a Linux kernel before, I recommend that you set aside an hour or more to peruse the options in each of these menus. If in doubt about what an option does, your safest course of action is usually to compile that option, at least as a module (M). On the other hand, this action can create a bloated kernel, particularly for features that provide no modular compilation option.

Optimizing Kernel Performance

One of the primary reasons to recompile your kernel is to improve your overall system performance. Because the kernel is responsible for handling so many critical system features, ranging from scheduling other processes to filesystem interactions, inefficiencies in the kernel can have an impact on every other program the computer runs. For this reason, improving the efficiency of the kernel is very important, and actions you take to this end can have greater-than-average payoffs. This isn't to say, though, that you're likely to see a huge performance boost when you recompile a kernel. Such improvements are likely to be modest, and they probably won't even be noticeable without running benchmarks; however, they will impact just about every program you run. Kernel performance tuning is most important on systems that are very limited in one way or another, such as an old system with little RAM that you want to use as a print server. These options can also have a substantial impact on systems with multiple CPUs, unusually large amounts of RAM, or other exotic features, as well.

This section describes three types of optimizations you can perform: Setting CPU options, removing unnecessary drivers, and tuning device drivers. Each of these options works in a different way and can help improve performance in different circumstances.

Selecting a CPU and Related Options

As noted in the earlier section, "An Overview of Kernel Options," one of the main areas of the kernel configuration system is the Processor Type and Features menu. This menu includes options that can influence the efficiency of the kernel when run on particular systems:

Subarchitecture Type　This option, which isn't available on 2.4.*x* kernels, tells the system which of several IA-32 designs the system uses. Most users should select PC-Compatible. Other options apply to exotic IA-32 computers that aren't compatible with standard IA-32 computers, such as some workstations from IBM and SGI.

Processor Family   As described in Chapter 1, many different models of IA-32 CPUs are available from several different manufacturers. The Processor Family option lets you specify which of these models you use. Most Linux distributions use kernels optimized for the 386 family, which means that the kernels work on just about any IA-32 CPU, but with most CPUs, the kernel could run a tiny bit faster with another optimization. Some distributions (notably Mandrake) optimize all code for more sophisticated CPUs, and some others (such as Red Hat and SuSE) offer kernels precompiled for other CPUs.

SMP Support   If your motherboard has more than one CPU, it's important that you select this option. If this option is not enabled, Linux will use just one of the CPUs, which is obviously not very efficient. If you enable this option when it shouldn't be enabled, the kernel will run on most, but not all, single-CPU systems, but won't run as quickly as it would if configured for single-CPU operation. In the 2.5.67 kernel, you can specify how many CPUs your system has after selecting this option.

Preemptable Kernel   This option can improve the perceived responsiveness of a Linux system by enabling user-mode programs to preempt running low-priority processes even when those low-priority processes are performing kernel calls. Enabling this option is generally desirable on workstations or other systems that interact directly with users. This option is present in the 2.5.67 kernel but not in the 2.4.20 kernel.

High Memory Support   This option changes the way the kernel maps physical RAM to the virtual memory spaces used by individual programs. Pick Off if your computer has 1GB of RAM or less, 4GB if the system has between 1GB and 4GB of RAM, and 64GB if the system has over 4GB of RAM. If you pick this final option, the kernel won't boot on CPUs that don't support Intel's Physical Address Extension (PAE) mode. In practice, you may need to select 4GB if you have over 896MB of RAM.

Math Emulation   *Floating-point units (FPUs)*, aka *math coprocessors*, perform floating-point (as opposed to integer) arithmetic, and Linux relies on this support to operate. Some very old CPUs (all 386, some 486, and some NexGen CPUs) lacked FPUs, and instead relied on optional FPUs that could be added separately. Not all such computers came with FPUs, and for the benefit of those that didn't, the Linux kernel provides an FPU emulator, which enables Linux to work on these systems. Omitting this support is the best choice on all modern computers, but the option is required if you have an ancient system that lacks a separate FPU. (If you add this support unnecessarily, it will go unused, but will make the kernel about 66KB larger than it needs to be.)

MTRR Support   Many CPUs (Intel Pentium Pro and above, Cyrix 6x86 and above, AMD K6-3 and some K6-2 CPUs, and a few others) support a feature that Intel calls the *Memory Type Range Register (MTRR)*. (Some manufacturers use other names for this feature.) This option can improve data transfers to video cards, but requires kernel support. Enabling this option can improve video performance if you have one of these CPUs. Enabling this option unnecessarily won't cause problems, except for increasing the kernel size by about 9KB.

NOTE   *Many CPU options vary depending on the CPU architecture (IA-32, PowerPC, etc.). This list emphasizes the IA-32 options, because they're the most common. Options on other architectures may be quite different.*

Setting some of these options incorrectly can prevent your system from booting, as just described. Other options (most notably the SMP option if you have multiple CPUs) won't prevent the computer from booting if set incorrectly, but will impair performance. Some options, such as the Processor Family, might yield small performance boosts once set for your CPU. All of these options deserve at least some attention.

Removing Unnecessary Drivers

A second procedure that can improve kernel performance is removing unnecessary drivers. Most distributions provide kernels that are configured to boot on as wide a range of hardware as possible. In many cases, this means that drivers are compiled as modules so that the modules can be accessed after the kernel has loaded, without bloating the kernel beyond usability. In other cases, though, creating a kernel that boots on many systems means that the kernel must include drivers that are *not* needed on your system. For instance, a distribution may include a large number of ATA or SCSI drivers. These drivers consume memory, but most of them go unused on any given system.

Removing unnecessary drivers has a benefit mainly in reducing memory consumption. Once a driver is gone, the kernel becomes a bit slimmer, giving more room in memory for user programs. On modern systems with hundreds of megabytes of RAM, this effect is likely to be modest. Most hardware driver modules' sizes are measured in the tens of kilobytes, so even taken together, a dozen or more drivers won't consume a huge amount of RAM. Removing unnecessary drivers can be a great boon on an older system or on specialized systems such as palmtop computers, which have limited amounts of RAM.

In addition to saving RAM, reducing the kernel's size can help at boot time. A smaller kernel loads more quickly. This effect is tiny if you boot from a hard disk; however, if the kernel is on a floppy disk, the effect can be more substantial. More important, a smaller kernel can *fit* on a floppy disk. A kernel loaded with all the drivers won't fit in the 1.44MB space of a conventionally formatted 3.5-inch floppy disk. This consideration is most important if you want to create a floppy boot disk for an emergency recovery system, as described in Chapter 17, "Protecting Your System with Backups." Having a bootable kernel on a floppy disk can also come in handy in case you accidentally damage your boot loader installation or if you want to test a new kernel without changing your boot loader configuration.

TIP   If you find that you can't create a kernel that's small enough to fit on a conventional floppy, you may be able to create a bootable CD-R disc instead. One way to do this is to create a 2.88MB file and treat it like a floppy disk image. You can then copy the kernel to this file, make it bootable, and use `mkisofs`'s *bootable CD option (*`-b`*) to create a bootable CD-R using the 2.88MB image file.*

To remove unnecessary drivers, you must peruse your configuration to locate them. What is unnecessary, of course, varies from one system to another. For instance, a computer without a SCSI host adapter doesn't need any of the SCSI device drivers. (Such a system might still need SCSI support if you enable SCSI emulation for ATA devices or if you use IEEE-1394 or USB disk devices, which look like SCSI disks to the kernel.) On the other hand, an all-SCSI system needs SCSI disk support and support for the SCSI host adapter, but it doesn't need ATA support at all. A system with both types of devices needs its boot device in the kernel proper, but chances are the other type of device can be compiled as a module. In fact, most Linux drivers can be compiled as modules.

These include network drivers, sound card drivers, CD-ROM drivers, floppy disk drivers, most filesystems (whatever you use for the root filesystem being a notable exception), USB drivers, RS-232 serial drivers, parallel port drivers, and more.

On the other hand, you may want to compile some devices into the kernel, despite the fact that the kernel size will increase unnecessarily. Placing a hardware driver in the kernel means that it will almost certainly be detected correctly when the system boots. A misconfigured /etc/modules.conf or other module configuration file can lead to a failure to identify hardware. For this reason, you may want to compile drivers for hardware that's always in use, such as network adapters, into the kernel itself. Placing such drivers in modules saves little or no RAM, and if you don't put too many such drivers in the kernel file proper, it should still fit on a floppy disk. In the end, you'll have to discover your own balance on this point.

Tuning Device Driver Options

Some device drivers support options. For instance, Figure 15.4 shows the SCSI Low-Level Drivers submenu of the SCSI Device Support menu, highlighting the SYM53C8XX SCSI Support option. When you activate this option, using either M or Y, the configuration tool presents a number of additional options that can fine-tune the driver's behavior.

Precisely what these options do is highly device-specific. Some of the possibilities include:

Activating Advanced Features Some device features are on the cutting edge, as far as the Linux driver is concerned. Such features may enhance performance, but because they're so new, they may also cause system crashes or other problems. Such options are usually marked as being new or experimental. Other features may improve performance and be reliable with some hardware, but some specific models of devices may not support the option.

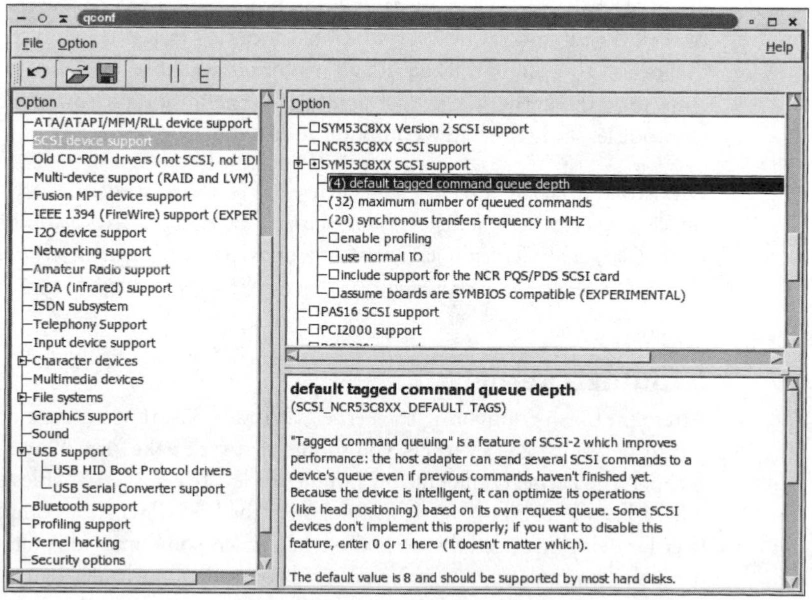

FIGURE 15.4

Some kernel options provide associated sub-options that fine-tune the driver's behavior.

Adjusting Parameters for Specific Devices   Some drivers support a wide array of devices, and the driver might work best with some tuning adjustments for specific devices. For instance, you might adjust the speed of the device or select an option that tunes assorted internal parameters based on the subclass of the device you're using.

Enabling Compatibility Modes   Some hardware supports both device-specific and more generic methods of operation. Ordinarily, the device-specific modes work best, but these modes may cause problems for some specific devices. For this reason, some drivers give you the option of using an older mode that works with more devices, albeit with a drop in speed.

Enabling Debugging Features   Some drivers support special debugging options. These may log extra information in the kernel message queue (accessible by typing **dmesg**) or in special files in the /proc filesystem, which can be useful if you're having problems. On the other hand, this activity is almost certain to degrade performance.

When you activate a driver, look for any driver-specific options that may be present. If it's not obvious what these options do, examine the help for each option. (If you use make xconfig for a 2.5.x or 2.6.x kernel, the help information appears in the lower-right pane. For 2.4.x or earlier kernels or if you use make menuconfig, you need to select the Help option.) In most cases, this description will provide guidance concerning how to pick the best option, although sometimes the descriptions can be confusing. If in doubt, leave the option set at its default value or pick what sounds like the more conservative option. Alternatively, you can experiment, selecting one option and using it and then trying the other option.

Compiling and Installing a Kernel

Picking all the kernel options is the most tedious part of creating a custom kernel. Given the hundreds of available options, it can take an hour or more to review the possibilities, particularly if you're diligent and review every option. Once this task is done, typing a few commands should finish the job of compiling the kernel and making it available for use. You issue separate commands for compiling the kernel file proper and your kernel modules. You must then install the new kernel and its modules and reboot the computer to use the new kernel.

WARNING   Building a kernel requires the presence of assorted development tools. Most distributions provide some easy way to install these tools during system installation (by selecting a development tools package). Tools required include the GNU Compiler Collection (GCC), make, procps, *possibly filesystem-specific tool kits, and so on. If you're missing a tool, you'll encounter an error message when you try to compile the kernel.*

Building a Kernel

After you finish configuring the kernel with make xconfig or some other command, it's time to build the kernel. With 2.4.x kernels, you should first type **make dep**. This command tells the system to search through the kernel configuration and files to locate *dependencies*—files that depend on other files to compile or link. If you fail to perform this step, the kernel may not compile completely. Most 2.5.x and later kernels don't need this step, though. Kernels sometimes also fail to compile if old files from previous failed compilations exist. You can rid yourself of such files by typing **make clean**, which removes these files. This command deletes intermediate compilation files, which can be helpful if you need to clear some space on the partition that holds the Linux kernel source code tree.

You actually compile the kernel by typing **make** followed by a name for the kernel. Several names are available, and they produce distinct results:

vmlinux   This make target is in many respects the simplest; it creates a kernel file called vmlinux in the kernel source root directory. This is the preferred target for some non-IA-32 platforms.

zImage   This target used to be common, but it is now rare. It creates a compressed kernel image for IA-32 systems, known as zImage and stored in arch/i386/boot. This kernel relies on a series of tricky operations during the boot process, though, and as a result there's a maximum size limit for such kernels. Most 2.4.*x* and later kernels are too large for these operations, so make zImage isn't used much any more.

bzImage   This target is the preferred one for IA-32 systems. It creates a compressed kernel image, called bzImage and stored in arch/i386/boot.

bzdisk   This target creates a bootable IA-32 floppy disk. The disk is formatted using the File Allocation Table (FAT) filesystem and uses the ldlinux.sys boot loader to boot Linux from floppy. To use this command, you should first insert a blank floppy disk in your floppy drive and type **make bzdisk**.

rpm   This target creates an RPM Package Manager (RPM) file containing the kernel, its modules, and a few support files. The resulting RPM file is stored in your RPM package directory, /usr/src/ *distname*/RPMS/*arch*, where *distname* is a distribution-specific name and *arch* is an architecture code, such as i386 or ppc. The main kernel file in this package is called /boot/vmlinuz-*a.b.c*. You can treat it like a vmlinux or bzImage kernel file. The rpm target is most useful if you want to build a kernel that you plan to install on several other RPM-based computers.

The most typical method of building Linux is to type **make bzImage** or, on some platforms, **make vmlinux**. You can then build the kernel's modules, as described in the next section, "Building Kernel Modules," and install the kernel and its modules, as described in the upcoming section, "Installing a Kernel."

When you use any of these methods, the make utility runs a series of commands to compile the kernel, link it, and possibly process it further. You'll see a series of compilation commands, most of which use gcc, scroll past on your display. If all goes well, these commands will complete with lines that describe where the kernel file has been stored. This process may take anywhere from a few minutes to many hours, depending on the speed of your CPU and the options you've picked. On modern computers, compilation is likely to take well under an hour.

Occasionally, compilation fails. If this happens, you'll see an error message. Such problems can be hard to track down. They're sometimes caused by errors in the source code itself, particularly if you're compiling a development kernel. More often, your configuration is strange—for instance, you might have added options without adding other options upon which the first depends. The configuration tools are designed to prevent such things from happening, but sometimes they fail. Another potential source of problems, at least with 2.4.*x* kernels, is the failure to type **make dep** before making the kernel. Missing development tools can also cause problems. Whatever the cause, sometimes typing **make clean** and then trying again will correct the problem, but sometimes you'll have to examine the error message and hope it presents a clue. You may have luck by removing a driver that's mentioned in the error message (assuming it's not really necessary for basic system functionality) or by reconfiguring how that module is compiled (setting it to compile into the kernel rather than as a module, for instance).

NOTE   An ordinary user can compile a kernel if the user has full write access to the kernel source directory tree. Installing the kernel normally requires `root` *access, though.*

Building Kernel Modules

To build kernel modules, you type a single command: `make modules`. Like the kernel compilation process proper, this command runs a series of `gcc` commands to compile the kernel modules. Unlike the main kernel compilation, though, the result is a series of module files rather than a single kernel file. The next section, "Installing a Kernel," describes how to install these module files. Making modules is likely to take about as long as making the kernel itself, although the details depend on how many features you've configured to compile into modules, versus into the kernel proper.

Installing a Kernel

Installing a new kernel is a three-step process, but the order in which you perform these steps is unimportant. These steps are as follows:

- Installing the kernel modules
- Copying the system map file to `/boot`
- Configuring the system to boot the new kernel

Installing the kernel modules is the simplest of these three tasks from your perspective, although in some sense it's the most complex. This is because the kernel `Makefile` provides a target for installing the modules: Type `make modules_install` as `root` and the system copies all the kernel modules to the `/lib/modules/a.b.c` directory, where `a.b.c` is the kernel version number. This command also performs other necessary housekeeping tasks. The bottom line is that the kernel modules should be available to the computer once you reboot with the new kernel.

Copying the system map file is also fairly straightforward. After building the kernel, you should find a file called `System.map` in your main kernel directory. This file contains data that can help various error-reporting tools identify the names of kernel routines in the event of problems. To use the file, though, it must exist in `/boot`. You can copy the file directly, as in `cp System.map /boot`; however, doing so may overwrite an existing system map file for a kernel you might want to use. Many systems use symbolic links to help manage these files. For instance, if you've just compiled a 2.5.67 kernel, you would type `cp System.map /boot/System.map-2.5.67`. You can then rename any existing `/boot/System.map` file or, if it's a symbolic link, delete it. Create a new `/boot/System.map` symbolic link that points to the system map file for the kernel you intend to boot. Mandrake and Red Hat attempt to create an appropriate symbolic link when they boot, as part of the `/etc/rc.d/rc.sysinit` startup script.

NOTE   The system map file isn't required for Linux to boot or run. It's more of a convenience for error reporting tools, system diagnostic tools, and the like.

Most systems place their kernels in the /boot directory, but some place their default kernels in the root (/) directory. In order to keep clutter in the root directory to a minimum, I recommend you use /boot for kernels you compile, even if your distribution places its default kernel in the root directory. I also recommend you rename your kernel as you move or copy it to /boot, in order to help you identify it. For instance, you might type the following command to place a 2.5.67 kernel in /boot:

```
# cp /usr/src/linux-2.5.67/arch/i386/boot/bzImage /boot/bzImage-2.5.67
```

WARNING *Do not overwrite your standard working kernel when you copy the new kernel. If something went wrong when you compiled the kernel or when you set up your boot loader, you want to have a known working kernel available as a fallback.*

If necessary, you can add more identifying information to the filename. For instance, you might call the kernel bzImage-2.5.67-scsi if you've included SCSI support. You can use such naming conventions to keep different kernels straight if you experiment with different options or features. If you plan to do such experiments, though, you may want to manually edit the Makefile generated by make when you create the kernel. The fourth line of this file sets the EXTRAVERSION variable, which adds information to the kernel version number. Adding your code (such as scsi) by setting it using this variable tells the system about your changes, and the build and install utilities will track the changes. For instance, when you type **make modules_install**, your extra code will be added to the kernel modules directory name, so you can keep separate kernel module directories for your different kernel builds.

Using a New Kernel

After you copy the kernel to /boot, you must reconfigure your boot loader to use it. Chapter 10 describes this process in detail for both the Linux Loader (LILO) and Grand Unified Boot Loader (GRUB). In brief, with either boot loader you should copy a working Linux option within the boot loader configuration file (/etc/lilo.conf or /boot/grub/menu.1st), change its name, and change the reference to the kernel file. Be sure to create a copy of a working entry and modify the copy; keep the original reference around, just as you keep the original kernel, so that you have a known-working fallback should you have problems with the new kernel. For LILO, you must then type **lilo** as **root** to install the changed configuration. In the case of GRUB, you don't need to type any special commands after modifying the configuration file.

WARNING *Many distributions use RAM disks as part of their normal boot process. These configurations may include highly kernel-specific features, though, so they may not work correctly after you upgrade your kernel. Be sure to eliminate references to RAM disks from your boot loader configuration for your new kernel. You may also need to eliminate options that change the video mode. Depending on the options you chose, these features may result in a blank screen as the system boots.*

If you don't want to modify your boot loader configuration, you can test a new kernel by using LOADLIN (also described in Chapter 10) to boot your new kernel. Alternatively, you can type **make bzdisk** to create a boot floppy with the new kernel. In either case, you must still copy the kernel modules to their target location by typing **make modules_install**.

Changing a kernel is one of the few software upgrades that necessitates a reboot of a Linux system. When you reboot, pick the new kernel from the boot loader's menu and pay attention to the boot messages as your system starts up. Chances are most of these messages will scroll by too quickly for you to read, but you may notice problems—drivers that report they can't find hardware, servers that don't load, and so on. If the system boots and allows you to log in, you might want to type **dmesg | less** to peruse the kernel messages at a more reasonable pace; however, this command won't display the SysV startup script messages. In extreme cases, the system may freeze during the boot process. If this happens, examine the error messages for clues, then reboot the computer and choose your old kernel. You can then try to track down the source of the problem in your kernel configuration. Perhaps you omitted an important driver or set an option too optimistically.

If all goes well, you should be greeted by a working Linux system. It should function much as did your original system, but it may include a better mix of options for your system, security or bug fixes, or other desirable improvements.

Summary

Building a custom kernel is usually not necessary to use Linux, but it can improve your system's performance. By including the appropriate features, setting the options to best suit your hardware, and excluding any unnecessary features, you can create a kernel that takes best advantage of your hardware. The tools for doing this task have changed in the 2.5.x development kernel, but the general procedure for making these optimizations is the same: You select the options you want to include using special tools, compile a new kernel, install it, and use it. Whenever you undertake these steps, you should be careful to preserve a known working kernel. An error during kernel compilation can create an unbootable system, so having a working fallback position is cheap insurance against a problem that could be tedious to correct.

Chapter 16

Optimizing X Configuration

THE X WINDOW SYSTEM, or X for short, is the standard GUI environment for Linux. Most Linux systems use XFree86 (http://www.xfree86.org) as the default X software, so configuring XFree86 is important if you want to use Linux in GUI mode. Fortunately, most Linux systems ship with tools that help configure XFree86, and these tools generally run at system installation time, so X usually works as soon as you finish installing Linux. Sometimes, though, the automatic tools yield a nonworking or suboptimal configuration. In these cases, you may need to dig into XFree86's configuration to fix matters yourself. You may also want to do this in order to activate advanced or unusual X features. This chapter covers these topics. It begins with an overview of the X configuration file. Fonts are one of the specific topics that frequently cause consternation under Linux, so they're up next. Configuring specific video card features can also cause problems. This chapter concludes with a look at custom video modes—running a display at a nonstandard resolution or refresh rate to get the most out of your monitor.

NOTE   *This chapter emphasizes XFree86 4.x, which is the version that ships with most Linux distributions in 2003. XFree86 3.x used a somewhat different configuration file format, used a very different driver architecture, and supported fewer font features. As a result, if you're using XFree86 3.x, much of the information in this chapter will not apply directly or it will be implemented in a slightly different way in the configuration file. Unfortunately, a few video cards are supported better by XFree86 3.x than by 4.x, so you may need to use 3.x if you have one of these cards. Commercial X servers, such as those from MetroLink (http://www.metrolink.com) and Xi Graphics (http://www.xig.com), also use their own configuration file formats and support their own unique mixes of features.*

The Structure of *XF86Config*

XFree86 uses a configuration file that's usually called one of three things:

1. /etc/X11/XF86Config-4

2. /etc/X11/XF86Config

3. /etc/XF86Config

XFree86 looks for the file in this order, so if your system has two or more of these files, edit the one that's earliest in the search order. Some distributions use /etc/X11/XF86Config-4 for the XFree86 4.*x* configuration file and /etc/X11/XF86Config for the XFree86 3.*x* configuration file, so the latter file's contents may not be suitable for XFree86 4.*x*. For simplicity's sake, I will refer to the XFree86 4.*x* configuration file as XF86Config throughout the rest of this chapter.

Broadly speaking, the XF86Config file contains three types of settings:

◆ Global settings that affect the overall behavior of the X server

◆ Sections that define the behavior of specific input/output components

◆ A layout section that merges together the component sections into a coherent whole

Each type of setting is contained within a section that's labeled, appropriately, Section, followed by a section name in quotes, as in Section "Files". Each of these sections ends with a line that reads EndSection. The order of sections in the file is unimportant.

Global Sections

Several XF86Config sections affect the entire server. These sections set global variables or features that aren't easily tied to just one display. These sections include:

Files   This section defines the locations of important files. Frequently, this section is dominated by FontPath lines. (Each FontPath line points either to a single directory [] in which fonts are stored or to a font server computer. (The upcoming section, "Improving the Appearance of Fonts," covers fonts in more detail.) Other directories may be specified by other lines, such as ModulePath (which sets the directory in which driver modules are stored) and RgbPath (which sets the location of the RGB color database).

ServerFlags   You can set miscellaneous server options in this section. For instance, specifying Option "AllowMouseOpenFail" "true" enables the server to run even if it doesn't detect a mouse; and Option "DontZap" "true" tells the server to ignore the Ctrl+Alt+Backspace keystroke, which normally terminates X.

Module   XFree86 4.*x* supports *modules*, which are similar to kernel modules—each provides support for some hardware or software feature. The Module section is likely to include several Load directives, each of which specifies a module that should be loaded. Common modules include those for various font formats, such as type1 and freetype; and X server extensions, such as glx, an OpenGL support tool. Many modules are loaded automatically, and so don't need to be specified in this section. Some modules accept parameters that can be specified in lines that reside between Subsection and EndSubsection lines.

DRI The *Direct Rendering Infrastructure (DRI)* is a 3D acceleration framework for X. This section of XF86Config includes options related to use of DRI. This topic is covered in more detail in the upcoming section, "Using 3D Acceleration."

Modes X uses *modes*, which are numerical descriptions of a monitor's timings, to set the resolution and refresh rate of the monitor. XFree86 4.*x* includes a number of built-in modes and can obtain more modes by communicating with modern monitors. You can also specify a custom mode by including a Modeline line in a monitor's section. Alternatively, you can create a Modes section and define a mode that can be used by multiple monitors. The upcoming section, "Creating a Custom Video Mode," describes custom video modes in more detail.

Not all XF86Config files will have all of these sections. The DRI and Modes sections are particularly likely to be missing. Unless you need to use the features implemented by these sections, don't be concerned if they're missing from your configuration file.

The Server Layout and Screen

XFree86 operates on the concept of a server *layout*. This layout combines several configurations that together define a unique user input/output system. A typical layout includes three components: a keyboard, a mouse, and a screen. The screen is itself composed of two components: a monitor and a video card (called a Device in XF86Config). This arrangement is illustrated in Figure 16.1.

FIGURE 16.1

XFree86 ties components together in a hierarchical manner.

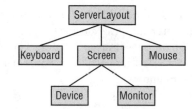

The ServerLayout section is often the last section of the XF86Config file, although it need not be. It includes pointers to the three core components that make up the layout:

```
Section "ServerLayout"
    Identifier "layout1"
    InputDevice "Keyboard1" "CoreKeyboard"
    InputDevice "Mouse1" "CorePointer"
    Screen "screen1"
EndSection
```

Note that each of the component sections is named, as is the layout itself. This feature enables one XF86Config file to define multiple layouts and devices. This feature can be important when using multiple monitors or if you want to have the option of using, say, two different keyboards or mice, as you might with a laptop computer. This section may also include additional options that can influence its behavior.

The Screen section ties together a monitor and video card. It's also likely to include several subsections, each devoted to a display running at a specific color depth. Each of these color-depth settings includes a list of supported modes, which are typically named after the resolution they implement. You can launch X with options to set the color depth, thereby switching between them, and perhaps setting a resolution as a consequence. A Screen section looks like this:

```
Section "Screen"
    Identifier "screen1"
    Device "device1"
    Monitor "monitor1"
    DefaultDepth 16

    Subsection "Display"
        Depth 8
        Modes "1280x1024" "1024x768" "800x600"
    EndSubsection

    Subsection "Display"
        Depth 16
        Modes "1280x1024" "1024x768" "800x600" "640x480"
    EndSubsection
EndSection
```

This Screen section defines just two color depths (8-bit and 16-bit), but it's not uncommon to see four or more defined. The Identifier line gives a name to this Screen section; note that it's the same name used in the Screen line of the ServerLayout section. The Device specification points to another named section that defines the video card, while the Monitor line points to a named section that describes the capabilities of the monitor.

Component Sections

You can configure four major hardware components in XF86Config. Each of these components has its own section:

Keyboard The keyboard is defined in an InputDevice section that uses the Keyboard driver. Chapter 3, "Using External Peripherals," includes information on configuring a keyboard in X.

Mouse X mouse configuration can be tricky sometimes; if you specify the wrong model, X may not start, or the mouse pointer might not move or might move erratically. Chapter 3 includes information on mouse configuration. You configure a mouse with an InputDevice section, just as you do a keyboard; but the mouse uses a driver called mouse and a different set of options.

Video Card In order to create a display, X needs to know what sort of video card your system uses. You give it this information in a Device section. The upcoming section, "Using Card-Specific Optimizations," describes this section in more detail.

Monitor XFree86 can tell a video card to create a display, but unless your monitor can handle whatever resolution and refresh rate X tells the card to create, the monitor may ignore the display.

You probably want to create the best display your monitor can handle. For instance, the higher the refresh rate the better, as a general rule. Therefore, XF86Config includes a Monitor section in which various monitor capabilities are described. The most important of these are the HorizSync and VertRefresh lines, which set the range of horizontal and vertical refresh rates that your monitor is capable of running, as in HorizSync 27.0-115.0. Both values can be obtained from most monitors' manuals, so consult your manual to set these values correctly. You can also create custom display modes, as described in the upcoming section, "Creating a Custom Video Mode."

WARNING   *Although most modern monitors ignore video modes outside of the range they can handle, models from the mid-1990s and earlier can be damaged if you try to feed them a display with a too-high refresh rate. Therefore, you should not guess at the* HorizSync *or* VertRefresh *values. Check your manual, the manufacturer's web page, or any other documentation you can find to enter these values correctly.*

You can configure more than one of each device type. For instance, you might have a laptop computer that you sometimes use with its built-in touchpad and sometimes use with a USB mouse. On such a system, you might specify two mice and reference them both from the ServerLayout section. Some systems have two video cards and two monitors, and XFree86 4.x allows you to use both simultaneously.

Improving the Appearance of Fonts

Historically, one common complaint about Linux on the desktop has been the poor quality of its font handling. This matter has been improving in recent years, and even when using traditional font tools, the appearance of fonts can be improved over what you might see by default. Linux font handling is still a bit tricky, though. Understanding the different font types and knowing where to go to get fonts are critical prerequisites. Beyond this, you can serve fonts by creating font directories and telling X about them via FontPath lines in XF86Config, or you can run a font server to deliver fonts to one or many computers. The latest Linux font development is in *font smoothing*, a technique to improve the appearance of fonts at screen resolutions. Unfortunately, font smoothing requires new font display techniques that are not yet fully integrated into X, so you may need to jump through some extra hoops to use smoothed fonts.

The Importance of Font Implementations

Broadly speaking, there are two types of fonts:

Bitmap Fonts   These fonts are described in terms of individual pixels in an array of pixels. For instance, Figure 16.2 shows a bitmap representation of the letter *A*. Bitmap fonts must be hand-drawn for every combination of text size and display resolution, which makes them inflexible. If a font isn't available in the right size, it won't be displayed or it will be scaled in a way that makes it look chunky. On the other hand, these fonts tend to be quick to draw, because they can be copied from memory to the display with little computation required. The fact that they're hand-drawn for specific resolutions also tends to make them look good at low resolutions because a human artist can optimize them for particular sizes. Many bitmap font formats are available, and X can handle many of them.

FIGURE 16.2

A bitmap font is
built from individual
pixels that may be
either on or off.

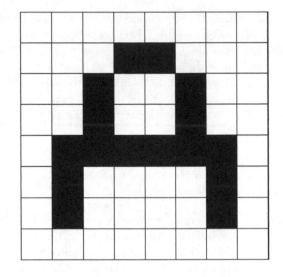

Outline Fonts   These fonts are built from mathematical descriptions of their outlines, using lines and curves. A font *rasterizer* (a component of X or some other program) can then create a bitmap for display at any resolution. This feature makes outline fonts very flexible, but they take more CPU time to display. They frequently don't look as good at screen resolutions as do bitmap fonts, because font rasterizers tend to be aesthetically challenged compared to human artists. The two most popular outline font formats are Adobe's *PostScript Type 1* (aka *Adobe Type Manager*, or *ATM*) and Apple's *TrueType*. Both formats are supported by XFree86, although TrueType support was added recently, with XFree86 4.0.

X ships with a modest assortment of bitmap fonts designed for both 75 dots per inch (dpi) and 100dpi displays. These fonts tend to look fairly good at the specified resolutions, but not nearly as good at other resolutions. All Linux distributions also ship with a wider assortment of outline fonts, mostly in Type 1 and TrueType format.

NOTE   Technically speaking, a font is a set of characters rendered at a specific size and (for computers) resolution. In common use, though, the word font *often refers to outline formats or a collection of bitmap fonts that work at several sizes—a meaning that better matches the term* typeface. *In this book, I use the word* font *in this less accurate but more popular sense.*

Most fonts you find on the Internet or on font CDs are in Type 1 or TrueType format. Type 1 fonts come as collections in several files. The most important of these are .pfb or .pfa files, which hold the font data proper; and .pfm or .afm files, which hold detailed information on the spacing between individual letters. X needs the .pfb or .pfa files but not the .pfm or .afm files. Some applications, such as some word processors, need these latter files, though. TrueType fonts come as single files with .ttf extensions.

TrueType fonts have acquired a reputation for looking good at screen resolutions; however, this reputation is due in part to the fact that a few popular TrueType fonts are very well designed. These exemplary fonts include extensive *hinting*—information embedded in the font on how to tweak the font display at low resolution. In particular, many of the fonts that Microsoft includes with its products are very well designed. When you use a randomly selected font from elsewhere, the TrueType version might or might not look any better than the Type 1 version.

The quality of the font rasterizer is also very important in determining the appearance of a font. Part of the reason for the historical complaints about Linux's font quality is that XFree86's Type 1 font rasterizers have not been the best. This situation is improving, though, particularly with new font libraries that handle font smoothing.

Fonts typically come in *families*. For instance, many fonts come in *normal* or *Roman* styles intended for most body text, along with an *italic* variant, a *bold* version, and a *bold-italic* version. Some fonts come with more variants, such as several gradations of boldness, narrow variants, and so on. Some programs can fake one or more of these styles using the normal variant, but the results are almost always superior if you use a custom font for each style. As a result, installing "a" font may actually require installing several fonts, one for each style.

Obtaining Third-Party Fonts

You may be satisfied with the selection of fonts available with your Linux distribution. If not, you must track down and install additional fonts. Fortunately, Linux can use most of the same fonts available for Windows, so obtaining new fonts is fairly straightforward. Some common sources of additional fonts include:

Commercial Font CD-ROMs   Many commercial font CD-ROMs are available in computer stores. Some of these CD-ROMs include very high-quality fonts from reputable font foundries, such as Adobe or Bitstream; but others are little more than amalgamations of freeware fonts collected from random websites.

Software Packages   Many software packages ship with font collections. This is particularly true of commercial word processors and graphics packages. In fact, you might want to peruse the closeout bin at your local computer store for old versions of graphics packages that come with good font collections. Even if you don't need the software, the fonts may be useful to you.

Web and FTP Sites   A wide variety of web and FTP sites deliver fonts. These fonts may be commercial, shareware, or freeware. One particularly large archive of free fonts is the one maintained by the Comprehensive TeX Archive Network (CTAN; `http://www.ctan.org/tex-archive/fonts/`). The MyFonts site, `http://www.myfonts.com`, is an excellent resource if you're looking for a particular commercial font or want to find a font that matches one you've seen elsewhere.

NOTE   *Macintosh Type 1 and TrueType fonts contain the same data as Windows Type 1 and TrueType fonts, but the file formats are different. Linux can easily use Windows-style outline font files, but fonts for Macintoshes must be converted to Windows format first. Many font CD-ROMs come with both Windows and Macintosh versions of the fonts. If you mount the CD-ROM in Linux using the `iso9660` filesystem type code, you'll automatically access the Windows fonts.*

Sometimes the lines between these font sources can be blurred; for instance, you may be able to purchase individual fonts from a commercial website or buy a CD-ROM with many fonts. Many of the fonts shipped with Linux distributions are also available from websites or FTP sites.

One tool that can be particularly helpful in dealing with flaky fonts or fonts that ship in the wrong format is PfaEdit (`http://pfaedit.sourceforge.net`). This program is an outline font editor for Linux. It can read Type 1 and TrueType fonts in either Windows or Mac OS files, and can write files to all of these formats. Therefore, PfaEdit can be a useful tool for converting fonts between formats. As a font editor, the program can also change font names, attributes, and so on, which can be handy if a font is misbehaving or is misidentified by other font tools.

Traditional X Font Configuration

Traditionally, X applications ask the X server to display text in a font that's specified using an *X Logical Font Descriptor (XLFD)*, a rather lengthy string that describes the font. In order to do this, X must know which XLFDs are associated with which font files. Therefore, installing a font is essentially a matter of linking these two pieces of data. You must set up a font directory with a mapping file and tell X about these directories.

NOTE *The upcoming section, "Serving Fonts to Many Computers," describes another way to serve fonts using the traditional X font display mechanism. The upcoming section, "Using Font Smoothing," describes alternative font-display techniques that are being used by an increasing number of programs.*

SETTING UP A FONT DIRECTORY

Fonts reside in one of a handful of directories on a Linux computer. Traditionally, they are subdirectories of `/usr/X11R6/lib/X11/fonts/`, but if you're installing your own fonts, you may want to use another directory, such as `/usr/local/fonts`. Copy your font files to this directory or subdirectories of it, such as `/usr/local/fonts/tt` for TrueType fonts. This is the easy part of the font installation task. Once you've done this, you need to create a file called `fonts.dir`. This file associates font files to XLFDs. It starts with a line that specifies the number of fonts mapped by the file. Each subsequent line is a font filename followed by an XLFD; for instance:

```
cour.pfa -adobe-courier-medium-r-normal--0-0-0-0-m-0-iso8859-1
```

NOTE *Many tools create both `fonts.dir` and `fonts.scale` files. Both files have the same format, and the contents will be identical for a directory that contains only outline fonts. The `fonts.dir` file describes all the fonts in a directory and is the most important file; `fonts.scale` describes only outline fonts, not bitmap fonts.*

This line specifies that the XLFD is to be tied to the `cour.pfa` font file. Because the XLFD is rather long and includes some repetitive sequences, typing it in manually would be tedious at best. Instead, you can create `fonts.dir` using special tools. These tools are listed here:

typelinst This program may or may not be installed by default. If not, look for it in a package called `font-tools`, `typelinst`, or something similar. You may need to track the package down using RPM Find (`http://www.rpmfind.net`). Once installed, change into the directory holding your Type 1 fonts and type **typelinst**. The program creates both a `fonts.dir` and a `fonts.scale` file summarizing the fonts it found in that directory.

ttmkfdir This program is the TrueType equivalent of `typelinst`. It may be available in a package called `ttmkfdir`, `freetype-tools`, or something similar. The program is more frequently installed than is `typelinst`. You use it in a similar way, but `ttmkfdir` sends its output to `stdout` by default, so you must redirect it by typing **`ttmkfdir > fonts.dir`** if you want to create a `fonts.dir` file directly. This program occasionally omits fonts from its output if they lack certain characters. You can force the program to include these fonts by adding the `-c` parameter.

mkfontscale   This program is a relative newcomer; it ships with Xfree86 4.3 and later. It does more-or-less what the combination of `typelinst` and `ttmkfdir` do—it creates a `fonts.scale` file that contains information on both Type 1 and TrueType fonts within a directory. You can then copy this file to `fonts.dir` or, if you prefer or if the directory also includes bitmap fonts, type **mkfontdir** to combine information on the outline and bitmap fonts in the directory into a `fonts.dir` file.

All of these tools are helpful, but none is without its flaws. You may want to examine the output files to be sure they include entries for all the fonts in the directory. If not, you may be able to copy an entry for another font and change the font name, weight (`medium`, `bold`, `light`, and so on), slant (`r` for Roman, `i` for italic, `o` for oblique, and so on), or other relevant features. Sometimes you'll find that different styles of the same font vary in important ways—for instance, one may have a typo in the name, or the font foundry may not match. Such problems can prevent you from using styles in word processors or the like. It's possible that the output will include more than one entry per font file. For instance, you may find several *encodings* for each font. These are the strings near the end of the XLFD, such as `iso8859-1`, which denote what characters are available in the font. Such duplication isn't normally a problem, but it can make the `fonts.dir` file much longer than it might otherwise be. Sometimes `mkfontscale` does a much better or worse job with particular fonts than do `typelinst` or `ttmkfdir`, so if you have problems with one tool, you may want to try another.

SETTING X'S FONT PATH

Once you've set up a font directory, you must add the directory to X's font path. With Mandrake and Red Hat, you do this by altering a font server's configuration, as described in the next section, "Serving Fonts to Many Computers." With Debian, Slackware, or SuSE, you edit the font path directly in the `XF86Config` file. Locate the `Files` section. It should contain a series of lines like this:

```
FontPath   "/usr/X11R6/lib/X11/fonts/Type1"
```

NOTE   *Some Debian systems, as well as some custom configurations for other distributions, use both font directories and font servers.*

The `FontPath` line indicates that the specified directory is part of the font path—X will check that directory for a `fonts.dir` file when it starts up, and deliver the fonts specified in that file to applications. To add your new font directory to the X font path, you can add a similar line pointing to your directory. X searches the font paths in order, so if a font appears in two directories, X uses the one from the earlier font path. If a directory doesn't exist, it's automatically removed from the font path. As a general rule, bitmap font directories appear first in the font path, with `:unscaled` added to the directory name. This string indicates that X is to use fonts in the directory only at their specified sizes, without attempting to scale them. Next up are outline fonts. The bitmap font directories often appear again at the end of the list, but without the `:unscaled` addendum. This placement allows X to scale a bitmapped font only as a last resort.

Once you've added your new font directory to `XF86Config`, you can tell X to begin using the changed font path by typing the following commands in an `xterm`:

```
$ xset fp+ /new/font/path
$ xset fp rehash
```

The first of these commands appends the new diectory to the font path dynamically, without restarting X. The second command tells X to rescan its font path, adding fonts as necessary.

WARNING   If you make a mistake, typing **xset fp rehash** *can cause X to misbehave. Typically, programs will hang or refuse to launch. Therefore, I recommend you type this command only after saving work in all your open applications. If you run into serious problems, you may have to terminate X by pressing Ctrl+Alt+Backspace.*

Serving Fonts to Many Computers

You can configure X to use a *font server*, which is a program that delivers bitmapped fonts to any X server on a network. The font server may deliver a bitmap font directly or it may create a bitmap from an outline font file. In fact, Mandrake and Red Hat both use font servers rather than X's built-in font rendering mechanisms. These distributions run a font server and tell X to use the font server running on the same computer. This practice arose when font servers to handle TrueType fonts became commonplace, but before TrueType support was integrated into X. If you must use a pre-4.0 version of XFree86, this remains the simplest way to use TrueType fonts, at least from applications that can't use Xft, as described in the next section, "Using Font Smoothing." To tell X to use a font server, you pass the name of the font server to X via a `FontPath` line in `XF86Config`'s `Files` section:

```
FontPath   "unix/:7100"
FontPath   "tcp/fontserv.example.com:7100"
```

The first of these two lines is the default configuration in Red Hat. It tells Linux to look at port 7100 on the local computer for a font server. Mandrake's configuration is similar, except that it uses -1 instead of 7100. The second line is not the default for any major Linux distribution. It tells the computer to look for a font server on another computer—port 7100 on the `fontserv.example.com` computer in this example. One computer can include several font servers in its font path.

Using a networked font server has certain advantages. Most importantly, it can simplify font configuration on a large network. Rather than install the same fonts on many computers, you can install them on one system and configure all the X servers on a network to use fonts from the font server computer. Unfortunately, this approach also has its disadvantages. One problem is that applications can misbehave or hang if the font server becomes inaccessible or is restarted. Another problem is that networked font servers don't work well with applications that do font smoothing. Such applications are becoming more common, so relying on a font server for important fonts is becoming increasingly undesirable. Note that these problems aren't as important for *local* font servers, as used by Mandrake and Red Hat. Network problems are unlikely to make their font servers inaccessible, and local programs can still find locally installed fonts for font smoothing, even if they're also delivered via a font server.

Whether you run a font server locally or in a network-accessible manner, you must configure it. The most common font server for Linux is `xfs`, which ships with X. This server is usually configured through the `/etc/X11/fs/config` file. You set the font path in this file through the `catalogue` line, which lists font directories separated by commas on one or more lines, as in:

```
catalogue = /usr/X11R6/lib/X11/fonts/URW,
            /usr/local/fonts/tt
```

If you're setting up a font server on a distribution that doesn't normally run one, you must launch the font server by creating a new startup script, as described in Chapter 9, "Bypassing Automatic Configurations to Gain Control;" or you may find a SysV startup script for the font server that's currently inactive and be able to activate it.

If your distribution uses a font server by default and you want to open it up for other systems to use, you should check for a couple of lines in the `/etc/X11/fs/config` file:

```
no-listen = tcp
port = -1
```

Either option makes the font server inaccessible to other systems. If you find the first, you should comment out the line. If you find the second option, change `-1` to `7100` and alter the `FontPath` entry in `XF86Config` appropriately. Mandrake overrides the port number in its `xfs` SysV startup script, `/etc/rc.d/init.d/xfs`. Therefore, you must also change the references to `-port -1` in this file to `-port 7100`. After making these changes, you must restart the font server. If you changed the `XF86Config` file, you must also restart X, or at least use `xset` to reset X's font path to reflect your changes.

In order to serve fonts, `xfs` requires that font directories be prepared just as they are for an X server. Therefore, you should consult the earlier section, "Setting Up a Font Directory," for information on this task.

NOTE   *Versions of* `xfs` *delivered with XFree86 3.x and earlier don't understand TrueType fonts. If you're using an older Linux distribution and want to serve TrueType fonts, you can use a version of* `xfs` *from a more recent distribution, or you can use a TrueType-enabled font server, such as* `xfsft` (`http://www.dcs.ed.ac.uk/home/jec/programs/xfsft/`) *or* `xfstt` (`http://developer.berlios.de/projects/xfstt/`). *If you're using a recent distribution that ships with XFree86 4.x but you must still use XFree86 3.x for your video card, you can use the* `xfs` *that ships with your distribution in order to use TrueType fonts.*

Using Font Smoothing

Font smoothing, aka *anti-aliasing*, is a font display technique in which some pixels that fall along the edge of a character are displayed as gray rather than black or white. The effect is that the text appears to be less jagged than it otherwise would. Some people like this effect, but others find that it makes text look blurry. Unfortunately, font smoothing in Linux is quite confusing because several approaches to the task have been developed since XFree86 4.0.2 was released. As a result, configuring font smoothing can be quite frustrating because what works on one system or environment doesn't work on another. What's more, the same tools that deliver smoothed fonts can also deliver fonts without font smoothing. An increasing number of programs are using these tools in addition to or even instead of X's traditional fonts, so configuring fonts to work with these tools can be important even if you don't want to use smoothed fonts.

FONT SMOOTHING PRINCIPLES

Until recently, X hasn't supported font smoothing at all. A few X applications, such as Adobe's Acrobat Reader, have implemented font smoothing by bypassing X's normal font-rendering mechanisms, but for the most part, Linux users have had no choice but to use unsmoothed fonts. This situation began to change with XFree86 4.0.2, which used a library known as Xft 1.0 to implement font smoothing. This library is an interface tool between X and the FreeType library (http://www.freetype.org), which was originally developed as a TrueType rendering system, although it now also handles Type 1 and other font formats. Unfortunately, Xft has undergone major changes with subsequent versions (1.1 and 2.0), which has contributed to font-smoothing chaos in Linux. Configuration methods vary greatly, and it's easy to find yourself with a system in which different applications deliver different sets of fonts because one program uses Xft, and hence Xft-delivered fonts, while another program uses X's traditional unsmoothed font-rendering mechanisms.

NOTE   *A few programs call FreeType directly, without the use of Xft. For instance, WINE (the Windows emulator) and OpenOffice.org both use FreeType independently of Xft. Such programs have their own font configuration systems, so you may need to install the same fonts half a dozen or more times. With any luck, Xft will become popular and obviate the need for some of these installations in the future.*

In order to use smoothed fonts, an application calls the Xft libraries, which are typically installed along with X in a package called xshared, xlibs, XFree86-libs, or something similar. These libraries require direct access to font files, so you must normally point them to your font directories, as described in the next section, "Configuring Fonts in Xft." Once that's done, you can access smoothed fonts; however, the procedure for doing so varies from one program to another. Both the KDE and GNOME environments provide tools to help configure fonts, but these settings may not apply outside of the target environments. What's more, some programs work *only* with fonts delivered via Xft. This shortcoming is particularly common in GNOME applications. The result is that these programs won't work with fonts served via a standard X font server, although if the same fonts are made available via Xft, you may not notice this problem. Other programs can serve both smoothed fonts delivered from Xft and unsmoothed fonts delivered via X or a font server. When you use such a program, you may notice that some fonts are smoothed and others aren't. Some programs provide program-specific smoothed font configuration outside of the GNOME or KDE settings, so if you find that some programs don't use font smoothing, you may want to check the configuration options for the programs that don't deliver smoothed fonts.

CONFIGURING FONTS IN XFT

Xft font configuration varies with the Xft version. No matter the version, the most important steps are similar to those required for configuring X's standard font access, but the details differ.

Configuring Fonts in Xft 1.x

Xft 1.0 and 1.1 are configured using a file called XftConfig, which is typically located in /etc/X11. The most important lines in this file set the Xft font path using the dir keyword:

```
dir "/usr/X11R6/lib/X11/fonts/Type1"
dir "/usr/X11R6/lib/X11/fonts/TrueType"
```

Typically, you point to all the directories on your normal X font path that hold outline fonts. Although Xft can deliver bitmap fonts, it's most frequently used only for outline fonts, so directories that hold bitmap fonts are usually omitted from the Xft font path. If you've added your own fonts to some other directory, such as `/usr/local/fonts/tt`, you can edit the `XftConfig` file to reflect this fact.

Individuals may also specify font directories in a file called `.xftconfig` in their home directories. Typically, this file contains just `dir` lines, formatted just like equivalent lines in the system-wide `XftConfig` file. This setup enables users to add fonts that other users might not want or need.

Xft 1.x uses a file called `XftCache` in each font directory as an index to the directory's font files. This file is similar in concept to the `fonts.dir` file used by XFree86 or `xfs`, but the two files have different formats. If your directory doesn't have this file, Xft will create a file called `~/.xftcache` in your home directory when you try to perform certain key operations; this file then substitutes for `XftCache` files in your font directories. If you prefer to create a global file for all users, type **xftcache ./** as root in each font directory; this command creates the requisite cache file. Alternatively, you can type **xftcache** with no directory specification to have it create the `XftCache` file in each directory on the Xft font path.

Xft tries its best to detect changes you make to your font directories as you make them, so you shouldn't need to restart X when you add fonts. Typing **xftcache** may help, but it isn't strictly required, because Xft will create an `~/.xftcache` file if necessary. Running applications may not notice changes to available fonts until you restart them, though.

Configuring Fonts in Xft 2.0

Xft 2.0 uses a completely different type of configuration than does Xft 1.x. The 2.0 version of the library uses a configuration file called `fonts.conf`, which is typically stored in `/etc/fonts`. This file is actually an Extensible Markup Language (XML) file, so if you're familiar with XML, you should be able to parse much of its content. Most of the file consists of aliases for and elaborated information about specific fonts—for instance, marking Times as a serif font and Helvetica as a sans serif font. Near the top of the file, though, you'll find several directories listed between `<dir>` and `</dir>` codes, like this:

```
<dir>/usr/X11R6/lib/X11/fonts</dir>
<dir>/usr/share/fonts</dir>
```

These lines tell Xft to look for fonts in the specified directories and all their subdirectories. For instance, the first line shown here handles all the standard X font locations, and the second line handles `/usr/share/fonts` and its subdirectories.

It's not uncommon to see a directory such as `~/.fonts` included in the `fonts.conf` file. This entry enables users to add fonts by placing them in their `~/.fonts` directories. Xft 2.0 also looks for a secondary configuration file called `~/.fonts.conf`, so users can fine-tune their configurations.

Xft 2.0 uses a configuration file called `font.cache-1`. This file's format is the same as that of the `XftCache` file used by Xft 1.x, and can be created with a utility called Fontconfig. Type **fc-cache /font/dir**, where `/font/dir` is the directory in which you've stored fonts, to generate a `fonts.cache-1` file in `/font/dir` that describes the fonts in the directory. If you don't do this, Xft will create a `.fonts.cache-1` file in each user's home directory that replaces the `fonts.cache-1` files. As with Xft 1.x, version 2.0 tries to spot changes to the font directories and implement them as soon as possible, so if you add or change files, you may see `~/.fonts.cache-1` files appear or grow.

If you want to use Xft, but don't want it to apply font smoothing, you can tell the system to deliver unsmoothed fonts. To do so, add the following lines to your `/etc/fonts/fonts.conf` file:

```
<match target="font">
    <edit name="antialias" mode="assign">
        <bool>false</bool>
    </edit>
</match>
```

If you want to use font smoothing for most, but not all, fonts, you can disable smoothing on a font-by-font basis using similar code. For instance, the following lines disable font smoothing for the Bitstream Vera Sans font:

```
<match target="font">
    <test qual="any" name="family">
        <string>Bitstream Vera Sans</string>
    </test>
    <edit name="antialias" mode="assign">
        <bool>false</bool>
    </edit>
</match>
```

Similar options are accessible from GUI tools for particular applications, as described in the next section, "Using Smoothed Fonts in Applications." Setting these options in the global `fonts.conf` file may be more convenient, though. The GUI methods also don't support font-by-font changes, as does the `fonts.conf` method.

USING SMOOTHED FONTS IN APPLICATIONS

KDE provides a pair of tools in its Control Center that relate to fonts. You can launch the Control Center from an item in the K Menu from the KDE Panel, or you can type **kcontrol** in an **xterm** to launch the program. The first tool is the Appearance & Themes ➤ Fonts tool, which is shown in Figure 16.3. (This tool may be accessed under a different name in some distributions' KDE implementations.) The upper portion of this tool provides settings for the font you want to use for assorted common elements, such as the default ("general") font, the font used in menus, and so on. Click Choose to change any of these fonts. The bottom portion of this tool provides font smoothing options, in the Anti-Aliasing area. Check the Use Anti-Aliasing for Fonts option to enable font smoothing in KDE applications. You can also select a couple of sub-options. First, you can exclude a range of font sizes from font smoothing. You might do this if you like font smoothing in general, but not at some font sizes. Second, you can check the Use Sub-Pixel Hinting box to use this technique, which can improve the appearance of fonts on some liquid crystal display (LCD) monitors.

The second tool available from the KDE Control Center is accessible from the System Administration ➤ Font Installer index option. This tool helps automate font management. By default, it allows you to install fonts in the `~/.kde/share/fonts` directory and its subdirectories. You can use this tool to copy fonts to this directory, whereupon the system automatically creates a `fonts.dir` file and tells various font systems, such as Xft and X, to use the fonts in this directory.

FIGURE 16.3

KDE provides tools to enable font smoothing for KDE applications.

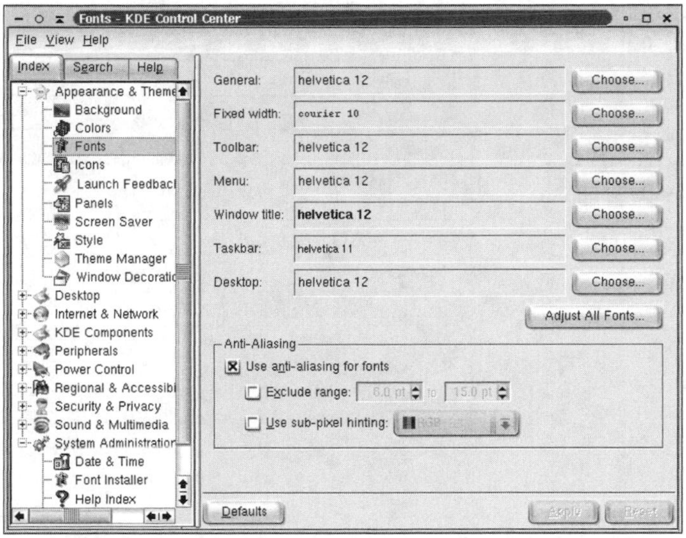

NOTE *The KDE Control Center's Font Installer sometimes holds files open after accessing them. This feature means that installing a font directly from a CD-ROM may make it impossible to unmount the CD-ROM. KDE typically closes the files after a minute or two, so this problem corrects itself if you give it some time.*

GNOME provides a font configuration tool known as Font Preferences. You can launch it by selecting the Applications ➤ Desktop Preferences ➤ Font menu item from the GNOME Panel or by typing **gnome-font-properties** in an xterm window. The result is the window shown in Figure 16.4. As with the equivalent KDE tool, this program enables you to set font preferences for applications that use it—mostly GNOME programs. You can set the default application font, the font used by desktop icons, and so on. The Font Rendering area includes options related to font smoothing, although that term isn't used. The Monochrome option disables font smoothing and the remaining options enable it, but with variations that work well for different types of displays. In particular, the Subpixel Smoothing (LCDs) option is worth trying on LCD monitors and notebooks. Clicking Details brings up another dialog box with more options, such as the extent to which GNOME applications use hinting and some details related to the subpixel smoothing option.

Other programs can use Xft independently of KDE or GNOME, and so they may have their own font configuration tools. Even KDE and GNOME programs may have application-specific font-setting tools. These options may set the font used in a document, as in a word processor's or web browser's display; or they may set display options, such as the font used in dialog boxes or menus. It's not always obvious whether a program is using Xft for such options, though; a program can use X fonts, Xft fonts, or even fonts it renders itself or by calling FreeType directly.

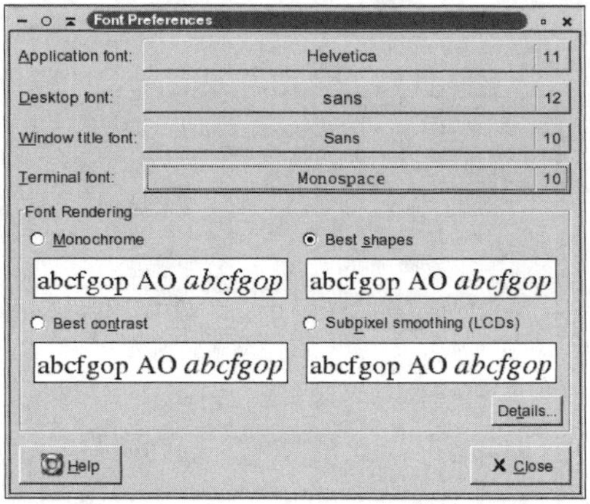

FIGURE 16.4

GNOME's Font Preferences dialog box enables you to select GNOME fonts and set font-smoothing options.

Using Card-Specific Optimizations

Chances are your distribution configured X well enough to run with your hardware when you installed it. If not, or if the configuration works but doesn't work as well as you'd like, you may need to tweak the XF86Config file, either directly or using a configuration tool. This section covers some of the configuration tools that are available as well as two types of tweaks you may need to make: changing the video card driver and activating 3D acceleration features. The next section, "Creating a Custom Video Mode," covers a more extensive tweak you may want to try.

Using an X Configuration Tool

Several X configuration tools exist to help you get X up and running. Most Linux distributions run one of these tools at installation time, but you can run them after this point if you're not satisfied with the initial configuration. These configuration tools are:

XFree86   The XFree86 4.x program itself, XFree86, can generate an initial configuration file. Type **XFree86 -configure** as root when X is *not* running, and the program will produce a file called /root/XF86Config.new, based on its probes of your hardware. This file will probably not contain an optimal configuration, though, so you may have to tweak it by hand or with another tool.

xf86cfg   This program, shown in Figure 16.5, is a popular GUI tool for configuring XFree86 4.x. To configure a component, right-click its icon and select Configure from the resulting context menu. If you launch the program with the -textmode option, it runs in text mode, so X need not be running to use the program.

xf86config   This program is a fairly simple and inflexible but effective text-based tool. It asks you a series of questions and generates an XF86Config file based on your responses. Unlike most X configuration tools, xf86config can generate configuration files for both XFree86 3.x and XFree86 4.x. Which one it generates is system-dependent. On most modern Linux distributions, it should create an XFree86 4.x file.

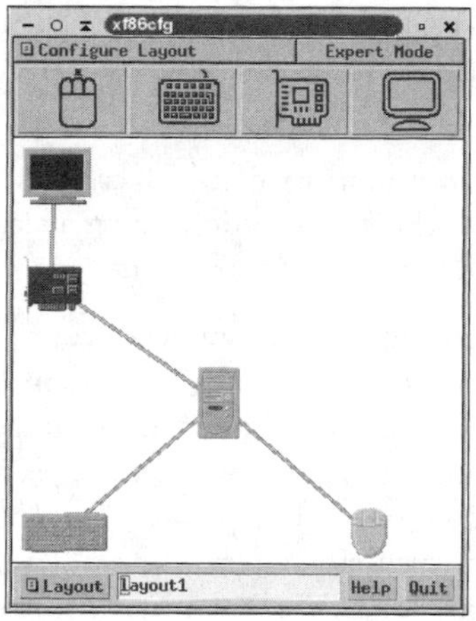

FIGURE 16.5

The xf86cfg program is a popular GUI tool for setting up XFree86 4.x.

There are also tools for configuring XFree86 3.x, such as Xconfigurator and XF86Setup. Some distributions include custom tools that run during system installation, but others use a standard tool for this task. In some cases, the installer starts X using a generic VGA or SVGA driver in order to let you use an X-based configuration tool during system installation.

In any event, X configuration tools ask you for the basic information described earlier, in "The Structure of XF86Config," such as your mouse type and video card model. This last option is particularly important; an incorrect video card selection will most likely result in the inability to start X. In some cases, X may start, but performance will be poor.

Using the Correct Video Driver

Under XFree86 4.x, you set the video driver in the Device section, which typically looks like this:

```
Section "Device"
    Identifier "device1"
    VendorName "ATI"
    BoardName "ATI Mach64 Utah"
    Driver "ati"
EndSection
```

The Identifier line names the device so that it may be referred to by name in the Screen section. The VendorName and BoardName options are names for your own use; you can set them to whatever values you like. The Driver line is the single most important line in the Device section because it sets the driver that XFree86 uses for the video card. To determine which driver to use for your card, consult the XFree86 documentation, and particularly the device page at http://www.xfree86.org /current/Status.html. This page includes links for many different video chipset manufacturers. For instance, if you have a Trident chipset, click the Trident Microsystems link. The resulting page provides information in three categories:

3.3.6 This section tells you how to use XFree86 3.3.6 (the last of the 3.x series) with the video card. Information includes the name of the X server executable to run and a list of cards or chipsets that work with that server.

4.3.0   This section's name is likely to change to reflect the current software version by the time you read this. It summarizes the driver name you provide on the `Driver` line and lists the cards or chipsets supported by the driver.

Summary   This section provides a summary of which cards or chipsets are supported by XFree86 3.3.6 and 4.x. Be sure to check this section; you may learn that your card has substantially better support in one version of XFree86 or another.

In most cases, you can get XFree86 4.x to work well with your card, but you must normally be able to identify the chipset the card uses, or at least the chipset's manufacturer. (Many drivers can identify the specific chipset model; for instance, the `ati` driver supports and can correctly identify most ATI chipsets, so you may not need to know your exact chipset model number.) Chapter 1, "Optimizing System Architecture Usage," provides pointers on identifying chipsets.

Because XFree86 4.x uses a modular driver system, some video card manufacturers have begun to provide XFree86 4.x drivers for their video cards. You may want to check with the manufacturer to see if this is true of your video card, particularly if the card is a new model. XFree86's developers usually can't produce accelerated drivers for a video card until several months after it's released, so manufacturer-provided drivers might produce better results initially.

Two drivers deserve special attention: `fbdev` and `vga`. These drivers enable Linux to work with a display even if a hardware-specific driver isn't available. The `fbdev` driver works with a *frame buffer* device, which is an abstraction of the video hardware provided by the Linux kernel. The `fbdev` driver isn't often used on IA-32 systems, but it's fairly common on other platforms. The `vga` driver works by using lowest-common-denominator hardware standards, much as full-screen games do. You might try one or both of these drivers if you can't get your video card to work in any other way, but these drivers are limited. Most importantly, they're likely to be slower than a regular driver. They may also support only a limited range of resolutions. The `fbdev` driver requires kernel support for your video card.

Using 3D Acceleration

If you have a video card with 3D acceleration features, you may want to enable those features in X. You won't see any improvement in performance when using most programs, though; 3D acceleration is most commonly used by first-person-perspective games. A few other programs, such as 3D modeling tools, may also use these features.

When displaying a 3D object, a video card must account for many visual effects. For instance, where is the light source? What is the object's texture, and how does this interact with the light? How reflective is the object? 3D video cards include circuitry to help compute these effects. If a card lacks that circuitry, the computer's CPU must take over part of the job. This will reduce the performance of the 3D application, and may yield inferior results, as well. Video cards may use a variety of techniques to render 3D objects, and these techniques may produce better or worse results.

As with many hardware features, a series of software layers exist between a video card's 3D acceleration features and software that uses these features. In the Linux world, the biggest chunk of this interface is implemented in one of several implementations of OpenGL (`http://www.opengl.org`). Specific OpenGL implementations for Linux include:

Xi Graphics' Summit   Xi Graphics (`http://www.xig.com`) markets a line of commercial X servers that can replace XFree86. Some of these products, known as the Summit series, include OpenGL support.

Mesa   This package is an open source implementation of the OpenGL specification. You can learn more from the project's web page, `http://mesa3d.sourceforge.net`. This package is used by XFree86's official 3D system, DRI.

If you want to use 3D acceleration features, you must configure both the Linux kernel and XFree86. In the kernel, you must add DRI support. This support is present in the Character Devices section. You must activate the main DRI support area and compile support for your specific card. If your card isn't supported, you'll get only unaccelerated 3D features from 3D applications, even if your video card includes 3D circuitry.

In `XF86Config`, you must load two modules in the `Module` section:

```
Load  "glx"
Load  "dri"
```

You can also configure a `DRI` section, which may look something like this:

```
Section "DRI"
    Group       "video"
    Mode        0660
EndSection
```

This section uses Unix-style permissions to control access to the 3D features. In this example, those features are given permissions of `0660` and ownership by the `video` group—in other words, only users who belong to the video group can use the 3D acceleration features. If you want to allow anybody to use those features, you could omit the `Group` specification and change `0660` to `0666`.

Once you've set up these features, you should install the Mesa package from your distribution or from the Mesa website. To test it, install the Mesa demo programs (they're often in a package called `Mesa-demos` or something similar) and try running one or more demos from this system, such as `bounce` or `gears`. Be sure to run the demos from an `xterm` window so that you can look for messages from the programs. For instance, if the program reports that the `XFree86-DRI` extension is missing, it means that your kernel's DRI module didn't load. Perhaps your video card isn't supported, or perhaps the module just didn't load for some reason. Try loading the module manually, as described in Chapter 1, or build the driver directly into the kernel and reboot.

Creating a Custom Video Mode

One problem that vexes some Linux users is getting X to display acceptably on a monitor. The issue here isn't one of graphics manipulation speed, color depth, or the like; it's getting the best resolution, getting the best refresh rate, or centering the display properly on the screen. Fortunately, X is very flexible in its handling of displays, so it's possible to get it to do just about anything you might want. Unfortunately, doing so can be tricky, because it involves editing the video configuration at a low level. Fortunately, there are tools to help you do this.

WARNING   *Creating a custom video mode poses many of the same risks as setting the horizontal and vertical refresh rates of your monitor at random. Monitors made in the late 1990s and beyond usually ignore incorrect inputs, but earlier monitors may be damaged if you feed them incorrect inputs. Be extremely cautious when you create custom video modes.*

Why Create a Custom Video Mode?

In most cases, X starts and works correctly at a reasonable resolution. If you just want to change to another common resolution (such as 1024 × 768 rather than 1280 × 1024), you can do so by editing the Modes line in the Display subsection of the Screen section of XF86Config. Remove an unwanted resolution, add a new one, or change the ordering. (XFree86 tries the resolutions in order, from left to right.) If your desired resolution appears before the one you're seeing and if it's a standard resolution, chances are your monitor can't handle it—or at least, X thinks that your monitor can't handle it, given the HorizSync and VertRefresh values you gave in the Monitor section. If you're sure your monitor is capable of handling the video mode, double-check those values and restart X if you change them.

Sometimes, though, the default video modes just aren't enough. You might want to create a custom video mode for several reasons, including:

Correcting Display Centering or Image Size One common problem, particularly on multiboot systems, is that the display may not be centered or may not be the proper size. (In this context, *size* refers to the physical size of the image, not its resolution in pixels.) For instance, if you adjust the display to be centered in Windows, and if you then boot to Linux, the display may appear physically shorter and shifted to the left. You can correct this matter by tweaking your configuration, as described in the upcoming section, "Tweaking a Modeline." If you're otherwise satisfied with the resolution and refresh rate, this is the simplest type of change you can make. Many monitors can remember multiple settings, though, which may obviate the need for this sort of adjustment.

Custom Resolution You may want to run X at an unusual resolution. For instance, I have a 19-inch monitor, and the standard resolution for a monitor of this size is 1280 × 1024; however, this resolution creates pixels that are slightly wider than they are high, which can distort graphics. To get pixels that are closer to square, I use a custom 1360 × 1024 display. You can set just about any resolution you like, though, within the limits of your monitor's and video card's capabilities.

Custom Refresh Rate Depending on your resolution, chances are that your monitor is capable of delivering a slightly higher overall refresh rate than a standard video mode delivers. XFree86 selects the highest refresh rate available from the modes it has at hand, but it's usually possible to get a slightly higher refresh rate from a system. For instance, on my monitor, the standard 1280 × 1024 display runs at 85Hz; but by creating a custom 1360 × 1024 display, I was also able to boost the refresh rate to 105Hz, reducing eye strain from looking at the display.

You should realize that these reasons for creating a custom video mode apply mostly to traditional cathode ray tube (CRT) monitors, not to the newer LCD monitors that are becoming popular on desktops and have long been the standard on laptops. LCDs have a fixed number of pixels, and so work best at a specific resolution, which is almost always a standard size. When they work with analog outputs, they support a very limited set of refresh rates, again including standard values, and there's little benefit to providing a different refresh rate to LCDs; they don't change their scan rate in the way that CRTs do. The main exception to this rule would be if you have an LCD with an unusual display size, but such screens are quite rare.

If you want to proceed with creating a custom video mode, the next step is in learning a bit more about *modelines*, which are numerical descriptions of the video display. You'll then be able to use a tool to help compute an appropriate modeline, insert it into your XF86Config file, and use it. You can then tweak the modeline so that it creates a display of the appropriate size and placement.

Creating a Modeline

The key to X video modes lies in the modeline, which may reside in either the `Monitor` section of `XF86Config` (in which case it applies to just one monitor) or in a separate `Modes` section (in which case any monitor can use it). A typical modeline looks like this:

```
# 1024x768 @ 85 Hz, 70.24 kHz hsync
Modeline "1024x768" 98.9  1024 1056 1216 1408  768 782 788 822  -HSync -VSync
```

The first line is a comment that describes the effect of the modeline—in this case, it creates a 1024 × 768 display at 85Hz, which is a common video mode. The second line is the modeline itself, and it's broken up into several parts:

Modeline   Every modeline begins with this keyword. An alternative form uses the keyword `Mode` and breaks the entry across multiple lines. This form is more readable but less common than the single-line `Modeline` entry.

Modeline Name   The modeline name appears in quotes—`"1024x768"` in this example. Modelines are typically named after the resolution they create, sometimes with a refresh rate appended, as in `"1024x768@85"`. You refer to the modeline by name in the `Modes` line in the `Screen` section. If two modelines have the same name, X uses the one that produces the maximum refresh rate, within your monitor's limits, as defined by the `HorizSync` and `VertRefresh` values in the `Monitor` section, and your video card's maximum dot clock.

Dot Clock   The number after the modeline name (`98.9` in this example) is the *dot clock*. This number is a measure of the rate of data flow through the video card when using the mode. All video cards have maximum supported dot clocks, and if a modeline exceeds this value, X won't use it.

Horizontal Timings   The next four numbers of the modeline (`1024 1056 1216 1408` in this example) represent the horizontal timings for the video mode. The first number is the number of pixels in the actual display. The next three numbers represent the start, stop, and total number of pulses sent to create a single horizontal line of the display.

Vertical Timings   The next four numbers of the modeline (`768 782 788 822` in this example) are analogous to the horizontal timings, but they provide vertical timing information. The first number is the vertical resolution and the next three numbers provide start, stop, and totals for vertical timing pulses.

Miscellaneous Flags   The modeline may include some miscellaneous flags, such as `-HSync -VSync` in this example. These particular flags tell XFree86 what polarity to use for the horizontal and vertical sync signals. Other common flags include `Interlace` (to set an interlaced video mode), `DoubleScan` (to set a mode in which every scan line is doubled), and `Composite` (to set composite sync). As a general rule, you shouldn't worry about these flags unless you're intimately familiar with your video hardware.

Creating a modeline by hand is a tedious proposition at best and involves crunching through numbers to create the desired timings and dot clock value. Fortunately, there are tools to help you do the job. One of these is the XFree86 Modeline Generator web page, `http://xtiming.sourceforge.net`, which is shown in Figure 16.6.

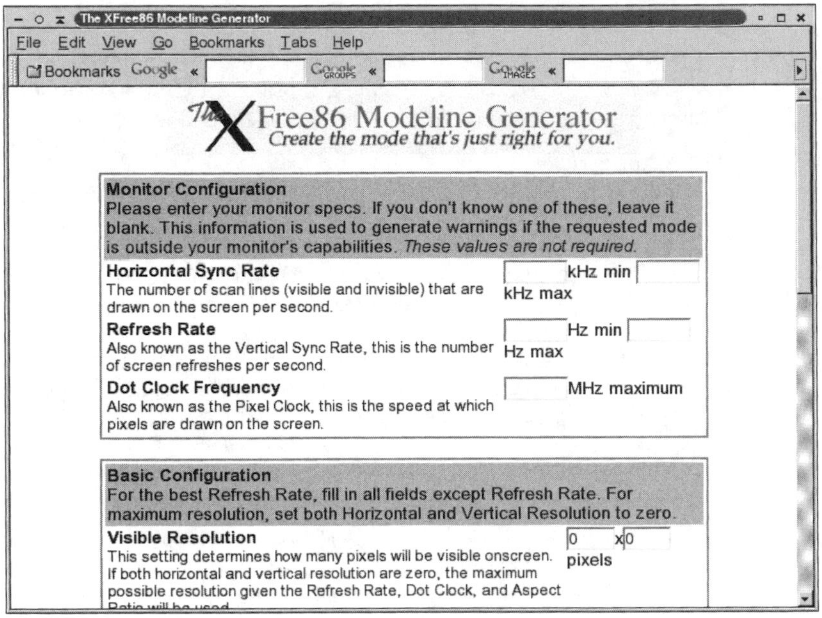

FIGURE 16.6

The XFree86 Modeline Generator page performs the tedious calculations required to create a custom video mode.

To use this tool, you need several pieces of information:

Monitor's Refresh Rates   These values are the ones provided on the HorizSync and VertRefresh lines in XF86Config. You need four numbers in total: the minimum and maximum for both horizontal and vertical timings.

Video Card's Maximum Dot Clock   The page needs to know the maximum dot clock value your video card can handle. To learn what your video hardware's maximum dot clock is, shut down X and type **X -probeonly &> probe.txt** and then peruse the probe.txt file for a line that specifies the maximum clock rate, such as Maximum clock: 199 MHz or PixClock max 80Mhz. Some systems place this information in a log file, such as /var/log/XFree86.0.log. Be sure to run the test with the video card connected to the monitor you intend to use; some configurations report the maximum dot clock the monitor can handle.

Desired Resolution   You may already know what resolution you want to use. Alternatively, you can provide your target refresh rate and let the tool compute the maximum resolution your system will support.

Desired Overall Refresh Rate   You may already know your target refresh rate. This value must be somewhere between the monitor's minimum and maximum refresh rates, but depending on your resolution, it's possible that your monitor won't be able to support anywhere near the high value of the VertRefresh range. Alternatively, if you know the resolution you want to support, you can have the tool compute the maximum refresh rate your hardware will support.

Once you have this information, enter it into the fields in the XFree86 Modeline Generator web page. You must enter values for all five fields in the Monitor Configuration area. In the Basic Configuration area, you can enter values for the Visible Resolution, Refresh Rate, or both. If you leave any value set at 0, the system computes the optimum value given other constraints. The lower half of the Basic Configuration area (not visible in Figure 16.6) provides some additional options. For instance, you can tell the system to constrain your aspect ratio to 4:3, 16:9, or some other ratio, to produce square pixels on common monitor sizes; and you can tell it to create an interlaced video mode. When you're done, scroll to the bottom of the page and click the Calculate Modeline button. The page refreshes, but this time it displays your custom modeline at the top. For instance, when I entered horizontal sync rates of 27 through 115, vertical refresh rates of 50 through 160, a maximum dot clock of 230, a desired refresh rate of 100Hz, and a 4:3 aspect ratio constraint, the system spat out the following modeline:

```
Modeline "1296x972@100" 230.00 1296 1328 2200 2232 972 988 1004 1021
```

Experience with your monitor might enable you to further tweak this modeline, but doing so requires experimentation. For instance, the system whose specifications I entered to create this modeline is the one I mentioned earlier, which runs at 1360×1024 with a 105Hz refresh rate—better than the modeline created by the web page. Creating this modeline took several hours of experimentation, though. If you're interested in such fine-tuning, consult the XFree86 Video Timings HOWTO (`http://tldp.org/HOWTO/XFree86-Video-Timings-HOWTO/`). Note that this HOWTO claims it's now obsolete except for certain limited situations. In my experience, though, XFree86 often doesn't optimize video modes as well as a person can, even when those conditions don't apply.

Using a Custom Modeline

Once you've obtained a new modeline, using it is fairly straightforward:

1. Copy the modeline into the `XF86Config` file. The simplest configuration is to put the modeline in the `Monitor` section for the monitor with which you'll use it. If you used the XFree86 Modeline Generator web page, you can use a cut-and-paste operation to move the modeline from the web page directly into `XF86Config`.

2. Add a reference to the new modeline in the appropriate `Display` subsection of your `Screen` section. For instance, if your Modes line reads `Modes "1024x768" "800x600"` and you want to add the modeline described earlier, you would change this line to read `Modes "1296x972@100" "1024x768" "800x600"`.

3. Save the `XF86Config` file and exit from X, if it's running.

4. From a text-mode login, type **startx** to test the new video mode.

If your video mode works, then you're in business. It may be that it works but produces a display that's misaligned, too large, or too small, though. You can probably use monitor controls to get the display to appear as you want, but you may want to adjust the modeline instead. If so, read on....

Tweaking a Modeline

If you don't want to use your monitor's controls to center your display or make it fill the screen, you can tweak the modeline to do so. Changing the video timing elements of the modeline will alter where on the screen the image begins and ends. You can experiment randomly, but a much better solution is to use a tool to help with the process. This tool ships with recent versions of XFree86, and it is called xvidtune. To use it, type its name in an xterm window. The result resembles Figure 16.7. The program also displays a warning concerning the possibility of damaging your monitor. I've already mentioned this possibility twice before in this chapter, so consider yourself amply warned. That said, minor tweaks to the position or size of your display are unlikely to cause problems.

FIGURE 16.7

The xvidtune program enables you to tweak your video mode.

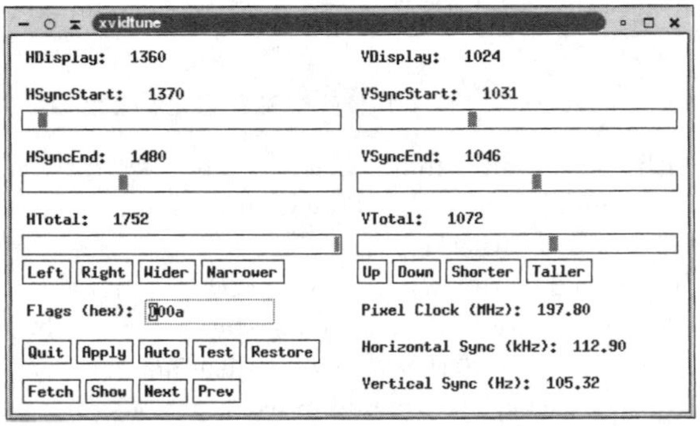

To use xvidtune, click the eight adjustment buttons—Left, Right, Wider, Narrower, Up, Down, Shorter, or Taller. You won't see your adjustments until you click the Test button, which initiates a five-second test of the new settings. Keep changing the settings and performing tests until you're satisfied with the results. You can then click the Show button to have xvidtune display a modeline for the modified settings in the xterm from which you launched it. You can copy that modeline into your XF86Config file, as described in the earlier section, "Using a Custom Modeline." You may want to give the modeline a slightly different name, such as "1024x768-tweak", so that you can be sure you use it rather than the original modeline.

Summary

X is a powerful GUI environment, and Linux distributions usually do a good job of implementing a basic X configuration. Some X details, though, may benefit from post-installation modification. Fonts represent one area of potential improvement, particularly if you have a personal collection of fonts you want to use. Video drivers, including 3D acceleration features, may also benefit from modification, although Linux usually sets the basic video driver correctly. Finally, X is very flexible in its video mode settings; you can create a custom video mode that runs at just about any resolution or refresh rate you like, within the limits of your hardware. Setting a custom video mode can be tricky, but some tools can help you accomplish these goals.

## Chapter 17

Protecting Your System with Backups

EVERYBODY WHO'S USED A computer for long has experience with Murphy's Law: "If anything can go wrong, it will." With computers, the worst thing that can happen is complete loss of the computer and all its data—say, from hardware theft, a fire, or what have you. One step down from this disaster is complete loss of the data, but not most of the hardware. For instance, the hard disk might go bad, or you might accidentally destroy the data through careless use of low-level disk utilities.

Fortunately, you can protect yourself from much of the pain associated with these events. Backing up your data is a critical part of this protection. You should put some time and effort into planning a backup strategy, though. This planning begins with picking a backup medium (tape, removable disk, and optical media are the three most popular choices). You must then pick software for creating your backups. Performing whole-system backups is usually fairly straightforward. If you want to minimize the time you spend on backups, you can perform incremental backups so that you don't need to back up the same unchanging files time and time again. Finally, no backup procedure will do you any good if you don't have a way to restore the backup, so you must plan for this eventuality, as well.

WARNING   *Making a backup is a good practice, but for the best security, you should make multiple backups and store at least one backup off-site. Doing so will ensure that you can restore a backup even if one backup fails or if a disaster such as a fire destroys everything in the building housing the computer.*

Picking the Right Backup Medium

The first choice in backing up your computer is picking an appropriate backup medium. Just about any data storage device can be used for backups, but some devices are more appropriate than others. Typically, the greater the capacity of the medium, the better—although for some purposes (such as backing up individual projects), a low-capacity medium may be just fine. I break backup media into three categories: tapes, removable disks, and optical media (CD-R and related formats).

NOTE   *Chapter 2, "Improving Disk Performance," includes a rundown of many specific media types. Pay particular attention to the "Moving Data via Sneakernet: Removable Media" section and especially Table 2.5, which summarizes many of the choices in specific products.*

Pros and Cons of Tape

Tape might be the most common backup medium. Tape drives vary in capacity from a few megabytes to 160GB uncompressed, so a single tape is often large enough to hold a backup of an entire computer. The tapes themselves are also usually fairly inexpensive, ranging in price from a few dollars to a few tens of dollars, depending on the type and capacity. The initial prices for tape drives can range from about $250 to several thousand dollars. Many of the multithousand-dollar drives are actually *changers*. They can automatically swap tapes in and out, effectively increasing the drive's capacity to several times the capacity of a single tape, often in the terabyte range. Even aside from the multi-tape needs of a changer, a typical tape backup system is likely to need between half a dozen and several dozen tapes, depending upon tape capacity, backup frequency, and how long you plan to keep the backups. Between a drive and enough tapes to last for a year or two, you should plan to spend the better part of $1,000 on a low-end tape system capable of storing 10–40GB uncompressed. The total cost goes up as the system's capacity does, but the cost to store 100GB or so probably won't be substantially over $1,500.

WARNING   Tape drive manufacturers often quote their drives' estimated capacities with compression enabled. The amount of compression you get varies depending on the data you back up, so take these estimates with a grain of salt. Uncompressed capacity is usually about half the claimed compressed capacity.

A variety of tape formats are available. These formats differ in capacity range, price, reliability, and features. Table 17.1 summarizes some of the characteristics of some of the more popular formats. The prices are typical of what I found advertised by several web merchants in early 2003; they might change by the time you read this. The capacities and prices (including media prices) are for drives that were available when I checked websites; most format families include older lower-capacity variants. Some drives can use these older media, and these media may cost less than indicated in Table 17.1. This table summarizes the prices for single-tape units; changers for most formats are available, but they cost more than indicated.

TABLE 17.1: VITAL STATISTICS FOR SEVERAL POPULAR TAPE FORMATS

DRIVE TYPE	UNCOMPRESSED CAPACITY	DRIVE COST	MEDIA COST	SPEED
8mm	20–60GB	$2,000–3,500	$40–80	3–12MB/s
AIT	35–100GB	$700–3,500	$55–120	3–12MB/s
DAT	4–20GB	$450–1,200	$6–30	1.5–5MB/s
DLT and SuperDLT	40–160GB	$1,000–$4,500	$50–170	3–16MB/s
Travan	10–20GB	$250–550	$35–50	0.6–2MB/s
VXA	33–80GB	$550–1,300	$70–100	3–6MB/s

Travan and its predecessor, Quarter-Inch Cartridge (QIC), have traditionally dominated the low end of the tape drive backup arena, in part due to the low cost of the drives. Although it's traditionally been aimed at a slightly higher market, Digital Audio Tape (DAT) is now attractive for low-end uses, due in part to the low cost of DAT media. Formats such as AIT and DLT, which are available in 100GB or higher capacities, are attractive for network backup servers and even workstations with unusually large storage needs, but the cost of these drives and their media can be prohibitive for smaller workstations.

Most tape drives use SCSI or ATA interfaces. Typically, higher-end units use SCSI, and a few low-end models use ATA. Some external drives also use USB or IEEE-1394. In the past, low-end drives sometimes used the floppy or parallel-port interfaces, but such devices are now relics. SCSI drives use two device files; `/dev/st0` causes the drive to rewind after each use and `/dev/nst0` doesn't. ATA drives use `/dev/ht0` and `/dev/nht0`, respectively, for these functions. In both cases, if your system has more than one tape drive, the trailing number increases from 0 to 1 and higher for the second and later drives. External USB or IEEE-1394 drives look like SCSI drives to Linux.

One of the problems with tapes is that they aren't extremely reliable. Individual experiences differ, but most people who use tapes find that the media fail on occasion. Drives sometimes have problems reading tapes written on other drives, too. Tape is also a *sequential-access* medium, meaning that you must read through all of a tape's contents to get to data toward the end of the tape. (Some formats provide shortcuts in some situations, though.)

Despite tape's problems, it remains a popular backup medium because of the high capacity of individual tapes and the low cost of tapes on a per-gigabyte basis. Given hard disk pricing trends, though, tape is starting to lose ground to removable disks.

Pros and Cons of Removable Disks

Instead of using tapes, many people use removable disks as backup media. Table 2.5 in Chapter 2 summarizes many of the available removable disk technologies. At the low end, common 3.5-inch floppy disks hold 1.44MB. At the high end, special mounts are available to turn ordinary hard disks into removable media. You can also buy external SCSI, USB, or IEEE-1394 hard disks.

One of the prime advantages of removable disks—especially removable hard disks—is their speed. Modern hard disks can easily exceed 20MB/s; manufacturers typically claim speeds of 30–75MB/s, although actual speeds are likely to be substantially less than this. Unlike tapes, disks permit random access to data, which can greatly speed data recovery. By copying files using commands such as `cp`, you can use a disk for backup much as you might use a fixed hard disk. For backup purposes, though, using `tar` or some other backup tool may be preferable because these tools can do a better job of preserving all the important characteristics of a file—its ownership, permissions, status as a symbolic link, and so on. You can also use the backup software's compression scheme to fit backups from a larger disk on a smaller medium. Depending on how you use the backup software, though, using it may deprive you of the random-access nature of the disk technology.

Over the past few years, hard disk prices have been dropping more rapidly than prices for tapes and tape drives. In early 2003, hard disks sell for about $1 per gigabyte, which is competitive with prices for blank tapes. This fact makes removable or external hard disks very attractive as a backup medium. Why buy a more expensive and slower tape when you can have a hard disk for the same price? One answer to this question is that removable disks tend to be delicate. A tape is likely to survive a drop from table height, but a hard disk might not. Most removable disk media, such as floppies and Zip disks, are a bit more rugged than hard disks, but they also store less data and are likely to cost more per gigabyte. The delicacy of hard disks can be an important consideration in backup storage, particularly when you take a backup off-site for safekeeping.

You might consider keeping a backup hard disk in the computer to avoid subjecting it to physical shocks. This approach has several drawbacks, though. For one thing, you'll be limited in the number of backups you can retain; one of the beauties of removable backups is that you can keep many backups from different times, which can be handy in reconstructing old work. Another problem is that a hard disk kept inside the computer may be rendered useless by the same problems that might take out the primary disk, such as a power surge or theft of the computer. Nonetheless, an internal backup disk can be part of an overall backup strategy. In fact, some types of Redundant Array of Independent Disks (RAID) configuration are designed as a type of backup with automatic data recovery features.

Another problem with removable hard disks is that they're bulkier and heavier than tapes or other removable disk technologies. This fact can make it more awkward to move the backup to an off-site location. This problem isn't likely to be insurmountable, though; a standard 3.5-inch hard disk is nowhere near as awkward to move as, say, a sofa. You might need to rent a bigger safety deposit box for off-site storage, though, if that's how you handle this task.

Overall, removable hard disks make an appealing backup option, given their falling prices and high speed. If their bulk and delicacy aren't major issues, hard disks are a good choice. For smaller backup jobs, such as archiving individual projects, keeping backups of your configuration files, or transferring individual files between computers, removable disk media such as floppies and Zip disks are good choices. These media are a bit more rugged and compact than hard disks, but they're lower in capacity and slower. Optical media can be a good choice for some of these duties, as well.

Pros and Cons of Optical Media

Optical media include Compact Disc Recordable (CD-R), CD-Rewriteable (CD-RW), and assorted recording Digital Versatile Disc (DVD) variants (DVD-R, DVD+R, DVD-RAM, DVD-RW , and DVD+RW). These media all use optical technologies—a laser burns data onto a light-sensitive substrate. The data can be read back by using a laser tuned to a lower power setting.

NOTE *Magneto-optical disks, which use a hybrid magnetic and optical recording technology, are also available. From a software perspective, these disks work like other removable disk technologies, such as Zip disks, so the comments in the preceding section, "Pros and Cons of Removable Disks," apply to them.*

Fundamentally, optical media are sequential access during writing but random access when being read. As described in Chapter 2, you write to these disks by creating a filesystem and then using software such as cdrecord to write that filesystem all at once. You can sometimes append to an existing filesystem. Software surrounding the Universal Disk Format (UDF) has made optical media access more closely resemble access to other disks on other platforms, but Linux's UDF support is still rudimentary, and doesn't yet take advantage of most of these features.

Optical media are very durable when properly stored—shelf life estimates range from 10 to 100 years. The media themselves have no moving parts, so they aren't likely to be affected by a fall from table height, unless they're scratched in the process. These media are common enough that software and hardware to read them are likely to be common for decades. They're also compact and so can be easily transported off-site, or you can store many media on a small bookshelf.

At the low end, CD-RW drives can be purchased for well under $100. (CD-R drives are no longer common.) CD-R media cost $0.30–$1.00 and can be used in CD-RW drives, but they can't be reused. Reusable CD-RW media cost $0.50–$1.50. Both CD-R and CD-RW media can store up to 700MB per disc, for a cost of well under $1/GB if you shop carefully. Recordable DVD drives cost $300–$4,000, while media cost $3–$25. These media store 4.7–9.4GB, so their cost hovers around $1/GB. New blue-light laser technologies are on the verge of being introduced.

These technologies will increase recordable DVD capacities to 23GB, but introductory prices will be several thousand dollars for the drive alone. Of course, these prices are likely to drop quickly in the next couple of years. In other words, optical media prices are potentially lower than those of hard disks, considering media alone, but you can't back up all the data from a modern hard disk onto a single recordable DVD, much less a CD-R or CD-RW. This limited capacity is the optical media's Achilles' heel from a system backup perspective.

Nonetheless, optical media can be useful for backups. You can back up individual projects, configuration files, and so on. If you don't mind swapping discs during the backup, you may be able to back up a small system onto just a handful of optical discs. If you plan your partitions appropriately, you may be able to fit one partition per optical disc.

TIP   If you run a multiboot system and you've installed the core components of each OS on 700MB or smaller partitions, you can record these boot partitions directly to CD-R or CD-RW discs and then restore them using dd. *The destination partition must be precisely the same size as the original partition for this procedure to work, though. If you compress the backup, you may be able to fit a 1.4GB partition onto a single CD-R or CD-RW disc.*

A Rundown of Backup Programs

You can back up a Linux system, or a portion thereof, using any of many different programs. Some of the more popular programs for creating backups include the following:

AMANDA   The *Advanced Maryland Automatic Network Disk Archiver (AMANDA)* is a powerful network-based backup tool. It builds on dump or tar to enable one computer to serve as a backup station for potentially dozens of other computers. The project's home page is http://www.amanda.org.

BRU   The Backup and Restore Utility (BRU) is a commercial backup package for Linux and other Unix-like systems. It creates an archive of backup files at the start of the backup, so you can easily view a list of backed-up files and select those you want to restore from the list. It can be used to back up individual systems or an entire network. The core utility is text-based, but BRU also comes with a unique GUI front-end. You can read more at http://www.bru.com.

cp   The standard Linux cp command can be used to create backups on disk media, but not on tapes. Ordinarily, cp modifies file characteristics, such as the owner; however, if you add certain options, such as -a, cp does a better job of preserving this information.

cpio   This program is a popular archiving tool for Linux. You can use it to create an archive directly on a tape, or you can pipe its output through cdrecord to create a cpio-format optical disc.

dump   This program works at the inode level, which means that the program does a better job backing up files without modifying characteristics such as last-access date stamps and hard links than do most other backup tools. This feature also means that the program is highly filesystem-specific, though. Versions for ext2fs/ext3fs (dump) and XFS (xfsdump) are available, but they produce incompatible archives; you can only restore to the type of filesystem from which you backed up. This program relies on a companion program, restore, to restore data.

smbtar The Samba package for file and printer sharing with Windows systems comes with a script called `smbtar`. This script combines the `smbclient` and `tar` programs, permitting a Linux system to back up Windows clients. The Windows clients must have file sharing enabled, though.

tar The `tar` program has long been a staple in the Linux world. It's conceptually very similar to `cpio`, but `tar` has become the standard archive format for exchanging file collections on the Internet. Its name stands for *tape archiver*, so as you might expect, it can be used to archive a filesystem directly to tape. You can also use it with `cdrecord` to create a `tar`-format optical disc.

As a general rule, `tar` is the most popular and lowest-common-denominator backup tool, but it's not always the best choice. AMANDA and BRU are particularly worthy of note for backing up a network. AMANDA includes automatic backup scheduling tools that can greatly simplify the backup and restore procedures. The cost is that AMANDA, on both the backup server and its clients, takes a great deal of effort to configure.

WARNING *Most backup programs don't encrypt their data. An unauthorized individual who obtains your backup can read sensitive data, even if the files have restrictive permissions on the original hard disk. Therefore, you should treat backup media as you would other sensitive documents. If you deal in unusually sensitive data, you may want to consider adding encryption to your backups to protect them in the event they're stolen or "borrowed."*

Using *tar*'s Features

Because it's the lowest-common-denominator backup tool and because it's used in nonbackup tasks, `tar` deserves a bit more attention. The basic syntax for this command is

```
tar command [qualifier[...]] [file-or-dir[...]]
```

This syntax is deceptively simple, because `tar` supports a very large number of commands and qualifiers, the most important of which are summarized in Tables 17.2 and 17.3, respectively. (Consult the `tar` man page for a more complete list.) Many qualifiers take options themselves, such as filenames. To use `tar`, you combine precisely one command with any number of qualifiers. The *file-or-dir* that you specify is the file or directory that is to be backed up or restored.

TABLE 17.2: tar COMMANDS

COMMAND	ABBREVIATION	DESCRIPTION
--create	c	Creates an archive
--concatenate	A	Appends tar files to an archive
--append	r	Appends non-tar files to an archive
--update	u	Appends files that are newer than those in an archive
--diff or --compare	d	Compares an archive to files on disk
--list	t	Lists archive contents
--extract or --get	x	Extracts files from an archive

TABLE 17.3: tar QUALIFIERS

COMMAND	ABBREVIATION	DESCRIPTION
--directory *dir*	C	Changes to directory *dir* before performing operations
--file [*host*:]*file*	f	Uses file called *file* on computer called *host* as the archive file
--listed-incremental *file*	g	Performs incremental backup or restore, using *file* as a list of previously archived files
--one-file-system	l	Backs up or restores only one filesystem (partition)
--multi-volume	M	Creates or extracts a multitape archive
--tape-length N	L	Changes tapes after *N* kilobytes
--same-permissions	p	Preserves all protection information
--absolute-paths	P	Retains the leading / on filenames
--verbose	v	Lists all files read or extracted; when used with --list, displays file sizes, ownership, and time stamps
--verify	W	Verifies the archive after writing it
--exclude *file*	(none)	Excludes *file* from the archive
--exclude-from *file*	X	Excludes files listed in *file* from the archive
--gzip or --ungzip	z	Processes archive through gzip
--bzip2	j	Processes archive through bzip2

As an example of tar in action, consider a backup of the root directory (/), /home and /usr. These directories are backed up to a SCSI tape drive (/dev/st0) with the following command:

```
# tar --create --verbose --one-file-system --file /dev/st0 / /home /usr
```

This command can be abbreviated as follows:

```
# tar cvlf /dev/st0 / /home /usr
```

NOTE *Some non-GNU versions of* tar *require a dash (-) prior to abbreviated commands. Linux's versions of* tar *don't require this feature, though.*

WARNING *Using* --one-file-system *and backing up each partition explicitly is generally a good idea. If you try to simply back up the root partition and all mounted partitions, your backup will include the contents of* /proc, *any removable media that happen to be mounted, and perhaps other undesirable directories. The extra data will consume space on your backup media and may cause problems when you restore the data. Alternatively, you can explicitly exclude such directories using* --exclude *or* --exclude-from.

USING *TAR* TO BACK UP TO A REMOVABLE DISK

Although cp may be the obvious choice for backing up to a removable disk, tar has certain advantages in this role. For one thing, tar can perform incremental backups, as described shortly in "Incremental Backups: Minimizing Backup Resources." How can you use tar to back up to another disk, though? There are three ways. First, you can archive data to a tar file (aka a *tarball*) on an ordinary filesystem. Second, you can use a partition or even a raw disk device as the tar destination, much as you can use a tape device as the destination. Third, you can create a pipe to copy files through tar. For instance, suppose you've mounted a backup disk at /mnt/backup, and you want to archive the contents of /home to this new location. You could type the following command to achieve this effect:

```
# tar clpf - /home | (cd /mnt/backup; tar xvlpf -)
```

This command creates an archive of /home on stdout (-) and pipes it to a pair of commands. The first of these commands changes to the target directory and the second extracts the archive from stdin into the new directory. This example produces results that are very similar to those of the much simpler cp -a command, but you can add more tar options—say, to perform incremental backups—which can make tar worthwhile for this task.

Incremental Backups: Minimizing Backup Resources

Frequent backups can help you immensely in the event of data loss, but creating backups can be time-consuming. A tape drive capable of 6MB/s data transfers takes close to 4 hours to back up 80GB of data. Media capacity is also an issue. As your storage needs grow, so do your backup needs, and changing from one backup medium to another can be costly. Therefore, you probably want to stretch the life of your media as much as possible, and that means minimizing the amount of data you back up on a regular basis. Finally, if you maintain a network of computers, backups can consume a great deal of network bandwidth, robbing you of the use of that bandwidth for other purposes. For all of these reasons, a technique known as *incremental backup* is popular. Incremental backups enable you to back up everything once and then back up only new or changed files on subsequent backups. Of course, sooner or later you'll want to perform a new full backup. Understanding the types of incremental backups and schedules for their use can help you to plan the backup strategy that's best for your needs. Most backup programs support incremental backups. As an example, I describe tar's incremental backup options.

NOTE *The Linux cp command doesn't provide any incremental backup options. On the other end of the scale, AMANDA provides extensive incremental backup tools; in fact, it's designed to work only in a special incremental backup mode that spreads network resource usage out over time.*

Types of Incremental Backup

In describing incremental backup schemes, three major types of backups come into play:

Full Backup   A full backup contains all the files on a system, or at least all the files that are important. (Full backups may deliberately omit the contents of temporary directories such as /tmp, for instance.) If you perform only full backups, you can restore anything or everything from the system using just one backup medium or set of media; but such backups take the most time and consume the most media space.

Incremental Backup An incremental backup contains only those files that have been added or changed since the last full backup. (As with full backups, you may deliberately omit certain files or types of files.) If you perform a full backup on Monday and incremental backups every other day of the week, the incremental backups will gradually increase in size over the week. Restoring data requires using two media or sets of media: the full backup and the latest incremental backup.

Differential Backup A differential backup contains only those files that have been added or changed since the last backup of any type. (Again, you can omit specific files or file types, if you like.) If you perform a full backup on Monday and differential backups every other day of the week, the differential backups are likely to vary randomly in size. Restoring data may require accessing the full backup and every differential backup made since the full backup.

Each backup type represents a different trade-off between backup convenience and restore convenience. All backup schedules include at least periodic full backups. Including incremental or differential backups (or both) in a backup schedule is usually beneficial. Precisely how often to perform each backup type is an issue that must be decided on a case-by-case basis, as described in the next section, "Creating a Backup Schedule."

WARNING Incremental and differential backups store new files, but most backup programs don't record the fact that deleted files have been deleted. Therefore, a full restore from a complete set of backups may include more files than were stored on the system at any given point in time. (A very new backup program, Duplicity, `http://www.nongnu.org/duplicity/`*, claims to record information on deleted files.) If disk space is tight, or if your users regularly create and delete very large files, be sure to consider this fact when designing a backup plan, lest you run out of disk space when you restore data.*

Creating a Backup Schedule

If your backups are to do you any good, they must exist. It's easy to overlook a backup procedure if it's something you do infrequently or irregularly. Thus, you should create a regular schedule of backups and a routine to implement them. Just how frequently the backups should be performed is up to you. You should consider factors such as the inconvenience of creating the backup (including system or network slowdowns while backing up), your budget for media, and the importance of work lost between the backup and a system failure.

The last factor is arguably the most important, particularly for a large multiuser system or a network. If a single Linux computer functions as a file server for two dozen people who store documents on it daily, a backup that's just one day out of date represents about 200 hours of lost work. On the other hand, a home system with a single user who creates few documents might do well with weekly backups; the number of truly vital files stored on such a system in a week is likely to be small.

Typically, you'll perform a full backup on a system once a week or once a month, and you'll perform incremental or differential backups on a weekly or daily basis. For instance, you might perform a full backup on the first day of each month, an incremental backup every Friday, and a differential backup every other weekday. Such a schedule might require accessing over half a dozen media for a full restore, though. Another plan might involve a full backup every Friday and incremental backups every day. Such a system would require accessing a maximum of two media for a full restore.

TIP   *Because incremental and differential backups typically consume much less space than do full backups, you can probably fit several of these smaller backups on a single backup medium. For instance, you might need one complete tape for a full backup, but you can fit an entire week's worth of differential backups on one tape. Be sure to consider this fact when purchasing backup media.*

Backups are best performed when system resources aren't being heavily used. Typically, this means late at night. Unfortunately, this also means that you're not likely to be physically present when the backup runs. (If it's a home system, you might try initiating a backup when you stop using the computer at night, though.) For this reason, backups are frequently handled via scripts called from `cron` jobs. You can place such a script in `/etc/cron.daily` on most distributions, and the system will run it automatically early in the morning. Of course, you must ensure that the backup medium is accessible; if it's not, the backup won't occur. You should also ensure that the backup script generates reasonable error reports in such a situation, and that the `cron` job mails these reports to your account or otherwise notifies you of the problem.

Creating Incremental Backups with *tar*

As an example of an incremental backup system, consider creating a backup to a SCSI tape device (`/dev/st0`) using `tar`. For the purposes of this example, suppose the computer has four partitions: root (`/`), `/home`, `/usr`, and `/var`. The initial full backup might be accomplished with a command such as this:

```
# tar cvplf /dev/st0 --listed-incremental /var/log/incr.dat / /home /usr /var
```

This command backs up all four partitions to `/dev/st0`. The `--listed-incremental /var/log/incr.dat` option tells `tar` to use `/var/log/incr.dat` as an index of previously backed-up files. When you run this command to create a full backup, this file should be empty or nonexistent; `tar` then populates it with a date code and information about each directory that's been backed up. If you later add files to a directory, `tar` can determine which files are new and back them up.

TIP   *You may want to use output redirection (>) to store the verbose output of* tar *in a file when backing up. This procedure will create a file that lists the contents of the backup, which can make it easier to locate files for restore. When you perform an incremental or differential backup, store the data to different files or use the appending output redirection operator (>>) so that you don't wipe out the full backup's file list.*

To perform an incremental or differential backup, you type the same command you use to perform the full backup; however, how you handle the backup log file differs:

Incremental Backups   Prior to making an incremental backup, you should make a copy of the initial incremental log file under a new name and refer to that copy when making the incremental backup. Alternatively, you could make an initial copy of the log file and then restore it after each incremental backup. In either case, the idea is to refer to the original backup log whenever you make a new backup, hence causing all files added or changed since that full backup to be included in the new backup.

Differential Backups   The simplest way to perform a differential backup is to keep using the same backup command, including the same log file, for every backup. Each time you run the command, `tar` modifies the log file, so a new differential backup is created the next time you run the command.

If you want to mix backup types, you might need to create copies of the log file and restore them only at certain times. For instance, to create a new incremental backup once a week and daily differential backups, you'd copy the full backup's log file, use the original name every day, and restore the full backup's log file from the copy you made on a weekly basis.

One other factor requires attention: Placement of incremental or differential backups on the backup media. If you use a random-access medium such as a removable hard disk, you can place these backups in directories named after the dates of the backups. With tapes, you can use the mt command to skip over some backups. You would then use a non-rewinding tape device, such as /dev/nst0 rather than /dev/st0, to access the tape. For instance, suppose you've created an initial full backup with the preceding command on Monday. On Tuesday, you want to create a differential backup using a fresh tape. You could use the same command to accomplish this task. On Wednesday, you want to create another differential backup on the same tape as you used on Tuesday, but without wiping out Tuesday's backup. You could type the following commands to accomplish this goal, after inserting the tape:

```
# mt -f /dev/nst0 rewind
# mt -f /dev/nst0 fsf 1
# tar cvplf /dev/nst0 --listed-incremental /var/log/incr.dat / /home /usr /var
# mt -t /dev/nst0 offline
```

The first of these commands probably isn't necessary, because most tape drives rewind the tape when you insert it. The second command tells the tape drive to skip over the first *file*. In this context, a tape file is a backup—think of it as a tar file stored directly on the tape. The third command is the backup command, but modified by using the non-rewinding device file, so as not to rewind the tape drive. The fourth command rewinds the tape and takes it offline. You could use the rewinding tape device (/dev/st0) instead of the non-rewinding one in the third command if you prefer; this would obviate the need for the fourth command, although this command does a bit more, such as ejecting the tape, on some tape drives.

For subsequent differential backups, you would increment the fsf counter in the second command—you'd make it **fsf 2**, **fsf 3**, and so on. These commands will skip over increasing numbers of backups. Of course, you must be careful not to exceed your tape drive's capacity.

Upon restore, you must mirror these commands; if you want to restore a file from the third backup file on a tape, you must precede the restore operation by an appropriate mt command, such as **mt -f /dev/nst0 fsf 2**. When doing a full restore using differential backups, you can restore data one tape file at a time, and type **mt -f /dev/nst0 fsf 1** between each restore operation. You presumably don't want to skip any files, so the fsf number never exceeds 1; you just want to use this command to get the tape drive to read from the start of each new tape file.

Emergency Restore Procedures

Restoring data from a backup is fairly straightforward when your system is fundamentally intact and you just need to recover a handful of lost files; you run the backup software in reverse, as it were. For instance, you use tar's --extract command rather than the --create command. In the case of tar, you must specify the files or directories you want to recover on the command line, or else the system will attempt to recover everything. For instance, you might type these commands to restore the /home/alice directory from a tape backup if you've accidentally deleted it:

```
# cd /
# tar xvplf /dev/st0 home/alice
```

NOTE *Unless you use the* --absolute-paths *option to* tar *when you create a backup, the program strips the leading slash (/) from directory names. Therefore, to restore data to its original location, you must first move into the root (/) directory. Alternatively, you can restore data to another location and then move it to its final destination. This latter approach is safer; if you mistype or forget to include a filename, restoring to another location guarantees that you won't overwrite newer files with older ones.*

A more troubling problem is what to do when a system is so badly damaged that you can't use it to recover itself. For instance, how do you recover if your hard disk dies or if your system is compromised by an intruder? In the first case, you must get a new hard disk, and you obviously can't boot it into Linux until you've restored Linux, and you can't restore Linux without booting Linux—a chicken-and-egg problem. In the second case, you can't trust the programs on the hard disk, and so you must use another installation to recover. In both cases, and in many others, the solution is to use an emergency recovery system. These systems enable you to boot a second Linux system in order to work on your primary Linux system. These emergency systems can be useful for work other than emergency file restores, too; for instance, you might use one to edit a boot script if you've accidentally damaged it. This section describes several emergency recovery systems. Of course, you should be sure to test your emergency recovery system so that you know it will work when you need it.

Types of Emergency Recovery System

The challenge in creating an emergency recovery system is in putting Linux on a bootable medium that's probably much smaller than a typical Linux system. Fortunately, most emergency recoveries require just a handful of utilities—fdisk, filesystem tools, an editor, tar or other backup and recovery tools, and so on. An emergency recovery system doesn't need big programs or sets of programs such as TeX, Mozilla, KDE, or the like. Nonetheless, some emergency recovery systems come on large media and include some of these tools. Common forms for emergency recovery systems include floppies, CD-ROMs, higher-capacity removable disks, and spare Linux installations. In all cases, you can either create your own custom emergency recovery system or use a ready-made system. (This distinction isn't very substantial in the case of spare Linux installations, though.)

EMERGENCY FLOPPY DISKS

The smallest medium for emergency recovery systems is a floppy disk. This fact makes floppy-based emergency recovery systems very Spartan; they're not likely to include the X Window System (X) or other large packages. Nonetheless, floppies have an advantage because they're available on almost all computers, particularly in the IA-32 world. (Some Macintoshes lack floppy drives, though.) What's more, computers that have floppy disk drives can almost always boot from a floppy disk. Systems made before the late 1990s may not be able to boot from anything but a floppy disk or a hard disk, which can complicate the use of some other recovery media.

A typical Linux kernel is roughly a megabyte in size—large enough that it fills most of a single 1.44MB floppy disk. This fact means that many floppy-based emergency systems come on two or more floppy disks. Some use unusual formats to squeeze a bit more capacity out of a floppy, such as 1.72MB rather than 1.44MB. These formats tend to be more delicate than normal formats, so you're more likely to find that these floppies have gone bad after a time than would be the case with normal 1.44MB floppies. Therefore, I recommend making at least three copies of any floppy-based emergency recovery system. You may also want to store these copies in different locations—say, one in your desk drawer, another in an office down the hall, and a third at an off-site location along with your off-site backups. You should test these floppies periodically to ensure that they're readable, and replace them when necessary.

You can create or find emergency floppy images in several different ways:

Create Your Own   Creating your own emergency floppy system requires intimate knowledge of how Linux boots, what tools are required to use it, and so on. Therefore, creating your own emergency floppies isn't for the faint of heart. One way to proceed is to use another system, such as the ones described next, as a starting point. Modifying a working system is almost always easier than creating a new one.

Distribution-Provided Emergency Systems   Many distributions provide an emergency recovery floppy disk image or images on their CD-ROMs. You can use these to perform basic recovery operations. Consult your distribution's documentation for details.

WARNING   Many distributions allow you to create an emergency boot floppy that's designed to boot the distribution in case of a failure of the boot loader. This tool isn't the same as a full emergency recovery system as described here; it won't do you any good if your installation is seriously damaged beyond a boot loader or kernel file problem. Don't assume you're protected just because you created such a floppy when you installed Linux.

Tom's Root/Boot Disk   This tool is a custom single-floppy emergency recovery disk for IA-32 systems. You can obtain it from `http://www.toms.net/rb/`. The system was designed from the start with emergency recovery in mind; it includes the smallest binaries available along with the tools needed for many emergency recovery situations.

μLinux   This tool is another single-floppy Linux distribution, similar in concept to Tom's Root/Boot Disk. Check its web page, `http://mulinux.nevalabs.org`, for more details.

Crash Recovery Kit   There are actually several Crash Recovery Kit packages based on different kernel versions and available in different sizes. These systems are built from a Red Hat core, and so should be familiar to Red Hat users. You can read more at `http://crashrecovery.org`.

BOOTABLE REMOVABLE DISKS

A step up from an emergency system on a floppy disk is an emergency system on a higher-capacity removable disk, such as a Zip disk, a Jaz disk, or even a removable hard disk. Depending on the disk capacity, you might or might not have room for such niceties as X or a hefty editor such as Emacs.

ZipSlack and BigSlack are a pair of distributions that are particularly well-suited for use on removable disks. (Both are headquartered at `http://www.slackware.com/zipslack/`.) These distributions are trimmed-down versions of Slackware Linux. ZipSlack is designed to fit in about 100MB, whereas BigSlack requires 850MB. Both install to FAT partitions using the Linux UMSDOS filesystem, so you can install them on an emergency medium from DOS or Windows in a pinch, although setting them up from Linux is easier.

You can try installing other distributions onto a removable disk. Linux treats such disks as removable hard disks, so in principle the installation process is much like installing to a regular hard disk. Many distributions have problems installing to anything as small as a Zip disk, though. You can accomplish the task with Debian or Slackware. There are also small distributions, such as Peanut Linux (http://www.ibiblio.org/peanut/), that are likely to work well on smallish removable media.

In order to boot Linux from a removable disk, you'll need one of three things:

BIOS Support for Booting from a Removable Disk   If your computer's Basic Input/Output System (BIOS) supports booting from a removable disk, you can configure it to do so and boot from your emergency system. Of course, that system must then have a working Linux Loader (LILO) or Grand Unified Boot Loader (GRUB) installation on its boot sector. Most modern computers can be configured to boot from a removable disk, but this support may work only with ATA disks.

Boot Loader on a Floppy   If your computer's BIOS doesn't support booting directly from a removable disk, you may be able to work around the issue by placing LILO or GRUB on a floppy disk and configuring the boot loader to redirect the boot process to the removable disk. This practice still relies upon the BIOS at least recognizing the removable drive, though, so it may not work with external drives.

Boot Floppy   If all else fails, you can put the Linux kernel directly on a boot floppy. You can either use a bootable DOS floppy and LOADLIN to load the kernel or save the kernel "raw" to the disk, in which case it boots and looks for Linux wherever it's configured to do so.

BOOTABLE EMERGENCY CD-RS

Because CD-Rs have so much capacity, Linux systems that run from a CD-R can include many niceties, such as X, GUI configuration tools, and so on. Bootable Linux CD-Rs have become common both as emergency systems and as demo systems. You can use a demo system as an emergency recovery system if you like.

One problem with emergency CD-Rs is that they can be difficult to modify. For instance, adding software such as BRU to a CD-R can be more difficult than adding BRU to a removable disk emergency recovery system, because you must copy the files that comprise the emergency system to your hard disk, add the BRU files, and burn a new CD-R. You must also ensure that the new system is bootable.

As with emergency recovery floppy disks and larger removable media, there are several sources of emergency CD-Rs, including:

Distribution CD-Rs   The CD-ROMs or CD-Rs that you use for installing Linux may boot into an emergency mode. Sometimes these modes are equivalent to emergency boot floppies. For instance, if you type **linux rescue** at the lilo: prompt in Red Hat's installer, it boots into what is effectively an emergency floppy system. Other distributions come with or make available fuller demo systems. For instance, SuSE makes a "live-eval" version of its distribution available on a downloadable CD-R image.

DemoLinux   This distribution is specifically designed as a demo version of Linux; it boots from CD-R and runs a substantial subset of normal Linux tools. DemoLinux is roughly equivalent to

SuSE's live-eval CD-R image. The English DemoLinux home page is
`http://www.demolinux.org/en/index.html`.

Crash Recovery Kit   This system, described earlier in "Emergency Floppy Disk," is available on a CD-R image as well as on a floppy disk. The CD-R version, of course, includes many more niceties.

Most computers made since the mid-1990s can boot from their CD-ROM drives, so booting these distributions shouldn't be a problem. If by chance you can't boot from the disc, you can probably create a boot floppy from files on the disc. Check its documentation for details.

SPARE LINUX INSTALLATIONS

A final approach for emergency systems is to create a spare Linux installation on your main hard disk. Instead of installing Linux once, you install it twice, once with a full complement of tools and again with a slimmer assortment. Your main system's `/etc/fstab` file shouldn't automatically mount the second system's partitions, so they won't be damaged should a software error wipe out the main system. In such an event, you can select the emergency system in your boot loader and be up and running fairly quickly, with any luck.

NOTE   *The effective difference between a spare Linux installation and an installation to a removable disk is very slim. From a logical standpoint, the two approaches are identical, aside from the fact that the removable disk is removable.*

The main problem with the spare installation approach is that it doesn't protect you against catastrophic hardware failure. If your hard disk dies or if the computer is stolen, a spare installation won't do you any good. Nonetheless, it can be a convenient approach for helping to recover from less drastic problems. For this reason, it's a good method to use on a system with which you frequently experiment—for instance, a test system on which you try new software and techniques. Such systems are more likely to suffer from problems such as damaged boot files, and so can benefit from the quick recovery possibilities that a spare Linux installation offers.

A variant on this approach, to be used only after disaster strikes, is to create a new minimal installation from which you can direct more extensive recovery efforts. For instance, suppose you've created a backup and tested an emergency system, and your computer is stolen or seriously damaged. You buy a replacement computer but find that your emergency system doesn't work with it—for instance, the emergency system's kernel might lack support for your hard disk controller. In such a case, you can create a small emergency system on the new disk by installing ZipSlack, BigSlack, a small Debian system, or some other small Linux system. This system should provide enough tools to enable you to restore your backup. With luck it will boot, but if not, the emergency system should give you the tools to build a new kernel or otherwise troubleshoot the problem and get the restored system up and running.

Testing Emergency Recovery Systems

No matter what emergency recovery system you use, you should check to be sure that it includes all the tools you need for an emergency recovery situation, including `fdisk`, filesystem-creation tools, an editor, and a copy of your backup program (or its restore companion, for systems that use two programs). Also be sure that the system supports whatever filesystems you use. Some of these tools (particularly floppy-based tools) use older kernels, and so lack support for newer filesystems, such as ReiserFS, JFS, and XFS. If your backup or restore system relies on network data transfers, be sure it includes the appropriate network hardware drivers and whatever clients or servers you need to perform the restore.

You should test your emergency recovery system as well as you can as soon as you create it. Ideally, you should use it to restore a complete and working system. This may be practical if you have a spare computer on which to test it, or even just a spare hard disk. If you're short on such hardware, though, try booting the system and recovering a few files into a temporary directory. Document the use of the system—write down the important recovery commands it supports, where important files and mount points are located, and so on.

Don't assume that the recovery system will continue to work indefinitely. Media can go bad—this is especially true of floppy disks. If you add, delete, or replace hardware, these changes may necessitate changes to the drivers or configuration of the emergency system. If the emergency system uses a password, be sure you remember it. You may need to keep it synchronized with the **root** password on your main system or make it particularly memorable.

WARNING *Emergency systems can be used by miscreants who gain physical access to your computers. Your own emergency system might be so abused, but intruders can bring their own boot disks, as well! Chapter 18, "System Security," covers security measures and physical access concerns.*

Summary

Backups are frequently overlooked, particularly on home or small office systems, but they're extremely important. Hardware can fail or be stolen, software bugs can destroy data, and human error can damage a system. Thus, the question isn't so much whether you'll find a backup helpful, but when you'll need it. Linux provides many backup tools, ranging from the standard cp command to specialized backup packages. These programs can be used with a variety of backup media, including tape, removable disks, and optical media. No matter how you use these programs, you should take precautions to ensure that you can recover the data when disaster strikes. Specifically, you should study emergency recovery tools and prepare one for your system.

## Chapter 18

System Security

IN THE MOVIES, BREAKING into a computer is usually an easy matter. The typical computer intrusion, as depicted by Hollywood, involves one character guessing another's password. Although password security is important, cracking a password is not the only method of attack. This chapter begins with a look at common methods of attack, such as social engineering, exploiting buggy software, and abusing physical access to a computer. This chapter then describes steps you can take to help secure your system. These steps include the proper selection of passwords, so movie-style villains can't get in on the third try, as they invariably do. Other steps involve removing unnecessary servers and keeping your software up-to-date. Chapter 21, "Detecting Intruders," covers another important security topic—discovering when intruders manage to break into your system. As you read this chapter, remember that security is best applied in layers, so that if one security measure doesn't stop an intruder, another may do the job.

Computer security is an extremely complex topic, and this chapter can provide just an introduction to the perils and the defenses available. For more information, consult a book on Linux security, such as Hontañón's *Linux Security* (Sybex, 2001) or Hatch's *Hacking Linux Exposed, 2nd Edition* (Osborne/McGraw-Hill, 2002). Note that specific security threats can change very rapidly, but the basic principles involved in securing a system remain constant over time.

Methods of Attack

In order to understand system security, you must know how crackers break into computers. Just knowing how they operate can often suggest obvious countermeasures; for instance, you can warn your users to be wary of popular social engineering attacks. Other approaches include taking advantage of software bugs, using break-ins of one computer to access another, guessing or breaking a password, probing networks for known weaknesses, performing denial-of-service attacks, and gaining special privileges via physical access to the hardware.

NOTE   *The media at large tends to refer to computer miscreants as* hackers. *In the computer world generally and in the Linux community specifically, this word has another meaning: A hacker is someone who enjoys working with computers, or especially programming them, and who uses computer skills in legal and productive ways. Because of this meaning of the word* hacker, *I avoid using it to refer to computer criminals; instead, I use the word* cracker *to refer to such individuals.*

Social Engineering

One method of attack is decidedly low tech: Manipulate users into revealing passwords or other information that can be used to compromise a computer. This approach is known as *social engineering*. On the surface, it seems unlikely to succeed; but social engineers use deception to trick users into divulging their passwords or otherwise performing actions that aid the social engineer. Sometimes they need only look on as users perform some common activity. Ultimately, social engineering relies on misplaced trust. Some specific examples of social engineering include:

Impersonating a Sysadmin   Social engineers sometimes pose as system administrators. The social engineer telephones, sends e-mail to, or otherwise contacts a user and claims to be a system administrator. The social engineer may ask for the user's password using some pretext, such as a need to re-initialize a password database. If successful, the social engineer may collect quite a few passwords in this way. The social engineer might use a similar ploy to get users to run software designed to compromise the computer.

Impersonating a User   Users aren't the only ones who can be scammed by social engineers. Social engineers can pretend to be users who've forgotten their passwords. System administrators and help desk personnel may then let the social engineer change a user's password. Unless you know all your users by sight, you should implement a policy requiring the presentation of photo IDs before you allow people to change the passwords on "their" accounts.

Dumpster Diving   Sometimes people throw away paper that contains passwords or other sensitive data. Social engineers may paw through the trash to find such scraps of paper, which may be worth many times their weight in gold to the cracker. Even less sensitive documents, such as organizational charts, can be used by social engineers in designing more elaborate attacks. Crackers may also obtain sensitive data from used hard disks or even floppies, so you should be cautious when discarding these items or sending them to others.

Shoulder Surfing   This technique involves peering over a user's shoulder as the user types a password or other sensitive data. This type of attack is particularly likely to occur in public settings such as university computer labs. A higher-tech variant of this approach uses devices that record information that users type on their keyboards. Some of these devices are small enough that they can be mistaken for keyboard adapters, such as those used to plug older keyboards into modern PS/2 keyboard sockets.

Trojan Horse Programs   Some programs claim to do one thing but in fact do another. For instance, a program might claim to be a tool to help you clean up unused files, but in fact e-mail your password or other sensitive data to the social engineer. An Internet-specific variant of this theme is a website that requires a password but that's run by a cracker. Because many users employ the same password on many websites, a social engineer can use the information gleaned from a fake website to gain access to users' accounts on more sensitive websites.

Fake Login Screens   In public computing centers, one specific type of program combines the features of a Trojan horse and shoulder surfing: a program that presents a fake login screen. Such a program looks like an ordinary login screen but in fact does nothing but record the username and password, present a fake error message, and then call the normal login routine. A miscreant can leave such a program running on a public terminal, and victims believe they've mistyped their passwords. A variant on this theme is a network-enabled popup window that requires a password. For instance, if your X server's security is lax, a miscreant can display such a window on your X terminal, making it look like a password request from a web page or user program.

Borrowed Accounts   A social engineer may befriend a legitimate user of a computer system and then ask to "borrow" the account—say, to browse the Web. In reality, the social engineer uses the account for a more sinister purpose, such as exploiting a local vulnerability or installing a fake login screen.

E-mail Viruses and Worms   In the past few years, a large number of viruses and worms have spread across the Internet via e-mail. Many spread by relying on users to run attached programs, which may be disguised as something else. This type of attack has almost always targeted Microsoft Windows systems, but in theory such an attack could target Linux users.

Social engineering is a very broad field, and the key to defending against such attacks is skepticism. Don't trust that the person on the other end of the phone is who he or she claims to be; don't trust that the e-mail attachment really is a great new song from your favorite band; don't trust that you mistyped your password when you see a login failure message. Buy a paper shredder to destroy paper documents with even slightly sensitive information. Do a low-level format on floppy disks (using `fdformat`) before sending them off-site, and wipe hard disks clean by using `dd` to copy zeroes to all sectors before discarding them. (Even more drastic measures may be in order when handling extremely sensitive data; for instance, some government agencies crush used hard disks to protect the data they once stored.)

Many social engineering techniques can be used to steal sensitive data unrelated to your Linux system. For instance, shoulder surfing for automatic teller machine (ATM) passwords is common, and dumpster diving is a popular means of obtaining social security numbers, credit card applications, and other data needed for identity theft.

Exploiting Buggy Software

A second method of attack is to exploit buggy software. One particularly common type of bug that often leads to security vulnerabilities is the *buffer overflow*. This condition occurs when a programmer doesn't set aside enough space to hold input data. Ordinarily, the result is odd program behavior or crashes; but a cracker who studies a buffer overflow bug may be able to exploit it to place new instructions in the program code itself. The result can be a system break-in.

Bugs are particularly sensitive in server software, which is accessible to the world at large; or when software is run as `root`, either directly or by being owned by `root` and having its set-user-ID (SUID) bit set. The worst case is the combination of the two. When this happens, a miscreant from the other side of the world can break into your computer, without using an ordinary account. The cracker may be able to set up a new account, replace existing software, and so on. (Chapter 21 describes how to detect when this happens.)

Even software run locally by ordinary users can be exploited in this way. Unfortunately, not all users are trustworthy, particularly at large sites. Even when all your users are trustworthy, a social engineering attack might be combined with software bugs to give the social engineer sensitive information or to otherwise do the cracker's bidding.

Two defenses against buggy software are described later in this chapter: Running as few servers as possible (covered in "Removing Unnecessary Servers") and installing the latest versions of software (covered in "Keeping Software Up-to-Date"). Both techniques reduce the chance that your system will be running vulnerable software.

Leveraging Break-Ins of Other Systems

Crackers sometimes take advantage of break-ins of systems other than your own in order to do damage. One method of doing so was already mentioned earlier, in "Social Engineering." Users frequently employ the same password on multiple systems. A cracker who obtains a username and password for one system may try it on other systems. Therefore, even if your own system's security is otherwise impeccable, it may be compromised through vulnerabilities in other computers.

A second type of leveraged break-in results from trust relationships between computers. One such trust relationship exists between servers and their clients; some servers are configured with a list of trusted clients. For instance, the Network File System (NFS) grants access to systems specified in /etc/exports. If the trusted client is compromised, the server may be compromised in turn, at least to a limited extent. A cracker who breaks into the client may be able to read sensitive data files from all users on the server and be able to plant Trojans in users' directories which might lead to further compromise.

A more subtle variant of this trust problem relates to trusting data provided by other servers. For instance, you can specify computers via hostname in /etc/exports. If you do so, then this means that your server is trusting data provided by your local Domain Name System (DNS) server. If a cracker compromises your DNS server, the cracker can alter those entries to gain access to your NFS server's files even without breaking into any of the trusted clients. Similar problems can exist in other systems, too; for instance, a Samba server that relies on user authentication by a domain controller is vulnerable to a compromise of the domain controller computer.

The usual protection against such problems is similar to the solution to social engineering problems: Trust as little as possible. For instance, whenever possible you should specify other computers by IP address rather than hostname. IP addresses can also be forged, particularly if the miscreant has physical access to your network, but by using IP addresses you've at least eliminated the DNS server as one potential vulnerability in your computer's security.

Password Cracking

One popular means of breaking into computers is to obtain legitimate users' passwords through illegitimate means. This task can be accomplished in several different ways:

Social Engineering   Many social engineering attacks are aimed at acquiring a password. These attacks may not technically be password *cracking*, but they create the same effect—compromised accounts.

Network Password Interception   Some types of network probes enable attackers to monitor traffic on a local network, as described in the next section, "Scanners and Sniffers." One of the features crackers look for is unencrypted passwords, as used by protocols such as Telnet and the File Transfer Protocol (FTP). One excellent defense against this threat is to use encrypted protocols, such as the Secure Shell (SSH), rather than unencrypted protocols. Another measure that can help, but that is less effective overall, is to use network switches rather than network hubs to connect computers. Switches don't echo data except to the target computer, so a miscreant must have compromised the sending or receiving computer to monitor data when the network uses a switch.

Dictionary Attacks   The type of activity that's most commonly meant by the phrase *password cracking* is discovering the original password from an encrypted form. Linux stores encrypted passwords in `/etc/shadow` (older systems used `/etc/passwd`). If a miscreant obtains a copy of that file, it's often possible to extract a few passwords by using a *dictionary attack*—encrypting every word in a dictionary using the same algorithm Linux uses and looking for a match to a stored encrypted password. The upcoming section, "Choosing Good Passwords," describes how to create a password that's both resistant to a dictionary attack and memorable to the user.

NOTE   Linux stores its passwords using what's known as a one-way hash, meaning that it's theoretically impossible to obtain the original input from the hashed (encrypted) form. When you type a password, Linux hashes it, and if the new hash matches the one it's stored, Linux gives you access. As a result, crackers can't technically decrypt passwords, but they can stumble upon them through a dictionary attack. On the other hand, encryption protocols such as SSH require that the data they transmit be recoverable at the other end. Therefore, if a cracker manages to decrypt such a data stream, a password sent via that stream could be recovered directly, without using a dictionary attack.

Crackers frequently try to obtain the passwords for ordinary user accounts. Many users think that such access isn't terribly important; "after all," a casual user might reason, "there's no sensitive data in *my* account!" Even if an account holds no sensitive data, crackers cherish such accounts because they can serve as launching points for further attacks. These attacks may be against the same computer—for instance, the cracker might exploit vulnerabilities in local software to acquire `root` privileges. Further attacks might also be against other computers—crackers often use network clients to attack third parties, using the compromised computers and accounts as shields to protect their identities. In fact, a small site is far more likely to be compromised to be used as a stepping stone in further attacks than to get at data on the site's computer itself. Crackers may also be interested in personal vendettas. A cracker who breaks into an individual's account can easily send offensive e-mail from that account, for instance, making the e-mails look very legitimate.

Many servers restrict network access directed at `root`. For instance, most Linux systems' Telnet server configurations don't permit direct logins as `root`. This practice reduces the odds of a successful breach of the `root` account; to break in via password cracking, the miscreant must have both an ordinary user password and the `root` password. Some servers do permit direct `root` logins, though. For instance, many distributions ship with their SSH servers configured to permit `root` logins. Whenever possible, you should change these configurations to be more restrictive. (In the case of SSH, check `/etc/ssh/sshd_config` and change the line that reads `PermitRootLogin yes` to read `PermitRootLogin no`, and be sure that line isn't commented out.)

Scanners and Sniffers

Crackers sometimes engage in information-gathering expeditions. These activities aren't designed to break into a computer by themselves; instead, they're intended to gather information that facilitates future break-in attempts. Common activities along these lines include:

System Scans   A system scan is designed to test a specific system's vulnerabilities. A simple scan checks for open *ports*—numbered access points used by network clients and servers. Most servers have assigned standard ports, as defined in /etc/services. For instance, web servers usually run on port 80. If a system probe detects that port 80 is open, the cracker infers that the computer is running a web server and may be vulnerable to any number of attacks associated with web servers. More detailed system scans may attempt to determine which web server is running, and hence what attacks might succeed. Other types of system scans may attempt to identify which OS the server is running, and hence identify any vulnerabilities unique to a specific OS.

Network Scans   Network scans are much like system scans, but they're directed against an entire network. For instance, a cracker might know of a newly discovered vulnerability in the Apache web server. The cracker will, therefore, launch a network scan designed to find systems running the vulnerable version of Apache. These scans will target hundreds of computers in a short period of time, but they'll look only for the vulnerable software; these scans may miss other vulnerable programs.

Network Sniffing   Network *sniffing* requires physical access to a network, either via a compromised computer on the network or by the cracker installing a new device on the network. A network sniffer monitors network activity and logs interesting data, such as unencrypted passwords. If an Ethernet network uses hubs or coaxial cabling, sniffers can monitor all the activity on the network. If the network uses switches, though, sniffers can normally only detect packets directed to or sent from the system that runs the sniffer, along with a handful of *broadcasts*—packets deliberately sent to all the computers on the network.

Scanning and sniffing are accomplished by way of programs, known generically as *scanners* and *sniffers*. These programs are handy tools for crackers, but they also have legitimate uses. For instance, you might use a scanner to check your systems for the presence of servers they shouldn't be running, as described in the upcoming section, "Using Remote Network Scanners." Network sniffers, such as tcpdump (http://www.tcpdump.org) and Snort (http://www.snort.org), are useful for diagnosing network problems. You can monitor network traffic on a packet-by-packet basis, and if you understand the low-level protocols, such monitoring enables you to determine why particular problems might be occurring. Some sniffers, including Snort, can also be configured to alert you whenever suspicious network activity occurs.

Worms and viruses frequently engage in network and system scans in an automated way. Unlike many other network scans, these scans are part of an automated attack; if a worm discovers a vulnerability, it attacks immediately. To date, most network worms and viruses attack Windows systems, not Linux systems; but this could change in the future.

Denial-of-Service

One type of attack isn't designed to give the attacker access to your computer; it's intended to deny you access to your own computer or network. This attack form is known as a *denial-of-service (DoS)* attack. DoS attacks can take several forms. One common one is to flood your network with garbage data. With your network overloaded, you can't use it for real work. Such attacks are frequently launched from many computers simultaneously—a variant known as a *distributed DoS (DDoS)* attack. Crackers sometimes use simple Trojan horse programs (known as *zombies*, *bots*, or *zombie bots*), installed on innocent individuals' computers through social engineering, to launch attacks on specified targets. Even if the zombie bots run on systems with low-speed dialup Internet connections, collectively they can saturate a high-speed Internet connection. Another technique is to use tricks to get the target computer to generate more in the way of reply traffic than it receives from the attacker, thereby allowing a poorly connected attacker to bring down a site with much greater network bandwidth. Configuring your system to not respond to certain common types of network accesses, such as pings, can at least keep your systems from aiding the attacker by generating return traffic.

DoS attacks are frequently targeted at the victims' Internet connections. Properly configured firewall computers can easily block these attacks, keeping them from affecting internal networks. Nonetheless, the damage done by loss of the Internet connection can be severe. There's very little you can do to protect yourself from such an attack. Once it's begun, you can contact your ISP, who may be able to take steps to block the attacking packets or change your IP address range.

DoS attacks aren't limited to network connectivity, though. Some attacks have been designed to take advantage of bugs in OSs or software to crash computers, or at least specific servers. Other attacks may rely on your own logging tools to cause problems by flooding your system logs so that they expand to fill the partitions on which they reside. You can prevent damage from DoS attacks designed to crash your computer by upgrading affected software, much as you would upgrade any other buggy software. Logging tools are increasingly using algorithms that are smart enough not to log many identical messages, so attacks aimed at your system logs are less likely to succeed than they once were. Nonetheless, you might want to forego logging of unimportant information. For instance, you can configure tools such as Snort or `iptables` to log every instance of a ping of your computer; but doing so opens you up to a simple DoS attack based on pings filling your logs. Unless you have a specific reason to log such access, it's probably better not to do so.

NOTE   Worms—even those targeted at non-Linux platforms—may have effects similar to DoS attacks. They consume network bandwidth and, if you've configured a firewall or intrusion detection software to log suspicious activities, the rapid-fire worm probes may bloat your log files to uncomfortable levels. Similar comments apply to unsolicited bulk e-mail (spam); ISPs sometimes see the same spam coming from many sites simultaneously, much as in a DDoS attack.

Physical Access

Perhaps the most serious threat is from a cracker who has physical access to a computer. Given such access, a few simple tools, and a few minutes alone, an intruder can open a computer and steal its hard disk, or even walk off with the entire computer. An intruder who wants to be a bit less obvious could reboot using a Linux emergency system, such as those described in Chapter 17, "Protecting Your System with Backups." Once the emergency system is booted, a cracker can copy otherwise protected data files or modify the system's configuration files to give the intruder remote **root** access in the future.

Physical access can also be an issue in storing backups and other removable media. Most backups are unencrypted, and ordinary file ownership and permissions are ineffective on backups. Likewise, these measures mean little on floppy disks, CD-Rs, and other removable media.

In order to guard against unauthorized physical access to a computer, you can take several steps, including:

Securing Building and Room Access   Be sure the building in which the computer resides has adequate security, such as locks and alarm systems. The rooms in which sensitive computers reside need extra security, as well. Be sure that people who are authorized to be in the building or machine room understand the importance of security and don't give unauthorized individuals entry. Social engineers may pretend to have lost keys or use other ploys to gain physical access to a computer.

Installing Antitheft Devices You can obtain locks and chains with which to tie a computer to a desk or, better, to a wall or floor. These devices can slow down would-be thieves who want to walk off with an entire computer, but a well-prepared thief can probably cut through such devices. Nonetheless, they can be important deterrents, particularly for computers in public areas.

Installing Antitamper devices Most computer cases open easily once a handful of screws are removed. You can replace these screws with ones that require special tools, such as Torx-head screws, for a modest increase in security. Better yet, some computer antitamper devices can seal a case closed with a lock. As with antitheft devices, such measures aren't foolproof, but they can act as a deterrent or slow down an intruder long enough to increase the chance of detection.

Setting BIOS Options Modern Basic Input/Output Systems (BIOSes) include security options. One of these is a BIOS password, which you must enter before changing the BIOS settings. A second option is the boot order. To prevent an intruder from booting an emergency system, configure the computer to boot *only* from the hard disk. Most BIOSes include a virus-detection option that might spot viruses or other unauthorized code on the hard disk's boot sector; however, such options sometimes misidentify a Linux boot loader as a virus, making them worthless. A few other hardware components, such as some laptop hard disks, can also be password-protected.

Using Encryption The last resort against physical access is data encryption. If you use data encryption tools, an intruder can't do much with the encrypted data—at least, not without the decryption password or some way to bypass it.

Like most other security measures, physical access protections should be applied in layers. No one measure is foolproof, and even a combination of all physical access protections can be overcome, given enough effort. The real question isn't whether your system is secure, but whether it's secure *enough*. This assessment is somewhat subjective and depends upon your comfort level and the amount of time and money you're willing to invest in security, versus your perceived risk and the potential damage that might be done by a breach.

Choosing Good Passwords

Many types of attack begin with a stolen password. Passwords can be compromised in many ways, and for some methods, such as finding a password with a sniffer program, all passwords are equally vulnerable. Some methods of attack, though, such as dictionary attacks, are more likely to succeed with some passwords than with others. For this reason, you should educate your users about how to select a good password. A perfect password from a security standpoint is a random selection of letters, numbers, punctuation, and any other characters that the system recognizes. Unfortunately, such passwords are hard for people to remember, so they tend to write them down—a practice that's at least as bad as using a poor password, as crackers may be able to find the paper on which the password is written. A good compromise is to create a password by starting from a memorable base and modifying that base so that it's not likely to appear in a cracker's dictionary.

WARNING   *Be extra careful when constructing the* **root** *password. This password is unusually sensitive, so you should be sure it's not guessable, and you should protect it from being discovered. For instance, you should* never *type the* **root** *password over an unencrypted protocol, such as Telnet or FTP.*

Selecting a Solid Base

The first step in generating a good password is to pick an appropriate *base*, which is a string that's memorable but that shouldn't appear in any language's dictionary as a single word. One reasonable procedure for picking a base is to use an acronym. For instance, you might use *yiwttd*, for *yesterday I went to the dentist*. (Of course, this specific example is a poor one because it's been used as an example in this book. A cracker who reads this book might add *yiwttd* to a dictionary, and it might spread from there.) Another option for a base is to use two short and unrelated words, such as *bunpen*. You won't find *bunpen* in a dictionary, although you will find its constituent words. (Again, this specific example is now a poor base because it's appeared in this book.) A variant on the multiword approach is to use fragments of multiple words, such as *asepho*, derived from *baseball* and *telephone*. As a general rule, an acronym is the safest choice, providing it doesn't happen to spell anything.

NOTE   *These examples are all six characters long. Subsequent modifications add characters, and passwords on some OSs are limited to eight characters in length, hence the six-character length. Modern Linux distributions are not so limited, and in fact eight characters is a more reasonable* minimum *safe password length than a maximum. You might need to generate short passwords for some purposes, though, such as for retrieving e-mail from your ISP or logging onto web pages.*

There are many common types of strings you should *never* use as a password, even as a base:

- The name of any relative, friend, co-worker, or pet

- The name of any character in a book, movie, or play; or the name of a favorite work of fiction or art

- Your own name or your username

- Any other personally relevant information, such as your Social Security number or street address

- Particularly for the **root** password, any word signifying great power, such as *deity* or *boss*

- Particularly for workstations, a name or word that appears in plain sight of the terminal, such as the monitor's model number

- Any single word in any language, even if it's spelled backwards

- Any obvious misspelling of a word, such as *r0cket*, where the number *0* replaces the letter *o* in the word

- Any ascending or descending sequence of numbers or letters, such as *54321* or *ghijk*

- Any string of identical characters, such as *mmmmm*

- Any string of characters that appears on the keyboard, such as *qwerty*

The first six prohibitions are designed to protect against targeted attacks—the sort that seem to have a 100 percent chance of working in the movies. The rest of the prohibitions are designed to protect against words that are likely to appear in cracker dictionaries. These dictionaries are larger than ordinary dictionaries; they can include words in many languages, common misspellings, and nonwords that people are likely to try using.

Modifying the Base

Once you've selected a base by creating an acronym or combining multiple words or word fragments, you should modify that base. These modifications move the base further from the original base and make it harder for a cracker to guess the password, even if the base appears in the cracker's dictionary. Modifications you can make include:

Adding Random Punctuation, Numbers, or Control Characters   You can add punctuation, numbers, or even control characters to the password. Ideally, you should place these features randomly within the base, as in *yi9wtt}d* or *b#unp0en*. The number of possible additions of even just two characters is so large that password-cracking programs can't check every possibility. One exception: many people start or end passwords with numbers, so crackers often try the hundred password variants that result from this change, rendering the change ineffective.

Changing Case at Random   Linux's passwords are case-sensitive, so randomly altering the case of passwords can be an effective strategy. For instance, your password might become *Yi9wTT}D* or *b#UNp0eN*. This modification isn't effective on all systems or password types, though. For instance, the passwords used by the Server Message Block (SMB)/Common Internet File System (CIFS), and hence by Linux's Samba server, are case-insensitive.

Reversing the Order of One Base Word   If you use a pair of words as the base, you can reverse the order of one of the two words, as in *NU#bp0eN*. By itself, this modification isn't extraordinarily effective, but it does increase the cracker's search space by a modest amount.

As a general rule, adding punctuation, numbers, or control characters is the single most effective modification you can make. Altering the case of random characters can also be an important modification, at least for Linux's primary passwords.

When you're done, the password should resemble gibberish, but be memorable to you personally. Automated password-cracking tools will very probably be unable to match your password, which is the goal of the exercise. As an ordinary user, you can then change the password by using the `passwd` command:

```
$ passwd
Changing password for user ferd.
Changing password for ferd
(current) UNIX password:
New UNIX password:
Retype new UNIX password:
passwd: all authentication tokens updated successfully.
```

This program asks for your current password and then asks you to type the new password twice, as protection against a typo. None of these passwords echoes to the screen, even as asterisks, in order to reduce the chance of a shoulder surfer gleaning information about the password. The superuser can add a username to the command, as in **passwd ferd**. The system doesn't ask for confirmation of the original password, enabling **root** to change the password even if the user has forgotten the original.

GUI tools for changing passwords are also available. For instance, Figure 18.1 shows **userpasswd**, which is part of the GNU Network Object Model Environment (GNOME) desktop environment. These tools work much like the text-mode **passwd**, although they often echo asterisks to the screen as you type a password, as Figure 18.1 shows.

FIGURE 18.1

GUI tools for changing passwords are accessible from menus in default desktop environment configurations.

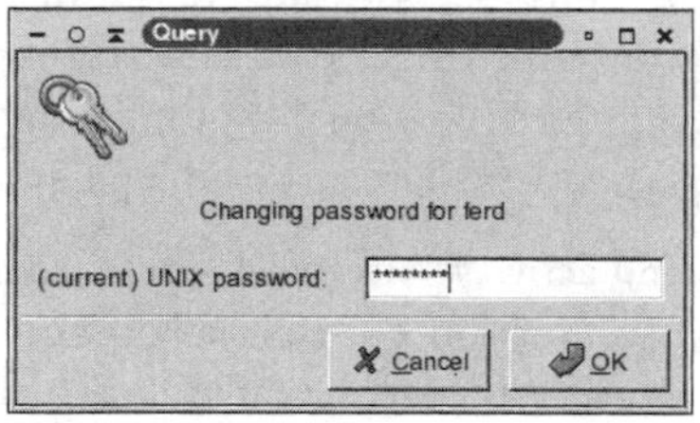

WARNING   *Try not to change your password over an unencrypted link such as a Telnet session. Doing so poses the same risks of sniffing experienced when entering your password for login. If some suspicious event compels you to change your password over an insecure link, change it again as soon as possible over a secure link.*

Protecting Passwords from Abuse

Once you've generated a password, you normally use it. Simultaneously, though, you must protect the password from discovery by means other than password cracking. Certain practices put passwords at risk of discovery by others, and other practices can help prevent this discovery, or at least minimize the risk if your password is found out. Steps you can take to improve your password security include:

Use Encryption   Whenever possible, use encrypted protocols, such as SSH, rather than unencrypted protocols, such as Telnet. This rule is particularly important on the Internet at large; when you send an unencrypted password over the Internet, it probably passes through about a dozen routers, any one of which could be compromised. Unfortunately, it's not always possible to use encryption. For instance, many ISPs provide only unencrypted tools for recovering e-mail using the Post Office Protocol (POP).

Change your password frequently   If you change your password often, you minimize the time period during which crackers can abuse it, should it be discovered. As the system administrator, you can enforce a password-change time by using the -x parameter to **passwd**. For instance, typing **passwd -x 30 ferd** enforces a 30-day maximum password lifetime on the **ferd** account.

Use unique passwords for each account   If you have multiple accounts, don't reuse the same password on each account. This practice will minimize the risk should the password for one account be discovered. Unfortunately, the proliferation of password-protected websites makes this advice practically impossible to follow for websites. You may need to categorize your sites according to sensitivity, and assign unique passwords only to sites that are particularly sensitive, such as online banking sites. Alternatively, many web browsers can now remember passwords for you; however, this approach has its own perils, which are described next.

Store passwords only in your head   Writing down passwords is potentially very dangerous; if the paper on which a password is written falls into the wrong hands, your account becomes instantly insecure. Likewise, storing your password in a computer file is risky; if your primary account is compromised, the secondary accounts protected by passwords stored in the primary account's files may also be attacked. (Some software, such as password managers on PalmOS handheld computers, can encrypt a list of passwords. If you must store passwords in a computer file, using such a system can reduce the risks.) Unfortunately, some tools are very awkward or impossible to use without storing passwords on disk; for instance, Fetchmail (`http://catb.org/~esr/fetchmail/`) is virtually worthless if it can't read a password from its configuration file.

Beware of suspicious notices and activity   If your login failed but you think you typed the password correctly, change your password at once—especially if you logged in using a public terminal. If somebody's lurking nearby when you log in, be careful to shield the terminal as you type the password. Never give your password to anybody else. As a general rule, odd occurrences—both in software and in human behavior—should be treated with suspicion. These events may have perfectly innocent explanations, but if in doubt, take appropriate actions to protect your account. Changing your password is cheap insurance against many types of attack.

Many of these protective measures are essentially defenses against social engineering. Others defend against network sniffing or other dangers. All of them must be practiced by ordinary computer users, which means that you, as a system administrator, must find a way to educate your users. In some cases this is easy; for instance, if you're running Linux on a personal workstation, you may be the only user. In other cases, you may need to include password education in a formal user training program.

One other step you may want to consider as a system administrator is auditing your users' passwords. You can run a password-cracking program, such as Crack (`http://www.crypticide.org/users/alecm/`), to discover weak user passwords. You can then notify users of their weak passwords and give them some time to correct the matter. For the best security, transfer the password file via floppy disk to a computer that's not connected to the network and run the password-cracker on it. This practice will minimize the chance that a miscreant will stumble upon your password cracking.

WARNING   Although discovering weaknesses in your system security in order to correct problems is an admirable goal, most organizations have strict policies forbidding activities such as password cracking. To avoid running afoul of such policies, even though you're doing it in the service of improving system security, be sure to clear password-cracking activity with somebody who has the authority to do so. Obtain this authorization in the form of a written and signed document, not merely a verbal approval. Failure to obtain permission to crack users' passwords may cost you your job or even result in criminal charges being filed against you.

Removing Unnecessary Servers

Servers are common sources of security problems. Because they're exposed to the network, and often to the Internet at large, bugs in servers may be exploited by a wide range of people. This fact makes servers unusually sensitive from a security point of view. It's best that no computer run any server that it doesn't absolutely have to run. In order to head off problems, of course, you must have some way to identify unnecessary servers—a task that's sometimes easier said than done. Once you've identified servers, you can reduce their risk in one of three ways: You can hide servers from unauthorized sites, you can shut servers down, or you can remove the server software from the computer.

Locating Unnecessary Servers

Before you can remove servers you're not using, you must locate them. You can go about this task in several ways, each of which has its specific advantages and disadvantages. Broadly speaking, three methods are checking for installed or running software, monitoring the local computer's network activity, and scanning one system from another.

CHECKING INSTALLED OR RUNNING SOFTWARE

Several Linux tools, which are described more fully in other chapters, can help you track down software that's installed or running. At a crude level, the `ls` command or a GUI file browser enables you to see what files exist in common program directories, such as `/bin`, `/sbin`, `/usr/bin`, `/usr/sbin`, `/usr/X11R6/bin`, `/usr/local/bin`, and `/usr/local/sbin`. (Many distributions also store program files in subdirectories of `/opt`.) Unfortunately, many of the files you'll find in these directories have cryptic names, so figuring out what these programs do can be time-consuming. As the `/usr/local` directory tree holds files you've installed without the benefit of your distribution's package management system, you may want to take the time to study its contents periodically to be sure there's nothing you've forgotten or that's suspicious in this directory tree.

TIP *If you don't recognize a program name, type* **man** **progname***, where* `progname` *is the program name. Many programs come with man pages describing their operation, so chances are good you'll find information on what the program does.*

Most software on most Linux systems is installed with the help of package management systems, as described in Chapter 11, "Managing Packages." This fact provides a means to study the software installed on your system. GUI package management tools, such as GNOME RPM, MandrakeUpdate, Red Hat's Package Management, SuSE's YaST2, or the Storm Package Manager for Debian, can be very useful because they enable you to quickly browse the installed packages, reading descriptions of what each package does. For instance, Figure 18.2 shows the Storm Package Manager in operation, including a description of an FTP server installed on the system. Using a package manager, you can uninstall any packages that aren't necessary.

Another approach to assessing the risk from installed programs is to examine the Linux process table using `ps`, as described in Chapter 14, "Programs and Processes." For instance, you might type `ps ax | less` to peruse the processes that are running on your system. Chances are many of these processes will be unfamiliar to you because their names are cryptic and they're programs that normally run in the background and don't require attention. When examining processes, pay particular attention to those whose names end in `d`. Servers' names often, but not always, end in that letter, which stands for *daemon*—a word derived from the Greek for "helper." Daemons run in the background and perform useful tasks. Most servers run as daemons, but not all daemons are servers.

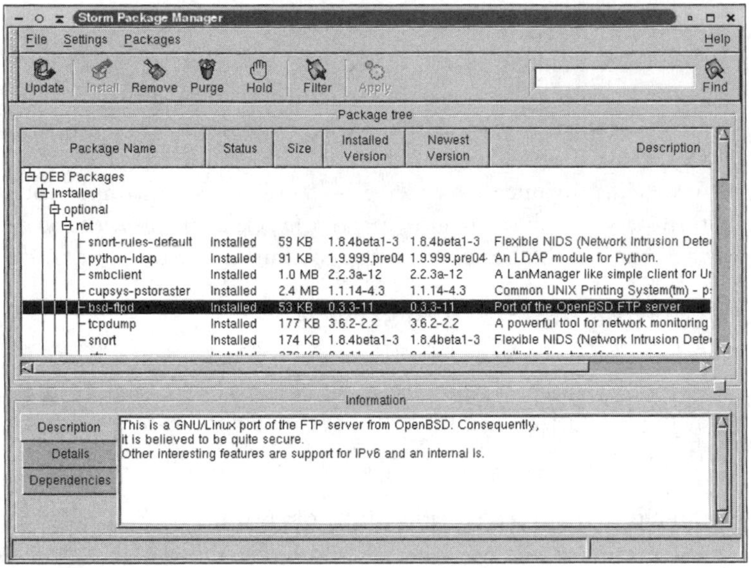

FIGURE 18.2

GUI package man-
agement tools enable
you to determine
what's installed on
your system and
remove unnecessary
packages.

One limitation of checking running processes is that this approach doesn't reveal servers that are launched by super servers (inetd or xinetd) unless somebody happens to be accessing the server in question at the time you use ps. Fortunately, you can assess the servers that are handled by the super server fairly easily—check the /etc/inetd.conf file for inetd or the /etc/xinetd.conf file and files in /etc/xinetd.d for xinetd. Chapter 22, "Running Servers," provides more information on the formats used by these configuration files.

USING LOCAL NETWORK ACTIVITY TOOLS

Unfortunately, checking installed and running local programs can be tedious, and it's easy to overlook a server, particularly if its name doesn't make it obvious that it's a server. One tool that can be helpful in spotting stray servers is netstat. This program is the Swiss Army knife of network status tools; it provides many different options and output formats to deliver information on routing tables, interface statistics, and so on. For purposes of spotting unnecessary servers, you can use netstat with its -a and -p options, as shown here:

```
# netstat -ap
Active Internet connections (servers and established)
Proto Recv-Q Send-Q Local Address          Foreign Address        State
➥PID/Program name
tcp        0      0 *:ftp                   *:*                    LISTEN
➥690/inetd
tcp        0      0 teela.rodsbooks.com:ssh nessus.rodsbooks.:39361 ESTABLISHED
➥787/sshd
```

I've trimmed most of the entries from this output to make it manageable as an example. The Local Address and Foreign Address columns specify the local and remote addresses, including both the hostname or IP address and the port number or associated name from /etc/services. The first of the two entries shown here isn't actively connected, so the local address and the foreign address and port number are all listed as asterisks (*). This entry does specify the local port, though—ftp. This line indicates that a server is running on the ftp port (TCP port 21). The State column specifies that the server is listening for a connection. The final column in this output, under the PID/ Program name heading, indicates that the process with a process ID (PID) of 690 is using this port. In this case, it's inetd.

The second output line indicates that a connection has been established between teela .rodsbooks.com and nessus.rodsbooks.com (the second hostname is truncated). The local system (teela) is using the ssh port (TCP port 22), and the client (nessus) is using port 39361 on the client system. The process that's handling this connection on the local system is sshd, running as PID 787.

It may take some time to peruse the output of netstat, but doing so will leave you with a much improved understanding of your system's network connections. If you spot servers listening for connections that you didn't realize were active, you should investigate the matter further. Some servers may be innocent or even necessary. Others may be pointless security risks.

TIP *When you use the* -p *option to obtain the name and PID of the process using a port, the* netstat *output is wider than 80 columns. You may want to open an extra-wide* xterm *window to handle this output, or redirect it to a file that you can study in a text editor capable of displaying more than 80 columns. To quickly spot servers listening for connections, pipe the output through a* grep LISTEN *command to filter on the listening state. The result will show all servers that are listening for connections, omitting client connections and specific server instances that are already connected to clients.*

USING REMOTE NETWORK SCANNERS

A final method of spotting unnecessary servers is to use a network scanner, such as Nmap (http://www.insecure.org/nmap/) or Nessus (http://www.nessus.org). These tools will scan another computer to locate open ports. More sophisticated tools, including Nessus, will check for known vulnerabilities, so they can tell you if a server might be compromised should you decide to leave it running.

WARNING *Network scanners are used by crackers for locating likely target systems, as well as by network administrators for legitimate purposes. Many organizations have policies forbidding the use of network scanners except under specific conditions. Therefore, you should check these policies and obtain explicit permission, signed and in writing, to perform a network scan, just as you should obtain permission before performing password cracking. Failure to do so could cost you your job or even result in criminal charges, even if your intentions are honorable.*

Nmap is capable of performing a basic check for open ports. Pass the -sT parameter and the name of the target system to it, as shown here:

```
$ nmap -sT teela.rodsbooks.com

Starting nmap V. 3.00 ( www.insecure.org/nmap/ )
Interesting ports on teela.rodsbooks.com (192.168.1.2):
(The 1581 ports scanned but not shown below are in state: closed)
Port       State       Service
21/tcp     open        ftp
22/tcp     open        ssh
```

NOTE   As with the output of `netstat` *shown in "Using Local Network Activity Tools," this output has been trimmed for brevity's sake.*

This output shows two open ports—21 and 22, used by `ftp` and `ssh`, respectively. If you weren't aware that these ports were active, you should log onto the scanned system and investigate further, using `netstat` or `ps` to locate the programs using these ports and, if desired, shut them down. The `-sT` option specifies a scan of TCP ports. A few servers, though, run on UDP ports, so you need to scan them by typing **nmap -sU *hostname***. (This usage requires `root` privileges, unlike scanning TCP ports.)

Nmap is capable of more sophisticated scans, including "stealth" scans that aren't likely to be noticed by most types of firewalls, ping scans to detect which hosts are active, and more. The Nmap man page provides details. Nessus, which is built atop Nmap, provides a GUI and a means of performing automated and still more sophisticated tests. Nessus comes as separate client and server components; the client enables you to control the server, which does the actual work.

When you use a network scanner, you should consider the fact that the ports you see from your test system may not be the same as those that might be visible to an attacker. This issue is particularly important if you're testing a system that resides behind a firewall from another system that's behind the same firewall. Your test system is likely to reveal accessible ports that would not be accessible from the outside world. On the other hand, a cracker on your local network would most likely have access similar to your own, so you shouldn't be complacent because you use a firewall. Nonetheless, firewalls can be important tools for hiding servers without shutting them down.

Hiding Servers from View

Once you've spotted servers, one approach to making them less of a risk is to hide them from most of the Internet. You can do this in several different ways:

Using External Firewalls   If your main concern is with outside access to a server, a separate firewall computer may be the best answer. Using such a firewall can permit local users to access the server while blocking outside access. Chapter 20, "Controlling Network Access," describes firewalls in more detail.

Using Local Firewalls   In addition to or instead of running a firewall on a separate computer, you can set up firewall rules on the same computer that runs the server. These rules can block access from any but specified computers. Again, Chapter 20 describes firewall configuration in more detail.

Using TCP Wrappers or `xinetd`   The TCP Wrappers package provides a screening service for incoming connections to servers that can use TCP Wrappers. One important TCP Wrappers-enabled program is `inetd`, so you can filter connections to any server run through `inetd`. The `xinetd` super server provides a similar set of access controls without using TCP Wrappers. Both of these tools are described in more detail in Chapter 20.

Using Server-Specific Controls   Some servers provide controls similar to those enabled by TCP Wrappers or `xinetd`. You should consult your server's documentation to learn what options it provides.

However you do it, hiding servers from view can greatly enhance security if servers should be accessible to some users but not to the world at large. As a general rule, firewalls do a better job of hiding servers than do TCP Wrappers, xinetd, or server-specific rules, but there are exceptions. For instance, if the computer has two network interfaces, xinetd can respond to queries on only one interface; it doesn't even listen for connections on the non-served interface.

TIP   If you have a choice of ways to implement a restriction, use them all! A misconfiguration or bug in one method might let an intruder through, so using redundant restrictions improves your system's security.

Shutting Down Servers

The next step in protecting yourself from server abuse is to shut it down entirely. Linux systems today ship with fewer servers active than did Linux systems a few years ago, so chances are you won't find many unnecessary servers running. You may find some, though, and if a server is truly unnecessary, the best course of action is to shut it down. Doing so not only protects you from abuse, but is also likely to reduce the memory load on the computer, thereby improving its performance at other tasks.

Chapter 22 covers methods used to start up servers. If you detect a truly unnecessary server, you may want to check each of these methods of startup and, when you find how the server is starting, disable it. The most common methods are listed here:

SysV Startup Scripts   Most distributions use SysV startup scripts, located in /etc/init.d, /etc/rc.d, or /etc/init.d/rc.d, to start servers. You can remove these startup scripts or rename the links to them in directories such as /etc/init.d/rc?.d so that the links' names start with K rather than S. These actions should cause the server to not start up when you next reboot the computer.

Super Servers   The inetd and xinetd super servers launch many servers. Reconfiguring these servers is a matter of editing the /etc/inetd.conf file for inetd, or the /etc/xinetd.conf file or files in /etc/xinetd.d for xinetd.

Local Startup Scripts   If you installed a server yourself from source code, it may be started through a local startup script, such as Mandrake or Red Hat's /etc/rc.d/rc.local or SuSE's /etc/init.d/boot.local.

The output of netstat can help you to localize the startup method. If inetd or xinetd controls a port, you can go straight to the super server's configuration file. If netstat shows that the server itself is listening on the port, you should investigate SysV startup scripts, and if you can't find anything there, look for local startup scripts.

After you change the configuration, you may need to shut down the server manually using kill, as described in Chapter 14. If a SysV startup script is present, you can pass the stop parameter to it, as in **/etc/init.d/ssh stop** to shut down the SSH server. If a server is launched from a super server, passing a SIGHUP to the super server should have it reread its configuration file, thereby stopping responses by the servers you've disabled. For instance, **killall -HUP inetd** tells inetd to reread its configuration file.

Shutting down a server is a very effective means of preventing it from responding to requests, and hence from being a potential security threat; however, there's always the chance that it will be run again. For instance, a software upgrade might restore configuration files that launch the server, or you might have misidentified the startup mechanism. You might be willing to tolerate this risk if you want to occasionally run the server; however, if you never want to run the server again, shutting it down isn't the best option. Instead, you should completely remove it from the system.

Uninstalling Servers

The most drastic measure to prevent a server from becoming a security risk is to uninstall it. The first step in uninstalling a server is usually to shut it down using its SysV startup script or `kill`, as described in the preceding section. Once this is done, you can use your partition's package management system to remove the server, as described in Chapter 11. Typically, removing the package also removes its SysV startup script or `/etc/xinetd.d` entry, if it has either of these. Thus, the computer can no longer even attempt to start the server. In some cases, the server may be started through other means, in which case the system may attempt to start the server, but it won't succeed. For instance, if you've got an `/etc/inetd.conf` entry for a server, `inetd` will not be able to launch the server. To prevent error messages from appearing in your logs, and to prevent accidental launches should you reinstall the package, you should track down and remove such entries.

If you installed the server from source code yourself, it may exist in `/usr/local` and not have an entry in your package database. Uninstalling such a package may be harder than uninstalling a packaged program, but it can be done. The most critical step is to delete the main server program. Check the server's documentation to determine what this file is. Many programs include an `uninstall` target for `make`, so you can uninstall the package by moving into the original source code directory and typing **`make uninstall`**.

Be aware that removing the software isn't a perfect guarantee that it'll never be run. You might accidentally install it again in the future, or one of your users might install the software for personal use. (Ordinary users can't run servers on privileged ports—those numbered below 1,024—but some servers are designed to run on unprivileged ports, and even normally privileged servers can run on unprivileged ports.) Crackers who obtain access to your system through other means might install additional servers for their own convenience.

Keeping Software Up-to-Date

Many security problems can be traced back to buggy software. Buggy servers—particularly if they must run as `root`—can give anybody on the Internet access to your computer. Servers aren't the only potential source of problems, either. Network clients can contain bugs that can be exploited by miscreants. Such problems have been documented in e-mail readers and web browsers, for instance. Under Linux, such problems are unlikely to give an attacker control of the computer, because these programs are normally run with ordinary user privileges. Nonetheless, buggy user software can give a cracker access to sensitive personal data. Some programs also run SUID `root`, and a bug in such a program could be devastating.

WARNING   *The risk of a security-related bug is one of many reasons you shouldn't browse the Web, read e-mail, or perform other routine tasks as* `root`. *A typo or slip of the mouse when performing a routine task as* `root` *could wipe out the entire system, whereas the same mistake as an ordinary user would, at worst, wipe out only your personal data.*

Fortunately, bugs in Linux software are usually fixed soon after they're discovered. Therefore, if you monitor such things closely, chances are you'll find fixes for problems before crackers can widely exploit them. The question is how best to watch for updated software. Chapter 11 describes one class of tools designed to help automate software updates: Tools such as Debian's Advanced Package Tool (APT), Red Hat's Update Agent, and SuSE's YaST can notify you of important updates soon after they become available, or at least make it easy for you to check for them. In some configurations, these tools can even update your system automatically, although this practice isn't without its risks— an update might damage a configuration file or break a delicate set of dependencies, for instance. Overall, these update tools are an invaluable security boon.

Whether or not you use automatic update tools, there are other sources of information you should monitor for important security notices. You may hear of a problem before an update becomes available. If the problem is serious enough, you might want to temporarily disable a server or remove the affected software. Important sources of security information include:

Security Websites   Many security websites exist. Three of the most important are the sites for the Computer Incident Advisory Capability (CIAC; `http://www.ciac.org/ciac/`), the Computer Emergency Response Team (CERT; `http://www.cert.org`), and the Center for Internet Security (CIS; `http://www.cisecurity.org`). All three sites offer information on the latest threats, pointers to additional information, and so on. CIAC, CERT, and CIS cover security for all platforms. A similar Linux-specific site is Linux Security (`http://www.linuxsecurity.com`). All of these sites are good places to look for more information if you hear of a new threat but need more details.

Security Mailing Lists   Many security websites offer companion mailing lists or e-mail newsletters. Check their web pages for details. You can subscribe to the CERT advisory mailing list by sending e-mail to `majordomo@cert.org` containing the text `subscribe cert-advisory`. Once on the list, you'll receive a copy of every CERT advisory in your e-mail, so you can respond quickly should the need arise.

Security Newsgroups   Several Usenet newsgroups cover security. Of particular interest to Linux users are `comp.security.unix` and `comp.os.linux.security`. Newsgroups devoted to specific security topics, such as `comp.security.firewalls`, also exist, as do groups for specific Linux distributions, such as `linux.debian.security`. These newsgroups can be a good place to go to ask advice or to lurk to watch ongoing discussions and notices of new problems.

Distributions' Websites   Most distributions have security-related pages on their websites. These may be accessible as links from the main page or buried under some other topic. If you don't see a *security* link, look for words such as *errata* or *updates*. Some distributions are now relying on their update tools and giving security web pages a less prominent position on their sites.

Individual Program's Website   If you run particularly visible or sensitive servers, you may want to monitor their home pages. This action is particularly advisable if you've replaced a standard package with one that normally doesn't come with your distribution, and therefore may not be handled by your automatic package update tools or mentioned on your distribution's web page.

Each of these sources of information has its advantages and drawbacks. For instance, certain mailing lists can alert you to problems soon after they're discovered; but these alerts may not provide you with the simplest upgrade path. For that, you may need to look to your distribution's or the program's website or an automatic upgrade tool. Newsgroups and security web pages are useful general education resources. In sum, these information sources are best used together to help you know when to upgrade your system, as well as how to deal with security threats generally.

Summary

As the world's computers become more tightly interconnected through always-up Internet links, system security becomes more important. Those who wish to do you harm or to use your system in harming others can attack in many different ways, ranging from tricking you or your users into revealing sensitive information to physically stealing your hardware to breaking in remotely using any of several techniques. Keeping one step ahead of the crackers in all these areas is a challenging task. You can make a good start by taking a few precautions, such as picking good passwords, removing unnecessary servers, and keeping your software up-to-date. You should also watch for news of security breaches so that you can update your system quickly when it becomes necessary.

Part IV

Networking Tools

## Chapter 19

Basic Network Configuration

CHANCES ARE YOUR LINUX installation program asked you a few questions in order to configure networking. If not, many distributions include network configuration tools that can help you get the network running, at least minimally. If yours didn't or if you want to optimize the network configuration beyond what the automated tools can do, this chapter will lead the way. It begins with a look at the lowest level—the network card. This information is likely to be important if you need to buy a new network card or if you're having problems with the network card's hardware. Next up is information on the Dynamic Host Configuration Protocol (DHCP), which is a popular tool for automatically setting basic network options on most computers on a network. (Chapter 27, "Miscellaneous Servers," covers DHCP server configuration—the other side of the DHCP equation.) If your system doesn't use DHCP, chances are it uses a static IP address, and methods of setting these options are covered next. Unfortunately, networks don't always work as they should, so the next section describes methods of testing your network's performance to help localize problems. Finally, this chapter covers some common optimizations you can employ to help improve network performance.

Getting the Most from a Network Card

Most networks today are built atop Ethernet, a set of hardware standards for network devices. Some Ethernet hardware, such as cables, hubs, and switches, reside outside the Linux computer. Most such devices are "OS-agnostic"—they work equally well with any OS. (There are a few exceptions, though, such as stand-alone network print servers, which must support the network printing protocol you use.) The network hardware component that requires the most attention from a Linux perspective is the *network interface card (NIC)*. This device requires support in the form of Linux drivers, and you may need to adjust Linux's configuration to use the card.

NOTE *Most NICs are actual plug-in cards; however, there are a few exceptions. Some motherboards include Ethernet circuitry on-board. Laptop computers frequently use PC Card Ethernet devices. Universal Serial Bus (USB) Ethernet devices are also becoming popular. With a few wrinkles, such as the location of drivers in the kernel configuration utility, all of these devices are treated alike from a software point of view. For simplicity, I refer to all of these devices as NICs in this chapter.*

Picking an Appropriate Network Card

If you're adding a computer to a network or if you need to replace a NIC, your first task is to pick one. Most network cards sold today are Ethernet models, which work only on Ethernet networks. For this reason, I focus on this type of hardware. If your network uses another type of network hardware, such as Token Ring, you must instead purchase a card for that type of hardware.

NOTE   Wireless networking technologies are becoming popular, particularly in homes and small offices where the cost or hassle of laying network wires is prohibitive. Wireless networking hardware works much like Ethernet or other wired network tools, but without the wires.

WARNING   When using wireless hardware, be particularly cautious about security. Someone parked in a car outside your building could easily snoop on your network traffic if you use a wireless protocol. Wireless protocols do include encryption tools, but these tools often slow down network accesses, and they may not be enabled by default. You might want to put a firewall between your wireless devices and your wired computers as a precaution in case an interloper abuses your wireless network.

Most Ethernet cards on store shelves today are 10/100 devices, meaning that they work at both 10 megabits per second (Mbps) and 100Mbps. Not coincidentally, most twisted-pair Ethernet networks today run at one or both of these two speeds. Earlier Ethernet standards used either thin or thick coaxial cabling and ran at 10Mbps. The up-and-coming standard is for *gigabit Ethernet*, which runs at 1,000Mbps (1 gigabit per second, or Gbps). Gigabit Ethernet variants that use twisted-pair and optical cabling are available. In early 2003, Gigabit Ethernet is starting to become affordable— gigabit Peripheral Component Interconnect (PCI) NICs sell for $50 to $200, as compared to $10 to $50 for most 10/100 PCI NICs. Therefore, you may want to at least consider gigabit hardware if you're upgrading an entire network or a large part of one. Gigabit hardware is also worthwhile for systems that transfer a lot of data, such as busy servers. (Such systems may need special support switches or routers to feed several 100Mbps connections into a single 1Gbps NIC, though.)

Fortunately, Linux includes drivers for the vast majority of network cards, especially in the 10/100 Ethernet realm. You're more likely to have problems with non-Ethernet hardware, including some wireless devices. Support for PC Card and USB adapters is also spottier than for PCI cards and Ethernet chipsets built into motherboards. For advice on specific models, perform a web search, including a search on Google Groups (http://groups.google.com). Be sure to click the link to sort responses by date so that you can spot the most recent responses. Chances are that somebody's asked about the compatibility of specific models or chipsets recently. You can also check your distribution's hardware compatibility page. Remember that Linux drivers are written for chipsets, and any given chipset may appear on dozens of manufacturers' cards. This fact is particularly true of Ethernet chipsets and Ethernet NICs sold under store brands or lesser-known labels. Chapter 1, "Optimizing System Architecture Usage," includes information on identifying the chipset that a board uses. Many of these techniques, though, work only after you've installed the board, or at least can examine it visually—you may not learn much by looking at the box in a store.

For use on a workstation or a light-duty server, you won't find much performance difference between NICs; these machines don't move enough data to make a noticeable difference. For use on heavily loaded servers, you may want to stick to well-known brand names, such as Intel and 3Com. Such products have mature Linux drivers, and the hardware is usually capable of sustaining heavy data transfer rates. Some other brands, and even many generic boards, also use good hardware. In particular, many NICs, including some models from Linksys and NetGear, use the original Digital Equipment Corporation (DEC) "Tulip" chipset or its clones. These chipsets perform well, and boards based on them are less expensive than many competing name-brand devices. Tulip-based boards have a drawback, though: Because there are so many Tulip clones, and because manufacturers change their hardware frequently, the driver authors have a hard time keeping up with new devices. There have been periods where a popular new Tulip-based board hasn't worked reliably until the Linux drivers have been updated. Boards based on some other low-end chipsets don't always perform very well on heavily loaded systems. NICs based on the RealTek 8139, for instance, sometimes yield worse speed than is possible with Intel, 3Com, or Tulip hardware, and may impose higher CPU loads, to boot. These deficiencies most likely won't be noticeable on a workstation or lightly loaded server, though.

Telling Linux to Recognize Your Card

In order to use a NIC, Linux must recognize it. This process is normally handled by your distribution's installation routines; the installer sets up an appropriate `/etc/modules.conf` entry, as described in Chapter 1, to load the driver as a module. If you recompile your kernel, be sure to compile the driver for your NIC, either as a module or built into the main kernel file. If you compile the driver into the kernel proper, the system should auto-detect the card. If not, you must have an appropriate `/etc/modules.conf` entry or load the driver with `insmod` or `modprobe`, either manually or in a startup script, as described in Chapter 9, "Bypassing Automatic Configurations to Gain Control."

Some NICs, particularly older Industry Standard Architecture (ISA) models, require special parameters to operate correctly. Chapter 1 describes how to pass such parameters to a card. You can find information in the drivers' documentation (usually in `/usr/src/linux/Documentation/networking`, although the `linux` directory name includes a version number on some systems) or on Donald Becker's website (`http://www.scyld.com/network/`; Donald Becker wrote many of the Linux Ethernet drivers). The Ethernet HOWTO document (`http://www.tldp.org/HOWTO/Ethernet-HOWTO.html`) also contains a great deal of card-specific information.

Checking Network Card Speed

Most Ethernet cards sold today are capable of operating at various speeds, such as 10Mbps or 100Mbps. Such devices typically auto-detect and configure themselves for the best possible speed, although a few older boards require driver parameters to set their speed. If you've got such a board and are operating at a lower speed than you believe your hardware should be using, consult your driver's documentation.

Most NICs include a series of light-emitting diodes (LEDs) near their connectors, and one of these LEDs usually denotes the link speed. For most 10/100 NICs, a lit LED indicates that it's connected at 100Mbps. If yours isn't lit and you believe it should be, you should first verify that the rest of your network is operating in 100Mbps mode. If you use hubs to connect your computers, even a single system operating at 10Mbps will bring down the speed of the rest of your components. Tracking down such a problem may be tedious; you may need to turn off or unplug every computer and then turn them on or plug them in one by one until you notice the speed drop. Remember that devices such as print servers qualify as computers and can drag down the transfer speed. Switches don't suffer from this problem. If you have only one 10Mbps device connected to a switch, it will communicate with other computers at 10Mbps, while interactions that don't involve the 10Mbps device will work at 100Mbps. Some "dual-speed" hubs exist. These operate separate 10Mbps and 100Mbps segments with hub-like interaction within each segment but switch-like interactions between them.

TIP *Hubs and switches typically include diagnostic LEDs that indicate active connections and often the speed of the connection. These LEDs can be as useful as NIC LEDs in diagnosing problems.*

Switches have another advantage over hubs: Switches enable NICs to operate in full-duplex mode, in which both computers involved in a transaction can send data simultaneously, much like a telephone conversation. Hubs use half-duplex mode, in which only one computer can send data at a time, much like using a walkie-talkie. Depending on the nature of your network traffic, full-duplex operation can improve performance substantially.

TCP/IP Basics

A *network stack* is a set of routines that link applications on one computer to the network hardware, and from there to applications on another computer. Network stacks are built in layers, each of which "packs" or "unpacks" data for transmission to the next layer in the stack. The top layer of the stack consists of applications—both *clients* (programs that initiate network data transfer, and with which humans usually interact) and *servers* (programs that respond to network data transfers, and that usually operate semi-independently).

Most networks today use the *Transmission Control Protocol/Internet Protocol (TCP/IP)* network stack. The Internet is built from TCP/IP, as are most native Unix and Linux networking tools. A few alternative network stacks, such as NetBEUI (used by Windows), IPX/SPX (used by Novell), and AppleTalk (used by Mac OS) also exist. These alternative stacks usually fill limited roles, such as delivering local file- and printer-sharing resources. All major operating systems today support TCP/IP, and many now use it even for local file and printer sharing.

In order to enable inter-computer communications, all network stacks provide some means of addressing. In TCP/IP, this takes the form of an *IP address*, which is a four-byte number usually expressed in base ten with dots separating each byte, as in 172.30.9.102. An IP address can be broken into two parts:

♦ A network part, which identifies a unique network

♦ A machine part, which identifies an individual computer on a network

In practice, the machine part is seldom used alone. This division is accomplished via the *network mask* (aka the *netmask* or *subnet mask*), which takes the form of a series of binary 1 values followed by a series of binary 0 values, totaling 32 bits (4 bytes). Each bit matches with a bit of the IP address. The IP address bits tied to netmask 1 values are part of the network address, and those tied to netmask 0 values are part of the machine address. This arrangement is illustrated in Figure 19.1. Network addresses have traditionally been broken on byte boundaries, yielding network masks that use either 0 or 255 values for each byte, as in 255.255.0.0, but this practice is no longer universal. Network masks can also be expressed as a number of *1* bits following the IP address and a slash, as in 172.30.9.102/16, which indicates an IP address of 172.30.9.102 in conjunction with a netmask of 255.255.0.0.

FIGURE 19.1

TCP/IP addresses are combined with a netmask to isolate the network address.

IP Address	172.30.9.102	`10101100 00011110 00001001 01100110`
Netmask	255.255.0.0	`11111111 11111111 00000000 00000000`
Network Address	172.30.0.0	`10101100 00011110 00000000 00000000`

On a lower level, network hardware also uses addresses. Ethernet NICs, for instance, have 6-byte *Media Access Control (MAC)* addresses, which are usually expressed as hexadecimal (base 16) values separated by colons or some other punctuation, as in 00:50:BF:19:7E:99. (These addresses are also sometimes called *hardware addresses* or *physical addresses*.) The network stack adds the MAC address to outgoing packets, and it discovers the MAC address associated with any given local IP address. MAC addresses are useful only for local networking tasks. For systems off of the remote network, TCP/IP relies on a *router*—a computer that's connected to more than one network and that directs packets between the networks to which it's connected. The Internet is a very large set of interconnected routers and the computers to which they're connected. You can operate an isolated local network without a router; however, if your computers are connected to the Internet, you must provide them with the IP address of a router (aka a *gateway* address).

At a higher level than IP addresses, TCP/IP supports *hostnames*—full alphanumeric names, such as www.sybex.com. These names are broken into parts separated by dots, with the earliest parts being the most specific. TCP/IP supports several mechanisms to tie hostnames to IP addresses, the most important of which is the *Domain Name System (DNS)*. DNS uses a series of servers, each of which is responsible for some part of the Internet. Your local DNS servers, which know about your local computers and how to make queries of other DNS servers to find IP addresses for other systems, are the most important DNS servers from a basic network configuration perspective. No matter how you configure your computers, you must normally give them the IP address for at least one DNS server. Providing two or three addresses creates redundancy, thereby improving reliability.

IPv4 VERSUS IPv6

This chapter emphasizes a particular variety of IP addressing known as *IP version 4* or *IPv4* for short. As with many computing protocols, of course, changing needs have challenged the limits of IPv4 addressing. One of the most important of these is the IPv4 address space. A 32-bit address is theoretically capable of handling 2^{32}, or 4,294,967,296 addresses. In practice, the total number of Internet addresses is lower than this because of inefficiencies in how they're doled out. Given the explosive growth of the Internet, IPv4 addressing is reaching its limits in the first years of the 21st century. Other problems, such as increased security threats, contribute to a need to upgrade IPv4.

The successor to IPv4 is *IPv6*. This version of IP supports a 128-bit address, which works out to a theoretical maximum of 2^{128}, or 3.40×10^{38}, addresses. This is enough addresses to assign 2.29×10^{20} addresses to each square centimeter of land on the Earth. Switching to IPv6 should therefore be adequate for a while. IPv6 also introduces changes that will help protocol developers to improve security. Unfortunately, the shift is taking quite some time to implement; as I write in early 2003, IPv6 Internet connections are still quite rare. Much of the pressure for a shift has been eased by the implementation of measures designed to minimize the need for new IPv4 addresses, such as widespread adoption of Network Address Translation (NAT), a technique whereby an entire subnetwork can "share" a single external IP address. Nonetheless, IPv6 is still likely to become common in the next few years. Fortunately, Linux already supports IPv6, so if and when you need to make the switch, you'll be able to do so. Configuring a system to use IPv6 addresses, though, is somewhat different than configuring the system to use IPv4 addresses.

DHCP: Promises and Perils

Many networks use DHCP to help simplify network configuration. On such a network, one computer (the DHCP server) delivers IP addresses and related configuration information to other computers (the DHCP clients). Instead of entering half a dozen pieces of information on each client, the clients need only be told to use DHCP. This simplification speeds up client configuration and makes it less likely that errors will creep in and cause problems. Unfortunately, what DHCP promises and what it delivers don't always match. You may find that you need to change your DHCP client's configuration to get it to work on any given network. In extreme cases, you may need to swap out one DHCP client and replace it with another. (Chapter 27 covers the related topic of DHCP server configuration.)

How DHCP Should Work

DHCP relies on *broadcasts* for its basic functionality. When a computer sends a broadcast, it addresses outgoing packets to all computers or to all computers on a network. For instance, a broadcast might be addressed to 255.255.255.255—a code that means all computers anywhere. Typically, routers don't pass broadcast traffic unless it's directed at a specific subnetwork, which keeps the Internet from being flooded by broadcasts.

When a computer that's configured to be a DHCP client boots or brings up its network interface, the computer sends a broadcast to the DHCP server port. The network's DHCP server computer hears this broadcast and replies to the sender with the basic information the sender needs to configure itself. The DHCP server sends this information to the client by using the client's MAC address, which was embedded in the DHCP broadcast, so the DHCP client doesn't need an IP address to receive the reply. Information that a DHCP server can deliver to its clients includes:

◆ The client's IP address

◆ The client's network mask

◆ The IP address of a router for the local network

◆ The addresses of one or more DNS servers

◆ The client's assigned hostname

◆ The length of the *lease* on the assigned IP address

◆ Miscellaneous protocol-specific information

Much of this information is the necessary data for operating on a TCP/IP network, as described earlier, in "TCP/IP Basics." DHCP can provide some protocol-specific information, though, such as the address of a Server Message Block/Common Internet File System (SMB/CIFS) Windows Internet Name Service (WINS) server, which fills much the same role in SMB/CIFS networking as a DNS server fills for most TCP/IP protocols.

The fact that DHCP assigns *leases* to IP addresses is important. If a computer crashes or shuts down without telling the DHCP server it's going down, the DHCP server must eventually be able to assign the address to another computer; otherwise, the DHCP server might eventually run out of IP addresses, as it might assign multiple addresses, in series, to the same computer. Typical lease times range from a few hours to several days. Ordinarily, a DHCP client contacts the DHCP server to request a lease renewal when the lease time is halfway up. If this contact fails, the client tries again closer to the lease renewal time. Therefore, a computer that's never shut down keeps the same IP address forever, assuming there are no network problems, such as an extended DHCP server outage. DHCP servers can be configured to give computers the same IP addresses repeatedly, based on the clients' MAC addresses or hostnames they pass to the server when they boot. This configuration is optional, though, and must be implemented in the server.

If some basic detail of your network changes, such as the IP address of the router, DHCP makes updating clients simple: You need only change the configuration in the DHCP server, and that change will propagate to all the DHCP clients when they renew their leases. If the change is an important one, such as a router address change, you may want to reduce the lease time on the server sometime prior to the scheduled change, so that clients will receive the updated information soon after you implement the change.

How DHCP Really Works

In theory, DHCP should greatly simplify network configuration for any network that has more than a handful of computers. In practice, of course, DHCP has a few problems:

Client/Server Incompatibility   Occasionally, a DHCP client and server simply don't get along well. This type of problem can be extremely frustrating when you're configuring a computer as a DHCP client, because you enter all the data you should enter and it simply doesn't work. Fixing this type of problem for Linux DHCP clients is described in the next two sections, "Tweaking DHCP Clients" and "Changing DHCP Clients."

Dynamic IP Addresses   Although computers that run continuously typically use the same IP address for extended periods of time if you use DHCP, this stability isn't guaranteed. A computer's IP address can change, particularly if you shut it down and its lease expires while it's shut down. This characteristic makes DHCP configuration a poor choice for servers unless the DHCP server is configured to deliver the same IP address to the server time after time.

Potential Server Loss   If the DHCP server becomes inaccessible, the resulting network problems can be quite severe, because the DHCP clients will drop off the network as their IP addresses expire. You can minimize the potential for such problems by using long lease times. A related problem that's not so easily fixed is the potential for problems should the DHCP server be down or inaccessible when you boot a DHCP client. Depending on the OS and its options, the DHCP client may refuse to bring up its network interface or it may assign itself an IP address—perhaps the last one it used, or possibly an address in a range commonly used for this purpose.

In general, DHCP works well when it's properly configured. If you're setting up a single Linux system or a few Linux systems on an existing network, chances are you have little choice about whether to use DHCP. If your network has a DHCP server and your computer isn't exempted from using it for some reason (say, because it's a server that must have a static IP address), you must use your network's DHCP server. If your network doesn't have a DHCP server, you use a static IP address, as described in the upcoming section, "Using a Static IP Address."

Tweaking DHCP Clients

Most Linux distributions ship with one or more of four DHCP clients: pump, dhclient, dhcpxd, or dhcpcd (don't confuse either of the last two with dhcpd, the most common Linux DHCP server). Table 19.1 summarizes which clients come with which distributions, along with information about the startup scripts and configuration files that call and configure these clients. This information is critical if you want to modify a DHCP client configuration using anything except your distribution's GUI configuration tools.

NOTE *Network configuration files sometimes bear the name of the network interface, such as* ifcfg-eth0 *for the* eth0 *interface. If you're using a non-Ethernet interface or if you have more than one NIC, these names will be different.*

If you configure your computer to use DHCP by using your distribution's standard tools, chances are the system worked when you started it (assuming your network has an appropriate DHCP server, of course). If it didn't work, you must edit your configuration in some way. You can take any of four approaches to this task:

Use Your Distribution's Configuration Tools   The most straightforward approach is to attempt to use your distribution's GUI configuration tools to fix the problem. Many tools provide some way to enter common details that you may need to provide to your DHCP client, such as a system name. (Some networks require DHCP clients to announce themselves by name.) Unfortunately, some GUI tools are extremely limited in the DHCP client options they enable you to adjust, so you may need to take another approach.

Edit the Extra Configuration Files   In most distributions, the files listed under the Extra Configuration Files column of Table 19.1 control DHCP client options. Peruse these files looking for options you can adjust, such as the hostname the DHCP client presents to the DHCP server.

TABLE 19.1: DHCP CLIENT CONFIGURATION INFORMATION

DISTRIBUTION	DEFAULT DHCP CLIENT	ALTERNATIVE DHCP CLIENTS	DHCP CLIENT STARTUP SCRIPT	EXTRA CONFIGURATION FILES
Debian GNU/Linux 3.0	dhclient	pump	/sbin/ifup[1]	/etc/network/interfaces, /etc/dhclient.conf
Mandrake Linux 9.1	dhclient	dhcpcd, dhcpxd, pump	/sbin/ifup	/etc/sysconfig/network, /etc/sysconfig/network-scripts/ifcfg-eth0, /etc/dhclient-eth0.conf
Red Hat Linux 9.0	dhclient	none	/sbin/ifup	/etc/sysconfig/network, /etc/sysconfig/network-scripts/ifcfg-eth0
Slackware Linux 9.0	dhcpcd	none	/etc/rc.d/rc.inet1	none
SuSE Linux 8.1	dhcpcd	dhclient	/sbin/ifup-dhcp	/etc/sysconfig/network/dhcp, /etc/sysconfig/network/ifcfg-eth0

[1] *Binary executable, not a script*

Edit the DHCP Startup Script   If you can't figure out what to change in the configuration files or if making these changes is ineffective, you can try editing the startup script. Consult the man page for your DHCP client to learn about options you can use, then modify the startup script to pass those options directly. Alternatively, examining the startup script may provide you with the information you need to edit the configuration file to get the job done. Unfortunately, Debian's /sbin/ifup "script" is really a compiled binary program, so this approach is impractical with Debian unless you want to track down, edit, and recompile the program's source code or replace /sbin/ifup with your own script.

Bypass Normal Network Startup Tools   Finally, if all else fails, you can try bypassing the normal startup script process, as described in Chapter 9. For instance, you could call your DHCP client from a local startup script.

Changing DHCP Clients

Sometimes tweaking a DHCP client configuration just isn't enough. A DHCP server configuration may be fussy enough to just plain not work with a client. As a general rule, pump is the most troublesome client. Fortunately, few modern distributions use pump (none of the five summarized in Table 19.1 use it by default). Some older distributions used pump, though, and you might have installed it by accident. It's also possible that your DHCP server doesn't get along with dhclient or dhcpcd. If that's the case, you must change your DHCP client.

Most distributions automatically detect DHCP clients and run them, no matter which client you have installed. Table 19.1 lists the clients that ship with each distribution. The DHCP startup script should recognize all of these clients and, in some cases, more. Therefore, the simplest way to reconfigure your DHCP client is to use your package system, as described in Chapter 11, "Managing Packages," to remove the DHCP client your system is configured to use and to install another one. When you reboot, the system should try to use the new DHCP client. To use the new DHCP client without rebooting, try using your distribution's SysV startup scripts. For instance, on Mandrake, you might type:

```
# /etc/rc.d/init.d/network stop
# /etc/rc.d/init.d/network start
```

The network, including the new DHCP client, should be up again a few seconds after you type the second command. Try using ps to verify that the new DHCP client is running, as in **ps ax | grep dhcpcd** to search for dhcpcd; and type **ifconfig eth0** to view the new network configuration and verify that your system has an IP address. (Both of these commands can be issued from non-root accounts.)

Using a Static IP Address

If you're running a server that requires a fixed IP address or if your network doesn't have a DHCP server, chances are you'll configure your network options the old-fashioned way—using a static IP address. Most distributions provide tools to help configure a static IP address at system installation time or from system configuration utilities after you've installed Linux. For instance, Figure 19.2 shows a tool that comes with Mandrake. Type **drakconf** or locate the Mandrake Control Center on your system's menus, then navigate to the DrakConnect option in the Network & Internet area. Click Wizard, and follow the prompts to answer this and other configuration questions.

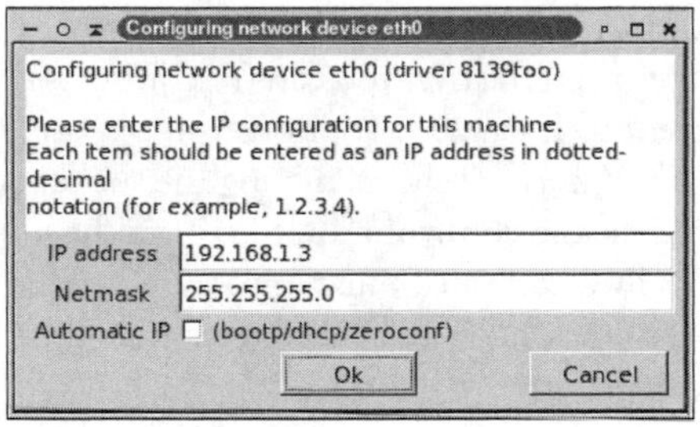

FIGURE 19.2

GUI tools enable you to set up a system for basic functionality using a static IP address.

Some configurations require going beyond the options supported by configuration tools such as drakconf. When you find yourself having to set unusual options, you may need to dig into configuration files. Knowing where to look can save you a lot of time and frustration. One situation that deserves special attention is configuring a computer with more than one NIC. Even if you use DHCP on one or more interfaces, such systems typically require manual adjustment to work correctly.

Files for Setting Network Options

In many cases, the files described in Table 19.1 control static IP address configuration as well as DHCP options. For instance, Listing 19.1 shows a SuSE system's static IP address configuration, as defined in /etc/sysconfig/network/ifcfg-eth0.

LISTING 19.1: TYPICAL OPTIONS IN A STATIC IP ADDRESS CONFIGURATION FILE

```
BOOTPROTO='static'
BROADCAST='192.168.1.255'
IPADDR='192.168.1.1'
NETMASK='255.255.255.0'
NETWORK='192.168.1.0'
REMOTE_IPADDR=''
STARTMODE='onboot'
UNIQUE='WL76.hvctWyU2jj4'
WIRELESS='no'
```

Most of the entries in Listing 19.1 are self-explanatory, at least if you know the terminology, as summarized earlier, in "TCP/IP Basics." Many distributions use the BOOTPROTO variable to set the method of network configuration—static for a static IP address or dhcp for DHCP. The STARTMODE option in Listing 19.1 tells the system to start networking when the system boots. UNIQUE is a system-specific ID code. You can change these options, or options such as the IPADDR and NETMASK, to change the static IP address configuration.

The computer's hostname often appears in a file called /etc/hostname or /etc/HOSTNAME. Many networking tools use the name in this file when announcing the system to other computers or in displays such as login prompts. The `/etc/hosts` file also sets the hostname, along with the computer's IP address, in lines like these:

```
127.0.0.1        localhost
192.168.1.1      trex.pangaea.edu    trex
```

This file serves as a sort of mini-DNS; it can provide static mapping of IP addresses to hostnames. This file usually contains both a mapping of `127.0.0.1` to `localhost` and an entry for the machine's network IP address and hostname. The latter entry includes both the fully qualified domain name (FQDN; `trex.pangaea.edu`) and a shorter "nickname" (`trex`). Small networks sometimes use `/etc/hosts` entries to enable users to type computer hostnames rather than IP addresses without running a full DNS server.

TIP *If your computer takes a long time to start up, including a pause when starting sendmail, check* `/etc/hosts`. *Some programs pause for long periods if they can't resolve the computer's hostname to an IP address. If DNS isn't working at that point in the boot process, a properly configured* `/etc/hosts` *file can bypass problems.*

Another important network configuration file is `/etc/resolv.conf`. This file holds information on DNS servers. Listing 19.2 shows a typical `resolv.conf` file. The `nameserver` lines are the most important ones; each of these lines points to one DNS server. If one DNS server doesn't respond, Linux tries the next one, and then a third, if defined. The `domain` line specifies the domain in which the computer resides. You can omit the name of the domain (`pangaea.edu` in Listing 19.2) from a hostname during a lookup; for instance, entering **http://trex** in a web browser will find the web server running on `trex.pangaea.edu`. The `search` line accomplishes a similar goal, but you can specify several search domains. Searching many domains can slow down name resolution, though, and may return the wrong IP address sometimes, if a name is duplicated in two domains.

LISTING 19.2: CONTENTS OF A TYPICAL /etc/resolv.conf FILE

```
domain pangaea.edu
search north.pangaea.edu south.pangaea.edu
nameserver 172.30.9.7
nameserver 192.168.1.1
```

One final but very important configuration file is your distribution's local startup file, as described in Chapter 9. Most network options can be set by calling networking programs, such as `route` or `ifconfig`, from a local startup file. For instance, the following lines bring up `eth0` and assign it a default route (the local gateway system) of 192.168.1.1:

```
ifconfig eth0 up
route add default gw 192.168.1.1
```

Configuring Multiple NICs

Most computers have just one network interface, but some have multiple interfaces—that is, they're *multihomed*. For instance, routers have multiple interfaces, one for each network. Occasionally a nonrouter will have multiple interfaces. One common example is a computer that has a local area network (LAN) connection for purely local networking and that uses the Point-to-Point Protocol (PPP) for Internet connectivity. You might also want to configure a server on a network with multiple subnets to use multiple interfaces, one for each subnet. This configuration can reduce the load on the router that resides between the subnets, it can reduce the traffic on at least one of the subnets, and it may make it easier to implement certain types of access controls—for instance, you can run some servers on one interface but not on the other.

If both of your NICs use static IP addresses and are Ethernet devices, configuring them is fairly straightforward, although your GUI tools might or might not be much help. Basically, most distributions place separate configuration files in `/etc/network`, `/etc/sysconfig/network`, `/etc/sysconfig/ networking`, or a similar location, one file per interface. Table 19.1 summarizes the locations of these configuration files. Examine these files, and if necessary copy one file to create a second interface's configuration, making the necessary changes for each network.

One detail that can be tricky when configuring a system with multiple interfaces is the *default route*, aka the *gateway address*. This is the IP address of the computer that should handle traffic destined for the Internet at large, as opposed to computers on either network to which the computer is directly connected. The default route is usually set in one of the configuration files outlined in Table 19.1, but sometimes another file handles the job. In SuSE, for instance, it's set in the `/etc/sysconfig/ network/routes` file. (SuSE also uses files named `/etc/sysconfig/network/ifroute-if`, where *if* is the interface name, for interface-specific routes.) Even a multihomed computer has just one default route. If by chance both your interfaces obtain IP addresses via DHCP, both DHCP servers may try to assign default routes to your computer. If this happens, you may want to use a local startup script to remove one of the two default routes, using a line like this:

```
route del -net default gw 192.168.1.1
```

This line removes the `192.168.1.1` gateway from the routing table. Of course, if you use a line like this to override a DHCP configuration, it must execute after the DHCP client runs. If your normal startup script sequence launches local scripts before the network is configured, you should create a new custom SysV startup script to execute a command like this one after the DHCP client runs, or modify your distribution's network startup script to do the job.

Another potential problem is the addition of routes. For instance, suppose one NIC links to the Internet and another links to a local network. If the local network has no ties to other networks, the configuration is fairly straightforward—`ifconfig` will create the appropriate local routes when the network configuration scripts launch it. If the local network has a small router that links to a second local network, though, you must add a route for that local network. Once again, a local startup script is the best solution. You can add a line like the following:

```
route add -net 192.168.7.0/24 gw 192.168.1.7
```

This line tells the system to add a routing table entry to pass all traffic destined for the `192.168.7.0/24` network to `192.168.1.7`. This computer must be configured as a router between its two networks (`192.168.7.0/24` and, presumably, `192.168.1.0/24`).

If you want to configure a Linux computer as a small router, such as the one just described, you must first set the system up with two network interfaces. You can then enable routing by entering the following command in a local startup script that executes after both network interfaces become active:

```
cat "1" > /proc/sys/net/ipv4/ip_forward
```

Thereafter, the computer functions as a router, assuming appropriate kernel options are available, as they are by default on most Linux distributions. You should be aware of the potential problems that come with this configuration, though—if your computer should *not* function as a router (say, because the two networks already have a router with extensive firewall features built in), you should check that this configuration is *not* enabled. Type the following command after the system has booted to be sure the system isn't a router:

```
$ cat /proc/sys/net/ipv4/ip_forward
0
```

The output value of 0 indicates that the system is not a router. If Linux responds with 1, the computer is a router. Check your network startup files for any call that accesses /proc/sys/net/ipv4/ip_forward and make any necessary changes.

TIP   An old computer (even a 486) can make a good Linux-based router for a small network. Load a small Linux distribution, such as a minimal Debian installation or ZipSlack (described in Chapter 17, "Protecting Your System with Backups"), onto the computer. Remove all unnecessary servers, configure the computer with two NICs, and set up routing functions. For added security, consult Chapter 20, "Controlling Network Access," for information on setting up iptables *firewall rules. Advanced router functions are available, but they are well beyond the scope of this book.*

Testing Network Performance

Network performance problems can sometimes be inscrutable. Why do you get 3MB/s transfer rates from one site but only 3KB/s from another site? Why do some web pages appear almost instantaneously while others make you wait for seconds before displaying anything at all? Unfortunately, many of these problems are due to deficiencies on the Internet at large, and you may not be able to fix them. Other problems are more localized, though. In order to tell these problem types apart, you must conduct tests or at least know the symptoms of different types of problems.

The two most fundamental measures of network performance are *throughput* and *latency*. These are measures of the overall data transfer rate and the time for a signal to pass from one site to another and back again, respectively. Throughput is important when you're downloading large files, such as Linux CD-R images. Latency is important when you're using a highly interactive protocol, such as a remote login tool. In addition to these two speed measures, diagnosing problems with specific hardware, such as routers and DNS servers, deserves some attention. When these devices malfunction, you can get sporadic or constant network performance problems.

NOTE   Network performance can vary over time. On a business's LAN, performance is likely to be worst during the workday, as employees go about their daily routines. Regional Internet transfers are likely to be slowest in the evening, when the Internet is clogged with home users browsing the Web. You may want to perform several tests over time to help determine the cause of problems and plan for future local network expansions.

Testing Throughput

The best measure of throughput is a large continuous data transfer. Ideally, you want the sending system to generate data instantly and the receiving system to discard it, to avoid complications such as disk-access bottlenecks. In practice, such tests are hard to run unless you control both computers. For this reason, I describe a good but imperfect stand-in: using a File Transfer Protocol (FTP) exchange to measure throughput.

To perform an FTP test, you must have an FTP client installed on one system and an FTP server on another system. This second system might not be under your direct control; for instance, you might use this technique to test data transfer between your network and some remote site on the Internet. If you want to perform a local speed test, consult Chapter 24, which includes information on FTP server configuration. Your task will be greatly simplified if the FTP client reports data transfer speeds, as do most text-based FTP clients. (A few GUI clients omit this report, forcing you to time transfers with a stopwatch.)

WARNING   *FTP programs report speeds in a variety of units. Megabytes per second (MB/s) and kilobytes per second (KB/s) are both common. Ethernet speeds are often stated in megabits per second (Mbps). If you miss the distinction between bits (b) and bytes (B), you can easily misinterpret your data transfer speeds by a factor of eight. Also, a few programs don't use the correct abbreviations for bits and bytes. If your speeds seem to be an eighth or a tenth what you expect, it may be that you're misinterpreting (or the FTP client is misreporting) the units.*

Connect from the FTP client to the server and locate a file to transfer. It's important that the test file be fairly large—at least a megabyte, and possibly larger if you're testing transfers on a fast network. Smaller files are likely to transfer so quickly that minor random variations in transfer times will translate into large differences in apparent throughput.

Once you've located a file of suitable size, try transferring it. If possible, direct the client to store the file as /dev/null. For instance, to transfer megfile.bin using the standard text-mode Linux ftp program, type **get megfile.bin /dev/null** in ftp. This practice will remove local disk-access delays from the equation. The first time you transfer a file, there may be delays due to disk accesses on the server system. You can't completely eliminate the possibility of server-side problems interfering with throughput estimates, but if you perform multiple transfers, chances are good that the second and subsequent transfers will be from an in-memory disk cache rather than from the disk itself. For this reason, you should disregard the first transfer speed and instead use the average of the next few transfers. In most cases, a total of just two or three estimates (not counting the initial one) should be sufficient to give you some idea of what the throughput is. If your estimates vary wildly, though (say, by a factor of 2 or more), you might want to try increasing the file size. It's also possible that varying network load or a flaky router is causing erratic performance. In addition to retrieving files, you should try sending files using put, as in **put megfile.bin**. This test will be possible only if you have write access on the server, of course.

On a lightly loaded 100Mbps Ethernet LAN, you should be able to achieve speeds of at least 7MB/s. In tests on my own LAN, most transfers run at between 8MB/s and 11MB/s. Systems with weak CPUs, sluggish hard disks, or heavy local or network loads may produce lower values than this. If a test comes in substantially below this value (or an adjusted value if your network runs at a different speed), you may want to investigate further. For instance, try reversing the client and server roles, or try another FTP client or server; the problem could be due to a misconfigured or poorly performing program. You can also try using a protocol other than FTP.

NOTE   Gigabit Ethernet is fast enough that its theoretical maximum transfer speed is faster than most hard disks in 2003. Thus, if you're using gigabit Ethernet, you must pay careful attention to your disk subsystem and perhaps implement a redundant array of independent disks (RAID) configuration. If you don't, you won't fully utilize the potential of gigabit Ethernet, at least not on individual transfers.

You might also want to check the output of `ifconfig`, which includes error counts:

```
$ /sbin/ifconfig eth0
eth0      Link encap:Ethernet  HWaddr 00:05:02:A7:76:DA
          inet addr:192.168.1.2  Bcast:192.168.1.255  Mask:255.255.255.0
          UP BROADCAST RUNNING MULTICAST  MTU:1500  Metric:1
          RX packets:196432 errors:2 dropped:0 overruns:0 frame:0
          TX packets:100753 errors:3709 dropped:0 overruns:3707 carrier:0
          collisions:0 txqueuelen:100
          RX bytes:220874752 (210.6 MiB)  TX bytes:59365177 (56.6 MiB)
          Interrupt:42 Base address:0xd000
```

Two receive (RX) errors and 3,709 transmission (TX) errors appear in this example's output. Such errors may be the result of driver bugs, a flaky NIC, bad cables, or defective switches, among other things. The sixth line of output includes a count of collisions (0 in this example). Collisions are an inevitable occurrence when your network uses a hub, but a network with switches should have few or no collisions. If the number of collisions is more than a few percent of the total number of packets sent and received, chances are you have too many computers connected on a hub. Try replacing the hub with a switch, or break the network into two parts, with a router or at least a small switch between the parts.

Internet throughput varies with a number of factors, including the speed of the server, the number of other connections to the server, the type of Internet connection used by the server, the load on the routers between you and the server, the nature of your own Internet connection, and the demand for Internet bandwidth from other users at your site. Assuming your LAN is involved in your Internet access, you won't exceed your LAN speeds for Internet throughput. In most cases, Internet transfer speeds are likely to be far lower than those on the LAN. Some sites may crawl along at 1KB/s or less, but others may exceed 1MB/s, assuming you have a fast enough Internet connection. In many cases, your own Internet connection will be a limiting factor. For instance, if you have an Asymmetric Digital Subscriber Line (ADSL) connection rated at 604Kbps, you probably won't get more than 60 to 70KB/s transfer rates from good sites.

NOTE   Some Internet connections, including ADSL and cable modems, yield asymmetric speeds—upstream speeds are much lower than downstream speeds. If you measure speeds in both directions, you may see a five- or tenfold difference in throughput.

One common problem is that some sites are much slower than others. Any of the Internet speed factors can be the cause. One issue can be distance. Accessing sites from the other side of the planet can be very sluggish because of the large number of routers between the sites. Each router is a chance for packets to be lost, which degrades overall performance. Large distances also increase latencies. Ordinarily, latencies aren't strongly correlated with throughput, but if latencies rise too high, the systems may pause their transmissions while they wait for acknowledgement of sent data, as described in the upcoming section, "Setting the Send and Receive Window Sizes."

Checking Latencies

The primary tool for checking latencies is ping. This program is a standard part of all Linux systems, and its basic use is fairly straightforward: Type the program name followed by a hostname or IP address. You can also use a number of parameters, such as -c, which sets the number of packets the program sends. The result is a series of checks of the remote system (which you terminate by pressing Ctrl+C if you didn't use -c):

```
$ ping -c 3 www.linux.org
PING www.linux.org (198.182.196.56): 56 data bytes
64 bytes from www.linux.org (198.182.196.56): icmp_seq=1 ttl=43 time=99.1 ms
64 bytes from www.linux.org (198.182.196.56): icmp_seq=2 ttl=43 time=84.4 ms
64 bytes from www.linux.org (198.182.196.56): icmp_seq=3 ttl=43 time=91.8 ms

--- www.linux.org ping statistics ---
3 packets transmitted, 3 received, 0% packet loss, time 2020ms
rtt min/avg/max/mdev = 84.431/91.801/99.144/6.006 ms
```

This test shows latencies in the form of ping times of between 84.4 and 99.1 milliseconds (ms). Unlike throughput, in which higher values are better, *lower* latencies are superior. As with throughput, latencies can vary substantially from one site to another. Some of the causes of this variation include:

Physical Distance　Information cannot travel faster than the speed of light (186,282 miles per second). As the Earth's circumference is 24,902 miles, this means that the theoretical minimum round-trip ping time between two computers on opposite sides of the planet is 134ms. By contrast, the theoretical minimum ping time over a 6-foot Ethernet cable is so small as to be negligible. In practice, distance has a more profound effect than a simple examination of physics and the speed of light would seem to suggest. This is partially because greater distance is associated with a larger number of intervening routers (the next factor in this list), and in part because Internet paths seldom take the shortest physical route.

Number of Intervening Routers　Every router that processes a packet takes a certain amount of time to do so. The result is that pinging systems that are separated from you by many routers can take a long time, even if those systems are physically nearby.

Load on Intervening Routers　Computers tend to do things more slowly when they're asked to do a lot of work. Routers are nothing more than computers configured to direct network traffic. Many of the routers through which your Internet traffic travels are dedicated to the task of routing—they do almost nothing else. As a result, when Internet traffic increases, the routers slow down. The result can be increased latencies or even lost packets.

Link Types　Some connection technologies produce higher latencies than others. The worst technology in this regard is satellite-based Internet access, which uses satellites hovering at 22,282 miles above the Earth. A packet traveling from a computer to that satellite, back down to the receiving station, and then the reply taking the reverse path must traverse at least 89,128 miles, for a minimum theoretical minimum ping time of 478ms. In practice, PPP links over telephone lines also tend to produce quite high latencies. Most dedicated Internet connections (cable modems, DSL, T1 lines, and so on) produce latencies of just a few milliseconds to the nearest router.

To get a feel for the latencies your network and Internet connection produce, try pinging a few systems, such as a computer on your LAN, the first router beyond your Internet connection (that is, the router provided by your ISP), some computers you know are operated in your geographic area, and some more distant systems. Computers on your LAN are likely to produce ping times of 1ms or less. My own ISP's routers yield ping times in the 10 to 20ms range. Computers geographically near me (in Rhode Island) are closer to 50ms. Those on the west coast of the United States or in England yield ping times of about 100ms. Australia and New Zealand take just under 300ms to ping. Hong Kong, Israel, and Russia all produce ping times of a bit over 300ms. One complication can involve routing paths. For instance, my own ISP routes all my packets through Georgia; therefore, my own latencies to sites in Georgia are about 40ms, compared to 50ms to sites a few miles from me. Also, sites may not be hosted where you believe them to be. For instance, my own personal website (`http://www.rodsbooks.com`) is hosted by a company in California. Most colleges and universities run their own web servers, so you can try pinging nearby schools' web servers as nearby systems. Once you're familiar with typical ping times for your connection, you'll be able to spot aberrant performers. If the issue is important enough, you may want to try looking for routers that aren't performing as they should.

NOTE *Some sites are configured to not respond at all to pings. Therefore, if you ping a site and it doesn't respond, you can't be sure if the site is down or if it's deliberately ignoring your pings. For purposes of learning about typical ping times, move on to another site. If you're trying to diagnose a problem with that particular site, though, a failure to respond to pings deprives you of some potentially useful information.*

Locating Flaky Routers

Many Internet connectivity problems can be traced to difficulties experienced by just one router in the path between you and your target site. Such problems may affect all sites, some sites, or even just one site. Using `ping`, you can identify which sites have latency problems, but `ping` doesn't tell you where the problem lies in the network. To do that, you need another tool: `traceroute`. This program traces the route that packets take going to a remote site and reports three latencies for each of these sites. For instance, here's a sample run of this program:

```
$ traceroute -n www.whitehouse.gov
traceroute: Warning: www.whitehouse.gov has multiple addresses; using 63.209.213.16
traceroute to a1289.g.akamai.net (63.209.213.16), 30 hops max, 38 byte packets
 1  192.168.1.254  1.899 ms  1.046 ms  1.047 ms
 2  10.1.88.1  14.334 ms  11.082 ms  12.477 ms
 3  68.9.8.253  15.875 ms  17.262 ms  13.846 ms
 4  68.9.14.5  14.644 ms  22.929 ms  25.401 ms
 5  68.1.0.44  20.196 ms  12.477 ms  17.781 ms
 6  68.1.0.43  15.880 ms  12.726 ms  14.658 ms
 7  68.1.0.51  30.978 ms  21.440 ms  26.877 ms
 8  67.29.170.1  27.167 ms  30.978 ms  26.993 ms
 9  209.247.9.173  28.867 ms  26.455 ms  23.185 ms
10  64.159.1.45  41.636 ms  46.747 ms  43.022 ms
11  64.159.3.70  39.151 ms  36.240 ms  41.194 ms
12  63.209.213.16  37.947 ms  46.459 ms  41.738 ms
```

TIP *The -n parameter causes* `traceroute` *to report computers' IP addresses rather than their hostnames. Although the hostnames can be informative, the DNS lookups can slow down the process.*

In this example, the first router (192.168.1.254) is my own LAN's router, and the second (10.1.88.1) is the router to which my router connects. The block of routers whose IP addresses start with 68 also belongs to my ISP. Subsequent addresses correspond to routers later along the path, until the final entry, which is the target system.

This example `traceroute` output shows no unusual problems. Most hops reveal a modest increase in latencies, although there are a few larger jumps. The increase in latency moving off of my LAN is quite substantial, for instance, as is the increase from the ninth to the tenth hop. Neither of these increases is truly aberrant, though. If you see an increase of more than 20 or 30 milliseconds, the later router could be overloaded. Another possibility is that the hop spanned an unusually great physical distance. For instance, when I traced a route to a Linux FTP site in Australia, I saw two big jumps in latencies: one increase of about 60ms from a router in Washington, D.C. to one in Los Angeles, and another increase of about 160ms from Los Angeles to Sydney.

Severe problems may show up in `traceroute` output as asterisks (*) in place of times. These marks denote a packet that wasn't acknowledged—in other words, packet loss. If a router loses many packets, the result is likely to be a severe degradation in throughput and unreliable operation. Although TCP/IP was designed to tolerate a certain amount of packet loss, the phenomenon requires the sender to request that a packet be resent after a period of time (the *timeout* period). This process takes time, and so degrades throughput.

In most cases, locating a flaky router will not accomplish much. If you happen to control the router, of course, you can investigate further—confirm that it's powerful enough to handle the load it receives, check that it's not suffering from some other problem such as runaway processes or a denial-of-service (DoS) attack, and so on. If you don't control the router, the best you can do is to contact whoever does control it. You can learn who this is by using the `whois` command:

```
$ whois 209.247.9.173
```

This command returns a lot of information, including contacts for whoever controls the IP address. (You can also use a hostname.) Sometimes `whois` returns two or more entry summaries instead of contact information:

```
$ whois 68.1.0.43
Cox Communications Inc. COX-ATLANTA (NET-68-0-0-0-1)
                          68.0.0.0 - 68.15.255.255
Cox Communications Inc. NETBLK-ATRDC-68-1-0-0 (NET-68-1-0-0-1)
                          68.1.0.0 - 68.1.127.255
```

If you see something like this, select one of the network blocks (typically the more specific one, such as `NETBLK-ATRDC-68-1-0-0` in this example) and perform a `whois` lookup on it. If you contact the router's operator, use a technical contact address in the `whois` output and include your `traceroute` output. I recommend contacting router operators only if a problem is persistent; many problems are transient and are well known to the router's operators when they occur, so sending them e-mail about such problems won't do any good.

One additional tool can sometimes be useful, or at least educational: Xtraceroute (`http://www`
`.dtek.chalmers.se/~d3august/xt/`). This program is an X-based tool that displays your network
traffic's route on a map in a window, as shown in Figure 19.3. To launch the program, type **xtraceroute**
after installing the package. Unfortunately, information on router locations in Xtraceroute's database
is sometimes wrong, so you may see network paths taking bizarre hops around the world.

FIGURE 19.3

If you want to see
how your data travels
the globe, use
Xtraceroute.

Diagnosing DNS Problems

The cry goes out around the office, "The network's down!" E-mail correspondence piles up in the
mail server and employees aren't able to browse the Web or transfer files with co-workers elsewhere.
This scenario is common, but it's also common for the problem to have an embarrassingly local
cause: DNS failures. If your local DNS servers go down, the entire network will *appear* to be down—
if you type an address into a web browser, no page will appear, to name just one symptom.

DNS failures leave certain clues. For instance, when you use `ping` or `traceroute`, these tools
report back the IP address of the site you are trying to contact before any other output:

```
$ ping trex.pangaea.edu
PING trex.pangaea.edu (198.168.1.1): 56 data bytes
```

If that line is present, name resolution is working, at least for the target site. (Remember that
`/etc/hosts` can provide name resolution, although this file normally only holds a handful of names

and IP addresses.) If the program hangs before reporting an IP address, chances are good that your DNS server has failed. You can verify the matter by trying to use host, which returns an IP address when given a hostname or a hostname when given an IP address:

```
$ host trex.pangaea.edu
trex.pangaea.edu has address 192.168.1.1
```

If this command returns an error message, you can be certain there's something wrong with name resolution. This problem can take several forms:

Broken Local DNS Configuration   The computer at which you're typing the command may have an incorrect DNS configuration. Review your /etc/resolv.conf file, as described earlier in "Files for Setting Network Options," and verify that it lists valid DNS servers on its nameserver lines.

Broken Network Connection to the DNS Server   It's possible that the DNS server is functioning but that a critical network link between your system and the DNS server has come down. The problem could be as simple as a network wire that's come loose, or it could be a damaged switch, router, or some other problem.

Crashed or Malfunctioning DNS Server   The DNS server itself might be misbehaving. If you run it yourself, verify that it's working locally. If somebody else operates the DNS server, and if the problem is persistent, contact the operator to report the problem. You may be able to work around the problem temporarily by specifying another DNS server in /etc/resolv.conf. You can also use IP addresses rather than hostnames with many network protocols to bypass the DNS server, but this solution isn't workable for most Internet accesses.

In addition to completely failing, DNS servers can also become sluggish. This can happen because of overloaded DNS servers or because of problems on the Internet generally. For instance, if the DNS server's Internet connection is sluggish, its own outside queries will become slow. DNS servers cache recent accesses, so these sluggish accesses will affect new queries for sites that are seldom visited. The result is that popular sites may come up very quickly, whereas less popular sites may take many seconds to connect, but will respond quickly thereafter.

TIP   *If you rely on an ISP's DNS servers, and if they don't perform well, you can run a caching-only DNS server locally, as described in Chapter 27. Of course, if your ISP can't manage to run a reliable DNS server, the ISP probably isn't very good, so you might prefer to switch ISPs!*

Optimizing Network Performance

Some of the diagnostic techniques described in the preceding section, "Testing Network Performance," suggest fixes for problems, such as contacting the operator of a router that's not performing well or fixing a misconfigured /etc/resolv.conf file. This section covers three additional measures you can take to improve performance. Two relate to low-level TCP/IP settings. These values are normally set reasonably, so tweaking them won't help in most cases, but it can help on some networks. The third option, running local servers, can improve performance when you rely on outside servers that you could as easily run closer to home.

Setting the MTU Size

Like most computer protocols, TCP/IP was designed with flexibility in mind. One negative consequence of flexibility is that when different systems implement a protocol using different defaults, the two systems may not interact as efficiently as when the two systems use the same defaults. One point of flexibility in TCP/IP is the *maximum transfer unit (MTU)* size, which is the maximum size of data packets it sends. You can learn the MTU for your system by using `ifconfig`:

```
$ ifconfig eth0 | grep MTU
          UP BROADCAST RUNNING MULTICAST  MTU:1500  Metric:1
```

This command displays the MTU, among other information. Ideally, all the computers on your LAN should use the same MTU. Linux's default value for Ethernet networks is 1,500 bytes, and this value is common on many other OSs, as well. If a device on your network uses an MTU smaller than others, transfers involving that device may be slowed down slightly, particularly if the devices communicate through another device (such as a router). Such communication may require packets to be broken up. For instance, some ADSL connections use an MTU of 1,492 bytes, meaning that 1,500-byte packets must be split into two: one 1,492-byte packet and another 8-byte packet. If the originating computer had used a 1,492-byte or smaller MTU, the split wouldn't be necessary. Of course, an 8-byte packet takes less time to send than does a 1,492-byte packet, so this conversion doesn't double transmission time, but the extra overhead does degrade performance somewhat.

For the most part, MTU size isn't a big deal in Linux, because Linux uses a technique known as *path MTU discovery* to determine the MTU on a site-by-site basis. If the initial MTU used for a connection is too high, Linux throttles it back until it works, thereby optimizing the connection. You can verify that path MTU discovery is enabled on your system by typing this command:

```
$ cat /proc/sys/net/ipv4/ip_no_pmtu_disc
0
```

A return value of 0 means that path MTU discovery is working; 1 means that this feature is disabled. You can use `echo` to copy a value into this pseudo-file if you want to change this option.

If you know that your system should use an MTU that's smaller than it does by default, you can alter the MTU by using the `mtu` option to `ifconfig`:

```
# ifconfig eth0 mtu 1492
```

This example sets the MTU to 1,492 bytes, as might be appropriate if your system is on a LAN that uses an ADSL account with an MTU of 1,492. Setting this option in a startup script may slightly improve performance, even when your computer performs path MTU discovery; it won't try a 1,500-byte MTU that's destined to fail.

Setting the Send and Receive Window Sizes

A TCP data transfer isn't a one-way affair; the sending computer sends data packets but expects to hear back from the recipient about the success of the data transfer. Suppose that these operations were to occur in serial—that is, the sender sends a packet, the recipient acknowledges receipt of the packet, and only then does the sender send a second packet. In this scenario, the transmission would be slowed down by the latencies involved in the connection. For instance, consider a 1Mbps connection with a 100ms round-trip latency and a packet size of 1,500 bytes. At time 0, the sender begins sending the packet. At 50ms (half the ping time), the recipient begins to receive the packet, but at 1Mbps, a 1,500-byte packet takes 12ms to arrive. Assuming an instantaneous response, that means the recipient can begin to send a response at 62ms. That response arrives at the sender's system at 112ms. (The response is likely to be much shorter than 1,500 bytes, so we can assume it arrives much more quickly than 12ms.) If the sender can't send a packet until receiving a reply, the sender will end up spending 12ms of every 112ms actually sending data, reducing the 1Mbps link to a 107Kbps (0.107Mbps) connection.

The solution to this problem is the negotiation of a *receive window*, which is the number of bytes that a system will accept before sending an acknowledgment, and a *send window*, which is the number of bytes it will send before requiring an acknowledgment. By setting these values high enough, you enable the sender to deliver data more-or-less continuously. Unfortunately, the optimum window size depends on the latency and throughput between the two computers—it should be at least as many bytes as your system can receive during the round-trip latency (that is, the ping time) between the systems. Table 19.2 summarizes the minimum window sizes you should use for different speeds and latencies. Entries in this table are derived from the formula $size = bandwidth \times latency$, where $size$ is the window size in bits, $bandwidth$ is the throughput speed in bits per second, and $latency$ is the ping time in seconds. (Table 19.2's rows and columns specify latencies in milliseconds, throughput in megabits per second, and window size in kilobytes, though.)

TABLE 19.2: MINIMUM SEND AND RECEIVE WINDOW SIZES

LATENCY (MS)	1MBPS THROUGHPUT	2MBPS THROUGHPUT	4MBPS THROUGHPUT	8MBPS THROUGHPUT
50	6KB	12KB	24KB	49KB
100	12KB	24KB	49KB	98KB
150	18KB	37KB	73KB	146KB
200	24KB	49KB	98KB	195KB
300	37KB	73KB	146KB	293KB
400	49KB	98KB	195KB	391KB
500	61KB	122KB	244KB	488KB

Linux's default window size is 64KB, which is enough for most connections. LAN speeds are off the chart as far as Table 19.2 is concerned, but consider a 100Mbps Ethernet network with 1ms latencies. The $size = bandwidth \times latency$ formula suggests a minimum receive window size of 12.2KB, so a 64KB window size is quite adequate. On broadband and other always-on Internet connections, latencies for connections on the same continent are usually 100ms or less, and connections seldom exceed 4Mbps. If your Internet connection is unusually speedy, though, you may want to consider a larger receive window size. Another extreme case is a satellite connection, which has very high latencies. Assuming a typical 500ms latency, a 61KB window size should be adequate for a 1Mbps connection.

If you believe your system's performance is suffering because of a window size that's too small, you can adjust it in either of two ways:

Using route Options The route command adds routes to the Linux routing table. You can locate your system's call to route (most likely in one of the scripts referenced in Table 19.1) and modify that call to include the window W parameter, where W is the window size in bytes.

Setting /proc Filesystem Options You can set the default and maximum send and receive window sizes using entries in the /proc/sys/net/core directory. Specifically, rmem_default and rmem_max set the default and maximum receive window sizes, while wmem_default and wmem_max set the default and maximum send window sizes. For instance, typing **echo "131072" > /proc/sys/net/core/rmem_max** sets the maximum receive window size to 128KB.

In order to be effective, both your system and the one with which it's communicating must support the larger size. For this reason, this adjustment may be ineffective if the remote system uses a 64KB or smaller window size.

Running Servers Locally

Accessing certain servers on the Internet at large is common, but running equivalents on your local network, or even on a workstation, can improve performance in some cases. Examples of servers you might want to run locally include:

Web Proxy Servers A *proxy server* is a stand-in for another server; it accepts requests for data transfers, processes them partially, and passes them on to other systems. Proxy servers exist for many reasons, including security, filtering unwanted content, and improving speed. Speed improvements in web proxy servers derive from two factors. First, proxy servers can cache access requests, speeding up second and subsequent requests for a document. The Squid proxy server (http://www.squid-cache.org) exists largely for this reason. Second, a proxy that filters content can remove large images that can take a long time to download. Proxies designed to remove ads, such as Privoxy (http://www.privoxy.org), have this effect.

DNS Servers Running your own DNS server can speed up DNS accesses for much the same reason that running a caching web proxy server can speed accesses. Chapter 27 covers DNS server configuration.

Mail Servers If you receive lots of e-mail from an ISP's mail server, you may wait for it to download into your mail reader. You can use a local mail server in conjunction with Fetchmail (http://catb.org/~esr/fetchmail/) to speed up local mail accesses. Fetchmail can periodically retrieve mail and store it locally, so that you don't need to wait so long when you load up your mail reader. The downside is that you won't see any mail that's arrived at your ISP between Fetchmail's last run and the time you launch your mail reader. Chapter 25, "Delivering E-Mail," covers both mail server and Fetchmail configuration.

News Servers If you read Usenet news, you can run a local news server that does for news what the combination of Fetchmail and a local mail server does for e-mail. An example of such a program is Leafnode (http://www.leafnode.org). News servers designed for this purpose are much smaller than full-blown news servers. In some configurations, the local news server may download much more data than you'll ever read, but it will do so quickly, so the total time you're connected to the news server can be much shorter than it might otherwise be. This approach is most appealing if you're charged by the minute for your Internet connect time.

WARNING *As described in Chapter 18, "System Security," running servers unnecessarily is a security risk. You should balance the benefits gained from running servers locally against the potential damage they might do. In some cases, the risk is very low. For instance, a server run behind a Network Address Translation (NAT) firewall is unlikely to be found and abused by an outside miscreant. If the system on which you run a server is directly exposed to the Internet, though, the risk of running such a server is much greater.*

Summary

Linux distributions are mature enough that they usually do a good job configuring your network at install time. Sometimes, though, it pays to know more about the network configuration in order to tweak a configuration to get better performance or even get it to work at all. Network hardware is seldom incompatible with Linux, but when it is you must know what to buy as a replacement. Both of the main methods of assigning IP addresses in Linux, DHCP and static IP addresses, pose certain challenges, particularly on a multihomed system. Once the network is up and running minimally, you may want to run performance tests, either to verify that you're getting reasonable network performance or to track down the cause of poor performance. You may also want to tweak a few settings to improve performance generally.

Chapter 20

Controlling Network Access

BEFORE YOU SET UP servers for real use, you should understand how to control who can access those servers. Failure to take this precaution is likely to lead to your servers being used by undesirables—perhaps to take over your system or perhaps just to use it to launch attacks on other people. This chapter begins with an overview of techniques you can use to block unwanted accesses. It then proceeds to cover several methods in greater detail: firewalls, TCP Wrappers, and xinetd. Finally, this chapter describes chroot jails, which are tools that can help prevent intruders from damaging anything if they do manage to take over a server.

NOTE *This chapter is effectively about security. Chapter 18, "System Security," introduces many important security concepts and measures; and Chapter 21, "Detecting Intruders," describes how you can monitor your system for signs of intrusion.*

Methods of Keeping Out the Bad Guys

As described in Chapter 18, *crackers* (those who attempt to break into or otherwise abuse others' computers) employ many different methods of attack. Countermeasures for some of these approaches are described in Chapter 18. This chapter is devoted to more in-depth coverage of network access controls. First, though, comes a summary of some of the techniques you can use to block unwanted access.

Running Only Necessary Servers

Every server you run is a potential doorway through which both legitimate users and crackers can enter your system. Ideally, servers are without flaws and are configured correctly. Unfortunately, our world isn't ideal; most servers have a history of bugs that can be abused by crackers. This history suggests that bugs in current software are common, although largely undiscovered by both the good guys and the bad guys. For this reason, you shouldn't run any server that you don't need to run. If a computer doesn't run a server, crackers can't exploit a bug in that server.

The "Removing Unnecessary Servers" section of Chapter 18 describes how to go about tracking down servers you don't need to run and how to disable or remove them.

Keeping Servers Up-to-Date

If you must run a server, try to run the latest version of it. Sometimes (but not always) server updates fix security bugs. For this reason, running old versions of a server can be risky—the old version may be susceptible to attack. In theory, you should be able to check the *change logs* (summaries of changes made to programs) to ascertain whether an old version you're running is a security risk. For updates that don't cross major version boundaries, though, it's usually much simpler to use your distribution's package system to update to a more recent version.

WARNING   *Package management systems sometimes replace server configuration files when you upgrade the package. There-fore, I recommend backing up the configuration files prior to performing such an upgrade. For that matter, keeping a backup of the entire /etc directory tree is a useful precaution.*

Chapter 11, "Managing Packages," includes information on using package management tools to help keep your system up to date. Automated or semi-automated tools, such as Debian's Advanced Package Tool (APT) and Red Hat's Update Agent, can be very helpful in this process, as well. The "Keeping Software Up-to-Date" section of Chapter 18 includes additional pointers to resources for helping in this endeavor.

Using Passwords on Servers

Many servers use passwords to control access to the computer. For such servers, password maintenance, as described in the "Choosing Good Passwords" section of Chapter 18, is extremely important. Most servers use the main Linux password database, so setting user passwords with `passwd` handles them all. A few servers, though, use their own password databases. For instance, Samba (covered in Chapter 24, "Sharing Files") can use either the Linux password database for unencrypted passwords or its own password database for encrypted passwords. Virtual Network Computing (VNC) is a remote login tool that normally uses passwords stored in users' home directories. VNC is covered in Chapter 26, "Providing Remote Login Access."

Some servers don't normally use passwords. For instance, web servers are often open to the public, and Simple Mail Transfer Protocol (SMTP) servers typically accept mail for local delivery without a password. Both of these server types can be configured to require passwords, but doing so defeats the purpose of using them in their most common configurations. You might want to require passwords for some limited-access systems. In some respects, servers that don't use passwords are actually *less* risky than are those that require passwords; servers that don't use passwords typically give very limited access to the system. Web servers, for instance, frequently only deliver documents stored in a few directories. Servers that use passwords, by contrast, frequently give the user much more complete access to the computer, often including the ability to run arbitrary programs. As a result, a compromised password can become an extremely powerful tool in the hands of a cracker. Of course, there are exceptions to this rule; a web server can be misconfigured to give too-broad access to a system without a password, for instance. Also, some types of security problems result in the server running the cracker's arbitrary code, with or without a password. Nonetheless, maintaining good passwords is extremely important for servers that use them.

Limiting Outside Access to the Server

Much of this chapter is devoted to a specific class of access restrictions based on the calling system's IP address or related information, such as the hostname or the port number used to initiate the connection. The theory behind these restrictions is that the IP address belongs to a known computer that can be trusted, at least to a limited extent. For instance, to prevent abuse, you might want to keep anybody but computers on your local area network (LAN) from accessing a VNC login server. You'd still implement password protections on this server; however, nobody from outside your LAN has any business even trying to access it, so you block any such attempts before they can even get the chance to enter a password. You can use similar restrictions to block only known troublemaker IP addresses or to grant access to specific systems outside of your LAN—for instance, to enable employees to use the VNC server to work from home if they have broadband Internet connections with static IP addresses. Several methods of implementing IP address restrictions are common:

Firewalls   Traditionally, a *firewall* has been a router that blocks access to a network based on IP addresses and similar criteria. Recently, the term has come to apply to certain programs that can run on a single computer to protect that computer alone. One common type of firewall tool is a *packet-filter firewall*, which blocks individual TCP/IP packets at a low level in the network stack. The upcoming section, "Blocking IP Addresses with a Firewall," is devoted largely to implementing packet-filter firewall rules.

TCP Wrappers   This program provides a means for programs to accept or reject connections based on the calling system's IP address or other criteria. It's frequently used in conjunction with the inetd super server, which mediates connections for many servers. The upcoming section, "Blocking IP Addresses with TCP Wrappers," covers TCP Wrappers in more detail.

xinetd   This program can be thought of as roughly equivalent to a combination of inetd and TCP Wrappers, although it's a unique package with its own strengths and weaknesses. Using xinetd can be particularly helpful on computers with multiple network interfaces, because it can listen to one interface but not another on a server-by-server basis. The upcoming section, "Enhanced xinetd Access Restrictions," covers xinetd security features. Chapter 22, "Running Servers," covers xinetd's nonsecurity configuration.

Server-Specific Restrictions   Many servers contain their own unique IP-based access restrictions. For many, these restrictions work much like TCP Wrappers restrictions; in fact, some use TCP Wrappers to implement these restrictions. A few servers, such as Network File System (NFS) servers, use IP-based restrictions as their primary security measure, so configuring these systems correctly is critically important.

NOTE   *Most of these access restriction tools enable you to specify computers by hostname instead of or in addition to using IP addresses. Some of these tools do a single lookup on the hostname when the program starts, though, making the lookup ineffective at tracking systems whose hostnames remain constant but whose IP addresses change. Using hostnames also opens these tools up to possible compromise of DNS servers. If a miscreant breaks into a network's DNS server and changes its entries, servers that use hostnames for security can be compromised.*

Limiting Server Access to the System

Because of the possibility that bugs might give a cracker full access to your system, you shouldn't completely trust any server. Even a seemingly harmless and trivial server, such as a font server (described in Chapter 16, "Optimizing X Configuration"), can theoretically be hijacked and abused. The preceding section summarized steps you can take to minimize the server's exposure to the outside world, and hence crackers' opportunity to abuse the server. Much of the rest of this chapter is devoted to expanding this discussion. A complementary approach is to limit the server's access to your computer. Two common ways to limit such access are:

Running a Server as a Minimum-Privilege User   Many servers don't need special privileges to run. For instance, a font server only needs to be able to access font files, process them, and pass the results over the network. Therefore, there's no reason to run a font server as `root`. Doing so only increases the odds that a cracker will be able to abuse a security flaw to gain `root` privileges on your system. On the other hand, some servers, such as most that accept user logins, need to run as `root`. Server documentation usually specifies the minimum privileges the server needs. Super servers provide tools to set the privileges with which a server runs, and Chapter 22 covers these options. Servers that don't run in this way, but that can run without `root` privileges, usually provide server-specific options to set the server's username. Many low-privilege servers can run as `nobody` (a special low-privilege account that's standard on most systems). Others may require or benefit from server-specific accounts.

Using a Jail   A *chroot jail* is a way of running a server in a special Linux subsystem. The idea is this: Set up a directory tree that contains all the files a server needs to operate, including library files, executables, configuration files, and so on. Once this is done, run the server in such a way that it can't access files outside of this special directory tree, even with `root` privileges. This approach isn't perfect, but it can slow down intruders, and it may present a high enough hurdle that a cracker will move on to another system rather than try to break out of your jail. The upcoming section, "Containing Access in a Jail," describes `chroot` jails in more detail.

These techniques serve as protection against the scenario of a server being compromised. By limiting the access that the server has to your computer, you limit the damage that an intruder can do. Neither approach is perfect, though. An intruder might be able to leverage the limited access provided by the `nobody` account or the access available from within a jail to do further damage. Indeed, if the cracker isn't targeting you personally, these measures may not matter; access as an ordinary user or from within a jail may be all the miscreant needs to use your system as a launch pad for attacks against others. Nonetheless, these techniques can be important components of an overall security plan.

Blocking IP Addresses with a Firewall

Firewalls come in many different forms. Even if you use just one type of firewall, you should be familiar with the options that are available to you. Linux provides tools to let you implement several different types of firewall, but packet filter firewalls are the most popular type of Linux firewall. In Linux, `iptables` configures a packet-filter firewall. Knowing how to use this tool will enable you to set up a firewall, either to protect one computer or on a router to protect an entire network.

Linux Firewall Tools

Broadly speaking, two types of firewall tools for Linux exist: proxy servers and packet-filter firewalls. Proxy servers accept connections from software running on the host computer or network, partially process them, and then pass the connections on to other computers. This approach enables proxy servers to perform sophisticated high-level filtering. For instance, a proxy server can remove ads from web pages. Proxy servers may interfere with or block certain legitimate transactions, though, particularly those requiring encryption. They also require more CPU power on the proxy server computer than do packet filters. In principle, a proxy server running on a computer with two network interfaces but not configured as a router can provide very strong protection of the computers behind the proxy server; only the protocols supported by the proxy server are enabled, and only through the proxy server's filtering. In practice, this type of configuration tends to be very constricting; users often find it necessary to use an unsupported protocol, so the proxy server becomes an obstacle. Some proxy servers also require special clients or client configuration. Proxy servers are also most often used to protect networks on which no servers or only local servers run; they aren't generally used to enhance the security of servers that should be publicly available. In practice, therefore, proxy servers are often used as an optional security measure or only on the most heavily protected part of a network. The "Filtering Content Using a Proxy Server" section of Chapter 8, "Miscellaneous User Tools," describes some popular proxy filters for web access.

Packet filter firewalls work at the level of individual packets; they permit or allow individual packets to pass through the system. This can be done either based on the contents of the packet alone or the packet in conjunction with other packets with which it's associated (so-called *stateful inspection*, which helps spot and block certain types of attacks that involve hijacking an established connection). This approach is speedy and doesn't require any special client or server configuration. Packet filtering can protect both clients and servers behind the firewall, and it can be used to limit outgoing client connections from potential troublemakers within your network. For these reasons, packet-filtering firewalls dominate Linux firewall discussions.

In 2.4.*x* through 2.6.*x* kernels, Linux uses the `iptables` tool to configure packet-filter firewalls. To use this tool, you tell it what type of packet you want to filter and how to do it. For instance, you can tell it to drop all packets directed at port 80 (used by web servers) from anything but the local network. You call `iptables` once for each rule that you want to implement, so `iptables` firewalls are frequently implemented in startup scripts that call the program dozens of times.

Unfortunately, `iptables` scripts can be tedious to write. For this reason, an assortment of GUI and non-GUI `iptables` front-ends exist. Some of the options include:

Shorewall   This package is a set of predefined `iptables` firewall scripts that you can use as a base for modification. Mandrake provides a simple GUI interface (`drakfirewall`, which is accessible from the Mandrake Control Center) to customize these rules, but this interface is decidedly limited. You can modify the scripts directly by editing them in the `/etc/shorewall` directory. Shorewall uses its own SysV startup script, and on some systems, it will call `/etc/sysconfig/iptables` for additional firewall rules. The main Shorewall web page is `http://www.shorewall.net`.

Red Hat Security Level Configuration   Red Hat ships with a pair of tools called `redhat-config-securitylevel` and `lokkit`, which are GUI and text-based `iptables` script generators. (A GUI version of `lokkit` is available as `gnome-lokkit`, as well.) These tools generate an `iptables` configuration file and place it in `/etc/sysconfig/iptables`, where the `iptables` SysV startup script reads it.

SuSE Firewall2   Like Shorewall and Red Hat's Security Level Configuration, this package is a set of firewall rules that you can modify to suit your needs. SuSE stores the rule set in /etc/sysconfig/SuSEfirewall2 and provides a means of modifying them in its YaST and YaST2 system configuration tools.

Knetfilter   This tool, headquartered at http://expansa.sns.it/knetfilter/, creates an iptables script and gives you fine-grained control over it using a GUI interface, as shown in Figure 20.1. If you want to edit the rules manually, you can do so by editing /etc/iptables_rules.cfg. Unfortunately, Knetfilter doesn't display rules after you've saved them, quit the program, and loaded them again, so editing an existing rule set with the program isn't practical.

As a general rule, the GUI tools can be helpful for setting up a quick rule set, but if you need to do anything more than a very basic configuration, you must dig into the text configuration files or write a firewall script. The next two sections, "Basics of iptables" and "Restricting Access with iptables," describe how to do this.

FIGURE 20.1

Knetfilter provides more fine-grained control over packet filter firewall rules than do most GUI tools.

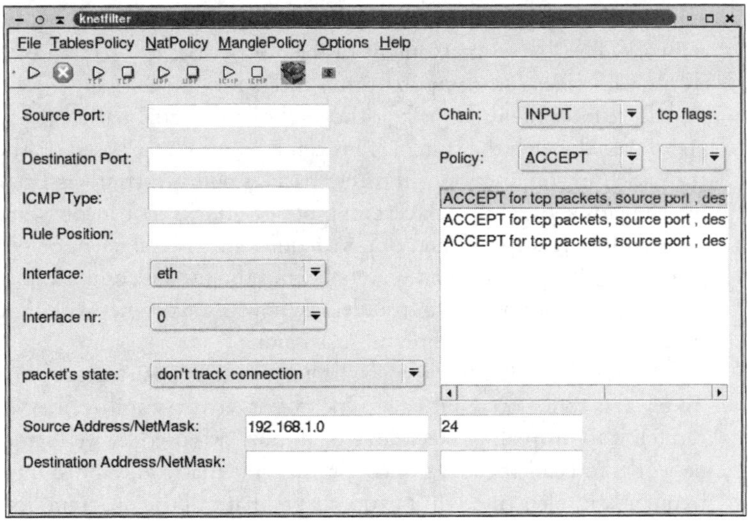

Basics of *iptables*

The Linux kernel uses a series of rules to determine what to do with any given packet it receives or that's generated by local processes. These rules are arranged in *chains*, which provide a series of patterns and actions to be taken should a packet match the pattern. The first rule to match a pattern determines what the system does with the packet—accept it, reject it, or pass it to another chain. The chains are in turn organized into *tables*, with relationships between them. The most important table is the filter table, which is illustrated in Figure 20.2. In this table, the INPUT chain processes packets destined for local programs, the FORWARD chain processes packets that the system is to forward (as in a router), and the OUTPUT chain processes packets that originate locally and are destined for outside systems. Any given packet passes through just one of these chains. Other standard tables include the nat table, which handles Network Address Translation (NAT), and the mangle table, which modifies packets in specialized ways.

FIGURE 20.2

Linux uses a series of rules, which are defined in chains that are called at various points during processing, to determine the fate of network packets.

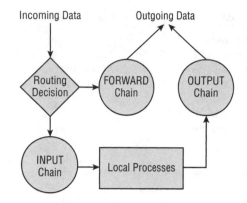

In order to create a packet-filter firewall, you must design a series of rules for specific tables and chains. For instance, you might tell the INPUT chain to discard any packets directed at port 80 (the web server port) that don't originate from the local network. Another set of rules might tell the OUTPUT chain to block all outgoing packets from local processes destined for port 25 (the SMTP mail server) except for those directed at your network's mail server computer. A router is likely to include a number of special rules for the FORWARD chain, as well, in order to control routing features independently of local programs' accesses.

Linux provides the iptables utility for manipulating firewall rules. This program relies on the presence of assorted options in the Linux kernel. Most importantly, you must enable the Network Packet Filtering option in the Networking Options configuration area (which is in the Networking Support area in 2.5.x and later kernels). Once you've done this, you can activate various options in the IP: Netfilter Configuration submenu off of the Networking Options menu. . Be sure the IP Tables Support option is active. I recommend that you build just about everything else, as well, at least as modules. You can probably ignore the ipchains and ipfwadm support options, and in fact you *must* omit them if you compile IP Tables Support into the main kernel file. Most Linux distributions ship with most of these options compiled as modules.

NOTE   *The* iptables *utility works with 2.4.x through 2.6.x kernels, and it may work with future kernels, as well. The 2.2.x kernel series used the* ipchains *tool instead, and 2.0.x used* ipfwadm. *You only need to support these tools if you have an old firewall script created with these tools.*

Restricting Access with *iptables*

Creating a packet filter firewall requires designing a series of rules, each of which corresponds to a single call to iptables in a firewall script. In addition, you must set the *default policy*, which is what the chain is to do when no rule matches. Before you embark on this task, though (and at various times during your firewall development), you may want to review the present configuration.

CHECKING THE CONFIGURATION

The iptables program responds to the -L parameter by displaying a list of the rules that make up a given table. You may optionally pass a table name by using the -t parameter. For instance, Listing 20.1 shows how to view the current filter table.

LISTING 20.1: SAMPLE USE OF iptables TO VIEW FIREWALL CONFIGURATION

```
# iptables -L -t filter
Chain INPUT (policy ACCEPT)
target     prot opt source              destination
DROP       all  --  172.24.0.0/16       anywhere

Chain FORWARD (policy DROP)
target     prot opt source              destination

Chain OUTPUT (policy ACCEPT)
target     prot opt source              destination
```

The default table is filter, so omitting -t filter from this command produces the same output. The table summarized by this output is nearly empty; the FORWARD and OUTPUT chains have no rules, and the INPUT chain has just one rule—it drops all input from the 172.24.0.0/16 network. Although the format of information presented by iptables -L isn't exactly equivalent to what you use when you create a rule, the similarities are strong enough that you should be able to interpret the output once you know how to create rules.

SETTING THE DEFAULT POLICY

One critically important consideration when designing a firewall is the *default policy*, which is what the firewall does with packets that don't match any rules in a chain. In fact, in the standard filter table, there are three default policies, one each for the INPUT, FORWARD, and OUTPUT chains. The default policy corresponds to an action that the system can take. Three options are common:

ACCEPT   An ACCEPT action causes the system to accept the packet and pass it on to the next chain or system. For instance, if the INPUT chain's default policy is ACCEPT, any packet that doesn't match a rule is passed on to the target program (assuming one is using the specified port).

DROP   This action causes the system to ignore the packet—to "drop it on the floor," as it were. To the system that sends the packet (which could be a remote system or a local program, depending on the chain involved), it appears that the packet was lost due to a routing error or the like.

REJECT   This action is much like DROP, except that the kernel returns a code to the calling system or program indicating that the packet has been rejected. This behavior is similar to what would happen if no program were using the target port. This action requires that you compile explicit support for it into the kernel, either in the main kernel file or as a module. Unfortunately, REJECT doesn't work as a default policy, but you can use it as a target for more specific rules.

Typing **iptables -L** reveals the default policy, as shown in Listing 20.1—in that example, the INPUT and OUTPUT chains have a default policy of ACCEPT, whereas the FORWARD chain has a default policy of DROP. To change the default policy, you should first flush the chain of all its rules by passing the -F parameter and the chain name to iptables. You can then pass the -P parameter to `iptables`, along with the policy name. In both cases, you can optionally include `-t` and the table name:

```
# iptables -t filter -F FORWARD
# iptables -F INPUT
# iptables -P FORWARD DROP
# iptables -t filter -P INPUT DROP
```

As a general rule, the safest default policy is a closed one—that is, to use `DROP`. When you use such a default policy, you must explicitly open ports with firewall rules. This means that if a server is running on your computer without your knowledge, it doesn't pose a security risk because packets can't reach it and it can't send packets. Likewise, if you close outgoing ports, malicious software or individuals may not be able to launch attacks on others unless they use the protocols you've approved for use. On the other hand, a default closed policy means that you must design your firewall rules very carefully; an oversight can cause an important client or server to stop working.

TIP   *Although you cannot set the default policy to* REJECT, *you can achieve much the same end by other means. Specifically, you can insert a rule at the end of the chain that uses* REJECT *on all packets not matched by previous rules. If you do this, the default policy as set via the* -P *option to* `iptables` *becomes irrelevant. The upcoming section, "Using* `iptables`," *describes how to create individual rules.*

If you want a default closed policy, you must decide between using `DROP` and `REJECT`. There are good arguments to be made in favor of both rules. `DROP` is the "stealthy" option. If you were to use `DROP` on every port and protocol, many network scanners would fail to detect your computer at all; it would appear not to exist. Of course, such an extreme policy would make the network useless; in practice, you must let *some* traffic through, and this frequently gives information to crackers. For instance, if a system drops everything but port-80 accesses, the cracker knows that you're running a web server (or something else) on port 80. Because computers don't normally drop packets, though, the cracker also knows that you're running a firewall with a default `DROP` policy. By contrast, `REJECT` does a poorer job of hiding your system's presence from casual scans, but once a cracker has found your system, it's less obvious that you're running a firewall.

On occasion, these different policies can have an effect on protocols. Specifically, many protocols are designed to keep trying to make connections if packets are lost. This behavior can sometimes result in connection delays for related protocols if you use a default `DROP` policy. For instance, a server might try contacting your computer's port 113, which is used by the `ident` (aka `auth`) server. This server provides information about who on your system is making connection requests to servers, the goal being to provide a trail in log files to help track abuse back to its source. (TCP Wrappers can also use an `ident` server as an authorization tool.) If your system uses an `INPUT` chain `DROP` rule on port 113, the result can be connection delays if a remote server tries to use your `ident` server. Of course, you can overcome such problems on a case-by-case basis by adding ordinary rules to the offending chain, overriding the default `DROP` rule with a `REJECT` rule, or perhaps even an `ACCEPT` rule.

TIP   *If your computer has two network interfaces but it should not function as a router, use a* `DROP` *default policy on the* `FORWARD` *chain. Doing so will prevent the computer from functioning as a router, even if you inadvertently configure it to forward packets in another way.*

USING *IPTABLES*

To add a rule to a chain, you call `iptables` with a command like this:

```
# iptables -A CHAIN selection-criteria  -j TARGET
```

The *CHAIN* in this command is the chain name—INPUT, OUTPUT, or FORWARD for the `filter` table. The *TARGET* is the firewall target that's to process the packet, such as ACCEPT, REJECT, or DROP. You can also specify a LOG target, which logs information about the packet and then tries to match the next rule. Various other targets are also available; consult the `iptables` documentation for details.

NOTE   The -A option appends a rule to the end of a chain. (A synonym is --append.) You can use other options, such as -D or --delete to delete a rule. Consult the `iptables` man page for details on this command; it's far more complex than I can present in just a few pages.

The tricky part of this command is in the *selection-criteria* component. You can specify many different criteria to match different features of a packet. If you specify more than one criterion, all of them must match in order for a rule to apply. Some of the possible criteria are listed here:

--protocol or -p   You can filter based on the type of low-level protocol used. Options are `tcp`, `udp`, `icmp`, and `all`. With the exception of `all` (which matches all protocols), these options match the like-named low-level TCP/IP protocols.

--sport or --source-port   All TCP and UDP traffic comes from programs that are linked to particular ports—that is, *source ports*. Every TCP or UDP packet includes the source port number, and you can match a rule on this information. For instance, to match all traffic from web servers running on the standard port (80), you specify `--sport 80`. You can also specify a range of ports by separating the port numbers by colons, as in `--sport 1024:65535`, which matches all ports between 1024 and 65,535, inclusive.

WARNING   It's possible to run servers on nonstandard ports, so filtering based on this information may not be perfectly reliable. Nonetheless, most servers do run on their standard ports, so such filters can be partially effective. Most clients run on unpredictable port numbers, so filtering based on client port numbers usually isn't practical.

--dport or --destination-port   Just as TCP and UDP packets have embedded source ports, they include destination ports. You can filter based on this information, just as you can with source ports.

--source or -s   This option filters based on the source IP address. You can provide either a single IP address or a network address and matching netmask specified as the number of bits, as in 172.24.17.0/24.

--destination or -d   Just as you can filter based on the source IP address, you can filter based on the recipient IP address. The form of the specification is the same as for the `--source` option.

--in-interface or -I   For computers with multiple network interfaces, you can filter based on the input interface name, such as `eth1` or `ppp0`. This option works with the INPUT and FORWARD chains, but not with the OUTPUT chain.

--out-interface or -o   The output interface specification works much like the input interface option, but it matches outgoing traffic destined for a particular interface. This option works with the FORWARD and OUTPUT chains, but not with the INPUT chain.

TIP   All Linux computers use a loopback or localhost interface, identified as lo, for certain local network activity. You can create a filter using this feature to enable your system to talk to itself, which is necessary for certain tools, such as X servers and print queues, to work.

--state   One of the more advanced iptables features (and one not present in ipfwadm or ipchains) matches based on the *state* of a connection—whether it's a new connection, an established one, a related packet (such as an error message), or potentially forged. To use this option, you must precede it with -m state on the same iptables command line. You can specify a state of INVALID, NEW, ESTABLISHED, or RELATED. The main intent of stateful packet inspection is to block packets that might have been forged (that is, ones that would match INVALID). You can also try blocking NEW connections to ports that aren't used by servers; this practice can foil users from running unauthorized servers on your system or network.

NOTE   This rule list is not complete. Consult the iptables man page for information on more matching criteria.

Many of these options are used in pairs that match packets traveling in opposite directions. You must remember that most networking connections involve two-way communications. One side sends a packet or a stream of packets to the other side, and the second side replies. Therefore, with a default DENY policy, it's not enough to simply unblock, say, packets directed at your web server (with the --destination-port and possibly other options) on your INPUT chain. You must also unblock packets coming from the web server (with the --source-port and possibly other options) on the OUTPUT chain. If you reverse the chains with which these rules are associated, you affect the ability of clients to communicate.

A SAMPLE CONFIGURATION

The options described in the preceding section may seem complex, and indeed they enable you to create a sophisticated set of firewall rules. In order to better understand these rules, consider Listing 20.2, which shows a simple firewall rule set as a bash script. (Chapter 4, "Mastering Shells and Shell Scripting," describes shell scripts in more detail.) This script is a very minimal script that might be run on a workstation or server. Aside from flushing and setting the default policy, this script doesn't touch the FORWARD chain. To configure a router as a firewall, you'd have to create rules for the FORWARD chain reflecting the types of traffic you want to allow to pass between networks.

LISTING 20.2: A SAMPLE iptables FIREWALL SCRIPT

```
#!/bin/bash

iptables -F INPUT
iptables -F FORWARD
iptables -F OUTPUT
```

```
iptables -P INPUT DROP
iptables -P FORWARD DROP
iptables -P OUTPUT DROP

# Let traffic on the loopback interface pass
iptables -A OUTPUT -d 127.0.0.1 -o lo -j ACCEPT
iptables -A INPUT -s 127.0.0.1 -i lo -j ACCEPT

# Let DNS traffic pass
iptables -A OUTPUT -p udp --dport 53 -j ACCEPT
iptables -A INPUT -p udp --sport 53 -j ACCEPT

# Let clients' TCP traffic pass
iptables -A OUTPUT -p tcp --sport 1024:65535 -m state \
        --state NEW,ESTABLISHED,RELATED -j ACCEPT
iptables -A INPUT -p tcp --dport 1024:65535 -m state \
        --state ESTABLISHED,RELATED -j ACCEPT

# Let local connections to local SSH server pass
iptables -A OUTPUT -p tcp --sport 22 -d 172.24.1.0/24 -m state \
        --state ESTABLISHED,RELATED -j ACCEPT
iptables -A INPUT -p tcp --dport 22 -s 172.24.1.0/24 -m state \
        --state NEW,ESTABLISHED,RELATED -j ACCEPT
```

Listing 20.2 begins with a series of six calls to iptables that flush the firewall rule chain and set the default policy. These lines ensure that when you run this script, you won't add to an existing rule set, which could bloat the chains, thereby degrading performance and causing unexpected effects. The remaining lines are broken into four parts, each of which has two iptables calls. These parts set rules relating to specific types of traffic:

Loopback Interface Traffic   The two lines that refer to 127.0.0.1 allow the computer to communicate with itself over the loopback interface (lo). The references to 127.0.0.1 and the associated -d and -s parameters are arguably a bit paranoid; anything coming over the lo interface should come from this address.

DNS Queries   Most systems rely on a Domain Name System (DNS) server to translate hostnames to IP addresses. In order to keep this system working, you must enable access to and from remote DNS servers, which run on UDP port 53. The DNS rules in Listing 20.2 are actually rather permissive, because they enable traffic to or from *any* DNS server to pass. In theory, a miscreant could run something other than a DNS server on UDP port 53 to use this rule to bypass your security. In practice, though, such abuse would be unlikely to work, because it would require something other than DNS on the local system to use the oddly configured external client or server. If you like, you could add IP address restrictions to these lines to improve the security.

Client Traffic   The next two calls to iptables create a broad set of acceptance conditions. Network clients generally use high TCP ports—those numbered between 1024 and 65535. These rules, therefore, open those ports to access in both directions, but with a twist: These rules use stateful packet inspection to ensure that NEW packets are allowed only on *outgoing* connections. The omission of the NEW state from the INPUT chain means that a server run on a high port (as an ordinary user might try in an attempt to get around your system's security) won't be able to accept connections. Both rules also omit the INVALID state, which can reduce the chance of a miscreant intercepting and "hijacking" an established connection.

Local SSH Server Traffic   The final two calls to iptables open a hole in the firewall to enable local computers to make connections to the SSH server. This server runs on port 22, so traffic to and from that port and originating from or destined to the local (172.24.1.0/24) network is accepted. As with the client traffic rules, these rules employ stateful inspection as an added precaution. INVALID packets are rejected in both directions, and NEW packets are accepted only on input packets.

Many firewall scripts define variables that contain the host machine's IP address and the address for the local network, and then they refer to these variables, rather than using them directly, as Listing 20.2 does. This practice greatly simplifies changing the script if your IP address changes or if the script is to run on multiple computers.

Blocking IP Addresses with TCP Wrappers

Packet-filter firewalls can be extremely effective at blocking access based on IP addresses and port numbers, but they aren't the only tools for doing so. TCP Wrappers (covered in this section) and xinetd (covered in the upcoming section, "Enhanced xinetd Access Restrictions") are two other tools that can block access based on IP addresses. In many respects, TCP Wrappers and xinetd are less flexible tools than are packet-filter firewalls. For example, they can't block access to servers that aren't launched from a super server or designed to use them, and they can't intercept traffic targeted at or sent by clients. Nonetheless, TCP Wrappers and xinetd can do a few things that packet-filter firewalls can't do, such as log and restrict based on the remote user's username (if the remote system is running identd or an equivalent server). For these reasons and because system security is best implemented in layers, you may want to use TCP Wrappers or xinetd instead of or in addition to iptables.

TCP Wrappers is most commonly used on systems that run the inetd super server, which is described in Chapter 22. A few stand-alone servers, such as the NFS server, can use it, as well. It's possible to use TCP Wrappers in conjunction with the xinetd super server, but for the most part there's no reason to do so, because xinetd includes functionality similar to that of TCP Wrappers. Distributions that use inetd by default, and for which TCP Wrappers is therefore most important, include Debian, Slackware, and SuSE.

Basics of TCP Wrappers

The most common use of TCP Wrappers is in conjunction with inetd. Instead of calling the server program directly, inetd calls TCP Wrappers (via its tcpd executable) and passes it the name of the ultimate server program, along with any parameters it needs. TCP Wrappers can then study the incoming connection and decide whether or not to accept it. If the connection is refused, TCP

Wrappers doesn't even call the server; it just drops the connection. If TCP Wrappers accepts the connection, it launches the server and hands it the connection.

In order to configure TCP Wrappers, you provide criteria for accepting or rejecting connections in two files: `/etc/hosts.allow` and `/etc/hosts.deny`. The first of these files defines computers that should be granted access to the system; the second specifies systems that should not be allowed to connect. If a system is listed in both files, `hosts.allow` takes precedence. If neither file lists a system, TCP Wrappers allows it to connect.

TIP   To run a system with the tightest possible TCP Wrappers security, include a line reading `ALL : ALL` *in* `/etc/hosts.deny`. *This line blocks all incoming accesses handled by TCP Wrappers. You can then open individual servers for specific client systems in* `/etc/hosts.allow`.

To use TCP Wrappers, you refer to a server by its filename, which may not be the same as its service name in `/etc/services`. For instance, an FTP server might be referred to as `in.ftpd`, `vsftpd`, `proftpd`, or various other names. When you use TCP Wrappers in conjunction with `inetd`, the server's filename appears immediately after the call to `tcpd` on the `/etc/inetd.conf` line for the server. Ordinarily, the server must reside somewhere on `tcpd`'s path. If you need to include the complete path to the server in your `/etc/inetd.conf` file, TCP Wrappers' restrictions may not work correctly. If necessary, you can create a symbolic link from a directory on your path to the actual server executable.

Restricting Access with TCP Wrappers

The formats for both `/etc/hosts.allow` and `/etc/hosts.deny` are identical, although the same entry has opposite effects in the two control files. The general format for these entries is as follows:

```
service-names : client-list [: shell-command ]
```

The *service-names* may be one server name, such as `in.ftpd` or `in.telnetd`; or it may be several names, separated by commas or spaces. You can also use the `ALL` keyword, which stands for all services. The optional *shell-command* is a command you can run when access is attempted. You can use this feature to mail a notification to an address, present a failure message on the port, or take some other action.

The *client-list* is potentially much more complex than the *service-names*. As with the *service-names*, the *client-list* may be a single entry or many, separated by commas or spaces. You can specify clients in any of several different ways:

IP Address   You can provide a single IP address, such as `172.24.45.102`, to block or allow access from that IP address.

IP Address Range   If you want to block or allow access by an entire network based on its IP address range, you can do so. The simplest approach is to provide a partial IP address (ending in a dot), such as `172.24.45.`, which matches all systems in the `172.24.45.0/24` subnet. You can also provide the complete network address and add the number of bits or a complete netmask after a slash, as in `172.24.45.0/24` or `172.24.45.0/255.255.255.0`.

Hostname   If you don't want to use IP addresses, you can block or authorize an individual computer by providing its hostname, as in `trex.pangaea.edu`. This approach is riskier than using an

IP address, though, because it relies on a successful and accurate DNS lookup. If a cracker compromises your (or potentially even somebody else's) DNS server or if your DNS server goes down, the TCP Wrappers rules may not work as you expect.

Domain Name   To block or authorize access based on a domain name, you list the domain name preceded by a dot. For instance, `.pangaea.edu` blocks or authorizes all computers in the `pangaea.edu` domain. As with hostname authentication, this approach is dependent upon accurate and reliable DNS resolution.

NIS Netgroup Name   If your network runs a Network Information Services (NIS) netgroup server, you can specify an NIS netgroup name by preceding it with an at sign (`@`). As with hostname and domain name specifications, this approach puts your system at the mercy of another system—in this case, the NIS server.

Wildcards   You can use any of several wildcards that match particular groups of computers. Examples of wildcards include `ALL` (all computers), `LOCAL` (all computers whose hostnames resolve without dots—normally those on the same domain as the server), `UNKNOWN` (computers whose hostnames or IP addresses aren't known, or users whose names can't be verified via `identd`), `KNOWN` (computers whose hostnames and IP addresses are known, and users whose names are returned by a client's `identd` server), and `PARANOID` (systems whose hostnames and IP addresses don't match). All of these options except for `ALL` are somewhat risky because they depend upon proper DNS functioning.

Usernames   You can match individual users by preceding a hostname or IP address by the username and an at sign, as in `sue@trex.pangaea.edu`.

In addition to these rules, you can use the `EXCEPT` keyword to create a list with exceptions. For instance, `172.24.45.0/24 EXCEPT 172.24.45.72` excludes `172.24.45.72` from the client list.

As an example of several of these rules in operation, consider Listing 20.3, which shows a sample `/etc/hosts.allow` file. This file should be used in conjunction with an `/etc/hosts.deny` file that restricts access for some or all servers. If Listing 20.3 were used with an empty `hosts.deny` file, it would have no effect, because no systems would be denied access.

LISTING 20.3: A SAMPLE `/etc/hosts.allow` FILE

```
in.telnetd : 172.24.45.2 trex.pangaea.edu
vsftpd : 172.24.45. EXCEPT 172.24.45.1
imapd : .pangaea.edu EXCEPT router.pangaea.edu
ipop3d : sue@trex.pangaea.edu
```

If used in conjunction with a very restrictive `/etc/hosts/deny` file (say, one containing the line `ALL : ALL`), Listing 20.3 grants access to only four servers, and it allows only a few hosts to access those services:

Telnet   The `in.telnetd` line tells the system to accept Telnet connections only from `172.24.45.2` and `trex.pangaea.edu`. Presumably, these are local hosts for which Telnet's risks are minor.

FTP   The vsftpd line tells TCP Wrappers to accept FTP connections from every computer on the 172.24.45.0/24 network except for 172.24.45.1. Perhaps 172.24.45.1 is a router or some other host that should never need to use an FTP client.

IMAP   The Internet Message Access Protocol (IMAP) is a mail retrieval protocol, and the imapd line restricts access to this protocol. All the computers in the pangaea.edu domain except for router.pangaea.edu may access this server.

POP   The ipop3d line enables sue@trex.pangaea.edu to use the Post Office Protocol (POP) to retrieve e-mail. Other users of that system and users of other systems (even sue on other systems) can't access the ipop3d server.

WARNING   *Remember that TCP Wrappers protects only those servers that use its features. Many servers aren't launched through* inetd *and don't use TCP Wrappers.*

TCP Wrappers provides more features than I can present here, and some of its features can have very subtle effects. For this reason, you should thoroughly test any /etc/hosts.allow and /etc/hosts.deny files you create. If you have problems, type **man 5 hosts_access** to read the official documentation on the TCP Wrappers control file format.

Enhanced *xinetd* Access Restrictions

Mandrake and Red Hat have abandoned inetd in favor of xinetd (pronounced "zi-net-dee"). This fact has changed the nature of access restrictions in these distributions compared to other distributions. Specifically, although it's possible to use TCP Wrappers with xinetd, doing so is not common. Instead, xinetd provides its own access control tools, many of which are very similar to those provided by TCP Wrappers. If you want to use these controls instead of or in addition to those provided by TCP Wrappers, you can replace inetd with xinetd even on distributions that use inetd by default.

xinetd in a Nutshell

The main xinetd configuration file is /etc/xinetd.conf. Both Mandrake and Red Hat use this file to set server defaults. You can enter the access restrictions described in the next section, "Restricting Access with xinetd," in the defaults section of this file, or you can enter restrictions in the files devoted to individual servers. These files reside in /etc/xinetd.d, and they are usually named after the server or service they control. For instance, swat handles the Samba Web Access Tool (SWAT) server. This file is likely to consist mainly of lines like the following:

```
service swat
{
    port        = 901
    socket_type = stream
    wait        = no
    only_from   = 127.0.0.1
    user        = root
    server      = /usr/sbin/swat
    disable     = no
}
```

These lines specify the port on which the server runs and other critical features. Chapter 22 covers most of these options in detail. This example demonstrates one access control option, though: the only_from line.

One important difference between restricting access with TCP Wrappers and with xinetd is that you must restart the xinetd server, or at least tell it to reread its configuration file after making changes to that file. You can do so by passing it the HUP signal, as in **killall -HUP xinetd**.

Restricting Access with *xinetd*

Many of the xinetd access control tools mirror those in TCP Wrappers, although xinetd uses different names. You'll also find these controls spread across files, which can make it harder to review your system's overall security settings. On the other hand, xinetd offers a few security options that TCP Wrappers doesn't offer. Broadly speaking, the xinetd options fall into several categories:

Host and Network Access Restrictions You can use the only_from and no_access options much as you would use entries in TCP Wrappers' /etc/hosts.allow and /etc/hosts.deny files, respectively. If you include an only_from line, though, all systems not explicitly listed are denied access. You can specify hosts by IP address, network address with or without netmask (as in 172.24.45.0 or 172.24.45.0/24), hostname, or a network name listed in /etc/networks. If you use a hostname, xinetd does a single hostname lookup whenever you start the server, so this option is likely to be unreliable if a client's IP address changes at all frequently. If a system matches both only_from and no_access lines, xinetd applies the rule associated with the more specific line. For instance, if only_from enables access from 172.24.45.0/24 and no_access denies access to 172.24.45.7, then 172.24.45.7 will not be able to access the system.

Interface Restrictions If your computer has multiple network interfaces, you can bind a server to just one of those interfaces with the bind or interface options, which are synonymous. These options take the IP address on the local computer associated with an interface as an option. For instance, bind = 172.24.45.7 ties the server to the interface with the 172.24.45.7 address. When you use this feature, xinetd doesn't even listen for connections on other interfaces, which can greatly enhance security; a miscreant can't take advantage of a bug, even in xinetd, if xinetd isn't listening on the interface the cracker is using.

Temporal Restrictions If you want a server to be available at some times of day but not others, you can configure temporal restrictions using the access_times feature. This keyword takes two times, separated by a dash (-), as an option. The times are specified in 24-hour format. For instance, access_times = 07:30-18:00 restricts the server's availability to between 7:30 A.M. and 6:00 P.M. This restriction applies to the original connection; users can continue using the server past the curfew period. For instance, if a user logs into a Telnet server that's restricted to 7:30 A.M. to 6:00 P.M. at 5:57 P.M., the person could remain connected well past 6:00 P.M.

As a general rule, xinetd can be an improvement over TCP Wrappers on systems with multiple network interfaces or if you want to implement temporal restrictions. The host-based restrictions in xinetd are slightly less sophisticated than those in TCP Wrappers, but for the most part you can accomplish the same goals with either system. If your distribution uses xinetd but you find you must use a TCP Wrappers feature, you can use TCP Wrappers in conjunction with xinetd, much as you can use TCP Wrappers with inetd. Specifically, you use server = /usr/sbin/tcpd to get xinetd to call TCP Wrappers; then pass the server name and arguments on the server_args line.

Containing Access in a Jail

No matter how carefully you shield your servers from potential abusers with tools such as packet-filter firewalls, TCP Wrappers, and xinetd, you can't block all accesses to the servers. Doing so would be pointless; servers exist to communicate with clients, and there's always some risk that an unfriendly party will control one of those clients. An environment in which the server program's root directory is changed—that is, a chroot jail—is one system you can use to minimize the risk to your computer should a misconfigured or buggy server be discovered by a cracker. Of course, you should know what a chroot jail can and cannot do to protect your system. Once you understand the jail's capabilities, you can set it up. Doing this requires both preparing the jail directory and running programs in the jail.

What Is a *chroot* Jail?

The basic idea behind a chroot jail is to isolate a server in a minimal virtual Linux system. This system is defined by a special directory tree you devote to the jail. For instance, you might set aside /jails/ftp to house the FTP server. As far as the FTP server is concerned, /jails/ftp is the root directory; when the FTP server tries to access files in /pub, it's really reading files from /jails/ftp/pub. This configuration has several important implications:

No Access Outside the Jail   The jailed application can't access potentially sensitive files that reside outside of the jail, such as configuration files in /etc. Even read access to these directories is unavailable. This fact makes it very difficult for jailed applications to abuse security flaws in other programs or to retrieve potentially unprotected but sensitive files.

Need to Reproduce Vital System Files   All the files a jailed application requires must be duplicated within the jail. For instance, if a server needs a particular library file, you must copy it to an appropriate subdirectory within the jail. (In some cases, a hard link will work; but using a hard link gives the jailed application access to the file outside of the jail.) Depending on how the jailed server is started, it may need configuration files within the jail. You may also need to create duplicates of device files and even the /proc filesystem for some servers.

Super Server Interactions   If a server is normally run from a super server, you must do one of three things: reconfigure the server or the super server to lock the server in the jail; run a copy of the super server in the jail along with the target server; or reconfigure the server to run without a super server.

Increased Maintenance Effort   Servers don't usually ship configured to operate within jails, although some servers are easier to configure in this way. Therefore, when you upgrade a server, you'll probably have to copy the upgraded files into the jail and restart the server.

Multiple Jails   You can set up multiple jail directories, one for each jailed server. Doing so can improve your security compared to operating just one jail. For instance, suppose two servers have security flaws that interact, enabling one server to be abused to modify another's configuration files, which in turn could give an intruder root access. If these two servers are run in separate jails, neither can see the other's configuration files, so the interaction vulnerability can't be abused without breaking out of the jail.

Unfortunately, `chroot` jails are imperfect. It is possible for `root` to break out of a `chroot` jail. Therefore, a server run as `root` might be able to break out of the jail if it's compromised. An intruder might also be able to do substantial damage even working from within a `chroot` jail. For instance, a mail server that's misconfigured as an open relay could be abused by a spammer to relay mail whether or not it's run from within a jail. Some servers may not work well within a jail. For instance, a file server might need access to users' home directories, which probably aren't in the jail. Of course, with some planning you could put users' home directories within the jail.

In sum, a `chroot` jail isn't a panacea, but it is a useful security tool. Some servers, such as many FTP servers, are designed to be run from within a jail and include configuration commands that make it easy to do so. Other servers aren't designed with `chroot` jail use in mind, but some of these can still be run from within a jail by calling them with the `chroot` command.

Setting Up a Jail Directory

If you want to run one or more servers from within a `chroot` jail, the first task you must undertake is to configure the jail directory. In principle, this directory could be anywhere. As an example, this section describes setting up a directory in which you can run a Network Time Protocol (NTP) server. I will describe NTP more fully in Chapter 27, "Miscellaneous Servers."

NOTE   *For this description, I used Debian 3.0 running on an iMac as a model. Distributions often ship with binaries compiled in unique ways, though. For this reason, you may need to perform slightly different steps than I describe to set up NTP to run in a jail if you're using a different system.*

Once you've decided where to place the jail directory, create it. For this example, I used `/jail/ntp`. Type **`mkdir -p /jail/ntp`** to create this directory. You must then populate this directory with files that the server will need:

Server Files   The most obvious file is the server file itself—ntpd in this case, from `/usr/sbin`. Typing **`mkdir -p /jail/ntp/usr/sbin`** creates the directory. You can then type **`cp -p /usr/sbin/ntpd /jail/ntp/usr/sbin`** to copy the original file to the jail.

Support Programs   Some servers launch support programs while they run. For instance, many FTP servers rely on `ls`. You must copy these files to their appropriate locations in the jail directory. Debian's NTP package ships with several support programs in `/usr/sbin`—a few whose names begin with `ntp` and one that doesn't (`tickadj`).

Support Libraries   Many programs rely on dynamic libraries. You can learn which libraries a server uses by typing **`ldd *server*`**, where *server* is the server's filename, complete with path. Debian's `ntpd` relies on five libraries, which must be copied to an appropriate location within the jail. Some libraries rely on other libraries, so you should repeat this test for every library you copy. Servers with explicit `chroot` jail support may be able to link with dynamic libraries in their normal directories before they lock themselves in the jail, so this step may not be necessary for such programs.

Configuration Files   NTP uses the `/etc/ntp.conf` file, which must be copied to the jail's `etc` directory (`/jail/ntp/etc` in this example). You must also configure the NTP server using this file, as described in Chapter 27. Debian stores its time zone in `/etc/timezone`, so copying this file is in order, as well.

Log and Temporary Directories   NTP keeps log files in /var/lib/ntp, /var/log/ntpstats, and optionally /var/log/ntpd. These directories must exist or you'll be unable to create and examine log files, which can be useful debugging resources. Some servers also create temporary files in /tmp, so you may want to create this directory. If a server must be able to write to a directory, be sure its permissions are set appropriately.

TIP   *Some servers can log data via* syslogd; *others log directly to a file. Some give you an option. As a general rule, logging directly to a file is simpler for servers run in a jail, because there's no need to copy* syslogd *into the jail. In the case of NTP, you can set the logging option with the* logfile *line in* /etc/ntp.conf.

User Database Files   Some servers need access to user database files such as /etc/passwd. Such programs often use the Pluggable Authentication Module (PAM), and so they may require that much of your PAM configuration be copied into the jail. As a general rule, servers that need user database files are poor candidates for running in a jail, because they often need access to users' home directories. The NTP server doesn't need any of these files.

Server Data Files   Some servers exist to deliver files to clients. For instance, users generally access an FTP server to retrieve files from the computer; and a font server delivers fonts to clients. You must move or copy data files into the jail for such servers to be effective. In some cases, you can use the --bind option to mount to make a virtual copy of a data directory within the chroot environment. For instance, **mount --bind /usr/X11R6/lib/X11/fonts /jail/xfs/fonts** makes the normal Linux fonts directory tree available to a font server run in a jail at /jail/xfs. This approach has some risks, though, because it effectively gives the jailed server access to some files outside of its jail. The NTP server doesn't deliver data files *per se*, so there's no need to copy such files to its jail directory.

Miscellaneous Support Files   Some servers rely on support files in odd locations. Try running the server and then examining the files it's opened with lsof, as in **lsof | grep ntpd**. In the case of ntpd, you should see the libraries it uses, possibly some log files, some network connections, and /dev/null.

Device Files   Some servers rely on device files, which you must re-create. For instance, ntpd uses /dev/null. You can copy a device file with cp and its -a option, as in **cp -a /dev/null /jail/ntp/dev/null**. Actually learning what device files, if any, a server uses can be trickier. Using lsof, as when finding miscellaneous support files, can help.

Special Filesystem Files   Some servers rely on files in the /proc or other special filesystems. If this is true of your server, you can mount a copy of the special filesystem in the jail by copying the original /etc/fstab entry for the filesystem but using a mount point within the jail. If your distribution uses DevFS, you can do this for device files, but this approach is overkill. It's safer to just copy the one or two device files the server needs. The ntpd server doesn't rely on any files in /proc.

WARNING   *The* /proc *filesystem and some device files give software extraordinary power over your computer. For this reason, you should be cautious about copying these files or creating a duplicate* /proc *filesystem in a jail. Sometimes a server doesn't really need these files, although it may benefit from them in some way.*

Once you've copied all of these files into your jail, that directory should contain several of the subdirectories and files found on a normal Linux system; essentially, it's like a miniature Linux installation. Precisely how many files you must copy depends on the server. My NTP system uses a dozen files and a similar number of directories and subdirectories. Once run, the server generates a few more files.

Running Programs in the Jail

Two methods of running a program in a `chroot` jail exist. The easiest method is to rely on an option in the server's configuration file. For instance, the ProFTPd server (`http://www.proftpd.net`) automatically locks the server in a `chroot` jail when you use the `<Anonymous>` directive in its configuration file. Such server packages sometimes ship with preconfigured jail directories. They also may be able to use libraries and configuration files outside of their jails, which can greatly simplify configuration.

Other servers require help to run from a jail, and this help is provided by the `chroot` command. This command's syntax is as follows:

```
chroot /new/root server-name [options]
```

In this command, */new/root* is the jail's location and *server-name* is the path to the server *relative to the jail*. For instance, to run `ntpd`, you would type:

```
# chroot /jail/ntp /usr/sbin/ntpd
```

This command looks as if it's running the original `ntpd`, but it's not—you can delete or rename that file and the command will still work. Of course, this assumes that everything about your `chroot` environment has been configured correctly. Chances are it won't work on your first attempt when configuring a new server. You may need to examine the server's log files and otherwise troubleshoot the server to discover why it's not working.

TIP   Configure the server to work outside of the jail before trying to get it to work inside the jail. You can then copy the working configuration files into the jail. If you try to run the server within the jail from the start, you won't be sure if the problems are due to a jail misconfiguration or to more ordinary server problems.

In order to run the server from the jail on a regular basis, you must alter or bypass the server's ordinary startup scripts, as described in Chapter 9, "Bypassing Automatic Configurations to Gain Control." Unfortunately, some distributions' startup scripts use special tools to run servers, such as `start-stop-daemon`. You may need to copy these tools into the jail, which is an added hassle. Worse, some of these tools rely on the `/proc` filesystem, which is an unacceptable security risk if the server itself doesn't need this facility. For this reason, you may want to disable the normal SysV startup script and use a local startup script, or you may want to replace the default SysV startup script with a much simpler one of your own devising.

Once your server is running in its jail, you must remember to take extra precautions to maintain it. Most importantly, remember to copy the server's files and support files whenever you upgrade any relevant packages. You may also need to take steps to rotate the server's log files.

Summary

Keeping crackers out of your system can be a full-time job, particularly if you run computers that are fully exposed to the Internet. Fortunately, assorted tools and techniques exist to help insulate your system from harm. Several of these tools—packet-filter firewalls, TCP Wrappers, and `xinetd` security settings—limit servers' (and, in the case of firewalls, clients') exposure to potentially malicious access attempts. If a server doesn't receive a malicious packet, the server can't be harmed by it. Another layer of defense lies in a `chroot` jail, which is a way of insulating a server from the rest of the Linux system. A server running in a `chroot` jail is less likely to be able to do any harm to the system than is a server running in a more conventional manner. Of course, none of these measures is perfect, which is why you should remain vigilant to signs of intrusion, as described in the next chapter, "Detecting Intruders."

Chapter 21

Detecting Intruders

THE SAYING GOES, "Eternal vigilance is the price of liberty." Something similar is true in computer security. It's not enough to create good passwords, eliminate unnecessary servers, configure a firewall, and so on, as described in Chapter 18, "System Security," and Chapter 20, "Controlling Network Access." You must be alert to signs of trouble—subtle or not-so-subtle clues that an intruder might be using your system. To some extent, you can detect intruders because they're often clumsy and leave traces that nobody can miss, such as broken servers. You shouldn't work on the assumption that a cracker will be so incompetent as to leave a figurative sign reading "you've been had" on your computer, though. Tools exist to help detect somewhat more competent miscreants. One of the most popular of these is Tripwire, which enables you to check for alterations in critical system files. Another tool is chkrootkit, which scans your system for known *root kits*— software packages crackers use to acquire root privileges. Finally, if you discover that your system has been compromised, you should know how to proceed—what to do (and what *not* to do) to fix your system and not make matters worse.

Noticing Suspicious Events

One method of detecting intruders is being aware of the normal operation of your system and noting deviations from this standard. You may notice something odd about the system, such as a higher-than-normal system load. You may also see unusual files or changes to configuration files. Finally, users other than you may notice problems and complain. All of these things may be symptoms of an intrusion—or they could have more mundane explanations. In any event, spending some time investigating odd occurrences can put you on the trail of an intruder, and that's the first step to correcting the problem.

Odd System Behavior

Linux systems vary greatly in how they operate. One system might normally run with a high CPU load, whereas another might normally run with little or no load. One computer might normally see little network traffic, whereas another might regularly transfer gigabytes of data every day. As a system administrator, you should have a good feel for how a system normally runs. You should investigate any deviation from normal behavior. Even if the deviation isn't due to a break-in, it may represent a problem that you should correct. Some possible oddities you should investigate include:

Unusual Load Averages   A *load average* is a measure of the demand for CPU time placed on the system by all the programs it runs. Chapter 14, "Programs and Processes," describes this concept in more detail. You can check your load average with uptime or top. Many GUI environments also provide load average meters. If you see the load average change from its usual range, a cracker could have broken in and be running CPU-intensive programs or could have caused CPU-intensive programs to crash. On the other hand, legitimate users could be demanding more CPU time than normal for legitimate reasons, or a CPU-intensive program might have crashed for mundane reasons or run out of data to process.

Unusual Network Traffic   Just as with load averages, a system normally sees a certain range of network traffic. One possible cause of changes in network traffic patterns is an intrusion. A cracker might be using your system as a node in a distributed denial-of-service (DDoS) attack, for instance, chewing up your network bandwidth. On the other hand, you could be seeing an innocent spike in demand for a server's services, or a user could be downloading unusually large files for legitimate reasons. One way to monitor network traffic is to watch the LEDs on a NIC—but they are usually not very visible, as they're on the back of most computers. Hubs and switches also have activity LEDs, and these LEDs may be more accessible. Similar comments apply to external modems—both telephone modems and broadband modems. Typing **ifconfig eth0** (or a similar command for an interface other than eth0) produces a measure of transmitted (TX) and received (RX) packets.

Strange Running Processes   If you use ps, top, or some other process-monitoring tool, you may see processes with which you're not familiar. If you are familiar with all of the processes that run on the computer, seeing something new can be a sign of a problem—or it could be something innocent, such as a user running a perfectly legitimate program that's not often run on your system. You should definitely take the time to peruse your process list to become familiar with what's normal for your system.

Odd Program Crashes   Unfortunately, programs sometimes crash, even on Linux. After you've used Linux for a while, you should be familiar with which programs are likely to crash on your system. If another program starts crashing, it could be that an intruder has changed a configuration file, support libraries, or even the program executable file itself, thereby causing the crashes. Alternatively, it could be that a routine system upgrade or an error on your part caused these problems. Program crashes can also be early signs of deteriorating hardware, such as RAM or a hard disk starting to go bad.

Changes in Program Behavior   In most cases, programs should behave in a very predictable manner. For instance, if your bash shell presents a plain dollar sign ($) prompt today, it should do the same tomorrow unless you change the configuration file. If a program's behavior changes suddenly and without your having updated it or changed its configuration file, an intruder might have fumbled a takeover by inadvertently altering a configuration file detail or by changing a program file. On the other hand, you might have forgotten a legitimate upgrade or change, or the program might be responding to some other change in the system that you don't realize is related. If you share administrative responsibility for the system, perhaps another administrator has made a change.

Peculiar Log Entries   All Linux systems maintain log files, most of which reside in /var/log and its subdirectories. These log files may contain clues concerning an attempted or successful intrusion, such as repeated login failures or reports of unusual server stop/start cycles. Crackers often try to cover their tracks by editing or deleting log files, so even missing log files or gaps in log files can be signs of trouble.

Filled Filesystems   If you notice that a filesystem has filled up, you should investigate the matter. Even if it's due to innocent causes, such as increased user demand for storage space, you must correct the problem. Sometimes an intruder might inadvertently or intentionally fill a filesystem. One type of DoS attack involves causing your system to create huge log files, filling your log file partition. Such attacks aren't intrusions *per se*, but they do require your attention.

Unfamiliar Usernames   If you notice unfamiliar usernames in ps or top listings or in /etc/passwd or other system configuration files, investigate immediately. Some servers require special accounts to operate correctly, but for the most part, if an account wasn't present when you installed the system and wasn't added by you or another authorized administrator, it's suspect. Make a backup of /etc/passwd right after you install the system, and keep it for reference.

Complaints from Other System Administrators   In many ways the worst-case scenario is receiving a complaint from another system administrator. You might receive a phone call or e-mail complaining of suspicious access attempts from your computer. Another common complaint concerns spam originating from your system. Sometimes these complaints are signs of an intrusion; the intruder is using your system to attack others. Other times these complaints indicate that you have a local user who's a "bad apple" and is attacking others. Sometimes (particularly with spam and e-mail worms) the complaint is spurious; it's easy to forge e-mail headers to indicate a false return address, and a spammer may be attacking you indirectly in this way.

All of these indications demand further investigation on your part. How you proceed depends on the nature of the peculiarity. Sometimes reading a few man page entries or contacting a user about an unusual process will clear up the situation. Other times you may need to do extensive web searches. Using chkrootkit, as described in the upcoming section, "Looking for Root Kits with chkrootkit," may be in order.

WARNING   *When dealing with a potential system intrusion, you shouldn't trust anything on the system that's under investigation. For instance, a cracker might have planted false man page entries to explain away an unusual program; and a compromised system's e-mail might not be trustworthy. Intruders sometimes alter common system tools such as ls to hide their tracks. Perform your investigations from another computer that displays no unusual symptoms.*

Unusual Files or File Contents

Crackers frequently leave behind odd files or file entries. Some of these have been alluded to already, in "Odd System Behavior." In particular, /etc/passwd may hold usernames it shouldn't contain, and log files may show odd behavior, be edited, or even be missing entirely. Other files are very sensitive, as well. Pay particular attention to the files in /etc and its subdirectories. Most servers use configuration files in this directory tree, and the system startup scripts reside here, as well. Keep a backup of this directory tree on a write-protected removable medium so that you can verify that files haven't been altered.

Crackers often add program files to normal program file directories such as /bin and /usr/bin. Sometimes these files are common misspellings of ordinary commands, intended to run when the system administrator mistypes the target command. Of course, a Linux system contains so many program files that you can't reasonably check every directory for files that shouldn't belong there. In part, tools such as Tripwire are designed to do this job.

User Complaints

As a system administrator, you should know how your systems normally operate. Your systems' users will also know how the systems they use operate, but from a different perspective. Sometimes this perspective will be helpful in discovering problems. Your users may complain of system slowdowns (indicating unusually high load averages, network traffic, or low-memory conditions), odd program behavior, or other issues described earlier, in "Odd System Behavior." Treat such complaints seriously. They may or may not turn out to be security problems, but whatever the cause, the problems should be fixed.

Users might also notice problems with physical security, such as suspicious individuals watching people log in on public terminals or open doors that should be locked. Investigate such reports. If necessary, contact appropriate physical security authorities or others responsible for the security features in question.

Monitoring for Intrusion with Tripwire

Although being on the lookout for suspicious events and configurations is always advisable, this approach is far from guaranteed to detect a break-in. A skilled or lucky cracker may be able to change your system in a subtle enough way that you'd be unlikely to notice the damage, and use few enough system resources that you wouldn't notice a degradation in performance. For this reason, tools exist to systematically scan your system for compromised components. One of the most popular of these tools is Tripwire (http://www.tripwire.org). This program is designed to detect modifications to files and directories and to alert you to these changes. As a security tool, Tripwire must attend to various security issues that greatly complicate its design and configuration. Issues of what files to monitor are also important. For these reasons, configuring and running Tripwire takes more effort than you might at first think. Modifying the configuration as you update your system also takes special effort. Despite these problems, using Tripwire is advisable, particularly on high-profile systems that are exposed directly to the Internet.

Tripwire: Detecting Modified Files

Tripwire's basic approach is fairly straightforward: The program scans important system directories and stores vital information about the files it finds in a database. Information can include the creation date and time, the file size, and various types of *checksums* (codes that are likely to change if any byte in the file is altered). Once this database is in place, it serves as a reference. You can run Tripwire automatically on a regular basis from a cron job or manually whenever you feel it's appropriate. On these subsequent runs, the program recomputes the information it stored in the database. If the new data doesn't match the stored data, Tripwire raises an alarm; the files have been altered.

For instance, suppose you configure Tripwire to run once a day from a `cron` job. If an intruder breaks into your system and manages to replace critical binary files, Tripwire will detect that fact and can send you an e-mail or otherwise notify you of the problem. Therefore, you're unlikely to go more than a day between an intrusion and your becoming aware of it, minimizing the period during which the cracker can do further damage.

Unfortunately, life isn't quite as easy as I've just described. The problem is this: An intruder who can replace critical system files can also alter Tripwire's configuration. For instance, the intruder could modify Tripwire's database so that it reflects the modified files. Several possible defenses against such actions exist. One that's very popular, and that's described in the coming sections, is to use encryption. If the database is encrypted in such a way that Tripwire can read it but not write to it without a password, chances are a cracker won't be able to modify the database. Another option is to store the database on a read-only medium—ideally one that's physically impossible to write, such as a CD-R disc in a CD-ROM drive. In both of these cases, of course, an intruder could theoretically replace the Tripwire executable itself. Therefore, you may want to manually monitor this file using other tools.

Configuring Tripwire

In order to use Tripwire, you must configure it much as you do many other programs. The most conventional part of this process is setting Tripwire options in its configuration file and in the *policy file.* The configuration file lists ancillary programs, additional configuration file locations, and the like. The policy file lists files and directories that Tripwire is to check and lists the methods Tripwire is to use to check these files and directories. After you've set up the Tripwire policy file, you must initialize the Tripwire database. Subsequent runs of Tripwire can check the installed files or update the database.

TIP   Ideally, you should install and configure Tripwire after setting up the Linux system but before connecting it to a network. This practice will ensure that Tripwire's initial check of your system reflects a computer that has not been compromised. If you delay configuring Tripwire, it could record an already-compromised system as its baseline, thereby making it worthless.

TRIPWIRE PACKAGES AND CONFIGURATION FILES

Unfortunately, not all Linux distributions ship with Tripwire. As I write, the current version of Tripwire is 2.3-47. Debian, Mandrake, and Red Hat all ship with recent versions of the program or make them available in a reasonable way. (For Debian, you must install it from the Non-U.S. package group.) SuSE makes an old 1.2 version of the program available, but this version doesn't support encryption, and its configuration file format is substantially different than described in this chapter. Slackware doesn't ship with Tripwire at all. For both SuSE and Slackware, I recommend that you download a Tripwire package from the main Tripwire website (`http://www.tripwire.org`). The RPM package works well for SuSE.

Most modern Tripwire installations place configuration files in /etc/tripwire. You're likely to find at least two files here initially: twcfg.txt and twpol.txt. These files are unencrypted versions of the main configuration file and the policy file, respectively. Subsequent configuration steps create files called tw.cfg and tw.pol from these plain-text files. Tripwire will use these encrypted files in operation.

Most Tripwire RPMs include a file called twinstall.sh in the /etc/tripwire directory. The binary tarball available on the Tripwire website includes a similar file called install.sh. Whatever the name, this file is a shell script that runs through many one-time configuration requirements. Its use is described in the next section, "Setting Tripwire Options." Instead of providing this file explicitly, Debian's Tripwire package runs a custom Tripwire configuration script when you install the package.

SETTING TRIPWIRE OPTIONS

You may need to edit one or both of two Tripwire configuration files. The first, which is usually called twcfg.txt, sets global configuration options, such as the location of the database file and various defaults. Chances are you don't need to edit this file, but you may want to look at it to verify that its options are reasonable. Some options you may want to modify or add include GLOBALEMAIL, a list of e-mail addresses to which reports should be sent; MAILNOVIOLATIONS, whether or not to send e-mail reports if no security problems are found; and EDITOR, the complete path and filename of the text editor you want Tripwire to use for certain operations.

The second Tripwire configuration file is usually called twpol.txt. This configuration file defines the files and directories that Tripwire should monitor, and which features of these files and directories it should use to do this monitoring. The Tripwire policy file format may seem confusing at first. At its core, this file consists of a handful of major elements. Most lines define directories that Tripwire is to scan, and have the following format:

```
[!] object-name [select-flags] [(attributes)] ;
```

The optional exclamation mark (!) symbol represents a *stop point*—if present, Tripwire stops scanning a directory tree at this point. For instance, you might want to tell Tripwire to scan /usr/local but to ignore /usr/local/fonts. You'd create an entry for /usr/local and another, preceded by an exclamation mark, for /usr/local/fonts.

The *object-name* is the name of the file or directory you want to be scanned. You can also use a variable, as described shortly, to stand in for a directory name.

The *select-flags* are methods of specifying what sorts of tests you want performed on a file or directory. The *select-flags* take the form of a plus sign (+) or minus sign (-) followed by one or more of the codes specified in Table 21.1. For instance, you might specify +tpug to check the file type, permissions, UID, and GID. Using a plus sign means to check the feature, and a minus sign indicates that the specified feature is *not* to be checked. The lowercase options are all quick and easy to check; information for these checks is accessible in the files' inodes, so the file itself doesn't need to be accessed. The uppercase options perform various types of checksums, which require reading the entire contents of the file. These checks, therefore, take much longer to perform, particularly on large files. Such tests are appropriate for the most critical configuration and executable files, but you might want to forgo them for many ordinary executables.

TABLE 21.1: TRIPWIRE FLAGS FOR CHECKING FILES AND DIRECTORIES

FLAG	MEANING
a	Last access time stamp
b	File size in blocks
c	Create/modify time stamp
d	Disk device number on which the inode resides
g	Group ID (GID) of file
i	Inode number
m	Modification time stamp
n	Inode reference count
p	File permissions
r	Device number
s	File size in bytes
t	File type (ordinary file, directory, etc.)
u	User ID (UID) of file
l	File is increasing in size
C	Cyclic Redundancy Check (CRC) 32-bit hash
M	Message Digest 5 (MD5) hash
S	Secure Hash Algorithm (SHA) hash
H	Haval signature

You can optionally include *attributes* within parentheses after the *select-flags*. For instance, `recurse=false` causes scanning of a directory but not its subdirectories, and `rulename=name` sets a name for the rule, which can help you identify it in Tripwire's reports.

Although many lines define how Tripwire is to handle directories and files, other lines perform other functions. These other lines include:

Comments Lines beginning with hash marks (#) are comments and are ignored. Comments can also appear after an otherwise valid entry on one line.

Directives These are keywords preceded by a pair of at signs (@), as in `@@section` to define a section of the policy file or `@@ifhost` to test whether Tripwire is running on a particular host. (You might use the latter to create one policy file that you can move easily across several hosts.)

Variable Definitions You can assign and use variables much as you do in a shell script. One difference is that variables are enclosed in parentheses when used. Tripwire variable definitions also end in a semicolon (;) character. For instance, some default scripts use a line reading SEC_INVARIANT = +tpug ; to set a variable, and then refer to $(SEC_INVARIANT) later in the file. Some variables are preset to reasonable flag values for particular directory types. Specifically, $IgnoreNone tests everything, $ReadOnly is good for read-only files and directories, $Dynamic works well for configuration files that are accessed often, and $Growing is good for files such as log files that grow in size.

Preceding Attribute Rules   You can define attributes in parentheses before a group of Tripwire rules, which are then enclosed in curly braces ({}). This approach can help you to define common attributes for a set of directories.

As an example of a Tripwire policy file, consider Listing 21.1. This file is a simple configuration that uses many of the features just described. A variable is defined on the first line ($TWBIN), and it is used in a set of rules given the name Tripwire Binaries using a preceding attribute section. Following this section, several rules define checks for specific directories—/usr/bin and /etc.

LISTING 21.1: SAMPLE TRIPWIRE POLICY FILE

```
TWBIN = /usr/sbin ;

# Tripwire binaries
(
  rulename = "Tripwire Binaries",
)
{
  $(TWBIN)/siggen        -> $(ReadOnly) ;
  $(TWBIN)/tripwire      -> $(ReadOnly) ;
  $(TWBIN)/twadmin       -> $(ReadOnly) ;
  $(TWBIN)/twprint       -> $(ReadOnly) ;
}

/usr/bin -> $(ReadOnly) ;
/etc -> $(Dynamic) ;
```

In practice, your Tripwire policy file is likely to be much longer and more complex than Listing 21.1. Most Tripwire packages ship with a sample policy file that's several hundred lines long, if not over a thousand lines. These lines specify the files and directories that Tripwire is to monitor in excruciating detail. You should back up this file, then go through it carefully. Remove references to files and directories that don't exist on your system. If you've added important packages that aren't reflected in the default file, create entries for them. You may want to do so by copying an existing entry set and modifying it to fit the new package's needs. Tripwire notifies you of files that are specified in the policy file but that don't exist on the system when you initialize the database, so you may end up revising this information after you initialize the database for the first time.

TIP   Don't delete lines from the policy file; instead, comment them out by adding a hash mark to the start of the line. This practice enables you to easily add a line back should the need arise in the future.

WARNING   *The unencrypted versions of both the configuration and the policy file could conceivably be useful to an intruder. For instance, the policy file could tell the intruder which directories and files are monitored, so an intruder could try hiding extra programs in unprotected directories. For this reason, after you convert these files to their encrypted formats, you should move the originals to a removable disk and delete them from the hard disk.*

INITIALIZING THE DATABASE

If your Tripwire installation didn't run its setup script when you installed the system, run it now. (This script is often called `/etc/tripwire/twinstall.sh`.) The script will ask for two *passphrases*, which are like passwords but are frequently longer. Create these passphrases carefully and protect them, as described in Chapter 18. The script will then ask for the site passphrase twice, as it creates encrypted versions of the configuration and policy files from your clear-text versions. If the script reports that it's failed, check the error messages. Chances are they'll report a bad line in the original configuration or policy file. For instance, you might have mistyped a variable name or specified an invalid flag. Correct the error and try again. (Subsequent runs of `twinstall.sh` won't require you to generate new passphrases, but you will have to enter the passphrases you created initially.)

If your Tripwire installation doesn't include a `twinstall.sh` script, you can create encrypted configuration and policy files by using `twadmin`, as described in the upcoming section, "Modifying the Tripwire Configuration." Before you do this, though, you must manually create key files. Type `twadmin --generate-keys -S /etc/tripwire/site.key` to generate the site key. Use the same command, but substitute -L *hostname*-`local.key`, where *hostname* is your hostname, for -S `site.key`, to generate the local key file. These filenames are referenced as SITEKEYFILE and LOCALKEYFILE in `twcfg.txt`, so check there if you're in doubt about the filenames.

Once you've finished initializing these configuration files, you can proceed to initializing the database. You do this by typing `tripwire --init`. The program will ask for your local passphrase. After you enter it, Tripwire will scan the directories specified in the policy file and generate the encrypted database file. This process can take a long time, particularly if you've configured Tripwire to perform MD5 sum scans or similar hashes on directories that contain very many or very large files. Even the minimal Listing 21.1 may take several seconds to initialize. Be patient. When it's finished, with any luck the system will respond that it has generated a database file. It will also report on files specified in the policy file but not found on the system. You may want to remove references to these files, re-create the encrypted policy file, and reinitialize the database to be rid of these notifications.

Verifying System Integrity with Tripwire

After all the work editing configuration files, performing system integrity checks is fairly straight-forward: Type `tripwire --check`. As with initializing the database, this process is likely to take several minutes. When it's done, it creates a report that it stores in the REPORTFILE directory, as specified in the configuration file. Tripwire may also e-mail the report to the account specified with the GLOBALEMAIL variable, but only if Tripwire found problems or MAILNOVIOLATIONS is set to `true`. The command also sends the report to `stdout`, so you can see it on the screen. The report is fairly verbose, but pay particular attention to the filesystem summary section. For the policy file shown in

Listing 21.1, the output should include lines like this if you've made no changes to the system except to add a single file to /etc:

```
  Rule Name                      Severity Level    Added    Removed  Modified
  ---------                      --------------    -----    -------  --------
  Tripwire Binaries             0                 0        0        0
  bin                           0                 0        0        0
  (/usr/bin)
* etc                           0                 1        0        0
  (/etc)

Total objects scanned:  5149
Total violations found:  1
```

The final line shown here reveals that one problem was found. The matrix makes it plain that the problem was a file added to /etc. Later in the report, you'll find lines that report on violations in more detail:

```
Added:
"/etc/strangefile"
```

If you see a report like this, you should investigate further. If the "problem" is really something innocent, you can either ignore it or modify the Tripwire database to reflect the valid change to the system.

WARNING   *If you choose to ignore the reported violation, be aware that Tripwire might then be unable to detect subsequent unauthorized changes to the file or directory in question. For instance, if you add a legitimate user, and if a cracker subsequently breaks in and adds an account, Tripwire won't be able to detect the cracker's activity unless you update its database to reflect the new valid user.*

TIP   *Before adding software, changing configuration files, adding users, or making any other change that would appear in a Tripwire report, you should run Tripwire to be sure there are no suspicious activities. You can then update the Tripwire database after making your changes and be confident that the database doesn't include any untoward changes. For still greater security, take down the network just before running Tripwire, to be sure the system isn't compromised as you make your own valid changes.*

Running Tripwire manually can be worthwhile at times, but as a general rule, Tripwire works best when run regularly. Typically, you'll create a cron job to have the program perform a check on a regular basis—typically daily. For instance, you might create a script to run Tripwire and drop it into /etc/cron.daily. In fact, the Debian, Mandrake, and Red Hat Tripwire packages all include scripts to do precisely this. If you're using one of these packages, you should see a Tripwire report appear in your e-mail every morning, depending on the setting of MAILNOVIOLATIONS in twcfg.txt.

If you want to examine a regular Tripwire report some time after it's been made, you must use the twprint utility to examine the binary report file. These reports are most likely to be stored in

/var/lib/tripwire/report/ and to be named after your computer, along with a date code and .twr extension, such as knox.luna.edu-20030703-040252.twr. Pass twprint the -m r -r options and the filename, as in:

```
# twprint -m r -r /var/lib/tripwire/report/knox.luna.edu-20030703-040252.twr
```

The result of typing this command should be much the same as having Tripwire check your system, except that the program displays the results of a check that's already been run. You might use this facility to compare a recent check against old ones, in order to ascertain when a particular change to the system occurred.

Modifying the Tripwire Configuration

Tripwire configuration involves two plain-text configuration files, encrypted variants of these plain-text files, and an encrypted database file. You may want to update any of these files. To do so, you must do more than just edit the original configuration files:

Modifying the Configuration File   To modify the configuration file (typically /etc/tripwire/twcfg.txt), you must first edit the original file and then use twadmin to create a new binary file (typically /etc/tripwire/tw.cfg). Type **twadmin --create-cfgfile -S /etc/tripwire/ site.key /etc/tripwire/twcfg.txt** to do the job.

Creating a new Policy File   If you've made particularly extensive changes or are initializing the database for the first time, you may want to create an entirely new encrypted policy file. You can do so by typing **twadmin --create-polfile -S /etc/tripwire/site.key /etc/tripwire/ twpol.txt** to replace the encrypted binary tw.pol file. After changing the policy, you should type **tripwire --init** to reinitialize the Tripwire database.

Modifying the Policy   To modify the policy, you use the tripwire utility itself and its --update-policy option. Specifically, if you've modified the policy stored in /etc/tripwire/twpol.txt, you can type **tripwire --update-policy -S /etc/tripwire/site.key /etc/tripwire/twpol.txt** to update the encrypted binary tw.pol file. Prior to issuing this command, you must update the database, as described next.

Updating the Database   If you've made changes to your system and want to update the Tripwire database to reflect these changes, you must pass the --update parameter to Tripwire to have it do this job. In practice, this command may also require you to pass it the name of a Tripwire report file, as in **tripwire --update --twrfile /var/lib/tripwire/report/knox.luna.edu-20031212- 155357.twr**. Tripwire displays a modified version of the report in the editor specified in the configuration file. Partway through this report, there will be lines showing the added, changed, or deleted files, such as /etc/strangefile in Figure 21.1. Be sure an X appears in the box next to each file whose changed status you want to update. If you don't want to update a file, remove the X next to its name. When you're done, save your changes and exit the editor. Tripwire asks for your local passphrase and changes the database. If you want to forgo the prompting phase, you can add the --accept-all parameter.

FIGURE 21.1

You use an editor to specify which changed files you want to add to the database.

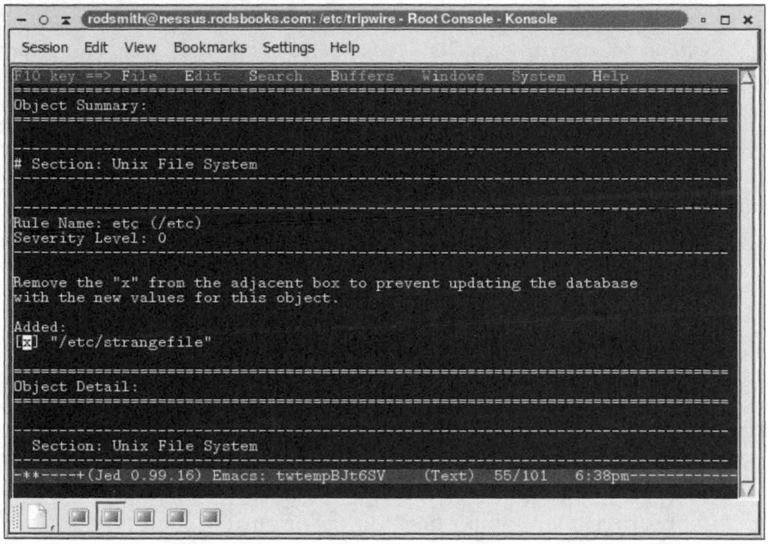

Imagine this scenario: You're administering a Linux system but you neglected to install Tripwire. You run across some suspicious activity, such as strange behavior from one of your programs. By itself, this activity isn't strong evidence of a security breach, but it is suspicious. What can you do to investigate the matter? If your system uses RPMs, one answer is to use the rpm utility—specifically its verify (-V) option. Because the RPM database includes MD5 sums and similar checks of package integrity, it can be used to verify the integrity of your packages, albeit with some important caveats. To verify a single package, type **rpm -V packagename**, as described in Chapter 11, "Managing Packages." Any files that have changed appear in a list, along with a string summarizing the ways in which they've changed. To verify every package on the system, type **rpm -Va**. This command is likely to produce copious output, though, so you may want to pipe it through less or redirect it to a file you can peruse later.

One big caveat concerning this approach is that a miscreant can easily defeat a simple test by installing a root kit named after a regular package but using RPM. The root kit's files will then appear to be valid to rpm. One possible countermeasure is to verify the suspect files against the original archive, ideally stored on CD-ROM. For instance, **rpm -Vp /path/to/packagename.rpm** will verify the installed package against the one in /path/to. For even better security, boot using an emergency boot system and test your system using the emergency system's version of rpm. This practice will protect against the possibility that the miscreant might replace your copy of rpm with one that ignores compromised files.

Overall, RPM can't come close to replacing Tripwire. At best, RPM is an awkward security tool compared to Tripwire. At worst, RPM's results aren't trustworthy. Nonetheless, it's better than nothing if you haven't installed Tripwire or some other security auditing tool.

Looking for Root Kits with *chkrootkit*

If you're familiar with Windows systems, chances are you're also familiar with virus scanners (aka antivirus tools). These programs scan a Windows system, or sometimes just specific files or e-mail attachments, for the presence of viruses, worms, Trojans, and other unfriendly programs. The Windows virus scanner market is large and supports several major commercial programs. There are even a few virus scanners for Linux, such as F-Prot Antivirus for Linux (`http://www.f-prot.com/products/`). Such scanners typically scan Windows programs stored on a Linux system, or they scan incoming e-mail for worms that affect Windows. Viruses and worms that infect Linux systems are very rare, so there's very little market for a Linux virus scanner for Linux programs.

Although Linux viruses aren't common, Linux security is far from assured. Crackers can utilize root kits, which often leave traces behind. Detecting root kits is very much like detecting the leavings of a virus, and a tool to detect Linux root kits does exist: `chkrootkit` (`http://www.chkrootkit.org`). This program is available for many distributions, or you can download the source code and compile it yourself.

TIP *Because* `chkrootkit` *works by examining specific files for specific symptoms of specific root kits, it's vitally important that you run the latest version of the program. If you can't find a precompiled package for the latest version, you should definitely download the source code and compile it on your system.*

Fortunately, `chkrootkit` is fairly easy to use—type its name, and the program scans your system and reports what it finds. With luck, this will be a series of `not infected`, `nothing found`, `not found`, and similar reassuring messages. If the program reports the presence of a root kit, though, you'll have to take action, as described in the next section, "What to Do in the Event of a Breach."

What to Do in the Event of a Breach

Suppose that the worst happens: Your system is compromised to the point that the intruder has gained `root` access. You may discover this through Tripwire reports, a `chkrootkit` run that reports problems, or some other means. What should you do? Unfortunately, in this situation you can't trust *anything* on your computer. Given `root` access, the cracker could have changed any file, including those you might use to restore the system to its normal state. Even if you've identified a root kit, you can't be sure those are the only files the intruder has changed. In broad outline, the procedure for dealing with an intrusion is as follows:

1. **Disconnect your system from the network.** Remove your system from the Internet and from your local network. You should literally unplug the network connection (if it's wired). This step ensures that your system can't be abused to attack others while you're trying to repair it.

2. **Make a backup.** Before you do anything else, make a backup of the system in its compromised state. This backup serves two main purposes. First, depending on how you choose to proceed, you may need to restore user data files from the backup. Second, you can use the backup for subsequent investigations. It may even prove to be helpful evidence if a criminal investigation ensues. Evidence that your system was compromised could help fix the blame where it belongs if the cracker used your system to attack others. You may want to make a separate backup of /etc for easy reference later in this procedure.

TIP   *The ideal backup is the original disk—you can then install a new replacement disk. Alternatively, you could copy compromised partitions to a spare disk using* dd. *Using the original disk or a full copy as the backup enables law enforcement to study the disk in detail, should the matter become a criminal investigation. Investigators might find traces of deleted files that could implicate the true culprit, and these traces would be lost if you were to use* tar, dump, *or other conventional backup tools.*

3. **Determine the method of entry.** This step is easier said than done. Your log files may provide clues concerning the method of entry, as might symptoms of system misbehavior. As you research the security of important servers and other programs, you may discover a server or two with known security bugs that might have been used to gain entry.

4. **Wipe the system clean.** Delete every system file on the computer—program files, libraries, configuration files, and so on. Do this by using an emergency Linux system and making new filesystems on the old partitions. If you've separated /home or other user data directories onto separate partitions, you can probably spare them, although it's possible that an intruder has left surprises even on these directories. As a minimal precaution, search any partitions you intend to keep for executable files (**find /home -perm -0111 -type f** should do the trick for /home) and evaluate whether they should be executable (or even present) yourself.

5. **Reinstall or recover the system.** Reinstall the system from scratch or restore it from a backup. (The latter option is covered in Chapter 17, "Protecting Your System with Backups.") If necessary, restore your system's configuration to its pre-intrusion state—for instance, set up your servers the way they were before the intrusion. If you restore either the entire system or configuration files from backups, be sure the backups were made before the intrusion. If you made a backup of /etc in Step 2, *do not* restore it in its entirety. You can use individual files as models for changes to your system, but blindly restoring these files may end up restoring an intruder's "back door." One possible exception is user database files, such as /etc/shadow and /etc/passwd; however, you should audit these files to be sure you aren't restoring any suspicious accounts.

6. **Upgrade system security.** Update old packages and fix any possible methods of entry you identified in Step 3. If you couldn't identify anything specific, you'll have to make do with package updates and increasing your general level of security. For instance, you might add a packet-filter firewall, as described in Chapter 20, or remove any servers you don't need to run. You should also change the root password and possibly ordinary users' passwords.

7. **Restore data files.** If you wiped out /home or other important data files, you can now restore them. If the intruder modified user files (say, defacing a website), you may need to restore from an older backup.

8. **Restore to the network.** Only after you've upgraded security should you contemplate returning the system to the network. At this point, your system should be clean and much harder to break into than it was before, so it's no longer a menace to others.

This procedure may seem tedious and paranoid, but it's better to err on the side of safety. If you don't take adequate precautions against fresh compromises, or if you don't clean every trace of the intruder from your system, you might see return visits, which will only give you more headaches.

On the other hand, some types of intrusion are not serious enough to merit this entire procedure. For instance, if you've found an old account that should have been deleted long ago but that's still being used, you can probably just delete the account. Likewise, if an authorized user has been abusing the system to attack others without gaining local `root` access, you can probably skip the long process. Basically, this procedure exists to protect you and your data from a cracker who's acquired `root` privileges. Those privileges mean that the intruder could have hidden away files in odd locations to be used after a partial cleaning, simplifying a future break-in—even if the system has improved security after the intruder's been discovered once.

In addition to the clean-up procedure, you may want to undertake other measures. For instance, you might want to initiate disciplinary action against an authorized user who has abused computing privileges. You might even want to contact the police. Unfortunately, small-time cracking activities are extremely common, and the police lack the resources to pursue all but the most damaging intrusions. For instance, the FBI most likely won't take an interest even in an interstate intrusion unless damages exceed several thousand dollars.

WARNING   *One thing you should* never *do in response to a break-in is to retaliate. As a practical matter, a misaimed retaliation can harm innocent people and land you in hot water. Even if you manage to attack the true perpetrator and don't get caught yourself, this activity only raises the general level of lawlessness on the Internet at large. It may invite a further retaliation from the original cracker, leading to an escalating spiral of attacks.*

Summary

You can take many steps to protect your system against intrusion, but security isn't a binary matter of being secure or not being secure; it's a matter of degrees. Even systems that are very well protected have vulnerabilities. For this reason, you should be alert to the possibility of intrusions. General awareness of your system's normal operating behavior can be invaluable because deviations from normal behavior can be an indication of trouble. Beyond this, security tools provide systematic methods of looking for intrusion. Taking the time to configure Tripwire is very worthwhile, and `chkrootkit` can help you identify an intrusion after it's occurred. Recovering from a breach can be a tedious undertaking, but doing the job right can save you a lot of grief caused by a repeat visit from an uninvited guest.

Part V
Server Tools

Chapter 22

Running Servers

MANY LINUX SYSTEMS RUN *servers*—programs that respond to network requests for data transfers. (The word *server* can also refer to a computer that exists mainly to run server programs.) Even if a computer isn't primarily a server system, it can run a server or two as a secondary role, or it can run a server in support of another function. For instance, Linux prints using software that is technically a server, but it can be configured to work only locally rather than over the network. The remaining chapters of this book are devoted to servers, and they describe several common Linux servers, including web servers, file servers, e-mail servers, remote access servers, and miscellaneous servers. This chapter begins the server coverage with a look at a very fundamental issue: configuring your system to run servers. Three methods of doing this are common: SysV startup scripts, super servers, and local startup scripts. Each of these methods has its advantages and disadvantages, and understanding how and when to use each method is a prerequisite for effective server configuration.

Demystifying SysV Startup Scripts

All major Linux distributions except Slackware use a collection of startup scripts inspired by the AT&T System V version of Unix. This startup script collection is known collectively as *SysV startup scripts*, and it's introduced in Chapter 9, "Bypassing Automatic Configurations to Gain Control." These scripts start individual services, which can be servers or nonserver system components such as basic networking or sound drivers. Many servers rely on SysV startup scripts to operate, so this topic requires more attention. In order to effectively change the operation of servers that launch via SysV startup scripts, you must know where the scripts are located and how to use them, both to start and stop servers on a one-time basis and to make more persistent modifications. You should also know that many distributions ship with tools designed to help you manipulate your SysV startup scripts.

SysV Startup Script Locations and Names

SysV startup scripts work in *runlevels*, which are numbered sets of servers and other important system components. Runlevel 0 shuts down the computer, runlevel 1 is a special single-user mode that can be used for emergency maintenance, and runlevel 6 reboots the computer. Runlevels 2 through 5 can be configured as you see fit. Most Linux distributions use runlevel 3 as a standard text-mode startup and runlevel 5 to start X and an X Display Manager Control Protocol (XDMCP) GUI login screen. Debian, though, attempts to start X and an XDMCP server in all runlevels between 2 and 5; and Slackware uses runlevel 4 rather than runlevel 5 to start X and an XDMCP server.

In order to implement runlevels, most Linux distributions place SysV startup scripts in one directory and then create symbolic links to these scripts in other directories named after the runlevel in question. Table 22.1 summarizes these locations. A question mark (?) in a directory name stands for a runlevel number between 0 and 6. Debian and SuSE also support an S in this position, which is used for startup scripts—servers that should run in all runlevels. In addition to these directories, some distributions create symbolic links. For instance, SuSE creates a link called /etc/rc.d that points to /etc/init.d, and Mandrake and Red Hat create links called /etc/init.d that point to /etc/rc.d/init.d. This practice can help you if you type a path to a script that's valid on one distribution but that might not work on the one you're using.

TABLE 22.1: SYSV STARTUP SCRIPT LOCATIONS

DISTRIBUTION	SYSV STARTUP SCRIPT MAIN DIRECTORY	SYSV STARTUP SCRIPT LINK DIRECTORIES
Debian 3.0	/etc/init.d	/etc/rc?.d
Mandrake 9.1	/etc/rc.d/init.d/	/etc/rc.d/rc?.d
Red Hat 9.0	/etc/rc.d/init.d/	/etc/rc.d/rc?.d
SuSE 8.1	/etc/init.d	/etc/init.d/rc?.d

NOTE *Slackware doesn't use SysV startup scripts in the same way as do most other distributions, but it does use runlevels. Instead of using SysV startup scripts as described here, Slackware uses startup scripts called /etc/rc.d/rc?.d, where ? is the runlevel number, to set the runlevel.*

Within the main startup script directory, SysV startup scripts are typically named after the servers or other programs they launch. For instance, on a Debian system, apache starts the Apache web server, exim starts the Exim mail server, and samba starts the Samba file server. These names aren't completely standardized across distributions, though. For instance, Mandrake, Red Hat, and SuSE all use smb rather than samba to start Samba. Also, distributions sometimes use different servers for the same function. For instance, Debian uses Exim as a mail server, Mandrake and SuSE use Postfix (started with a postfix SysV startup script), and Red Hat and Slackware use sendmail (started with a sendmail SysV startup script in the case of Red Hat). You can override these defaults by removing the standard package and installing another one. You can also add and remove servers; most server packages ship with one or more SysV startup scripts. For all of these reasons, the contents of the main SysV startup script directories vary a great deal from one distribution or installation to another.

WARNING *Installing a package intended for one distribution on another distribution often works without problems. SysV startup scripts, though, tend to be very distribution-specific, which complicates their installation across distributions. If you must do this, you may need to remove the SysV startup script that came with the package and create a new one or bypass the SysV startup procedure and use local startup scripts. Chapter 9 describes how to create a new SysV or local startup script.*

The SysV startup script link directories contain symbolic links to the original SysV startup scripts. These links are named after the original scripts, but they begin with three new characters: an S or a K and a two-digit number. For instance, a link might be called S91apache and link to the main apache startup script. The leading S or K characters stand for *start* or *kill*, respectively—they're codes for whether the server should or should not run in the specified runlevel. The two-digit number is a sequence code. Scripts are executed in the sequence specified by those numbers. You can use this feature to control the order in which servers run. For instance, Apache is a high-level server that relies on other features, such as basic networking. For this reason, it has a high number. Unfortunately, sequence numbers aren't standardized across distributions, so if you're used to one distribution and must work on another, you may find the sequence numbers unfamiliar.

Starting and Stopping Servers

Starting and stopping servers is a matter of calling the SysV startup scripts and passing them the appropriate parameters. You can do this on a one-time basis to make temporary changes, or you can make permanent changes by changing the names of the links in the startup script link directories for your default runlevel. You can also modify the order in which your servers start or stop.

MAKING TEMPORARY CHANGES

Most SysV startup scripts accept several parameters that affect the run status of the servers or other programs they handle. The most important of these parameters are start and stop, which start and stop the service, respectively. You can call these scripts as root and pass them these parameters. Most distributions respond by displaying the status of their efforts; for instance, to start Samba on a Mandrake system, you might type the following command and see the specified output:

```
# /etc/rc.d/init.d/smb start
Starting SMB services:                                    [  OK  ]
Starting NMB services:                                    [  OK  ]
```

The precise nature of the feedback depends on the distribution and the startup script. This specific example starts two servers, smbd and nmbd, and tells you that the servers have both been started. Chances are these displays will look familiar; most distributions display these messages during the system boot process.

WARNING   *Startup messages aren't entirely trustworthy. Sometimes the SysV startup script will tell you that it's done what you told it to do, when in fact the server has crashed during startup or has failed to shut down when told to stop. If in doubt, use* ps *or some other process monitoring tool to look for evidence of a running server.*

In addition to start and stop, most SysV startup scripts accept a few other parameters. Examples include restart, which restarts a service; reload, which causes the service to load changes to its configuration file; and status, which reports on the status of a service. Check individual scripts to learn what parameters they accept. Frequently, typing the script name with no parameters creates a usage summary:

```
# /etc/rc.d/init.d/smb
Usage: /etc/rc.d/init.d/smb {start|stop|restart|status|condrestart}
```

Any changes you make by calling SysV startup scripts after booting the computer won't persist across boots; when you shut down and restart, the computer will come up in the same state it was in when you last booted. In order to make a change permanent, you must either change the runlevel or change the SysV startup script links.

MAKING PERSISTENT CHANGES

One way to make changes permanent is to change the runlevel. If two runlevels' SysV startup script link directories contain different mixes of links, changing the runlevel will change the services available. You can change the runlevel on a one-time basis by typing **telinit *runlevel***, where *runlevel* is the runlevel number. To make this change permanent, you must edit the /etc/inittab file and change the number in the line that begins id:

```
id:3:initdefault:
```

Change 3 to 5, for instance, to have the computer start up in runlevel 5. Typically, runlevels between 2 and 5 don't vary except in their handling of X startup methods; most runlevels are text-mode runlevels, whereas runlevel 5 starts X and displays a GUI login prompt. You can, however, create custom runlevels if you like, in order to easily switch between different run states. For instance, you might set aside a runlevel as a means of shutting down certain servers for maintenance. Of course, in order to make those changes, you must alter the SysV startup script links.

You can create SysV startup script links just as you can create any other link. For instance, suppose you've found that the apache startup script has no link in the runlevel 3 directory on a Debian system. You might type the following command to create this link:

```
# ln -s /etc/init.d/apache /etc/rc3.d/S91apache
```

Thereafter, when you boot the system into runlevel 3, Apache should start. Likewise, if you want to ensure that Apache does *not* start in runlevel 3, you might type the following command:

```
# ln -s /etc/init.d/apache /etc/rc3.d/K20apache
```

Of course, you should be sure that a given runlevel directory doesn't have both a start and a stop script. This condition is potentially confusing at best. (SuSE's configuration tools often create this condition, though.) As a general rule, you should create matching scripts for all of the runlevels between 2 and 5, so that if you change your runlevel, you won't find your servers starting or stopping when you didn't intend them to do so. In practice, if you don't change your runlevels frequently, having the appropriate links only in your default runlevel directory should work well.

SETTING SERVER STARTUP ORDER

The preceding discussion ignored an issue that's very important but that can be perplexing: What do you use as a sequence number? As a general rule, there is no single correct number; for a single service, it varies from one distribution to another. For instance, Debian uses a sequence number of 20 to start the X Font Server (xfs), whereas SuSE uses a sequence number of 15 for this server. Ultimately, the startup sequence depends on the needs of the individual servers. For instance, many servers work best when started after the network interface is brought up (often by a script called network or networking).

The server shutdown order is similarly constrained by the needs of individual servers. If you shut down a service before the servers that depend on it, those dependent servers might not shut down as smoothly or as cleanly as you like.

If you want to create a new startup or shutdown script, try looking for other scripts of the same type to ascertain a good number. For instance, suppose your Mandrake system isn't starting Postfix in runlevel 5. You might type the following command to learn what numbers are used for the Postfix startup script in other runlevels:

```
$ find /etc/rc.d/rc?.d -name "*postfix*"
/etc/rc.d/rc0.d/K30postfix
/etc/rc.d/rc1.d/K30postfix
/etc/rc.d/rc2.d/S80postfix
/etc/rc.d/rc3.d/S80postfix
/etc/rc.d/rc6.d/K30postfix
```

This result reveals that the startup number of 80 is appropriate for Postfix on this system. You can then create an appropriate link using that number and starting with the letter S. If you wanted to shut down Postfix in runlevel 5, you'd use a K30 prefix to the link's filename.

Mandrake and Red Hat both include suggested startup sequence numbers in their default SysV startup scripts, as comments near the start of the scripts. For instance, Mandrake's `postfix` script includes the following line:

```
# chkconfig: 2345 80 30
```

This line tells the system that the server should be active in runlevels 2 through 5, that the startup sequence number is 80, and that the shutdown sequence number is 30. This information conforms to that returned by the previously presented `find` command, except that for some reason the startup script links for runlevels 4 and 5 had been deleted.

Many of SuSE's SysV scripts contain similar information, but it's stored in a different format—specifically, in lines between comments that read `BEGIN INIT INFO` and `END INIT INFO`. Information provided in these comments includes prerequisite SysV startup scripts and default start and stop runlevels.

You may find scripts with the same sequence numbers. These scripts are run in alphabetical order, but the order in which they're run shouldn't matter. Some configuration tools don't enable you to create SysV startup script links with identical sequence numbers.

Using Distribution-Specific Tools

SysV startup scripts are very flexible, but they can be awkward to configure. Creating multiple symbolic links and determining the appropriate sequence numbers make the task of changing your servers' startup configurations difficult. For this reason, many distributions ship with tools to help simplify this task. These tools include `chkconfig`, `ntsysv`, `ksysv`, Red Hat's Service Configuration Tool, and YaST.

USING *CHKCONFIG*

The `chkconfig` utility is a fairly straightforward command-line tool that ships with Mandrake, Red Hat, and SuSE. It supports changing both SysV startup script configurations and servers started from xinetd. It can be used to report on the SysV configuration, add or delete services, or modify the runlevels in which a service is active.

To view a configuration, pass the `--list` parameter to the program, optionally followed by a service name. For instance, to learn about the Postfix server configuration, you might type:

```
$ /sbin/chkconfig --list postfix
postfix          0:off   1:off   2:on    3:on    4:off   5:off   6:off
```

NOTE *Ordinary users can run* chkconfig *to examine server configurations, but not to change those configurations. Most ordinary users must specify the* /sbin *directory when launching* chkconfig. *To change startup scripts, you must run the tool as* root.

This report reveals the runlevels in which SysV startup script links are set to start or stop the server. Servers that are launched by xinetd produce much shorter output lines; these servers are reported as being either on or off, with no runlevel information. In reality, they run only when xinetd is running, and hence only in the runlevels in which xinetd is active. If a link is missing, chkconfig reports its status as off.

To add or delete SysV startup script links for a script that exists in the main script directory, pass the `--add` or `--del` parameters, followed by the name of the service you want to modify. This command requires that a SysV startup script exist in the main directory, and it uses the chkconfig comment in that script to determine the appropriate sequence numbers and in which runlevels the service should run. For instance, to add Postfix to the system, type the following command:

```
# chkconfig --add postfix
```

To modify the runlevels in which a service is active in Red Hat or Mandrake, pass chkconfig the `--levels` parameter, followed by the runlevel numbers, the SysV startup script name, and the code on, off, or reset. The `--levels` parameter and runlevel numbers are, of course, unnecessary when dealing with servers started via xinetd. For instance, to deactivate Postfix in runlevels 4 and 5, type the following command:

```
# chkconfig --levels 45 postfix off
```

SuSE's version of chkconfig doesn't support the `--levels` option; instead it uses `--set`, which has a slightly different syntax. To use `--set`, you pass it the runlevels in which you want the service to run. If you want to disable the server in specific runlevels, you must pass chkconfig the runlevels in which you *do* want the service to run, omitting the runlevels you want to disable. For instance, if Postfix is currently active in runlevels 3, 4, and 5 and you want to disable it in runlevels 4 and 5, you might type:

```
# chkconfig --set postfix 3
```

USING *NTSYSV*

The chkconfig utility fits nicely in the tradition of text-based Linux tools that require options passed to them on the command line. If you prefer something that's a bit more interactive, you might want to consider ntsysv, which is depicted in Figure 22.1, running within an xterm. This tool ships with Mandrake and Red Hat and uses a text-based interface to acquire information on which services should be started. If you type **ntsysv** and nothing else, the program enables you to select which servers should be started in the current runlevel. Use the arrow keys to position the cursor in a box to the left of the service name, and press the spacebar to toggle the service on or off. Services that are on have asterisks (*) in their boxes; those that are off don't have asterisks in their boxes. When you're done, press the Tab key to highlight the OK button and press the Enter key.

By default, ntsysv enables you to modify only the current runlevel. To edit another runlevel or runlevels, you can pass the runlevel numbers using the --level option, as in **ntsysv --level 4** to edit runlevel 4, or **ntsysv --level 345** to edit runlevels 3, 4, and 5.

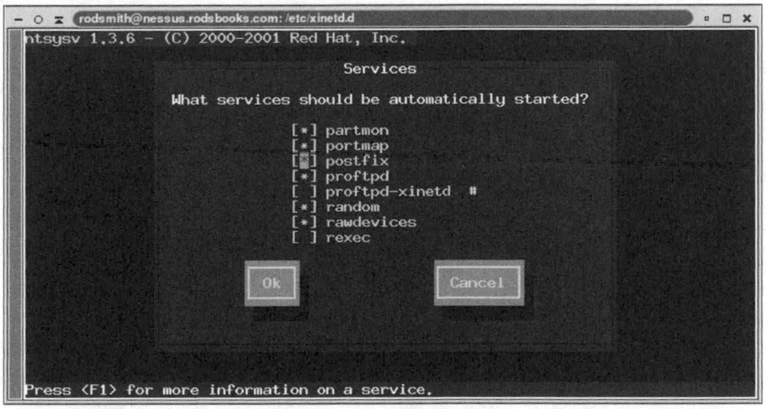

FIGURE 22.1

The text-based ntsysv program enables you to inter-actively edit which services are active.

USING RED HAT'S SERVICE CONFIGURATION TOOL

Red Hat's Service Configuration tool (redhat-config-services), as shown in Figure 22.2, is essentially a fully GUI version of ntsysv. Select a service, and the tool displays information about it, including whether or not it's active. Click the Start or Stop buttons to change the current running status, or click Restart to restart an already running server. To activate or deactivate the server, check or uncheck the box next to the server's name. This change affects only the current runlevel. You can change which runlevel is affected by selecting a new one from the Edit Runlevel menu. (The tool only supports editing runlevels 3 through 5.) After you've made changes, be sure to select File ➢ Save Changes. The program doesn't ask for confirmation; it saves the changes immediately.

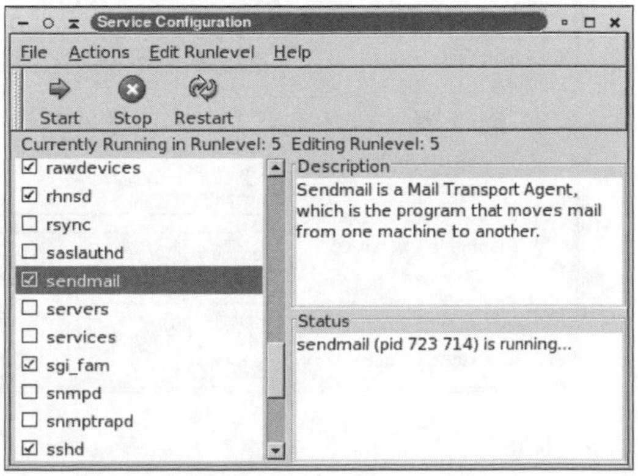

FIGURE 22.2

Red Hat's Service Configuration tool is essentially a GUI version of ntsysv.

USING YaST OR YaST2

SuSE's text-based and GUI configuration tools, YaST and YaST2 (which I refer to collectively as *YaST* for simplicity) provide the means to edit SuSE's SysV startup sequences. From the main YaST menu, go to the System area and then select the Runlevel Editor option. The default is the Runlevel Editor tool, from which you can set the default runlevel. If you click the Runlevel Properties button, YaST opens a display of services started in various runlevels, as shown in Figure 22.3.

To change a configuration, scroll to the name of the service you want to modify and select it. The check boxes below the main service display will change to reflect the current configuration. Check or uncheck boxes as you see fit. YaST keeps its own record of the proper sequence numbers for starting and stopping services, so you don't need to attend to this detail when using YaST. When you're done making changes, click Finish to activate them.

USING *KSYSV*

Unfortunately, `ntsysv`, Red Hat's Service Configuration tool, and YaST don't work in all distributions. One option for cross-distribution GUI server control is `ksysv`, which is part of the K Desktop Environment (KDE). This tool can be used on any Linux distribution that uses a typical SysV startup script system, although it's missing from Red Hat's default installation. The first time you launch the program, it may ask you which distribution you're using so that it knows where to look for the scripts and links. Once you give it this information, it displays a window similar to the one shown in Figure 22.4. You can adjust which runlevels are displayed by clicking the boxes in the lower-right corner of the window (Figure 22.4 omits runlevels 0 and 6).

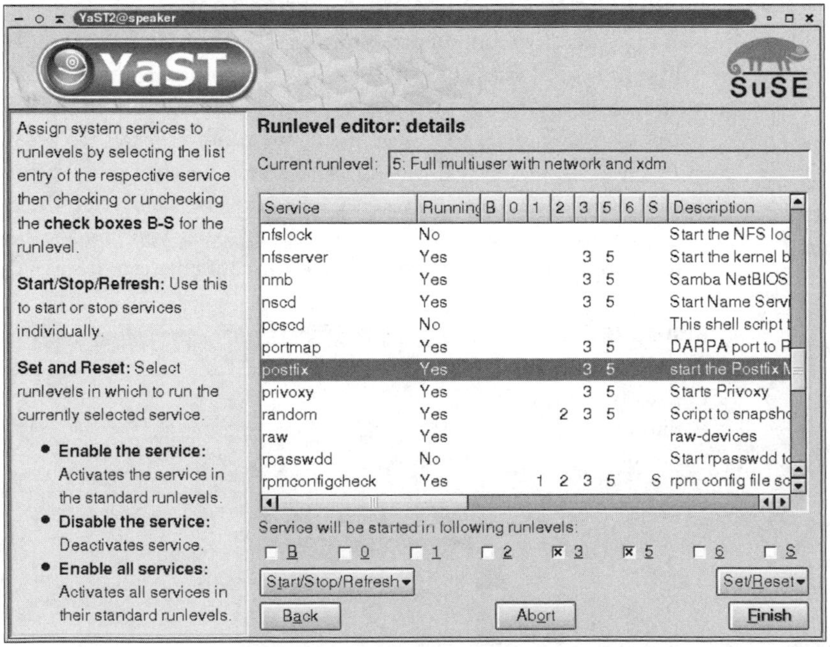

FIGURE 22.3

YaST2 enables you to change startup script runlevels.

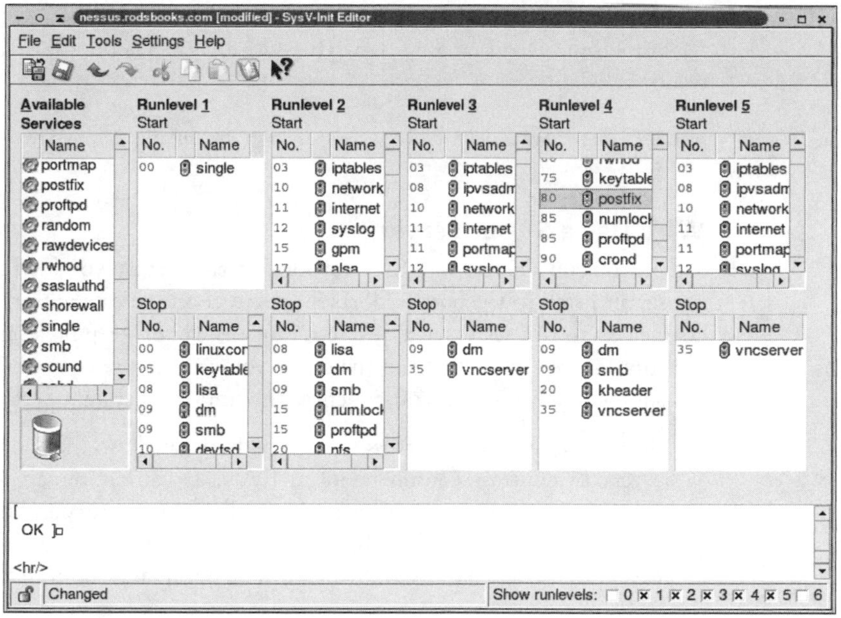

FIGURE 22.4

The ksysv runlevel configuration tool enables you to drag and drop services between runlevels.

The ksysv window displays a close analog to the structure of the SysV startup script directories. The Available Services area displays all of the available SysV startup scripts, and each Runlevel area displays scripts for both starting and stopping services in a given runlevel, along with the sequence numbers for these scripts. You can drag and drop services between these areas and to the trash can icon beneath the Available Services area. When you drag a service to a runlevel, ksysv tries to generate a sequence number in-between the two services above and below the position to which you drag the service. If these services have the same number or if the numbers differ only by one, ksysv can't generate a unique number and refuses to create an entry. You must then edit at least one of the surrounding services. You can do this, as well as change other features of a service, by clicking it. The program pops up a dialog box from which you can change the service number, start or stop the service, and so on.

When you're done making changes, select File ➢ Save Configuration. The program displays a warning that making incorrect changes to SysV startup scripts can cause boot problems. Click Save if you're sure your changes are valid, or click Cancel otherwise.

Unfortunately, ksysv can't take advantage of the chkconfig information stored in Mandrake and Red Hat SysV startup scripts. This fact means that chkconfig and ntsysv do a better job of automatically assigning series numbers in these distributions. Nonetheless, ksysv can be a useful tool if you understand how to handle these features.

Running Small Servers Optimally with Super Servers

Many servers typically run from SysV startup scripts, but this isn't the only way to launch servers. One common alternative is to use a *super server*, which is a server that launches other servers on request. This approach has certain advantages over launching servers from SysV startup scripts (or from other types of startup script), but it's not without its problems, either. Two super servers are common in Linux: inetd and xinetd. Ordinarily, Debian, Slackware, and SuSE all use inetd, whereas Mandrake and Red Hat use xinetd; but you can change the super server a distribution uses if you want to do so.

NOTE   Super servers are themselves servers, and they are generally launched from SysV startup scripts.

Why Use a Super Server?

When you run a server via a SysV or local startup script, you load that server into memory and have the server listen to the port or ports it uses to communicate with the outside world. Super servers enable you to run servers in a different way. Instead of keeping a server permanently loaded, you load the super server and have it run the server you want to use only when an incoming call requests it. This approach has several consequences that influence system performance and security:

Memory Use   Super servers tend to be fairly small, so they consume little memory. Many servers, by contrast, consume a lot of RAM. If you can replace a dozen RAM-hungry servers with one super server, overall demand for RAM will drop, and hence system performance will improve. This analysis, though, assumes that the servers are used only sporadically. If servers are constantly in use, the RAM savings will be minimal or nonexistent.

Request Response Time   Launching a server takes a certain amount of time, and so servers run from a super server tend to respond more slowly than do servers that are run directly. This effect tends to be very small for small servers, but it can be noticeable for larger servers. For instance, Apache 1.x can be run from a super server, but doing so can add a lag of roughly half a second (depending on disk speed, system load, and other factors) to Apache's responses. Small servers that run and then maintain a connection, such as most login servers, show only a tiny fraction of a second's lag at launch, and then they perform as well as if they'd been run directly.

Maintaining Information Across Calls   Some servers must maintain information across calls, or they must run continuously in order to maintain information. For instance, a Network Time Protocol (NTP) server (as described in Chapter 27, "Miscellaneous Servers") must run continuously in order to monitor the drift in your system's clock and so that it can periodically synchronize itself with other NTP servers. Domain Name System (DNS) servers maintain caches of prior name lookups. Running such a server from a super server loses this cache, which increases name lookup times.

Server User IDs   All Linux processes run with the authority of a specific user. Most servers must be started as root in order to connect to the privileged ports (those numbered below 1024). Some such servers spawn subprocesses that run with lower privileges, but the initial connection as root poses at least a theoretical vulnerability. When you use a super server, you can launch a server using any user ID (UID) you like, providing the server can function under that UID. This approach means that server bugs are less likely to result in system compromise. On the other hand, security bugs in the super server itself become a potential threat.

Runlevel Considerations   Super servers don't enable you to configure servers to run only in particular runlevels, except by the very crude standard that all the super server–mediated servers run in precisely the runlevels in which the super server itself runs. If you want a server to run only in a particular set of runlevels, you must run it via a SysV startup script.

Security Screening   As described in Chapter 20, "Controlling Network Access," you can use features of super servers to block incoming accesses that don't meet certain criteria. You can use TCP Wrappers in conjunction with either `inetd` or `xinetd` to accomplish this goal, or you can use `xinetd`'s own controls to much the same effect.

On the whole, super servers are good for small and seldom-used servers, as well as those that lack security features you want to implement via TCP Wrappers or `xinetd`'s security tools. Super servers are less ideal for large servers that should respond quickly to incoming requests and for those that work best when they can maintain their state across calls. Many servers work best when run in a particular way; consult your server's documentation for details. Some servers can be run in either way, but some of them must be told how they're being run via a configuration file entry or a parameter passed on the command line.

RPM Package Manager (RPM) and Debian packages for servers frequently include either SysV startup scripts or `xinetd` configurations. (Because `inetd` is configured through a single file, distributions that use `inetd` don't usually include `inetd` configuration files in their packages, although Debian packages sometimes include scripts that can enable `inetd` configurations.) For this reason, explicitly configuring a server to start up when you next boot is seldom necessary, although you may need to start the server once or restart the super server to get the server to respond immediately after you install it.

Using *inetd*

The traditional Linux super server is `inetd`. Debian 3.0, Slackware 9.0, and SuSE 8.1 all use `inetd` by default. Earlier versions of Mandrake and Red Hat also used `inetd`, but recent versions of these distributions have switched to `xinetd`. The `inetd` super server is configured via the `/etc/inetd.conf` file. This file contains comment lines that begin with hash marks (#) and server definition lines that take the following form:

```
service-name socket-type protocol flags user server args
```

Each field is separated from its neighbors by spaces or tabs. The meanings of these fields are listed here:

service-name   This field is the name of the protocol, as defined in `/etc/services`. For instance, `ftp` stands for an FTP server and `telnet` is a Telnet server.

socket-type   The *socket type* is normally either `stream` or `dgram`, although a few other options, such as `raw`, `rdm`, and `seqpacket`, are also possible. The appropriate value varies from one server to another, so consult the server's documentation to learn which you should use.

protocol   Most servers use the `tcp` protocol, but a few servers use `udp`, and an even smaller number use other protocols. Servers that use the Remote Procedure Call (RPC) system to mediate connections specify a protocol of `rpc/tcp` or `rpc/udp`. In any event, the protocol must be listed in `/etc/protocols`. You should consult your server's documentation to learn which it uses.

flags You can pass a wait or nowait flag, which tells inetd whether the server is single-threaded or multithreaded, respectively. This option is only relevant for datagram (dgram socket type) servers; others use a nowait entry by convention. You can append a dot and a number to this entry to limit the number of instances of a server that inetd will allow to run at once. You can use this feature to limit the number of simultaneous connections your system will accept, thereby heading off potential CPU, memory, or network bandwidth use problems. If you omit the maximum connections number, it defaults to 40.

user This entry specifies the user under whose name the server is run. This value is frequently either root or nobody, but any user listed in /etc/passwd is valid. You can append a group name after a dot, as in ftp.servers to run the server as the ftp user in the servers group.

WARNING *Never run a server with higher privilege than is required. Doing so can pose a security risk in the event of a bug, or sometimes even when a server is operating normally. The privileges a server requires vary from one server to another, so consult its documentation for details.*

server This field points to the server itself, such as /usr/sbin/vsftpd to launch vsftpd. The inetd server also supports a few protocols by itself. For these, the *server* field should read internal. If you use TCP Wrappers to launch a server, this field should read /usr/sbin/tcpd (of course, the path should be adjusted if tcpd resides somewhere else on your system).

args Many servers rely upon arguments passed to them on the command line. The final field is where you specify these arguments, separated by spaces, if necessary. If you launch a server via TCP Wrappers, the first argument is the name of the server you want to launch.

As an example, consider the following entry, which is from a SuSE system:

```
imap stream tcp nowait root /usr/sbin/tcpd imapd
```

This entry tells inetd to listen on the imap TCP port (143) and to launch imapd via TCP Wrappers whenever a connection appears. This server is run with root privileges because it's an Internet Message Access Protocol (IMAP) server, which requires root privileges to process logins from any user who wants to retrieve e-mail via IMAP.

Most distributions that use inetd ship with many predefined entries for common servers; however, most of these entries are commented out by placing hash marks before each deactivated server. This practice ensures that a server won't be launched accidentally just because you've installed it; you must take active steps to activate the server by uncommenting the relevant line before it will work. Some protocols are represented by multiple entries, one for each server that can handle the protocol. If you want your system to use the protocol in question, you must decide which server to use and uncomment the correct inetd.conf entry. If you uncomment the wrong entry, the server won't respond. Some servers—particularly those that don't ship with a distribution—don't have default entries in inetd.conf. To use such a server, you must add the entry. The simplest way to do this is usually to copy a sample entry from the server's documentation. If the documentation doesn't provide such an entry, it may not have been designed to run from a super server, but you can try creating an entry by modifying another. You may have to guess at the *socket-type*, *protocol*, and *flags* fields, though.

Changing the `inetd.conf` settings will not change the way your currently running `inetd` process responds to incoming requests. Restarting the computer will accomplish this change, but much simpler methods are to restart `inetd` or to pass the server a HUP signal. You can restart `inetd` by stopping it and starting it again via its own SysV startup script, or usually by passing the script the `restart` option. For instance, you might type **/etc/init.d/inetd restart** on a SuSE system. You can do this manually by using `kill` and then launching `inetd` manually, as well, but using the SysV startup scripts is better if your system uses them. This approach has a major drawback, though: It's likely to kill any open connections mediated by `inetd`. To avoid this problem, pass the HUP signal, as in **killall -HUP inetd**. Some distributions support a `reload` option to their `inetd` SysV startup scripts to accomplish this goal, as well. For instance, **/etc/init.d/inetd reload** will do the job on Debian and SuSE systems.

If you implement changes to your `inetd` configuration and can't connect to the new server, check the system log files. You may find entries from `inetd` concerning an inability to find the program file, a socket already being open, or various other error conditions. Knowing what's causing a problem may suggest corrections, such as double-checking the filename in /etc/inetd.conf to correct a typo.

Using *xinetd*

The `xinetd` (pronounced "zi-net-dee") super server can be thought of as a souped-up version of `inetd`. This server incorporates two major improvements that make it appealing:

♦ You can break the super server's configuration into multiple files, one for each server. This fact means that server packages from a distribution's maintainer can include `xinetd` configurations as ordinary files in their packages, which is a boon for distribution maintainers.

♦ The `xinetd` super server incorporates security features similar to those provided by TCP Wrappers. This fact is particularly important on systems with multiple network interfaces, because `xinetd` can listen for connections to a server on only one interface, improving security over the `inetd`/TCP Wrappers approach. Chapter 20 describes `xinetd`'s security features in more detail.

The `xinetd` super server includes some less dramatic improvements over `inetd`, some of which are detailed shortly. The main `xinetd` configuration file is /etc/xinetd.conf. Both Mandrake and Red Hat use a minimal xinetd.conf file, though. This file sets only a few defaults and calls the files in /etc/xinetd.d to handle individual servers. A configuration that's equivalent to the one presented for an IMAP server in the previous section, "Using `inetd`," is as follows:

```
service imap
{
    socket_type    = stream
    protocol       = tcp
    wait           = no
    user           = root
    server         = /usr/sbin/imapd
    server_args    =
    disable        = no
}
```

This entry contains all of the information present in the inetd configuration for the same server, except that it's split across multiple lines and each line is labeled. In practice, xinetd isn't very fussy about the order of these options, so you may see them in different orders. You may also see empty options, such as server_args in this example, omitted.

You can use assorted options to xinetd that aren't available in inetd. One of these options is disable, which takes a yes or no parameter. If this option is set to yes, xinetd ignores the server. You can use this feature to temporarily or permanently disable a server without uninstalling it. Many servers ship with a disable = yes entry so that you must explicitly enable the server before it will work. A few other options that may be of interest include:

group   Instead of specifying the group under whose name a server is launched after a dot in the user specification, xinetd uses a separate group line to do this job.

instances   You can limit the number of servers that xinetd will allow to be simultaneously active for a given service type. Specify a number or UNLIMITED (which is the default) if you don't want to use this feature. This feature can be useful to prevent problems caused by a server becoming too popular.

per_source   This option works just like instances, except that it specifies a limit per source IP address. It can be useful in preventing problems from certain types of denial-of-service (DoS) attacks or to ensure that a system's server resources aren't monopolized by a handful of legitimate but heavy users.

nice   You can specify a priority for a server's process by using the nice option, which works much like the nice command for launching programs, as described in Chapter 14, "Programs and Processes."

max_load   To protect your system's performance from degrading too far because of CPU load imposed by servers, you can have xinetd refuse connections when the CPU load rises too high. For instance, max_load = 3.5 tells xinetd to refuse connections if the one-minute load average equals or exceeds 3.5.

log_on_success AND log_on_failure   Like inetd, xinetd logs information about connections. You can fine-tune what information the super server logs on successful and unsuccessful connection attempts with these options. For successful connections, you can specify PID (the server's process ID), HOST (the client's address), USERID (the remote username, if the client is running an auth/ident server), EXIT (an entry when the connection was terminated), and DURATION (the length of the connection when it's terminated). For unsuccessful connections, only HOST, USERID, and ATTEMPT (a mere notice that an unsuccessful connection attempt was made) are available. In either case, you can specify a list of options separated by spaces, or you can change the default by using plus (+) or minus (-) prefixes to the assignment operator to add or subtract the options from the default. For instance, log_on_success = HOST PID tells the system to log the client hostname and the server's PID. The line log_on_success += USERID tells xinetd to log the remote username in addition to whatever the default is.

log_type   This option tells xinetd how to log information. You can specify SYSLOG *log-facility*, where *log-facility* is a code for the syslog facility to be used, such as daemon, auth, authpriv, user, mail, lpr, news, uucp, or ftp. You can also specify the logging level after the *log-facility*, such as emerg, alert, crit, err, warning, notice, info, or debug. If you prefer to log information to a file independently of the syslog facility, you can do so by specifying log_type = FILE *filename*, where *filename* is the log filename. You can append two numbers to a FILE log type, specifying the number of events that must occur to trigger a logging event and the number of events beyond which xinetd stops logging (to prevent the log file from filling with identical log messages).

redirect   You can tell xinetd to pass TCP connection attempts on to another computer. For instance, redirect = 172.19.201.78 143 redirects the connection attempt to port 143 on 172.19.201.78. Firewall rules can also be used to achieve this effect, and they're generally more efficient. You might want to use this feature in conjunction with other xinetd features, though, such as temporal restrictions, as described in Chapter 20.

Security Options   You can configure xinetd with an assortment of access control tools based on IP address, time, and so on. Chapter 20 describes these options in more detail.

Just as with inetd, you must tell xinetd to restart or reread its configuration file after making changes to that file. This is also necessary if you add a new configuration file to /etc/xinetd.d, such as after you install a new server. You can use the same methods to restart xinetd or have it reread its configuration file that you can use with inetd. As with inetd, the method that's least likely to cause disruption is to pass the server a HUP signal, as in **killall -HUP xinetd**.

On Mandrake and Red Hat, some of the tools described earlier for modifying SysV startup script configurations also work with xinetd configurations. Most importantly, chkconfig, ntsysv, and Red Hat's Service Configuration tool can handle xinetd-mediated servers. All xinetd-mediated servers run in the same runlevels in which xinetd runs, though, so it's not possible to modify the runlevels for individual xinetd-mediated servers.

When All Else Fails: Local Startup Scripts

Local startup scripts, which are described in more detail in Chapter 9, are not used by default for any servers in any Linux distribution. (One partial exception is Slackware, which could be thought of as using local startup scripts instead of SysV startup scripts; but the Slackware approach doesn't really fit cleanly in either category.) As a review, Table 22.2 presents information on local startup script names and when these scripts run during the boot process.

TABLE 22.2: LOCAL STARTUP SCRIPT INFORMATION BY DISTRIBUTION

DISTRIBUTION	LOCAL STARTUP SCRIPT	RUN TIME OF LOCAL STARTUP SCRIPT
Debian 3.0	Files in /etc/rc.boot	After basic /etc/rcS.d scripts but before runlevel-specific scripts
Mandrake 9.1	/etc/rc.d/rc.local	After SysV startup scripts
Red Hat 9.0	/etc/rc.d/rc.local	After SysV startup scripts
Slackware 9.0	/etc/rc.d/rc.local	At end of /etc/rc.d/rc.M startup script
SuSE 8.1	/etc/init.d/boot.local	After basic /etc/init.d/boot.d scripts but before runlevel-specific scripts

Local startup scripts have most of the same advantages and disadvantages as SysV startup scripts. Specifically, local startup scripts result in the server running (and consuming memory) at all times, so servers respond quickly to client accesses. Local startup scripts don't normally provide any scripted method of shutting down or restarting servers, though, as SysV startup scripts do; and local startup scripts provide no simple means of starting a server only in specific runlevels. Of course, you could write scripts that support these features, but the effort involved would be comparable to the effort involved in writing your own unique SysV startup scripts.

The effectiveness of local startup scripts for specific tasks varies from one distribution to another, depending on when the local startup script runs. This script may be a good way to launch high-level servers for those distributions that run the local startup script after most or all of the normal SysV startup scripts. If one of those tools that's launched via a SysV startup script depends on features provided by a server launched via a local startup script, though, a local script run time before the relevant SysV script is preferable.

Deciding Which Method to Use

For the most part, you'll do well to use whichever startup method is implemented or assumed in the server package you install. If a package ships with a working SysV startup script, use it; if it ships with a `xinetd` definition file in `/etc/xinetd.d`, use it; and if it ships with no such file but the documentation refers to uncommenting an `/etc/inetd.conf` entry, do so or create an equivalent entry in a file in `/etc/xinetd.d`. Using the default or expected configuration involves the least effort on your part and involves following the advice of the server author or distribution maintainer. These people probably know more about the server than you do, so unless you have good cause to do things differently, following their lead makes sense.

Some servers, though, run equally well stand-alone or from a super server, and you may have a reason to run a server in a nonstandard way. Sometimes you may be forced to do things differently, particularly when installing a server from a source tarball or from a package intended for a distribution other than the one you're using. Some specific cases in which you may want to do things differently include:

Saving Memory on Little-Used Servers   If a server is seldom used, you may want to try running it from a super server even if it's normally run stand-alone. Doing so involves disabling the server using the normal SysV runlevel tools and enabling a super server configuration.

Applying Extra Security   If you want to apply security features offered by TCP Wrappers or `xinetd`, running the server via a super server makes sense. Some servers, though, support TCP Wrappers directly, or they include similar features of their own. You can also use packet-filter firewall rules to protect any server. Of course, extra security can be good, but the security you gain by using a super server may be marginal if you're already using other measures.

Using Runlevel-Specific Options   If you want to run the server only in some runlevels, the simplest approach is to use SysV startup scripts. You must disable the super server configuration and write a SysV startup script.

Installing from a Nonnative Package   If you install a server from a package intended for a distribution other than the one you're using, it may include SysV startup scripts in the wrong location, or worse, the startup script may not work on your distribution. In this case, the simplest solution is generally to use a local startup script. Sometimes a super server configuration is the next-best solution. If you want to retain the SysV startup script benefits, you must write one yourself, modify one intended for another server, or modify the one that came with the server so that it works with your distribution.

Installing from Source Code   The problems of installing a nonnative package are largely the same as those of installing a package from source code. One exception is that source tarballs seldom come with sample SysV startup scripts, so you may not have a base script to even try.

Remember that some servers have very specific needs. For instance, Apache 2.0 and later can't run from a super server, and Samba runs poorly from a super server. Other servers, such as many FTP and Telnet servers, are designed to run from a super server and may not work correctly if run from a SysV or local startup script. Consult your server's documentation for details. You may also want to experiment to learn how the server performs when it is run in different ways.

Summary

Aside from starting servers manually, most Linux distributions support three methods of launching servers: via SysV startup scripts, via a super server, and via local startup scripts. Each method has its advantages and disadvantages. Server packages frequently ship with SysV startup script files or `xinetd` configuration files, so activating a server once you've installed it takes little or no effort. When you do have to change a configuration, tools such as `chkconfig` and `ksysv` can help, particularly with servers run from SysV startup scripts. More extensive changes may require creating unusual super server configurations or local startup script entries for your server.

## Chapter 23

Getting More from a Web Server

IN ONLY ABOUT TEN years, the World Wide Web (WWW or Web for short) has exploded from nothing to a vital part of our daily lives. Most computer users are familiar with the Web and with web browsers—the client side of the Web's client/server structure. Web servers, also known as *Hypertext Transfer Protocol (HTTP) servers*, are the programs with which web browsers most commonly communicate. (Most web browsers can also use a few other protocols, but HTTP dominates web page delivery.) Naturally, Linux supports web servers, including the single most popular web server program, Apache. Other options are available and may be preferable in some cases, though.

A default Apache installation takes remarkably little effort to function as a basic web server. A few tweaks to the configuration can enable or disable common features, though. More complex uses of a web server are delivering dynamic content and delivering secure content. These practices require careful preparation of the server or the content. You should also know at least a little about creating web pages.

Web Server Choices for Performance and Security

In March of 2003, a survey conducted by Netcraft (`http://news.netcraft.com`) of active websites showed that Apache ran on 62.51 percent of the web server computers surveyed. Apache's nearest competitor, Microsoft's Internet Information Services (IIS), ran on 27.44 percent of the server computers. (IIS is not available for Linux.) Thus, it should come as no surprise that discussions of web servers in Linux, including most of this chapter, focus on Apache. Nonetheless, there *are* alternatives to Apache, and many of them have advantages over Apache. Some servers are smaller and, therefore, consume less RAM; some are optimized to serve web pages more quickly than Apache can; and some offer features that Apache doesn't offer.

Perhaps one of the strongest reasons to use an alternative to Apache is to diversify the Internet's installed base of web servers. When an important infrastructure component, such as web server software, comes to be dominated by just one product, the result is known as a *monoculture*. Monocultures are risky because a security problem can quickly lead to a huge number of servers being compromised. For instance, a worm written to take advantage of a hypothetical Apache vulnerability could quickly spread to most web servers, crippling the Web as a whole. If fewer server computers ran Apache, this same worm would spread less quickly and infect fewer computers.

If you want to run a Linux web server, you have surprisingly many choices. A very incomplete list includes:

Apache Naturally, Apache heads the list of Linux web servers. Most of this chapter focuses on Apache. Check its web page at `http://httpd.apache.org` for more information, or read a book on the server, such as Charles Aulds' *Linux Apache Server Administration, 2nd Edition* (Sybex, 2002). As I write, Apache 2.0.44 is the current version, but the 1.3.*x* series remains popular. The differences between the two are small by the standards of this chapter's coverage, but many Apache administrators have carefully tweaked their configurations and don't want to disrupt their setups with an upgrade that modifies the way Apache handles features that are key for them but may not be critical for others.

Roxen This web server is one of Apache's closest competitors in terms of features. It includes a web-based configuration tool, which may make it more appealing than Apache to some new administrators. Although Roxen is a commercial product, a free version with some limitations is available. Consult its web page, `http://www.roxen.com`, for more information.

thttpd The Tiny/Turbo/Throttling HTTP Server (`thttpd`; `http://www.acme.com/software/thttpd/thttpd.html`) is designed as a lightweight server for sites that don't need all of Apache's features. By shedding support for features such as Secure Sockets Layer (SSL) security, `thttpd` can be much smaller than Apache—roughly 90KB, versus about 300KB for Apache. The `thttpd` developers claim that their server can outperform Apache by a wide margin, but this comparison was to the older 1.3.*x* Apache, and they also point out that few sites need that sort of speed.

Zeus This product is a fairly popular commercial web server for Linux. It's pricey, at $1700 for the standard version in early 2003, but its developers claim it's faster than Apache. Read more on its web page, `http://www.zeus.co.uk/products/zws/`.

Kernel-Based Web Servers At their core, web servers perform a very simple task: They transfer data from the disk to the network. This task is so simple that various projects exist to implement web server features in the Linux kernel. This approach can greatly improve web server efficiency by cutting out a user-level process (the traditional web server). One of these projects, kHTTPd, is a standard part of 2.4.*x* and later kernels. Kernel-based servers, though, can't handle complex tasks such as dynamic content. Furthermore, by moving extra code into the very sensitive kernel, they have the potential to reduce the reliability of the computer.

NOTE *Search on Sourceforge (`http://sourceforge.net`) or perform a web search to locate many additional web server options for Linux. The* `thttpd` *website includes some performance statistics on various web servers at* `http://www.acme.com/software/thttpd/benchmarks.html`, *although as I write, these results aren't very recent.*

Overall, Apache is the simplest choice for most users. All major Linux distributions ship with Apache, and it works with few or no modifications for many simple sites. The `thttpd` server can also be a good choice if you don't need Apache's features or if you're running on a particularly underpowered computer; however, you may need to hunt it down and install it. Although `thttpd` isn't harder to configure than Apache, distributions don't support it as well, and because few people use it, you may find it harder to get support on Usenet newsgroups or the like. Kernel-based servers also offer advantages when your server is straining under the load and you can't afford to upgrade the hardware. Roxen and Zeus are both worthy competitors to Apache at the high end, but their commercial or semicommercial nature makes them less practical for sites operating on a tight budget.

Apache Configuration File Basics

The primary Apache configuration file is called `httpd.conf` or (for Apache 2.0 on some Linux distributions) `httpd2.conf`. This file is usually located in `/etc/apache`, `/etc/httpd`, or `/etc/httpd/conf`. Whatever the filename or location, most of the lines in this file are either comments that begin with hash marks (#) or options lines that take the following form:

```
Directive Value
```

The `Directive` is the name of a parameter you want to adjust, and the `Value` is the value given to the parameter. The `Value` may be a number, a filename, or an arbitrary string. Some directives appear in named blocks begun and ended with codes enclosed in angle brackets, such as this:

```
<IfDefine APACHEPROXIED>
    Listen 8080
</IfDefine>
```

This particular example sets the `Listen` directive to `8080` if the `APACHEPROXIED` variable is defined. Note that the final line uses the name specified in the first line, but preceded by a slash (/). This arrangement signifies the start and end of a block of options, albeit one that contains just one option in this example.

Apache is designed in a modular way—many of its features can be compiled as separate modules that can be loaded at run time or left unloaded. Precisely which features are compiled as modules and which are compiled into the main Apache executable (typically called `apache`, `httpd`, or `httpd2`) varies from one distribution to another. To load a module, you use the `LoadModule` directive, and many Apache configuration files have a large number of these directives early in the file. With Apache 1.3.*x*, you may also need to use the `AddModule` directive to activate the module after you've loaded it, or to activate the features of a module that's compiled into the main binary. You may want to peruse these modules to see what features are enabled by default.

TIP *Commenting out the* `LoadModule` *directives for unused features can be a good security measure. For instance, if you have no need to deliver dynamic content, commenting out the* `cgi_module` *can reduce the chance that an accidental misconfiguration or intentional cracking will cause damage. Unfortunately, it's hard to know what each module does, so I recommend caution in commenting out module definitions.*

In addition to the main configuration file, a handful of additional files are important:

access.conf Not all Apache configurations use this file, which is essentially a supplemental file that tells Apache how to treat specific directories. Many systems roll this information into the main configuration file. For those that don't, an `AccessConfig` directive in the main file points to the `access.conf` file.

mime.types or **apache-mime.types** This file defines assorted *Multipurpose Internet Mail Extension (MIME)* types, which are codes that help identify the type of a file. HTTP transfers identify files by MIME type, but Linux filesystems don't store MIME type information natively. Therefore, Apache uses this file to map filename extensions (such as .html or .txt) to MIME types. The default file handles most common files you're likely to deliver on your web server, but you may need to add MIME types if you place exotic file types on the server.

magic This file exists in support of a second method of determining a file's MIME type. Rather than rely on filename extensions, this file includes "fingerprints" for many file types based on the files' contents. You shouldn't try to adjust this file unless you have precise instructions on doing so for a particular file type or if you possess a deep understanding of the file's internal format.

These files typically reside in the same directory that holds the main Apache configuration file. You're most likely to need to adjust access.conf, but only on systems that use it by default or if you choose to use this configuration option. If you deliver unusual file types, the best way to associate MIME types with those files is usually by adjusting the mime.types or apache-mime.types file; modifying the magic file is much trickier.

Common Apache Configuration Tweaks

A default Apache configuration file usually works at least minimally. You can test your installation after installing it by entering **http://localhost** as the URI in a web browser running on the same computer. You should see a generic page appear, as shown in Figure 23.1, which depicts the default page on a Mandrake 9.1 system. You should also test access to the server from other computers to be sure firewall rules (described in Chapter 20, "Controlling Network Access") or other problems aren't blocking access to the server. If you can't access the server, check that it's running. It should appear as apache, httpd, or httpd2 in a ps listing. Apache 1.3 can also be run from a super server, although this configuration is not common.

Once the server is running, you may want to adjust some of its defaults. Some common features you might want to change include the server's user and group, the location of web pages the server delivers, and virtual domains. Two still more advanced options—delivering secure web pages and serving dynamic content—are covered in upcoming sections of this chapter.

Setting the Apache User and Group

Like most servers that start via SysV or local startup scripts, Apache starts running as root. Apache supports two directives that adjust the username and group name under which the server runs after it's started. These directives are User and Group. For instance, you might include the following lines to have Apache run as the user apache in the group called agroup:

```
User apache
Group agroup
```

Once you've set these options, a check of these features using ps should reveal that most instances of Apache are running as the specified user and group. The first instance, though, will continue to run as root. This instance doesn't directly respond to incoming requests, though.

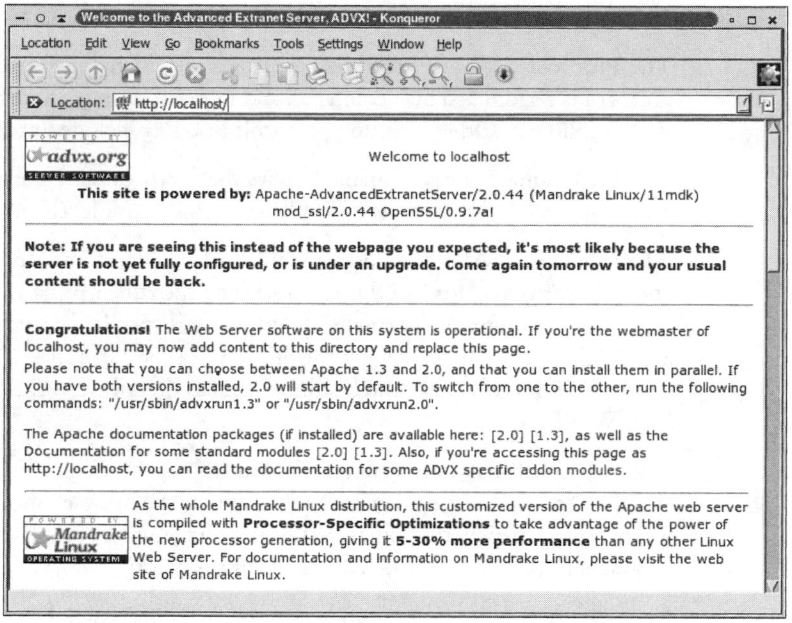

FIGURE 23.1

Once installed and run, a default Apache configuration displays a generic Apache web page or a page for your distribution.

Another option is to run Apache from a super server, as described in Chapter 22, "Running Servers." You can then specify Apache's user and group using the super server's mechanisms. This approach only works with Apache versions prior to 2.0, and was discouraged even with 1.3.*x* releases. Apache 2.0 and later must be run directly. If you want to run an earlier version of Apache from a super server, you must set the ServerType inetd directive to tell Apache that it's running from a super server. (The default value is standalone, meaning that the server is run directly.)

Changing Web Page Locations

As a general rule, Apache supports two types of static web pages: a site's web pages and individual users' web pages. A site's web pages are maintained by the system administrator or a designated webmaster; most ordinary users can't modify these pages. Multiuser systems sometimes provide users with web space. These pages are typically served from subdirectories of the users' home directories. Naturally, Apache provides tools for changing the locations of both site web pages and individuals' web pages.

URI COMPONENTS

To understand how Apache returns web pages, it's helpful to look at how an HTTP request is structured. The usual form of this request, as typed by a person in the Address or Location field of a web browser, is as a *Uniform Resource Identifier (URI)*, which looks like this:

```
http://www.threeroomco.com/products/biggie.html#orig
```

NOTE *The URI acronym is the official replacement for another acronym, Uniform Resource Locator (URL). Although URL is still in common use, it's officially an "informal" term.*

This URI consists of four components:

The Protocol   The first few characters of a URI specify the protocol—http in this case. The protocol is terminated by a colon (:), and in many cases (including URIs for HTTP transfers) two slashes follow it. Other common protocols in URIs include https (secure HTTP), ftp, and email.

The Hostname   The hostname follows the protocol name in HTTP URIs, as well as some other types of URIs, such as FTP URIs. In this example, the hostname is www.threeroomco.com.

The Filename   After the hostname in HTTP URIs comes the filename that's to be retrieved—/products/biggie.html in this example. The filename can be a single file or a complete path to a file, as in this example. Normally, the filename is specified relative to the server's document root, as described next, in "Changing the Site's Web Page." If a tilde (~) leads the filename, though, it's relative to a specified user's web storage area, as described in the upcoming section, "Enabling User Web Pages."

Additional Information   Some URIs include additional information. The preceding example specifies #orig after the filename, meaning that the browser should locate a tag called orig within the page and display the text at that point. Dynamic content uses this part of the URI to enable browsers to pass data to the web server for processing.

Many of these components can be omitted or abbreviated. For instance, most web browsers assume an HTTP transfer if you start the URI with the hostname. If you omit the filename, the web server assumes a default filename. In Apache, you can set this default with the DirectoryIndex directive. If you provide more than one value for this directive, Apache searches for them all. Most installations create a default that searches for one or more of index.htm, index.html, or index.shtml. If you're moving an existing set of web pages to Apache and that set includes a different default index filename, you may want to change the default.

CHANGING THE SITE'S WEB PAGE

One of the earliest directives in the Apache configuration file is probably a DocumentRoot directive, which tells Apache where to look for the web pages it delivers. You'll find the default web pages, such as the one displayed in Figure 23.1, in this location. In order to use Apache to deliver your own site's pages, you can do one of two things:

◆ Change the DocumentRoot directive to point to another directory in which you've stored your website's pages.

◆ Replace the files in the default DocumentRoot directory with ones you create.

The first option is slightly preferable because it reduces the odds that your web pages will be accidentally overwritten when you upgrade your web server installation. When you create a new directory to house your website, you should be sure that it's readable to the user under whose name Apache runs. This username is often specified with the User directive in the main Apache configuration file. The group may also be important; that's set via the Group directive. Because public websites seldom contain sensitive data, it's not uncommon to make the directories and the files within them readable to the world.

Typically, a user known as the *webmaster* is responsible for maintaining the website. The webmaster may also be the system administrator, but this isn't always the case. The webmaster normally has full write access to the site's web page directory, and the webmaster may in fact be the owner of this directory tree and all the files within it. The default document root directory isn't normally the webmaster's home directory, though; configuring the system in this way would enable anybody to download files such as the webmaster's `.bashrc` file.

ENABLING USER WEB PAGES

In addition to a site's main web pages, Apache can deliver web pages belonging to individual users. In order to activate this feature, you must set the `UserDir` directive, which takes the name of a directory within a user's home directory as an argument. For instance, you might use the following definition:

```
UserDir public_html
```

Once this directive is set, users can create subdirectories called `public_html` and store their personal web pages in that directory. For instance, suppose a remote user enters **http://www.threeroomco.com/~charlotte/apage.html** as a URL. If the server is configured with `UserDir` set to `public_html` and if the user `charlotte` has a home directory of `/home/charlotte`, then Apache will attempt to return `/home/charlotte/public_html/apage.html` to the client.

TIP   Delivery of user web pages relies on the `userdir_module` module. If your site shouldn't deliver user web pages, you may want to remove the `LoadModule` directive that loads this module. If you remove this directive, an attempt to use the `UserDir` directive will cause Apache to fail at startup, unless it's surrounded by an `<IfModule mod_userdir.c>` directive to test for the module's presence.

WARNING   Be sure when you set up the `UserDir` directive and the `root` user's home directory (typically `/home`) that outsiders can't retrieve files from `root`'s home directory. Such a configuration is a potential security threat.

Serving Virtual Domains

A single Apache web server can deliver pages for multiple domains. This configuration is extremely important for web hosting ISPs, who run web servers that respond differently to requests for each client. For instance, one ISP might deliver web pages for www.threeroomco.com, www.pangaea.edu, and many more. In order to do this without devoting an entire computer and IP address to each domain, the ISP must configure the web server to respond differently depending on the hostname part of the URL. This practice is known as configuring *virtual domains*. Of course, if you're an ISP hosting virtual domains, this chapter is inadequate for your job; you should read several books on Apache or hire a system administrator with substantial experience running Apache or some other web server. Nonetheless, virtual domains can be useful even on some smaller sites. For instance, a small company might change its name and want its web server to respond differently to two hostnames— say, displaying a message about the name change when called by the old name and displaying the full website under the new name. An individual or small business might also partner with another individual or small business to set up websites on a broadband connection, minimizing the costs associated with running their websites in this way. Two methods of delivering virtual domains are common: `VirtualDocumentRoot` and `VirtualHost`.

USING *VirtualDocumentRoot*

The idea behind the `VirtualDocumentRoot` directory is to tell Apache which directory to use as the document root directory based on the network interface or hostname used by the client. `VirtualDocumentRoot` works much like the standard `DocumentRoot` directive, except that you include variables, as specified in Table 23.1, in the directive's value.

TABLE 23.1: VARIABLES USED IN CONJUNCTION WITH `VirtualDocumentRoot`

VARIABLE	MEANING
%%	A single % in the directory name.
%p	The server's port number (normally 80, but secure sites run on port 443).
%*N.M*	Parts of the name. *N* is a number that refers to the dot-separated name component. For instance, if the name is www.threeroomco.com, %1 means www, %2 means threeroomco, and so on. Negative numbers count from the back; %-1 means com, %-2 is threeroomco, and so on. An *N* of 0 refers to the entire hostname. The optional *M* refers to the number of characters within the name. For instance, %2.4 would be thre. Negative *M* values count from the end of the component, so %2.-4 would be omco.

The `VirtualDocumentRoot` directive is most useful when you want to host a large number of domains or when the domains change frequently. You can set up a domain merely by creating a new subdirectory. For instance, suppose you want to create a directory structure of the form /home/httpd/*tld*/*domain*, as in /home/httpd/com/threeroomco as the document root directory for www.threeroomco.com. A configuration accommodating this layout would look like this:

```
VirtualDocumentRoot /home/httpd/%-1/%-2
```

Alternatively, suppose you want to alphabetize your domains, so that www.threeroomco.com's document root directory would be in /home/httpd/t/threeroomco. This arrangement could be achieved using the following entry:

```
VirtualDocumentRoot /home/httpd/%-2.1/%-2
```

WARNING *Some configurations could create duplicate entries. For instance, the preceding entry will try to place both* threeroomco.com's *and* threeroomco.org's *document roots in the same directory. This may not be a problem if you host just a few domains. To avoid the problem, use the* %0 *variable in the path, which uses the entire hostname.*

Whenever you use `VirtualDocumentRoot`, you should set the following line in your Apache configuration file:

```
UseCanonicalNames Off
```

Ordinarily (or when `UseCanonicalNames` is set to `On`), Apache tries to use the hostname of the machine on which it runs when performing relative accesses within a website—that is, when a web page omits the protocol and hostname portions of a URI in a link and provides only the document filename. This practice is likely to lead to "file not found" errors or incorrect pages returned, because Apache will look up the wrong site's documents. Setting `UseCanonicalNames` to `Off`, though, tells Apache to instead use the hostname provided by the client with the original access, which results in a correct lookup.

USING *VirtualHost*

Another approach to defining virtual domains is to create `VirtualHost` directive blocks. These blocks must be preceded in the file with a line that defines the interfaces on which you want to define virtual hosts:

```
NameVirtualHost *
```

This example tells the system to create virtual hosts on all interfaces. If the system has multiple interfaces and you only want to create virtual hosts on one interface, you can specify the IP address rather than an asterisk as the value of this directive. At some point after the `NameVirtualHost` directive in the Apache configuration file are `VirtualHost` directive blocks for each hostname:

```
<VirtualHost *>
    ServerName www.threeroomco.com
    DocumentRoot /home/httpd/business
</VirtualHost>

<VirtualHost *>
    ServerName www.luna.edu
    DocumentRoot /home/httpd/loonie/html
    ScriptAlias /cgi-bin/ "/home/httpd/loonie/cgi-bin/"
</VirtualHost>
```

As with a `VirtualDocumentRoot` configuration, you should be sure to set `UseCanonicalNames` to `Off` in the main Apache configuration file. Failure to do so is likely to result in spurious "document not found" errors and possibly failures to retrieve documents when web pages use relative document references in URLs.

One of the big advantages of `VirtualHost` definitions over `VirtualDocumentRoot` is that you can customize each server to respond differently. For instance, the preceding example uses document root filenames that are unique but that aren't systematically related to the hostnames. The definition for `www.luna.edu` also activates a dynamic content directory via the ScriptAlias directive, which is described in more detail in the upcoming section, "Serving Dynamic Content with CGI Scripts." These advantages can be very important for many servers that handle just a few domains. The drawback to this approach is that you must change the configuration file every time you add or delete a domain, which can be a hassle if you change the domains you handle on a regular basis.

Serving Dynamic Content with CGI Scripts

No doubt you've encountered web pages that are composed of dynamic content. The hallmark of such a site is that its content varies from one user to another. For instance, the "shopping cart" page on a web merchant's site is dynamic content. Web search engines rely on dynamic content—after all, your search may be entirely unique. Given the popularity of both Apache and dynamic content, it shouldn't be surprising that Apache supports delivering dynamic content. Doing so requires telling

Apache how to deliver dynamic content, as well as creating that content. Unfortunately, dynamic content is one of the riskier web server configurations, so you must be aware of the dangers it poses.

NOTE *This section focuses on configuring Apache to deliver dynamic content. Creating that content is potentially very complex—more complex than telling Apache how to deliver it. The upcoming section, "Creating CGI Scripts," introduces the topic, but doesn't cover it in great detail.*

Types of Dynamic Content

Dynamic content comes in several different forms. A traditional static web server delivers the same file in response to every incoming data request. A dynamic site need not respond in this way, though. Instead, a client's request for a page causes the server to process data in some way. Two common types of dynamic content are:

CGI Scripts The *Common Gateway Interface (CGI)* is a means of enabling the web server to run an outside program to generate a web page, rather than directly deliver an unchanging web page. The program in question is frequently a script, so these programs are often called *CGI scripts*. In principle, the external program could be written in a compiled language such as C, Pascal, or FORTRAN, though. In practice, Perl is a very popular CGI scripting language.

SSIs Compared to CGI scripts, *Server Side Includes (SSIs)* are very primitive. This mechanism enables the web server to modify a template of a web page. You might use this feature to change the date on an otherwise static web page, for example. This chapter doesn't describe SSIs in more detail, but you should be aware of their existence.

Another dynamic content element is important: *web forms.* These are web pages that include text-entry fields, buttons, selection lists, and so on. Most dynamic content relies on web forms to enable users to enter information to be delivered to the web server for use in generating dynamic content. For instance, a web search engine includes, at a minimum, a text entry field and a button to initiate a search. Like other web pages, web forms are created using HTML. Effective use of GCI scripts requires some knowledge of web forms.

Telling Apache to Serve CGI Scripts

To configure Apache to serve CGI scripts, you must do two things: Load the CGI module and tell Apache which directories may contain CGI scripts. Some approaches also require additional configuration steps. Telling Apache to support CGI is done via lines like the following:

```
LoadModule cgi_module modules/mod_cgi.so
AddModule mod_cgi.c
```

The first line loads the CGI module, if it's compiled as a separate module. The module filename specification (`modules/mod_cgi.so` in this example) may need to be changed for your system. Use other `LoadModule` lines in your default configuration file as a guide. The second line may be required in Apache 1.3.*x* when the module is built into the main Apache binary, and sometimes when it's not. If your configuration file doesn't have other `AddModule` lines, chances are this second line is unnecessary. The default Apache installations of many distributions include the appropriate lines to enable Apache's CGI features, so you may not need to do anything.

TIP   *If you do not want to deliver CGI scripts, you may want to comment out the lines that enable Apache to deliver CGI scripts. Doing so will reduce the risk that an accidentally enabled CGI scripting directory could lead to abuse of your server's CGI capabilities.*

Once you've enabled Apache's basic CGI scripting capabilities, you must tell it where to look for CGI scripts. This configuration is the equivalent of the `DocumentRoot` or `UserDir` directives telling Apache where to look to deliver static content. Some ways in which you can do this are:

ScriptAlias   This directive is roughly equivalent to `DocumentRoot` for CGI scripts; it tells Apache to treat files in a specific directory as CGI scripts and to enable execution of CGI scripts within that directory. This directive takes two values: A name that's to appear in the URL's filename as a CGI script indicator and a local path. For instance, `ScriptAlias /cgi/ "/home/httpd/cgi-bin/"` tells Apache to look in `/home/httpd/cgi-bin` for CGI scripts when the requested filename begins with `/cgi`. For instance, if a user enters a URL such as **http://www.threeroomco.com/cgi/info.pl**, Apache on the server computer runs `/home/httpd/cgi-bin/info.pl`. This configuration also requires the presence of the `mod_alias.so` module (loaded as `alias_module`), so be sure it's present. Some distributions include a default `ScriptAlias` configuration, so check your existing configuration file for one.

Options +ExecCGI   Including the `Options +ExecCGI` directive in a configuration file enables CGI script execution globally or within the specified directory. This approach is best used within a `<Directory>` directive block to limit its scope to the specified directory. Using `Options +ExecCGI` globally is potentially quite risky.

AllowOverride Options and .htaccess   If you include the `AllowOverride Options` directive in your configuration file, Apache will examine the directories it serves for a file called `.htaccess`. (If this option is used within a `<Directory>` directive block, Apache looks for this file only in the specified directory.) If present, this file may contain options to override the configuration specified in the main Apache configuration file, including an `Options +ExecCGI` line. Using this approach may be helpful if you want to enable individuals to activate CGI scripting for the directories they control.

WARNING   *The* `AllowOverride Options` *directive is potentially risky. When this directive is in force, users may set up* `.htaccess` *options, including CGI script execution options, that result in security holes. For instance, a user might enable CGI scripting and then write a CGI script that results in a security breach. Of course, poor CGI scripts pose this risk no matter how they're run, but at least if you use* `ScriptAlias`*, you can firmly control the directories from which CGI scripts may be run.*

No matter how you configure Apache to run CGI scripts, you should remember that these scripts are programs. They must have their execute permission bits set. If you obtain a script from a website that hosts such scripts, you may need to type **chmod a+x** *scriptname*, where *scriptname* is the name of the script, before the script will execute.

WARNING   *Don't trust CGI scripts obtained from any random source. Try to evaluate the credentials and trustworthiness of any person or website that delivers CGI scripts, or study the script carefully to be sure it doesn't contain malicious code. The upcoming section, "CGI Scripting Perils," describes potential security problems with CGI scripts in more detail.*

Creating CGI Scripts

CGI scripts are computer programs. Chapter 4, "Mastering Shells and Shell Scripting," describes one type of programming language: shell scripts. You can use a shell script as a CGI script, although Perl is a more common CGI scripting language. I can't provide a complete guide to writing CGI scripts in this chapter, but I can provide a brief overview of the process. For more information, consult a book on Apache or your scripting language of choice. The Apache website also includes pages on CGI scripting, at `http://httpd.apache.org/docs/howto/cgi.html` and `http://httpd.apache.org/docs-2.0/howto/cgi.html`. Four key points about CGI scripts are:

♦ CGI scripts use standard input (`stdin`) and standard output (`stdout`) for interaction with the user.

♦ Prior to the bulk of the output, CGI scripts should generate a header that identifies the output's MIME type. For standard HTML, this line should read `Content-type: text/html\r\n\r\n`. (The \r\n codes stand for new lines—use two of them to separate the `Content-type` header from the bulk of the document.)

♦ Typically, you should generate output that's in HTML format. Of course, you *can* create other formats, but as the Web is mostly based on HTML, that's the preferred format. If you create a CGI script to generate graphics or specialized file types, you must change the `Content-type` header appropriately.

♦ If your CGI script accepts input, the input appears as field/value pairs, where the field is the name of the field in a web form and the value is the value entered by the user. The field and value are separated from each other by an equal sign (`=`), and field/value pairs are separated from each other by ampersands (`&`). For instance, your script might receive back input such as `fname=Elwyn&lname=White`, telling you that the user entered `Elwyn` in the `fname` field and `White` in the `lname` field.

CGI Scripting Perils

The prototypical web server requires very little in the way of user authentication. The server is accessible to the public at large and delivers content to anybody who wants it. This configuration is at least theoretically low in security risk because static web servers deliver unchanging data, provide very limited client-to-server data transfer facilities, and don't enable users to run arbitrary programs locally. Therefore, if a web server has no bugs and if it's properly configured (two very big *ifs*), a miscreant is unlikely to be able to abuse a web server.

Dynamic content adds an entirely new dimension to this equation, though. CGI scripts enable outsiders to run programs that aren't part of the web server. These programs are often written by individuals who don't have extensive knowledge of how to write secure software. As a result, CGI scripts sometimes contain severe security flaws, which might be exploited by crackers. These problems are exacerbated if you run Apache with a too-high privilege level. Most default installations set the server to run as a low-privilege user, such as **apache** or **nobody**. Doing so minimizes the risks associated with CGI scripts, but a poorly written script in conjunction with local security flaws could still enable intruders to do a great deal of harm even with these limited privileges. The same is true if the scripts need to be able to change critical data, such as customer information databases; with such access, a bug in a script or a limited intrusion via Apache could irreparably damage the databases.

Another approach to limiting the potential of scripts to do serious damage is to run them in a chroot jail, as described in Chapter 20. As with using limited-access accounts, though, this approach isn't perfect. Any data that a script must be able to manipulate will be accessible to the server even within the jail. As noted in Chapter 20, it's possible to break out of a jail, given root privileges.

Overall, CGI scripting is risky. This risk is offset by its flexibility. You may have no choice but to run a web server that can handle CGI scripting. If so, you may want to use physically separate servers for CGI scripts and for static content. Doing so will help you isolate any potential harm from a compromise of the CGI scripting system. This approach may also help you balance the load to your website as a whole. A web server that handles primarily static content doesn't need to be as powerful as one that handles CGI scripts. This is because delivering static content requires little in the way of CPU power, whereas CGI scripts must be run, and therefore consume at least some extra CPU time. Depending on your site's size and traffic level, you may be able to use an older computer to deliver static content and place CGI traffic on a more capable system that's devoted entirely to this task.

Serving Secure Content

Secure HTTP is denoted by an https:// header in the URI. This protocol is an HTTP variant that uses encryption to keep data transfers private. Apache supports secure HTTP transfers, but configuring it to do so is a three-step process:

1. You must install a special version of Apache or add-on package that enables encryption.

2. You must obtain or create a *certificate*, which is an encryption key.

3. You must configure Apache to listen on the secure HTTP port and respond to requests on that port using encryption.

Why Serve Secure Content?

Crackers who install packet sniffers on the server's network, the client's network, or an intervening router may be able to read the traffic sent between the web server and the web browser. Submitting sensitive information, such as credit card numbers, over such a link is therefore risky. Secure HTTP makes such sniffing pointless; the cracker sees only encrypted traffic, and therefore can't extract sensitive data from the exchange. In theory, a cracker could decrypt the traffic, but the CPU requirements of breaking the encryption schemes used are enormous—it would take years of CPU time to do the job, at least with today's CPUs and encryption algorithms.

In addition to securing the content of data transfers, secure HTTP provides an authentication benefit. The encryption protocols used enable one or both sides to authenticate the identity of the other side. In secure HTTP, this is most often used to enable the browser to verify the server's identity. Doing this provides some protection against a miscreant setting up a fake website, breaking into a DNS server, redirecting traffic intended for the legitimate site to the fake one, and stealing sensitive data. If this happens, the user's web browser displays a warning dialog box, such as the one shown in Figure 23.2, which is presented by Opera when an unknown certificate crosses its path. Assuming the user knows what this message means, the user is then alerted to the possibility of a hijacked website and won't blindly reveal sensitive information. Unfortunately, many users *don't* understand what dialog boxes such as the one shown in Figure 23.2 mean, and they approve the transactions without further checks. Many browsers, including Opera, make accepting the suspicious certificate the default action—a dubious practice from a security point of view.

NOTE   Web browsers alert their users to unknown certificates using dialog boxes that vary substantially in form and style. Most don't present much of the information shown in Figure 23.2 unless you click a button to reveal details.

FIGURE 23.2

Secure HTTP provides authentication and warnings when a server's identity can't be verified.

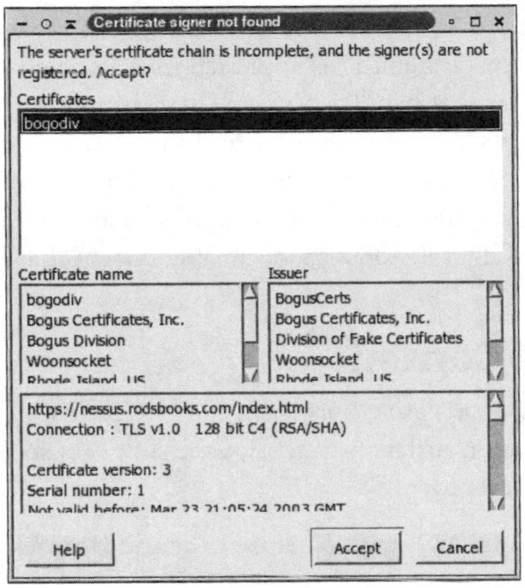

Secure websites are most commonly associated with financial transactions—web merchants and online banking are two very high-profile and common uses of these techniques. If you intend to set up such a site, do not rely on this chapter alone; there are many security issues you must consider. Hire somebody who's experienced with such configurations. This chapter's coverage of secure content is most useful for a webmaster who wants to use encryption on somewhat less sensitive data, probably on a private website. For instance, you might want to use secure HTTP to encrypt data delivered via a web server to employees, as a precaution against local sniffing; or possibly to encrypt somewhat sensitive data on a public website. You'll have to judge for yourself when the data become sensitive enough to require calling in an outside expert to help configure the system.

NOTE   Part of the reason for bringing in a security expert is to help secure all of the systems around the web server— the databases it uses, other server programs running on the web server computer or other computers near it on the network, and so on.

Web servers normally respond to connection attempts on port 80. In order to avoid confusion, secure web servers normally respond to another port: 443. (The `https://` header in a URI tells the web browser to connect to this port.) As described in the upcoming section, "Changing the Apache Configuration," you may need to tell Apache to listen to this port for secure connections. One server can listen to both the secure and normal HTTP ports, or you can run different server programs on the different ports. Using firewall rules, you can even redirect traffic so that one computer serves one port and another computer serves another port, with the same apparent outside IP address.

Installing Secure Apache

Secure HTTP relies on an encryption protocol known as the *Secure Sockets Layer (SSL)*. In order to implement SSL, your system needs an SSL library. In the past, SSLeay (`http://www2.psy.uq.edu.au/~ftp/Crypto/ssleay/`) was a common SSL library for Linux. Today, SSLeay has been largely superseded by OpenSSL (`http://www.openssl.org`), which is based in part on SSLeay. OpenSSL ships with many Linux distributions, so you can probably install it from your main installation medium. If you use SSLeay instead of OpenSSL, the following description will still be relevant.

In addition to SSL, you must install an SSL-enabled version of Apache or an SSL module for Apache. Two popular implementations are Apache-SSL (`http://www.apache-ssl.org`) and mod_ssl (`http://www.modssl.org`). The original mod_ssl works with Apache 1.3, but a variant for Apache 2.0 is documented at `http://httpd.apache.org/docs-2.0/mod/mod_ssl.html`. Distributions that ship with Apache 2.0 often include this module as a separate package. In Mandrake 9.1, for instance, it's `apache2-mod_ssl`.

Obtaining or Creating a Certificate

SSL uses two *keys* on each side of the connection: a public key and a private key. Each of these keys can be used to encrypt data such that its paired key can decrypt it. Each side gives its public key to the other side, which uses its partner's public key to encrypt data. Each side then uses its private key to decrypt data. Because only a public key's matching private key can decrypt the data, the sender can be certain that only the intended recipient can decrypt the data.

The use of keys does not, by itself, ensure that the data's sender is the person or computer claimed. Hypothetically, a miscreant could fake transmissions from the sender using the recipient's public key. SSL uses *certificates* as a way of verifying the other side's identity. Certificates are digital codes used to create keys. The sender's identity is verified by using certificates that are issued and "signed" by one of a handful of *certificate authorities (CAs)*. Every modern web browser has a list of CA signatures, and so can verify that a website's keys have been signed by an appropriate CA and that the website is, therefore, what it claims to be. This system isn't absolutely perfect, but it's reasonably reliable.

NOTE *Secure web servers normally need certificates, but web browsers don't normally use them. A prototypical secure web server processes financial transactions, and for these, customers are concerned about the identity of the merchant to prevent exploitation. Positively identifying customers is less critical in this application, because a web merchant normally obtains a credit card number, physical address, and other identifying information. To be sure, fraudulent credit card use is a problem; however, without additional (and potentially intrusive) infrastructure linking various databases, personal certificates probably would not eliminate such abuses.*

In order to deliver secure content, you need a certificate. For many purposes, the best way to do this is to buy one from a CA. A list of about two dozen CAs is available at `http://www.apache-ssl.org/#Digital_Certificates`. Before obtaining a certificate from a CA, you should research the companies' policies and determine how widely recognized their certificate signatures are. There's no point in buying a cut-rate certificate if your users' browsers generate alerts such as the one shown in Figure 23.2. You could create your own certificate that would create the same result.

Creating your own certificate makes sense if you don't care about authenticating the identity of the server or if this authentication is only required on a few systems. For instance, if you want to encrypt certain web server accesses on a small local network, or even between offices that are geographically separated, you don't need to go to a CA. You can tell your web browsers to accept your own locally generated certificate. Of course, telling your users to accept your personal certificate but not to accept suspicious certificates from other sites may be confusing.

Some Apache SSL extension packages automatically run a script that creates a new certificate when you install the package. If yours doesn't, check the package files for a script or instructions on doing the job. Unfortunately, precisely how you do this varies from one package to another, and given the number of distributions and number of packages, I can't describe all the possibilities. As an example, though, Mandrake 9.1's `apache2-mod_ssl` ships with a script that does the job, and you can launch it as follows:

```
# /usr/lib/ssl/apache2-mod_ssl/gentestcrt.sh
```

This script will ask a series of questions, such as your geographical location, company name, and e-mail address. This information may be presented to the user when the browser complains about the unknown certificate, as shown in Figure 23.2. For a small site with local users, your exact answers to these questions are largely unimportant.

Whether you obtain your certificate from a CA or generate it locally, you must make it available to Apache. Typically, this is done by copying the certificate to a special certificate directory somewhere in `/etc`, such as `/etc/ssl/apache`. If you use a script to generate a certificate, the script may do this automatically, or it may place the certificate in another directory, such as the main Apache configuration directory. The certificate consists of two files: a certificate file (which often has a `.crt` extension) and a key (which often has a `.key` extension).

WARNING *Be sure you protect the certificate and key from prying eyes. The default configuration when utilities create these files uses* **root** *ownership and* **0600** *permissions to accomplish this task. If you copy the files, be sure these features are preserved. A miscreant who copies these files can impersonate your (formerly) secure web server!*

Changing the Apache Configuration

Some SSL-enabled Apache packages ship with their own configuration files. Others use the regular Apache configuration file. Apache 2.0 systems tend to need only very minimal configuration file changes to support SSL. With these systems, you may only need to load the SSL module with a line like this:

```
LoadModule ssl_module /usr/lib/apache2-extramodules-2.0.44/mod_ssl.so
```

This example works on a Mandrake 9.1 system; it may need adjustments to the location of the SSL module on other systems. Once activated in this way, an Apache 2.0 system will respond to both ordinary HTTP and secure HTTP requests.

Apache 1.3 systems may require more configuration file changes. Some features you may need to adjust include:

Port This option, which has been replaced by `Listen` in Apache 2.0, binds the server to a particular port. The secure HTTP port is 443, and you may need to set this value with Apache 1.3 systems. Some secure Apache variants automatically bind to both the regular and the secure HTTP ports.

SSLEnable This directive takes no options. When it's present, it merely enables the server's SSL features. This option is required to use SSL in Apache 1.3, but it isn't recognized by Apache 2.0. Instead, Apache 2.0 supports the SSLEngine directive, which takes on or off values to enable or disable SSL.

SSLRequireSSL Ordinarily, Apache will deliver files to both ordinary HTTP and secure HTTP clients. Using this option tells Apache to deliver files only to clients that have made secure connections. This directive takes no value, and it is normally placed within a <Directory> directive block.

SSLCACertificatePath This directive points to the directory in which the SSL certificate resides, such as /etc/ssl/apache.

SSLCertificateFile This directive identifies the SSL certificate file, such as /etc/ssl/apache/server.crt.

Some of these directives may be used on Apache 2.0 systems, as well as on Apache 1.3 systems. The SSLRequireSSL directive is particularly noteworthy, because it can help keep your web server from inadvertently delivering sensitive data over an unencrypted link.

Designing Web Pages

Whether you deliver them statically or via scripts, unencrypted or via a secure server, websites are typically composed of documents (*web pages*) created in the *Hypertext Markup Language (HTML)*. This section serves as a brief introduction to the design of web pages, but it's far from a complete guide. For more information, consult a tutorial such as http://www.cwru.edu/help/introHTML/toc.html or http://www.mcli.dist.maricopa.edu/tut/. The official guide to HTML is available at http://www.w3.org/MarkUp; consult this page for many links to additional information. As a general rule, you have two choices for how to create web pages: Use an HTML editor or HTML export feature in a program designed for the task or create an HTML file "by hand" using an ordinary text editor.

Using an HTML Editor

Many programs can create HTML output. In practice, HTML editors cover a continuum. At one extreme are editors that attempt to work like what-you-see-is-what-you-get (WYSIWYG) word processors. These editors display features such as bold or italic text, fonts, inline graphics, and lists more or less as they'll appear in a web browser. At the other extreme are basically ordinary text editors with a few features to ease creation of HTML, such as menus from which you can insert HTML codes.

NOTE True WYSIWYG in HTML editors is impossible because you can't know how a reader's web browser will render the HTML you create. Features such as fonts, browser window width, and graphics capabilities vary substantially from one system to another. Therefore, you shouldn't take such features as displayed in an HTML editor's window very seriously.

Many word processors can export in HTML format. Abi Word, KWord, OpenOffice.org, Word-Perfect, and others all support creation of HTML documents. Typically, you can create a file just as you would any other and the program generates suitable HTML when you save it. Word processors, though, are not usually designed for creating or editing HTML. Some lack good mechanisms for inserting important HTML features such as links, for instance. Some word processing features may be lost in the conversion to HTML. For these reasons, I recommend using a word processor for HTML creation only in a pinch or if you want to convert an existing word processing document to HTML.

Other editors are designed to create HTML. Examples include ASHE (`http://www.cs.rpi.edu/pub/puninj/ASHE/`), August (`http://www.bostream.nu/johanb/august/`), Bluefish (`http://bluefish.openoffice.nl`), Quanta (`http://quanta.sourceforge.net/`), and WebSphere Studio Homepage Builder (`http://www.ibm.com/software/webservers/hpbuilder/`). Most of these programs are open source, but WebSphere is commercial. Many of the open source editors are far from WYSIWYG; for instance, Figure 23.3 shows Quanta displaying the default Mandrake Linux Apache web page shown in a web browser in Figure 23.1. Nonetheless, these editors typically include menu options and button bars designed to help you create HTML. Some also include preview modes so you can get some idea of how a web browser might render the page. With a little basic familiarity with HTML (as described in the next section, "Creating HTML by Hand"), you can do a lot with one of these basic editors.

Some web browsers ship with built-in HTML editors. Netscape and Mozilla, for instance, provide an HTML editor component called Composer. These editors tend to be more GUI-oriented than most Linux HTML editors; they hide HTML tags and instead display text as a web browser is likely to display it. Of course, even this display isn't truly WYSIWYG, because another browser, or even the same browser on a different system, might display the text in a very different way than Composer does.

FIGURE 23.3

Many HTML editors are basically just ordinary text editors with highlighting and special tools to help manipulate HTML tags.

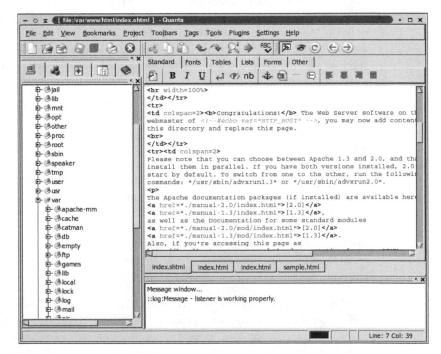

One problem with HTML editors, and especially with the ones that hide HTML tags, is that they often produce poor HTML. Such documents may display correctly on most web browsers, which tend to be remarkably tolerant of HTML errors; but they may cause problems on a few browsers. If you use such an editor, careful testing is particularly important. This topic is described in the upcoming section, "Testing Web Pages."

Creating HTML by Hand

HTML is basically nothing but plain American Standard Code for Information Interchange (ASCII) text in which certain characters have special meaning. These character sequences are known as HTML *tags*, and most are enclosed in angle brackets (<>). For instance, Listing 23.1 shows a short HTML file.

LISTING 23.1: A SAMPLE HTML FILE

```
<!DOCTYPE HTML PUBLIC "-//W3C//DTD HTML 4.01 Transitional//EN"
➥"http://www.w3.org/TR/html4/loose.dtd">
<HTML><HEAD>
<TITLE>Sample Web Page</TITLE>
</HEAD>
<BODY BGCOLOR="#FFFFFF" TEXT="#000000">
<P>This is a sample web page. It can include features such as
<A HREF="http://www.threeroomco.com/sample/">links</A>.</P>
</BODY></HTML>
```

Most tags come in pairs. The first begins a formatting feature and the second ends it. The second tag is named like the first, but the name is preceded by a slash (/), as in <P> to start a paragraph and </P> to end it. Tags are not case sensitive. The tags demonstrated in Listing 23.1 include:

<!DOCTYPE>   Most HTML files begin with a line such as the first line of Listing 23.1, which identifies the version of the HTML standard that the file follows. Most HTML editors give you several choices of document type. For simple pages, the document type isn't very important, so you should use whatever is the default. This tag has no matching closing tag.

<HTML>   The actual HTML is enclosed within an <HTML> tag. Normally, the closing </HTML> tag signifies the end of the file. (Some HTML editors create incorrect tag nesting order, though, so sometimes closing tags for features within the file come after the </HTML> tag.)

<HEAD>   An HTML header defines certain features of the file. The header isn't displayed in the browser's window, although parts of it may be accessible from the browser or displayed in the title bar.

<TITLE>   The <TITLE> tag appears within the header and gives a title to the page. Many browsers display the title in the browser's window. When users add pages to their bookmarks, the pages' titles are the default text for accessing the pages.

<BODY>   The bulk of the web page begins with the <BODY> tag, which closely follows the closing </HEAD> tag. Information within the body may be displayed in the reader's web browser window. Listing 23.1's <BODY> tag includes options within it to set the text and background colors. This example uses numeric color codes for white background and black text, but you can use name codes for common colors if you prefer.

<P> The <P> tag delineates a paragraph. Because web browsers ignore line breaks, these tags are necessary to mark where one paragraph begins and another ends.

<A HREF> This tag denotes an HTML link—a hypertext reference to another web page, an FTP site, an e-mail address, or the like, expressed as a URI. The text within quotes in the opening tag (`http://www.threeroomco.com/sample` in Listing 23.1) is hidden from the reader. The text between the opening and closing tags (`links` in Listing 23.1) typically appears in color, and it is often underlined, to signify that it's a link.

You can generate web pages, albeit not very flashy ones, with knowledge of just a few tags. In fact, you may not need many more tags than Listing 23.1 uses if you just want to display paragraphs of plain text. In addition, though, there are tags to create bulleted and numbered lists, to embed graphics within web pages, to create tables, and so on.

TIP   If you want to generate an effect but don't know how to achieve it, you can probably learn by examining the HTML for a page that uses the effect. Most web browsers include an option accessible as View ➤ Page Source or something similar so that you can examine a web page's underlying HTML.

Testing Web Pages

After generating a web page, you should test it. What looks good in your editor may not render well on a web browser. What's worse, different web browsers render HTML in different ways, so what works well with one browser may work poorly with another. I recommend performing two types of test:

HTML Validation Tests A variety of automated tools exist to check an HTML file for common errors. Examples include HTML::Lint (`http://sourceforge.net/projects/html-lint/`), the Weblint Gateway (`http://ejk.cso.uiuc.edu/cgi-bin/weblint`), and Bobby (`http://bobby .watchfire.com/bobby/html/en/`). Some of these tools, including the latter two, are web-based, and so require that your page be accessible from a web server. If you run your web page through such a test and discover that it has problems, you may want to correct them. Be aware, though, that some of these tools are very conservative and may report issues that won't cause problems with any common web browser. Some, such as Bobby, are intended to help you design pages that are not only good HTML, but that are also accessible to those with impaired vision or other problems.

Multibrowser Viewing Tests You should try viewing your web page in several different web browsers. The most important of these is arguably Microsoft's Internet Explorer, which is the single most popular web browser by a wide margin. Others you may want to try include Netscape, Mozilla, Galeon, Konqueror, Opera, and lynx. (Chapter 8, "Miscellaneous User Tools," describes web browsers in more detail.) Many browsers, including Netscape, Mozilla, and Galeon, use the same underlying rendering tool, and so should render pages in much the same way. If possible, you should test your page from at least two or three operating systems and using a variety of system settings, such as different color depths and screen sizes. Note also that the features available to a browser vary greatly across software versions. For instance, a page that displays well in Netscape 6.0 might not display well in Netscape 4.5.

TIP The `lynx` *browser is unusual because it's entirely text-based. As such, it's a good test of how your page will work if a user has shut off automatic graphics loading or for users with visual impairments, who browse the Web using text-to-speech software.*

As a general rule, simple web pages are more portable than are complex web pages. Some sites create very complex designs—complex enough that their web servers may deliver web pages customized for particular clients. This approach to web page design is risky because it's likely to cause problems for users with unusual browsers or browser settings. For more information on creating websites that are accessible to all users, consult the Bobby web page or the Any Browser Campaign site, `http://www.anybrowser.org/campaign/`.

Summary

The Web is the most visible part of the Internet, and it's built atop HTTP. The most common HTTP server is Apache, and Linux is a good platform for running this server. Other web servers for Linux do exist and can be good choices in some cases, but Apache's broad installed base makes it appealing for both new and experienced system administrators. A default Apache installation on Linux works well, but you may want to tweak the installation to modify the locations of web pages the server delivers, to handle multiple domains, or to perform other tasks. Serving CGI scripts and delivering secure content via SSL are two more demanding tasks to which Apache can be put. Both of these tasks require more extensive changes to the Apache configuration. Finally, a web server is useless without content to serve. You can create web pages by hand, or you can use any of several tools to help in this task.

Chapter 24

Serving Files

MANY NETWORK SERVERS DEAL with files in one form or another. Web servers deliver files to clients, which usually display them directly to their users. Mail servers send and receive files, which may be stored, forwarded, or delivered to users' mail readers. One of the most direct forms of file transfer, though, occurs in a class of servers known generically as *file servers*. This class of server can be thought of as consisting of two subclasses: *file-transfer servers* (which transfer files using special clients) and *file sharing servers* (in which the clients access files as if they were stored on local disks). This distinction is somewhat slippery, because the same protocol may be handled in different ways by different clients. The most common file-transfer protocol is known, quite descriptively, as the *File Transfer Protocol (FTP)*. For a long time, it was the master of the Internet file transfer seas, and it remains popular for this purpose. (Many links from web pages for downloading large files lead to FTP sites.) Among file-sharing servers, two important protocols are the *Network File System (NFS)* and the *Server Message Block/Common Internet File System (SMB/CIFS)*. NFS is a common file-sharing protocol between Unix and Unix-like systems, whereas SMB/CIFS is most popular on networks dominated by Windows systems. Linux includes servers (and clients) for handling both protocols—NFS through any of several NFS servers and SMB/CIFS through the Samba server.

NOTE *Some file exchange protocols and servers are very complex. Samba, in particular, provides dozens of options to help it overcome cross-platform differences and integrate well with Windows systems. If you're setting up a Linux system to function as a Samba server, you may want to consult a book on the subject, such as my* Linux Samba Server Administration *(Sybex, 2001) or Ts, Eckstein, and Collier-Brown's* Using Samba, 2nd Edition *(O'Reilly, 2003). (The first edition of the latter title comes with Samba in electronic form.) Erez Zadock's* Linux NFS and Automounter Administration *(Sybex, 2001) covers NFS in more detail than I can describe in this chapter. Some FTP servers are also very complex, but books about them are uncommon.*

FTP: Delivering Files to Any Client OS

FTP has long been a popular server. The protocol has some peculiarities, but every OS that has a serious TCP/IP stack has an FTP client. FTP is typically used in one or both of two ways:

◆ Users must authenticate themselves to the server by providing a username and password. They can then read, and often write, files to their home directory or to common areas on the computer.

◆ Users provide a username of anonymous and any password (conventionally their e-mail addresses). They can then read, but usually not write, data stored in public directories. This *anonymous FTP access* is a popular means of delivering public files such as software upgrades, multimedia files, and so on.

Both configurations share many features, but certain details differ. How you set up an FTP server to use either system depends on the server you choose. Several such servers exist for Linux. This section describes your choices and then covers two popular FTP servers, ProFTPd and vsftpd, in more detail.

WARNING   One of FTP's major problems when used for authenticated user access is that FTP sends all data, including passwords, in an unencrypted form. This fact means that miscreants on the server's network, the client's network, or intervening networks can use packet sniffers to steal users' passwords. This issue isn't as much of a problem for anonymous access, which is supposed to be public.

Choosing the Right FTP Server

FTP is an old protocol, and numerous implementations of it have sprung up over the years. These servers vary in many details; however, they all serve the same protocol, and they all look very much alike to their users. FTP server options for Linux include the following:

ProFTPd   This server, headquartered at http://proftpd.org, is one of the more popular of the very complex FTP servers. It ships with most major Linux distributions. Its configuration file is modeled after that of Apache, and the server supports many advanced features.

vsftpd   This server aims to excel at security, stability, and speed. In doing so, its developers have chosen to eschew some of the more advanced features of servers such as ProFTPd and WU-FTPD. If you don't need those features, this tradeoff may be more than acceptable. You can learn more from its website, http://vsftpd.beasts.org. It's available with a growing number of Linux distributions.

WU-FTPD   The Washington University FTP Daemon (WU-FTPD) is an old standard in the Linux world. Unfortunately, it's collected more than its fair share of security problems and isn't the speediest FTP server available. For these reasons, it ships with fewer Linux distributions today than in years past. Its main website is http://www.wu-ftpd.org.

BSD FTPD   The BSD versions of Unix use their own FTP server, which has been ported to Linux and made available in Debian (in the bsd-ftpd package) and SuSE (in the ftpd package). This server is generally considered quite secure.

PureFTPd   This server, headquartered at `http://www.pureftpd.org`, is another FTP server that emphasizes security. SuSE ships with a version of this server.

oftpd   This server is unusual because it's designed to function *only* as an anonymous FTP server; it doesn't support logins using ordinary user accounts. This feature can be appealing if you only want to run an anonymous server, but it makes this server unsuitable for many other purposes. It's available from `http://www.time-travellers.org/oftpd/`.

NOTE   This list of FTP servers is far from complete. The `oftpd` *web page describes the primary developer's search for a name for the server. He wanted a name of the form* `xftpd`, *where* `x` *was a single letter. Starting with* `aftpd`, *he found that* `oftpd` *was the first name that wasn't already in use!*

Because FTP can potentially provide users with substantial access to the system—the ability to read or write any file, within limits imposed by Linux file ownership and permissions—FTP servers are unusually sensitive from a security point of view. As a result, the web pages for many of the servers in the preceding list emphasize their developers' attention to security. Most FTP servers provide explicit support for locking themselves in `chroot` jails, as described in Chapter 20, "Controlling Network Access."

For a small FTP site, chances are any of the servers in the preceding list will work well, with the exception of `oftpd` if you want authenticated user logins rather than anonymous access. Given its poor security history, WU-FTP might be best avoided, as well. Because they both ship with multiple Linux distributions, the next two sections focus on ProFTPd and `vsftpd`. ProFTPd is best suited to installations requiring complex configurations. If your needs are simpler or if your site handles a lot of traffic, `vsftpd` might be a better choice. The remaining servers are also worth considering if they happen to be easily installed on your distribution or (in the case of `oftpd`) if you want to run an anonymous-only site.

ProFTPd Configuration

ProFTPd is available with many Linux distributions, including Debian, Mandrake, and Slackware. You can install it on other distributions by using another distribution's package or by installing from source code. In either of these cases, though, you'll need to deal with server startup issues, as described in Chapter 22, "Running Servers." Most distributions run ProFTPd from a SysV startup script. It can be run from a super server, though, and some configurations (such as Slackware's) run it this way by default.

ProFTPd is configured through the `proftpd.conf` file, which normally resides in `/etc`. This file's syntax closely resembles that of the Apache configuration file, described in Chapter 23, "Getting More from a Web Server." Lines may be comments that begin with hash marks (`#`) or directives, which take the following form:

```
Directive Value
```

ProFTPd also supports directive blocks, which are denoted by leading and trailing directive block names in angle brackets (`<>`). The leading directive block name often includes a value, and the trailing directive block indicator usually begins with a slash (/). For instance, the following lines appear in the default Mandrake ProFTPd configuration:

```
<Directory />
  AllowOverwrite  on
</Directory>
```

These lines tell the system to apply the AllowOverwrite on directive within the root (/) directory—in other words, to apply it everywhere, unless another directive overrides this one in a specific subdirectory. Directive blocks usually define *contexts*, which support different sets of directives. Table 24.1 summarizes some of the directives you might want to adjust. This table is far from a complete listing of ProFTPd options, though. Consult the documentation on the ProFTPd website for more details.

TABLE 24.1: IMPORTANT PROFTPd DIRECTIVES

DIRECTIVE	VALUE	MEANING
ServerName	String	Sets a descriptive name that ProFTPd delivers to clients when they connect.
ServerType	standalone or inetd	Tells ProFTPd if it's running from a SysV or local startup script (standalone) or from a super server (inetd).
User	Username	The username that ProFTPd uses to run.
Group	Group name	The group that ProFTPd uses to run.
AllowUser	Username list	Gives the specified user or users access to a directory.
DenyUser	Username list	Denies the specified user or users access to a directory.
UseFtpUsers	on or off	Specifies whether or not to deny access to the users listed in /etc/ftpusers. The default value is on, which is a useful security measure.
UserAlias	Two usernames	Tells ProFTPd to accept logins using the first specified username as if they were from the second specified username.
RequireValidShell	on or off	Specifies whether or not the user's account requires a valid shell specification.
AllowOverwrite	on or off	Enables users to overwrite existing files, assuming they have write privileges to the target directory.
<Directory>	Directory name	Begins a context that applies to the specified directory tree.
<Anonymous>	Directory name	Begins a context that grants anonymous access to the specified directory tree. ProFTPd locks itself in a chroot jail within this directory tree.
<VirtualHost>	Hostname or IP address	Begins a context that enables ProFTPd to respond differently to different network interfaces associated with the specified hostname or IP address.

The default ProFTPd configuration typically enables authenticated logins, so individuals who have accounts on the computer can use the system's FTP server. If you want to enable anonymous access, you may need to add an <Anonymous> directive block similar to this one:

```
<Anonymous /var/ftp>
    User ftp
    Group ftp
    RequireValidShell off
    UserAlias anonymous ftp
</Anonymous>
```

This configuration tells the system to accept logins as anonymous using the ftp account and to run as the user and group ftp. The RequireValidShell off line is necessary if the /etc/passwd entry for the ftp user specifies a shell that's not listed in /etc/shells. If the /etc/ftpusers file includes the ftp user, you may need to remove that entry from the ftpusers file.

Once you've changed the ProFTPd configuration, you must restart the server. This topic is covered in more detail in Chapter 22. Typically, you use a SysV startup script's restart option, as in:

```
# /etc/rc.d/init.d/proftpd restart
```

NOTE   *If you run ProFTPd from a super server, you don't need to explicitly restart it when you change its configuration. You must restart the super server or tell it to reload its configuration file if you want to enable or disable ProFTPd or change options you pass to it on the command line.*

vsftpd Configuration

The ProFTPd server is extremely powerful, but sometimes a simpler server is in order. Such a server provides at least the potential for greater security and speed. An FTP server that's rapidly gaining prominence for these features is vsftpd, which is available for Debian, Mandrake, Red Hat, and SuSE.

Ordinarily, vsftpd is run from a super server, as described in Chapter 22; however, it can be run from a SysV or local startup script if you prefer. The vsftpd configuration file is /etc/vsftpd.conf. This file contains comment lines, which begin with hash marks (#), and directive lines that take the form:

```
option=value
```

There must be no stray spaces surrounding the equal sign in vsftpd directives. Table 24.2 summarizes some of the most important vsftpd directives. This table doesn't cover all of the available directives; check the vsftpd.conf man page for information on additional directives.

TABLE 24.2: IMPORTANT vsftpd DIRECTIVES

OPTION	VALUE	MEANING
listen	YES or NO	If YES, vsftpd binds itself to the FTP port. Set this value to YES if vsftpd is run from a SysV or local startup script; leave it at its default value (NO) if it's run from a super server.
ftpd_banner	String	Sets a welcome message that appears in the user's FTP client program when connecting.

Continued on next page

TABLE 24.2: IMPORTANT vsftpd DIRECTIVES *(continued)*

OPTION	VALUE	MEANING
nopriv_user	Username	The username vsftpd uses for unprivileged operations.
ftp_username	Username	The username vsftpd uses for anonymous access. The default is ftp.
local_enable	YES or NO	Whether or not to accept authenticated local user logins.
anonymous_enable	YES or NO	Whether or not to accept anonymous logins.
anon_root	Directory name	The directory to be used as the root directory for anonymous access. This directory must normally not be writeable to the anonymous user, unless anon_upload_enable is YES. The default is the anonymous user's home directory, as specified in /etc/passwd.
chroot_local_user	YES or NO	Tells vsftpd whether or not to use chroot when accepting local user logins.
userlist_enable	YES or NO	If YES, vsftpd checks the file specified by userlist_file and denies logins to these users before asking for a password.
write_enable	YES or NO	Grants or denies the ability to write files—that is, for users to upload files as well as download them.
anon_upload_enable	YES or NO	Grants or denies anonymous users the ability to upload files. If YES, write_enable must also be YES.

The default vsftpd configuration file often supports both authenticated local user logins and anonymous logins. Typically, vsftpd performs a chroot for anonymous users, but it does not do so for authenticated local users. If you want to verify or change these features, check the configuration file for the following lines, and change them as necessary:

```
anonymous_enable=YES
local_enable=YES
```

You can also change additional options related to these, such as the location of the anonymous root directory (anon_root) and whether or not to chroot into authenticated users' home directories when they log in (chroot_local_user).

NFS: Sharing with Linux or Unix

NFS has long been the standard file-sharing protocol among Linux and other Unix-like OSs. NFS supports Unix-style ownership and permissions, which is an important consideration on many Linux installations. It's also well supported in the Unix world generally, so sharing files across Unix-like OSs usually poses no serious problems.

Linux's NFS servers have changed substantially over the years. Simple configurations tend to work much as they always have, but many more advanced specific options have been quite ephemeral. In order to function as an NFS server, a computer must have a configuration file defining the directories you want to export. (The word *export* is often used as a noun to refer to a served directory). To access a remote NFS server's files, you mount the exports using the same mount command you use to mount local filesystems.

NFS Kernel and Package Options

Every major Linux distribution ships with an NFS server called rpc.nfsd. In most distributions, this server is part of the nfs-utils package, but Debian places it in the nfs-kernel-server package. These standard servers rely on NFS server support that's built into the kernel, as described shortly. Older NFS servers did not rely on this support, and such servers are still available on some distributions. For instance, Debian's nfs-user-server runs entirely in user space without taking advantage of the kernel NFS server support.

Many distributions present options to activate the NFS server at system installation or when you install the NFS server package. For others, you may need to create or activate a SysV or local startup script, as described in Chapter 22. The startup script is called nfs-kernel-server (or nfs-user-server for the user-mode server) in Debian, nfs in Mandrake and Red Hat, and nfsserver in SuSE.

In order to use a kernel-based server, your kernel must include the appropriate options to support NFS features. Other kernel features are required to mount another computer's NFS exports. Both sets of options are accessible from the File Systems ➤ Network File Systems kernel configuration menu, as shown in Figure 24.1 for a 2.5.67 kernel. (Chapter 15, "Creating a Custom Kernel," describes Linux kernel configuration in more detail.) The NFS File System Support option enables support for NFS *client* functionality, and the NFS Server Support option activates NFS server functionality.

FIGURE 24.1

The Linux kernel provides NFS support options in its configuration tool.

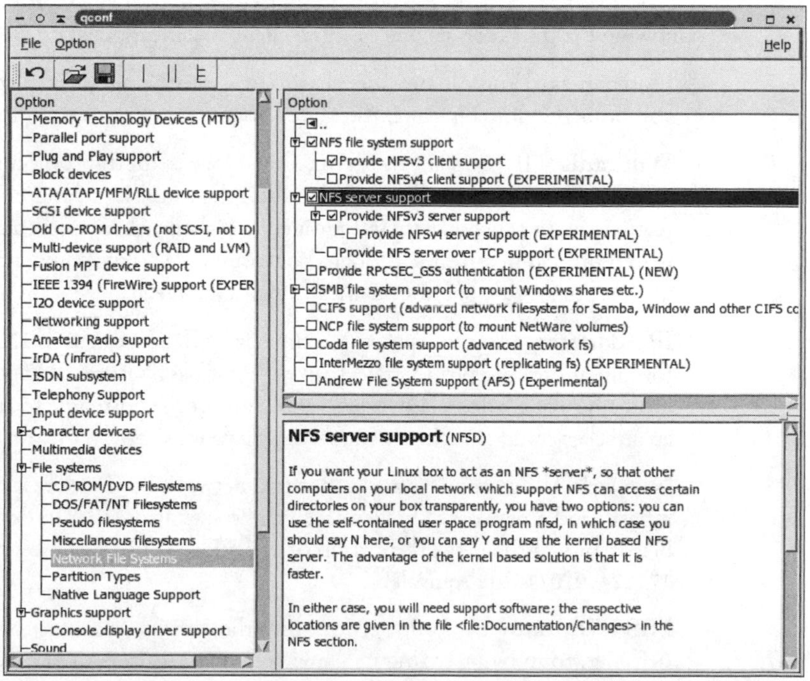

NOTE *The 2.4.x kernel series uses a GUI configuration tool that looks different than the 2.5.67 tool shown in Figure 24.1. Most of the options are the same, though, with the exception of the NFSv4 options, which aren't present in 2.4.x kernels.*

NFS has undergone several revisions over the years. These NFS version numbers are often appended to the *NFS* acronym, as in *NFSv2* for NFS version 2. This level is the default in the Linux kernel options; to use NFSv3 or NFSv4, you must activate extra features, which are visible in Figure 24.1's menu. As of the late 2.4.x and 2.5.x kernels, NFS support through NFSv3 is reasonably stable and complete. NFSv4 support is still considered experimental as of the 2.5.66 kernel (the latest as I write). I recommend avoiding the use of an experimental NFS driver; it may result in poor performance, lost files, or other problems.

All Linux distributions' default kernels support NFS, although it's sometimes compiled as separate modules—`nfs.o` for the NFS client and `nfsd.o` for the NFS server. The appropriate module should load automatically when you try to mount a remote export or start the NFS server. If it doesn't, consult the "Subtle and Flexible: Loading Drivers as Modules" section of Chapter 1, "Optimizing System Architecture Usage." Although the NFS support modules aren't hardware drivers, loading them is done using the same tools you use to load hardware driver modules. Some distributions ship with this support compiled into the main kernel file rather than as a module.

Setting Up Exports

Linux uses the `/etc/exports` file to describe the directories that an NFS server exports. Lines in this file may be comments, which begin with hash marks (#), or they may be export definitions. Each export definition takes the following form:

```
/directory client(options) [client(options)[...]]
```

The `/directory` is the directory that's to be made available, such as `/home` or `/opt/OpenOffice.org`. Following the directory are one or more client specifications. You can list clients in any of several ways:

Hostnames   You can provide a computer's hostname, such as `collins.luna.edu` or `collins`. If you omit the domain name, the server assumes you're referring to a computer in its own domain.

Wildcards   If you want to export a directory to all the computers in a domain, or to certain subsets of them, you might be able to use the asterisk (*) and question mark (?) wildcards. These features work much like their equivalents in shells when used to specify filenames. They don't match dots in hostnames, though. For instance, `*.luna.edu` matches `collins.luna.edu` and `gordon.luna.edu`, but not `bean.surveyor.luna.edu`.

IP Addresses   You can specify a computer by IP address, as in `172.24.202.7`. This method is harder for humans to interpret than hostnames, but it has a security advantage because it doesn't rely on a Domain Name System (DNS) server to convert the hostname to an IP address. If you use hostnames, an attacker could conceivably gain access to your NFS server by first taking over a DNS server.

Network Addresses   You can specify a network by IP address range by providing the IP address, a slash, and a netmask. The netmask can be specified either in dotted-decimal form or as the number of bits in the network portion of the address. For instance, `172.24.0.0/255.255.0.0` and `172.24.0.0/16` are equivalent.

NIS Netgroups   If your network uses the *Network Information System (NIS)*, you can specify an NIS netgroup by preceding its name with an at sign, as in `@tranquility`.

Following each client specification is a comma-separated list of options. Table 24.3 summarizes the most common of these options. You can find additional options in the exports man page.

TABLE 24.3: COMMON NFS EXPORT OPTIONS

OPTION	MEANING
secure or insecure	Specifies that the client must connect (secure) or need not connect (insecure) from a secure port (one numbered below 1024). The default value is secure.
rw or ro	Specifies read/write (rw) or read-only (ro) client access to the export. The default in recent Linux NFS servers is ro, but some versions have used rw. I recommend making your choice explicit to avoid the possibility of confusion.
sync or async	The async option can improve performance at the cost of a risk of data corruption in the event of a system crash. In kernel NFS servers up to and including version 1.0.0, async was the default; but more recent versions use sync as the default.
hide or nohide	Ordinarily or when you use the hide option, the NFS server "hides" filesystems mounted inside an exported directory. For instance, if you export /usr and if /usr/local is a separate partition, clients won't see /usr/local's contents. If you specify nohide, clients will see files and subdirectories in /usr/local. The nohide option can confuse some clients, and works only with single-host specifications (hostnames and IP addresses). Instead of using nohide, you can export each partition individually and mount each export on the NFS clients.
root_squash or no_root_squash	For security reasons, the NFS server normally "squashes" access from root on the client, substituting a low-privilege user ID for the root user ID. You can grant the remote root user full root access to the exported directory by using the no_root_squash option. This option is potentially very dangerous, though.
all_squash or no_all_squash	This option specifies whether or not to apply "squashing" to accesses from ordinary users. Squashing such accesses can be desirable as a means of providing a modest security increase on read-only exports.

NOTE   The options available in the NFS server have changed between NFS server versions in the past, and they may change in the future. Consult the exports man page for details if you have problems with any of these options.

As an example of an NFS /etc/exports file, consider Listing 24.1. This file defines three exports—for /home, /opt, and /exports. The /home export is fairly straightforward. The clients of this export (collins, gordon, swigert, roosa, and worden) are defined using hostnames without domain names. All of these clients have read/write access to the share. All except gordon must connect from a secure port, but gordon is granted an exception to this rule. Perhaps gordon is running a non-Unix OS that uses a high-numbered port for NFS access. The /opt export is made available to two clients, mattingly.luna.edu and evans.luna.edu. The first of these clients has full read/write access to the share, and root access from this client is not squashed. You might use this configuration if mattingly's administrator needs to be able to add software to the /opt export, but this configuration is risky—a security problem could allow a miscreant to change files in this potentially sensitive directory. Finally, the /exports directory is exported to all computers in the lm.luna.edu domain (but not its subdomains) and to all computers in the 172.24.0.0/16 network. In the case of the lm.luna.edu domain, all user accesses are squashed. In both cases, no client can write to the export.

LISTING 24.1: EXAMPLE /etc/exports FILE

```
/home collins(rw) gordon(rw,insecure) swigert(rw) roosa(rw) worden(rw)
/opt mattingly.luna.edu(rw,no_root_squash) evans.luna.edu(ro,nohide)
/exports *.lm.luna.edu(ro,all_squash) 172.24.0.0/16(ro)
```

You should keep in mind the fact that NFS relies on its clients to handle some security tasks. In particular, note that NFS doesn't require a password for access. If the client is authorized in /etc/exports, the client can access the directory or directories in question. A couple of decades ago, only professionally administered Unix workstations would have such access, so risks were low. Today, anybody who can fake a DNS entry or gain physical access to a network to hijack an IP address can break into a regular NFS server and read files under any assumed username. For this reason, you should be very conservative about authorizing remote access via the exports file. In some environments, read/write access to home directories may be required, but read/write access to most other directories is most likely an undue risk. Listing 24.1's read/write and no_root_squash access to /opt for mattingly is particularly risky; I presented it only to give an example of no_root_squash in action.

If you make changes to your /etc/exports file, you can tell the NFS server about those changes with the exportfs program. Specifically, type **exportfs -r** as root to update the server's list of available exports to match the exports file. You can also use this utility's -u option to make a specific export unavailable, or various other options to have other effects. Consult the exportfs man page for details.

Mounting NFS Exports

Linux's NFS client is, essentially, the Linux kernel itself. The kernel treats another computer's NFS export as a filesystem that can be mounted via the mount command or an entry in /etc/fstab. Chapter 5, "Doing Real Work in Text Mode," Chapter 10, "Using Multiple OSs," and Chapter 12, "Filesystems and Files," all describe these tools to varying extents and in different contexts. The rules for using NFS exports are similar to those for using regular filesystems on partitions, although some details differ. To mount an NFS export, you specify the nfs filesystem type. In some cases, Linux can determine from context that you mean nfs, so you can sometimes omit this option. Instead of specifying a Linux device filename, you specify the host and export name. (For protection against a DNS server compromise or as a matter of preference, you can use an IP address rather than a hostname.) For instance, to mount /home from kranz.luna.edu at /mnt/morehome, you might type the following command:

```
# mount -t nfs kranz.luna.edu:/home /mnt/morehome
```

TIP *If you don't know what exports a server makes available, you can type* **showmount -e *servername***. *The result is a list of exports available on* **servername**, *along with the clients that can connect to each export.*

In the case of the preceding example, you can omit the -t nfs specification, and if your client is in luna.edu or is configured to search that domain via a search line in /etc/resolv.conf, you can specify the export as kranz:/home rather than kranz.luna.edu:/home. If you want to mount an export whenever the computer boots or give ordinary users the power to mount an export, you can do so by adding an entry to /etc/fstab. For instance, the following line mounts this export at boot time:

```
kranz.luna.edu:/home  /mnt/morehome  nfs  defaults  0  0
```

You can add many standard mount options, as well; for instance, specifying an option of ro causes a read-only mount, even if the server has granted your system read/write access. (You cannot use rw to gain read/write access if the server gives you only read-only access, though.) There are also a few NFS-specific mount options. The most important of these may be hard and soft. Ordinarily or if you explicitly specify hard, a program trying to access an NFS server will hang if the server doesn't respond. When the server becomes available, the program will continue where it left off. If you specify soft, though, the kernel's NFS client will eventually time out and deliver an error message to the client. If your network or NFS server is flaky, you may prefer soft, because you'll be better able to kill processes that hang because of an inability to access NFS exports. If your network is functioning normally, though, hard is the preferred behavior, because specifying soft can cause occasional problems on a well-behaved network.

Once an export is mounted, all ordinary users can access that export, within limits imposed by file ownership and permissions. One potential caveat is that NFS uses user ID (UID) and group ID (GID) numbers in handling ownership and permissions. If users have accounts on both the client and the server computer, the users' UIDs and GIDs on those two systems must match, or the users won't be able to access their own files. A similar problem can arise if users have accounts on two or more clients that access the same server. Various workarounds have been deployed to fix this problem, but most aren't current. For instance, some older NFS servers supported options to map UIDs and GIDs between client and server; but the current Linux NFS server doesn't support this option. Your best bet is to synchronize UIDs and GIDs whenever necessary. Note that this practice isn't required for fundamentally public read-only exports, such as exports of directories holding software or shared read-only templates, unless some users should be restricted from accessing these files. Also, if an NFS server holds home directories but users don't need to log into that computer directly, you don't need to synchronize UIDs and GIDs because the users don't need accounts on the server. (You do still need to synchronize UIDs and GIDs across multiple clients in this case, though.) If the server doesn't have accounts for its NFS users, be sure any directory to which users should be able to write has permissions to enable world writing, or at least writing by the appropriate group, which in this case must be mapped appropriately.

Samba: Sharing with Windows

Ironically, Linux has become a popular addition to many networks in order to fill the role of a Windows file server, using a protocol (SMB/CIFS) that's most strongly associated with Microsoft. This situation has developed because Linux's SMB/CIFS server, Samba (http://www.samba.org), is extremely robust, is by some measures faster than Windows NT/2000 SMB/CIFS servers, and can do some tasks better than can Windows servers. The flip side is that, because Samba must mediate between two different computing worlds, it's more complex. It needs options to specify how to handle filename case, for instance. Fortunately, Samba's default configuration works reasonably well, once a handful of options are set to customize the server for your network.

Installing Samba Packages

All major distributions ship with Samba, but they differ in how they break up the package. Some ship separate packages for clients, servers, and common support programs. Others combine two or all three of these packages. Some distributions provide ancillary packages, such as documentation. The distribution-by-distribution details are listed here:

Debian This distribution provides a shared `samba-common` package, separate client (`smbclient`) and server (`samba`) packages, a `samba-doc` package holding documentation, and a package holding the Samba Web Administration Tool (SWAT, in the `swat` package).

Mandrake This distribution provides a breakdown of Samba packages similar to Debian's, but the packages are named differently: `samba-common`, `samba-client`, `samba-server`, `samba-doc`, and `samba-swat`.

Red Hat Red Hat has chosen a split much like Mandrake's, except that its Samba server is in a package called `samba` instead of `samba-server`. Red Hat also provides a GUI configuration tool in `redhat-config-samba`.

Slackware Unlike most distributions, Slackware distributes Samba in one monolithic package called `samba`.

SuSE SuSE's main `samba` package includes most Samba functionality, including those features present in Samba common, Samba server, and SWAT packages in most other distributions. The `samba-client` package provides client functionality.

NOTE *The Samba client functionality provided with Samba is for both an FTP-like client and a tool called `smbmount` that can mount SMB/CIFS shares. The `smbmount` program requires support in the Linux kernel in order to work, though. Figure 24.1 shows this option, called SMB File System Support. The Samba client package also includes tools to enable a Linux computer to print to a printer shared via SMB/CIFS.*

Most Linux distributions' Samba packages include SysV startup scripts to launch the Samba server. These scripts are typically called `smb`, but Debian calls its script `samba`. Slackware ships with a separate `rc.samba` startup script for Samba. You can configure the server to start using the procedures described in Chapter 22. The Samba server actually consists of two main programs, `smbd` and `nmbd`, and the SysV scripts start both servers. After you make changes to your Samba configuration, you must restart the Samba server, typically by typing a command such as **/etc/rc.d/init.d/smb restart**. (The exact path and filename will vary depending on your distribution, of course.) The `smbd` server handles the actual file sharing tasks, while `nmbd` provides an interface to the NetBIOS name resolution tools used by SMB/CIFS. (These tools partially duplicate ordinary TCP/IP name resolution procedures, and they exist for historical reasons.) Although smbd can run effectively from a super server, nmbd operates poorly in this mode. For this reason, you shouldn't try to run Samba from a super server.

The SWAT package provides a web-based means of configuring Samba. SWAT normally runs from a super server. Once it's running, you can browse to http://localhost:901 on the server computer, or possibly browse to the server computer's port 901 from another system. SWAT will prompt for a username and password (enter **root** and the root password) and then display the main page, as shown in Figure 24.2. The Globals link enables you to set global options, which are introduced in the next section, "Setting Global Samba Options." The Shares and Printers links provide the means to set up file and printer shares, as described in the upcoming sections, "Creating File Shares" and "Creating Printer Shares." The SWAT configuration options closely mirror those in the main Samba configuration file, so using SWAT should be fairly straightforward once you've read the next three sections.

> *WARNING   Using SWAT from a remote computer (particularly one off of your local network) is potentially very risky because of the possibility that a miscreant might sniff your root password. Indeed, running SWAT at all poses some risks, because a miscreant with the root password could then modify your Samba configuration to grant access to /etc, and from there the cracker could do anything. Some distributions implement measures to reduce the risk. For instance, the Mandrake and Red Hat /etc/xinetd.d/swat files tell xinetd to accept connections for SWAT only from the localhost interface (127.0.0.1). If your distribution doesn't implement such restrictions by default, you should configure them yourself. Chapter 20 describes how to do this using packet-filter firewall rules, TCP Wrappers, or xinetd.*

FIGURE 24.2

SWAT is a powerful web-based tool for configuring Samba.

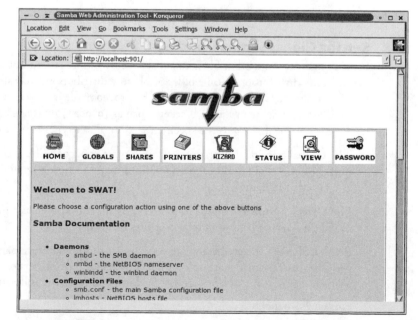

In addition to the main Samba packages, various ancillary tools exist. Some of these are GUI SMB/ CIFS network browsers akin to the My Network Places or Network Neighborhood tools in Microsoft Windows. LinNeighborhood (`http://www.bnro.de/~schmidjo/`), which is shown in Figure 24.3, and Kruiser (`http://devel-home.kde.org/~kruiser/`) are two examples. Some distributions provide distribution-specific Samba configuration tools, such as Red Hat's `redhat-config-samba`. You can install such packages, but they aren't required for basic Samba functionality.

FIGURE 24.3

GUI SMB/CIFS browsers such as LinNeighborhood enable you to browse the contents of a Windows network.

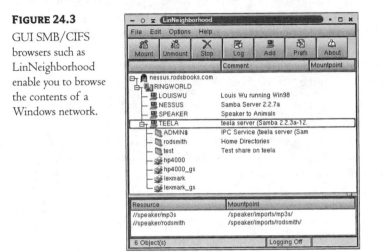

Setting Global Samba Options

Samba's main configuration file is called `smb.conf`, and it's stored in the `/etc/samba` directory on all major Linux distributions. Some older or obscure distributions may store this file in another directory, such as `/etc/samba.d` or `/etc/smb`. The `smb.conf` file is broken down into sections, each of which is led by a name in square brackets, such as `[global]` or `[home]`. Subsequent lines, up until the next section name, belong to the specified section. Three types of section exist:

The Global Section　The first section in most `smb.conf` files is the `[global]` section. This section defines global defaults and sets options that affect the overall performance of the server, such as its NetBIOS name.

File Shares　Samba's equivalent to an NFS export is known as a *share*. File shares enable Samba to deliver files to clients and to accept files from clients.

Printer Shares　Printer shares are very similar to file shares in many respects, but Samba sends the files that a printer share accepts into Linux's local print queue, so they end up being printed. Within each section, options are assigned using lines of the following form:

```
option = value
```

Options and most values are case-insensitive. (Some values are Linux pathnames or other inherently case-sensitive strings, though.) Boolean values of `1`, `True`, and `Yes` are equivalent, as are `0`, `False`, and No. Hash marks (#) and semicolons (;) are both comment characters; lines beginning with these characters are ignored.

The [global] section is particularly important to Samba's functioning. In fact, your Samba server probably won't be useable by your Windows clients until you've made one or two changes to this section. Table 24.4 summarizes some of the features you might want to change in this section. As with similar tables throughout this chapter, Table 24.4 is far from complete. You may need to consult the Samba documentation or a book on the server to learn about additional options if you have problems.

TABLE 24.4: COMMON GLOBAL SAMBA OPTIONS

OPTION	VALUE	MEANING
workgroup	String	NetBIOS workgroup or NetBIOS domain name. Often, but not always, related to the network's TCP/IP domain name.
netbios name	String	Computer's NetBIOS name. Often, but not always, the same as the computer's TCP/IP hostname without the domain portion. This is also the default value.
printing	String	Name of the printing system, such as LPRng or CUPS. Samba adjusts its printing command to suit the printing system.
printcap name	Filename	Name of the /etc/printcap file or a stand-in for it. This option is necessary for the [printers] share to operate correctly.
load printers	Boolean	Whether or not to load printers defined in the /etc/printcap file or its equivalent when a [printers] share is present. The default value is Yes.
hosts allow and hosts deny	Hostnames or IP addresses	Host-based access controls, similar to those provided by TCP Wrappers or xinetd.
security	user, share, server, or domain	Specifies how Samba authenticates local users— by using usernames and passwords (user), by mimicking the method used by Windows 9x/Me (share) on a share-by-share basis, by sending an authentication request to another computer (server), or by deferring to a domain controller (domain).
encrypt passwords	Boolean	Specifies whether or not to require encrypted passwords.
smb passwd file	Filename	Encrypted password file.

Two of the options in Table 24.4 are very important for most systems. The first of these options is `workgroup`. SMB/CIFS networks are built atop NetBIOS workgroups or domains. If your Samba server's workgroup name isn't set correctly, your Windows clients won't be able to find it—at least, not easily. If you don't know what your workgroup name is, try typing the following command (note the trailing dash in the command):

```
$ nmblookup -MS -
querying __MSBROWSE__ on 192.168.1.255
192.168.1.1 __MSBROWSE__<01>
Looking up status of 192.168.1.1
        SPEAKER          <00> -          M <ACTIVE>
        SPEAKER          <03> -          M <ACTIVE>
        SPEAKER          <20> -          M <ACTIVE>
        ..__MSBROWSE__.  <01> - <GROUP> M <ACTIVE>
        RINGWORLD        <00> - <GROUP> M <ACTIVE>
        RINGWORLD        <1b> -          M <ACTIVE>
        RINGWORLD        <1c> - <GROUP> M <ACTIVE>
        RINGWORLD        <1d> -          M <ACTIVE>
        RINGWORLD        <1e> - <GROUP> M <ACTIVE>
```

The output includes information on both the *master browser* computer (which manages lists of computers for browsing with tools such as LinNeighborhood, as shown in Figure 24.3) and on the workgroup. In this case, SPEAKER is the master browser for the RINGWORLD workgroup. Compare this information to the information in Figure 24.3; it also shows the SPEAKER computer and the RINGWORLD workgroup.

The second option you'll most likely have to adjust is the `encrypt passwords` option. All versions of Windows since Windows 95 OEM Service Release 2 (OSR2) and Windows NT 4.0 Service Pack 3 use encrypted passwords by default. If `encrypt passwords` is set to `No`, Samba uses the Linux username and password database. In this case, recent Windows clients won't connect to Samba unless the Samba or Windows client configuration is changed. When `encrypt passwords` is set to `Yes`, Samba requires its own password database, which is independent of the standard Linux password database. In this case, recent Windows clients will connect to the Samba server. In practice, it's usually easiest and safest to use encrypted passwords. To do so, follow these steps:

1. If necessary, set `encrypt passwords` to `Yes`.

2. As `root`, type **smbpasswd -a *username*** at a command prompt, where *username* is a username for a user who should have access to the Samba server. The program will prompt for a new password, and then it will prompt you to type it again. The first time you issue this command, it will complain that the `passdb` database doesn't exist. You can ignore this complaint.

3. Repeat Step 2 for all the users who should have Samba access.

If you have many users, the process of adding them all to Samba's encrypted password database can be tedious, but it's necessary. Many distributions include a script called `mksmbpasswd.sh` that can create a Samba password file from a Linux `/etc/passwd` file. Unfortunately, Linux and Samba use different methods of encrypting passwords, so it's not possible to convert actual passwords. The resulting Samba password file includes usernames but no passwords. As a result, `mksmbpasswd.sh` saves little or no effort. If you can run with unencrypted passwords for a time, though, you could use this script and use the `update encrypted = Yes` option. Samba will then add passwords to its encrypted database as users log on using unencrypted passwords. (You must run with `encrypt passwords = Yes` for this process to work.) This practice might be useful if you were migrating a network from unencrypted to encrypted passwords, but for most existing installations, it's not an option.

TIP *Although Samba is most commonly used to deliver files to Windows clients, it can serve files to other platforms, including Linux. Using* `smbmount`*, a Linux client can mount a Samba share. In most cases, NFS is preferred for Linux-to-Linux file sharing, but on occasion Samba is better. For instance, Samba's support for passwords and individual user accounts gives it an edge if you need to exercise this sort of user-by-user access control.*

SAMBA AND WINDOWS XP

Unfortunately, Windows XP has changed the way it handles encrypted passwords, and so is incompatible with Samba's encrypted password system as delivered. To fix the problem, you can use REGEDIT on Windows XP. Change the following entry's value from 3 to 2:

```
HKEY_LOCAL_MACHINE\System\CurrentControlSet\Control\lmcompatibilitylevel
```

Samba 3.0, when released, should not need this change to the Windows XP Registry. If you want to use a Windows XP system with a domain controlled by Samba, you may also need to change another Windows Registry setting. Most Samba distributions ship with a file that will do the job: `WinXP_SignOrSeal.reg`, usually stored in `/usr/share/doc/samba-doc-`*version*`/docs/Registry` or a similar directory, where *version* is the Samba version number. Copy this file to the Windows XP system and double-click it. This should launch REGEDIT, which will make the necessary changes.

Creating File Shares

File shares begin with the share name in square brackets and continue until the next share definition or until the end of the file. Typically, lines after the share name line are indented, although this isn't required. A fairly basic file share looks like this:

```
[test]
    comment = Test share on %L
    path = /exports/shared
    writeable = Yes
```

This share delivers the contents of `/exports/shared` under the share name `test`. (Figure 24.3 shows this share, among others, accessible from TEELA.) Most of these options aren't actually required; they provide extra information to clients (the `comment` option) or set features of the share (the `writeable` option). Even the `path` option can be omitted—the default value is `/tmp`, except in one special case, described shortly. Table 24.5 summarizes some of the most common file share options.

TABLE 24.5: COMMON FILE SHARE SAMBA OPTIONS

OPTION	VALUE	MEANING
comment	String	A one-line description of the share, which appears in some views of the share from the client.
path	Directory name	The directory to be shared.
browseable	Boolean	Whether or not the share appears in browsers. The default value is Yes.
writeable	Boolean	Whether or not users can write to the share, given the appropriate permissions. The default value is No.
create mask	Octal permission string	The Linux permissions assigned to new files created by clients. (Execute permission bits may be modified by other options, though.)
directory mask	Octal permission string	The Linux permissions assigned to new directories created by clients. (Execute permission bits may be modified by other options, though.)
nt acl support	Boolean	Whether or not to map Linux file ownership and permissions onto Windows NT-style ACLs. The default value is Yes.
force user	Username	An override to the username assigned to new files created by users. Also affects the files the user can read or write.

NOTE *Many Samba options are available with alternative spellings or synonyms. For instance,* writeable, writable, *and* write ok *are all synonymous. An antonym for all of these is* read only; read only = True *is the same as* writeable = False.

Many Samba file share options affect how Samba handles the translation between Linux ownership, permissions, filenames, and other filesystem details and features that DOS and Windows expect on their filesystems. DOS and Windows 9x/Me don't support Linux ownership and permissions, so Samba uses create mask and directory mask to set default permissions. Samba uses the username of the individual who mounted the share to set the owner of new files, unless force user overrides that setting. Windows NT, 2000, and XP support ownership and access control lists (ACLs). When such a client connects to Samba, the server maps Linux ownership and permissions onto limited ACLs. If you use an ACL-enabled filesystem, such as XFS, with a recent Samba package, you get better ACL support from your clients.

One special Samba file share comes predefined in many distributions' smb.conf files: [homes]. This share is unusual because it maps to the user's home directory. For instance, if the user buzz has a home directory of /home/buzz, and if this user opens a browser onto the server from a Windows machine, a [homes] share will appear under the name buzz. If this user opens this share, he'll find files from his home directory available in the share.

NOTE   *In order to display a* [homes] *share with the user's username, the user must have logged into the server. A few non-Windows SMB/CIFS browsers don't prompt for a password, and hence aren't fully logged in, until after the user selects the share to open. In these browsers, the* [homes] *share appears by that name, but when the user accesses the share, it opens on the user's home directory.*

The [homes] share is unusual in a couple of configuration details. First, it normally includes a browseable = No option, which would ordinarily make the share disappear from browse lists. In the case of [homes], this option makes the share name homes disappear from browse lists, but a share named after the user remains in the browse list. Second, [homes] shares usually lack a path option. Samba knows to map this share to the users' home directories rather than to a fixed location.

Creating Printer Shares

Samba printer shares are very similar to file shares. The primary distinguishing characteristic is the printable = Yes option, which tells Samba to treat the share as a printer share. If this option is set, Samba tries to send files destined for the printer to a local print queue of the same name as the Samba printer share. (If you want to use another print queue name, you can set it with the printer option.)

Rather than define printers one by one, many Samba configurations rely on a special printer share name that's akin to the [homes] share for file shares: [printers]. This share might look something like this:

```
[printers]
   comment = All Printers
   browseable = no
   path = /tmp
   printable = yes
   create mode = 0700
```

If this share is present, and if the [global] section does *not* include a load printers = No option, Samba scans /etc/printcap (or another file defined by printcap name in the [global] section) and creates a printer share for every print queue on the system. This feature can be a convenient way to share all of your printers at once.

Samba delivers the print job via the local printing system—BSD LPD, LPRng, CUPS, or something more exotic if that's what you use. The global printing option defines how Samba submits print jobs, so be sure this option is set correctly. In all cases, the format of the job Samba submits must be something that the print queue can handle. Because Samba simply passes a file it receives from the client on to the server's printing system, this means that the client must have a print driver that generates output the Linux print queue can process. In most cases, Linux print queues are designed to handle PostScript input, so using a generic PostScript driver on the client is in order. As a general rule, drivers for Apple LaserWriter models work well for monochrome printers, and QMS magicolor PostScript drivers work well for color printers. Adobe also provides generic PostScript drivers at http://www.adobe.com/support/downloads/, but these drivers are licensed only for use with printers that use genuine Adobe PostScript interpreters. If your printer is a PostScript model, you can try using the driver provided by the manufacturer. On occasion, though, these drivers create output that includes mode-switching codes that confuse Linux print queues, so you may need to use another driver. Alternatively, you can include the `postscript = Yes` option; this tells Samba to tack a PostScript identifier onto the start of the file, causing the Linux print queue to correctly identify the output as PostScript.

If your printer is a non-PostScript model, you can try using its native driver. This practice will only work if the Linux print queue recognizes the format and passes print jobs unmodified to the printer, though. If necessary, you can create a "raw" print queue, as described in Chapter 13, "Managing Printers," to pass data through without changes.

NOTE   *Many, but not all, printers that can't be made to work from Linux can still be served to Linux clients using Samba and a raw print queue. A few such printers rely on two-way communication between the printer and Windows printer driver. Such printers won't work via Samba unless they're supported in Linux.*

In practice, it's hard to say which is better—to use Windows PostScript drivers with a Linux print queue that interprets PostScript using Ghostscript or the printer's native drivers in Windows and a raw queue. The PostScript approach is likely to reduce network traffic when printing text, but it imposes a greater CPU load on the print server. The native driver approach is likely to increase network traffic when printing text and shifts the CPU load onto the clients. The PostScript approach may be desirable if you use applications that work best with PostScript printers, such as some desktop publishing and graphics tools. Native drivers often give more convenient access to printer features such as resolution adjustments. Either approach could produce superior output; the best approach depends on the drivers in question and the type of printing. I recommend you try both approaches. You may want to create two queues, one for each method. (If your Linux queue is smart enough to recognize the file type, you'll need only one Samba printer share; you can create multiple queues on the clients that print to the same Samba share.)

File Serving Security Concerns

Serving files is an extremely important function for many Linux systems. Both file-transfer servers and file sharing servers are very popular and play vital roles on many networks. Unfortunately, these server types necessarily give clients fairly broad access to your server computer. The ability to read and, often, write arbitrary files, even within a limited set of directories, can be abused if your configuration is sloppy or if the server contains a bug. For this reason, you should be very cautious when configuring your file server.

Whenever possible, apply multiple layers of protections based on hostnames and IP addresses. You can use packet-filter firewalls, TCP Wrappers, `xinetd`, or server-based restrictions. Chapter 20 describes most of these techniques. The idea is to limit access to the server to individuals who have legitimate reasons to interact with it. Thinking out these restrictions is particularly important in the case of NFS servers, which have no other access-control tools. Of course, some servers, such as anonymous FTP servers on the Internet as a whole, shouldn't be restricted in this way. Their exposure is part of the risk of running such servers.

You should always be very cautious about what directories you make available through file servers. You should *never* share critical directories such as /etc through a file server. Even read-only access to such a directory could be risky. If miscreants can read your configuration files, they can better plan an attack against you based on problems they might find in your configurations, even of servers other than the file server. Limit users to read-only access whenever possible. By its nature, FTP normally gives users access to any directory on the computer, within limits imposed by normal Linux ownership and permissions rules. Most FTP servers use `chroot` jails to limit this access for anonymous users, but such limits for authenticated user logins are rarer. You may want to use a server, such as `vsftpd`, that can lock users into `chroot` jails in their own home directories. Of course, if users can log in through other means, they may be able to use those logins to do damage, as well, so using `chroot` jails for ordinary users may be pointless.

FTP sends passwords in unencrypted form over the network, which can be a huge security risk for authenticated user logins. For this reason, I recommend limiting authenticated FTP access to your local network. You may want to consider eliminating the FTP server altogether and instead using secure protocols. For instance, the Secure Shell (SSH), described in Chapter 26, "Providing Remote Login Access," provides encrypted file-transfer tools. Specifically, the `scp` client can copy files between a client computer and a server running SSH. A handful of FTP client programs, such as gFTP (`http://gftp.seul.org`), can connect to an SSH server and perform transfers just as they would using an FTP server. An SSH client known as `sftp` also provides FTP-like access via SSH. If you can use such clients, SSH makes a superior replacement for FTP.

Although most Windows networks now use encrypted passwords for SMB/CIFS transfers, non-password data pass over these networks in unencrypted form. As such traffic is usually local and passwords are usually encrypted, the security risks are lower than they are with FTP or Internet transfers, but nonetheless you should exercise diligence with Samba passwords and encryption.

Summary

Linux supports several protocols that are designed for two-way file transfer. Three of the most popular of these protocols are FTP, NFS, and SMB/CIFS. Each of these tools has its place. FTP is most useful in making files available to anonymous users or for two-way file transfers with clients of any OS. Several FTP servers are available for Linux, ranging from small specialized tools to complex servers that support very advanced options. NFS is a file-sharing server for Unix and Unix-like OSs. It relies on the client for some security features, so its use is best restricted to a very limited set of (probably local) computers. SMB/CIFS is conceptually similar to NFS, but it is used primarily on Windows networks. Linux's SMB/CIFS server, Samba, supports a huge number of options for helping integrate Linux and Windows systems. With all of these servers, you should be mindful of potential security problems associated with file servers.

Chapter 25

Delivering E-Mail

E-MAIL HAS BECOME ONE of the most important communications mediums for both businesses and individuals. As with most networking tools, e-mail relies on the presence of both clients and servers. Chances are you're familiar with e-mail clients (aka *mail readers*) generally. Chapter 8, "Miscellaneous User Tools," describes Linux mail clients specifically. Most individuals and many small businesses run mail clients locally but rely on others to run mail servers. Some individuals, some small businesses, and most large organizations run their own mail servers, though. Doing so gives them greater control over their mail delivery options, but it requires an investment in time and effort to configure and run the server. Even small sites might want to use a local mail server to increase mail delivery options.

Before configuring a mail server, you should understand a bit of how mail delivery works. After you understand the theory, the first step you must take when running a mail server is configuring your Internet domain to accept the mail. You must also decide which mail server to run. Most distributions ship with mail server configurations that work reasonably well. This chapter covers three popular servers: sendmail, Postfix, and Exim. These servers accept incoming mail from your own or other sites. Another type of mail server delivers mail to mail clients. Two specific protocols and some popular packages for handling them are covered in this chapter. Unfortunately, the mail environment has become increasingly unfriendly, with unwanted messages polluting the e-mail waterways. Controlling such flow is an important consideration when you run your own mail server, so this chapter covers this topic. Finally, this chapter looks at a tool called Fetchmail, which enables you to acquire mail from an ISP's mail server and inject it into your local mail queue. This tool can be very helpful for individuals and small sites who use an ISP for mail delivery but who want the benefits of running a local mail server.

NOTE *Mail server configuration is a complex topic. If you need to handle mail delivery for more than a few dozen users, or if advanced configurations are important, you should consult a book on the subject. Many titles are available, most on specific servers. Examples include Craig Hunt's* Linux Sendmail Administration *(Sybex, 2001), Richard Blum's* Postfix *(Sams, 2001), and Philip Hazel's* Exim: The Mail Transfer Agent *(O'Reilly, 2001).*

Understanding Mail Protocols

Internet mail delivery today is dominated by a protocol known as the *Simple Mail Transfer Protocol (SMTP)*. This protocol is an example of a *push protocol*, meaning that the sending system initiates the transfer. A user writes a message using a mail reader and then tells the mail reader to send the mail. The mail reader contacts a local SMTP server, which may run on the same or another computer. The SMTP server accepts the message for delivery, looks up the recipient address, and delivers the message to the recipient system. In some cases, the recipient system may forward the mail to another system, which handles the mail account for the addressee. Depending on how the recipient reads mail, that person may use the destination mail server computer directly or run a mail client on another computer. In the latter case, the mail client uses a protocol such as the *Post Office Protocol (POP)* or the *Internet Message Access Protocol (IMAP)* to retrieve the mail from the local mail server. POP and IMAP are both examples of *pull protocols*, in which the recipient, rather than the sender, initiates the data transfer. This configuration is outlined in Figure 25.1. The Internet's mail system is flexible enough that the total number of links between the sender and recipient may be more or less than the number depicted in Figure 25.1, though. As already mentioned, users may read mail on the final SMTP server (`inbox.pangaea.edu` in Figure 25.1). The upcoming section, "Using Fetchmail," describes software you can use to further extend the chain beyond the pull mail link, as well.

Three of the computers in Figure 25.1—`mail.example.com`, `smtp.pangaea.edu`, and `inbox .pangaea.edu`—must run SMTP servers. These servers can be entirely different products running on different platforms. For instance, one might be sendmail on Linux, another might be Postfix on FreeBSD, and a third might be Microsoft Exchange on Windows. In addition to running an SMTP server, Figure 25.1's `inbox.pangaea.edu` must run a POP or IMAP server. The two endpoint computers—`client.example.com` and `franklin.pangaea.edu`—need not run mail servers. Instead, `client.example.com` connects to the SMTP server on `mail.example.com` to send mail, and `franklin.pangaea.edu` connects to the POP or IMAP server on `inbox.pangaea.edu` to retrieve mail.

FIGURE 25.1

E-mail typically traverses several links between sender and recipient.

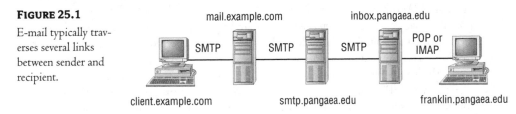

Configuring a Domain to Accept Mail

Internet e-mail addresses can take one of two forms:

◆ *username*@*host.name*, where *username* is the recipient's username and *host.name* is a computer's hostname. (The address can also use an IP address, typically surrounded by square brackets, in place of a hostname.) For instance, mail might be addressed to ben@`smtp.pangaea.edu`. This form of addressing is likely to work so long as the target computer is configured to accept mail addressed to it.

- *username@domain.name*, where *username* is the recipient's username and *domain.name* is the domain name. For instance, mail might be addressed to ben@pangaea.edu. Such addressing is usually shorter than an address that includes the mail server computer's full hostname, and it can be more reliable, depending on the domain's configuration.

In order for the second sort of address to work, the domain requires a special Domain Name System (DNS) entry. This entry is known as a *mail exchanger (MX) record*, and it points sending mail servers to a specific mail server computer. For instance, the MX record for pangaea.edu might point to smtp.pangaea.edu. Therefore, mail addressed to ben@pangaea.edu is delivered to the smtp.pangaea.edu server, which may process it locally or forward it to another computer.

Chapter 27, "Miscellaneous Servers," describes configuring the Berkeley Internet Name Domain (BIND) DNS server. In brief, an MX record belongs in the domain's control file, which is usually in /var/named and is usually named after the domain, such as named.pangaea.edu for pangaea.edu. (The exact name is arbitrary, though.) An MX record for pangaea.edu, pointing external SMTP servers to smtp.pangaea.edu for mail delivery, would look like this:

```
@   IN   MX   5   smtp.pangaea.edu.
```

The leading at sign (@) is a stand-in for the domain name. The IN is a standard part of most host definitions. MX, of course, refers to the fact that this is an MX entry. The number 5 in this example refers to the priority of the server. One of the advantages of using a domain name for mail delivery is that you can specify several mail servers, using one as a primary mail server and one or more as backups in case the primary server goes down. Outside SMTP servers try the MX entry with the lowest priority code first. The final field in this entry is the hostname of the mail server itself. Note that this entry ends with a dot (.). If the name doesn't end with a dot, the system attempts to add the domain name to the name specified; therefore, if you include the domain name but no dot, the domain portion will be doubled, and chances are the mail won't be delivered.

If another system administrator runs your domain's DNS server, consult that individual about MX record administration. If you use an outside provider, such as a domain registrar's DNS server, you may need to enter the MX record information in a web-based form. These forms may attempt to mirror the layout of information you'd find in a DNS server's configuration, as just described, but they may not allow you to change fixed information. Alternatively, the form may present simplified data entry fields, such as fields for the server priority code and hostname alone.

It's possible for a computer on one domain to function as a mail server for an entirely different domain. For instance, mail.threeroomco.com could be the mail server for pangaea.edu. This configuration requires setting up the server to accept mail addressed to the domain in question, and of course entering the full path to the mail server in the target domain's MX record.

Picking the Right Mail Server

As with many types of servers, Linux systems offer a wide variety of SMTP servers. The most popular Linux mail servers are all very powerful programs that are capable of handling large domains' mail needs, when paired with sufficiently powerful hardware. The most popular servers are:

Sendmail This server, headquartered at http://www.sendmail.org, has long dominated Internet mail delivery. Daniel Bernstein, the author of the competing qmail software, conducts periodic surveys of SMTP servers. The most recent of these was conducted in September and October of 2001, and it is reported at `http://cr.yp.to/surveys.html`. This survey shows sendmail running on 42 percent of systems—the most of any server, by a wide margin. Sendmail has earned a reputation for a difficult-to-master configuration file format. Fortunately, tools to create a configuration file from a simpler file are common. In the 1990s, sendmail suffered from a series of serious security bugs, but such problems have been less common since the late 1990s. Red Hat and Slackware both use sendmail as their default mail server.

Postfix   The Mandrake and SuSE distributions both use this server as their default mail server. Although it was used on only 15 of 958 servers in Bernstein's 2001 survey, its presence as the default on two major Linux distributions makes it a very important server in the Linux world. Postfix uses a series of small programs to handle mail delivery tasks, as opposed to the monolithic approach used by sendmail. The result is greater speed and, at least in theory, less chance of serious security flaws. (In practice, Postfix has a good security record.) Its configuration is much easier to handle than is sendmail's. You can learn more at `http://www.postfix.org`.

Exim   This mail server, described at `http://www.exim.org`, is the default for Debian. Bernstein's survey shows it in use on 14 of 958 servers. Like sendmail, Exim uses a monolithic design, but Exim's configuration file is much more intelligible. This server includes extensive pattern-matching tools that are very useful in fighting spam.

qmail   This server is the second most popular Unix mail server in Bernstein's survey, with 167 of 958 server computers running the program. Despite this popularity on the Internet, qmail isn't the default server for any major Linux distribution, perhaps because its license terms are peculiar—they don't permit distribution of binaries except under limited conditions. Like Postfix, qmail uses a modular design that emphasizes speed and security. Check `http://www.qmail.org` for more information.

TIP   If you want to run qmail, you can find links to binaries, including RPMs and Debian packages for many popular distributions, on the qmail web site. You needn't compile and install the software from source code unless perhaps you're running an unusually new, old, or exotic distribution.

For light duty—say, for a small business or personal mail server—any of these programs will work quite well. For such cases, I recommend sticking with whatever software is the standard for your distribution. Using the default server means you'll be less likely to run into strange configuration problems or incompatibilities. For larger installations or if you need advanced features, you may want to investigate alternatives to your distribution's default server more closely. You may find particular features, such as Exim's pattern-matching tools or the modular design of Postfix and qmail, appealing. All of these servers are capable of handling large or busy domains, although sendmail may require speedier hardware than the others to handle a given volume of mail. For small sites, even sendmail won't stress any but the weakest computers.

The following sections describe the configuration of sendmail, Postfix, and Exim in more detail. I've omitted qmail because it's not the default server for any major distribution, but it's certainly worth considering if you want to change your mail server.

Running Sendmail

Red Hat 9.0 and Slackware 9.0 both use sendmail for mail delivery, as do older versions of many other Linux distributions. If you want to run sendmail, you can use it with distributions that normally use other mail servers, but doing so requires removing the standard mail server and installing sendmail. Unfortunately, sendmail configuration file locations and names vary somewhat from one distribution to another, so you must know where to look to find these files. Once found, you can change many sendmail options, such as the addresses the server considers local and relay options.

NOTE   Many programs rely on the presence of an executable file called sendmail. *For this reason, mail servers other than sendmail usually include an executable called* sendmail, *which is often a link to the equivalent program file for the other mail server.*

Sendmail Configuration Files

The main sendmail configuration file is called sendmail.cf, and it's typically located in /etc/mail (both Red Hat and Slackware place the file in that directory). Unfortunately, this file is both very long (well over 1,000 lines for both Red Hat and Slackware) and difficult to understand. You should *not* attempt to edit this file directly; instead, you should edit a configuration file that can be used to generate a sendmail.cf file. This source configuration file is written using the m4 macro processing language, which is more intelligible than the raw sendmail configuration file format. To edit and compile an m4 configuration file for sendmail, you might need to install additional packages:

The m4 Macro Language   You must install the m4 macro language itself. This software usually comes in a package called m4. Look for a program file called m4 (often stored in /usr/bin) to ascertain whether or not it's already installed on your system. If it isn't, look for and install the package that came with your Linux distribution.

Sendmail m4 Configuration Files   You need a set of m4 configuration files for sendmail in order to modify your configuration. These files are installed from the sendmail-cf package in both Red Hat and Slackware.

Both distributions ship with default m4 configuration files that can be used to rebuild the standard sendmail.cf file that ships with the distribution. (In both cases, if you rebuild the default file, a few comments differ, but the rebuilt file is functionally identical to the original.) For Red Hat, the default file is /etc/mail/sendmail.mc. (This file actually ships with the sendmail package rather than sendmail-cf.) Slackware's default file is /usr/share/sendmail/cf/cf/linux.smtp.mc. To make changes to your configuration, follow these steps as root:

1. Back up your default /etc/mail/sendmail.cf file.

2. In a bash or other command shell, change to the directory in which the original m4 configuration file resides.

3. Copy the original file to a new name; for instance, you might call it myconfig.mc.

WARNING   Slackware's linux.smtp.mc *file uses a relative file reference (*../m4/cf.m4*) in an* include *statement in the first line of the file. If you copy the file to another directory, you must change that line to refer to the file in another way, such as the absolute filename* /usr/share/sendmail/cf/m4/cf.m4.

4. Edit the configuration file as described in the next few sections or to achieve other ends.

5. Type the following command to create a new /etc/mail/sendmail.cf file:

```
# m4 < myconfig.mc > /etc/mail/sendmail.cf
```

If all goes well, the m4 command won't display any messages in your command shell, but if you check, you should find that the /etc/mail/sendmail.cf file is new. You can then tell sendmail to read the new configuration file:

```
# killall -HUP sendmail
```

This command tells all running sendmail instances to reread their configuration files and implement any changes. You can then test those changes in whatever way is appropriate—by sending or receiving mail and checking whether the changes you set are implemented.

In addition to the main sendmail.cf file, several other files are important in sendmail's configuration. Most of these files reside in /etc/mail, but some may reside in /etc. Two of the most important of these files are:

access.db   This file, which usually resides in /etc/mail, controls access to the sendmail server. By listing or not listing particular systems in this file in specific ways, you can adjust which systems can use sendmail to relay mail to other systems. This file is a binary database built from the plain-text access file using the makemap program.

aliases.db   Like access.db, this file is a binary database file built from a plain-text file (aliases) using newaliases. In Red Hat, this file appears in /etc, but in Slackware, it's stored in /etc/mail. This file lists *aliases* for particular usernames or addresses. For instance, if you set up an alias linking the name postmaster to root, all mail addressed to postmaster is delivered to root.

Configuring the Hostname

E-mail messages have names embedded in them. These names identify the computer, so in theory they should be the same as the computer's hostname. Sometimes, though, the names in the header may need to be changed. For instance, you might want outgoing mail to be associated with your domain name rather than with the mail server name. Configuring your mail server in this way can head off problems down the road—say, if you change your mail server system. If your outgoing mail had used the mail server's true hostname, replies to old messages might continue to be addressed to this system and, therefore, bounce. To set the name that's used in the From: headers in mail messages, you should add lines such as the following to the m4 configuration file and rebuild your main configuration file:

```
MASQUERADE_AS(`target-address')
FEATURE(masquerade_envelope)
```

NOTE   *The* MASQUERADE_AS *line includes two types of single quote characters. The lead character is a back-tick, accessible on most keyboards on the key to the left of the* 1 *key. The close quote is an ordinary single quote character, which is on the key to the left of the Enter key on most keyboards. If you use the wrong characters, these lines won't work.*

Of course, you should change the *target-address* in these sample lines to the address you want to use, such as `pangaea.edu`. The `MASQUERADE_AS` line changes only the address displayed in the `From:` mail header line. It also changes this configuration only if the mail reader doesn't specify a different address. Many clients enable users to set arbitrary return addresses, and these values override whatever option you set in sendmail. The `FEATURE(masquerade_envelope)` line goes further; it overrides the settings users enter in their mail clients. You might use this option if you want to limit users' ability to set bogus return addresses in their mail readers.

Accepting Incoming Mail

In order to accept incoming mail, sendmail must be configured to accept incoming network connections. Slackware's default sendmail configuration does this, so you shouldn't need to modify it. Red Hat, though, configures its sendmail to accept only local connections. This configuration is good for workstations that may need to send outgoing mail or send mail between local users but that shouldn't receive mail from outside systems. If you want to receive mail from other computers, though, you must modify this configuration. To do so, edit the /etc/mail/sendmail.mc file or your localized copy of it. Look for the following line, which is about halfway through the file:

```
DAEMON_OPTIONS(`Port=smtp,Addr=127.0.0.1, Name=MTA')dnl
```

Comment this line out by adding the string dnl and a space to the start of the line. (Unlike most configuration files, sendmail m4 files use dnl as a comment indicator.) You can then create a new sendmail.cf file, as described in the earlier section, "Sendmail Configuration Files." Restart the server by typing **killall -HUP sendmail** or **/etc/rc.d/init.d/sendmail restart** and the server should accept connections from remote systems.

Another aspect of accepting remote connections is telling sendmail what hostnames to recognize as local. For instance, consider Figure 25.1. If `smtp.pangaea.edu` is the computer to which the `pangaea.edu` domain's MX record points, then `smtp.pangaea.edu` must know to accept mail addressed to *user*@pangaea.edu. Ordinarily, sendmail rejects messages addressed to anything but the computer's own hostname. You can change this behavior by adding any aliases for the mail server computer itself to a special configuration file. This file is called /etc/mail/local-host-names, and its use is enabled by default in Red Hat's configuration. In Slackware, you must first add a line to the sendmail m4 configuration file and create a new sendmail.cf file, as described earlier in "Sendmail Configuration Files." The line you need to add is:

```
FEATURE(use_cw_file)
```

Be sure this line appears before the two `MAILER` lines at the bottom of the default file. After you've rebuilt the sendmail.cf file, create or edit /etc/mail/local-host-names and add the names you want sendmail to recognize as local. For instance, you might add lines such as the following:

```
pangaea.edu
mail.pangaea.edu
```

Once this task is done, the server will accept mail to these domains as local mail, even if the server's hostname doesn't bear any resemblance to these names. For instance, entering these two lines on `mail.example.com`'s local-host-names file will cause it to deliver mail addressed to `sue@pangaea.edu` to any local account with a username of `sue`.

Sendmail Relay Configuration Options

Mail servers must often be set up as *relays*. In such a configuration, the server accepts mail from one system and passes it on to another. One common relay configuration is that of a departmental mail server, which accepts mail from many clients and passes the mail on to destination systems. For instance, Figure 25.1's mail.example.com is configured in this way. Another relay configuration involves telling sendmail to use another system as a relay. For instance, if Figure 25.1's client.example.com were a Linux system, you might configure it to use mail.example.com as an outgoing relay. Using outgoing relays enables you to use the relay computer as a control point for mail. In some cases, you must configure your system in this way. For instance, your LAN or ISP might be configured to block outgoing SMTP connections except to the authorized mail server.

CONFIGURING SENDMAIL TO RELAY MAIL

Sendmail provides many relaying options. The most common configuration involves a feature that can be defined in the sendmail m4 file using a line such as this:

```
FEATURE(`access_db')
```

Red Hat's default configuration adds some extra options to this definition. Slackware's standard configuration doesn't define this option; therefore, if you want to use it, you must add it to the m4 configuration file and rebuild the sendmail.cf file, as described earlier, in "Sendmail Configuration Files." Once the option is present, you can edit the /etc/mail/access file. A typical file might resemble the one shown in Listing 25.1.

LISTING 25.1: A TYPICAL access FILE FOR CONTROLLING MAIL RELAYING

```
# Allow relaying from localhost...
localhost.localdomain    RELAY
localhost                RELAY
127.0.0.1                RELAY
# Relay for the local network
172.25.98                RELAY
```

Red Hat's default file resembles Listing 25.1, except that Red Hat's default lacks the final entry. Listing 25.1 first approves relaying for the local computer, using three methods of identifying that computer—by two names (localhost.localdomain and localhost) and by IP address (127.0.0.1). If you activate the access_db feature, your /etc/mail/access file must contain these entries if your system is to reliably handle mail from the local computer. (Some programs call sendmail in such a way that these entries aren't necessary, but others use the loopback network interface, which requires that sendmail relay for localhost or its aliases.) To relay for more systems, you must add them to the list, as Listing 25.1 does. That example relays for the 172.25.98.0/24 network. If you prefer, you can specify individual computers or list them by domain name or hostname, but using IP addresses ensures that an attacker won't be able to compromise a DNS server to abuse your system's relaying abilities.

Because this section is about relaying, all of the examples in Listing 25.1 specify the RELAY option. You can provide other words, though, to achieve different effects:

OK   You can tell sendmail to accept mail for delivery even if another rule would cause it to be rejected. For instance, you might override a block on a network for specific hosts using OK.

RELAY   This option enables relaying. Although this section emphasizes relaying for clients in the specified network, this option is actually bi-directional. For instance, Listing 25.1 enables outside systems to relay mail to servers in the 172.25.98.0/24 network.

REJECT   This option blocks mail coming from or addressed to the specified hostname or network. Sendmail generates a bounce reply when an attempt is made to send to or from the forbidden systems. You might use it to block a known spammer's domain, for example.

DISCARD   This option works much like REJECT, but sendmail won't generate a bounce message.

ERROR:*nnn text*   This option also works like REJECT, but instead of generating a standard bounce message, it replies with the error code number (*nnn*) and message (*text*) that you define.

After you modify the /etc/mail/access file, you must create a binary database file from the plain-text file. To do so, you use the makemap command:

```
# makemap hash /etc/mail/access.db < /etc/mail/access
```

Some configurations, including Red Hat's, include this command in their sendmail SysV startup scripts, so you can skip this step if you restart the server using these scripts. When you're done, restart sendmail and test the new relaying configuration.

In addition to the access_db feature, sendmail supports a variety of additional relaying options. Most of these options include the word relay in their names, such as relay_entire_domain or relay_local_from. Most of these options implement relay rules that can be implemented through the /etc/mail/access file, though, so chances are you won't need them.

WARNING   One relay option you should avoid is called promiscuous_relay. *This option configures the system to relay from any host to any server. Such a configuration is dangerous because spammers can easily abuse it. In fact, you should be cautious when configuring relaying to prevent your system from relaying from any untrusted source. The upcoming section, "Stopping Outgoing Spam," covers this topic in more detail.*

Configuring Sendmail to Use a Relay

If your system must relay mail through another server, you can configure sendmail to accommodate this requirement. To do so, add the following line to the sendmail m4 configuration file and recompile the sendmail.cf file:

```
FEATURE(`nullclient', `relay.mail.server')
```

The procedure to modify the m4 configuration file is described earlier, in "Sendmail Configuration Files." Replace *relay.mail.server* with the hostname of the mail server that's to function as a relay, such as your departmental or ISP's mail server. You may also need to delete a couple of lines or comment them out by preceding the lines with dnl:

```
MAILER(local)dnl
MAILER(smtp)dnl
```

These lines duplicate the functionality included in the relay configuration, so including them along with the relay configuration may cause m4 to complain when you try to build a new sendmail.cf file. Not all configurations use these lines in their default files, though. For instance, Red Hat's configuration lacks the MAILER(local)dnl line but adds a line for Procmail.

TIP Some people use Linux computers, and especially notebooks, with multiple ISPs. In such a case, you may need to configure sendmail to relay through one ISP's mail server at some times and another ISP's mail server at other times. One trick that can help you do this is to prepare two sendmail.cf *files, one for relaying through each ISP's mail server. You can then copy the appropriate file to* /etc/sendmail.cf *and restart sendmail whenever you need to switch the outgoing mail relay. This same trick works with Postfix and Exim configurations, as well.*

Running Postfix

Mandrake 9.1 and SuSE 8.1 both ship with Postfix as the default mail server. Compared to sendmail, Postfix is simple to configure. Postfix uses a primary configuration file, /etc/postfix/main.cf, that has a relatively straightforward syntax. This file is also usually very well commented, so you can learn a lot about your configuration by perusing the main configuration file. One problem with Postfix configuration is that it relies heavily on variables, such as myhostname. One variable may be used to set another, which may be used to set another, and so on. Therefore, you may need to trace your way back through several layers of variable assignments to learn how an important variable is set. As with bash shell scripts, Postfix variable names are preceded by a dollar sign ($) when accessed, but not when you assign values to them. As with sendmail, some default settings may need to be changed, even on a fairly simple configuration.

Configuring the Hostname

Several Postfix parameters affect the name of the Postfix server computer or the hostname that appears in mail headers. The most common of these options are summarized in Table 25.1. In a simple configuration, you needn't adjust anything; Postfix acquires its hostname automatically and builds everything else from there. You can override the configuration if necessary, though—for example, if your computer has multiple hostnames and you want to use the one that Postfix doesn't auto-detect on the mail server, or if obtaining your domain name requires stripping more than one component from the hostname. The masquerade_domains option requires special explanation: This option strips away hostname components if and only if they'll match the specified reduced name. For instance, consider a case in which you've set masquerade_domains = pangaea.edu. If the server is told to send mail with an address of sue@trex.pangaea.edu, it will reduce this address to sue@pangaea.edu. If the system is told to send mail with an address of sue@example.com, it won't change the address.

TABLE 25.1: COMMON POSTFIX HOSTNAME OPTIONS

OPTION	DEFAULT VALUE	MEANING
myhostname	Computer's hostname, as returned by the hostname command	Computer's hostname; used as a default in many subsequent options. Must be fully qualified (that is, include both the hostname and the domain name).
mydomain	$myhostname stripped of its first component	Computer's domain name; used as a default in many subsequent options.
myorigin	$myhostname	The hostname that's appended to outgoing mail if one is omitted by the mail client.
masquerade_domains	None	Domains to which an address should be reduced. Domains are tried from left to right in the list until the first match is found.
masquerade_classes	envelope_sender, header_sender	Types of addresses that are affected by masquerade_domains. Possibilities are envelope_sender, envelope_recipient, header_sender, and header_recipient. If all four options are used, mailing to individual machines in the specified domains will become impossible.
masquerade_exceptions	None	Usernames that should not be masqueraded. For instance, if you set this value to root, root's mail headers won't be altered.
sender_canonical_maps	None	Changes sender address using a flexible lookup database.

The ultimate in address remapping is accomplished through the sender_canonical_maps option. Point this option at a file using a line such as the following:

```
sender_canonical_maps = hash:/etc/postfix/sender_canonical
```

You can then specify hostnames you want changed in the /etc/postfix/sender_canonical file. For instance, to change localhost and the misspelled pangea.edu to pangaea.edu on outgoing addresses, use the following two lines:

```
@pangea.edu @pangaea.edu
@localhost @pangaea.edu
```

You can also include usernames in order to make changes only for particular users' mail. After creating this file and referencing it in /etc/postfix/main.cf, you must convert the file to a binary format. Type **postmap sender_canonical** from the /etc/postfix directory to do this job. You can then tell Postfix to reload its configuration files by typing **postfix reload**.

Accepting Incoming Mail

Ordinarily, Postfix accepts local mail addressed to *$myhostname* or localhost.*$myhostname*, where *$myhostname* is your hostname or whatever value you've set for this variable. You can broaden or narrow the range of accepted local addresses by changing the mydestination setting. For instance, you might set this value as follows for a domain's mail server:

```
mydestination = $myhostname, localhost.$myhostname, localhost, $mydomain
```

You can add more names if you like, and in fact such a change may be required if the server should handle several domains or mail addressed to many specific clients on the network. If you specify many target destinations, you can break them across lines without using backslashes. Instead, indent the second and subsequent lines with one or more spaces or tabs. Postfix uses such indentation as a signal that the line is a continuation of the previous line's configuration.

Another option you may need to change is the inet_interfaces setting. This option sets the interfaces to which Postfix listens. For instance, setting it to $myhostname tells the server to listen on the network interfaces associated with the primary hostname—or whatever value $myhostname uses. If you change this value or if you want Postfix to listen more broadly, you can set the option to all to have the server listen to all network interfaces.

Postfix Relay Configuration Options

Naturally, you can configure Postfix to relay mail in various ways or to send mail through an outgoing relay. Postfix's default relay configuration is more open than that of sendmail, but it's closed enough to not be a big risk, at least for a typical office computer.

CONFIGURING POSTFIX TO RELAY MAIL

Several options influence how Postfix treats an attempt to relay mail. Table 25.2 summarizes these options. Postfix's relay configuration is built on the concept of *trust*; the server relays mail for machines that it trusts. Defining relay authorization, therefore, becomes a matter of defining what systems to trust.

TABLE 25.2: COMMON POSTFIX RELAY OPTIONS

OPTION	DEFAULT VALUE	MEANING
mynetworks_style	subnet	Type of networks Postfix trusts. subnet means the same IP address subnet as the server, class means the same IP address class as the server, and host means to trust only the server computer itself.
mynetworks	Network list as specified by $mynetworks_style	List of networks to be trusted. Networks may be specified as IP address/netmask pairs, or you may provide a filename for a file in which the information is stored.
relay_domains	$mydestination	Machines and domains listed explicitly by name.

When run from Linux, the default `mynetworks_style` setting means that Postfix will relay mail from any computer with an IP address in the same subnet as the server itself. For instance, if the mail server computer has an IP address of `172.25.98.7` with a netmask of `255.255.255.0`, the server will relay mail from any computer on the `172.25.98.0/24` network. In addition, the `relay_domains` default means that the server will relay mail from any computer specified in the `mydestination` option or in computers within the specified domain. For instance, if you have a `mydestination` specification that includes `pangaea.edu`, Postfix will relay from any computer in the `pangaea.edu` domain.

WARNING   If you're running Postfix on a computer that uses a dial-up Internet connection, its default configuration enables it to relay for all users of the ISP's subnet. This configuration is a spam risk, so you may want to tighten your Postfix settings.

As an antispam measure, you might want to limit Postfix's relaying capabilities. This might be particularly important if you've set `mydestination` to include a domain for which the server shouldn't serve as a relay, or if that domain's systems are already covered by IP address in the `mynetworks` or `mynetworks_style` options. To do so, you might provide a restrictive `relay_domains` configuration, such as:

```
relay_domains = $myhostname, localhost, localhost.localdomain
```

If you're running Postfix on a workstation, you might want to prevent the server from relaying mail for anything but the workstation computer itself. (This configuration accepts mail both from the local computer to anywhere and from anywhere to the local computer.) For this configuration, you must combine the tight `relay_domains` limit with a tight `mynetworks_style` definition:

```
mynetworks_style = host
```

If Postfix is running on a larger mail server and you want to expand the computers for which it will relay, the simplest way is usually to create an expanded `relay_domains` definition. For instance, to relay mail for the default systems plus `threeroomco.com`'s systems, you might use the following line:

```
relay_domains = $mydestination, threeroomco.com
```

CONFIGURING POSTFIX TO USE A RELAY

If you're configuring Postfix on a workstation or other system that should relay mail through another mail server, the configuration is fairly straightforward. Typically, you need to set the `relayhost` option to the name of the mail server you should use. For instance, to set your system to use `mail.example.com` as the mail relay, you would use the following line:

```
relayhost = mail.example.com
```

Alternatively, if you want to use the computer to which a domain's MX record points, you can provide the domain name rather than the hostname. Postfix then does an MX record lookup and sends mail to the domain's mail server. This configuration may be preferable if the name of the outgoing mail server is likely to change; you needn't adjust your Postfix configuration when this happens.

Running Exim

Although it's not used by as many major Linux distributions as sendmail or Postfix, Exim is roughly comparable to its competing mail servers in capabilities. Like Postfix, Exim uses a single major configuration file that's well commented. This file is called /etc/exim/exim.conf on Debian, the one major distribution to use this server. When you install Exim on Debian, the package management system runs a script, eximconfig, that asks a series of questions to set the default values in the Exim configuration file. Naturally, you can change the configuration at a later time, either by editing exim.conf directly or by running eximconfig manually.

Configuring the Hostname

The primary setting in /etc/exim/exim.conf that affects the apparent hostname is qualify_domain. This option sets the domain name that's added to mail from local users if the mail reader program doesn't provide one. You set this and other Exim options much as you set options in Postfix, using an equal sign:

```
qualify_domain = pangaea.edu
```

Exim doesn't provide quite the sort of options for altering the hostname in outgoing messages that sendmail and Postfix provide. Instead, Exim provides a generalized address rewriting mechanism. This system is called from /etc/exim/exim.conf using lines like the following, which appear near the end of the file:

```
*@pangaea.edu      ${lookup{$1}lsearch{/etc/email-addresses}\
                               {$value}fail} frFs
```

This line tells Exim to use /etc/email-addresses as a file that contains substitution pairs for the pangaea.edu domain. If you like, you can duplicate this line and change the domain at the start of the line and the lookup file in order to support changes for additional domains. The lookup file contains lines such as the following:

```
ben: bfranklin@pangaea.edu
sally: sally@threeroomco.com
```

These lines tell the system to change any outgoing mail originating from ben to appear to come from bfranklin@pangaea.edu, and to change mail from sally to appear to come from sally@threeroomco.com.

Accepting Incoming Mail

Exim can be configured to accept mail addressed in a variety of ways as local mail. The three primary options for doing so are summarized in Table 25.3. After installing Exim on Debian, chances are the local_domains option will be set to include localhost, your computer's hostname, and possibly your computer's domain name. Given this configuration, setting local_domains_include_host to true is redundant; the inclusion of the hostname in local_domains does the job.

TABLE 25.3: COMMON EXIM LOCAL DELIVERY OPTIONS

OPTION	DEFAULT VALUE	MEANING
local_domains	value of qualify_ recipient option	Colon-delimited list of names of domains or hosts that Exim is to treat as local.
local_domains_include_host	true	Whether or not to accept mail addressed to the computer's host-name as local.
local_domains_include_host_literals	true	Whether or not to accept mail addressed to the computer's IP address as local.

Exim Relay Configuration Options

Exim's mail relay options are roughly comparable to those of sendmail or Postfix. You can tell Exim to accept mail for relay based on an assortment of criteria, and you can tell Exim to send outgoing mail through another mail server configured as a relay.

CONFIGURING EXIM TO RELAY MAIL

The main Exim relay configuration option is host_accept_relay. This option accepts a colon-delimited set of host and network specifications. You can list systems by hostname, IP address, network/netmask combinations, or domain names preceded by an asterisk (*) wildcard. For instance, you might use the following line:

```
host_accept_relay = localhost:*.pangaea.edu:172.25.98.0/24:172.25.97.6
```

This line tells the system to accept relayed mail from localhost, the pangaea.edu domain, the 172.98.0/24 network, and 172.25.97.6. Several other methods of authorizing relaying also exist, although some of these alternatives partially duplicate functionality present in host_accept_relay. For instance, relay_domains enables you to specify domains for which Exim should relay mail, but using an asterisk wildcard with host_accept_relay accomplishes the same goal.

As with other mail servers, you should be cautious about authorizing relays. A too-broad configuration can be abused by spammers and lead other servers to refuse to accept mail from your server.

CONFIGURING EXIM TO USE A RELAY

Configuring Exim to use an outgoing mail relay involves more than a single configuration line. The Debian Exim configuration script (eximconfig), which is run when you install Exim, can optionally create the necessary configuration. If you prefer, you can enter the configuration in /etc/exim/exim.conf yourself. Although you'll have to alter the name of the outgoing mail server, the relevant lines look like this:

```
smarthost:
  driver = domainlist
```

```
    transport = remote_smtp
    route_list = "* mail.example.com bydns_a"
end
```

These lines appear near the end of the `exim.conf` file, between sections that control directors and retry configuration. The section is preceded by a series of comments specifying that the section controls routers. This configuration directs all outgoing mail to pass through `mail.example.com`. Mail addressed to systems that match the `local_domains` specification isn't passed through the relay mail server, though; that mail is delivered locally.

Delivering Mail to Clients with POP or IMAP

In years past, users often logged onto mail server computers using remote login protocols such as Telnet in order to read mail locally using mail readers such as Pine (`http://www.washington.edu/pine/`) or ELM (`http://www.instinct.org/elm/`). Such configurations are still workable today, but a more common configuration involves mail clients running on desktop or workstation systems. These clients connect to the mail server computer using a pull protocol such as POP or IMAP. This configuration allows users to run mail readers that utilize whatever GUI environment the users prefer. A POP or IMAP server can handle clients that run under Windows, Mac OS, Linux, OS/2, BeOS, or almost any other OS.

If you choose to run POP or IMAP, your first decision regards the POP or IMAP server. You must pick which protocol you want to support as well as the specific server package. Once that's done, you must install and configure the pull mail server and test it to be sure it works as intended.

Choosing the Right POP or IMAP Server

Before rushing to install a pull mail server, you must understand the differences between the major pull mail server protocols and the individual products that are available in this arena. In some cases, it doesn't much matter which protocol or server you select, but in others, the differences can be quite important.

POP VERSUS IMAP

The two major pull mail protocols are POP and IMAP. Although some more exotic protocols also exist, these two protocols dominate the field. Most modern mail clients support one or both of these protocols, and a few support more exotic protocols. Both POP and IMAP perform basically the same task: Client programs connect, retrieve e-mail, and disconnect. The client programs display a list of available messages and enable users to read these messages, archive them, reply to them, and so on.

NOTE   POP and IMAP are both pull mail protocols, so a mail client can retrieve mail from the POP or IMAP server. To send mail, a mail client uses another protocol—typically SMTP. Small networks are often configured such that mail clients use the same computer for an outgoing SMTP server that they use for incoming POP or IMAP mail. Larger networks sometimes use physically separate computers for these two functions in order to better spread the mail-delivery load. There can also be security advantages to separating these two functions, as well. For instance, pull mail servers use passwords that might be compromised. Running your network's world-accessible SMTP server on a system that doesn't have many ordinary users minimizes the risk that it could be abused by a cracker using a stolen password. You can block external access to your pull mail server, minimizing the chance that it could be abused.

Although they fill roughly the same role, POP and IMAP aren't identical protocols. Some of their important differences include:

Mail Storage   POP users typically retrieve their messages from the server and then immediately delete the messages from the server. Long-term archival of messages occurs on client systems. IMAP, on the other hand, was designed to enable users to store messages in folders on the IMAP server computer. As a result, an IMAP server may need to devote more disk space to user mail directories than a POP server. IMAP may also require more network bandwidth in the long run, although IMAP's partial retrieval options (which are described next) can mitigate this need or even give IMAP an advantage, depending on how your users interact with their mail systems. One big advantage to IMAP's system is that it enables users to access mail using different mail client programs or even different computers, without having to copy mail files between systems.

Partial Retrieval Options   POP mail retrieval is all-or-none. Clients can either retrieve a message in its entirety (using nothing but a number to identify it) or leave the message on the server. IMAP is more flexible; it supports retrieving various parts of a message, such as its header separately from its body. Therefore, with IMAP, users can delete messages they know they don't want without retrieving the bulk of the message text. With obvious spams and worms, this feature can save your network substantial amounts of bandwidth.

Client Support   Although POP and IMAP are both widely supported, POP support is more common than that for IMAP. If your users already have preferred mail clients, you may want to check their configuration options to learn what pull mail protocols they support.

Your decision of whether to support POP, IMAP, or both will boil down to a study of these factors. As a general rule, IMAP is the more flexible protocol, but you may prefer to force mail off of the mail server and onto clients as quickly as possible. In that case, using POP makes sense. If your users frequently use multiple computers, IMAP has a certain advantage in convenience for users. This advantage may be negated if users must call in on slow dial-up lines, though; in that case, local mail storage will result in quicker mail reading, at least after the first reading.

Both POP and IMAP are available in several different versions. In 2003, the latest versions are POP3 and IMAP4. Earlier versions of both are still in use at some sites, and you may need to support earlier versions for some older clients. In the case of IMAP, support for earlier versions is usually automatic. POP2, though, uses a different port (109) than does POP3 (110). IMAP uses port 143.

PICKING THE RIGHT PACKAGE

Pull mail servers tend to be much simpler than push mail servers. Essentially, pull mail servers are local mail clients, much like Pine or ELM. The difference is that they deliver mail to another computer using their own pull protocols instead of displaying mail to users who are logged in on the console, via SSH or the like. As a result, pull mail servers tend to lurk almost unnoticed. Nonetheless, several different pull mail servers are available for Linux:

UW IMAP   Despite its name, the University of Washington IMAP server (`http://www`
`.washington.edu/imap/`) supports POP2, POP3, and IMAP. The POP servers use the IMAP server behind the scenes. This set of servers is extremely common; it ships with most Linux distributions, usually in a package called `imap` or `uw-imapd`. The IMAP server stores user mail

folders in users' home directories, which can be awkward if users also log into their accounts and store nonmail files there.

Cyrus IMAP   Like UW IMAP, Cyrus IMAP (`http://asg.web.cmu.edu/cyrus/imapd/`) supports more than just IMAP. Specifically, Cyrus IMAP supports IMAP, POP3, and a Kerberos-enabled POP3 variant (KPOP). This server stores IMAP mail folders in a proprietary file format in its own directory tree, so it can be a good choice if users store nonmail files in their home directories.

nupop   This server is designed for quick and efficient handling of POP3 requests. Its goals are accomplished, in part, by discarding support for IMAP and other protocols. You can learn more at `http://nupop.nuvox.net`.

popa3d   This server, like `nupop`, is a POP-only server designed for efficiency. Its website (`http://www.openwall.com/popa3d/`) also emphasizes the developers' attention to security.

Courier   The Courier mail server (`http://www.courier-mta.org`) is an integrated set of SMTP, POP, and IMAP servers. Although the Courier SMTP server isn't very popular in Linux, the IMAP server can be installed separately, and it has a modest following.

Qpopper   This POP3 server was originally a commercial product released by the same people who developed the popular Eudora client and server packages. With version 4.0, though, Qpopper has gone open source. You can learn more at `http://www.eudora.com/qpopper/`.

qmail-pop3d   This POP3 server ships with the qmail SMTP server (`http://www.qmail.org`). As such, it can be a good choice if you use qmail as your SMTP server, but isn't a good choice if you use another SMTP server.

One critical consideration when picking a pull mail server is the message file formats the server supports. All of the major mail servers covered in depth in this chapter (sendmail, Postfix, and Exim) use a format known as *mbox*, in which messages in a mail folder are stored in a single file. Typically, SMTP servers or their helper programs store users' files in `/var/spool/mail/`*username*. IMAP servers that use mbox format use files of the same type for mail directories in users' home directories, subdirectories thereof, or special IMAP mail server directories.

The qmail server, by contrast, stores its incoming mail in another format: a *maildir*. The maildir format devotes one directory to each mail folder and puts each message in its own file. Typically, incoming maildirs are stored in users' home directories. IMAP servers that use maildirs typically store them in users' home directories. Although qmail uses maildirs by default, it can be configured to use the mbox format. Similarly, Postfix and Exim can both be configured to use maildirs.

The UW IMAP, Cyrus IMAP, and Qpopper servers all use mbox format for incoming mail. UW IMAP also uses mbox for IMAP mail folders. Cyrus IMAP uses its own unique format for mail folders. The `nupop`, Courier, and `qmail-pop3d` servers all use the maildir format. If a given pull server looks appealing but uses the "wrong" mail storage format compared to your SMTP server, you'll have to replace your SMTP server, reconfigure your SMTP server, or pick a different pull mail server.

One issue you should consider when installing and configuring a pull mail server is password security. In a typical configuration, the traditional POP and IMAP servers require password authentication—users must enter their usernames and passwords. Most servers authenticate users against the normal Linux username and password database. The basic protocols deliver the username and password over an unencrypted link. As a consequence, a miscreant with the appropriate access can sniff the password, as described in Chapter 18, "System Security." Some servers support encrypted variants of the standard protocols, but these variants require support in the mail clients. Another approach is to use the Secure Shell (SSH) to *tunnel* the pull mail protocol over an encrypted link—that is, to encrypt the pull mail data and pass it over an encrypted connection. This approach requires configuring SSH on the server and on all the clients, though. If you don't want to go to this effort, you may want to consider setting aside special mail-only accounts and instruct users to create unique passwords for these accounts. Ideally, you can create these accounts on a dedicated pull mail server computer. This practice will at least minimize the damage that a miscreant might do if pull mail passwords are compromised. You may also want to restrict access to your POP or IMAP ports using firewall rules, TCP Wrappers, or xinetd access restrictions, as described in Chapter 20, "Controlling Network Access."

Installing UW IMAP

Because it's readily available, ships with all major Linux distributions, and supports both POP and IMAP, this section describes the installation and configuration of UW IMAP. This server should work well with only a few tweaks in conjunction with sendmail, Postfix, or Exim. If you use qmail, though, you'll have to reconfigure qmail to use the mbox format. Consult the qmail documentation for details. Alternatively, you could use qmail-pop3d, Courier, or some other pull mail server instead of UW IMAP.

The first step in using UW IMAP is to install the package. Do so using whatever method your distribution supports, as described in Chapter 11, "Managing Packages." Most distributions ship UW IMAP under the name imap or uw-imapd. Unfortunately, Debian's uw-imapd package doesn't include support for POP, so if you want to use POP with Debian, you must either install UW IMAP from another source or use another server. Debian ships with the popa3d server, which works much like UW IMAP's POP support, except that the filenames are different (popa3d versus ipop3d).

Once the server is installed, you must activate it. UW IMAP's servers are designed to be run from super servers, as described in Chapter 22, "Running Servers." If you're using Debian, Slackware, or SuSE, this means editing /etc/inetd.conf. The lines that will activate the POP2, POP3, and IMAP servers, respectively, are:

```
pop2 stream tcp nowait root /usr/sbin/tcpd ipop2d
pop3 stream tcp nowait root /usr/sbin/tcpd ipop3d
imap stream tcp nowait root /usr/sbin/tcpd imapd
```

You may find lines like these in your /etc/inetd.conf already, but they may be commented out with a hash mark (#) at the start of each line. If so, you should uncomment the lines to activate the configuration. Some systems ship with multiple POP or IMAP configurations, one for each of several servers. If you find more than one for each server type, be sure to uncomment the correct line.

WARNING *If you want to support only one pull mail protocol, don't activate any others! Doing so would pose a potential security risk. For instance, if you don't want or need to support POP, uncommenting the* ipop2d *or* ipop3d *servers' configurations would leave your system vulnerable if a security flaw in these servers, but not in the* imapd *server, were found.*

If you use Red Hat or Mandrake, the imap package installs five files in /etc/xinetd.d: ipop2, ipop3, pop3s, imap, and imaps. Each of these files launches one pull mail server. (The files whose names end in s launch versions with encryption enabled.) With the exception of Mandrake's ipop3 file, all of these files ship with a disable = yes line, which has the effect of disabling the server. To activate a server, you must change yes to no on this line, comment the line out, or use a tool such as chkconfig (as described in Chapter 22) to enable the server.

Whether you use inetd or xinetd, you must restart the super server or tell it to reload its configuration file after you change your super server configuration. In most cases, typing **killall -HUP inetd** or **killall -HUP xinetd** should do the trick.

The UW IMAP servers are very simple; they don't read configuration files or accept arguments to alter their behavior. Once you've configured your super server to launch these servers, they should work. Try configuring a mail client to use your pull mail server to test the server's behavior. Figure 25.2 shows the relevant dialog box from KMail. To access this dialog box, select Settings ➤ Configure KMail, select the Network icon in the list on the left side of the dialog box, click the Receiving tab, and click the Add button or select an existing account and click Modify. (If you select Add, KMail asks what type of account you want to add. Figure 25.2 corresponds to modifying an IMAP account.) Precisely how you adjust the accounts in other mail clients varies by client; consult your mail reader's documentation for details.

WARNING   *Most mail clients enable you to store pull mail passwords locally. In Figure 25.2, this option is called Store IMAP Password in Configuration File. Such options are convenient, but potentially risky, because your password may be compromised if a miscreant gains access to your account. Indeed, if the configuration file is readable to other users, a miscreant might be able to steal your password from another person's account. For these reasons, I recommend you use your pull mail password only for mail retrieval, particularly if you store it in your mail reader's configuration file.*

FIGURE 25.2

Mail clients must be told where to find a POP or IMAP server.

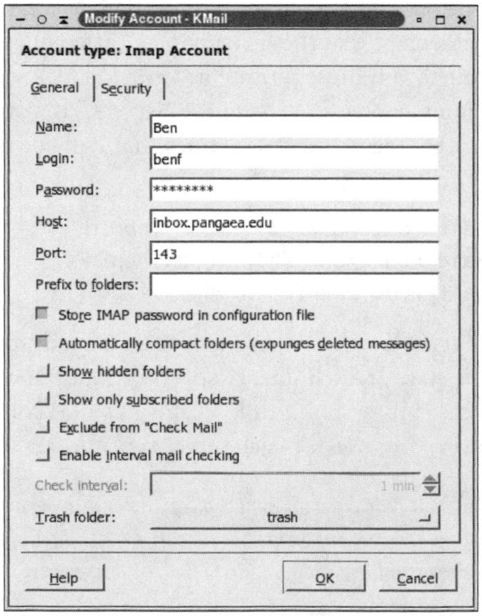

If you have problems, I recommend you try several diagnostic procedures:

◆ Try using Telnet to connect to the relevant port (109 for POP2, 110 for POP3, or 143 for IMAP). For instance, you might type `telnet inbox.pangaea.edu 143`. You should be greeted by some sort of prompt. If you can connect, you know that the problem is with client/server handshaking, authentication, or the like. If you can't connect, the problem could be a bad super server configuration or interference from a firewall or other security measure.

◆ Try using a mail client on the pull mail server itself, or at least try the Telnet procedure from the pull mail server. This test will help uncover problems that are due to security settings that affect local and remote systems differently, as is common with firewall security settings.

◆ Check the pull mail server's log files. Frequently, `/var/log/messages`, `/var/log/mail`, or a similar file will hold messages from the pull mail server that may give a clue about the source of the problem, such as an authentication error.

Stopping the Junk Mail

The bane of every e-mail administrator's existence is *unsolicited bulk email (UBE)*, more commonly known as *spam*. Spam is usually, but not always, commercial in nature. (Commercial spam is sometimes called *unsolicited commercial e-mail*, or *UCE*.) Whatever its contents, spam is a growing problem. Spam clogs mail servers' hard disks, consumes network bandwidth, and causes system administrators to waste valuable time answering questions about and otherwise combating it. Worse, some forms of spam are actually harmful to individuals. Spam is now a popular means of propagating illegal pyramid schemes, advertising child pornography, and worse. One particular type of spam, so-called *419 scams*, named after the Nigerian law they violate, has been associated with murders perpetrated against some of its victims. (See `http://www.crimes-of-persuasion.com/Crimes/Business/nigerian.htm` for details.)

Although spams that lead to loss of life are extremely rare, controlling spam is nonetheless a desirable goal, and one you should consider when you run a mail server. The type of spam upon which you're probably most focused is incoming spam—you want to keep the spams from clogging your hard disk and consuming your network bandwidth. Just as important, though, is controlling outgoing spam. If all mail server and network administrators kept their systems from sending spam, the problem would vanish. By securing your system against abuse, you can help reduce the severity of the problem for others.

Stopping Incoming Spam

As a mail server administrator, you probably want to minimize the amount of spam your system processes. Numerous techniques for combating spam have been developed over the years. Unfortunately, none is perfect. All spam-fighting techniques miss some incoming spam (so-called *misses*) or misclassify some legitimate e-mail as spam (so-called *false positives*). You can select one or more spam-fighting techniques to minimize one or both of these types of errors, and you may be able to adjust a spam criterion to decrease one type of error at the expense of increasing the other. It's usually better to let a spam through than to delete a legitimate e-mail, so most antispam tools are weighted in favor of producing misses compared to false positives.

This section begins with a summary of the most popular techniques used to fight spam. It continues with more information on two of the most popular techniques: blackhole lists and Procmail filters.

A RUNDOWN OF SPAM-FIGHTING TECHNIQUES

Spam-fighting techniques range from tools designed to stop spam before it reaches your mail servers to those that scan message contents in an effort to identify spams based on the language they contain. As a general rule, spam-fighting tools fall into one or more of several categories:

Blackhole Lists   Spammers tend to send spam from the same computers time after time. The spammer may control the IP address or may be abusing a server that's misconfigured as an *open relay*, meaning that it will relay from any computer to any other computer. In any event, this characteristic means that your mail server can reject mail based on its originating IP address. This technique generally uses one of dozens of *blackhole lists*, which are accessible from servers that use the DNS protocols in a unique way. If the blackhole list's DNS server returns a special name for an IP address, that address is on the blackhole list and the mail may well be a spam. Check `http://www.declude.com/junkmail/support/ip4r.htm` for a very long list of blackhole lists and a brief description of the criteria each uses for listing IP addresses.

Mail Server Pattern Matches   Some mail servers support pattern matching tools that can be used to spot suspicious data in mail headers or even in message texts. For instance, if your system regularly receives mail with a forged return address of `we@spam4u.com`, you can have the mail server refuse such mail, independently of the IP address of the sending system. Exim has very extensive pattern matching tools, and Postfix's tools are not far behind in this respect.

Post-Server Pattern Matches   Many mail configurations use a program known as Procmail (`http://www.procmail.org`) to add filtering capabilities to e-mail after the fact. Procmail uses a pattern-matching file built on *recipes*, which are descriptions of patterns and actions to be taken in response to those patterns. You can use Procmail to filter message headers or bodies. You can also use Procmail to "glue together" other spam-fighting tools.

Spam Databases   One unusual spam-fighting tool is Vipul's Razor (`http://razor.sourceforge.net`). This system uses an online database of known spam messages. The database includes a checksum for each message. Your computer computes a checksum for each message it receives and looks for that checksum in the database. If a match is found, the message is presumed to be spam and can be discarded or flagged. If no match is found, the message is either legitimate or is a very recent spam. (Vipul's Razor relies on rapid addition of spams to its database.)

Statistical Filters   The latest spam-fighting craze is *statistical* (or *Bayesian*, after the statistical rule they most commonly employ) spam filtering. Statistical spam filtering took off after Paul Graham described an effective statistical filter in his "Plan for Spam" essay (`http://www.paulgraham.com/spam.html`). This field is rapidly changing and includes both stand-alone filters, such as Graham's original filter and Bogofilter (`http://sourceforge.net/projects/bogofilter/`), and filters implemented in individual mail clients.

Each of these techniques has its strong and weak points. Blackhole lists and mail server pattern matches can block spam before the bulk of the spam is transmitted to your system, which can conserve bandwidth and CPU time. On the other hand, these techniques tend to be fairly indiscriminate; they produce a lot of false positives. (In-server pattern matches can be tuned, of course; a conservative set of rules may produce few false positives, but it probably won't catch much spam, either.) The remaining techniques require that spams be received in full before they can be analyzed, so they can't help to conserve your network bandwidth. Statistical filters and pattern matches can be tuned very well for individual users, but when applied to a large site, they're more likely to miss spam or produce false positives, because different individuals receive different legitimate and spam e-mail. Spam databases can be very effective, but they are also subject to "poisoning"—a widely distributed but legitimate e-mail (such as a legitimate mailing list's posting) can be added to the database in error or in malice, causing problems for many users.

For these reasons, many sites employ several antispam techniques. For instance, a conservative blackhole list or set of in-server pattern matches might block some of the most egregious spam, while Procmail filters or a statistical filter can be used to block more spam. These filters might be supplemented by filters customized for individual users. One very popular tool that attempts to combine many spam-fighting techniques, but that emphasizes pattern matches, is SpamAssassin (`http://spamassassin.org`).

Using Blackhole Lists

Blackhole list configuration varies greatly from one mail server to another, but all of the major mail servers support this method of fighting spam. In all cases, you need the address of a blackhole list's server to begin, so consult the list at `http://www.declude.com/junkmail/support/ip4r.htm`, or some other list, to locate one.

If you're using sendmail, you must add a line to your `m4` configuration file and rebuild the `sendmail.cf` file in order to use a blackhole list. The line in question looks something like this:

```
FEATURE(dnsbl, `blackhole.list.address', `Rejected - see
    ➥http://blackhole.list.website')
```

This line tells sendmail to use the blackhole list whose server is located at *blackhole.list.address*. It also includes a message in bounced mail to check *http://blackhole.list.website* for further information. This message can be important for users whose legitimate mail runs afoul of the spam filter. These users can read the website and send mail from another account or complain to their own mail administrators, who should be in a position to take corrective measures.

The Postfix blackhole list configuration involves two lines. The first sets the address or addresses of blackhole list servers and the second tells Postfix to use those servers:

```
maps_rbl_domains = blackhole.list.address
smtpd_client_restrictions = reject_maps_rbl
```

NOTE   The `smtpd_client_restrictions` *option can take additional values, such as* `reject_unknown_client`, *to implement additional types of antispam measures. Consult the Postfix documentation for details.*

Exim provides extensive support for blackhole lists. The most important `exim.conf` option is `rbl_domains`, in which you list the blackhole list server:

```
rbl_domains = blackhole.list.address
```

Ordinarily, an entry like this causes the server to reject mail from sites in the blackhole list. You can append the string `/warn` to the address, though, to cause Exim to add a warning header to the mail rather than reject it outright. Other filters, such as a Procmail filter, might use this header to flag a message for stricter spam-detection processing. Consult the Exim documentation for details on additional blackhole list options.

USING PROCMAIL FILTERS

Most Linux mail servers either use Procmail by default or can be configured to do so by setting a configuration file option. If you follow the instructions outlined in the next few paragraphs and find that Procmail isn't working, you can try creating a `.forward` file in your home directory that contains the following line:

```
"|/path/to/procmail"
```

Replace `/path/to` with the name of the directory in which the `procmail` binary resides. If even this doesn't work, you may need to consult the documentation for Procmail or for your mail server. Once Procmail is in the picture, the system reads the global `/etc/procmailrc` configuration file and the `.procmailrc` file in users' home directories. These files contain Procmail recipes, which take the following form:

```
:0 [flags] [:[lockfile]]
[conditions]
action
```

WARNING   *The system-wide `/etc/procmailrc` file is usually read and processed as* `root`. *This fact means that a poorly designed recipe in that file could do serious damage. For instance, a typo could cause Procmail to overwrite an important system binary rather than use that binary to process a message. For this reason, you should keep system-wide Procmail processing to a minimum and instead focus on using `~/.procmailrc` to process mail using individuals' accounts.*

Each recipe begins with the string `:0`. Various flags may follow, as summarized in Table 25.4. You can combine these flags to produce more complex effects. For instance, using *flags* of HB causes matching to be done on both the message headers and the body. The *lockfile* is the name of a file that Procmail uses to signal that it's working with a file. If Procmail sees a lockfile, it delays work on the affected file until the lockfile disappears. Ordinarily, a single colon (`:`) suffices for this function; Procmail then picks a lockfile name itself. You can specify a filename if you prefer, though.

TABLE 25.4: COMMON PROCMAIL RECIPE FLAGS

FLAG	MEANING
H	Matching is done to the message headers. (This is the default.)
B	Matching is done to the message body.

Continued on next page

TABLE 25.4: COMMON PROCMAIL RECIPE FLAGS *(continued)*

FLAG	MEANING
D	Matching is done in a case-sensitive manner. (The default is a case-insensitive match.)
c	Matching is done on a "carbon copy" of the message. The "original" is passed on for matching against subsequent recipes. This flag is generally used within nesting blocks (described shortly).
w	Procmail waits for the *action* to complete. If it doesn't complete successfully, the message is matched against subsequent recipes.
W	The same as a flag of w, but it suppresses program failure messages.

The *conditions* in a Procmail recipe are essentially ordinary regular expressions, but each *conditions* line begins with an asterisk. Most characters in a regular expression match against the same characters in the message, but there are exceptions. For instance, a caret (^) denotes the start of a line, a dot (.) matches any single character except for a new line, and the combination of a dot and an asterisk (.*) denotes a string of any length. A regular expression may include a string in parentheses, often with a vertical bar (|) within it. This condition denotes a match against the string on either side of the vertical bar. A backslash (\) effectively undoes special formatting in the following character; for instance, to match an asterisk, you would specify the string *. An exclamation mark (!) reverses the sense of a match, so that a recipe matches any message that does *not* meet the specified criteria. Each recipe can have no, one, or more *conditions*. (Using no *conditions* is usually done within nesting blocks or for backing up messages when you experiment with new recipes.) If a recipe includes several *conditions*, all must match for the recipe to apply. The Procmail man page describes these regular expressions in more detail.

Finally, a Procmail recipe ends with a single line that tells it what to do—the *action*. An *action* line may be any of several things:

A Filename Reference   Procmail stores the message in the named file in mbox format. To store messages in the maildir format, append a slash (/) to the end of the filename. For spam fighting, one effective but drastic measure is to store spam in /dev/null. This action effectively deletes the spam.

An External Program   If the *action* line begins with a vertical bar (|), Procmail treats the line as a program to be executed. You can use this feature to pass processing on to another tool, such as a statistical spam filter.

An E-Mail Address   An exclamation mark (!) at the start of a line denotes an e-mail address; Procmail sends the message to the specified address instead of delivering it locally.

A Nesting Block   An *action* line that begins with an open curly brace ({) denotes a nested recipe. The nested recipe takes the same form as any other recipe, but it is used only if the surrounding recipe matches the message. The nested recipe ends with a close curly brace (}).

As an example, consider Listing 25.2, which demonstrates many of the features of Procmail recipes. I have found variants of these recipes to be effective at blocking many spams, but of course your experience may differ.

LISTING 25.2: SAMPLE PROCMAIL RECIPES

```
# Don't apply recipes to postmaster
:0
*!^To:.*postmaster@(pangaea\.edu|smtp\.pangaea\.edu)
{
    # Block mail with more than five spaces in the Subject: header,
    # unless it's from the local fax subsystem
    :0
    *^Subject:.*        .*
    *!^From: root@fax\.pangaea\.edu \(Fax Getty\)
    /dev/null

    # Pass mail with bright red text through a custom spam blocking script
    :0 B
    *^.*\<html
    *^.*\<font color.*ff0000
    |/usr/local/bin/spam-block "mail with bright red text"

    # Stuff that's not to me.
    :0
    *!^(To|Cc):.*(pangaea\.edu|ben@example\.com)
    !sam@iwantspam.org
}
```

NOTE   *Listing 25.2 indents recipes within the nesting block. This practice improves readability, but isn't required.*

Listing 25.2 includes four recipes. Three of them are embedded within the fourth:

◆   The surrounding recipe matches any To: header that does *not* include the string postmaster@pangaea.edu or postmaster@smtp.pangaea.edu. This recipe uses the open curly brace ({) character to cause the included recipes to be applied only if the mail is not addressed to postmaster. The intent is to protect the postmaster's mail from the antispam rules. After all, users might forward spam to the postmaster account to complain about it, and such complaints should not be ignored.

◆   A great deal of spam includes five or more consecutive spaces in the Subject: header. The first true spam rule discards such messages. This rule matches all messages with five or more spaces in the Subject: header except for messages that are from the fax subsystem on the fax.pangaea.edu computer, which presumably generates nonspam fax delivery reports that would otherwise match this criterion. This recipe discards the spam by sending it to /dev/null.

◆ The second spam rule matches all messages that contain Hyptertext Markup Language (HTML) text that sets the font color to `ff0000`—that is, bright red. A great deal of spam uses this technique to catch readers' eyes, but in my experience, no legitimate mail uses this technique. This recipe passes the spam through a special program, `/usr/local/bin/spam-block`, which is not a standard program. I use it in Listing 25.2 as an example of using Procmail to pass a message through an outside program. This example includes a message string that's passed to the outside program along with the spam.

◆ The final spam rule matches messages that do not contain the local domain name (`pangaea.edu`) or a special exception username (`ben@example.com`) in the `From:` or `Cc:` headers. A rule like this one can be very effective at catching spam, but it can be dangerous when applied system-wide. The problem is that mailing lists, newsletters, and the like may not include the recipients' names in these headers, so the rule needs to be customized for all the mailing lists and other subscription e-mail a recipient receives. Doing this for a large site is a virtual impossibility. This rule will also discard most mail sent to a recipient using a mailer's blind carbon copy (BCC) feature, which causes the recipient name not to appear in any header. This rule uses the exclamation mark action to e-mail the suspected spam to `sam@iwantspam.org`. In practice, you're unlikely to e-mail your spam to any site, though; this use in Listing 25.2 is meant more as a demonstration of what Procmail *can* do than as a practical suggestion of what you *should* do with spam.

WARNING *Some spam-fighting tools include provisions to send "bounce" messages to the spam's sender. This practice is reasonably safe when applied in a mail server; the bounce message is generated while the sender is still connected, so the bounce message's recipient is likely to be the correct recipient. You should not attempt to bounce spam from a Procmail recipe or a mail reader, though. Doing so will usually send the bounce message to the wrong address—often a completely bogus address, but sometimes an innocent individual whose address was forged in the spam. Thus, bouncing spam once it's been accepted by your SMTP server will only add to the spam problem.*

Overall, Procmail is an extremely useful and powerful tool for combating spam. Because many pattern matches are best applied to individual accounts, I recommend using it in this way rather than as a system-wide filter. There are exceptions, though; some rules are general enough that you may want to apply them system-wide. Also, some tools build on Procmail in a way that's useful when they're applied system-wide.

Stopping Outgoing Spam

Stopping incoming spam is largely a matter of configuring your mail server and ancillary programs to detect spam and block it. Stopping outgoing spam presents a different set of challenges. In principle, you could apply tests similar to those used to detect incoming spam to messages your server relays for authorized hosts, or to mail that originates on the server itself. In fact, large ISPs may employ such tests. Most smaller sites, though, use two methods to minimize the risk that they'll become spam sources:

Clearly Stating Acceptable Use Policies The first step in preventing your system from becoming a spam source is to clearly articulate an acceptable use policy (AUP) and to ensure that all of your users understand this policy. On a very small network, such as a home network, this task can be done informally. For most business sites, it's best done through a formal document of some sort. Users must understand that any mail sent to more than a handful of recipients is suspect. (Of course, not all mass e-mail is spam; true opt-in newsletters, mailing lists, and so on are not spam. Unfortunately, many spams claim to be these legitimate forms of mass e-mail, which muddies the waters.) Your policy should state what action will be taken in case of an AUP violation.

Anti-Relay Configurations   One source of spam is hijacked mail servers. Spammers frequently look for open relays, which they can use to send mail to any recipient. Spammers do this because they can rely on the open relay to do most of the work, limiting their connect times and keeping their own ISPs' mail servers out of the loop, minimizing the chance that they'll be caught before their spam run is complete. The preceding sections, "Running Sendmail," "Running Postfix," and "Running Exim," all described relay configurations. You should use as limited a relay configuration as your system can manage. For workstations, this means that the system should relay only local e-mail. For most small networks' mail servers, the system should be configured to relay only the local network's mail.

Many websites offer advice on helping you keep your mail server from becoming a source of spam. One of the best of these is the Mail Abuse Prevention System (MAPS) Transport Security Initiative (TSI) site, `http://mail-abuse.org/tsi/`. One helpful test you can perform is a third-party relay test of your system. MAPS operates an automated relay test. To use it, type `telnet relay-test.mail-abuse.org` *from the system you want to test.* Initiating a Telnet connection in this way causes the MAPS server to perform a series of relay tests on your mail server. You'll see them run in your Telnet session, followed by a summary of any problems found. The MAPS TSI website also provides advice on securing a variety of mail servers.

If you become a spam source, chances are you'll hear complaints quickly enough. Correct the problem immediately. If necessary, take your mail server offline while you fix the server. Note, though, that a complaint doesn't necessarily mean your system is really to blame. Most spammers routinely forge their return addresses, and some deliberately or accidentally pick valid hostnames as return addresses. Recipients who don't look at the mail headers, or who don't know how to interpret them, may complain to the forged return address.

If you find that mail from your site is bouncing because your system is on a blackhole list, investigate further. It's possible that your system is an open relay or one of your users has been abusing your server. It's also possible that your server's IP address used to belong to a spammer. In this case, contacting the blackhole list maintainer should result in quick removal from the list, clearing up problems. A few blackhole lists don't contain actual spammer IP addresses, but just addresses that the list maintainers believe shouldn't be sending mail directly. The largest such class of addresses is those assigned by ISPs to end users, typically as dial-up IP addresses for Point-to-Point Protocol (PPP) connections. The reasoning is that end users should relay mail through their ISPs' own mail servers, which should not appear on blackhole lists. If you're using such an account, the easiest solution is to configure your mail server to relay through your ISP's mail server. Of course, if your ISP's mail server is unreliable or appears on another blackhole list, you have a problem. This problem's roots, though, are firmly planted in your ISP's soil, so the best solution may be to change to another ISP.

Using Fetchmail

Most of this chapter assumes that you're installing an SMTP server, and possibly a POP or IMAP server, on a computer that's part of an ordinary SMTP mail path, as depicted in Figure 25.1. Sometimes, though, you may want to extend that mail path beyond the end point as shown in Figure 25.1. For instance, if you use an external ISP for some or all of your incoming mail, chances are you must retrieve that mail via a POP or IMAP client. In some cases, though, you might not want to use a conventional mail reader to do that retrieval. For instance, you might want to use an IMAP client, but your ISP might support only POP; or you might want to combine several ISPs' mail streams into one; or you might want to take mail addressed to one account and deliver it to several local users. To accomplish these goals, you must effectively extend the SMTP mail path as shown in Figure 25.1 beyond the initial POP or IMAP connection. Figure 25.3 shows one possible configuration.

FIGURE 25.3

Fetchmail enables a computer to retrieve mail with a pull mail protocol and inject it into an SMTP queue for further processing.

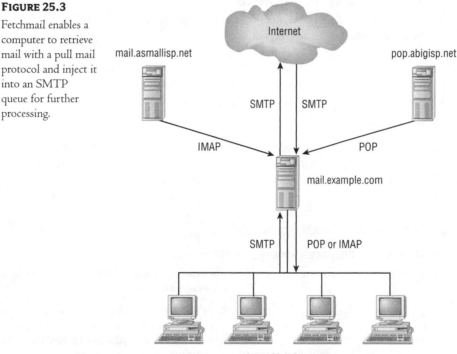

In this network, the local mail server (`mail.example.com`) has a direct connection to the Internet and can send and receive mail like any other mail server. It serves mail to a series of local mail clients using POP or IMAP, and it can relay mail from these clients. In addition to these conventional roles, though, `mail.example.com` pulls mail from two ISPs' mail servers using pull protocols and merges that mail into the local mail stream. This configuration, or a subset of it, is most useful for individuals and small businesses that use an ISP for receipt of some or all of their external mail. You can inject mail into a local queue for reading with mail readers running on the mail server itself, omitting the local mail client computers in Figure 25.3; or you can use the full local network as depicted in the figure. You can add or delete external mail servers, accept or not accept direct incoming SMTP connections from the Internet, send outgoing SMTP mail directly or via one of the ISP's mail servers, and make other changes. In any event, the goal is the same, and the Linux tool to accomplish this goal is the same: Fetchmail (`http://catb.org/~esr/fetchmail/`).

Fetchmail acts like a pull mail client, but instead of displaying the mail to users, it uses SMTP or other delivery mechanisms to send the mail on to other mail servers. Typically, Fetchmail passes the mail it pulls on to a mail server that runs on the same computer on which it runs. In order to accomplish this task, you must configure Fetchmail with information on both the servers to which it talks—the pull mail server and the push mail server. Once you've configured an account, you must run Fetchmail. Typically, you configure it to retrieve mail at regular intervals—say, once a day or once an hour.

Setting Global Fetchmail Options

Fetchmail runs as an ordinary user, and so uses a configuration file in an ordinary user's account. This file is called `.fetchmailrc` by default, but you can use another name if you prefer. As with many configuration files, a hash mark (#) denotes a comment line. Other lines perform one of two tasks: setting global options or configuring an account. The latter lines are covered in the next section, "Configuring an Account." Global options begin with the keyword `set` and are followed by an option name and (for many options) its value. For instance, a line might resemble the following:

```
set postmaster ben
```

This line sets the `postmaster` option to `ben`. If a value contains a space, you should enclose it within quotes. Using quotes when they aren't required does no harm for string values, but values that should be numbers should *not* be quoted. Table 25.5 summarizes some of the more important global Fetchmail options.

TABLE 25.5: COMMON FETCHMAIL GLOBAL OPTIONS

OPTION NAME	POSSIBLE VALUES	DESCRIPTION
postmaster	Local username	Forwards mail, including certain error messages, to this address as a last resort.
bouncemail or no bouncemail	None	Tells Fetchmail to send bounce messages or not to send bounce messages to the apparent sender for undeliverable mail. If you use no bouncemail, the user specified with the postmaster option receives bounce messages.
daemon	Time interval in seconds	Tells Fetchmail to run in daemon mode and poll the servers at the specified interval. If this option is omitted, Fetchmail retrieves mail once whenever it's called. The upcoming section, "Running Fetchmail Automatically," covers Fetchmail scheduling in more detail.
logfile	Filename	Configures Fetchmail to log its activities in the specified file.
syslog	None	Configures Fetchmail to log its activities via the system logger.

Configuring an Account

In order to retrieve e-mail from a remote pull mail server, Fetchmail must know about that server, your account on that server, and how to inject mail into the local mail queue. You give this information to Fetchmail in a `poll` line (which, in fact, can extend for several lines; the second and subsequent lines are indented). Broadly speaking, the format of a `poll` line is as follows:

```
poll server.name server-options user-descriptions
```

The *server.name* is, as you might expect, the hostname of the remote pull mail server. The *server-options* define features of the server, such as the protocol to be used in accessing the server. The *user-descriptions* section describes your account on the server and what Fetchmail is to do with messages it retrieves from the server. Tables 25.6 and 25.7 describe some of the common *server-options* and *user-descriptions*, respectively. These lists are not complete, though; Fetchmail supports many obscure options, so you should consult its man page if you don't see the information you need in these tables. It's important that you not intermix the *server-options* and *user-descriptions*; you *must* present all of the *server-options* before you begin with *user-descriptions*. In creating a `poll` line, you can intermix various words that Fetchmail ignores but that can help you (as a human) parse the configuration file. These words include `and`, `with`, `has`, `wants`, and `options`. The punctuation symbols colon (:), semicolon (;), and comma (,) are also ignored.

TABLE 25.6: COMMON FETCHMAIL SERVER OPTIONS

OPTION NAME	POSSIBLE VALUES	DESCRIPTION
`proto` or `protocol`	Protocol name	Name of the pull mail protocol. This is most commonly POP3 or IMAP, but Fetchmail also supports POP2, APOP, and KPOP. The AUTO option tries the IMAP, POP3, and POP2 protocols in sequence.
`interface`	Interface name/ IP address/netmask triplet	Specifies an interface that must be active before Fetchmail will attempt to poll a server. For instance, `interface ppp0/172.25.0.0/16` specifies that the system must have an address in the 172.25.0.0/16 network on ppp0 before Fetchmail will attempt to poll a server.
`monitor`	Interface name	Tells Fetchmail to look for activity on the named interface and to not attempt to poll a server if there's been no activity between the previous poll and the current time. This option works only in daemon mode, and it is most useful for dial-on-demand PPP configurations, which might otherwise be kept up by Fetchmail activity.
`interval`	Integer	Only check the site at certain poll intervals. For instance, `interval 3` causes Fetchmail to check the site at every third poll time. This option is only useful in daemon mode, and it is typically used when you want to poll several sites, but some more frequently than others.

TABLE 25.7: COMMON FETCHMAIL USER OPTIONS

OPTION NAME	POSSIBLE VALUES	DESCRIPTION
user or username	Username	A local or remote username. The default is for a remote username; however, if the username is followed by here, it's a local username.
pass or password	Password	Specifies the password on the remote server system.
ssl	None	Forces connection using Secure Sockets Layer (SSL) encryption. Many pull mail servers don't support SSL; however, if yours does, this option will improve mail transfer security.
sslcert	Filename	Specifies the file in which an SSL certificate is stored.
sslkey	Filename	Specifies the file in which an SSL key is stored.
is or to	Username	Links a remote account to a local username.
here	None	Follows a local username to clarify that it's local.
smtphost	Hostname	The SMTP server that Fetchmail uses for sending mail it retrieves from the remote server. The default value is localhost.
keep	None	Fetchmail normally deletes messages from the server when it retrieves them, but using this option causes Fetchmail to leave the messages intact. This is a useful debugging option to prevent loss of messages. The -k command-line option to the fetchmail program has the same effect.
fetchall	None	Fetchmail normally retrieves only the messages that it hasn't already retrieved. You can force it to retrieve all of the messages on the server by passing this option.
forcecr	None	Lines in mail messages should end in carriage return/line feed (CR/LF) pairs. Most mail servers tolerate messages that lack the CR, but qmail doesn't. Using this option fixes messages and, therefore, might improve reliability if you use qmail.

Creating a Complete Configuration File

The preceding description of Fetchmail options may seem quite abstract. To help clarify the matter, Listing 25.3 presents a sample .fetchmailrc file. This file begins by setting a few global options: the Fetchmail postmaster account, the option to send bounces to the original sender, the option to use the system logger, and the option to run in daemon mode with a poll interval of 1,800 seconds (30 minutes). The file continues with two source definitions: mail.asmallisp.net and pop.abigisp.net. Mail from the example account on mail.asmallisp.net is retrieved using IMAP and delivered to the local user ben. This account is polled only once every four intervals—that is, four times the 30-minute daemon interval, or once every two hours. Mail from the samplemail account on pop.abigisp.net is retrieved using POP3 and delivered to the user sally on mail.example.com, which might or might not be the same computer on which Fetchmail runs.

LISTING 25.3: SAMPLE FETCHMAIL CONFIGURATION FILE

```
set postmaster "ben"
set bouncemail
set syslog
set daemon 1800

poll mail.asmallisp.net with proto IMAP
        user "example" there with password "p3iY^oQB" is ben here
        options fetchall forcecr interval 4

poll pop.abigisp.net with proto POP3
        user "samplemail" there with password "I*uy9|bBj" is sally here
        options fetchall forcecr smtphost mail.example.com
```

Chances are that a file similar to Listing 25.3 will suit your needs, although of course you must modify various features, such as mail server names, usernames, and passwords. Save the configuration file in an ordinary user account and give it 0710 (-rwx--x---) or more restrictive permissions; in order to discourage you from storing your mail password in a file that's readable to anybody but you and root, Fetchmail refuses to run if anybody but the file's owner can read the configuration file.

WARNING   *Because Fetchmail requires your mail password to be stored in the clear in a file in your account, this file is extremely sensitive. Don't make a backup of the file that can be read by anybody else. If possible, use your mail passwords only for your mail account, not for any other purpose.*

If you prefer to use GUI configuration tools, you may want to look into fetchmailconf, which is a GUI tool for generating Fetchmail configuration files. When you launch the program, it gives you options to configure Fetchmail, test Fetchmail, or run Fetchmail. If you opt to configure the program and then pick expert mode, it displays a dialog box similar to the one shown in Figure 25.4. You set global options in the area entitled Fetchmail Run Controls. Type a pull mail server's hostname in the New Server field and press the Enter key to bring up a large dialog box in which you enter the information that will appear on a single poll line.

FIGURE 25.4

People who like GUI configuration tools can configure Fetchmail with one.

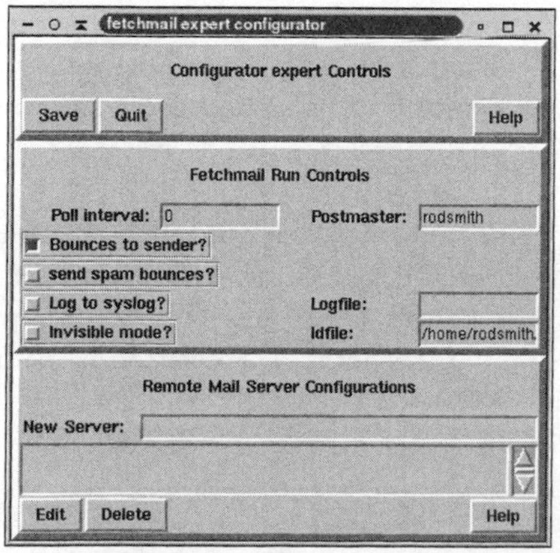

When you believe you have a configuration that should work, you can test it. For testing purposes, I recommend commenting out any daemon line you may have entered. As the user who created the configuration, type **fetchmail -k** to retrieve messages while leaving the originals on the mail server. If all goes well, Fetchmail should respond by displaying a series of dots (.), indicating its progress in retrieving messages. Your messages should then appear in your local mail queue. Try using a local mail reader to see if the messages are available.

TIP   *The account used to run Fetchmail is unimportant, except insofar as the account owner must be the only ordinary user with read privileges on the Fetchmail configuration file. For instance, the user* ben *may run Fetchmail, which then delivers local mail to* ben, sally, *and other users. Running Fetchmail as* root *is definitely not necessary, and in fact is a potential security risk. In theory, a bug in Fetchmail could enable a miscreant to write a mail message that would cause Fetchmail to misbehave and do things with* root *privileges that you don't want done.*

Running Fetchmail Automatically

You can run Fetchmail manually by typing **fetchmail** at a command prompt. If you have multiple configuration files, you can specify the one you want to use by adding -f and the filename to the command. Manual Fetchmail runs may be appropriate in some situations, but most users want to have Fetchmail automatically retrieve mail on a regular basis. Two ways of doing this exist: You can use Fetchmail's built-in daemon mode or you can run Fetchmail using a timed-run tool such as cron.

The preceding sections and Listing 25.3 describe and demonstrate the use of daemon mode. Add a set daemon *interval* line to the Fetchmail configuration file, and it will run in the background, checking mail at the specified interval. You can then start Fetchmail automatically in a SysV or local startup script, as described in Chapter 9, "Bypassing Automatic Configurations to Gain Control." In order to run Fetchmail as an ordinary user with the approach, you must use su, as in:

```
su -c '/usr/bin/fetchmail -f ~/.fetchmailrc' ben
```

This command launches Fetchmail using the username ben. Alternatively, if your Internet connection isn't up at all times, you could add commands to launch Fetchmail to your PPP dial-up script and to kill Fetchmail to the PPP shutdown script. The interface and monitor options could also be used to keep Fetchmail from trying to retrieve mail when your network connection is down.

Unfortunately, Fetchmail isn't always completely reliable when run in daemon mode. In my experience, the program occasionally hangs, causing it to stop checking mail. In order to avoid this problem, you can launch Fetchmail from a cron job *without* using daemon mode. For instance, Listing 25.4 shows a crontab file that might run Fetchmail. If you don't already have a crontab for the user who will be running Fetchmail, type Listing 25.4 into a file called crontab, making changes to the username, HOME directory specification, and time listing. When done, type **crontab crontab** as that user. Linux should enter the script as the user's crontab. If the user already has a crontab file, add the final line of Listing 25.4 to that file and type **crontab crontab**. If the user already has crontab entries but you can't find them, type **crontab -l > crontab** as that user to regenerate the original file, which you can then edit.

LISTING 25.4: A SAMPLE crontab FILE FOR LAUNCHING FETCHMAIL

```
SHELL=/bin/bash
PATH=/sbin:/bin:/usr/sbin:/usr/bin
MAILTO=ben
HOME=/home/ben

17,37,57 7-20 * * * /usr/bin/fetchmail > /dev/null
```

Listing 25.4 causes the /usr/bin/fetchmail program to be run at 17, 37, and 57 minutes past every hour between 7:17 A.M. and 8:57 P.M. This configuration demonstrates one of the advantages of a crontab configuration: You can schedule Fetchmail runs more flexibly than you can with Fetchmail's own daemon mode. Listing 25.4, for instance, doesn't run Fetchmail late at night, minimizing the exposure of your mail passwords when nobody is around to read the retrieved mail. On the other hand, using daemon mode enables you to more easily schedule retrievals from different servers at different intervals by using the interval keyword. You can achieve the same effect using cron, but to do so, you must create two Fetchmail configuration files (say, .fetchmailrc-1 and .fetchmailrc-2) and call them at different intervals using two lines in the crontab file.

WARNING   If you use a crontab line to run Fetchmail, do not include a daemon line in the .fetchmailrc file. If you attempt to use both methods, the first time Fetchmail is run from cron, Fetchmail will kick itself into daemon mode and, as a result, error messages will be generated on all subsequent attempts to run the program from cron.

Summary

Mail server configuration is a very important aspect of many Linux systems' configurations. This setup begins with the mail server configuration in your network's DNS server, which normally points callers to your network's mail server computer. The various default Linux mail servers, sendmail, Postfix, and Exim, have their own specific configuration details, but the basic configuration tasks are the same for each. You must configure these servers to insert the appropriate hostnames in outgoing mail, accept incoming mail addressed to your domain, and relay the mail they should relay but not relay the mail they shouldn't relay. Part of this relay configuration is intended to prevent your system from becoming a source of spam, and you may want to use any of several programs to block incoming spam, as well. Many networks require their own pull mail servers, which enable users to read mail using programs on their desktop computers. Naturally, Linux provides several options for pull mail servers. Finally, if you need to retrieve mail from external pull mail servers for delivery in your own mail server's mail queue, you can use a program called Fetchmail to serve as a bridge.

## Chapter 26

Providing Remote Login Access

ONE OF LINUX'S STRENGTHS compared to many other OSs is that Linux provides extensive support for remote logins. You can use a Linux server from remote systems that sit on the same desk as the target system or that are as distant as the opposite side of the globe. Linux has long provided this support, and in fact there are many different types of tools for handling it. These tools fall into two basic categories: text-mode and GUI. Text-mode tools are fairly straightforward, although some provide an assortment of configuration options. GUI tools are more complex. Some of these GUI tools work best in conjunction with a text-mode login, complicating their use. With a bit of planning, though, you should be able to create a GUI login method that end users can operate with minimal fuss.

Providing Text-Mode Remote Access

Using a text-mode access tool, you can run text-based programs on a Linux computer from a remote location. These tools can include examples of most major software types, such as text editors (Vi, Emacs, etc.), mail readers (Pine, Mutt, etc.), web browsers (Lynx), compilers (GCC), and more. Of course, many modern programs require the use of a GUI environment, and such programs need more sophisticated remote login tools, as described in the upcoming section, "Providing GUI Remote Access." Text-mode protocols have a speed advantage, though; passing a few characters back and forth is much quicker than passing fonts, lines, bitmaps, and so on, as GUI tools require.

The two most common text-mode remote login tools available today are the *Secure Shell (SSH)* and *Telnet*. SSH is definitely the preferred tool, particularly for use on the Internet at large, because it uses encryption to prevent miscreants from listening in on a transfer and stealing passwords or other sensitive data. You can also use SSH to encrypt GUI logins, as described in the upcoming section, "Tunneling GUI Logins through SSH." Despite these advantages, the unencrypted Telnet lingers as a popular protocol. It's simpler than SSH, and Telnet clients ship with all major OSs that support TCP/IP. Telnet's security risks may be minor on well-protected wired local networks. (Wireless networks that don't use encryption are subject to easy eavesdropping.)

Using SSH

Two versions of SSH are available for Linux, although only one is in common use. Whichever version you use, the configuration process is similar, and it is handled by configuration files stored in `/etc/ssh`. Using SSH is fairly straightforward, but you can enable more advanced options that can improve security or convenience by passing command-line options or performing special configuration tasks.

SSH IMPLEMENTATIONS

Two major implementations of SSH exist for Linux:

SSH The original SSH was developed by SSH Communications Security (`http://www.ssh.com`). This product is commercial, but source code is available with some packages. As I write, the latest version is 3.2.

OpenSSH This product was originally affiliated with the OpenBSD OS, but versions for many other OSs, including Linux, have since emerged. This is an open source re-implementation of the SSH protocols, and it is compatible with the original SSH product. The latest version is 3.6.1. You can learn more at `http://www.openssh.org`.

Most Linux distributions ship with OpenSSH. Debian calls its OpenSSH package `ssh`. Mandrake and Red Hat both split the software into three packages: `openssh`, `openssh-clients`, and `openssh-server`. Slackware and SuSE both ship the software in a single package called `openssh`.

NOTE   Because the original SSH is commercial and isn't included with any major Linux distribution, whereas OpenSSH is open source and comes with all major Linux distributions, this chapter uses OpenSSH as a model. Most of the information applies to the commercial version, though. For brevity, I usually refer to the software as SSH, except when the distinction between the commercial SSH and OpenSSH is important.

CONFIGURING SSH

You can run an SSH server via SysV startup scripts, local startup scripts, or a super server. (Chapter 22, "Running Servers," describes these methods of starting servers.) The SSH server must perform some encryption computations whenever it starts, so running the server from a super server can cause brief delays when connecting to the server. These delays are more noticeable with older CPUs than with modern ones. All of the major Linux distributions, except Slackware, launch SSH via SysV startup scripts. Slackware launches the server using the `/etc/rc.d/rc.sshd` script, which is called from `/etc/rc.d/rc.inet2`. After you make a change to the SSH configuration, you should tell the server to reread its configuration file. The `ssh` or `sshd` SysV startup scripts accept a `reload` option to do this job.

The SSH server is configured through the `/etc/ssh/sshd_config` file, and the SSH client is configured through the `/etc/ssh/ssh_config` file. These filenames are very similar, so be sure not to confuse them! Both files consist of comments (indicated by hash marks, #) and keyword/argument pairs, such as:

```
PermitRootLogin no
```

For the most part, both the client and server configurations are reasonable with most distributions. You might want to change a few options, though. Table 26.1 summarizes some SSH server options (in `sshd_config`) that you might want to change, and Table 26.2 summarizes some SSH client options (in `ssh_config`) you might want to change. Pay particular attention to the `PermitRootLogin` server option and to the X forwarding options on both the client and the server. As described in the upcoming section, "Tunneling X through SSH," using SSH to initiate a connection that supports X-based applications can be a convenient method of remote GUI access, but this configuration requires support in the client and server.

TABLE 26.1: COMMON SSH SERVER CONFIGURATION OPTIONS

KEYWORD	ARGUMENT TYPE	DESCRIPTION
Protocol	Integer	SSH protocol version number. OpenSSH 3.6.1 supports versions 1 and 2. To specify both versions, separate them with a comma, as in Protocol 1,2.
ListenAddress	Hostname or IP address and optional port number	Binds the server to listen only to the network interface associated with the specified address. If a port number is specified, it follows the address and a colon, as in ListenAddress 172.26.7.3:22. (The default SSH port number is 22.)
PermitRootLogin	Boolean, without-password, or forced-commands-only	Whether or not to accept direct logins as root. This option defaults to yes. Changing it to no will improve your system's security by requiring intruders to log in using an ordinary account and then using su, thereby requiring two passwords. The without-password option disables password authentication, meaning that another authentication method must be available. This option does *not* mean that users can log into the root account without any authentication. The forced-commands-only option enables public key authentication only for running commands remotely, which may be useful for performing remote backups or the like.
RhostsAuthentication	Boolean	If set to yes, the server accepts authentication based on the rhosts trusted-hosts authentication model for protocol level 1 sessions. This authentication method is inherently dangerous, as described in the upcoming sidebar, "Just Say 'No' to rlogin," so I strongly recommend you leave this option at its default value of no.
RsaAuthentication	Boolean	If set to yes (the default), the server accepts *Rivest/Shamir/Adleman (RSA)* authentication for protocol level 1 sessions. This approach can improve security or eliminate the need to type a password, depending on how it's configured.

Continued on next page

TABLE 26.1: COMMON SSH SERVER CONFIGURATION OPTIONS *(continued)*

KEYWORD	ARGUMENT TYPE	DESCRIPTION
PubkeyAuthentication	Boolean	If set to yes (the default), the server accepts public key authentication for protocol level 2 sessions. This approach can improve security or eliminate the need to type a password, depending on how it's configured.
AuthorizedKeysFile	Filename	Name of the file in which clients' keys for public key authentication are stored.
KerberosAuthentication	Boolean	If set to yes, this option enables SSH to accept Kerberos tickets and to authenticate users via a Kerberos server. This option is useful if your network uses Kerberos, but is set to no by default. Additional options that begin with Kerberos can fine-tune the configuration; consult the sshd_config man page for details.
X11Forwarding	Boolean	If set to yes, this option enables the server to forward X session data, as described in the upcoming section, "Tunneling X through SSH." The default value is no.
Compression	Boolean	If set to yes (the default), the server accepts requests from the client to enable compression. This option consumes CPU time but reduces network bandwidth use.

TABLE 26.2: COMMON SSH CLIENT CONFIGURATION OPTIONS

KEYWORD	ARGUMENT TYPE	OPTIONS
Protocol	Integer	This option works much like its namesake in the SSH server configuration file. The protocol levels are tried in the order specified.
ForwardX11	Boolean	If set to yes, the SSH client authorizes forwarding of X session data. The default is no. This option is similar to the X11Forwarding option in the server configuration, but it is named differently.
Compression	Boolean	This option works much like its namesake in the SSH server configuration file, except that the default value is no.
CompressionLevel	Integer	Specify a value for how much compression you want to apply. A value of 1 is fast but compresses data little; a value of 9 is slow but achieves higher compression ratios. The default value is 6.

USING SSH CLIENTS

In Linux, the primary SSH client is called, naturally enough, `ssh`. In its simplest form, you type the program name followed by the system to which you want to connect. Ordinarily, the remote server then prompts you for a password. The first time you connect, the system also informs you that it can't verify the authenticity of the remote site. Overall, your connection request will look something like this:

```
paul@bunyan:~$ ssh blueox.luna.edu
The authenticity of host 'blueox.luna.edu (192.168.1.6)' can't be established.
RSA key fingerprint is 4b:68:c1:a8:75:5e:b4:76:7b:a6:a2:0d:3a:8b:5f:48.
Are you sure you want to continue connecting (yes/no)? yes
Warning: Permanently added 'blueox.luna.edu,192.168.1.6' (RSA) to the list of
➥known hosts.
paul@blueox.luna.edu's password:
[paul@blueox paul]$
```

Some configurations automatically add previously unknown sites to the key file, so you may not have to authorize a connection. Either way, subsequent connections to the same system will lack the prompt and need to type **yes** to authorize a connection. You will have to type a password, though, unless you modify the configuration as described shortly. (The password doesn't echo to the screen.)

Linux's `ssh` client passes the current username as part of the connection protocol. If your username on the server system is different from your username on the client system, you must pass this information. You can do so by preceding the hostname with the username and an at sign (`@`) or by using the -l parameter. For instance, both of the following two commands log you onto the `jack` account on `blueox.luna.edu`:

```
$ ssh jack@blueox.luna.edu
$ ssh -l jack blueox.luna.edu
```

If you want to access a Linux system from a non-Linux system, you can do so. OpenSSH is available for many Unix-like systems, so you can use it from them. For other platforms, consult `http://www.freessh.org`. This site provides information about free SSH clients on a variety of platforms. Many commercial and shareware network access tools also support SSH.

In addition to remote login tools, SSH ships with clients to perform file transfers. The `scp` program works much like Linux's standard `cp`, but it operates over an encrypted SSH link. You can use a colon (`:`) to separate a hostname from the filename, and you can use an at sign (`@`) to separate a username from a hostname. For instance, to copy `somefile.txt` to the `jack` account on `blueox.luna.edu`, you might type:

```
$ scp somefile.txt jack@blueox.luna.edu:somefile.txt
```

You can omit parts of this command. For instance, you can omit `somefile.txt` from the destination, because the filename is identical to the source filename. (You must still include the colon, though.) You can omit the username and at sign if the remote username is the same as your username on the client system. A more sophisticated file-transfer tool is `sftp`, which works much like a text-mode File Transfer Protocol (FTP) client, but using the encrypted SSH connection. Using `sftp`, you can view a list of files available on the server system, transfer multiple files, and so on.

In a default configuration, SSH prompts for a password when making a connection. You can use alternative authentication tools, though; several such options are summarized in Table 26.1. When you activate these methods, they're tried before a password prompt. As an example, consider using public key authentication. As described here, this method will enable you to log into the remote system without typing a password. Instead, SSH will use private and public keys stored on the client and server. As a result, an interloper won't be able to masquerade as you without breaking into your computer and stealing your public key. You can use a similar approach, but with some modifications, to require use of an SSH-specific passphrase rather than the client's normal password for logins. To implement a public key system that requires no password, follow these steps:

1. Log into the SSH client system (say, bunyan.luna.edu).

2. Type the following command to generate public and private keys for the client system:

   ```
   $ ssh-keygen -q -t rsa -f ~/.ssh/id_rsa -C '' -N ''
   ```

NOTE   Omitting the -N '' parameter from this command causes the program to prompt for a passphrase. You will then need to use the passphrase instead of a password when you connect to the server. If you press the Enter key twice when prompted for the password, the effect is the same as including -N ''.

3. Copy the ~/.ssh/id_rsa.pub file from the client computer to the server computer. You can transfer this file via floppy disk, using scp, or by any other means you choose. If you use scp, you'll have to enter a password.

4. Log into the SSH server system (say, blueox.luna.edu). You may use SSH to do this, but at this point you'll still have to use a password.

5. Ensure that the ~/.ssh directory exists and has 0700 (-rwx------) permissions. If necessary, type **mkdir ~/.ssh** to create the directory or **chmod 0700 ~/.ssh** to set appropriate permissions on the directory

6. Add the id_rsa.pub file you've transferred from the client to the ~/.ssh/authorized_keys file on the server. (This filename may differ; check the AuthorizedKeysFile option in your SSH server configuration.) If this is the first client you've added, this file may not exist. Whether or not this is the first client, the following command should do the job (you may need to adjust paths or filenames for the public key file):

   ```
   $ cat ~/id_rsa.pub >> ~/.ssh/authorized_keys
   ```

7. Ensure that the keys file has the correct ownership and permissions. Permissions should be no more than 0600 (-rw-------). If necessary, type **chmod 0600 ~/.ssh/authorized_keys** to set these permissions.

Once you've completed these steps, you should be able to log in from the client (bunyan) to the server (blueox) without typing a password. Depending on the order in which the protocol levels are listed in your /etc/ssh/ssh_config file's Protocol line, though, you may have to specify that you want to use level 2 of the SSH protocol:

```
$ ssh -2 blueox.luna.edu
```

Using Telnet

SSH is a far more secure and flexible protocol than is Telnet, but Telnet remains popular. Telnet is easy to implement and configure, so many small network appliances use this protocol. Even certain Internet applications sometimes use Telnet—typically specialized applications in which authentication isn't an issue. Because Telnet clients come with almost every major TCP/IP-enabled OS, running a Telnet server can be an appealing way to enable remote logins. Because the basic Telnet protocol doesn't support encryption, though, it's a poor choice when security is an issue. Crackers can too easily eavesdrop on a Telnet session to obtain passwords or other sensitive data. For this reason, I recommend you completely disable Telnet and use SSH instead whenever possible. If you must support Telnet logins for very old or exotic client computers, though, you can do so. In such cases, I recommend you at least limit your Telnet access to your local network; the risks of sending login passwords unencrypted over the Internet are simply too great.

NOTE   *The Kerberos suite (`http://web.mit.edu/kerberos/www/`) provides an encrypted Telnet variant. This variant doesn't suffer from the same problems as the basic version of Telnet. Mandrake's default Telnet server supports Kerberos; however, it doesn't use Kerberos encryption unless your network hosts a Kerberos server and the client computers use Kerberos-enabled Telnet client programs. Debian also ships with an SSL-enabled Telnet (`telnetd-ssl`). This server supports encryption when communicating with a matched SSL-enabled client (`telnet-ssl`).*

All major Linux distributions ship with Telnet clients and servers. Debian ships its server in a package called `telnetd`. Mandrake calls its server package `telnet-server-krb5`. Red Hat and SuSE both call their server packages `telnet-server`. Slackware embeds its server in the `tcpip` package. For the most part, these packages are not installed by default, but Slackware is an exception to this rule—the `tcpip` package contains many critical TCP/IP tools. Mandrake's default Telnet server handles both the original unencrypted Telnet and the Kerberos-enabled variant.

Telnet servers are almost always run via super servers. The default Debian, Slackware, and SuSE `/etc/inetd.conf` files include configurations for Telnet servers, but Slackware's and SuSE's are commented out by default. Mandrake and Red Hat both use `xinetd` by default, and their Telnet server packages include `/etc/xinetd.d/telnet` configuration files. Red Hat's file disables the server via a `disable = yes` line in this file, but Mandrake's configuration enables the server. In all cases, after you make a change to the super server configuration or install the server, you must restart or reinitialize the super server, as described in Chapter 22, to activate or deactivate the Telnet server. Typing **`killall -HUP inetd`** or **`killall -HUP xinetd`** should do the trick.

The default Telnet servers have no configuration files. The servers do accept some command-line options, though; consult the `telnetd` man page for details. Kerberos-enabled Telnet servers require extensive configuration to support Kerberos features, but Kerberos configuration is beyond the scope of this book.

Once the Telnet server is running, you can use a Telnet client to access the server system. Type **`telnet`**, followed by the name of the server system. Typically, you'll be asked for a username and password:

```
paul@bunyan:~$ telnet blueox.luna.edu
Trying 192.168.1.6...
Connected to blueox.luna.edu.
Escape character is '^]'.
Telnet Server
login: paul
```

```
Password:
Last login: Tue Apr  8 18:20:57 from bunyan
[paul@blueox paul]$
```

The exact information displayed during a Telnet login varies from one system to another, so what you see may differ from what's displayed here. As a general rule, though, you'll see at least the `login:` and `Password:` prompts, followed by your shell prompt. Other information may appear amidst these components, as shown in the preceding example.

*TIP   You can add a port number to a `telnet` call, as in **`telnet blueox.luna.edu 25`** to connect to port 25 on `blueox.luna.edu`. This option can be useful in debugging non-Telnet protocols. For instance, you might check whether a mail server is running by trying to connect to its port, and you might even manually issue commands to send mail. This technique doesn't work for all protocols, though. Some, such as most Domain Name System (DNS) transfers, use User Datagram Protocol (UDP) packets rather than the Transmission Control Protocol (TCP) packets used by Telnet. Other protocols rely on encrypted or binary data that's not easily generated via Telnet.*

If you're using a non-Linux client computer, consult its documentation to learn where to find a Telnet client program. Telnet clients are available for almost all major OSs with TCP/IP stacks. One of the few that doesn't ship a Telnet client with its base OS or TCP/IP stack is Mac OS Classic. Several shareware and freeware Telnet clients are available for this OS, but it's better to bypass Telnet in favor of SSH if you must add software to the client. The more recent Mac OS X ships with a Telnet client.

JUST SAY "NO" TO `rlogin`

Linux systems support a third popular text-mode remote login tool, known as `rlogin` (the server is called `rlogind`). This program works on the *trusted hosts* authentication model, meaning that the server trusts hosts with specified IP addresses. As a user, you can create a file called `.rhosts` in your home directory, or root can create a file called `/etc/hosts.equiv`. These files contain lists of trusted client systems. Users of these clients can connect using no password or other authentication system.

The lack of passwords makes using `rlogin` convenient. Unfortunately, the trusted hosts security model is extremely risky. IP addresses can be spoofed, particularly if an attacker has physical access to your local network. The lack of any form of authentication means that if a network relies heavily upon `rlogin`, a compromise of one system translates quickly into a compromise of all systems. In addition, `rlogin` doesn't encrypt data, so it has all of the security problems of Telnet in addition to its own unique flaws. For these reasons, I strongly recommend that you not use `rlogind`. Look for a file called `rlogind` or `in.rlogind` on your system (it's most likely to be in `/usr/sbin`). If it's present, delete the file, or delete the package that installed it. (Unfortunately, Slackware ships its `in.rlogind` in the same `tcpip` package that holds so many critical TCP/IP programs, so deleting this entire package isn't advisable for Slackware.)

Providing GUI Remote Access

Although text-mode remote access is a powerful tool with an OS such as Linux that provides a wide array of text-based programs, some applications demand remote GUI access. You can't run programs such as graphics editors via a text-mode login, for instance. In addition, some users aren't comfortable with text-mode tools. For these reasons, Linux provides several GUI remote access tools.

One key GUI remote access method is the X Window System (X) itself. Unlike most GUIs, X is inherently network-enabled. X's network operations can be a bit hard to understand if you're not used to the terminology, though, and some methods of using X remotely can be tedious. Typically, you use X remotely by first logging in with another protocol. This may be a text-based protocol such as SSH or Telnet, or it may be a specialized X login tool, the X Display Manager Control Protocol (XDMCP). A second GUI remote access tool is Virtual Network Computing (VNC), which operates differently than does X. You can either launch a VNC server from an individual account or integrate X with an XDMCP server to provide login access for any authorized user. Finally, if you want to improve the security of your remote X accesses, you can tunnel either X or VNC through an SSH login.

NOTE   Linux GUI programs are increasingly making use of the X Render Extension, which was introduced with XFree86 4.0. Some non-Linux X servers and most VNC servers do not yet support this option. As a result, some X programs, including many GNOME applications, won't run with these tools.

Basic X Remote Logins

To understand X in a networked environment, you should first understand a peculiarity of X. Most servers, such as web servers, FTP servers, SSH servers, and so on, run on computers that are at a distance from the user who accesses them. The user sits at a computer that runs a client program. This relationship is reversed for X; individuals interact most directly with the server computer. The client may reside on the same computer (in a non-networked configuration) or on a distant system. This relationship is outlined in Figure 26.1. To understand this arrangement, think of it from the point of view of the client program. A web browser (client) uses a network protocol to exchange data with a server program. When you run a user program, such as a web browser, via a remote X connection, *you* become one of the remote sources of information. The program queries the X server to obtain your input (in the form of keystrokes and button presses) and delivers information to the X server (in the form of text and graphics to display). The web browser client is simultaneously a client for the Hypertext Transfer Protocol (HTTP), with which it interacts with the Web, of course.

FIGURE 26.1

An X server functions as a way of transferring data between a user and a user's programs.

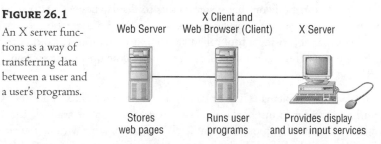

Because clients initiate contact with servers, the arrangement just outlined means that the remote computer must initiate the contact with the local one. This configuration presents a challenge: How do you, working on the server computer, tell the client that you want to work with it? The most straightforward solution is to use a conventional text-mode login tool, such as SSH or Telnet. The full procedure involves the following steps, using `bunyan.luna.edu` as the local computer and `blueox.luna.edu` as the remote system:

1. Log into `bunyan` as you normally would. If necessary, start X on this system.

2. Tell `bunyan` that you want its X server to accept connections from `blueox`. If `bunyan` is running Linux or another Unix-like OS, you do this by typing **xhost +blueox.luna.edu** in an `xterm`.

3. Use your remote-access tool to log into `blueox`. For instance, you might type **ssh blueox.luna.edu** and then enter your password.

4. On `blueox`, type **export DISPLAY=bunyan.luna.edu:0**. This command tells X programs on `blueox` to use the first display (that is, display 0) on `bunyan` rather than a local display.

5. Type the name of any program you want to run. For instance, type **galeon** to launch the Galeon web browser.

6. When you're done, use an `xterm` on bunyan to type **xhost -blueox.luna.edu**. This command tells bunyan's X server to stop accepting data from `blueox`. This action is a precaution, in case a miscreant with an account on `blueox` wants to cause you trouble by opening windows on your system.

This procedure works in most cases, but it leaves room for improvement. Some problems with this procedure include:

Tedium   Compared to a simple text-mode login, this process is tedious. It can be simplified in various ways, and in fact most of the rest of this chapter is devoted to describing methods that can be used to reduce the number of steps involved in obtaining remote access.

Security   X doesn't normally encrypt any data. Even if you used SSH in Step 3, data passed via X will not be encrypted. Of course, if you use SSH to log in, your password will at least be protected, provided you don't type it again in any X windows. Step 2 tells your local system to accept X data from the remote system, regardless of who's sending it. Therefore, if the remote system is a multiuser system, and if somebody on that system wants to display bogus windows on your system or perhaps even intercept your X-based keystrokes, you have no protection. More sophisticated authentication is possible using a tool called `xauth`, but it's tedious to configure and isn't as secure as using SSH to tunnel the connections, as described in the upcoming section, "Tunneling X through SSH."

Non-Unix Local Machine Problems   If your computer doesn't run Linux or another Unix-like OS, you may not have an X server installed on it. Numerous X servers are available for Windows, Mac OS, and other computers, but most are commercial products, some with hefty price tags. Versions of XFree86 are available for Windows (`http://www.cygwin.com/xfree/`), Mac OS X (`http://www.apple.com/macosx/x11/` or `http://www.mrcla.com/XonX/`), and OS/2 (`http://os2ports.com`), among others. Low-cost commercial products such as Mi/X (`http://www.microimages.com/freestuf/mix/`) and Xmanager (`http://www.netsarang.com/products/xmanager.html`) may also be good options. Most non-Unix X servers don't require explicit authorization in Step 2. Some provide procedures to help automate the login process; for instance, they may be able to use Telnet to log in and launch an `xterm` window without requiring you to launch a Telnet client.

Firewall Problems   The method just described requires client/server connections that run in both directions: An SSH, Telnet, or other text-mode login session running from you to the remote system and an X session running from the remote system to you. This configuration can require extra effort to pass through a firewall. The problem is particularly acute if one or both systems lie behind Network Address Translation (NAT) routers, which complicate configuration of servers on their protected networks.

Full-Screen Sessions   This procedure works best to enable you to run individual programs. As presented, it probably won't work to run an entire desktop environment, because your local computer probably already runs one, or at least a window manager, and one screen won't easily support two window managers.

For all of these reasons, this procedure is best applied on a short-term basis or for occasional use. For regular, ongoing use, chances are you'll want to employ another method. Using an XDMCP server, as described in the next section, is a good choice if you want to dedicate a computer to doing little but running another computer's programs. Using SSH, as described in the upcoming section, "Tunneling X through SSH," is a good choice for security or if you need to regularly run programs from several computers. Using VNC instead of X, as described in the upcoming sections, "Basic VNC Logins" and "Linking VNC to XDMCP," is a good way to run an entire desktop environment, and it may be a superior choice when running a server on your local computer is impractical. VNC may also be less expensive or easier to configure on non-Unix systems than an X server.

Using X via an XDMCP Server

You can think of XDMCP as a streamlined replacement for an SSH, Telnet, or other remote login protocol. You can run an XDMCP server on the remote system (the X client computer) to accept logins. When contacted, the XDMCP server uses X protocols to display a login screen. When you enter a valid username and password, XDMCP runs an X startup script. This configuration makes XDMCP a good choice for remote logins in which the remote system completely or almost completely controls the X server's display, such as when using a non-Linux X server or when you want to turn a Linux system into little more than a remote GUI terminal. XDMCP also happens to be used in a purely local way on most workstations. When you boot Linux and see a GUI login screen, you're really seeing an XDMCP server in action; this server just manages the local display.

Three XDMCP servers are common on Linux: The X Display Manager (XDM), the KDE Display Manager (KDM), and the GNOME Display Manager (GDM). Your first task in setting up an XDMCP server to handle remote logins is to pick between these three servers. Each has its own configuration quirks, so you must know how to handle each of these. Finally, you must know how to configure an XDMCP client (that is, an X server) to talk to the XDMCP server.

PICKING AN XDMCP SERVER

If your computer already boots into GUI mode, it's already running an XDMCP server. To find out which one it's using, type the following command:

```
$ ps ax | grep [gkx]dm
```

The result should be a list of any of the standard XDMCP server processes that are running—gdm-binary, kdm, or xdm. (This command may also turn up a few hits on unrelated programs, but these should be obvious.) In most cases, the easiest course of action is to modify the configuration of your default XDMCP server. If necessary, though, you can change which server your system uses. First, of course, you must ensure that it's installed. Search for the files involved and, if you can't find them, install the relevant package for your distribution. How you proceed thereafter depends on your distribution:

Debian   Edit the /etc/X11/default-display-manager file, which contains the full path to the XDMCP server you want to run. For instance, enter /usr/bin/X11/xdm in this file to use XDM. This path must match one in the DAEMON variable in the SysV startup script for the server in question.

Mandrake   Edit the /etc/sysconfig/desktop file, which holds variable assignments. Locate the DISPLAYMANAGER variable and set it to the name of the XDMCP server you want to use, such as gdm to run GDM. Mandrake supports two versions of KDM. Setting DISPLAYMANAGER to KDE uses the mdkkdm XDMCP server, while setting DISPLAYMANAGER to KDM uses the kdm XDMCP server. The mdkkdm server provides a stripped-down appearance compared to the regular kdm server.

Red Hat   Edit the /etc/sysconfig/desktop file, which holds variable assignments. Locate the DISPLAYMANAGER variable and set it to the name of the environment that's associated with the XDMCP server you want to use, such as "GNOME" to use GDM. Use "XDM" to launch XDM.

Slackware   The /etc/rc.d/rc.4 file controls starting X, including launching an XDMCP server. This file tests for the presence of the three major servers and launches the first one in the list it finds, using the sequence GDM, KDM, and then XDM. You must remove higher-ranking servers, remove their execute bits, or edit the startup script file to change which one launches.

SuSE   The /etc/sysconfig/displaymanager file sets several variables related to XDMCP operation, including the DISPLAYMANAGER variable, which specifies which server to use. Set this variable to the appropriate name, such as "kdm" to use KDM.

In practice, XDM is the simplest of the display managers; it only provides a login prompt. KDM and GDM both support additional user options, such as a choice of which desktop environment to run. They may also provide shutdown options and the like, although these are usually disabled for all but local users. KDM configuration is basically a superset of XDM configuration, but GDM uses its own unique configuration files. GDM lacks a few of XDM's and KDM's IP-based auditing features, so if you use GDM, you may want to be particularly diligent about setting up packet filter firewall rules (as described in Chapter 20, "Controlling Network Access") to prevent outside computers from reaching the XDMCP port (UDP port 177).

In some cases, particular servers may be very finicky on certain systems or distributions. If you have problems getting one server to work, try another. It may prove more amenable to modification to accept remote logins than is the default server.

In all cases, you must restart the server after you change your XDMCP configuration. In theory, passing a SIGHUP signal to the process should do the job, but in practice this sometimes doesn't work. You may need to log out, switch to a text mode runlevel (typing **telinit 3** should do this on all distributions except for Debian), and then return to the GUI login runlevel (5 for most distributions, but 4 for Slackware).

WARNING   *Don't pass a SIGHUP signal to the XDMCP server unless you're prepared to have the X server terminate, shutting down any programs you're running locally.*

In all cases, XDMCP normally runs only when the system is configured to start X and present a GUI login screen on the console. If you want the system to accept XDMCP logins from remote users but not run X locally, you can do so; however, you must alter the XDMCP configuration, as described in the following sections.

CONFIGURING XDM

Configuring XDM to accept remote logins begins with the /etc/X11/xdm/xdm-config file. The key change is in the following line, which usually appears near the end of the file:

```
DisplayManager.requestPort:    0
```

This line tells XDMCP not to listen on its usual port. Such a configuration is common on workstations, which normally manage their local X servers more directly. Change the 0 in this line to 177 or comment out the line by placing a hash mark (#) or exclamation mark (!) at the start of the line.

In addition to xdm-config, you must edit the /etc/X11/xdm/Xaccess file, which controls what XDMCP clients may access the XDMCP server. This file is likely to contain lines such as the following, but they'll probably be commented out:

```
*
* CHOOSER BROADCAST
```

These lines tell the system to accept logins from any host and to provide a *chooser* (a list of available XDMCP servers on the local network) to any client that asks for one. The default commented-out configuration denies access to all computers, so uncommenting the lines enables access. Instead of using an asterisk (*), though, you may want to specify computers by name. An asterisk can stand in for part of a name. For instance, *.luna.edu grants access to any computer in the luna.edu domain.

The /etc/X11/xdm/Xservers file lists the displays that XDM should manage. A typical configuration includes a line like the following:

```
:0 local /bin/nice -n -10 /usr/X11R6/bin/X -deferglyphs 16
```

NOTE   *This line varies greatly from one system to another. The* :0 local *part is the least likely to vary, and the line will also include a call to your X server program. Other details may differ.*

This line tells XDM to run /usr/X11R6/bin/X and to display an XDMCP login prompt on this server whenever the XDMCP server itself runs. If you don't want to start X locally but you do want to accept remote XDMCP logins, comment this line out. When you restart runlevel 5, the system should not start X, but it should accept remote XDMCP logins.

CONFIGURING KDM

KDM's configuration files are the same as those used by XDM, except that some KDM configurations place those files in new locations and under new names. Specifically, kde-config may replace xdm-config, and it may reside in /opt/kde/bin/ or /usr/bin. Xaccess and Xservers may reside in /opt/kde/share/config/kdm, /etc/kde/kdm, /etc/kde3/kdm, or some other directory. If you can't find these files, try using your package manager's tools to locate the package from which KDM was installed and then review the package contents. For instance, on a Red Hat system, you might type the following commands:

```
$ whereis kdm
kdm: /usr/bin/kdm
$ rpm -qlf /usr/bin/kdm | grep Xaccess
/etc/kde/kdm/Xaccess
```

In addition to these configuration files, which you can adjust much as you would XDM's configuration files, KDM provides KDM-specific configuration files. The most important of these files is kdmrc, which may be stored in /etc/kde/kdm, /etc/kde3/kdm, /etc/X11/xdm, or some other location. This file points to other configuration files—possibly including, directly or via links, XDM configuration files. The file also includes a section called [Xdmcp] in which various XDMCP options are set. Be sure that the following lines exist in this file:

```
Enable=true
Port=177
```

This file also includes a line called SessionTypes in the [X-*-Greeter] section. This line sets the names of the desktop environments or window managers that XDMCP can launch. This file doesn't define what to do with each session type, though; that task is handled by the Xsession script, which may be included with the KDM package or with another package.

CONFIGURING GDM

GDM uses an entirely unique configuration system. The GDM configuration files usually reside in /etc/X11/gdm, so check that directory first. If you can't find the files there, use your package manager to try to locate them, as described for KDM in the previous section. The main GDM configuration file is called gdm.conf, and the section that's most relevant to XDMCP server operation is called [xdmcp]. To enable remote logins, be sure that this section includes the following lines:

```
Enable=true
Port=177
```

If you want to accept remote XDMCP logins without starting X locally, locate the [servers] section of gdm.conf. This section normally contains a line such as the following:

```
0=Standard vt7
```

Comment out this line by adding a hash mark (#) to the start of the line and GDM won't start X on the local system when it's restarted. (You may need to switch to runlevel 3 and then back to runlevel 5 to restart GDM without X.)

Instead of editing the configuration file in a text editor, you can use a GUI tool. Type **gdmsetup** in an xterm window or select the option for the GDM configuration tool, often called Login Screen, GDM Configurator, or something similar, from a desktop environment menu. The result is the GDM Setup window, as shown in Figure 26.2. The XDMCP tab includes the XDMCP options, the most important of which is the Enable XDMCP check box. Be sure the program is set to listen on UDP port 177, as well.

FIGURE 26.2

GDM provides a GUI configuration tool in which you can activate XDMCP options.

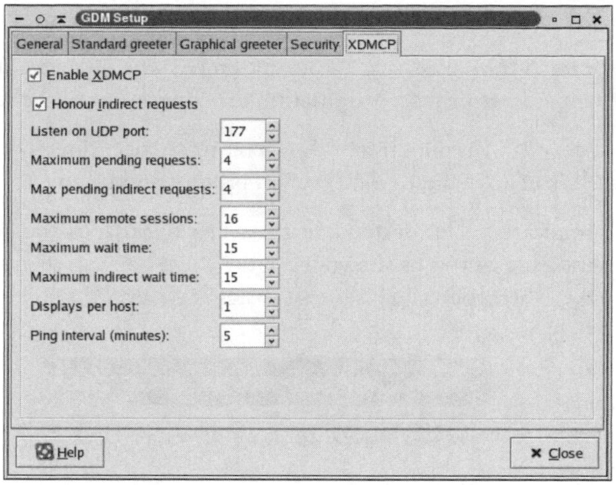

If you want to make additional login environments available to GDM users, you can add scripts to the `/etc/X11/gdm/Sessions` directory. Once you add a script, it becomes available as an option on the Session menu in the login dialog. If a user selects that option, the script you created runs as the user's login script. The default scripts usually call `/etc/X11/xdm/Xsession` with the name of the environment that's to be run.

USING AN XDMCP CLIENT

Once you've reconfigured and restarted the XDMCP server, it's time to try it with an XDMCP client—that is, an X server. The simplest configuration is usually from a Windows X server. For instance, Figure 26.3 shows the configuration utility for Xmanager.

FIGURE 26.3

Windows X servers typically provide a GUI tool for setting XDMCP server options.

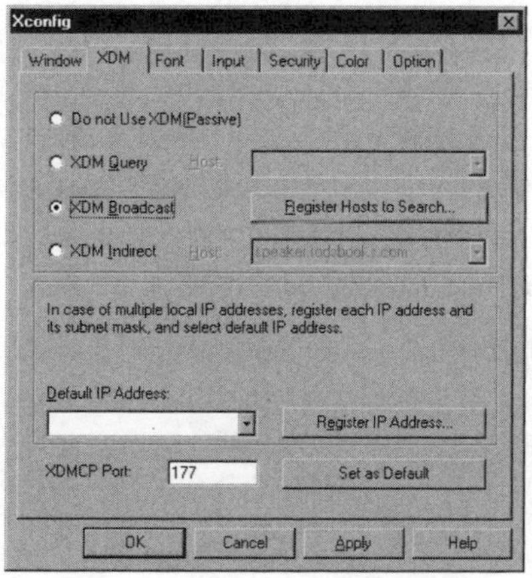

The XDM tab shown in Figure 26.3 provides several options relating to XDMCP use:

Do Not Use XDM (Passive) This option tells the server not to use XDMCP at all. Instead, you use some other method of initiating the connection to the remote system.

XDM Query This option tells the server to connect directly to a single XDMCP server. If all works well, you'll see the XDMCP login prompt and be able to access the system.

XDM Broadcast This option tells the server to broadcast a query for available XDMCP servers and present a list to you, as shown in Figure 26.4. You can then select which remote system you want to use, whereupon you'll see that system's XDMCP login prompt.

FIGURE 26.4

XDMCP clients frequently enable you to pick which XDMCP server to use from a list.

XDM Indirect This option works much like XDM Broadcast, except that the server doesn't send a broadcast itself; instead, it asks the host you specify to send the broadcast and display a chooser. This option is most useful if you're trying to select from machines that reside behind a firewall that blocks broadcasts but not XDMCP logins or other X-related activity.

NOTE *All of these options apply when you start the X server after configuring it. For instance, with Xmanager, the XDMCP option applies when you launch the program from the Xmanager icon.*

If you want to use a Linux system with XDMCP as a dumb GUI terminal for another system, you can do so. The trick is to not start X in the normal way, which launches a local window manager and may present the system's own XDMCP login prompt. Instead, you launch X from a text-mode login or custom startup script and pass it the `-query` *host.name*, `-broadcast`, or `-indirect` *host.name* options, which work much like the options of similar names just described for Xmanager. For instance, with X *not* running, you might type the following command at a text-mode prompt:

```
$ /usr/X11R6/bin/X -indirect blueox.luna.edu
```

This command starts X, tells the system to obtain a list of accessible systems from `blueox.luna.edu`, and presents that list on the display. One important difference between XFree86's handling of these options and those of most Windows X servers is that XFree86 doesn't present a list of available servers if you use the `-broadcast` option. Instead, it connects directly to the first available server.

TIP *If you have slow computers that you want to continue using, one way is to convert them into X terminals—computers that do nothing but run X in order to run programs on other systems. Install Linux on these systems, configure them to start in text mode, and create custom SysV or local startup scripts to launch X. Users can then log into other systems, using the old systems only for their displays, keyboards, and mice.*

Basic VNC Logins

Although X is inherently network-enabled, Linux supports a second remote GUI access protocol: VNC. This protocol operates under a very different network model than does X. Instead of running a server on the user's system, VNC runs as a client on the user's local computer. The VNC server then runs on the remote computer. This VNC server also doubles as an X server, which connects to the X clients (user programs). Figure 26.5 illustrates this arrangement.

FIGURE 26.5

VNC's network model is complex, but in practice it can be easier to use.

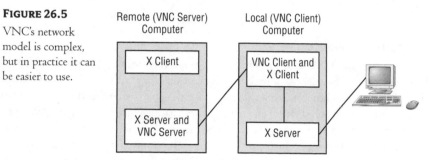

VNC is a cross-platform tool. Figure 26.5 depicts its use when both the client and server run Linux or another Unix-like OS, but in fact the client computer, server computer, or both could run Windows, Mac OS, or some other OS. Under Linux, individual users traditionally run the VNC server. This section describes this configuration. The upcoming section, "Linking VNC to XDMCP," describes a way to run VNC that's more akin to a conventional Linux server, so that it can process logins from arbitrary users.

VNC's Operating Model

Unlike X, which works on fairly high-level data structures such as fonts, text, lines, and curves, VNC operates on bitmaps. When a VNC client connects to a server, the server sends a bitmap to the client representing everything on the screen. This arrangement tends to be slower than X's system when network bandwidth is an issue, but VNC's system involves fewer back-and-forth data exchanges, so VNC can be faster if network latencies are high. VNC also supports various data compression options, which can reduce the demand for bandwidth.

Most X servers place windows from the remote system side-by-side with local windows. This arrangement can be convenient when you want to use programs from both systems simultaneously, but it complicates the use of complete desktop environments on the remote system. Some X servers, particularly those for Windows, support placing the X *root window* in a single local window, enabling you to run desktop environments from the remote system. This arrangement is often called a *rooted* X server. VNC works like a rooted X server: It creates a single window in which the remote system's environment appears. One of VNC's complications is that you must set the size of this window on the VNC server, but the optimum size might vary depending on the client you use.

Ordinarily, a VNC server's X process is entirely independent of other X servers running on the system. VNC can run a desktop environment that may be different from any other running on the computer at that time, and it can be used by a user who isn't logged into the console. On most non-Unix platforms, though, VNC merely echoes whatever session is displayed on the screen. KDE includes a tool that operates in this way, too, as described in the upcoming section, "Using KDE's VNC Options." In either of these cases, the VNC session is *persistent*—a client can connect, disconnect, and connect again later, and the system will be in the same state it had been in prior to the first disconnection. If you left programs running when you disconnected, they'll still be running when you reconnect. The method of running VNC described in the upcoming section, "Linking VNC to XDMCP," though, makes VNC work more like a normal login session: If you terminate a session and connect again later, the system will bring up a new session, and chances are you'll lose any unsaved changes.

USING VNC AS AN INDIVIDUAL

The first step to running VNC is to install it. Most modern distributions ship with VNC, but Slackware is an exception to this rule. Most modern distributions ship with a VNC variant known as Tight VNC. Typically, separate client and server packages are available, often called `tightvnc` and `tightvnc-server`. Some distributions omit the `tight` part of these package names, though. Debian calls its VNC client package `xvncviewer`. If you're not sure if VNC is installed on your system, use `whereis` to look for the `vncviewer` and `Xvnc` files, which are present in VNC client and server packages. (Debian uses `xvncviewer` rather than `vncviewer`.) If these files aren't present, look for the appropriate packages in your distribution, or check the original VNC website (`http://www.uk.research.att.com/vnc/`) or the Tight VNC website (`http://www.tightvnc.com`). Tight VNC provides additional data compression options, which can improve the performance of the VNC protocol. After you install VNC, follow these steps *as an ordinary user* on the VNC server system:

1. Create a directory called `.vnc` in your home directory. This directory will house your VNC configuration files.

2. Type **vncpasswd**. The program prompts you for a password and for a verification of this password. VNC doesn't, by default, use the normal Linux password database. You will need this password to gain entry to the system.

3. Type **vncserver**. This command is actually a script that performs various checks and then starts a VNC server (using the `Xvnc` program file) in your name. The program displays some summary information, including a VNC session number:

```
New 'X' desktop is blueox.luna.edu:1
```

You should now be able to access the VNC server system, as described in the upcoming section, "Using a VNC Client." When you try this, though, you may run into problems. One common issue is that the server fails to start, or it starts and then crashes. Check for log files in `~/.vnc`. These files may include clues to the problem. One common problem relates to font paths; the VNC server is very sensitive about its font paths, and it will crash if you specify font directories that don't exist or that are misconfigured. You can add the `-fp` option and a comma-separated list of font directories to the command line to work around this problem. Alternatively, you can adjust your configuration files.

A second problem—or series of problems, really—is that various default options may be set strangely. Most configurations use two types of configuration files:

The VNC Startup Script The `vncserver` script includes within it various options, such as the default desktop size, the default font path, and so on. For the most part, these defaults are equivalent to X server defaults you would set in your local X server's `XF86Config` file. You can edit this script to change these defaults.

User Configuration Files   Most VNC servers use `~/.vnc/xstartup` as a user's local startup script. This script may call `/etc/X11/xinit/xinitrc` or some other local default startup script, or it may launch a bare-bones window manager, such as `twm`. In any event, you can edit this script much as you'd edit any other X startup script, as described in Chapter 9, "Bypassing Automatic Configurations to Gain Control."

Debian's configuration is unusual because it uses `/etc/vnc.conf` and `~/.vncrc` as configuration files for both of these functions. (The file specifies a default startup script file, which you can change if you like.)

USING KDE'S VNC OPTIONS

KDE 3.1 includes built-in support for VNC. To use it, open the KDE Control Center by typing **kcontrol** in an **xterm** window or by selecting the Control Center from KDE's Kicker. Locate the Desktop Sharing item in the Network area, as shown in Figure 26.6. (On some distributions, the Network area may be called something else, such as Internet & Network.) This option enables you to activate or deactivate KDE's VNC server. This server is independent of the normal VNC server, and it operates in a different way. Rather than set up a unique VNC login session, KDE echoes its own environment. This feature enables you to "share" your current desktop with others, which can be convenient when doing demonstrations over a network.

FIGURE 26.6

KDE enables you to share your desktop using VNC.

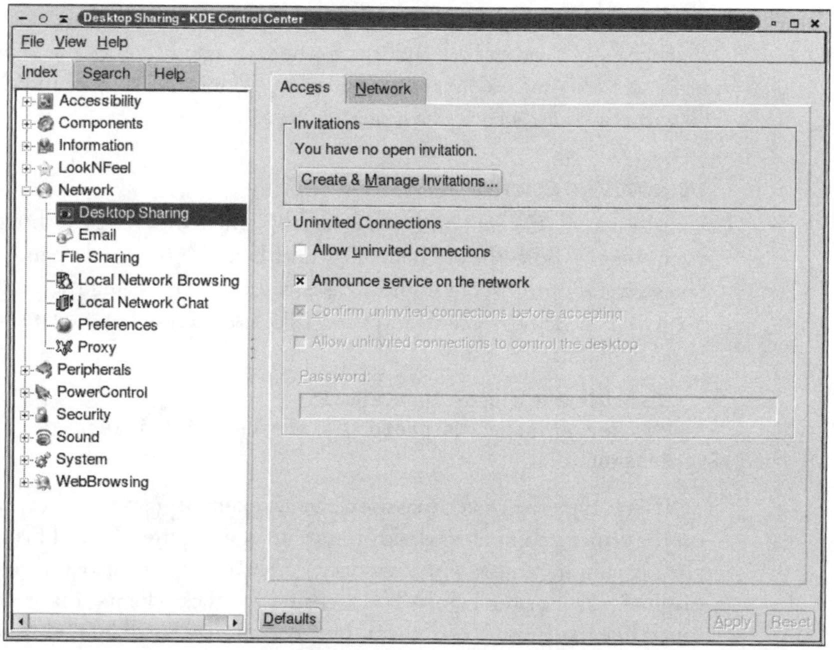

KDE supports two methods of authorizing clients to connect:

Uninvited Connections If you authorize uninvited connections, you specify a password and it remains valid until you change this option. You might use this feature if others have an ongoing need to control your computer, or merely to see what you're doing with it.

Invitations Click Create & Manage Invitations to set up a time-limited authentication. KDE displays a dialog box that summarizes any existing invitations and enables you to create new ones. You can create both *personal* and *e-mail* invitations, which are mostly alike; the difference is that KDE uses KMail to send information on the invitation to the recipient for e-mail invitations. An invitation expires one hour after it's been issued, and it uses a randomly selected password.

WARNING Sending passwords via e-mail is potentially dangerous. I recommend avoiding this invitation method if at all possible. If necessary, use a telephone to give your guest a password. On the other hand, the passwords are time-limited, and KDE informs you of connections, so e-mailing KDE VNC invitation passwords isn't as dangerous as e-mailing most other type of passwords.

You can use a KDE-created VNC session just as you would any other VNC session, as described in the next section, "Using a VNC Client." One important difference is that the KDE server displays a dialog box asking if you want to accept remote access whenever a connection attempt is made. You can then accept or refuse the connection, as well as allow or disallow remote users to control your system. This feature also makes the KDE VNC server useless for remote access if nobody is sitting at the server system. Overall, KDE's VNC support is most useful for remote training or debugging rather than remote control by ordinary users. Another difference between KDE's and the regular VNC server's sessions is that KDE's sharing method means that a user who connects actually controls your own desktop (assuming you grant that access). If you sit back and watch while somebody connects and uses your system, it will appear to be possessed—the mouse pointer will move, windows will open and close, text will type into windows, all without your touching the mouse or keyboard.

USING A VNC CLIENT

The Linux VNC client program is usually called `vncviewer`, although Debian calls its program `xvncviewer`. (Both the original VNC and Tight VNC use the same executable names.) This tool takes several options, but in most cases you use it by typing the program name followed by the VNC server name, a colon, and the VNC session number. For instance, you might type the following command:

```
$ vncviewer blueox.luna.edu:1
VNC server supports protocol version 3.3 (viewer 3.3)
Password:
```

If you type the correct password, `vncviewer` displays more text in your `xterm` and opens a window on the remote computer's desktop, as shown in Figure 26.7. (This figure shows several programs already running in the VNC window.) VNC clients are also available for many other OSs; check the original VNC or the Tight VNC websites for these clients. These non-Linux VNC clients work much like the Linux VNC client, but they emphasize dialog boxes for entry of the server's hostname and password.

FIGURE 26.7

A VNC client displays a remote system's desktop within a single window—note the window border surrounding this desktop image.

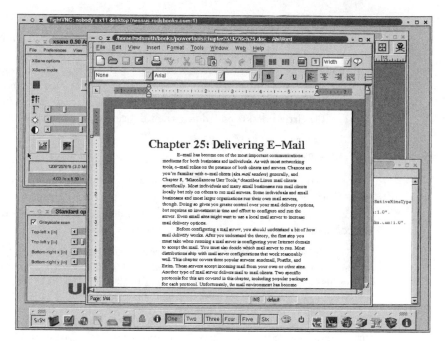

One important drawback of VNC is that the user must ordinarily launch the VNC server from the server computer before running the VNC client program from the client computer. In some cases, this requirement isn't a major issue. For instance, if you're sitting at a workstation and know you'll want to use it from another location in the near future, you can launch the server before leaving the workstation. In other cases, though, you may need to log into the VNC server computer using a text-mode login tool in order to launch the VNC server. This procedure requires two logins, which is a nuisance. What's more, this means you must run two login protocols on the server computer, increasing its security exposure.

Linking VNC to XDMCP

In order to simplify the VNC login procedure and eliminate the need for users to explicitly configure and launch the VNC server, you may want to link VNC to XDMCP. In this configuration, the VNC server's built-in X server contacts the computer's own XDMCP server to present a GUI login prompt using the VNC link to the VNC client. This configuration obviates the need to use a VNC-specific password or user configuration, but it poses certain challenges. Most importantly, you as a system administrator must link these components together. Doing so requires some effort, but it's effort that's well spent for a multi-user system.

To begin, review the earlier section, "Using X via an XDMCP Server." You must configure your XDMCP server to accept remote logins. One minor modification to the configuration described earlier is possible and even desirable, though: You can use the Xaccess control file (for XDM or KDM) or packet-filter firewall rules to block access to the XDMCP server and prevent it from accepting connections from anything except the localhost interface (127.0.0.1). Doing so can improve security by limiting the ways into the computer.

Once you've configured the XDMCP server, you must tell the VNC server to run in an unusual way. Rather than launch the server via the vncserver script, you configure it to run via your super server. The first step in doing this is to create an entry in /etc/services for the VNC service, which normally runs on a port between 5900 and 5999—port 5900 corresponds to VNC session 0, 5901 is VNC session 1, and so on. You can use a single port, or you can assign different ports to different functions. For instance, you might use two ports, one for 760 × 530 virtual desktops and another for 950 × 700 virtual desktops. Adding the following lines to /etc/services will do this job:

```
vnc-760x530     5900/tcp
vnc-950x700     5901/tcp
```

After you've done this, you must create a super server configuration to pass VNC logins onto the VNC server, Xvnc. This configuration must pass any options to the server that it needs in order to operate at the appropriate resolution, color depth, and so on. For instance, the following /etc/inetd.conf entry works on a Debian system:

```
vnc-760x530 stream tcp nowait nobody /usr/sbin/tcpd /usr/X11R6/bin/Xvnc :1
➡-inetd -query localhost -geometry 760x530 -depth 24 -once -fp
➡/usr/X11R6/lib/X11/fonts/Type1,/usr/X11R6/lib/X11/fonts/misc,
➡/usr/X11R6/lib/X11/fonts/75dpi,/usr/X11R6/lib/X11/fonts/100dpi
```

This entry is extraordinarily long because of the large number of options passed to Xvnc. In reality, it should all go on one line in your inetd.conf file. The options include:

:1   This option tells the server to use X session 1. (The local X server's session number is 0.) If you run VNC on more than one port, you must use a different X session number for each VNC session.

-inetd   This option tells Xvnc that it's being run via a super server.

-query   The -query localhost option tells the X server side of Xvnc to contact localhost for an XDMCP login prompt. You can also use the -broadcast or -indirect hostname options, as described earlier, in "Using an XDMCP Client."

-geometry   This option sets the size of the virtual desktop that VNC presents to clients. It can be just about anything you like, although geometries that are too large or too small aren't likely to be useable.

TIP   *You may want to use a geometry that's slightly smaller than a typical screen resolution. This will enable you to run a VNC window that nearly fills a client's screen without requiring the user to scroll to see elements along the edge of the virtual screen.*

-depth   This option sets the color depth used for transfers between the VNC server and client. In practice, 24 usually works well, but you can try other values, if you like.

-once   This option tells Xvnc to quit once the connection is terminated.

-fp   You set the font path with this option. On most systems, the font path will be quite lengthy, as in this example. You can copy the font path from your XF86Config file, except for the fact that

Xvnc requires its font path to be on a single line, with each element separated by commas. Xvnc is very finicky about its font path, so if you have problems, this is one of the first features you should investigate.

As with most servers, Xvnc supports additional options that I don't have space to describe. Consult the Xvnc man page for information on these parameters.

If you run Mandrake or Red Hat, you must create a xinetd configuration that's equivalent to the preceding inetd.conf line. For instance, the following /etc/xinetd.d/vnc file works in Red Hat:

```
service vnc-760x530
{
    disable      = no
    socket_type  = stream
    protocol     = tcp
    wait         = no
    user         = nobody
    server       = /usr/bin/Xvnc
    server_args  = :1 –inetd –query localhost –geometry 760x530 –depth 24
➥-once -fp unix/:7100
}
```

This configuration is almost exactly equivalent to the /etc/inetd.conf entry presented earlier, except for the font path. Red Hat uses a local font server to handle its fonts, so you can pass a pointer to that server (unix/:7100) as the font path. Mandrake's configuration is similar, except that the font path specification should be unix/:-1.

Once you've reconfigured your super server, tell it to reload its configuration file by typing **killall -HUP inetd** or **killall -HUP xinetd**. You should then be able to use a VNC client to access the relevant port. The vncviewer program won't prompt for a password; instead, you'll see an XDMCP login screen, as shown in Figure 26.8. You can enter your username and password and log in, selecting the environment you want to run.

NOTE *Each XDMCP server has its own unique look, and most distributions customize their XDMCP login screens. For this reason, your login screen probably won't look exactly like Figure 26.8, which shows KDM from KDE 3.1 running on Debian GNU/Linux 3.0.*

Using XDMCP in conjunction with VNC gives the user what appears to be a single-protocol GUI login tool. Users needn't log in with SSH or Telnet prior to making the VNC or X connection, and a single VNC session number works for all users. If you want to support multiple virtual desktop sizes, you assign one to each VNC session number. When users log out, their sessions are closed, so you lose the persistence feature of conventional VNC logins.

Tunneling GUI Logins through SSH

Unfortunately, neither X nor VNC was designed with great attention to security. With the exception of VNC passwords, which are delivered over the network in encrypted form, data sent via both of these protocols isn't very well protected. These protocols, therefore, make poor choices for use in high-security environments or over the Internet at large. The solution in both cases is to enlist the help of SSH in encrypting data transfer sessions.

FIGURE 26.8

Linking VNC to
XDMCP gives you
a traditional Linux
GUI login over
VNC.

NOTE *Enabling the use of encryption is only part of the GUI login security puzzle. To improve security further, you should restrict access to the nonsecured ports. You can use firewall rules, as described in Chapter 20, to do this job. X servers run on ports 6000 and up, while VNC servers run on ports 5900 and up (5800 and up for versions that accept HTTP logins with Java). In both cases, the first session is on the lowest numbered port (6000, 5900, or 5800), the second session takes over the next-higher port, and so on. For the best security, block the entire range from 5800 to 6099 to anything but local access.*

TUNNELING X THROUGH SSH

X is a very easy protocol to use in conjunction with SSH, at least if you've configured it appropriately. Ideally, both the client and the server should be configured to tunnel X sessions. To tell the SSH server to do so, be sure that the `/etc/ssh/sshd_config` file includes the following line:

```
X11Forwarding yes
```

The equivalent line in the `/etc/ssh/ssh_config` file for the SSH client is as follows:

```
ForwardX11 yes
```

In the case of the client, you can override a `no` setting by launching the `ssh` client with the `-X` option. Be sure that you pass an uppercase `-X`; the lowercase `-x` option *disables* X forwarding!

Once you've enabled these options, a remote text-based SSH login automatically enables the use of X-based programs from the remote system, at least if you're running an X server locally. Referring to the six-step procedure presented earlier, in "Basic X Remote Logins," you can skip Steps 2, 4, and 6.

This procedure works very well with Linux SSH clients. Some SSH clients for non-Unix OSs may not tunnel X, though. If you use such a client, you might not be able to get this procedure to work. If so, you might want to try another SSH client.

TUNNELING VNC THROUGH SSH

Another SSH tunneling option is to use SSH to tunnel VNC. To do this, you must have an SSH server running on the VNC server computer and an SSH client on the VNC client computer. The easiest way to use this option is to use the `-via` option of Tight VNC's `vncviewer`:

```
$ vncviewer -via proxy.luna.edu blueox.luna.edu:2
```

This command tells `vncviewer` to connect to the computer specified by the `-via` option using SSH and to use that link to initiate a connection to the ultimate target system. Normally, you would provide the same host twice on the command line—once for the SSH tunnel and again as the ultimate target of the VNC connection. If you're only concerned about Internet encryption, though, you could use an SSH server on a remote network (such as `proxy.luna.edu` in the preceding example) to link up to another system on that network (such as `blueox.luna.edu`) that has a VNC server but not an SSH server. For instance, you might connect to a Windows VNC server via an SSH server running on a Linux system on the same local network as the Windows system. This configuration would encrypt your Internet traffic, but not the traffic local to the destination network. If necessary, you can provide a username in addition to the SSH server computer's hostname, as in `paul@proxy.luna.edu`.

In a default configuration, `vncviewer` will ask you for your password on the SSH server system as well as your password on the target VNC server system. If you configure the SSH server to use keys without passphrases, as described earlier, in "Using SSH Clients," `vncviewer` won't prompt for the SSH password. If you tie VNC and XDMCP together, as described earlier, in "Linking VNC to XDMCP," `vncviewer` won't prompt for a VNC password, but you'll still see the XDMCP server and its username and password prompts.

The `vncviewer` program from the original VNC package doesn't support the `-via` option. In order to create an SSH tunnel using this package, you must type an extra command and change the way you address the VNC server system:

```
$ ssh -N -f -L 5910:blueox.luna.edu:5902 proxy.luna.edu
$ vncviewer localhost:10
```

The `ssh` command creates an SSH tunnel between the local computer and `proxy.luna.edu`, telling the SSH server on `proxy` to forward data to port 5902 on `blueox.luna.edu`. The 5910 that precedes the ultimate target system's name and port tells the SSH client to listen on port 5910 for data to send through this tunnel. The second line connects to this port (`localhost:10` in VNC nomenclature, or port 5910 on `localhost`), and SSH does the rest, tunneling the data to `proxy`'s port 5902. In practice, you're likely to use the same hostname twice on the `ssh` line, and you may use the same port number twice.

Preventing Remote-Access Security Problems

Remote login access can be a security nightmare waiting to happen. As described in Chapter 18, "System Security," login servers are unusually high-risk servers because they give users unusually complete access to the computer. If a password is compromised, a miscreant can abuse that password to cause problems for local users and perhaps to exploit purely local security problems to acquire `root` privileges. For this reason, ensuring adequate security is very important with these servers.

A good first step to this end is to use encryption. If possible, disable Telnet, and certainly `rlogind`. The unencrypted nature of these protocols makes them high-risk, especially for use over the Internet at large. Tunneling GUI protocols through SSH can also help a lot. As further protection against abuse, restrict any but the local computer from connecting to your local GUI server ports, as described earlier, in "Tunneling GUI Logins through SSH."

You may be able to use TCP Wrappers, `xinetd`, or packet-filter firewall rules to limit who can connect to your login servers. For instance, perhaps only local users should be able to use a VNC login server, and you might have configured it to run via `xinetd`, as described in the earlier section, "Linking VNC to XDMCP." In this case, you can use `xinetd`'s access restriction tools, as described in Chapter 20, to keep those from outside your local network from touching the local VNC server. Of course, if you tunnel these connections through SSH, even local users shouldn't be able to access the VNC server directly; they should use SSH to do the job.

Chapter 18 included information on the importance of selecting good user passwords. If you haven't already read that section, do so, and be sure you convey the information it contains to your users. Even if you use encryption and access control tools, poor passwords can be a threat, particularly if you have a local "bad apple" or a breach in one local computer that an outside miscreant might be able to exploit.

Summary

Linux provides a plethora of remote-access tools. Text-based login protocols, such as Telnet and SSH, enable you to run text-based programs from a distance. Telnet has long been a popular tool, but its lack of encryption features makes it a risky choice for any but very insular environments. SSH adds encryption and many more sophisticated features, making it the text-based remote login protocol of choice. Among GUI tools, Linux's native GUI, X, is inherently network-enabled. X works well for Linux-to-Linux or Linux-to-Unix connections, but it can be awkward to use in some situations. It's also not as well supported outside of the Linux and Unix worlds as might be hoped. For such situations, VNC offers a good alternative. Ordinarily, normal users run the VNC server, but you can configure it to run in conjunction with Linux's normal GUI login tool, XDMCP. Neither X nor VNC provides encryption support by default, but you can combine either tool with SSH to tunnel connections in an encrypted manner. No matter how you enable remote login access, you should pay careful attention to encryption and other security concerns, lest a cracker invade your system.

Chapter 27

Miscellaneous Servers

THE PRECEDING SEVERAL CHAPTERS covered specific server types or coherent groups of server types, such as mail servers and remote access servers. Many servers, though, don't fall neatly into coherent categories but nonetheless deserve some description. This chapter covers them, or at least three of them:

♦ Dynamic Host Configuration Protocol (DHCP) servers, which enable a computer to dole out IP addresses and related information to other computers. Running a DHCP server can reduce the administrative burden of a network with more than a handful of computers.

♦ Domain Name System (DNS) servers, which deliver IP addresses to computers when given hostnames, or vice versa. You may need to run a DNS server if you run your own domain or have a fairly plain type of Internet access. Even if you don't need to run a DNS server, doing so can be helpful if you want to give names to your local computers or if you want to improve the speed of DNS lookups.

♦ Network Time Protocol (NTP) servers, which help keep computers' clocks synchronized with each other and with an external time source. NTP is helpful or even necessary for some protocols, such as Kerberos, that assume different systems' clocks don't deviate significantly from each other. It can also be important when comparing log files across computers in the event of a security breach or other problem; if both systems use NTP, time stamps shouldn't vary between them by more than tiny amounts, thereby simplifying log comparisons.

Configuring a Network's IP Addresses with DHCP

Chapter 19, "Basic Network Configuration," describes the use of DHCP to configure a Linux system's networking options. If you want to use DHCP in this way, consult that chapter. This section is devoted to the other side of the coin—configuring Linux to deliver IP addresses to other computers.

Before embarking on setting up a DHCP server, you should know when it is and is not appropriate to use one. If you've decided to use the server, you must know where to find it and how to install it. You can then set general network-wide options. You must also tell the server what IP addresses it can deliver. The easiest configuration is to deliver *dynamic* IP addresses, meaning that clients aren't guaranteed the same IP address time after time. If necessary, you can also configure your DHCP server to deliver *static* IP addresses, meaning that any given client receives the same IP address whenever it asks for one.

TIP   Small office and home networks often use broadband routers. These devices are small boxes that include simple Network Address Translation (NAT) routers, switches, and often additional functionality in small and easy-to-configure packages. These devices can usually function as DHCP servers. Using them for this purpose can result in easier DHCP administration than is possible with a Linux DHCP server. On the other hand, a Linux DHCP server is far more flexible than the DHCP servers that come with small broadband routers.

When to Use DHCP

Chapter 19's description of DHCP advised using that protocol for configuring computers' network settings if your network uses DHCP—that is, if a DHCP server is available. In turn, the question of whether to run a DHCP server is answered by whether you want to use DHCP to configure most of your computers' networking features. This logic is somewhat circular, though, and the way to break out of the cycle is to consider the network as a whole. Which is better, configuring each computer's IP address and related information individually or setting up an extra server to handle the job?

One of the considerations in determining DHCP's value is the amount of effort invested in administering systems. All other things being equal, the break-even point for setting up a DHCP server is somewhere between half a dozen and a dozen computers. Below that number, it's generally simpler to use static IP addresses. Above that number, the effort invested in DHCP configuration is less than the extra effort of maintaining static IP addresses. Of course, other issues can intervene. Factors that tend to favor DHCP include ordinary users maintaining their computers' network settings, high turnover rates in computers or the OSs installed on them (such as networks with lots of laptops or simply OS reinstallations), the presence of multiboot systems, a network with odd or tricky configurations, and a network dominated by clients that don't need fixed IP addresses. Static IP address assignment is most useful when your network includes many servers that operate best on fixed IP addresses. Some factors can swing either way. For instance, consider a network with a diverse population of OSs. Maintaining such a system with static IP addresses can be tricky because you must know how to assign static IP addresses to each OS, including any quirks each OS has in this respect. DHCP can help simplify this configuration, although perhaps not dramatically—you must still know how to tell each OS to use DHCP, after all. On the down side, specific DHCP clients and servers may have interactive quirks, so you might run into problems configuring some of the more exotic OSs using DHCP. (In my experience, though, Linux's standard DHCP server works without problems with Linux, FreeBSD, Solaris, MacOS X, MacOS Classic, Windows 9x/Me, Windows NT/2000/XP, OS/2, and BeOS DHCP clients. It should work with additional OSs, too, but I haven't tested them.)

TIP   If your network includes some systems that must operate with fixed IP addresses and some that don't need fixed addresses, you have three choices. You can assign all IP addresses statically, you can assign some addresses via DHCP and assign others statically, or you can use DHCP for all computers and configure the DHCP server to provide fixed addresses to at least some clients. Mixing DHCP and static IP addresses isn't a problem; you must simply use a range of addresses for fixed IP addresses that DHCP won't try to assign. In fact, the DHCP server itself is likely to be assigned a fixed IP address.

Basic DHCP Installation

The main DHCP server package for Linux is written by the Internet Software Consortium (ISC; http://www.isc.org/products/DHCP/). This server usually ships in a package called dhcp, dhcp-server, or dhcp3-server (the current version is 3.0p2), and it is a widely distributed reference DHCP server. ISC also makes available a DHCP client, dhcpcd, which ships with many Linux distributions. The client, though, doesn't have the dominant position in the Linux world that the ISC dhcpd server holds. Other DHCP clients, most notably dhclient, run on many systems. The ISC dhcpd server works with these non–ISC DHCP clients, as well as with DHCP clients on other OSs.

Typically, a DHCP server has a static IP address itself. When it comes time to declare a range of IP addresses the server should deliver, you must be careful to exclude the server's own IP address from this range.

You can install the DHCP server using your usual Linux package management tools, as described in Chapter 11, "Managing Packages." If you prefer, you can download the source code, compile it, and install the server that way. Installing the package for your distribution is likely to be simpler, though, because it includes the necessary startup scripts. The DHCP server is best run from SysV or local startup scripts.

Recent versions of the DHPC server rely on the presence of a couple of specific kernel features that you might overlook if you rebuild your kernel yourself. These options are the Packet Socket and Socket Filtering features, which are accessible from the Networking Features submenu. This submenu is accessed from the Networking Support menu (as shown in Figure 27.1 for a 2.5.66 kernel) when you configure a kernel. (These options are in the main Networking Options menu in 2.4.*x* kernels, which also use a different configuration tool than is shown in Figure 27.1.)

The DHCP server configuration file is /etc/dhcpd.conf. This file can contain comments, denoted by a leading hash mark (#). Lines that aren't comments are either *parameters*, which describe general configuration features; or *declarations*, which describe the network's computers and the IP addresses the server

FIGURE 27.1

You must enable certain kernel options to run a recent DHCP server.

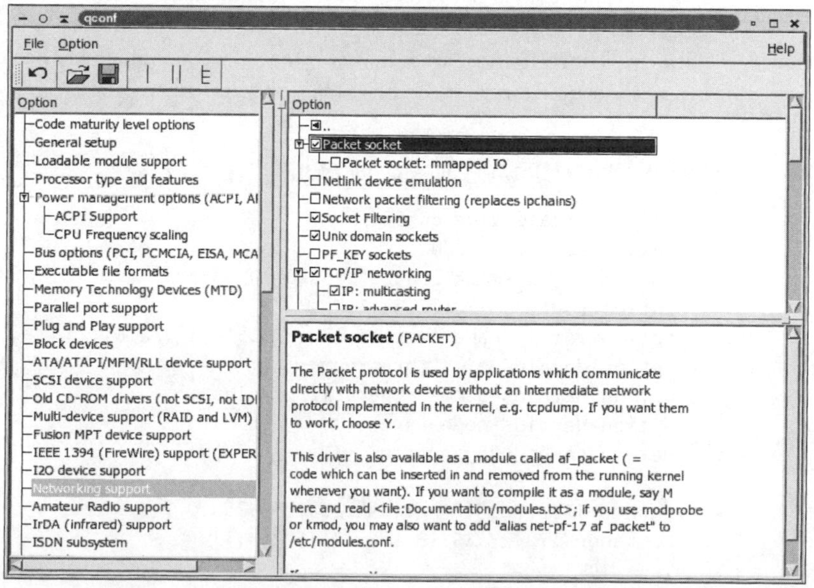

can deliver to those computers. The upcoming section, "Setting Network-wide Options," describes parameters in more detail. The following two sections, "Configuring Delivery of Dynamic Addresses" and "Configuring Delivery of Fixed Addresses," describe declarations in more detail. Some declarations are fairly complex and include parameters within them. These declarations indicate their multiline nature by using curly braces ({}). The opening curly brace marks the beginning of a block of parameters that make up the declaration, and the closing curly brace marks the end of this block.

Some DHCP clients (particularly some Windows systems) require responses from the DHCP server to be addressed to 255.255.255.255. Unfortunately, Linux sometimes changes such replies to have a return address corresponding to your network's broadcast address, such as 172.27.255.255 for the 172.27.0.0/16 network. If some of your clients don't seem to pick up network configurations when you use DHCP, you can change the Linux server's behavior by adding an appropriate route for the 255.255.255.255 address:

```
# route add -host 255.255.255.255 dev eth0
```

Of course, you should adjust this command if the device isn't eth0. This problem is particularly likely to occur if your DHCP server has multiple network interfaces. Some DHCP configurations add this route by default. If yours doesn't, you can modify the DHCP startup script or add the command to a local startup script, as described in Chapter 9, "Bypassing Automatic Configurations to Gain Control." You can verify whether or not this route is present by typing **route -n**. If the route is present, it should appear at the top of the output, as follows:

```
Destination      Gateway        Genmask          Flags Metric Ref    Use Iface
255.255.255.255 0.0.0.0         255.255.255.255 UH    0      0        0 eth0
```

Setting Network-wide Options

Most DHCP configuration files begin with a series of parameters that set global options. Listing 27.1 shows a typical small dhcpd.conf file, including many of the global options you might use. Many, but not all, of these global options begin with the keyword option. Whether or not a parameter begins with this keyword, most are followed by a value. This value may be an IP address, a hostname, a number, a Boolean keyword (true or false), or some other data.

LISTING 27.1: SAMPLE dhcpd.conf FILE

```
default-lease-time 86400;
max-lease-time 172800;
option subnet-mask 255.255.255.0;
option routers 172.27.15.1;
option domain-name-servers 172.27.15.2,10.72.81.2;
option domain-name "threeroomco.com";
option netbios-name-servers 172.27.15.2;
option netbios-node-type 8;
get-lease-hostnames true;

subnet 172.27.15.0 netmask 255.255.255.0 {
    range 172.27.15.50 172.27.15.254;
}
```

Table 27.1 summarizes some of the more common global options you might want to set. Many of these options are demonstrated in Listing 27.1. All parameter lines end with semicolons (;). Some parameters take more than one value. For instance, the `option domain-name-servers` line in Listing 27.1 provides two IP addresses, separated by commas. In most cases, you can substitute hostnames for IP addresses. Doing so puts your server at the mercy of the DNS server, though; if it goes down or is compromised, your DHCP server may be unable to provide the information, or it may provide incorrect information.

TABLE 27.1: COMMON GLOBAL DHCP SERVER PARAMETERS

PARAMETER	VALUE	DESCRIPTION
default-lease-time	Integer	Sets the default lease time in seconds. Clients may request a specific lease time that can override this value. Typical lease times are between a couple of hours and several days—tens or hundreds of thousands of seconds. Shorter lease times are in order if you're planning major network changes in the near future or if the network sees a lot of changes—for example, if laptop computers are being connected for a few hours and then disconnected.
max-lease-time	Integer	Sets the maximum lease time, in seconds, the server will grant. If a client asks for a lease time longer than this value, the server grants a lease of this value.
min-lease-time	Integer	Sets the minimum lease time, in seconds, the server will grant. If a client asks for a lease time shorter than this value, the server grants a lease of this value.
get-lease-hostnames	Boolean	If true, the server looks up the hostname associated with an IP address and returns that hostname to the client, which may use this value in setting its own hostname. By default or if this parameter is false, the server doesn't do this lookup.
use-host-decl-names	Boolean	If true, the server returns the hostname provided by the client as the client's assigned hostname.
ping-check	Boolean	If true, the server pings an address before assigning a lease on that address to a client. If the server receives a response, the server doesn't assign that address. This may be used to ensure that the server doesn't assign addresses that are already in use (say, by systems misconfigured with static IP addresses they should not be using). If the pinged system is also configured to ignore pings, this check won't work as intended.
option subnet-mask	Subnet mask (dotted quad format)	Sets the subnet mask to be assigned to clients.

Continued on next page

TABLE 27.1: COMMON GLOBAL DHCP SERVER PARAMETERS *(continued)*

PARAMETER	VALUE	DESCRIPTION
`option routers`	IP addresses	The IP address or addresses for the subnet's router.
`option domain-name-servers`	IP addresses	The IP address or addresses of DNS servers the clients may use.
`option domain-name`	Domain name	The name of the domain in which the clients reside.
`option netbios-name-servers`	IP addresses	The IP address or addresses of NetBIOS Name Service (NBNS) servers, aka Windows Internet Name Service (WINS) servers. These servers can be an important part of Server Message Block/Common Internet File System (SMB/CIFS) file sharing on Windows-dominated networks.
`option netbios-node-type`	Binary code	A code for how NetBIOS clients should attempt name resolution. Values are: 1 to use broadcasts, 2 to use a WINS server, 4 to try broadcasts first followed by a WINS server, and 8 to try a WINS server first followed by a broadcast. The best option is 8 if you provide a WINS server with the `option netbios-name-servers` parameter and, of course, configure the specified system as a WINS server.

NOTE Table 27.1 is far from complete, but it describes the most common options. For information on more options, consult the `dhcp-options` *and* `dhcp-eval` *man pages. Some of the options, such as the NetBIOS options in Table 27.1, set values that DHCP clients may ignore.*

Notably absent from Table 27.1 is any method of setting the IP address that clients are to receive. This option does appear in Listing 27.1, though, as part of the subnet declaration. The next two sections cover options for assigning IP addresses in more detail.

Configuring Delivery of Dynamic Addresses

Listing 27.1 is adequate for assigning dynamic IP addresses to no more than 205 computers. The lines that accomplish this task are the final three lines of the listing:

```
subnet 172.27.15.0 netmask 255.255.255.0 {
    range 172.27.15.50 172.27.15.254;
}
```

These lines make up a declaration. In this case, the declaration applies to the 172.27.15.0/24 network, as defined on the first line of the declaration. The parameters that appear between the curly braces apply only to machines in that block of addresses. You can create multiple subnet declarations if you like, and in some cases you might need to do this. For instance, the server might have multiple network interfaces and need to assign different IP addresses to machines on different physical subnets. For a network with a single physical subnet, a declaration similar to the one in Listing 27.1 should work just fine. This declaration's second line, consisting of a `range` parameter, defines the IP address range that the server delivers: 172.27.15.50 to 172.27.15.254. When you turn on a DHCP client computer, it might receive any address in this range, depending on which addresses the server has already assigned. If you have more computers than this range permits, then you should expand it (if possible) or create another `subnet` declaration that provides additional addresses. If you need significantly more than 205 addresses, expanding the declaration will probably require changing the netmask. For instance, using a `netmask` of `255.255.240.0` enables you to assign addresses ranging from 172.27.0.1 through 172.27.15.254. (You'd specify a `subnet` of `172.27.0.0` rather than `172.27.15.0` in this case.) Of course, you must have the right to use whatever addresses you pick. The addresses I use as examples in this chapter are parts of private address blocks that anybody can use, but they aren't routed on the Internet.

TIP *If possible, define a range that's substantially larger than the number of computers on your network. Doing so will give your network room to grow, and it will provide a buffer against addresses being claimed and not released, thereby consuming a lease unnecessarily.*

Given the 172.27.15.0/24 network block, Listing 27.1's reservation of only 205 IP addresses means that the first 49 addresses are available for static assignment. Typically, at least one of these addresses will be assigned to the network's router (172.27.15.1 in Listing 27.1), and one will go to the DHCP server itself. Others might go to a name server, mail server, or other servers that are best run with static IP addresses. Alternatively, you can run some of these servers using DHCP and assign them fixed addresses, as described in the next section.

WARNING *An address with a machine portion, in binary, of all 0s or all 1s has special meaning in TCP/IP addressing. All-0 addresses refer to the network itself, and all-1 addresses are used for broadcasts. You should never attempt to assign such an address using DHCP, nor should you attempt to assign it statically for that matter. If you use a 24-bit netmask, this means that the final byte of an address should never be 0 or 255.*

Configuring Delivery of Fixed Addresses

If you want to run servers but configure them to acquire their IP addresses and other information via DHCP, you can do so. This practice normally requires that you do one of two things, though:

- Link your network's DHCP and DNS servers so that the DNS server delivers the correct IP address for a given hostname. This practice may be reasonably reliable on a local network, but it may not be reliable if your systems should be accessible from the outside world, because your DNS server's entries will be cached by clients' DNS servers. Clients may, therefore, end up using an out-of-date DNS entry. Even if you configure the DNS server with a short lifetime for these entries, some DNS servers may ignore this information, possibly resulting in mismatched hostnames and IP addresses. This configuration also requires making intricate changes to both the DHCP and DNS servers' configurations. For these reasons, I don't describe this approach in this book.

- Configure your DHCP server to assign an unchanging IP address to the server computers. This goal can be achieved in several ways. The method I describe in this section involves using the *Media Access Control (MAC) address*, aka the *hardware address*, of the DHCP client computer to identify that system and enable the DHCP server to assign a specific IP address to that system each time it boots.

LOCATING THE MAC ADDRESS

The first step in providing a fixed address, at least when using the MAC address approach described here, is to locate the DHCP client's MAC address. For Ethernet devices, this address is a 6-byte number that's usually expressed in hexadecimal (base 16), typically with colons, dashes, or some other punctuation separating bytes. You can locate the MAC address in several different ways:

Hardware Stickers   Some network interface cards (NICs) have stickers affixed to them with MAC addresses. Similar stickers may exist on the external case of computers that ship with built-in Ethernet interfaces, such as some laptops. Locating the MAC address in this way is straightforward if you haven't yet installed the NIC, but it may not be convenient if it's already buried inside a computer. Many NICs also lack this sticker.

Linux DHCP Clients   On a Linux client, you can type `ifconfig eth0` (changing eth0 to another interface name, if appropriate). This command produces information on the network interface, including the hardware address (labeled `HWaddr`) on the first line of the output. This command requires that the interface be activated, although it need not be assigned an IP address.

Windows 9x/Me DHCP Clients   Windows 9x/Me provides a network configuration and information tool that you can access by typing `WINIPCFG` in a DOS prompt window. The result resembles Figure 27.2. Be sure you select the correct adapter in the selection box (with the high-lighted label of ISA Ethernet Adapter in Figure 27.2). The Adapter Address field shows the MAC address.

Windows NT/2000/XP DHCP Clients   Windows NT, 2000, and XP provide a tool similar to Linux's `ifconfig` for displaying information about the network interface. Type `IPCONFIG /ALL` in a DOS prompt window to learn about your interfaces. A line labeled `Physical Address` should reveal the MAC address.

Mac OS DHCP Clients   Both Mac OS Classic and Mac OS X reveal the MAC address in their GUI network configuration tools. In Mac OS Classic, open the TCP/IP Control Panel and click the Info Button. The Hardware Address line shows the MAC address. In Mac OS X, open the System Preferences tool and click the Network option. Be sure you select the correct network device in the Show list button. The display should resemble Figure 27.3. The MAC address is called the Ethernet Address in this tool.

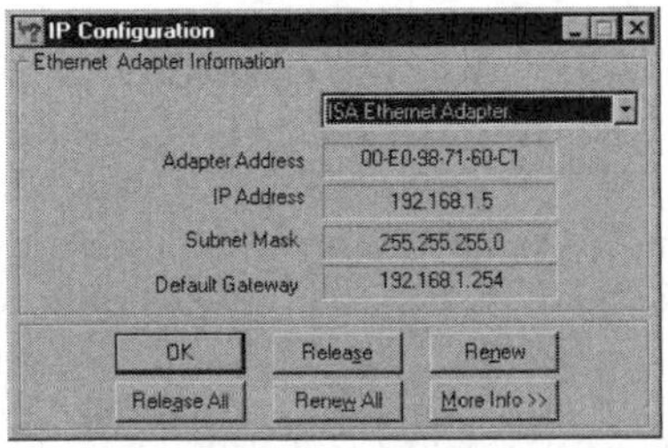

FIGURE 27.2

Windows 9x/Me provides a GUI tool for displaying the MAC address and other network information.

FIGURE 27.3

Mac OS X calls the MAC address the Ethernet Address in its GUI configuration tool.

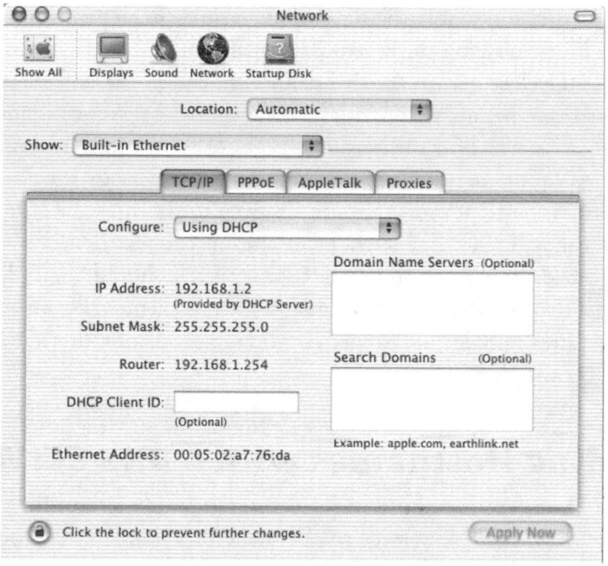

Locating the Address from the DHCP Server   No matter what OS the client uses, there are several ways you can locate the MAC address from the DHCP server. One method is to configure the DHCP client to use DHCP and then activate its network interface. Assuming the server is configured to deliver addresses as described in the earlier section, "Configuring Delivery of Dynamic Addresses," the DHCP client should pick up an address. You can then examine the DHCP server's logs for evidence of a lease granted for that address. The DHCP leases file (typically /var/lib/dhcp/dhcpd.leases) should include a multiline entry identifying the IP address and MAC address. Typing **grep dhcpd /var/log/messages | tail -n 1** as root should also reveal an entry with the IP address and MAC address in question. (If some other DHCP activity occurs between the target system's lease being granted and your typing this command, though, that activity will show up instead. Increase the number from 1 to 2 or higher to reveal earlier entries.) Finally, you can type **ping -c 1 *ip.addr*; /sbin/arp *ip.addr***, where *ip.addr* is the IP address, to learn the MAC address of the computer. This last approach will also work if you temporarily configure the future DHCP client with a static IP address.

DHCP SERVER FIXED ADDRESS OPTIONS

Once you have the MAC address of a DHCP client, you can add an entry to the DHCP server's /etc/dhcpd.conf file for that client. This entry can go within the subnet declaration, as shown in Listing 27.1, or the entry can go after the subnet declaration. Either way, the entry looks like this:

```
host calvin.threeroomco.com {
    hardware ethernet 00:80:C6:F9:3B:BA;
    fixed-address 172.27.15.2;
}
```

The host declaration tells the server that you're defining parameters for a specific computer. Place the computer's hostname after the keyword host, and end the line with an open curly brace. Lines between this one and the close curly brace that defines the end of the declaration apply only to this host.

The hardware parameter provides a means for the server to identify the host. This parameter is followed by a keyword for the hardware type (ethernet in this example, but token-ring is also valid) and the MAC address, using colons (:) to separate bytes of the address. The fixed-address line, of course, defines the IP address that's to be given to this host. Be sure that the address is not also specified in the range line for any subnet declaration!

After you add this entry and restart the server, it should begin delivering the fixed IP address you specify with the fixed-address parameter to that client. Of course, this will only work as long as the hardware address remains unchanged. If you replace a computer's NIC, you must update the hardware line to reflect the change.

Providing Hostnames with a DNS Server

Running a Domain Name System (DNS) server can be useful for several reasons. One important reason is to provide DNS service to outsiders for a domain that you operate. For small sites, though, it's usually much easier and safer to rely on an outside source, such as your domain registrar, to provide DNS service. A second reason to run a DNS server is to provide DNS services for local computers. These services can include a caching DNS server to improve DNS lookup speeds and the handling of a local domain for a private network.

Basic BIND Installation

The most popular DNS server in Linux is the Berkeley Internet Name Domain (BIND), which is usually installed in a package called bind or bind9 (the current version is 9.2.2). The actual server program within the package is called named.

Although BIND is the most popular DNS server, it's not the only one that's available. Others include djbdns (http://cr.yp.to/djbdns.html), dnscache (http://cr.yp.to/djbdns/dnscache.html), and pdnsd (http://home.t-online.de/home/Moestl/; see also http://www.phys.uu.nl/~rombouts/pdnsd.html for some updates). The first of these programs can do much of what BIND can do, but the remaining two are intended primarily as caching DNS servers only. They may be useful if you just want to provide a local DNS cache, but they can't function as authoritative DNS servers for your domain. (The pdnsd server provides some very limited local domain-handling features, but not enough to serve a real domain.)

Assuming you want to run BIND, you can install the server much as you would any other. BIND normally runs from a SysV or local startup script; it maintains a cache of recent requests in memory, so it works best when it can run continuously. Running the server from a super server would cause it to lose that cache, thereby degrading performance.

The main BIND configuration file is /etc/named.conf. A basic named.conf file consists of an options section, in which global options are defined, and a series of zone sections, in which specific DNS *zones* are defined. Each zone corresponds to one domain or subdomain for which the server is *authoritative*—that is, for which the server is the final authority. Both the options section and the zone sections span multiple lines, using curly braces ({}) to mark the beginning and end of each section.

Configuring a Forwarding-Only Server

Listing 27.2 presents a basic /etc/named.conf file that configures the server to function as a forwarding-only server—that is, a server that forwards DNS requests to other DNS servers. You might create such a configuration to speed up local DNS lookups. If you regularly use certain sites, your local server can cache these sites' addresses, thereby delivering the addresses to your DNS clients immediately, without sending the DNS request to your ISP's DNS servers.

LISTING 27.2: A FORWARDING-ONLY /etc/named.conf FILE

```
options {
   directory "/var/named/";
   forwarders {
      192.168.202.1;
      10.72.81.2;
   };
   listen-on {
      172.27.15.2;
   };
   forward first;
};
zone "." {
   type hint;
   file "named.ca";
};
zone "0.0.127.in-addr.arpa" {
   type master;
   file "named.local";
};
```

Listing 27.2 includes an `options` section that sets four options or sets of options:

directory   This line sets the directory in which zone configuration files and other ancillary configuration files appear. This directory is typically /var/named, but you can change it to something else if you prefer.

forwarders   This series of lines is very important; it specifies the IP addresses of the name servers to which BIND is to forward the name resolution requests it receives. You should obtain the IP addresses of your ISP's name servers and enter them here. (Don't try to use the addresses in Listing 27.2; they're fictitious.) You must enter these addresses as IP addresses, not as hostnames.

listen-on   This block of lines is optional. It tells the server to bind itself to the network interface with the specified IP address (172.27.15.2 in Listing 27.2). If the computer has multiple network interfaces, the server won't listen on any but the addresses you specify. This option is particularly important if you run the server only for the benefit of the computer on which it runs. You could bind to 127.0.0.1 to keep any other computer from using it and possibly exploiting bugs in the server.

`forward first`   This option tells the server to forward DNS lookup requests and then to attempt a full recursive lookup (that is, to try to resolve the address as regular nonforwarding servers do, by querying a chain of servers until an answer is found). This option contrasts with `forward only`, which tells the server to ask the forwarders about an address but not to try a full lookup if the initial query fails. The `forward first` option is desirable if your forwarders are unreliable, because it provides a fallback means of name resolution. This fallback takes time, though, and so `forward only` can produce speedier failures for mistyped hostnames if the forwarders are reliable. If you want to configure a nonforwarding DNS server, you should omit both the `forwarders` subsection and the `forward` line.

The zone blocks in Listing 27.2 tell BIND where to go to find information about the *root servers* (as described in the `zone "."` section) and to find information for the 127.0.0.0/24 netblock (the `zone "0.0.127.in-addr.arpa"` section). Root servers are the starting point for a full recursive lookup, and the 127.0.0.0/24 netblock is associated with the loopback interface. Both of these zones reference files (`named.ca` and `named.local`) that should exist in the directory specified on the `directory` line. These files normally exist in a default installation, but their names may not be the same as the ones specified in Listing 27.2. Consult your own default file.

With the exception of the IP addresses specified in the `forwarders` subsection, the `listen-on` interface address, and possibly the filenames of the default zone files, Listing 27.2 is a reasonable `named.conf` default file for a typical forwarding-only configuration. Change these details as appropriate for your system and BIND should function as a forwarding-only name server. Start it, reconfigure your clients to use this server, and it should work. After running the server for a few hours or days, you may see a modest improvement in name lookup times. This effect can manifest itself most noticeably in web browsing—web pages are likely to appear slightly more quickly when you or somebody else on your network accesses a site whose name is in the BIND cache. Retrieval of less commonly accessed sites isn't likely to improve. Performance may drop slightly if you restart BIND, as it will lose its cache.

Adding a Local Domain

If you want to have the DNS server convert hostnames to IP addresses for machines on your local network, you must set up a domain. This task involves setting up a zone and creating a domain control file. You should also remember to create a configuration for the reverse lookup, which maps IP addresses to hostnames. These tasks involve making changes to the main DHCP server configuration file and to zone files that are stored elsewhere.

SETTING UP A ZONE

The basic zone configuration is handled through a `zone` definition in the main DHCP configuration file (typically `/etc/named.conf`). Listing 27.2 includes two such definitions. One of these is for the *root zone* (`zone "."`), which tells the server how to locate the *root servers*, which are at the core of full recursive lookups. The second zone (`zone "0.0.127.in-addr.arpa"`) is for reverse DNS lookups on the localhost (127.0.0.0/24) network block. These are both specialized zones and shouldn't be adjusted unless you understand their intricacies. The reverse lookup on the localhost network is much like any other reverse lookup zone, though, as described in the upcoming section, "Handling Reverse Lookups."

A typical zone definition looks like this:

```
zone "threeroomco.com" {
   type master;
   file "named.threeroomco.com";
};
```

This definition includes three components:

Zone Name The zone name appears between quotation marks immediately after the `zone` keyword. For a forward lookup zone, the zone name is the same as the domain name or subdomain name. (It's possible to configure different servers to function as name servers for different subdomains of one domain. For instance, you might use three different name servers for the `threeroomco.com`, `room1.threeroomco.com`, and `room2.threeroomco.com` domains.) For reverse lookup zones, the zone name is the network portion of the subnet's IP address *in reverse order* followed by `.in-addr.arpa`. For instance, the zone name for the 172.27.15.0/24 subnet is `15.27.172.in-addr.arpa`.

Server Type The `type` line specifies whether or not the server is the absolute final authority for the domain. This chapter describes setting up a master server (`zone master`), which holds the original and fully authoritative files for a zone. It's also possible to run a slave server (`zone slave`), which retrieves its configuration files from the domain's master or from another slave. To configure a slave, you must include a `masters` line within the zone definition, such as `masters { 172.27.15.2; };`. This line tells the slave what computer holds the master files. You may also need to include an `allow-transfer` block on the master system to specify what servers can request zone transfers—that is, copy domain control files. This sort of configuration can simplify running a backup DNS server, which is a requirement when you register a domain on the Internet at large. For a small subnet in a home, small business, or department of a larger business, running multiple DNS servers may not be required, so using only master zones on the single DNS server is usually appropriate.

Domain Control Filename You must tell BIND where to look for the file that defines the mapping of hostnames and IP addresses for the zone. The filename you provide with the `file` option resides in the directory specified with the `directory` option in the `options` section. The name you use for this file is arbitrary, but it's conventionally named after the zone itself, such as `named.threeroomco.com` in this example. The next section of this chapter, "Configuring the Zone Control File," describes this file in more detail.

Assuming you want to run a DNS server for a single domain or subdomain, you should add a zone configuration for that domain's forward lookups. You can add a reverse zone definition at the same time, or you can put that task off so that you don't need to create the reverse zone definition file until you've gotten the forward lookups to work properly. There's little point in restarting the DNS server at this point; before it can do anything with the zones you define, you must create the zone control file.

OBTAINING A DOMAIN NAME

If you want to set up your own domain on a private subnetwork that's either not connected to the Internet or that's connected via a NAT router, you can use any domain name you like, albeit with some caveats. The main risk is that your fictitious domain name might match a domain that's already being used by somebody else. Even if it's unused today, it might be registered tomorrow. In this case, you'll be unable to reach that other domain's computers unless you reconfigure your network in some way. If your domain name creeps into outgoing network traffic, such as e-mail you send, the result can be confusion or even failures of the network protocols. For these reasons, if you use a made-up domain name, you should use one that's in a top-level domain (TLD) that's completely fictitious, such as .invalid. For instance, you might call your domain mydomain.invalid.

Another approach to obtaining a domain name is to register one. Dozens, if not hundreds, of domain registrars exist. These companies register a domain you select in your name, so you can use the domain in question for any purpose. Registering a domain is a necessity if you want to use your domain name on the Internet at large. If you register a domain, you can, of course, use names in that domain on your own network, including any segment or segments that aren't visible to the Internet as a whole. The cleanest way to do this is to use separate DNS servers for local use compared to Internet use. For instance, you might contract with a DNS service provider to handle your domain on the Internet, but run your own local DNS server that includes additional local-only entries.

To find a domain registrar, consult a list, such as those maintained at http://www.newregistrars.com and http://www.icann.org/registrars/accredited-list.html. You'll be able to obtain a domain in a popular TLD such as .com, .net, or .org. Some countries have made their TLDs available commercially, so you can obtain a domain in .cc, .tv, or others fairly easily, as well. If you want a domain in a specific country's TLD, consult http://www.iana.org/cctld/cctld-whois.htm for contact information. In the past, domain registration cost $70 for a two-year lease on a domain, but with so many competing registrars today, domain name lease times vary and costs seldom exceed $20 a year. Most registrars offer DNS services, either as part of domain registration or in a low-cost add-on package. Of course, these DNS services don't provide the advantages of running a DNS server on your own network, but they're usually quite adequate to enable users on the Internet at large to locate your servers.

A final option lies in between these first two options, and is appealing for those with broadband Internet connections that provide variable IP addresses: You can use a *dynamic DNS service*. These services enable you to use a hostname or a subdomain name within the range provided by the dynamic DNS provider. If you run appropriate software, you can keep forward lookups pointing to your IP address, even if it changes frequently. For lists of dynamic DNS providers, consult http://www.technopagan.org/dynamic/, http://www.geocities.com/kiore_nz/, or http://dns.highsynth.com. Once you're registered, you can then run a local DNS server as authoritative for your subdomain, but let the dynamic DNS service handle external lookups, which would normally all point to your single external IP address.

CONFIGURING THE ZONE CONTROL FILE

Listing 27.3 shows a typical small zone's control file, such as the named.threeroomco.com file specified in the zone configuration described in the previous section, "Setting Up a Zone." This file begins with a line that reads $TTL 1W, which sets the default *time-to-live (TTL)* value at one week. The file continues with two main parts. The first is the *start of authority (SOA)*, which begins the file and defines various features of the domain as a whole. The SOA line begins with the domain name, followed by a dot. The next characters are IN SOA, which define this record type. The record continues with the name of the zone's primary name server (donovan.threeroomco.com. in this example—again, note the trailing dot). The next entry looks like a computer's hostname, but it's not—it's an e-mail address, with the at sign (@) replaced with a dot. This e-mail address belongs to the person who's responsible for maintaining the zone. Therefore, Listing 27.3 specifies that susan@threeroomco.com should receive administrative e-mail.

LISTING 27.3: SAMPLE FORWARD LOOKUP ZONE CONTROL FILE

```
$TTL 1W
threeroomco.com.  IN  SOA  donovan.threeroomco.com.  susan.threeroomco.com. (
        2003092602 ; serial
        28800 ; refresh
        14400 ; retry
        3600000 ; expire
        604800 ; default_ttl
        )
calvin              IN  A      172.27.15.1
donovan             IN  A      172.27.15.2
powell              IN  A      172.27.15.3
mail.threeroomco.com.  IN  A   172.27.15.4
bigben              IN  CNAME  powell.threeroomco.com.
@                   IN  NS     donovan.threeroomco.com.
@                   IN  MX     10  mail
threeroomco.com.    IN  MX     50  purple.abigisp.net.
```

WARNING *Hostnames in zone control files usually have trailing dots. The trailing dot marks the end of a hostname. If it's omitted, the server appends the domain's name to the hostname. For instance, if the dot were omitted from* powell.threeroomco.com. *in the CNAME record in Listing 27.3, systems that tried to contact* bigben *would be directed to* powell.threeroomco.com.threeroomco.com, *which is almost certainly incorrect. The domain name itself in the SOA record must also have a trailing dot. Omitting the trailing dot from a domain name or hostname is a prime cause of problems in DNS zone configurations, so check this detail first if something doesn't work as you expect!*

The SOA record continues across the next several lines, using parentheses to group together several numeric entries. These entries frequently have comments associated with them describing their function, as in Listing 27.3. The meanings are, in order, a serial number, the refresh period, the retry period, the zone expiration period, and the default *time-to-live (TTL)* period for individual entries. The serial number is used by slave DNS servers to identify when a record has changed. You should increase this value whenever you change a record. Administrators frequently use a date-based code for the serial number. Listing 27.3's serial number of 2003092602 might indicate the second change on September 26, 2003, for instance. The remaining entries all specify times in seconds. The refresh, retry, and expire values all relate to master/slave zone transfer timings—how frequently the slave should check back with the master for updated files, how long it should wait before checking again if the first attempt fails, and how long it should wait before discarding a zone entirely if the master doesn't respond. The TTL value tells other DNS servers how long they should cache DNS entries. TTL values between a day and a week are common, but you may want to reduce your TTL value some time before making major changes to your domain. None of these values is very important if you're operating a single DNS server for a small private zone.

Entries after the SOA relate to individual computers or network features. These records begin with a machine name. You may omit the domain name, in which case the name specified in the SOA record is appended. If you include the domain name, be sure to include a trailing dot, as was done for `mail.threeroomco.com.` in Listing 27.3. An entry name of an at sign (@) specifies the domain name itself. This usage is common in certain types of entries that apply to the domain as a whole.

The record types have names that appear in the individual entries following the IN code. These record types specify the function of the record, and include:

A   An *address (A)* record defines an individual host on the domain. (You can assign an A record to the domain name itself, in which case the domain name is tied to an individual computer and the domain can have component computers as well.) The data following the A code is an IP address.

CNAME   A *canonical name (CNAME)* record lets you set up an alias, in which one hostname points to another computer by name. These entries list a computer by hostname rather than by IP address. Another way of accomplishing a similar goal is to create multiple A entries that point to the same IP address. CNAME configurations are most useful when the target computer's hostname is fixed but when the IP address may change in a way that's not under your control. For instance, if you use an outside web hosting service, you might use a CNAME record to point users at the outside provider's hostname.

PTR   A *pointer (PTR)* record is used in configuring a reverse DNS zone, as described in the next section, "Handling Reverse Lookups." Because it defines a forward lookup zone, Listing 27.3 contains no PTR records.

NS   A *name server (NS)* record points to a domain's name server. In Listing 27.3, the single NS record points to the same system specified as the primary name server in the SOA record. NS records normally begin with an at sign or the domain name. A domain may have multiple NS records if more than one DNS server is authoritative for the domain.

MX   A *mail exchanger (MX)* record points to a domain's mail server. As with NS records, MX records typically begin with at signs or the domain name. Following the MX code is a priority code. Outside mail servers attempt the send mail to servers in the order of this code. For instance, an outside mail server sending mail to `threeroomco.com`, as described in Listing 27.3, will first try to contact `mail.threeroomco.com`. If this contact fails, the outside server will try sending mail to `purple.abigisp.net`. Of course, the mail server must be configured to accept mail to the `threeroomco.com` domain. This topic is described in more detail in Chapter 25, "Delivering E-Mail." You specify a server by name in an MX record, either by hostname alone (in which case the SOA's domain name is added) or complete with domain name and trailing dot.

With this information in hand, you should be able to begin crafting your domain's zone file. Use Listing 27.3 as a starting point and make the appropriate substitutions for your system's hostnames, IP addresses, and so on. When you're done, double-check that the `/etc/named.conf` file points to the correct zone file and then tell `named` to reload its configuration by typing `killall -HUP named` as root. You should then be able to resolve hostnames into IP addresses using host or regular networking tools. For instance, you might type the following command and see the specified output:

```
$ host calvin.threeroomco.com 172.27.15.2
calvin.threeroomco.com has address 172.27.15.1
```

This command queries the DNS server at 172.27.15.2, even if your system isn't yet configured to use it by default. If you see an error message, review your configuration files. Be sure you've included all the elements in the SOA record, as well as the preceding $TTL line. Check that the record for the host you're testing exists and is properly formatted. Try testing other hosts; perhaps your entry includes a typo that's not present for other hosts. Try typing hostnames that don't exist, or specify as a DNS server an IP address that you know doesn't run a DNS server to compare the error messages. Perhaps these comparisons will provide a clue about what's wrong. Check log files such as /var/log/messages for error messages relating to the server.

HANDLING REVERSE LOOKUPS

Reverse lookups are handled in zone files that work much like forward lookup zone files. You must define a zone for these files in /etc/named.conf, much as you define a zone for forward lookups. For instance, to serve the 172.27.15.0/24 network, you might include a zone definition like this:

```
zone "15.27.172.in-addr.arpa" {
    type master;
    file "named.172.27.15.0";
}
```

Note that the order of the bytes in the IP address block is reversed on the zone line, the machine address portion is omitted, and .in-addr.arpa is appended. You can name the zone file whatever you like, but using the IP address in the name is common.

The zone control file looks much like the forward lookup zone control file, except that the reverse lookup zone control file is dominated by PTR records, which aren't present in the forward lookup zone file. You most likely won't find A or MX records in the reverse lookup zone file, but you will find an SOA record and one or more NS records. Listing 27.4 shows a reverse lookup zone file that matches Listing 27.3's forward lookup zone file.

LISTING 27.4: SAMPLE REVERSE LOOKUP ZONE CONTROL FILE

```
$TTL 1W
15.27.172.in-addr.arpa. IN SOA donovan.threeroomco.com.  susan.threeroomco.com. (
        2003092602 ; serial
        28800 ; refresh
        14400 ; retry
        3600000 ; expire
        604800 ; default_ttl
        )
1.15.27.172.in-addr.arpa.  IN  PTR  calvin.threeroomco.com.
2.15.27.172.in-addr.arpa.  IN  PTR  donovan.threeroomco.com.
3                          IN  PTR  powell.threeroomco.com.
4.15.27.172.in-addr.arpa.  IN  PTR  mail.threeroomco.com.
@                          IN  NS   donovan.threeroomco.com.
```

Most of the entries in Listing 27.4 begin with the full IP address (with byte order reversed), followed by `.in-addr.arpa.`. As with forward lookups, these pseudo-hostnames end in dots to prevent name completion on the pseudo-domain name, `15.27.172.in-addr.arpa`. The exception is the name 3 in Listing 27.4. This name omits the pseudo-domain name, which is added to the 3 name. Another exception is the NS record, which uses an at sign. All of the PTR and NS entries point to computers by name, complete with domain name and trailing dot. Because the domain this zone file defines is the `15.27.172.in-addr.arpa` pseudo-domain, you can't omit the domain name or dot from the regular hostname, as you can with a CNAME, MX, or NS record in a forward zone definition if the host resides in the main domain.

As with defining forward zones, you should tell `named` to reread its configuration file by typing **`killall -HUP named`** after you've finished your changes. You can then use `host` to look up IP addresses and verify that the correct hostname is returned. If it isn't, check your entries again, paying attention to trailing dots and other features that might cause problems, as described in the previous section.

NOTE　*If you're running a DNS server for a network that's accessible on the Internet at large, you might not need to configure it with a reverse lookup zone. Instead, that task may be handled by your ISP, which is responsible for the IP addresses in question. On the other hand, your ISP might hand that responsibility off to you, particularly if you've acquired a large block of IP addresses. Consult your ISP to determine who's responsible for handling this detail. If you're configuring a DNS server for a private network, you should probably configure the reverse DNS zone for that block yourself. Failing to do so won't cause problems for most networking tools, but a few may gripe about the lack of reverse lookups or even fail to work properly.*

Keeping Clocks Synchronized with a Time Server

If you deal with more than a couple of computers on a regular basis, you've no doubt become frustrated with *clock drift*, which is a computer clock's inability to maintain an accurate time. Clock drift exists for many reasons, but the end result can be maddening, as you attempt to keep all your clocks synchronized. Worse, clock drift can cause serious problems for some network protocols and troubleshooting procedures. These protocols and procedures require clocks on two systems to be synchronized to within a few seconds of each other, at most. For instance, the Kerberos security suite embeds time stamps in its packets, and it relies on this data as a security measure. As a result, if two systems' clocks are set differently, Kerberos may not work. If you're trying to track down a cracker, comparing log files from multiple systems can help, but this procedure is complicated if each system's clock is set differently. For these reasons, Linux supports various methods of synchronizing systems' clocks across a network. One of the most popular of these methods is the Network Time Protocol (NTP). By installing an NTP server on every computer on your network, you can keep the systems' clocks synchronized to each other, with well under a second's difference between them.

NOTE　*A typical NTP installation places a server on every computer. In reality, an NTP server functions as both a client and a server, as described shortly. Although there are client-only NTP packages, the full NTP server does the best job of maintaining a system's clock at an accurate value.*

Installing a Time Server

Common Linux NTP servers are all derived from the NTP reference software, which is housed at http://www.ntp.org. This server ships with all major Linux distributions, usually in a package called ntp or xntp. The current stable version of the NTP server as I write is 4.1.1, although development versions number up to 4.1.74. Older distributions ship with earlier versions of NTP. For the most part, these versions work in the same way as recent NTP packages, although a few details differ.

NTP servers typically include SysV startup scripts to launch the server at system start time. NTP servers should always be run through SysV or local startup scripts. They continuously monitor the system clock and check its value every few minutes against a reference clock. If the NTP server were run periodically, as from a super server, the server would do a much poorer job of maintaining the system's time. In some cases, you might want to use a client-only NTP program, such as ntpdate, to set a client's clock periodically, such as once a day. The ntpdate program is being abandoned, though, and may or may not even be available with specific distributions' NTP packages.

Once installed, the NTP server package provides a configuration file called /etc/ntp.conf. All major distributions include ntp.conf files that work reasonably well as they're shipped, with the exception of one critical detail: They must be told where to look to set their clocks. This detail is handled by a server line, which looks like this:

```
server bigben.threeroomco.com
```

This line tells the server to synchronize its clock with bigben.threeroomco.com. You can include multiple server lines, in which case the NTP server uses various algorithms to determine which server provides the most accurate time signal and synchronizes itself to that source.

Another pair of options you may want to use, particularly on large networks, are broadcast and broadcastclient. You can have your primary NTP server periodically broadcast the current time by using the line broadcast a.b.c.d, where a.b.c.d is the server's own IP address or a multicast address of 224.0.1.1. Other computers on the network then use the line broadcastclient yes to tell them to listen for these broadcasts. This configuration can reduce local NTP-related network traffic, particularly when you have many clients. Ordinarily, clients synchronize themselves with servers every few minutes, and with many local NTP clients, this traffic might become an issue. On a typical small network, though, the local NTP traffic is tiny compared to other network transfers, so this type of configuration isn't required.

Pointing to an External Time Source

Although you can operate NTP locally without referring to an external time source, the usual means of operation is to synchronize your local network's time to that of an outside time signal that's known to be accurate—that is, a *veridical* time source. Doing so requires understanding a bit about how NTP and various veridical time sources operate. You must then locate an external time source, configure one of your local computers to use it, and test NTP operation on that system.

UNDERSTANDING THE NTP STRATUM HIERARCHY

A handful of sites around the globe maintain highly accurate and precise atomic clocks that are the official time source for the entire world. Ultimately, a typical computer whose time is set via NTP traces its clock's settings back to one of these official time sources. NTP is designed to permit computers to set their clocks to a time signal maintained by an outside source. An NTP server does this, and in turn allows other computers to set their clocks to its own signal. This arrangement creates an expanding pyramid of clocks that trace their setting back to some accurate source, as shown in Figure 27.4. The peak of this pyramid is known as a *stratum 0* time server. Such a server is not a computer in the traditional sense; instead, it's an atomic clock, a radio that receives time signals broadcast from an atomic clock, or some similar device. A *stratum 1* time server sets its clock based on this veridical time source. A *stratum 2* time server sets it clock to a stratum 1 server's signal, and so on.

Figure 27.4 demonstrates another important feature of NTP: Individual NTP clients and servers can synchronize themselves to multiple time sources. Some of the computers in Figure 27.4 tie into two higher-stratum servers. In a configuration like this, the server that synchronizes to multiple sources uses various means to determine which source is more accurate.

If for some reason you need a highly accurate local time, you can obtain your own stratum 0 time source. The least expensive of these are radio devices that read time signals broadcast from Global Positioning System (GPS) satellites or via AM radio. The Linux Clock Mini-HOWTO document (`http://www.tldp.org/HOWTO/mini/Clock-4.html`) includes pointers to a few hardware manufacturers of such devices, which cost about $100. Using such a clock requires installing special drivers and pointing your NTP server to the device by using a special server configuration. You might need your own stratum 0 source if you're doing scientific experiments that require not just very precise but very accurate time measurements, for instance. Fortunately, few people need this sort of accuracy; configuring one of your systems as fairly low-stratum devices will work just fine for most purposes.

FIGURE 27.4

NTP enables an expanding pyramid of computers to set their clocks to a highly accurate original source signal.

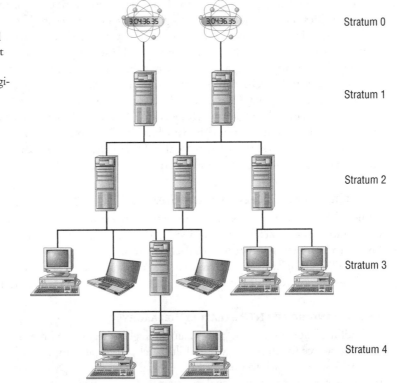

Typically, you'll set up one of your systems (or perhaps more, if your network is very large or split across many subnets) as your network's main time server. This server will synchronize itself with an outside time server, and all your other computers will use your main time server as a time source. This configuration minimizes the load placed on an external time server and the amount of NTP-related traffic between your site and other sites on the Internet. You can dedicate a computer to the task of being the NTP server, but this task imposes very little CPU or network load, so you may want to run the NTP server on some other convenient system, such as a print server or DHCP server. Keep in mind that the NTP server *is* a server, and it poses at least some security risk, so you shouldn't run it on a particularly sensitive system. Heavy network loads for other services could also degrade the accuracy of the NTP server's clock.

Because the number of publicly accessible stratum 1 time sources is limited, chances are you'll point your primary server at between one and three stratum 2 or lower NTP servers. Therefore, most of the computers on your subnet will be at stratum 3 or lower. Even with several intervening layers, these computers' clocks should be accurate to within less than a second.

LOCATING AND USING AN EXTERNAL TIME SOURCE

You can find lists of public stratum 1 and stratum 2 NTP servers at `http://www.eecis.udel.edu/~mills/ntp/servers.html`. The U.S. Naval Observatory operates a set of public stratum 1 servers; check `http://tycho.usno.navy.mil/ntp.html` for a list. In theory, you can use any of these servers as a source for your own main NTP server. In practice, some work better than others, and there's an etiquette involved in using these servers. All other things being equal, the best server to use is the one closest to you in a network sense. NTP works, in part, by measuring the round-trip latency between two systems. When the latency is low, the accuracy of the protocol is improved. As a general rule, network latency increases with physical distance, although there are exceptions to this rule. Therefore, if you're located in, say, California, you're almost certainly better off using an external server in the western half of the United States than you would be using a server in Australia or Europe.

TIP   *You can use* `ping` *to determine the round-trip latency between your network and a potential external time source. You may also find* `traceroute` *to be informative in determining the number of network hops between yourself and another site.*

After perusing the lists, you should have a set of potential external time sources. Be sure to read the website and especially the description of the sites you might use. Many sites are open to public use but request that potential users contact the NTP server maintainer before using the server. Be sure to do so if a site asks this courtesy. Also, as noted on the main NTP servers page, you shouldn't use a stratum 1 server as a source unless your site serves many computers—the most frequently cited cutoff value is 100 clients.

In addition to the public servers listed on the NTP servers page, you may be able to find other servers. One potentially very good source is your own ISP. Many ISPs operate NTP servers and are happy to let their customers point to them. This feature is seldom widely advertised, though, so you may need to ask about it. An ISP's server is likely to be an excellent candidate because it's likely to be close to you in network topology. If you're configuring an NTP server for a department in a larger organization, consult with your colleagues within the organization; it's possible that another department is running an NTP server to which you could synchronize.

However you locate external servers, you enter them in the /etc/ntp.conf file using server lines:

```
server time.abigisp.net
server ntp.pangaea.edu
```

You can use just one server, but listing two or three may be beneficial in case one server goes down or produces an inaccurate time source. Using three or more enables NTP to spot and exclude *false tickers*—NTP servers whose time signal is just plain wrong. If you trust your main external time source, though, using just one will help to reduce the load on other servers.

TESTING NTP OPERATION

Once you've configured your NTP server and restarted it, you should wait at least a few seconds, and ideally several minutes. You can then study the operation of the server by using the ntpq program. Type **ntpq** at a bash prompt and the program should respond with an ntpq> prompt. This program supports many commands; type **?** to obtain a list of them. The most important command for testing basic operation is peers:

```
ntpq> peers
     remote           refid      st t when poll reach   delay   offset  jitter
==============================================================================
 LOCAL(0)        LOCAL(0)        10 l   34   64  377    0.000    0.000   0.031
*time.abigisp.ne tock.luna.edu    2 u  957 1024  377   60.899    5.873   9.742
+ntp.pangaea.edu ntp2.carbon.ati  2 u   54 1024  357   34.832   -6.425   1.658
+ntp.example.com 172.27.0.19      2 u  999 1024  377   43.758    1.519   0.831
```

This output reveals several pieces of information about the local server and the computers to which it synchronizes. This particular system ties itself to three peers—time.abigisp.net (the t at the end of the hostname is truncated), ntp.pangaea.edu, and ntp.example.com. The asterisk (*) next to time.abigisp.net's name indicates that it's the system to which the local server has tied itself, based on the quality of various measures, such as the delay, offset, and jitter values. The plus signs (+) next to the remaining two servers indicate that they're producing reasonable time values, but they aren't the servers that provide the signals that NTP considers best. Other information in this display includes the stratum of the source server (in the st column), when the server was last polled (under when), and the polling interval in seconds (poll).

If you use ntpq soon after starting your server, you won't see a main source server selected for a few minutes. This is because NTP must take several time readings to determine which source provides the best signal. Once it has done this, NTP's operation, and the output of the peers command inside ntpq, stabilizes. The polling interval is short (usually 64 seconds) in the beginning, but it grows to a value of several minutes (typically 1,024 seconds, or about 17 minutes).

If ntpq returns a connection refused message, this means that the NTP server isn't running on the system. The NTP server may abort if the system's clock differs from that of the servers to which it synchronizes by more than 1,000 seconds (just under 17 minutes). The reason for this is that such serious differences usually indicate a seriously incorrect clock or a server that's a false ticker. Either situation requires manual adjustment. In the case of a system clock that's set incorrectly, you can launch ntpd with the -g option, which overrides the 1,000-second rule. You can also set the clock in a one-time fashion manually (via the `date` command) or by using `ntpdate`. The `ntpq` program may also display a summary that indicates it's not obtaining reliable data from its upstream servers. If no server acquires an asterisk after a few minutes of running, that may be a sign of problems. Perhaps you've selected servers that aren't reliable or to which the network path is flaky, for instance.

Setting Up NTP Clients

You configure most of the computers on your network in much the same way you configure your main NTP server. The main difference is that you specify just one system using a single `server` line: your network's main NTP server. When you use `ntpq` to verify the server's operation, it should display a summary that points to your network's main NTP server. If it doesn't, it could be that your main NTP server's NTP port (123) is blocked by a firewall, or the server may be misbehaving.

If you prefer not to expose most of your clients by running NTP servers on them, you can protect their NTP ports with firewall rules, as described in Chapter 20, "Controlling Network Access." Another option is to run `ntpdate` in a `cron` job instead of running the full server. This latter option may result in some clock drift between calls, but on most systems this drift will be minor. The NTP developers are discouraging use of `ntpdate`, though, and it may eventually disappear. (In Debian, it's in a separate package from the main NTP server.) To use `ntpdate`, call the program along with the hostname or IP address of your network's main NTP server:

```
# ntpdate bigben.threeroomco.com
```

NTP clients and servers are available for many OSs. Therefore, you can use a Linux NTP server to coordinate the time for just about any OS on your network. Try a web search to locate clients for more obscure OSs. Many OSs include NTP clients by default. For instance, in Windows NT or 2000, you can type **NET TIME /SETSNTP:***ntp.server* in a DOS prompt window, where *ntp.server* is your NTP server system.

If you have Windows 9*x*/Me clients and run a Samba server, you can use a time protocol that's part of SMB/CIFS. Include the following line in the `[global]` section of the Samba configuration file (`/etc/samba/smb.conf` on most systems):

```
time server = Yes
```

You can then type **NET TIME ***SERVER* **/SET /YES** in a DOS prompt window to set the clock on the Windows client to match the clock on the Samba server called *SERVER*. The Samba server need not be your domain's main NTP server, but if you want all your systems' clocks synchronized to an outside source, the Samba server should run an NTP server. The SMB/CIFS time protocol doesn't provide the precision or accuracy of NTP, but it's good enough for most purposes when setting Windows clients.

TIP *Try creating a DOS/Windows batch file (one whose name ends in* `.BAT`*) that calls* NET TIME *in either of the ways just described, and then copy the batch file to the Windows StartUp folder. Doing so will cause the Windows system to synchronize its clock whenever it boots, which for most Windows systems is frequently enough to keep their clocks set to within a few seconds of the veridical time, even if the clock drifts badly.*

Summary

Many networks rely on a handful of fairly unglamorous protocols that nonetheless make everything work. DHCP servers deliver IP addresses and related information to most clients on many networks, easing the task of configuring networking on individual clients. DNS servers convert hostnames to IP addresses and vice versa, making Internet naming what it is. Both of these protocols are widely used on many networks, although you may not need to run a DNS server yourself. A somewhat less popular tool is NTP, which enables you to keep many systems' clocks synchronized. Running one or more of these servers locally can help ease the burden of administering a network, and Linux serves as an excellent platform for all of these tools.

Glossary

/root

The system administrator's home directory. *See also* root and root.

419 scam

A type of *spam* that violates section 419 of the Nigerian Criminal Code. Such spams purport to be ways to make money by brokering shady funds transfers from Nigeria or other countries. Those who respond actually encounter increasing demands for cash to facilitate the promised funds transfers, which never occur.

access control list (ACL)

An access control list (ACL) is an advanced file-access control tool that's growing in popularity. ACLs permit finer-grained control of who may access a file than do the older (and still more popular) Unix-style ownership and permissions.

ACL

See access control list (ACL).

Advanced Linux Sound Architecture (ALSA)

An alternative sound protocol to the standard *Open Sound System*. ALSA drivers are being integrated into the 2.5.*x* kernel series.

Advanced Technology Attachment (ATA)

The most common means of connecting hard disks to IA-32 and other small computers. *See also* ATAPI and SCSI.

AGP bus

The *Accelerated Graphics Port* bus, a standard for interfacing video cards to motherboards. Most video cards sold since 2000 use AGP interfaces.

Alpha

The Alpha CPU architecture was moderately popular among Unix workstations in the 1990s, but its future is uncertain.

ALSA

See Advanced Linux Sound Architecture (ALSA).

American Standard Code for Information Interchange (ASCII)

The most common encoding method for plain text. ASCII assigns a single 8-bit number to each symbol (uppercase and lowercase letters, numbers, punctuation, and so on), as well as to some special functions, such as a "bell" (a tone played when the character is displayed on the screen).

anti-aliasing

See font smoothing.

API

See application programming interface (API).

application programming interface (API)

A set of functions provided by an operating system, user interface, driver, or the like for the benefit of other programs.

ASCII

See American Standard Code for Information Interchange (ASCII).

ATA

See Advanced Technology Attachment (ATA).

ATA Packet Interface (ATAPI)

A software extension to the ATA interface that supports commands for CD-ROM drives, tape drives, and other non–hard-disk devices.

ATAPI

See ATA Packet Interface (ATAPI).

Bayesian spam filters

See statistical spam filters.

binary

1: A number system in which only two digits exist: 1 and 0. Computers work on binary numbers at their lowest levels. **2:** A file format in which data are encoded in a way that's not readily interpretable by humans. Binary data files may be raw dumps of in-memory representations, compressed data, or otherwise hard to interpret. This contrasts to an *ASCII* file. **3:** A program file generated by a *compiler*.

bitmap

A type of graphic format in which individual pixels are mapped one-to-one onto the computer display. Bitmap graphics formats include GIF, JPEG, TIFF, and PNG. Bitmap fonts are also common, although they're losing ground to *outline fonts*.

block device

A hardware or simulated hardware device that performs input/output operations in multibyte groups, such as 512 bytes or 2,048 bytes at a time. Disk devices are examples of block devices. This contrasts with *character devices*.

boot loader

A small program, often stored in the *boot sector*, that directs the boot process. Simple boot loaders can boot just one OS, but more complex boot loaders enable you to select which OS to boot. These complex boot loaders often rely on files outside of the boot sector. Sometimes a primary boot loader in the boot sector calls upon a secondary boot loader stored elsewhere to finish the job.

boot sector

The first sector of a disk, which contains code that directs the computer's boot process. *See also* MBR.

broadcast

In networking, a type of network packet that's addressed to many or all computers. At a low level, computers use broadcasts to locate each others' hardware addresses. Some protocols, such as *DHCP*, also rely on broadcasts to provide basic functionality.

buffer overflow

A type of programming error in which input data exceeds the space used to store it. The result can be that the excess data ends up in other data's storage space, or even in the space used by executable code. Typically, the result is a program crash; but clever *crackers* may use buffer overflows as a way of getting their own code to run on a computer, thereby giving them access to the system.

bug

1: An error in a program or, less commonly, hardware design. **2:** A tool used to track who reads e-mail and when they read it. The sender incorporates a reference to a tiny graphics file as a *URI* in an *HTML*-enabled e-mail message and checks server log files to see when that graphics file is accessed.

bus

A hardware system for passing data between components. The *PCI*, *AGP*, and *ISA* busses are common internal busses. The *ATA* and *SCSI* busses connect computers to hard disks; and the *USB* bus connects computers to some external devices.

central processing unit (CPU)

The computer component that runs the OS and most programs.

CF

See Compact Flash (CF).

CGI script

A *Common Gateway Interface* script is a program that a web server runs to generate a web page to be delivered to the client. CGI scripts enable web servers to deliver dynamic content based on user input.

character device

A hardware or simulated hardware device that performs input/output operations a byte at a time. Examples include serial ports, parallel ports, and the keyboard. This contrasts with *block devices*.

child

In reference to Linux processes, the process that was launched from a specific *parent* process.

chipset

A set of one or more chips that together provide the core functionality of a circuit board. Linux drivers are typically written for chipsets, because one chipset may be used in dozens of boards sold by different manufacturers.

CHS geometry

The *cylinder/head/sector* geometry is a way of addressing a specific *cylinder* on a hard disk by using three numbers. This contrasts with *LBA mode*. The IA-32 BIOS uses CHS geometry in its oldest modes, and this method is used for some low-level disk data structures. *See also* head and sector.

CISC

See complex instruction set computer (CISC).

client

A network program that initiates a data transfer with a *server*. People often run and directly control network clients, such as web browsers and e-mail readers.

CMYK

See cyan/magenta/yellow/black (CMYK).

Common Unix Printing System (CUPS)

The printing software that's emerging as the new printing standard in the Linux world, pushing aside the older *LPD* systems. CUPS uses the *IPP* standard for network printing.

Compact Flash (CF)

A hardware format for solid-state data storage. It's commonly used by MP3 players, digital cameras, and other portable consumer electronics that may or may not interface with a computer. CF readers for computers are available, and Linux can treat them like hard disks.

compiled program

A program that's transformed from its original human-readable *source code* form into instructions that can be executed directly by the CPU. Compiled programs run quickly, but are more tedious to develop than *interpreted programs*.

compiler

A program that converts *source code* into a *compiled program* (aka *object code* or a *binary* file).

complex instruction set computer (CISC)

A CPU that can perform a wide range of operations using a single CPU command for each operation. CISC CPUs tend to be large and complex compared to *RISC* CPUs. The IA-32 architecture is a CISC architecture.

CPU

See central processing unit (CPU).

cracker

A computer miscreant. Crackers break into computers they're not authorized to access. Often referred to as *hackers* by the general media.

CUPS

See Common Unix Printing System (CUPS).

cyan/magenta/yellow/black (CMYK)

A color encoding scheme that describes every color as a combination of the four colors cyan, magenta, yellow, and black. CMYK color encoding is common on printers. This contrasts with *RGB* color encoding.

cylinder

In disk technology, a cylinder is a collection of matching *tracks* from multiple disk platters. Each track in a cylinder lies directly atop or below others in a collection of platters. *See also* sector and head.

daemon

A program that runs in the background to perform some helpful task. (The word *daemon* is derived from the Greek for "helper.") Most *servers* run as daemons.

DDoS attack

A *distributed denial-of-service attack* is a type of network attack that uses many computers to saturate your network's bandwidth, effectively shutting down your Internet access.

Debian package

A *package* format used by Debian GNU/Linux and its derivatives. Debian packages are roughly comparable to *RPM* files, but the two file formats aren't directly compatible.

default policy

In firewall configuration, this is what the firewall does with packets that don't match any explicit rules.

desktop environment

An integrated software package that includes a *window manager, file manager*, and assorted small utilities such as calculators, image viewers, text editors, and so on. GNOME and KDE are the two most popular desktop environments for Linux.

DHCP

See Dynamic Host Configuration Protocol (DHCP).

direct memory access (DMA)

A method of transferring data between memory and peripherals such as hard disk interfaces, Ethernet cards, and sound cards. DMA uses little CPU overhead, so it's better for multitasking OSs such as Linux than the competing *PIO* mode.

dirty bit

A flag on a disk *filesystem* that indicates whether the filesystem is currently in use (that is to say, it's "dirty"). When a computer unmounts the filesystem, it clears the dirty bit flag; when it mounts the filesystem, it sets the flag. If the computer detects the dirty bit when mounting a filesystem, that's an indication that a system crash or other problem happened, and that the filesystem may be in an unstable state.

DMA

See direct memory access (DMA).

DNS

See Domain Name System (DNS).

Domain Name System (DNS)

A method of converting *hostnames* to *IP addresses* and vice versa. DNS relies on a series of distributed DNS server computers, which know the mappings for their own subset of the Internet.

DoS attack

A *denial-of-service attack* is a type of *cracker* activity designed to prevent you from using your computer or network. *See also* DDoS attack.

driver

A software component that manages a hardware device or filesystem. Using drivers enables user software to access hardware with differing designs using the same commands. For instance, a CD-R package doesn't need to know whether you've got an Adaptec or Initio SCSI adapter.

Dynamic Host Configuration Protocol (DHCP)

A popular method of assigning IP addresses and related information to clients on a network.

ECP

See enhanced capabilities port (ECP).

emulator

A program that runs one operating system's programs inside another OS. Some emulators run an entire OS within another OS, and a few even emulate the target OS's hardware, enabling you to run, say, Microsoft Windows on a Macintosh.

enhanced capabilities port (ECP)

The most recent standard for parallel printer ports. *See also* SPP and EPP.

EPP

See enhanced parallel port (EPP).

enhanced parallel port (EPP)

An improved parallel printer port design capable of higher speeds than the original *SPP* design. *See also* ECP.

export

Used as a noun, refers to directories served to other computers via an *NFS* server.

ext2fs

See Second Extended Filesystem (ext2 or ext2fs).

ext3fs

See Third Extended Filesystem (ext3 or ext3fs).

Fast File System (FFS)

A filesystem used by FreeBSD and related OSs. It's supported in Linux through the ufs driver. *See also* UFS.

FAT

See File Allocation Table (FAT).

FFS

See Fast File System (FFS).

File Allocation Table (FAT)

The filesystem used by DOS and Windows 9*x*/Me. It can also be used by many other OSs, including Windows NT/2000/XP, OS/2, BeOS, Mac OS, Linux, and most other Unix-like OSs. The filesystem is named after an important data structure it uses internally.

file manager

A program that provides a GUI or menu-based interface for manipulating files. A file manager is an important component of most *desktop environments*, but stand-alone file managers are also available.

filesystem

1: A set of data structures written to a disk to support accessing files by name. Common Linux filesystems include *ext2fs*, *ext3fs*, *ReiserFS*, *JFS*, and *XFS*. *FAT* is a common filesystem from the Windows world. **2:** A directory tree, such as /usr and all the directories and subdirectories it contains.

File Transfer Protocol (FTP)

An old but popular protocol for transferring files across *TCP/IP* networks.

firewall

A router that's configured to restrict access between two networks as a security measure. The word can also be applied to software that protects a single computer from the outside world.

font

A collection of characters rendered in a particular style; a typeface.

font server

A network server that delivers *font* data to the same or other computers. Font servers can simplify font configuration on large networks.

font smoothing

A technique for font display in which some pixels are gray rather than black or white. The result is an illusion of higher resolution than the monitor can deliver. Some people like this effect, but others say that it makes characters look blurry. Also called *anti-aliasing*.

fork

The act of creating a new process. One process *forks* another one, enabling one program to start another one running. *See also* spawn.

format

Applied to disks, refers to the data structures written on the disk to support holding and accessing data. The word *format* may be used as a verb to refer to the process of writing this data to the disk. *See also* low-level format and high-level format.

FPU

A *floating-point unit*. *See* math co-processor.

Free Software Foundation (FSF)

An organization devoted to developing and promoting free software. In this context, *free* refers to freedom (as in "freedom of speech") more than to price. Free software is a specific type of *open source* software.

frame buffer

1: A buffer that holds a single image, as in a video processing system. **2:** A method of abstracting video hardware, allowing a single XFree86 driver, `fbdev`, to handle many video cards.

FSF

See Free Software Foundation (FSF).

FTP

See File Transfer Protocol (FTP).

gateway

A *router* computer.

Ghostscript

A program that converts PostScript into various other formats, including bitmap formats useable by many non-PostScript printers, common bitmap graphics file formats, and Adobe's Portable Document Format (PDF). Ghostscript is an integral part of many Linux systems' printer queues.

GNU's Not Unix (GNU)

A recursive acronym referring to a software project sponsored by the *FSF* to develop a free Unix-like OS. Many Linux components derive from the GNU project, but the Linux kernel was developed independently.

Grand Unified Boot Loader (GRUB)

One of two common *boot loaders* for Linux.

GRUB

See Grand Unified Boot Loader (GRUB).

hacker

1: A person who's skilled with computers, and especially with computer programming, and who uses that skill for productive and legal purposes. **2:** A computer miscreant; a *cracker*. The media generally uses this second definition, but the first is more common in the Linux community.

head

In disk technology, a head is a device that reads data from and writes data to a disk. Heads rest at the ends of pivoting arms so that they can be moved over any *track* on a hard disk. On most disks, heads are stacked so that they mark out *cylinders* built from tracks. *See* also sector.

high-level format

A type of disk *format* that holds *filesystem* data.

hostname

A name assigned to a computer, such as `www.sybex.com`. Hostnames consist of a machine portion (the part before the first dot—`www` in this example) and a network portion (`sybex.com` in this case).

HTML

See Hypertext Markup Language (HTML).

HTTP

See Hypertext Transfer Protocol (HTTP).

Hypertext Markup Language (HTML)

A file format used by most web pages. HTML is plain *ASCII* text with certain characters and character groups assigned special meanings.

Hypertext Transfer Protocol (HTTP)

The protocol upon which the *Web* is based. Its most common use is in transferring files from a web server to a web browser.

IA-32

See Intel Architecture 32 (IA-32).

IA-64

See Intel Architecture 64 (IA-64).

IMAP

See Internet Message Access Protocol (IMAP).

inode

A low-level data structure in a *filesystem*. The inode points to a specific file and holds information such as the file's creation time, owner, and permissions.

Intel Architecture 32 (IA-32)

A 32-bit CPU architecture designed by Intel. IA-32 CPUs have dominated the market from the late 1980s through the early 2000s. Also known as *x86*.

Intel Architecture 64 (IA-64)

A 64-bit CPU architecture designed by Intel. In 2003, its market penetration is slim, but Intel aims to wean consumers from the older *IA-32* architecture onto IA-64.

Internet Message Access Protocol (IMAP)

A popular *pull protocol* for mail transfer. IMAP transfers are initiated by mail readers so that users can retrieve their mail from mail servers. IMAP is more complex than the competing *POP*.

Internet Printing Protocol (IPP)

The printing protocol used by CUPS, the printing system that's becoming the Linux standard.

Internet Protocol (IP)

A key component of *TCP/IP* networking.

interpreted program

A program that's run by an *interpreter*, which reads the program file as created by the programmer and interprets it line-by-line. Interpreted programs run slowly, but they are relatively easy to develop. This approach contrasts with *compiled programs*.

interpreter

A program that runs *interpreted programs*.

IP

See Internet Protocol (IP).

IP address

A 4-byte address, such as 172.30.108.9, assigned to a computer on a *TCP/IP* network.

IPP

See Internet Printing Protocol.

IPv4

See Internet Protocol version 4.

IPv6

See Internet Protocol version 6.

Internet Protocol version 4 (IPv4)

Currently the most common version of *IP*. It is the basis for most of the Internet as it's implemented in 2003. IPv4 supports 32-bit addressing, for a theoretical maximum of 4,294,967,296 addresses.

Internet Protocol version 6 (IPv6)

The next-generation version of *IP*. The Internet will most likely shift to IPv6 sometime this decade. IPv6 supports 128-bit addressing, for a theoretical maximum of 3.4×10^{38} addresses.

ISA bus

The *Industry Standard Architecture* bus is a standard for connecting components such as parallel ports, sound cards, and modems to computers. In 2003, the ISA bus has been largely abandoned in favor of the *PCI bus* and *AGP bus*, but you may still have ISA devices on older computers.

ISO-9660

Named after the International Standards Organization document that defines it, this filesystem is the standard cross-platform lowest-common-denominator filesystem for CD-ROM, CD-R, and similar media. The Linux `mkisofs` program can create an ISO-9660 filesystem.

JFS

See Journaled File System.

journal

A data structure used by a *journaling filesystem*.

Journaled File System (JFS)

One of four *journaling filesystems* that are available for Linux. JFS was originally developed by IBM, has been added to the 2.4.20 kernel, and it can be added after the fact to older kernels. Some distributions, such as SuSE, ship with it and make it available as an install-time option.

journaling filesystem

A type of filesystem that maintains a *journal*, or a data file that holds information on pending operations. After a power outage or crash, the computer can use the journal to speed up checking the disk contents, thereby greatly reducing the startup time after a crash. Linux supports four journaling filesystems: *ext3fs*, *ReiserFS*, *JFS*, and *XFS*.

kernel

The core of an OS. The kernel assigns memory to programs, dishes out CPU time, provides an interface between programs and hardware, and manages filesystems. Technically, Linux is just a kernel; everything else, including X, user programs, and so on, runs atop the kernel. *See also* module.

key

In cryptography, a number that's used along with a precisely defined algorithm to encrypt or decrypt data.

latency

1: The time required for a data packet to pass from a sender to its recipient on a network. In practice, round-trip latency—the time for a packet to travel to its destination and a reply to be received by the original sender—is frequently measured. **2:** The time required for a data block to rotate under a read/write head on a disk device.

LBA mode

Logical (or *Linear*) *Block Addressing* is a method of specifying an individual sector to be read from a hard disk by using a single number. This method contrasts with *CHS geometry*. Most systems favor LBA mode once booted, but CHS mode is still required for some operations.

LILO

See Linux Loader (LILO).

Line Printer Daemon (LPD)

A printing system that's long been dominant in the Linux world, but that's losing ground. Two common LPD systems for Linux are the original BSD LPD and LPRng. Both are still available, but most distributions have switched to *CUPS* and its *IPP*.

Linux Loader (LILO)

One of two *boot loaders* for Linux.

load average

A measure of the demand for CPU time placed on a system. A load average of 0.0 means few or no programs are actively using the CPU. A load average of 1.0 means the demand for CPU time is exactly equal to the available CPU time. Load averages above 1.0 mean that the kernel must ration CPU time delivered to individual programs.

lossy compression

A compression scheme in which the decompressed data doesn't exactly match the input data. Lossy compression is useless for storing program files, databases, and so on, but it is often useful for audio, graphics, and video files. In these applications, humans are unlikely to notice the lost data, assuming the compression ratio isn't set too high.

low-level format

A type of disk *format* that defines low-level data structures such as *sectors* and *tracks*. Hard disks are low-level formatted at the factory, but floppy disks may need to be low-level formatted with `fdformat` before they can be used.

LPD

See Line Printer Daemon (LPD).

MAC address

The *Media Access Control* address is a low-level address associated with network hardware. Network hardware responds to packets addressed to its MAC address or to *broadcast* packets. The *network stack* converts an *IP address* into a MAC address when sending data.

Master Boot Record (MBR)

The MBR is closely related to the *boot sector*; it's the code in the boot sector that directs the boot process. The MBR frequently holds the primary *boot loader*.

math co-processor

A chip or part of a CPU that handles floating-point arithmetic—arithmetic that involves numbers that might not be integers, such as 208.3 or –0.00005. Also known as an *FPU*.

MBR

See Master Boot Record (MBR).

MIME

See Multipurpose Internet Mail Extension (MIME).

mixer

A program that adjusts the volume levels of various sound inputs and outputs. You can use a mixer to get good sound levels from such varied audio sources as audio CDs and MP3 file playback.

module

A software component that can be loaded into another one. The word is frequently applied to kernel modules, which contain hardware *drivers* or other components of the Linux kernel.

mount

The process of making a removable disk or partition available as a directory in the Linux directory tree. A command of the same name accomplishes this task. *See also* mount point.

mount point

A directory that serves as an access point for a partition or removable disk. For instance, if /mnt/cdrom is the CD-ROM mount point, then files on the CD-ROM are available in /mnt/cdrom or its subdirectories, once the CD-ROM is mounted.

Multipurpose Internet Mail Extension (MIME)

A code that identifies the type of data a file contains. File managers, Web browsers, e-mail clients, and other tools all rely on MIME types to tell them what application should handle particular file types.

MX record

A *mail exchanger record* is a type of entry in a *DNS* server that points to a domain's mail server.

NAT

See Network Address Translation.

netmask

See network mask.

Network Address Translation (NAT)

A technique used by some routers that enables an entire network to "share" a single external IP address. NAT is particularly popular among home broadband users and to stretch a limited supply of IP addresses in businesses that don't want to pay for more than they must.

Network File System (NFS)

A popular protocol for sharing files among Unix-like OSs. NFS *exports* can be mounted like local filesystems, giving remote systems convenient access to a server's files.

network mask

A numeric code that separates the network and machine portions of an *IP address*.

network stack

A set of kernel routines that interface between programs and a network. To communicate on a network, two computers require compatible network stacks to pack and unpack data. The most common network stack today is *TCP/IP*.

Network Time Protocol (NTP)

A network protocol for synchronizing two or more computers' clocks.

NFS

See Network File System (NFS).

NTP

See Network Time Protocol (NTP).

object code

A type of computer program file consisting of code that's been compiled by a *compiler*, usually into *binary* format for the target *CPU*.

open relay

A mail server that's configured to relay mail from any site to any other site. Open relays were once common, but in the past decade, their abuse as a tool for sending *spam* has driven all responsible mail server administrators to close their mail servers.

Open Sound System (OSS)

The primary sound standard for Linux. Two sets of OSS drivers are available: standard drivers that come with the kernel and an expanded commercial set available from 4Front Technologies.

open source software

Software for which the *source code* is readily available and for which users have the right to modify and redistribute both the source code and compiled *binaries*. The Linux kernel and most or all programs that ship with Linux distributions are open source.

orphan

A *process* whose parent has terminated. Orphans are "adopted" by init, the first regular process.

OSS

See Open Sound System (OSS).
See open source software. (Microsoft frequently uses the OSS acronym in this way, but its use elsewhere is rare.)

outline font

A font that's described in terms of lines and curves. To display such a font on the screen, the system must *rasterize* it into a *bitmap* font format.

package

A collection of files that provides a logically related set of features, such as a family of related fonts or a program file along with its documentation, configuration, and other support files. Linux packages are often distributed as *tarballs*, *RPM* files, or *Debian packages*.

packet-filter firewall

A type of *firewall* that operates by examining and passing or discarding individual *TCP/IP* packets.

pager

A tool that enables you to switch between *virtual desktops*, typically by clicking one square in a line or array of squares representing the different virtual desktops.

parallel port

A type of *port* that uses several signal lines, enabling transmission of an entire byte (or more) at one time. The term may be used generically to refer to any type of parallel interface or specifically to the port that's present on most IA-32 computers as a printer interface.

parent

In terms of Linux processes, a relative term describing the process that launched another process. *See also* child.

patch

A short file that can be merged with a larger file or set of files to modify the larger file or files. Patches are a common way of distributing changes to *source code*.

PC Card

A hardware interface standard most commonly used by laptop computers. PC Card devices plug into the computer and provide functionality such as network interfaces, modems, or external hard disk interfaces. Also known as *PCMCIA*.

PCI bus

The *Peripheral Component Interconnect* bus, a hardware standard for plug-in cards such as video cards, EIDE controllers, and Ethernet adapters. PCI is the dominant bus type on IA-32 systems in 2003, except for video cards, which generally use the *AGP bus*. *See also* ISA bus.

PCMCIA

See Personal Computer Memory Card International Association (PCMCIA).

Personal Computer Memory Card International Association (PCMCIA)

An industry association that developed a hardware standard, which is also sometimes referred to by the same acronym. *See* PC Card.

PID

See process ID (PID).

PIO

See Programmed Input/Output (PIO).

pipe

A tool for linking programs together. The first program's standard output (*see* stdout) is directed to the second program's standard input (*see* stdin). In a shell, you create a pipe by separating the program names with a vertical bar (|).

POP

See Post Office Protocol (POP).

pop-up ad

A type of ad delivered via web pages or HTML-enabled e-mail. Pop-up ads create new browser windows that display advertisements, requiring you to close the window to get rid of the ad.

port

1: A hardware interface, frequently to an external device, such as a *USB* port or an *RS-232 serial* port. 2: A number associated with a specific network-enabled program. Servers run on specific well-known ports, and clients also use ports for outgoing connections.

Post Office Protocol (POP)

A popular *pull protocol* for mail transfer. POP transfers are initiated by mail readers so that users can retrieve their mail from mail servers. POP is simpler than the competing *IMAP*.

PowerPC

A CPU architecture used primarily in Apple Macintoshes, some IBM workstations, and some embedded systems. Linux support for PowerPC (or *PPC*) is good, but not as good as for IA-32.

PPD file

A *PostScript Printer Description* file is a standardized file that describes a PostScript printer's capabilities—its page size, margins, resolution, and so on. Some applications can use PPD files to optimize their output for specific printers.

print filter

A program that processes printed files as part of a Linux print queue. A print filter may convert text to PostScript, PostScript to another format, or perform other transformations.

process

A running program, identified by a *PID* number.

process ID (PID)

A number that uniquely identifies a *process*.

Programmed Input/Output (PIO)

A method of transferring data between peripherals such as disk interfaces, Ethernet adapters, and sound cards. PIO mode requires extensive CPU intervention, and so slows down normal programs during I/O operations.

proxy server

A server that functions as a stand-in for another *server*. Typically, a proxy server partially processes a data-transfer request, sends a copy of the request to the true destination, receives a reply, partially processes the reply, and forwards it to the original client. Proxy servers can function as security filters or can improve network performance by caching replies from popular servers.

pull protocol

A protocol in which the recipient of data initiates the transfer. This term is often applied to the *POP* and *IMAP* mail protocols.

push protocol

A protocol in which the sender of data initiates the transfer. This term is often applied to the *SMTP* mail protocol.

RAM disk

A technique whereby a section of random access memory (RAM) is set aside and treated like a disk device. Many Linux distributions use RAM disks during system installation and even as part of the normal boot process.

random access

A method of data storage that enables reading or (if supported) writing any stored data without reading intervening data. Hard disks, floppy disks, and memory are all random access devices. This contrasts with *sequential access* devices.

rasterize

The process of converting an image into a format that can appear on a bitmapped computer display. This term is often applied to converting *outline fonts* into a bitmap format.

red/green/blue (RGB)

A color encoding system that describes every color as a combination of the three colors red, green, and blue. Computer monitors use RGB encoding. This contrasts with *CMYK* color encoding.

reduced instruction set computer (RISC)

A CPU that provides a limited set of operations. This reduces CPU complexity, allowing the CPU to perform tasks more quickly; but multiple commands may be required to perform some tasks that can be performed with a single command in a *CISC* CPU. The *PowerPC* and *Alpha* are both RISC CPUs.

ReiserFS

A *journaling filesystem* that's been included in the Linux kernel since early in the 2.4.*x* kernel series. Most distributions make ReiserFS an option for the default filesystem at install time.

RGB

See red/green/blue (RGB).

RISC

See reduced instruction set computer (RISC).

root

The system administrator's username. In this book, the name always appears in a monospaced font, or italicized in some headings. *See also* root and /root.

root

1: The lowest-level directory on a Linux system, referred to in shell commands or directory specifications with a single slash (/) character, as in **cd /**. All directories and files can be referred to relative to the root directory. **2:** The lowest-level directory in a specific directory tree or on a removable media, as in "you'll find the file in the CD-ROM's root directory." *See also* /root and root.

root kit

A software package that *crackers* use to acquire root privileges on a computer to which they have access as ordinary users.

router

A computer that links two or more networks together, passing network packets between the networks. The Internet is a collection of a very large number of networks tied together through a series of routers.

RPM Package Manager (RPM)

A recursive acronym referring to a file format and tool for distributing software *packages*. RPM files provide dependency and summary information that the RPM utilities store in a local database, enabling easy upgrades or removal of the package at a later date.

RS-232 serial port

A type of interface with external devices, such as modems, printers, or mice. Most RS-232 serial ports are limited to speeds of 115,200 bits per second, which is very slow by today's standards but still adequate for low-speed devices such as mice and telephone modems.

Samba

A popular Linux server for the *SMB/CIFS* protocol. Samba enables Windows (and other operating systems') clients to use a Linux server for storing files and as a print server.

SANE

See Scanner Access Now Easy (SANE).

scan code

A numeric code sent from a keyboard to the computer to represent the key that a user has pressed.

Scanner Access Now Easy (SANE)

The primary scanner software for Linux.

SCSI

See Small Computer System Interface (SCSI).

Second Extended Filesystem (ext2 or ext2fs)

Linux's primary native filesystem through the late 1990s. Since then, development of several *journaling filesystems* has reached a point where they're taking over as the standard Linux filesystem.

sector

A discrete unit of data storage on hard disks and similar devices. Most hard disk sectors are 512 bytes in size, but some devices use other sector sizes. CD-ROM sectors are 2,048 bytes. *See also* track, cylinder, and head.

Secure Shell (SSH)

An increasingly popular means of establishing a secure data transfer connection between two systems. SSH is commonly used as an encrypted remote text-based login tool, but it can also *tunnel* other protocols. Used in this way, SSH can add encryption to just about any network protocol.

Secure Sockets Layer (SSL)

An encryption protocol that's used by secure websites, *SSH*, and other secure Internet protocols.

sequential access

A type of data storage device in which data are read in sequence from start to end. These devices don't allow quick access to most data, so they're best used for backups or archival storage. Tape drives are the most common sequential access devices. *See also* random access.

server

1: A network program that responds to network data transfer requests from *clients*. Examples include web servers and e-mail servers. Servers usually run in the background, without direct human intervention, as *daemons*. **2:** A computer that exists mainly to run server programs.

Server Message Block/Common Internet File System (SMB/CIFS)

The protocol upon which Windows' file- and printer-sharing tools are built. Linux supports SMB/CIFS through the *Samba* package.

SGID bit

The *set group ID* bit is a special permission bit that tells the system to run a program with the group permissions associated with the file rather than those of the user who runs the program.

shell

A program that accepts commands and that performs actions or launches programs in response to those commands. The most common shell on Linux systems is bash.

Simple Mail Transfer Protocol (SMTP)

The protocol that dominates mail delivery on the Internet today. SMTP is a *push protocol* for mail delivery, and it is used by common mail servers such as sendmail, Postfix, Exim, and qmail.

Small Computer System Interface (SCSI)

A method of connecting hard disks and similar devices to computers. SCSI supports more devices per chain than does the more common *ATA* interface, and it has some other technical advantages, but SCSI is also more expensive than ATA.

SMB/CIFS

See Server Message Block/Common Internet File System (SMB/CIFS).

SMTP

See Simple Mail Transfer Protocol (SMTP).

social engineering

The process of tricking users into divulging their passwords or other sensitive computer data. Some *crackers* engage in social engineering as a method of breaking into computers.

source code

The original form of a computer program, before it's compiled by a *compiler*. Source code is relatively easily interpreted by humans, compared to the *binary* format into which it's ultimately converted. (Some programs are *interpreted*, meaning that they're never changed from their original source code form.)

spam

"Junk" e-mail, sent in bulk to recipients who, by and large, don't want it. Also called *UBE* or *UCE*.

spawn

The mechanism one *process* uses to start a *thread* running. *See also* fork.

SPP

See standard parallel port (SPP).

SSH

See Secure Shell (SSH).

SSL

See Secure Sockets Layer (SSL).

standard parallel port (SPP)

A term that applies to old-style parallel printer ports. This hardware is limited in speed, but remains adequate for many purposes. *See also* EPP and ECP.

statistical spam filters

Spam filters based on a statistical analysis of the words or other components of a message. A message with too many words that appear mostly in other spams is flagged as a probable spam message.

stderr

Standard error is an output stream used for high-priority messages from programs—frequently error messages. It's normally sent to your text-mode console, but it can be redirected.

stdin

Standard input is an input stream that text-mode programs use to accept input. It's normally linked to your keyboard, but it can be redirected.

stdout

Standard output is an output stream used for normal output from text-mode programs. It's normally sent to your text-mode console, but it can be redirected.

sticky bit

A special permission bit that alters the way Linux treats permissions within a directory. Without the sticky bit set, users can delete any files in a directory so long as they have write permission to the directory. With the sticky bit set, users need to own the files in a directory before they can delete them.

subnet mask

See network mask.

SUID bit

The *set user ID* bit is a special permission bit that tells the system to run a program with the permissions associated with the program's owner rather than the user who runs the program. *See also* SGID.

SysV startup scripts

A method of starting a Unix-like OS via many small startup scripts, one for each server or subsystem. Most Linux distributions use a SysV startup script system.

tarball

A file created by the tar program, and typically compressed with gzip or bzip2. Tarballs are commonly used for distributing source code or distribution-neutral binary programs.

TCP/IP

See Transmission Control Protocol/Internet Protocol (TCP/IP).

Telnet

An old but popular text-based remote-access protocol. Telnet doesn't encrypt data, unlike *SSH*, so Telnet is a poor choice on the Internet at large, on wireless local networks, or even on wired local networks where security is important.

terminal

A hardware device consisting of a keyboard, monitor, and perhaps a mouse, which enables access to a computer. Terminals have little memory, storage space, and CPU power. Unix (and hence Linux) systems support many terminals and hence many simultaneous users. Software (a terminal program or terminal emulator) can make a computer function as a terminal.

Third Extended Filesystem (ext3 or ext3fs)

A *journaling filesystem* derived from *ext2fs*. It's now the default filesystem for many distributions' standard Linux installations.

thread

A subprocess of a main *process*. Threading can improve an interactive program's apparent performance by placing lengthy noninteractive actions, such as formatting a print job, in the background.

throughput

Overall data transfer rate.

time-to-live (TTL)

A number that corresponds to how long a data structure should survive. TTL values are used in several protocols, including low-level *TCP/IP* packet transport and *DNS* server caches.

track

A ring-shaped collection of *sectors* on a hard disk platter. Disks contain multiple tracks in concentric rings. *See also* cylinder and head.

Transmission Control Protocol/ Internet Protocol (TCP/IP)

The most common *network stack*. The Internet is built atop TCP/IP, as are most Linux networking tools.

TTL

See time-to-live (TTL).

tunnel

1: (noun) A network protocol implemented inside another network protocol. Tunnels may exist to pass protocols over otherwise incompatible network types (for example, to pass NetBEUI traffic over the Internet) or to add features to a protocol (for example, using *SSH* to add encryption to otherwise unencrypted protocols). **2:** (verb) The process of creating and using a tunnel.

UART

See universal asynchronous receiver/transmitter (UART).

UBE

Unsolicited bulk e-mail. *See* spam.

UCE

Unsolicited commercial e-mail. A variety of *spam* that contains a commercial message. *See* spam.

UFS

See Unix File System (UFS).

uniform resource identifier (URI)

A method of describing an Internet resource. URIs include a protocol definition, a hostname, a filename, and additional information. In some instances, some of these components may be omitted. The most common type of URI is for a site on the *Web*. These URIs begin with http://, as in http://www. sybex.com.

universal asynchronous receiver/ transmitter (UART)

A key component of an RS-232 serial port. Several different models of UARTs exist, the 16550A being the most common on *IA-32* hardware.

Universal Serial Bus (USB)

A hardware standard for connecting a wide array of external devices, such as keyboards, mice, modems, scanners, and removable disk drives, to computers.

Unix File System (UFS)

An early filesystem for Unix systems. It is still supported by some Unix variants. Linux supports it with the ufs driver. *See also* FFS.

URI

See uniform resource identifier (URI).

URL

A uniform resource locator. *See* URI.

USB

See Universal Serial Bus (USB).

Virtual Network Computing (VNC)

A program and protocol for remote GUI access. VNC clients and servers are available for Linux, other Unix-like OSs, Windows, Mac OS, OS/2, and other platforms.

virtual terminal

A display that Linux manages, supporting input/output streams independent of other displays. Linux supports multiple virtual terminals using a single keyboard and monitor; you use Alt+F*n* keystrokes to switch between them.

VNC

See Virtual Network Computing (VNC).

Web

The *World Wide Web* (*WWW* or *Web* for short) has been the most visible part of the Internet since the mid-1990s. It's built largely upon *HTTP* and is accessed using a web browser program such as Netscape, Mozilla, or Konqueror.

web form

A type of web page that includes text entry fields, buttons, or other elements that users can manipulate. *CGI scripts* often use web forms as a method of acquiring user input.

widget set

A programming toolkit that enables programmers to easily create buttons, menu bars, dialog boxes, and so on for GUI applications.

window manager

A program that controls the outer edges of windows and provides window sizing and moving functions. There are literally dozens of window managers available for Linux, each with its own unique features.

WWW

The *World Wide Web*. *See* Web.

WYSIWYG display

A *what-you-see-is-what-you-get* display creates printed output that's identical to the on-screen display—or at least, as near to identical as can be achieved given differing resolutions, aspect ratios, and so on. Most word processors released since about 1990 have been WYSIWYG.

X

See X Window System.

x86-64

This CPU architecture is AMD's entry into the 64-bit CPU arena. It competes with Intel's *IA-64*, but it is more closely related to the *IA-32* architecture.

XFS

One of four *journaling filesystems* available for Linux. XFS was originally developed by Silicon Graphics. It isn't a standard part of the 2.4.19 kernel, but it is available as an add-on. XFS is arguably the most technically advanced Linux filesystem.

XLFD

See X Logical Font Descriptor (XLFD).

X Logical Font Descriptor (XLFD)

A string that describes a font—its name, its size, and so on. Programs use XLFDs to specify fonts to display, and you must provide an XLFD when installing a font in X.

X server

A program that mediates the interaction between X-based GUI programs and the screen, keyboard, and mouse used by the user. The X server includes or accesses a video driver and responds to local or network-based accesses from programs to display windows, accept keyboard input, and so on.

X Window System

Linux's primary GUI environment, called X for short. X is a network-enabled GUI, and in Linux it's usually implemented by a program called XFree86.

zombie

A *process* that's been killed but not removed from the process table by its parent. Zombies can only be killed by killing their parents; init should then automatically do away with the zombie.

Index

Note to the Reader: Throughout this index boldfaced page numbers indicate primary discussions of a topic. *Italicized* page numbers indicate illustrations.

Essential Linux Files

XFree86 Configuration Files and Directories *(see Chapter 16 for details)*

Main XFree86 configuration file	`/etc/XF86Config`, `/etc/X11/XF86Config`, or `/etc/X11/XF86Config-4`
Font server (`xfs`) configuration file	`/etc/X11/fs/config`
Xft 1.x configuration file	`/etc/X11/XftConfig`
Xft 2.0 configuration file	`/etc/fonts/fonts.conf`
Font directories	subdirectories of `/usr/X11R6/lib/X11/fonts` and `/usr/share/fonts`

Web Server Configuration Files *(see Chapter 23 for details)*

Main Apache configuration file	`httpd.conf` or `httpd2.conf`, in `/etc/apache`, `/etc/httpd`, or `/etc/httpd/conf`
MIME types file	`mime.types` or `apache-mime.types`, in same directory as main Apache configuration file

File Server Configuration Files *(see Chapter 24 for details)*

ProFTPd configuration file	`/etc/proftpd.conf`
vsftpd configuration file	`/etc/vsftpd.conf`
NFS exports definition file for NFS server	`/etc/exports`
NFS exports mounted from NFS client	`/etc/fstab`
Samba configuration file	`/etc/samba/smb.conf`
Samba encrypted password file	`/etc/samba/smbpasswd`